SHAKESPEARE SURVEY

## ADVISORY BOARD



(1) Shakespeare and his Stage
(2) Shakespearian Production
(3) The Man and the Writer
(4) Interpretation
(5) Textual Criticism
(6) The Histories
(7) Style and Language
(8) The Comedies
(9) *Hamlet*
(10) The Roman Plays
(11) The Last Plays (with an index to *Surveys 1–10*)
(12) The Elizabethan Theatre
(13) *King Lear*
(14) Shakespeare and his Contemporaries
(15) The Poems and Music
(16) Shakespeare in the Modern World
(17) Shakespeare in his Own Age
(18) Shakespeare Then Till Now
(19) *Macbeth*
(20) Shakespearian and Other Tragedy
(21) *Othello* (with an index to *Surveys 11–20*)
(22) Aspects of Shakespearian Comedy
(23) Shakespeare's Language
(24) Shakespeare: Theatre Poet
(25) Shakespeare's Problem Plays
(26) Shakespeare's Jacobean Tragedies
(27) Shakespeare's Early Tragedies
(28) Shakespeare and the Ideas of his Time
(29) Shakespeare's Last Plays
(30) *Henry IV* to *Hamlet*
(31) Shakespeare and the Classical World (with an index to *Surveys 21–30*)
(32) The Middle Comedies
(33) *King Lear*
(34) Characterization in Shakespeare
(35) Shakespeare in the Nineteenth Century
(36) Shakespeare in the Twentieth Century
(37) Shakespeare's Earlier Comedies
(38) Shakespeare and History
(39) Shakespeare on Film and Television
(40) Current Approaches to Shakespeare through Language, Text and Theatre
(41) Shakespearian Stages and Staging (with an index to *Surveys 31–40*)
(42) Shakespeare and the Elizabethans
(43) *The Tempest* and After
(44) Shakespeare and Politics
(45) *Hamlet* and its Afterlife
(46) Shakespeare and Sexuality
(47) Playing Places for Shakespeare
(48) Shakespeare and Cultural Exchange
(49) *Romeo and Juliet* and its Afterlife
(50) Shakespeare and Language
(51) Shakespeare in the Eighteenth Century (with an index to *Surveys 41–50*)
(52) Shakespeare and the Globe
(53) Shakespeare and Narrative
(54) Shakespeare and Religions
(55) *King Lear* and its Afterlife
(56) Shakespeare and Comedy
(57) *Macbeth* and its Afterlife
(58) Writing About Shakespeare

Aspects of *Macbeth*
Aspects of *Othello*
Aspects of *Hamlet*
Aspects of *King Lear*
Aspects of Shakespeare's 'Problem Plays'

# SHAKESPEARE SURVEY

## AN ANNUAL SURVEY OF SHAKESPEARE STUDIES AND PRODUCTION

---

58

# Writing About Shakespeare

EDITED BY

PETER HOLLAND

CAMBRIDGE UNIVERSITY PRESS
Cambridge, New York, Melbourne, Madrid, Cape Town, Singapore, São Paulo

Cambridge University Press
The Edinburgh Building, Cambridge CB2 2RU, UK

Published in the United States of America by Cambridge University Press, New York

www.cambridge.org
Information on this title: www.cambridge.org/9780521850742



First published 2005

Printed in the United Kingdom at the University Press, Cambridge

*A catalogue record for this book is available from the British Library*

ISBN 13 978 0 521 85074 2 hardback
ISBN 10 0 521 85074 6 hardback



*Shakespeare Survey* was first published in 1948. Its first eighteen volumes were edited by Allardyce Nicoll.
Kenneth Muir edited volumes 19 to 33.
Stanley Wells edited volumes 34 to 52.

# EDITOR'S NOTE

Volume 59, on 'Editing Shakespeare', will be at press by the time this volume appears. Volume 60 will be on 'Theatres for Shakespeare' and include papers from the 2006 International Shakespeare Conference. The theme of Volume 61 will be Shakespeare, Sound and Screen.

Submissions should be addressed to the Editor at The Shakespeare Institute, Church Street, Stratford-upon-Avon, Warwickshire CV37 6HP, to arrive at the latest by 1 September 2005 for Volume 60. Pressures on space are heavy and priority is given to articles related to the theme of a particular volume. Please send a copy you do not wish to be returned. Submissions may also be made via e-mail attachment to pholland@nd.edu. All articles submitted are read by the Editor and at least one member of the Advisory Board, whose indispensable assistance the Editor gratefully acknowledges.

Unless otherwise indicated, Shakespeare quotations and references are keyed to *The Complete Works*, ed. Stanley Wells, Gary Taylor *et al.* (Oxford, 1986).

Review copies should be addressed to the Editor as above. In attempting to survey the ever-increasing bulk of Shakespeare publications our reviewers inevitably have to exercise some selection. We are pleased to receive offprints of articles which help to draw our reviewers' attention to relevant material.

P. D. H.

# CONTRIBUTORS


JULIA BRIGGS, *De Montfort University*
SARAH ANNES BROWN, *Lucy Cavendish College, Cambridge*
MARK THORNTON BURNETT, *Queen's University, Belfast*
CLARA CALVO, *University of Murcia, Spain*
JANET CLARE, *University College, Dublin*
MICHAEL DOBSON, *Roehampton University*
TOBIAS DÖRING, *Freie Universität, Berlin*
HEATHER DUBROW, *University of Wisconsin-Madison*
RICHARD DUTTON, *Ohio State University*
CHARLES EDELMAN, *Edith Cowen University, Australia*
EWAN FERNIE, *Royal Holloway, University of London*
R. A. FOAKES, *University of California, Los Angeles*
PETER HOLLAND, *University of Notre Dame*
ANNA KAMARALLI, *Trinity College, Dublin*
DAVID KATHMAN, *Independent Scholar*
TINA KRONTIRIS, *Thessaloniki University*
JILL L. LEVENSON, *Trinity College, Toronto*
RUTH MORSE, *Université Paris 7, Denis-Diderot*
ANDREW MURPHY, *University of St Andrews*
LOIS POTTER, *University of Delaware*
ERIC RASMUSSEN, *University of Nevada*
FIONA RITCHIE, *King's College, University of London*
JAMES SHAPIRO, *Columbia University*
JAMES SHAW, *The Shakespeare Institute, University of Birmingham*
EMMA SMITH, *Hertford College, University of Oxford*
MARION WELLS, *Middlebury College*

# CONTENTS

CONTENTS

# ILLUSTRATIONS

# HAVING OUR WILL: IMAGINATION IN RECENT SHAKESPEARE BIOGRAPHIES

LOIS POTTER

'The biographer begins, of course, with the town of Stratford-upon-Avon, where Mr. Shakspere was born and died, giving a lengthy, nostalgic description of Stratford in Shakespeare's time, refulgent with the glow of small-town boyhood.'[1] As Joseph Sobran sarcastically indicates, there is indeed something 'almost comically formulaic' about Shakespeare biographies. Of course, this is equally true of other biographies; what the Renaissance would call *copia* is perhaps inevitable in Shakespeare's case, when there are so many books and so few facts. Since Sobran is an Oxfordian, he naturally makes a distinction between the 'Shakspere' of Stratford and the 'Shakespeare' who wrote the plays. He is right about this too: there is a gap between the biographical and the literary figure, though not, I think, because they were two different people. After two decades of writing about Shakespeare's life, Sir Sidney Lee concluded that 'The literary history of the world proves the hopelessness of seeking in biographical data, or in the fields of everyday business, the secret springs of poetic inspiration.'[2] This view, famously insisted on by T. S. Eliot, was once taken for granted in literary criticism. It is now largely superseded, on the one hand, by cultural materialism, which wants to know all it can about those 'fields of everyday business', and, on the other, by the postmodern taste for indeterminacy, which has readmitted legendary and anecdotal evidence in order to play with alternative life stories. And so Stephen Greenblatt argues, in his recent contribution to the biographical tradition, 'to understand how Shakespeare used his imagination to transform his life into art, it is important to use our own imagination'.[3]

Certainly, a depiction that appeals to the imagination may well stimulate a new reader of the plays and poems more than any amount of accurate documentation. It is becoming common for writers on Shakespeare to refer at some point to *Shakespeare in Love*, not because they believe its deliberately fantastic version of events but because it is the only one they can expect their readers to know. My own favourites among fictional Shakespeares are the actor briefly sketched in one chapter of John Arden's *Books of Bale*, the enigmatic figure, possibly a spy, in Peter Whelan's play *The School of Night*, and the hard-working writer – whose notes for *Twelfth Night* we get to read – in Grace Tiffany's *My Father had a Daughter*. The question is how much imagination a book can contain and still be taken seriously as a biography. To my mind, Gary O'Connor's *Shakespeare: A Popular Life* (2000) falls on the wrong side of the borderline. Russell Fraser's two-volume critical biography (1988 and 1992) allows itself a mixture of fictionalizing, or imagining, alongside detailed factual information and very full, sometimes frankly

[1] Joseph Sobran, *Alias Shakespeare: Solving the Greatest Literary Mystery of all Time* (New York and London, 1997), pp. 57–8.

[2] *A Life of William Shakespeare* (Oxford, 14th edn, 1931), p. 634. This comment first appears in the 1916 edition; the brief 'General Estimate' of the author in the 1898 edition was more vaguely adulatory.

[3] Stephen Greenblatt, *Will in the World: How Shakespeare became Shakespeare* (New York and London, 2004), p. 14.

idiosyncratic, critical analyses.[4] Anthony Holden's *William Shakespeare: His life and work* (1999) is more problematic.[5] Rather than get bogged down in questions of probability, Holden often simply accepts such traditions as that Shakespeare played Adam in *As You Like It* or that he 'was godfather to one of Ben Jonson's sons' (310). But he can be constructively imaginative too: citing the comparisons Mercutio and Falstaff make to the alderman's thumb-ring, he suggests that John Shakespeare's official ring had made an impression on his son (22). As long as strict accuracy isn't a prime consideration, this book can be recommended, but it suffers from Holden's lack of real inwardness with the literature of the period which sometimes leads him to misunderstand its tone. His own tone sometimes surprises as well. Many have suggested that Shakespeare's mother may have taken the baby William to her family home in Wilmcote while plague infested Stratford in 1564; by referring to her as Mary and to him as 'her first-born son' (20), Holden recreates the Holy Family's flight into Egypt.

Few biographies of Shakespeare can avoid being critical biographies, since to leave out the works is to make the life meaningless. But there is often not much distinction between a critical biography and a general book on Shakespeare that discusses the works in chronological order. Dennis Kay's very readable critical biography (1991) emphasizes the works more than the life, but brings in other interesting pieces of contextual information – for instance, he found that only one of the twenty-six male babies christened in Stratford in 1564 went on to attend university (a William Smith, who later became a schoolmaster in Essex).[6] His critical approach is independent: he thinks the epitaph on Elias James, found in the same MS as 'Shall I die?', is a possible Shakespeare composition (327). He and Russell Fraser are the only recent biographers who respond sympathetically to *The Two Noble Kinsmen*, probably because they are the only two who know anything about its effect in performance; Kay even argues that it, rather than *The Tempest*, is Shakespeare's farewell to his profession (335).

Apart from the major book-length biographies, a number of more general works have made biographical contributions. After at first ignoring the anti-Stratfordians, some scholars have found it worthwhile to do the kind of contextual work that was needed to put their objections into proportion. Irvin Matus's *Shakespeare, in Fact* (1994) is one of the best of these.[7] For instance, in answer to the common question of why so little remains in Shakespeare's own handwriting, he points out that even a work recognized at the time as of the utmost importance, the Authorized/King James Bible, left virtually no manuscript evidence behind (50–1). Alan Nelson's careful archival work has resulted in a filling-in of many contextual details, and his biography of the Earl of Oxford, though it carefully avoids mentioning Shakespeare, gives a detailed analysis of this nobleman's written English as well as his financial incompetence. A different kind of context is provided by Stanley Wells's *Shakespeare: for all Time*, which looks like a coffee table book, but is much more.[8] The main objection to the lavishly illustrated book is that the availability of pictorial material often dictates the emphases of the writing. Here, however, illustrations do an important part of the work of creating the visual background – those evocations of Stratford about which Sobran is so sarcastic, for example. Wells's book is not primarily a biography – about half of it is devoted to the dramatist's afterlife in the theatre and in the fictions of others – but its first section is closer to one than his *Shakespeare: a Life in Drama* (revised as *Shakespeare: The Poet and His Plays*). It contains, almost as asides, some directions in which further research might go: since those who learned Latin in school (like Richard Quiney and Thomas Greene)

4 Russell Fraser, *Young Shakespeare* (New York, 1988), and *Shakespeare: The Later Years* (New York, 1992).

5 *William Shakespeare: His Life and Work* (London, 1999).

6 Dennis Kay, *Shakespeare: His Life, Work and Era* (London, 1992), pp. 30–1. Kay also wrote a shorter, more streamlined biography, *William Shakespeare: His Life and Times*, for the Twayne's English Authors series (New York, 1995).

7 Irvin Leigh Matus, *Shakespeare, in Fact* (New York, 1994).

8 Stanley Wells, *Shakespeare for All Time* (Oxford, 2003).

continued to use it, 'It is quite possible that, if letters written by Shakespeare ever turn up, they will be in Latin' (14). Maybe the 'broad silver and gilt bowl' bequeathed to Judith will turn up some day too although it's hard to see how we would recognize it if it did (43).

Theatre historians have likewise made important contributions to the biography, though Andrew Gurr's most widely accepted suggestion is of a quite different kind: that Sonnet 145, with its apparent pun on 'hate away', is a youthful poem written during the poet's courtship of Anne Hathaway.[9] Richard Dutton's *Shakespeare: A Literary Life* (1989) does not offer a complete biography, but the author's knowledge of theatre and censorship history makes it valuable.[10] Almost alone among biographers, he takes the sonnets to be primarily literary exercises, playing sophisticated games and perhaps deliberately subverting all sonnet conventions (43). Meredith Skura's study of Shakespeare in terms of the psychology of the actor, though not based on fresh research in theatre history, offers interesting readings of the texts as reflecting such actorly concerns as fear of the hostile audience and the importance of the generous patron.[11] Robert Southworth, an actor, deals in *Shakespeare the Player* with the professional career.[12] Some of his suggestions about casting of the plays and doubling charts are interesting, but of course they have no more validity than any other speculations of this type.

However, most biographies of the last twenty years have been influenced, to one degree or another, by the work of Ernst Honigmann – who, ironically, has refused to write a book-length biography of Shakespeare on the grounds that there are already too many in existence. In particular, his *Shakespeare: The 'Lost Years'* (1985) is responsible for an increasing emphasis on the possibility that Shakespeare was a Catholic.[13] The Shakeshaft theory, going back as far as E. K. Chambers, takes a servant of that name to be an alias for a teenage Shakespeare, living in Lancashire with Alexander de Hoghton, the head of an aristocratic Catholic family; Robert Bearman's research has indicated the prevalence of the name Shakeshafte in Lancashire,[14] and there has always been good sense in the argument that it would seem odd to choose so transparent an alias. But many of the other connections traced by Honigmann are persuasive – the Stratford schoolmasters with Lancashire and Catholic origins; the satirist John Weever, who knew all the parties involved and wrote several epigrams on Shakespeare; the fact that Shakespeare wrote his only commendatory verse, 'The Phoenix and the Turtle', for a poem by Robert Chester dedicated to Sir John Salusbury, whose wife was an illegitimate daughter to the Earl of Derby, a friend of Hoghton. In fact, so many of the people that he mentions seem to have been related to each other or to other major players in the Shakespeare story that after a while one wants to invoke the Six Degrees of Separation principle. Honigmann connects a good many dots, but he is careful to indicate where the gaps are, and he is open both about his own research practices and about what might be done by others.

Honigmann has made two other contributions to the biographical debate. The first, his argument that Shakespeare's literary career began considerably earlier than the first recorded allusion in the *Groatsworth of Wit* (1592), has won general acceptance in principle. It is hard to see how a writer's talent could lie fallow for so long, especially in the theatre world of the 1580s, with its insatiable demand for new plays. Scholars are less certain what

9 Andrew Gurr, 'Shakespeare's First Poem: Sonnet 145', *Essays in Criticism*, 21 (1971), 221–6.

10 Richard Dutton, *William Shakespeare: A Literary Life* (Basingstoke, 1989).

11 Meredith Skura, *Shakespeare the Actor and the Purposes of Playing* (Chicago, 1993).

12 John Southworth, *Shakespeare the Player: A life in the theatre* (Stroud, 2000).

13 E. A. J. Honigmann, *Shakespeare: The 'Lost Years'* (Manchester, 1985).

14 See Robert Bearman, '"Was William Shakespeare William Shakeshafte" Revisited', *Shakespeare Quarterly*, 51 (2002), 83–94. For Honigmann's reply, 'The Shakespeare/ Shakeshafte Question, Continued', see *Shakespeare Quarterly*, 54 (2003), 83–86.

to do with the idea in practice, though some have taken it as a reason to treat, e.g., *King Leir* and *The Taming of A Shrew* as early works by Shakespeare, later revised by him. Going further, Eric Sams has identified many anonymous works of the 1580s, such as *Edmond Ironside*, *Fair Em*, *Locrine*, and *The Troublesome Reign of King John* as apprentice work by Shakespeare, arguing vehemently against once received views that explained Quarto versions of Folio plays as the result of memorial reconstruction and textual corruption.[15] Honigmann's other contention – that Shakespeare, as exemplified particularly in the legal documents he left behind, really did have a tiger's heart inside his 'gentle' manner – is developed both in *Shakespeare's Impact on His Contemporaries* and in the essay, 'Shakespeare's Will and Testamentary Traditions'.[16] It seems somewhat inconsistent with the Shakeshafte argument, which assumes that the seventeen-year old Shakespeare was charming and impressive enough to get a special bequest from a nobleman in whose service he had been for only a few months, but perhaps such a person could deceive his master about his true nature; in any case, people often become less nice as they get older. Understandably, the negative view of Shakespeare's character has had less general appeal than Honigmann's other arguments, with one exception that I'll discuss later. Eric Sams accepts the arguments for Shakespeare's Catholicism and the 'early start' but his Shakespeare is a sympathetic figure, largely self-educated, poor, and persecuted by snobbish university men. Honigmann's work on wills, incidentally, enables him to say with authority that Shakespeare's failure to mention books in his will does not mean he didn't have any: other wills with the same failure include those of such unlikely people as the schoolmaster John Cottom and the writer John Weever.[17]

Among recent biographers, Kay stands out for his relative lack of interest in the Catholicism theory, not so much because he finds the Lancastrian argument implausible as because it seems inconsistent with the traditions surrounding Shakespeare in the first hundred years after his death. These, Kay notes, seem patriotic in inspiration, designed to make the dramatist, by contrast with the refined French writers to whom he was so often compared, a hearty, typically English man's man (38). Of course, this may be the point. A Shakespeare riddled with doubts and neuroses is more to our taste than the lighthearted lecher and poacher of the early anecdotes, the happy and successful man chronicled in Rowe's 1709 biography, the respectable one of Malone,[18] or the selfish and perhaps embitter one that Honigmann seems to envisage. Thus, many biographers have been willing to believe that the apparent lack of excitement in Shakespeare's life is the result of deliberate concealment – that he was, in the title of Richard Wilson's book, *Secret Shakespeare*.[19] The Catholicism theory has obvious attractions, since it can explain the plays' inconsistent treatment of religious issues, as well as the dramatist's low profile (by comparison with Jonson), and even the lack of personal documents concerning him. Though Honigmann doesn't note this, another of its attractions is that it helps to justify some of the less pleasant traits that he identifies in Shakespeare: a deep sense of insecurity might well lie behind an obsession with saving money and buying property, perhaps even behind his apparent determination not to leave his wife a rich, and therefore remarriageable, widow. On the other hand, Ben Jonson does not seem to have felt that his conversion to Catholicism required him to lie low, and a comparative study of other playwrights reveals that many of them, for instance John Fletcher, left even fewer handwritten documents than Shakespeare.[20]

---

[15] Eric Sams, *The Real Shakespeare: Retrieving the Early Years, 1564–1594* (New Haven, 1995).

[16] E. A. J. Honigmann, *Shakespeare's Impact on his Contemporaries* (London, 1982) and 'Shakespeare's Will and Testamentary Traditions' in Tetsuo Kishi, Roger Pringle and Stanley Wells, ed., *Shakespeare and Cultural Traditions* (Newark and London, 1994), pp. 127–37.

[17] Honigmann, *The Lost Years*, p. 131.

[18] For an analysis of Malone's account, see Margreta de Grazia's *Shakespeare Verbatim: The Reproduction of Authenticity and the 1790 Apparatus* (Oxford, 1991), esp. pp. 134–41.

[19] Richard Wilson, *Secret Shakespeare: Studies in Theatre, Religion, and Resistence* (Manchester, 2004). This book appeared too late for review.

[20] See Matus, *Shakespeare, in Fact*, p. 265.

Though Honigmann assumes that Shakespeare was converted to Protestantism in the early 1580s, a view which makes sense of his writing *King John* as well as the apparent lapses into the older beliefs in some parts of *Hamlet*, Wilson, Wood and Greenblatt (in descending order of certainty) base their accounts of Shakespeare on the likelihood that he was the product of a Catholic upbringing, with a background of secrecy and persecution.

Park Honan's biography is a thoroughly professional piece of work, for which one's respect only increases with use.[21] This is a writer who scrupulously attempts to trace the numerous received opinions about his author back to their ultimate source and who, committed as he is to a full biography, is obliged to work in all the facts, not just those that he finds interesting or that happen to fit his argument. Honan has taken the trouble to chase up the kinds of legal and financial records that most of us find boring, and manages to integrate all the details into his story, documenting them properly, and quoting the appropriate sources, without losing momentum. For instance, he examines a record of a sale of land to which Mary Arden set her mark in 1579 and finds evidence of her ability to use a pen (14); he takes Judith Shakespeare's witnessing a deed of sale for one of the Quiney family in 1611 as evidence of a close relationship with them well before her marriage with Thomas Quiney in 1616 (391). Honan's Shakespeare is a genial, comfortable conformist, who enjoyed his education while making jokes about it, and whose behaviour as a writer was characterized above all by professionalism. He is quick to discount a picturesque but impossible story, though willing to give it in the first place, and he draws on a sort of common sense psychology where it seems appropriate. For instance, with reference to the plague of 1564, he thinks that John Shakespeare, as a town official, could not have left town or have allowed his wife to leave. Further, he suggests that Mary's care for her son must have been particularly intense in that troubled period and that perhaps the sense of being loved in his first year gave Shakespeare the confidence that kept him from the need to show off that afflicted some of his contemporaries (18). Though he takes the Catholic argument seriously, he does not unreservedly accept it but offers (in a surprising, almost postmodern moment) a 'method of alternative narrative' to explain what Shakeshafte's life would have been in Lancashire, whether or not he was Shakespeare. Though understandably dismissive of so-called biographies that are really extended critical surveys of an author's work, interspersed with snippets of second-hand biography and history, Honan makes literary judgements on all the works and even on those tentatively ascribed to Shakespeare (he has been proved right in the case of *The Funeral Elegy*). These are conscientious surveys of current critical views, sometimes with comments on the plays in performance, but are likely to date sooner than anything else in the book. Useful appendices give family trees and 'A Note on the Shakespeare Biographical Tradition and Sources for his Life' (415–24), which will be a starting point for many other biographers. Despite the vast amount of material he covers, Honan is concise because he does not pad out his facts with more speculation than they can bear. Moreover, he can be called the cause that conciseness is in others. His immediate successors have been able, after acknowledging the existence of his comprehensive narrative, to move quickly on to more exciting and selective narratives emphasizing sexuality, religious persecution, psychological abnormality and greed.

Of these, certainly the most stimulating is Katherine Duncan-Jones's *Ungentle Shakespeare: Scenes From his Life*.[22] Its title may derive from Richard Wilson, who, paraphrasing Dylan Thomas, describes the 1616 will as Shakespeare 'going ungently into night'.[23] Though sceptical about all the evidence relating to Shakespeare's possible Catholicism, this book is a far more negative evaluation of his character than Honigmann's. It starts from a contextual approach: 'I don't believe that any Elizabethans, even Shakespeare, were what might now be called 'nice' – liberal, unprejudiced,

21 Park Honan, *Shakespeare: A Life* (Oxford, 1998).

22 Katherine Duncan-Jones, *Ungentle Shakespeare: Scenes from his Life* (London, 2001).

23 Richard Wilson, *Will Power* (London, 1993), p. 185

unselfish'(x). Duncan-Jones compares the Stratford dramatist unfavourably with another Stratfordian who was much more generous than he, the great late fifteenth-century benefactor Sir Hugh Clopton (xi). Shakespeare's bequest of £10 for the poor of Stratford certainly sounds mean, but, as a member of a theatre company he had been making regular contributions for poor relief in the parish throughout his stay in London, and Honigmann, comparing Shakespeare's will with others of the period, calls this provision generous ('Shakespeare's Will', 128). She admits that most people in the period used their wealth for themselves and their families alone and that when Shakespeare was hoarding malt in the bad years of the 1590s he was only doing what the rest of the Stratford maltsters did. The question is where to place the playwright on a rather long continuum of human behaviour. At the opposite end of the scale from Clopton, for example, one might compare Duncan-Jones's account of the appalling Garter King of Arms, Sir William Dethick, whose past included the accusation, by a fellow Herald's wife, that he had kicked her, poured her chamber pot over her head and rubbed hot ashes into her hair (99–100).

What makes *Ungentle Shakespeare* really worth reading is Duncan-Jones's superb knowledge of the literary and courtly context. She can say, for instance, that Sir George Carey and his daughter Bess (for whose wedding she thinks the dramatist wrote *A Midsummer Night's Dream*) took a special interest in dreams, about which the father wrote his daughter in a letter of 1593 (88–9). Whereas most other biographers know only Shakespeare's works, she is able to insert the two narrative poems dedicated to Southampton into a conversation with others similarly dedicated (among other things, she notes the puns on 'Vere' that might refer to Anne Vere, the woman Burghley wanted Southampton to marry). Arguing that Southampton supported the poet's application for a coat of arms, she notes the terse hint in the *Lucrece* dedication, 'Were my worth greater, my duty would show greater', and the presence in the Shakespeare escutcheon of the falcon from the Southampton coat of arms (91–6). She thinks Scoloker's *Diaphantus* not only refers to *Hamlet* but indicates some of the stage business Burbage might have used in it, such as smoking his pen and drinking from his ink-horn (180). In short, there are enormous numbers of intertextual points, which, in the end, make this book more valuable as literary criticism than as biography. But even in the area of textual evidence, Duncan-Jones raises issues that need further examining: for instance, she is very suspicious about the authenticity of that part of Simon Forman's diary that refers to the plays he saw in 1611 (xii–xiii).

Michael Wood's television series, *In Search of Shakespeare*, made brilliant use of visual material and of performance to do exactly what television can do and a book cannot. His beautifully produced book does what television cannot: that is, develops an argument at some length.[24] It is slightly less sensational than the series, though still inclined to create tenuous chains of connections, to make disconcerting leaps from 'perhaps' to 'we know', and to accept what is convenient for the narrative, particularly when it allows for the use of an effective visual record – for example, that the Cambridge portrait is indeed of Marlowe. Still, it must be said that the visual side of the book is wonderful, though it makes less use than the television series of those surprising glimpses of the back streets and cellars of a previously unknown, largely unchanged, ancient London. It would be worth buying just for the detailed maps of the theatre districts and the areas in which Shakespeare lived (Wood seems also to have benefited from Alan Nelson's admirable work on Shakespeare's neighbors). It will be plundered for PowerPoint illustrations. This book offers a major argument for the Catholic reading of Shakespeare's life, less conspiracy-driven than the television series. But it deals also with the other major questions in Shakespeare's biography and is in fact an extremely up-to-date summary of the current state of knowledge.

Unfortunately, the collaboration and editing that enabled Wood to incorporate so much recent work also make it impossible to track down some of the

[24] Michael Wood, *Shakespeare* (London, 2003).

sources. The publishers assume that readers won't follow up the quotations or want to know their authors, much less their act, scene and line numbers. The practice of giving only general acknowledgements in miniscule type at the back of a book may be allowable when one is drawing largely on secondary sources likely to be familiar to any competent scholar, but this is not that kind of book. It is full of detail, of fascinating illustrations (many of them identified only by the picture library from which they came), and of claims that cry out for more investigation. Wood's statement that 'we now know' that *The Phoenix and the Turtle* was about the martyrdom of a Catholic woman in 1601 is based on an article that appeared in the *Times Literary Supplement* on 18 April 2003, only six months before the book's publication (the 'we' of this statement is thus a pretty small group, and the documentation that would clinch the argument has yet to appear as I write).[25] His comments on the penmanship of Shakespeare's mother (48) are based on Honan's (see above); his arguments for the Earl of Pembroke as the young man of the sonnets (178–80) are not, of course, new, but their wording sometimes comes close to Katherine Duncan-Jones's in the introduction to her Arden edition of the Sonnets and almost anticipate the further bolstering by Jonathan Gibson in another *TLS* article.[26] Occasionally there are signs of careless note-taking: the statement that Shakespeare never blotted a line is attributed to Ben Jonson rather than, as Jonson himself does, to 'the players' (221). Like all too many biographers, Wood makes a practice of stating a fact about, say, the scenery of Stratford, and then quoting a few lines from the poet, as if to suggest that the one led inevitably to the other. Virtually everyone, for instance, after referring to the painted cloths in Mary Arden's childhood home, quotes the lines about painted cloths in *The Rape of Lucrece*. Wood goes even further, using the word 'uncanny' for some of the echoes that he thinks he detects. The phrase about those who have 'defaced the precious image of our dear Redeemer' in *Richard III* (2.1) refers in context to murdering or maiming the image of God as seen in a human being but Wood wants it to be an uncanny reflection of the adult Shakespeare's unconscious sense of guilt over an event that occurred several months before he was born, his father's supervision of the whitewashing of the religious paintings in the Stratford Guild Chapel (13).

On the other hand, Stephen Greenblatt's *Will in the World: How Shakespeare Became Shakespeare* searches for echoes of more than words, especially the words of high culture.[27] His first quotation is from a nursery rhyme and his last chapter is called 'The Triumph of the Everyday'. Greenblatt's Shakespeare is never ashamed of his roots and can easily and happily retire to live among ordinary people at the end of his life. But ordinariness is beautiful, by contrast with the tragic world of English Catholicism from which Greenblatt sees the poet as emerging. His first chapter opens 'Let us imagine', and one of his invitations to 'imagine' involves a meeting between the young Shakespeare and Edmund Campion. Campion's works are looked at in some detail, although Greenblatt goes on to admit that the meeting probably never happened, and his reading of the plays suggests that mysticism and martyrdom meant little to the poet outside an erotic context. To explain the apparent contradiction, he, like Wood and Wilson, invokes the traumatic effect of the torturing of members of the persecuted minority to which Shakespeare belonged. Entering London for the first time, the future dramatist could have seen on London Bridge the heads of several Catholics – some from his part of the world, some possibly

[25] See John Finnis and Patrick Martin, 'Another turn for the *Turtle*: Shakespeare's Intercession for *Love's Martyr*', *Times Literary Supplement* (18 April 2003), pp. 14–16, and subsequent correspondence. The source, not named in Wood's book, was pointed out by some reviewers and noted by Finnis in a message to the Shaksper Listserv (www.shaksper.net/archives/2003/2125.html).

[26] Jonathan Gibson, 'Cherchez la femme: Mary Wroth and Shakespeare's Sonnets', *Times Literary Supplement* (13 August, 2004), pp. 12–13. Gibson suggests, in the light of her affair with Pembroke, her brunette appearance and her participation in *The Masque of Blackness*, that she might have been the Dark Lady.

[27] Stephen Greenblatt, *Will in the World: How Shakespeare Became Shakespeare* (New York and London, 2004).

even known to him. This, Greenblatt thinks, would have encouraged him to cover his tracks as much as possible, avoid leaving a paper trail and keep his feelings to himself – revealing them, paradoxically, in those purchases of land, which give us several of his signatures (58). His will, ungracious as it sounds in many respects, can also be seen as a final expression of love for his eldest daughter and her husband (389). Greenblatt offers a clear and beautifully written narrative, interpretation more than biography, though, like Duncan-Jones, he achieves clarity in part by omission (of, e.g., most of the early histories and late romances, the non-narrative poems that aren't in sonnet form and the possibility of collaboration).

E. K. Chambers, in 1930, mentioned the speculations on where Shakespeare got the books that were sources for his plays: 'Did he borrow from the Earl of Southampton, or from Jonson or from Camden, or did he merely turn over their leaves on the stationers' stalls?' These, he declared, were 'foolish questions, to which I propose no answers'.[28] Most people now would think that they are very good questions, and the years since Chambers wrote have brought other equally interesting ones. Did Shakespeare visit the printing house of his fellow Stratfordian, Richard Field? Did the theatre company think it worthwhile to invest in copies of Plutarch and Holinshed, given the extensive use made of them by the house dramatist? What these questions don't lead to, or at least have not yet led to, are answers and this is why Chambers thought they were foolish. Modern biographers of Shakespeare would be lost if they were not allowed to ask unanswerable questions. It is the sheer number of these – or sometimes the tentative answers offered by bolder authors – that swells a chronology into a book.

Should they be asking other questions? At the conference on 'Writing About Shakespeare', on which this *Survey* volume is based, James Shapiro argued for a rethinking of the form of the Shakespeare biography. His own decision – to focus on a single year in the writer's life – produced marvellous results. However, I would guess that most biographies are the product of a publisher's desire for a book that will supersede, rather than complement, all previous ones. This usually means a cradle-to-the-grave structure, critical accounts of the works and as much information about context, afterlife and the current state of criticism as the word limit allows. Of course, the project is both ridiculous and redundant. The one question that all biographers want to answer, and cannot, is the source, not of the plays, but of what Lee called 'the secret springs of poetic inspiration'. Mapping the human genome may seem simple by comparison. Yet, given the complex encoding involved in both, the multiplication of questions, contexts and micro-facts, for all its repetition and wild experimentation, may after all be the right approach to take.

---

[28] E. K. Chambers, *William Shakespeare, a Study of Facts and Problems*, 2 vols. (Oxford, 1930), vol. 1, p. 23.

# TOWARD A NEW BIOGRAPHY OF SHAKESPEARE

JAMES SHAPIRO

Shakespeare biography hasn't changed much in the past hundred years. With few exceptions, those who write about his life continue to obsess over a handful of issues that have little to do with what or how he wrote – from his sexual inclinations to his pursuit of status to his decision to leave his wife a 'second best' bed. Because most of his biographers accept as a matter of faith the Wordsworthian notion that 'the child is father of the man,' a disproportionate amount of attention has also been devoted to finding in Shakespeare's early and 'lost' years – rather than, say, the first few years of his writing and acting career in London – the key to what made Shakespeare Shakespeare. Over time, the emphasis has changed, though the premise that his early years were crucial has not: Shakespeare the poacher, butcher's apprentice, soldier, lawyer's clerk and schoolteacher have all had their day and are currently supplanted by Shakespeare the crypto-Catholic. Given the absence of hard evidence to support such claims, the biographer's search has usually begun not in the archives but in the plays themselves, which are ransacked for clues that can be read back into anecdotal accounts of his early years (and since the plays contain a vast range of experiences, this is not as hard to do as it may sound). Unless one believes that the plays are two-way mirrors, it is difficult not to conclude that this approach is ultimately circular and arbitrary.

Traditional cradle-to-grave biographies of Shakespeare also share the unspoken assumption that what makes people who they are now also made people who they were back then. I'm not so sure. Because almost nobody thought to write a memoir or keep a personal diary in Shakespeare's day – revealing enough facts in themselves – we don't know whether the emotional lives of early modern English men and women were like ours. Their formative years certainly weren't. Childhood was brief, and adolescents, rich and poor, were sent from home to live and serve in other households. Plague, death in childbirth, harvest-failures and high infant-mortality rates may have diminished the intensity of family bonds. And these bonds didn't last as long: people lived, on the average, until their mid-forties (only one of Shakespeare's seven brothers and sisters made it past forty-six). Eldest sons like Shakespeare inherited all, creating friction among siblings. Though life was shorter, most Elizabethans delayed marriage until their mid-twenties (and a surprising proportion, including Shakespeare's three brothers, never married at all). Given the extremely low illegitimacy rates at the time, premarital desire must have either been sublimated or found an outlet in non-procreative sex – perhaps both. Even the meaning of such concepts as individuality was different. Writers, including Shakespeare, were only beginning to speak of 'individual' in the modern sense of 'distinctive' or 'special', the exact opposite of what it had long meant, 'inseparable'. This was also an age of faith, or at the least one in which church attendance was mandatory; religion, too played a greater role in shaping how life, death and the afterlife were imagined.[1] All this suggests that, as much as we might want Shakespeare to have been like us, he wasn't. We call this period early modern or pre-modern for good reason.

We know all this, yet collectively remain reluctant to ask whether the time has come to abandon the questionable assumptions and stale conventions that govern the writing of Shakespeare's life. It didn't have to turn out this way – and probably wouldn't have if Thomas Heywood's ambitious Jacobean 'Lives of All the Poets Modern and Foreign' had not vanished without a trace[2] or if seventeenth-century antiquarians like John Ward bothered to speak with Shakespeare's younger daughter, Judith, who was still alive after the Restoration (Ward made a note to contact her in 1662 but she died before he managed to do so and, with her, a direct and intimate sense of the kind of man Shakespeare was and how he spent his time).[3] A few more facts – or even anecdotes that weren't so obviously second or third-hand – might have put the lie to current, often wild, speculation about how Shakespeare became Shakespeare.

Unfairly or not, I blame John Heminges and Henry Condell for the ossified state of Shakespeare biography and for the difficulties we now face in accounting for Shakespeare's development as a writer. Having spent most of their adult lives performing in Shakespeare's plays they knew the sequence in which all but the earliest plays had been written. But when they put together the 1623 Folio they abandoned the chronological order of their model, Ben Jonson's 1616 Folio, choosing instead to shoehorn Shakespeare's plays into the categories of Comedies, Histories and Tragedies (which made for a very uncomfortable fit for 'tragedies' like *Cymbeline* and *Troilus and Cressida*). Even within these categories they ignored the order in which the plays were written, so that, for instance, *The Tempest* is the lead comedy in the First Folio. And, unlike Jonson, they made no mention of where and by whom each play had been performed. Heminges and Condell's decision to take Shakespeare out of time and place made it much easier for subsequent critics to conclude, as Coleridge did, that a transcendent Shakespeare wrote 'exactly as if of another planet'.[4] Some of the most popular one-volume editions of Shakespeare's works still organize the works by genre, and most of us, in our teaching, are more likely to speak of *Henry V* as part of an historical tetralogy that began four years earlier with *Richard II*, than we are to emphasize its connections to plays like *Julius Caesar* or *As You Like It*, written at much the same time, with which it shares a different set of preoccupations.

Shakespeare himself seems to have taken for granted that 'the purpose of playing' was to show, as Hamlet put it, 'the very age and body of the time his form and pressure' (3.2.20–4). But to see how Shakespeare's plays managed to do so depends upon knowing when each one was written. And with the deaths of Richard Burbage, Thomas Pope, Heminges and Condell, that knowledge too disappeared. Over a century and a half passed before Edmond Malone tried to tackle the question of Shakespeare's development in his 'Attempt to Ascertain the Order in Which the Plays of Shakespeare were Written'. Few were more steeped in Shakespeare scholarship than Malone, and yet the best that he could initially determine was that Shakespeare wrote *Hamlet* in 1596 and *Henry VIII* in 1601, that *The Winter's Tale* (1604) preceded *Lear* (1605), while *Julius Caesar* (1607) followed both *Cymbeline* (1605) and *Macbeth* (1606).

---

[1] The literature on early modern social history is vast. See, for example, Ralph A. Houlbrooke, *The English Family, 1450–1700* (London, 1984); J. A. Sharpe, *Early Modern England: A Social History, 1550–1760* (1987; 2nd edn, London, 1997); Martin Ingram, *Church Courts, Sex and Marriage in England, 1570–1640* (Cambridge, 1987); and David Cressy, *Birth, Marriage, and Death: Ritual, Religion, and the Life-Cycle in Tudor and Stuart England* (Oxford, 1997).

[2] See S. Schoenbaum, *Shakespeare's Lives*, new edn (Oxford, 1991), p. 83. Heywood's book was mentioned in 1614 and again in 1635.

[3] See E. K. Chambers, *William Shakespeare: A Study of Facts and Problems*, 2 vols. (Oxford, 1930), vol. 2, pp. 249–50.

[4] As cited in C. J. Sisson, *The Mythical Sorrow of Shakespeare*. Annual Shakespeare Lecture of the British Academy, 1934. From the Proceedings of the British Academy, vol. 20 (London, 1934), p. 6.

Malone's Shakespeare ended his career with a curious trio of plays: *Othello* (1611), *The Tempest* (1612) and *Twelfth Night* (1614).[5] It comes as no surprise that he made so little headway in linking the plays more securely to their times. Two centuries later we are still unsure of the exact order of the plays, especially the earliest ones. And for all that has been written about Shakespeare, we remain almost as far as ever from answering the question of how, in the course of a year or so, the author of competent but unspectacular plays like *Much Ado* and *The Merry Wives of Windsor*, went on to write *Hamlet*.

We need alternative approaches to writing Shakespeare's life and in the past few years we've begun to see a few that in important ways break with convention, such as Katherine Duncan-Jones's emphasis on scenes from his life.[6] I'd like to propose another approach, an experiment that risks a different kind of arbitrariness and circularity but that at least has the advantage of making use of a great deal of information that is currently overlooked. I'm urging that we begin writing partial or micro-biographies that focus intensely on specific years (or even shorter periods) of Shakespeare's creative life.[7] These studies would ignore Shakespeare's early and retirement years and focus exclusively on the years that matter most, the quarter-century in which he wrote and acted. Because biographers are led by convention to take us from birth to death and beyond, these years are almost always given short shrift. Any biography that devotes to each of these years more than twenty pages or so would quickly swell to an unpublishable length. Yet a period like 1595–6, when Shakespeare wrote, at the least, *Romeo and Juliet*, *A Midsummer Night's Dream*, *Richard II*, *The Merchant of Venice*, *1 Henry IV* and probably some sonnets as well, or 1605–1606, when Shakespeare appears to have written *Macbeth*, *Lear* and *Antony and Cleopatra*, deserve considerably more attention than biographers traditionally have given them.[8] Other years, especially early on his career, cry out for more patient unpacking of what Shakespeare read, wrote and acted in, the circles he moved in, the places he is recorded to have visited either in London or on tour, and, most of all, his engagement in what was going on in the world around him that shaped his plays and poems.

Such an approach could begin to address questions that biographers habitually sidestep: did Shakespeare come to London as an aspiring poet seeking patronage, as an actor, or as a hopeful playwright? Did he write plays in inspired bunches or contract with his playing company for a couple of plays a year? Were there relatively fallow periods in his career, such as the years between the completion of *Hamlet* and the accession of the King of Scots? How did the nature of his collaboration with other dramatists change over time? What do changes in his writing style – from metrics and rhetorical figures like hendiadys to his use of prose and of soliloquy – reveal? And to what extent did his plays engage topical concerns and did the nature of this engagement change over time? I suspect that scholars, freed of existing teleologies of Shakespeare's development and focusing on different moments in his career, would arrive at markedly different answers to these questions – and there would be, for the first time in a while, a basis for constructive debate about the contours of Shakespeare's writing life.

I urge this approach having spent much of the past decade or so researching Shakespeare's life and times in the course of 1599. One thing I learned by simply keeping a calendar of what happened in the course of a year is that dates we have long taken

[5] Malone's essay was first published in 1778. I have consulted a reprint of it in Edmond Malone, ed., *The Plays and Poems of William Shakespeare*, 16 vols. (Dublin, 1794), vol. 1, pp. 225–6.

[6] Katherine Duncan-Jones, *Ungentle Shakespeare: Scenes from his Life* (London, 2001).

[7] I am indebted here to Simon Jarvis, who first argued in the pages of the *Times Literary Supplement* (in a review of Claire Harman's biography of Fanny Burney, 10 June 1999) against the 'deadening convention' of 'total' biography, in favour of 'partial lives'. For Jarvis, cradle-to-grave biography is 'a genre which has become quiescent to the point (if we can hope for so much) of its demise'.

[8] Though for the latter group of plays, see the instructive discussion in Leeds Barroll, *Politics, Plague, and Shakespeare's Theatre: The Stuart Years* (Ithaca, NY, 1991).

for granted may be suspect. That truth universally acknowledged – that the Swiss tourist Thomas Platter saw a play about Julius Caesar on 21 September 1599 – is almost certainly off by ten days. While Platter himself says he saw it on the twenty-first, his journal indicates that he mistakenly assumed that England, like France, which he had just visited, followed the so-called 'new style' or Gregorian calendar. It may seem a minor detail that he saw it on 11 September, rather than the twenty-first, but it is valuable information to theatre historians eager to know when the Globe was completed as well as to historians interested in what Platter witnessed at court later that month.[9]

My calendar of events revealed other serendipitous connections. I would not have otherwise known that Edmund Spenser was at Whitehall when Shakespeare performed there, twice, in the closing days of 1598 or that a desperate Earl of Essex was riding home from Ireland to confront Elizabeth at Nonsuch Palace in late September 1599 at the very moment that the cream of England's merchant class was gathering in London to establish the East India Company. Without a calendar, I'd also never have known that Shakespeare and his fellow players performed at Richmond Palace on Shrove Tuesday (for which Shakespeare wrote a special epilogue) the evening before one of England's leading preachers, Lancelot Andrewes, gave an Ash Wednesday sermon 'before Queen Elizabeth at Richmond . . . at What Time the Earl of Essex was Going Forth, upon the Expedition for Ireland'.[10] If Shakespeare were still revising *Henry V*, Andrewes's war sermon could be seen as a new source; even if *Henry V* was completed by this time, the sermon clarifies what contemporaries expected from 'the General of our gracious Empress' (*Henry V*, 5.0.30).

Micro-biography that attends to time and place is likely to enlarge our understanding of what besides printed sources and earlier plays inspired Shakespeare. *Julius Caesar* offers a useful example. Though most of the royal residences where Shakespeare performed are no longer standing, we know from contemporary accounts of their treasures that Shakespeare would have encountered at these palaces many artistic renderings of Caesar's story. Foreign visitors who toured Nonsuch at this time were struck by its exterior, 'built entirely of great blocks of white stone on which are represented numerous Roman and other ancient stories'. Continuing this architectural theme, 'above the doors of the inner court' stood 'stone statues of three Roman emperors'. Elizabeth's palace at Greenwich housed a bust of Julius Caesar. And when Shakespeare and his fellow players visited Hampton Court, they would have seen displayed in the room next to Elizabeth's quarters 'a gold embroidered tapestry on the walls' which 'told the history of the murder of Julius Caesar, the first emperor'. If that were not enough, by 'the door stood three of the emperor's electors in customary dress painted in life-like fashion'. It seems that the desired effect of the *trompe-d'oeil* was to make viewers feel as though they were momentarily transported back in time. As they stood near the large tapestry of Caesar's assassination and faced the three life-like Roman electors painted by the door, did onlookers feel like co-conspirators or witnesses to a heinous political crime? And at Whitehall, Shakespeare could have seen yet another portrait of Caesar.[11] This evidence, largely ignored by

[9] When Platter left his native Switzerland and began his travels he used the Old Style dating of that Protestant country; when he arrived in France he was careful to switch to New Style (Seán Bennet, trans., *Journal of a Younger Brother: The Life of Thomas Platter as a Medical Student in Montpellier at the Close of the Sixteenth Century* [London, 1963]). But Platter fails to do the same when leaving France for England or returning to France (*Thomas Platter's Travels in England, 1599*, Clare Williams, ed. and trans. [London, 1937]). Platter's consistent mention of the days of the month on which Sundays fall while he is in England (it is the only day of the week that he ever mentions) confirms (despite a few dates that he clearly gets wrong) that Platter assumed that the English followed the Gregorian or New Style calendar – and that we need to adjust his dating accordingly.

[10] The sermon was first printed in Lancelot Andrewes, *Ninety-Six Sermons* (London, 1629).

[11] On images of Julius Caesar, see, for example. *The Diary of Baron Waldstein: A Traveller in Elizabethan England*, G. W. Groos, trans. and ed. (London, 1981), pp. 45, 71, 147, 149; and *Thomas Platter's Travels in England, 1599*, pp. 202, 223, 224.

biographers and editors, offers an opportunity to revisit the extent to which Shakespeare's play was inspired by, and perhaps reacted to, visual representations of Caesar and his 'murder'.

Another example, again from 1599, stands as a model of how much information the smallest of details can yield. I'm indebted here to the detective work of Alan Nelson.[12] Around 1599, George Buc – government servant, Member of Parliament, writer, and theatregoer – sought out Shakespeare's advice about the authorship of an anonymous play he had recently purchased. Like everyone in the theatre world, Shakespeare knew that Buc was next in line for Edmund Tilney's job as Master of the Revels, so we can assume he would have done his best to help him. Buc was also one of the first serious collectors of Elizabethan drama. And though Buc's play collection has since broken up, his handwriting has been identified in copies of sixteen plays now scattered in archives around the world. We know from his marginalia that Buc purchased at least four old plays belatedly published in 1599: *Alphonsus King of Aragon*, *Edward I*, *Sir Clymon and Clamydes*, and *George a Greene, the Pinner of Wakefield*. While all were published anonymously, Buc was well enough informed to write on their title pages that Robert Greene was the author of *Alphonsus* and George Peele of *Sir Clymon* and *Edward I*. He was stumped, though, by *George a Greene*. The group of plays overlaps with those Shakespeare may have consulted this year – for in the course of writing *As You Like It*, he probably looked at the depictions of Robin Hood in *George a Greene* and *Edward I*, and may have lifted the name of the old shepherd Corin from *Clymon and Clamydes*.

After purchasing *George a Greene*, probably at Cuthbert Burby's shop near the Royal Exchange, Buc went about finding out who wrote it, at which point he either ran into or sought out Shakespeare. Shakespeare recalled that the play had been written by a minister, though at this point his memory failed him: he couldn't remember the minister's name. The oversight was excusable. It had been over a decade since the play was first staged. But Shakespeare was able to volunteer an unusual bit of information: the minister had acted in it himself, playing the pinner's part. A grateful Buc scribbled on the play's title page his findings: 'Written by —— a minister, who acted the pinner's part in it himself. *Teste* [i.e., witnessed by] W. Shakespeare'. He'd have to fill in that blank another time. Buc's note offers a glimpse, if only a fleeting one, of a Shakespeare in 1599 who was recognized as an authority on the increasingly distant Elizabethan theatrical past – he alone of all the dramatists at work at the end of the previous decade was still writing plays. This is also one of the earliest indications that authorship mattered and plays were worth collecting. But more than this, it's a flesh and blood encounter that tells us something about Shakespeare's habits, his approachability, what it was like to talk with Shakespeare, what kinds of details stuck in Shakespeare's memory, even where he may have spent time and collected ideas for his plays. Not all of Shakespeare's encounters have to be invented.

All the examples that I've offered appear in printed texts or facsimiles long available to scholars. Indeed, because of the Internet, scholars can now easily access virtually every book published in Shakespeare's lifetime. And there is a great deal more information that can illuminate Shakespeare's life and work in standard sources like the Acts of the Privy Council, the voluminous published state papers and the Stationers Register. Even Henslowe's *Diary* can be usefully revisited to tease out the comings and going of various playwrights. Should we take the extended disappearance of Anthony Munday, Robert Wilson, Richard Hathaway and Michael Drayton from Henslowe's records in the early months of 1599 as an indication that they were now writing for the Chamberlain's Men?[13] And if so, what does that in turn

[12] See Alan H. Nelson, 'George Buc, William Shakespeare, and the Folger *George a Greene*', *Shakespeare Quarterly* 49 (1998), 74–83. For more on Buc, see Mark Eccles, 'Sir George Buc, Master of the Revels', in *Sir Thomas Lodge and Other Elizabethans*, ed. C. J. Sisson (Cambridge, Mass, 1933), pp. 409–506. And for Buc's books, see Alan Nelson's website: http://socrates.berkeley.edu/~ahnelson/BUC/quartos.html.

[13] See the relevant entries in R. A. Foakes and R. T. Rickert, eds., *Henslowe's Diary* (Cambridge, 1961).

suggest about their collaborative *Sir John Oldcastle*, performed after their return to the Admiral's Men in November 1599, which so explicitly challenges Shakespeare's portrait of the Lollard martyr in the two parts of *Henry IV*? And might this in turn indicate that members of this team of playwrights were responsible for the otherwise anonymous plays Shakespeare's company performed at this time, including *Thomas Lord Cromwell*?

Unpublished records have the potential to yield even more valuable connections. I'm not suggesting that scholars will stumble on new allusions to Shakespeare – though it's likely that some are still out there. Rather, when the vast trove of surviving and unprinted materials from the period are sifted and examined within a chronological framework, details that once seemed insignificant can prove illuminating. Take for example Simon Forman's casebooks. Scholars have naturally focused on Forman's fascinating dreams or plot summaries of plays he saw. But other, less exciting entries have much to tell us as well, such as Forman's notes for April 1599, which describe how he eagerly and unsuccessfully sought the hand of 'Sara Archdel' three times in the course of ten days at the Curtain Theatre. Forman writes how on the '20 of aprill her Unkell & I met at the Courtean and went into the feld together', and two days later 'met at the Curtean againe and after walked in the fild'. A week later, on 29 April, Forman returned to 'the Ceurtren and ther she came & her Vnkell & frinds and sate before me and after the play we wente in to the filds together and soe I had some *p*ly with her but nothing of Any thinge totching the matter and she semed very kind & courteouse & I led her by the hand . . .'[14] Forman's notes should be of interest to theatre historians and biographers, for they strongly suggest that the Chamberlain's Men had not yet moved into the Globe and were still playing in the Northern suburbs in late April – and were popular enough to draw playgoers to the Curtain this frequently (though admittedly, the wooing plot unfolding in the field outside the Curtain mattered a great deal more to Forman than those of the unnamed plays staged within). His story also invites us to consider how the theatre had by this time become a convenient and eroticized space where such encounters could occur, where an excited Forman could sit behind and observe the object of his affections, and even, after the play, take her hand strolling outside the theatre. It wouldn't take many more such stories to deepen our sense of the place of Shakespeare's stage in Elizabethan culture.

Ben Jonson famously claimed in his poem in that First Folio that Shakespeare was 'for all time'. But before he wrote those words he first acknowledged that Shakespeare was the 'soul of the age' whose plays spoke with such immediacy to contemporary concerns. Jonson understood, far better than those who have since taken his claims for a timeless Shakespeare out of context, that the only way to be for all time was first to be of an age. If we are to grasp Shakespeare's personality, and his universality, we had best begin by putting him back in his time and place.

---

[14] Simon Forman's Casebooks, Bod. MS Ashmole 219/56r–58v. I am indebted to Robyn Adams for this transcription of Forman's difficult hand.

# JONSON, SHAKESPEARE AND THE EXORCISTS

RICHARD DUTTON

In *The Puritan* (published in 1607), there is a delightfully tongue-in-cheek moment when Captain Idle (a highwayman pretending to be a conjurer) explains his supposed scruples about conjuring to Sir Godfrey Plus, the principal target of his trickery:

> I understand that you are my Kinsmans good Maister, and in regard of that, the best of my skill is at your service: but had you fortunde a mere stranger, and made no meanes to me by acquaintance, I should have utterly denyed to have beene the man; both by reason of the *Act past in Parliament against Conjurers and Witches*, as also, because I would not have my Arte vulgar, trite, and common. (F2V)[1]

In other words: we all know what you are asking me to do is illegal (I can even cite the precise statute), but seeing as you are a gentleman and vouched for by my kinsman, I am prepared to employ my skills for you *in private*. The statute referred to dated from 1604 and was not against conjuring and witchcraft *per se* (which were covered by other laws) but was aimed at persons 'taking upon them by witchcraft &c., to tell or declare in what place any treasure of gold or silver should or might be found or had in the earth or other secret places'.

That is, it was a law against pseudo-supernatural con-trickery, which is doubly funny in context, because the whole point of this con is to *restore* to Sir Godfrey a gold chain that has previously been 'borrowed'. The con itself is splendidly theatrical (4.2. in modern editions), with Idle laying out a 'circle' that might have been taken from the props for *Dr Faustus*, to the accompaniment of timely 'thunder' and 'lightning'. So the text and its players tacitly acknowledge the parallels between their own art (which God forbid anyone should dismiss as 'vulgar, trite, and common') and pseudo-supernatural con-trickery. They also acknowledge the laws by which such practices are supposedly contained. There is a parallel sequence of self-referentiality earlier in the play, which almost certainly dates the play in 1606. At the entry of Corporal Oath (described in the stage direction as 'a Vaine-glorious fellow') he encounters the dim-witted servants of the play's eponymous puritan widow:

> NICHOLAS What Corporall Oth? I am sorry we have met with you next our hearts; you are the man we are forbidden to keepe company withal, wee must not sweare I can tell you, and you have the name for swearing. (B4V)

This is of course familiar anti-puritan satire, mocking their insistence on the letter and show of divine law, while often ignoring its substance and spirit. But it is surely overlaid here with reference to the Act to Restrain Abuses of Players (May 1606), which forbade the jesting or profane utterance on stage of the name of God or members of the Trinity. In such a context, the very introduction of a character called Corporal Oath cocks a snook at Parliament's prissy legislation, while the

[1] Quoted from the Huntington Library copy of the 1607 quarto of *The Puritaine, or the Widdow of Watlingstreete*, as reproduced in *Early English Books Online*. The text is anonymous but often ascribed to Middleton.

subsequent jokes about him ('if you swear once, we shall all fall down in a swoon presently!') play with the audience's half-expectation that the law is about to be broken – and that they are supposed to feel suitably outraged by this.

*The Puritan* is an entertaining context in which to reconsider the issue of exorcism in *King Lear*, and alongside that the same subject in Jonson's *Volpone*. It neatly demonstrates that the early Jacobean players knew all too well about the legal framework (and other official sanctions) governing matters of divinity and supernatural con-trickery, and also how these related to the theatrical profession. And that they had their ways of commenting about these matters. This seems to me an important consideration in revisiting that most influential discussion of exorcism and *King Lear*, Stephen Greenblatt's 'Shakespeare and the Exorcists'.[2] This is a characteristically subtle and wide-ranging essay, with a fascinating thesis about the relationship between the suppression of Roman Catholic religious practices and the role of theatre in early modern England, issues which Greenblatt has developed in subsequent work.[3] Yet the essay itself is very narrowly focused, dealing almost exclusively with the relationship between Shakespeare's play and Samuel Harsnett's *A Declaration of Egregious Popish Impostures* (1603, reprinted 1604, 1605) and, to a lesser extent, his earlier *Discovery of the Fraudulent Practices of J. Darrel* (1599). There is no discussion of other plays that deal with exorcism (as *Volpone* does), or with other measures dealing with exorcism (such as James I's own interventions in this fertile field), or with legislation such as the 1604 Act discussed above dealing with other 'supernatural' matters. Greenblatt wants to keep this very much a textual exchange between Harsnett's books (in particular their widespread use of theatrical metaphor to expose and characterize the nature of the 'impostures' with which they deal) and Shakespeare's play; and he wants to focus exclusively on exorcism, rather than other supernatural dabblings, because its practice is especially theatrical in nature, in a context where he argues that theatre is 'the indelible mark of falsity, tawdriness, and rhetorical manipulation' (p. 112).[4]

Observing that *King Lear* is 'haunted by a sense of rituals and beliefs that are no longer efficacious, that have been emptied out' (p. 119), Greenblatt argues that 'at the moment when official religious and secular institutions are, for their own reasons, abjuring the ritual they themselves once fostered, Shakespeare's theatre moves to appropriate it' (pp. 125–6). We pass from the age of miracles and magic to a liberal humanist world that is haunted only by the echoes and memories of dead sacraments. Shakespeare's quite limited quotation of Harsnett is a remarkably narrow basis for a reading of a shift in the culture of such proportions. In support of that reading Harsnett is cast as a centrist representative of 'the established and state-supported Church of England' (p. 96), while Shakespeare becomes the representative of an institution which plays into that state's agenda: 'The official church dismantles and cedes to the players the powerful mechanisms of an unwanted and dangerous charisma; in return the players confirm the charge that those mechanisms are theatrical and hence illusory' (p. 120). This is how the thesis is phrased at its most provocative: 'When in 1603 Harsnett was whipping exorcism toward the theatre, Shakespeare was already at the entrance to the Globe to welcome it' (p. 115).

This powerfully seductive thesis has been challenged from a number of angles, not least by Gary Taylor, who demonstrates that actual ritual

[2] Quotations will be from the version of the essay printed in *Shakespearian Negotiations* (Berkeley, 1988), pp. 94–128.

[3] I am thinking in particular of *Hamlet in Purgatory* (Princeton, 2002).

[4] For a detailed recent account of the Roman Catholic threat to which Harsnett responded – 'the way in which Counter Reformation priests sent to England after 1574 cultivated and harnessed the culture of the miraculous in their efforts to reform and evangelize the populace and to defend doctrines and practices assaulted by Protestant polemicists' – see Alexandra Walsham, 'Miracles and the Counter-Reformation Mission to England', *The History Journal*, 46.4 (2003) 779–813, abstract. Although Harsnett wrote about Jesuit practices in the 1580s, largely because such full documentation was to hand, Roman Catholic claims to supernatural powers continued to be an issue well into the seventeenth century. John Darrell, whose activities Harsnett first exposed, was a Puritan.

by no means disappeared from the stage as Greenblatt argues, nor was it necessarily travestied, even if it took on alien forms: 'the divine presence most often incarnate on the early modern English stage was not Protestant or Catholic, but pagan'.[5] While conceding that 'Greenblatt's essay is our most sophisticated critical account of the relationship between early modern religion and theatre, and it fits Middleton well', he nevertheless resists its totalizing thrust: 'The absence from *King Lear* of real demonic possession, or real devils, does not prove that the essence of the divine has been emptied out of Shakespeare's theatre' (p. 21). On the contrary, he suggests that pagan ritual – singling out as a key instance the sacrificing to Fortuna in Jonson's *Sejanus* – provides a powerfully coded analogue for old Catholic rites: 'Shakespeare acted in Jonson's *Sejanus*, and his own late plays follow Jonson's lead: they give us, not a Brechtian emptying out of Christian mythology, but the commodification of a specifically Catholic affect' (p. 24).

Taylor does not pursue the point, but his argument concurs in significant ways with those who believe that Shakespeare was a life-long covert Catholic, and that his quotation in *King Lear* of Harsnett's virulent anti-Jesuit, anti-Catholic propaganda is in the spirit of a repudiation of it, rather than collusion with it.[6] Greenblatt is notably cagey on this point, and particularly the fact that in 1610 *Lear* was, with *Pericles*, in the repertoire of travelling players in Yorkshire who catered for recusant audiences.[7] With some apparent surprise, he suggests: 'It is difficult to resist the conclusion that someone in Stuart Yorkshire believed that *King Lear*, despite its apparent staging of a fraudulent possession, was not hostile, was strangely sympathetic even, to the situation of persecuted Catholics' (p. 122). Some Jacobeans, it would seem, were not attending properly to the text!

There are other possible flaws in Greenblatt's argument. One may well lie in casting Harsnett as an apparatchik in the state machine, when actually he was a rather more complex character, and very far from being a Calvinist iconoclast. An Arminian *avant la lettre* he had preached (when the Calvinist influence on the Anglican Church was as high as it ever would be) at St Paul's Cross against the Calvinist doctrine of double predestination, earning a stinging rebuke from Archbishop Whitgift. Later in his career, as a bishop, he was to face complaints from Calvinists about his insistence on matters of church protocol, such as the wearing of vestments, which would eventually be identified with the reforms of Archbishop Laud.[8] Since it was the Calvinists who were leading the drive within the Church of England to minimize 'popish' ritual and superstition, Harsnett is an odd man to cast as their agent. He was also the hapless press censor who passed for the press – without much more than a glance, he claimed – Dr John Hayward's *Life and History of Henry IV*, which became such an issue during the Essex crisis.[9] It was surely only Richard Bancroft's patronage which kept him secure, but Bancroft too was not the hard-line Calvinist his

[5] Gary Taylor, 'Divine [ ]Sences', *Shakespeare Survey 54* (Cambridge, 2001), pp. 13–30, 14.

[6] See, notably, Richard Wilson, *Secret Shakespeare: Studies in Theatre, Religion and Resistance* (Manchester, 2004).

[7] See most recently on this Phebe Jensen; 'Recusancy, Festivity, and Community' in *Region, Religion and Patronage: Lancastrian Shakespeare*, ed. R. Dutton, A. Findlay and R. Wilson (Manchester, 2003), pp. 101–120.

[8] Harsnett's career is most fully outlined in F. W. Brownlow, *Shakespeare, Harsnett, and the Devils of Denham* (Newark, DE, 1996). The Devon Puritan, Walter Yonge, was appalled in 1624 to hear from afar of Harsnett's Arminian practices: 'the Bishop of Norwich, Doctor Harsnett . . . silenced all the preachers that preached in the forenoon, and caused images to be set up in churches, and the picture of the Holy Ghost over the font; and excommunicated many, and would not absolve them under 20 £ a piece. The King commended him for it': *The Diary of Walter Yonge, Esq*, ed. George Roberts, Camden Society 41 (1848), p. 75. Yonge is a useful witness to several features of my argument precisely because he was so far removed from London and only caught wind of some of the most lurid and persistent rumours. My point is very often what was *thought* to be happening, rather than necessarily what *was* happening – all of which he filters through his Puritan sensibility.

[9] See 'Buggeswords: the Case of Sir John Hayward's *Life of Henry IV*' in Richard Dutton, *Licensing, Censorship and Authorship in Early Modern England* (Basingstoke, 2000), pp. 162–91.

predecessor Whitgift had been, or indeed his successor George Abbot was to be.[10]

More critically perhaps, I think Greenblatt is wrong to ascribe Harsnett's satirical denunciations of Jesuit (and, remember, Puritan) exorcisms to a pre-Enlightenment desire to take the rituals of exorcism out of the religious equation altogether. He certainly did want to confine the spiritual authority to conduct exorcisms to the Church of England and to reduce the incidence of such events from the disturbing frequency with which they had occurred in recent years – an aim doubtless largely achieved in the canons emanating from the 1604 Hampton Court conference, which severely restricted the freedom of even Anglican clerics to conduct such rituals.[11] The point, however, was not quietly to forget exorcism but (in line with Harsnett and Bancroft's proto-Arminianism) to exalt it to a high mystery, a rare remedy for rare occurrences, which only the highest authority of the Anglican church could sanction – nothing 'vile, trite, and common', as Captain Idle says of his pseudo-conjuring. So, for example, James I himself took an interest, notably in the case of Anne Gunter of Windsor, who in October 1605 was 'strangely possessed and bewitched, so that in her fits she cast out of her nose and mouth pins in great abundance, and did divers other things very strange to be reported'.[12] As in cases of witchcraft, James became more sceptical with experience than he had been when he wrote his *Daemonologie* (1597) – Harsnett's writing may have had an influence here – and he took satisfaction in uncovering frauds rather than conducting exorcisms. But this too could be a distinctly theatrical procedure, with the king at centre stage. And the point is that he ruled in such matters as Supreme Governor of the Church of England, one of the Anglican elite to whom Harsnett and his sympathetic superiors wanted such authority confined.

My critical differences with Greenblatt, however, focus most particularly on questions of tone and intention in the 'welcome' which Shakespeare (and Jonson) may be said to have extended to exorcism at the entrance to the Globe. In his reading of the appropriation of passages from the *Declaration* in *King Lear*, Greenblatt fails to acknowledge that Shakespeare drops the *language* of theatricality (to which Harsnett attaches most of the stigma) even as he translates them into theatrical form. That is, there is nothing *self-evidently* satirical or dismissive about the possession material as it appears in the play at all. This is a point noted by Amy Wolf, for example, when she argues that Shakespeare transmutes the strain of callousness in Harsnett's account of those who were subjected to quasi-theatrical exorcisms into something much more humane: 'Shakespeare uses the symbols, language, and details of Harsnett's *Declaration* to undermine the message of that pamphlet by contrasting possession with true madness, offering a sympathetic portrayal of demoniacs, and drawing a tragic portrait of human

10 On Harsnett and the stirrings in the early Jacobean period of what later might be called Arminianism or Laudianism, even affecting such a key figure as Robert Cecil, Earl of Salisbury, who made Harsnett one of his chaplains, see Pauline Croft, 'The Religion of Robert Cecil', *The Historical Journal*, 34.4 (1991) 773–96. Bancroft, hitherto Bishop of London, succeeded Whitgift as Archbishop of Canterbury in 1604 and was himself succeeded by George Abbot in 1608. Walter Yonge is typically revealing about the popular perception of Bancroft: 'In this parliament the archbishop Bancroft moved the higher house that the papists might have a toleration for four years; whereunto the bishop of Worcester replied, that it was pity they should be tolerated for seven days' (*Diary*, p. 6).

11 The Millenary Petition presented to King James by Puritans within the Church of England, who wanted its more thorough reformation, spoke of his godly subjects 'all groaning as under a common burden of human rites and ceremonies'. The Hampton Court conference was a response to the Petition, which however brought little about that the petitioners wanted. The restriction on officially sanctioned exorcisms was less a doctrinal issue than an attempt to rein in practices which had a habit of getting out of control.

12 Quoted from Yonge's *Diary*, p. 12. Yonge, away in Devon, does not actually mention James. See also *Hatfield House MSS*, XVIII, p. 450, and *The Journal of Sir Roger Wilbraham* (Camden Miscellany, X, London, 1902) for the end of October 1605. This episode is commonly cited in editions of *Volpone*, but less commonly in those of *King Lear*.

cruelty and evil that Harsnett's cynical politics do not admit.'[13]

Theatricality in *Lear* is not in fact marked by 'falsity, tawdriness, and rhetorical manipulation', unless we wish to argue in some reductive way that these are the inescapable hallmarks of the medium. Indeed, theatricality in this play is almost always a virtuous mode, not a vicious one – whether in the form of Kent's disguise, the Fool's brave 'performance' in the face of adversity, or Lear's 'trial' of Goneril and Regan. And this is particularly true in the case of Edgar, the character with whom the Harsnett exorcism material is most closely associated. His role as Poor Tom is not fraudulent in the way that the 'possessions' described in the *Declaration* are: it is not staged to enhance either his own authority or that of anyone who would rid him of his devils. It is an act of self-defence, which (ironically) is put on with the aim of becoming as anonymous as possible – and categorically not the centre of attention, as the poor devils in Harsnett inevitably are. Although he talks the language of possession, there is no evidence that he manifests startling physical symptoms – induced or otherwise – such as those of the *histerica passio* that Lear fears, or in the Anne Gunter case described above.[14] (This, as we shall see, is a major difference between *King Lear* and *Volpone*.)

And in the play's nearest equivalent to an actual exorcism – Gloucester's supposed leap off Dover Cliff – Edgar as Poor Tom (or perhaps as 'the foul fiend') is the exorcist, rather than the subject of ministration. His father is possessed by no exotic spirit, such as Flibbertigibbet, Modo or Mahu (11.97, 122), but by a black despair to which all mankind may be subject. Though this 'exorcism' is a notoriously absurd or 'absurdist' piece of theatre and only partially successful – Gloucester slumps back into 'ill thoughts' later (23.9), not without cause – it is, like Cordelia's subsequent revival of Lear from his sleep of madness, an act of love. Tough love, as some would say today, and palpably not an attempt to generate false spiritual authority. What Greenblatt's analysis most crucially leaves out is the possibility that the artifice of theatre is not always a matter of *emptying out*, of disillusionment, as Harsnett does indeed imply; it is often an act of compassion and sometimes (not least in Shakespeare) of magic. That is surely the issue of those 'pagan' religious rites identified by Gary Taylor in the late plays, and not entirely forgotten – if muted – even here. If those recusants in Yorkshire were off-message about *King Lear*, the text gave them good reason to be.

A comparison with *Volpone* is instructive here, though it is striking that the critical traditions associated with these two great plays have rarely made much of their closeness in time (they cannot be more than a year apart, and may well be much closer) or of their common themes – one of which is diabolic possession.[15] This may well be because, although Jonson is in some respects much closer in spirit to Harsnett than Shakespeare is, he does not quote directly from his works, a fact which may be telling in itself. The notion of possession is consistently associated with the intensely theatrical fraud perpetrated by Volpone and Mosca, and Mosca's very name links him with Beelzebub, the Lord of the Flies. If the theme of possession recurs throughout the play (cf. 2.6.85, 96; 3.7.46–7, 277; 5.2.24, 28; 5.9.8; 5.10.10, 5.12. 9–10), it surfaces in all its theatrical splendour at the very end.[16] It is in fact the very last twist of a famously convoluted plot that the lawyer, Voltore, feigns possession in a bid to prevent the truth coming to light:

---

[13] Amy Wolf, 'Shakespeare and Harsnett: "Pregnant to Good Pity"?' *Studies in English Literature*, 38 (1998), 251–64, p. 252.

[14] *The History of King Lear*, 7.222. Quoted from *The Norton Shakespeare*, ed. Stephen Greenblatt *et al.* (New York, 1997).

[15] *Volpone* is certainly a response to the Gunpowder Plot, as I discuss; *King Lear* may well be too: see Nina Taunton and Valerie Hart, '*King Lear*, King James and the Gunpowder Treason of 1605', *Renaissance Studies*, 17 (2003) 695–715. See Stephen Musgrove's *Shakespeare and Jonson*, The Macmillan Brown Lectures 1957 (Auckland, 1957), pp. 21–39, for an ahistorical account of the close thematic links between the two plays.

[16] References are to the R. B. Parker's Revels Plays Edition, *Volpone, or the Fox* (rev. edn, Manchester, 1999).

VOLPONE Sir, you may redeem it.
They said you were possessed: fall down and seem so.
I'll help to make it good. *Voltore falls.*
God bless the man!
[*Aside to Voltore.*] Stop your wind hard, and swell.
[*Aloud.*] See, see, see, see!
He vomits crooked pins! His eyes are set
Like a dead hare's hung in a poulter's shop!
His mouth's running away! [*To Corvino.*] Do you see, Signor?
Now 'tis in his belly –
CORVINO Ay, the devil!
VOLPONE Now in his throat –
CORVINO Ay, I perceive it plain.
VOLPONE 'Twill out, 'twill out! Stand clear. See where it flies
In shape of a blue toad with a bat's wings!
[*To Corbaccio.*] Do not you see it, sir?
CORBACCIO What? I think I do.
CORVINO 'Tis too manifest.
VOLPONE Look! he comes t'himself!
VOLTORE Where am I?
VOLPONE Take good heart, the worst is past, sir.
You are dispossessed.
1 AVOCATORE What accident is this?
2 AVOCATORE Sudden, and full of wonder!
3 AVOCATORE If he were
Possessed, as it appears, all this is nothing.
[*He indicates Voltore's statement.*]
CORVINO He has been often subject to these fits.
(5.12.21–38)

Here we have the precise clinical depiction, not of possession but of the theatrically generated illusion of possession (and Volpone's vain last bid to retain authority by command by it). This is the stuff of Harsnett's book and what Shakespeare consistently fails to reproduce. But this is neither to say that Jonson agrees with Harsnett nor that he sets himself in opposition to Shakespeare: on the contrary, I think we may say that both men repudiate the authority which Harsnett represents, but they do so by characteristically different inflections of the theatrical medium.

*Volpone*, I suggest, is an anti-Cecil play, written in the wake of the Gunpowder Plot, where Jonson himself was one of those who suffered under the crack-down on recusants that followed. I have developed some of the argument for this suggestion in a recent article, exploring the play's distinctive use of beast fable (and most specifically of fox-lore) in relation to the repeated use of such material to satirize the *regnum Cecilianum*, the rule of father and son – William Cecil, Lord Burghley and Sir Robert Cecil, Earl of Salisbury – in the period.[17] Both men were commonly nicknamed 'the fox', and were repeatedly characterized by their enemies as self-seeking upstarts who, with a hypocritical show of Protestant zeal, lined the family nest by the exactions placed on recusant Catholics. This charge surfaced with renewed ferocity after the Gunpowder Plot, which Robert Cecil was widely seen as fomenting in his own interest. Walter Yonge (no friend of recusants) records the charge: 'there were divers pasquils and libels cast about in London by a certain papist against the Earl of Sarum, Sir Robert Cicell, charging him to be the only match which kindled the King's displeasure against the Roman Catholics, wishing him to desist if he tendered his own life and safety. One of which he himself answered, and is extant in print' (*Diary*, pp. 2–3).[18] My argument in brief is that, in the play, Jonson represents the Plot itself as an enormous

---

17 '*Volpone* and Beast Fable: Early Modern Analogic Reading', *Huntington Library Quarterly*, 67 (2004), 347–70. I have developed the more general argument for *Volpone* being an anti-Cecil play in my edition for the forthcoming *Cambridge Ben Jonson*.

18 Cecil's response to the libel is *An answere to certaine scandalous papers, scattered abroad vnder colour of a Catholicke admonition* (Imprinted at London . . . by Robert Barker, printer to the Kings most excellent maiestie, 1606). Shortly after this entry, Yonge reports: 'About this time there was a pestilent libel in many men's hands, which challenged promises of the King, in behalf of the Papists, which no subject can believe' (*Diary*, p. 3). In the wider context there is no doubt that James had raised expectations that repressive measures against the Catholics would be reduced after he came to the throne: Jonson himself stopped attending Anglican communion in 1603 on that expectation. The Gunpowder Plot definitively put an end to such hopes, and Cecil was blamed for this as for much else. Pauline Croft suggests that Cecil was not personally ill-disposed toward the Catholics ('The Religion of Robert Cecil', p. 783ff); my point is the perception of Cecil at the time, especially by recusant Catholics themselves.

'red-herring' (4.1.51), the warped imaginings of Sir Politic Would-Be, whose 'plot / To sell the state of Venice to the Turk' (like all his politicking) proves most ironically to be 'notes / Drawn out of play-books' (5.4.37–8, 41–2). Meanwhile the *real* plot proves to be the 'reign' of Volpone and Mosca (not unlike that of the Fox and the Ape in Edmund Spenser's proscribed anti-Cecil satire, *Prosopopoia, or Mother Hubberd's Tale*), which represents the systematic subversion and exploitation of the state by the Cecils, under the guise of care for the general good.[19]

In this context, Voltore's patently false fit of possession is a perfect paradigm of the subverted state: an officer of the law, in a court of law, showing all the signs of being possessed by devils, in the interests at all costs of preventing the truth from emerging. It is the perfect riposte to Harsnett, in whose works such scenes provide evidence of false authority everywhere (Puritan, Jesuit), except in the hands of the Anglican state. Here the entire state – saving only the innocents-at-sea, Celia and Bonario, but including the Avocatori (only too anxious to welcome the 'heir', Mosca, as a son-in-law) – are credulous audience to what is palpably a piece of theatre. Theatre may sometimes empty ritual of its significance, but it is also a mechanism by which power is exercised: Volpone has ruled his world by one bravura piece of role-playing after another. It is only when he passes on that authority to his parasite/stooge, Mosca, and in this last gasp to Voltore, that his exercise of power comes to an end, with the 'mortifying' of the Fox.

It is helpful here to return briefly to *King Lear*, and in particular to Dan Brayton's recent reading of 'the multiple senses of possession' in the play, 'Angling in the Lake of Darkness: Possession, Dispossession, and the Politics of Discovery in *King Lear*'.[20] Brayton demonstrates that the search for hidden demons, for monstrous nothings supposed by those with power inside those they would rule, is a feature of the mindset of power in the play:

Immediately before Lear 'arraign[s]' (3.6.18) his daughters, Edgar exclaims, 'Frateretto calls me, and tells me Nero is an angler in the / lake of darkness' (3.6.6–7) . . . 'angler in the lake of darkness' does not simply refer to one who inhabits hell, but what we might call the thematic economy of the play: its persistent inquiry into the discovery of the monstrous as a political strategy. For Lear, Gloucester, Goneril, Regan, and Edmund are all anglers in the lake of darkness, and Edgar's cryptic, seemingly mad exclamation exposes them as such at the same time that it exposes his own possession by demons as a strategy of evasion and disguise. By choosing this phrase for my title, I would emphasize the remarkable fact of *King Lear*'s metatheatrical commentary on its own thematic obsession with darkness and discovery. *King Lear* itself is a tragedy angling in the lake of darkness.

(p. 420)

If so, Shakespeare does not simply welcome exorcism at the entrance of the Globe: he subjects it, and the whole mindset it represents, to the most sceptical scrutiny. As Brayton explains: 'What is at stake in my reading of *King Lear* in terms of the cultural poetic of possession . . . is not merely a demonstration that the play borrows from the language of witchcraft, or that it figures possession as the condition of kingship in a spectacular display of map-reading. What *King Lear* does with possession is much more radical: it turns the political apparatus of discovery on the very agency that it serves – sovereign power' (pp. 421–2). Harsnett's attempts to expose and put an end to exorcisms are small beer in a world where those in power so

[19] Other suggestive features which point to the topical anti-Cecil material in the play: the first congratulatory poem in the 1607 quarto is by Edmund Bolton, who was arraigned for recusancy with Jonson in 1606, setting a clear context; the second is by John Donne and alerts us to Jonson's development of Donne's unfinished 'Metempsychosis' – itself an anti-Cecil satire – in the show staged by Volpone's 'children' (1.2); those freaks of nature – the hermaphrodite, the eunuch and most particularly Nano the dwarf – almost certainly drew attention to the deformities in the Cecil family: Robert was small and hunch-backed, as was his daughter, Frances. Nano describes his forte as 'pleasing imitation / Of greater men's action, in a ridiculous fashion' (3.3.13–14).

[20] Dan Brayton, 'Angling in the Lake of Darkness: Possession, Dispossession, and the Politics of Discovery in *King Lear*', *ELH*, 70 (2003), 399–426.

obsessively seek to discover demons within their subjects in so many different contexts.

It is difficult to believe that a sceptic like Jonson would have set much store by a process like exorcism at the best of time. But it is very easy to believe that he would have objected to a state run by the Harsnetts, Bancrofts and Cecils of the world telling him whether he should believe in it or not. So, as a man always embroiled in a love-hate relationship with theatre itself, he parodically mirrors Harsnett's anti-theatricality as a way of registering his resistance to such authority – and to its wider attempts to control his own faith. Shakespeare is characteristically less confrontational than Jonson, but no less clear about where he draws the line in respect of power. Like Cornwall's servant, who tries to save Gloucester's second eye, he knows when authority turns to tyranny. So he turns Harsnett on his head by showing theatre as a form of compassionate magic, which helps to hold things together as society falls apart. As Carol Thomas Neely puts it: 'While Greenblatt sees spiritual rituals as "*emptied out*" in *King Lear*, in fact, through [Edgar's] invented mad discourse, sacred meaning is resituated: grief, guilt, anger, and punishment are understood within human psychological parameters, and supernatural rituals are adapted for therapeutic purposes'.[21] I would add that it is surely significant that new authority in the play grows through the deliberate impersonation of diabolic possession. If Edgar is indeed the one who is to 'Rule in this kingdom, and the gored state sustain' (24. 314), he does so by a curious reversal: he acquires the state authority of the exorcist by representing the very condition his office (in Jacobean England) seeks to remove from common view.

In *The Puritan, King Lear* and *Volpone* alike, for all their differences, theatre finds within itself varied voices to express its less than total compliance with a state that finally lacks the resources to be as univocal as it would like to be.

---

[21] Carol Thomas Neely, *Distracted Subjects: Madness and Gender in Shakespeare and Early Modern Culture* (Ithaca, NY, 2004), p. 61. Neely makes a similar point about Greenblatt and *Twelfth Night*: 'Although the supernatural underpinnings of exorcism are parodied and theological debates about possession are turned into a joke, the social, exclusionary uses of such a ritual in everyday life are affirmed' (pp. 154–5). I am grateful to Marisa Cull for bringing these passages to my attention.

# 'LENDING SOFT AUDIENCE TO MY SWEET DESIGN': SHIFTING ROLES AND SHIFTING READINGS OF SHAKESPEARE'S 'A LOVER'S COMPLAINT'

HEATHER DUBROW

## I

Often dismissed as a mere purveyor of mellifluous trifles, Samuel Daniel crafts an extraordinary passage that anticipates and elucidates some of the most provocative issues in Shakespeare's 'A Lover's Complaint'. In Daniel's 'Complaint of Rosamond', the ghost of Rosamond describes her seduction by a monarch, preceding that story by addressing a plea for sympathy and help to the narrator. Seductive itself, the language of her opening appeal draws attention to the instability of the role of auditor and the interplay of cooperation and collusion it potentially entails – problems central to Shakespeare's contribution to the same genre, to many of his other texts, and to our own lives within and outside the academy.

The work of those students of conversational interaction known as discourse analysts, which has received far too little attention thus far from literary critics, aptly glosses the interaction between auditors and speakers in both Daniel's and Shakespeare's complaints. Most practitioners of this discipline are linguists by training, but such thinkers as the sociologist Erving Goffman and the psychologist Richard J. Gerrig have also contributed influentially.[1] Although analyses by the discourse analysts are sometimes compromised by a positivistic and inappropriately benign model of the workings of conversations, their classifications of the various positionalities participants may assume are germane to many other kinds of language as well. Discourse analysts compellingly alert us, for example, to the ways even listeners who appear to be largely silent may participate, a phenomenon we will encounter in both Daniel's and Shakespeare's poems. Particularly valuable to students of those texts are the subdivisions in the roles of both author and listener mapped in varying ways by discourse analysts. Thus, borrowing one of several comparable systems, the terminology proposed by Erving Goffman, we can distinguish the *animator*, or the person who fulfils a kind of ambassador role by speaking someone else's ideas, from the original *author* of the sentiments.[2] These categories, we will find, gloss numerous relationships in 'A Lover's Complaint', as well as in Daniel's poem: the connections between and among characters within each text; the links between each poet and his non-diegetic audiences; and the ties of poet, printer and publisher.

Similarly, students of discourse analysis have subdivided the position of listener. It is common to separate the person or persons directly addressed

For valuable assistance with this essay, I am indebted to the audience at the International Shakespeare Association meeting in Stratford-upon-Avon in July 2004, where it was first presented, and to Kimberly Huth, Harold Love and Donald Rowe.

[1] See Richard J. Gerrig, *Experiencing Narrative Worlds: On the Psychological Activities of Reading* (New Haven, 1993); Erving Goffman, *Forms of Talk* (Philadelphia, 1981).

[2] Goffman, *Forms of Talk*, ch. 3.

from the other hearers termed by Herbert H. Clark and Thomas B. Carlson 'side participants'. Emphasizing the value of further subdivisions, Clark and Carlson also distinguish participants, addressees and overhearers; Goffman's system disjoins the ratified listeners, who are directly and openly addressed, from bystanders, whose presence is assumed even though it is not acknowledged through direct address, and from eavesdroppers.[3] Such distinctions as well are frequently germane to Shakespeare's and Daniel's complaints.

## II

Intriguing in its subtleties, tantalizing in its apparent contradictions, a passage from Daniel's 'Complaint of Rosamond' deploys diction in particular to stage the two overlapping category crises that we will subsequently trace in Shakespeare's poem.[4] First, in Daniel's lines we see the erosion of distinctions among cooperation, critique and complicity. And second, the text also stages the erosion of distinctions between and among audience, animator and author.

As importunate as she is unfortunate, Rosamond

> Comes to sollicit thee, since others faile,
> To take this taske, and in thy wofull Song
> To forme my case, and register my wrong.
> (33–5)[5]

'Sollicit' (33) of course mainly means 'petition', and, although its specific application to the invitations of a prostitute was not present in the period in question, it did carry with it the suggestion of inviting someone to perform illegal actions – a suggestion that Rosamond almost immediately attempts to play down with the mundane, pleasingly alliterative and conventionally metrical phrase, 'To take this taske' (34).

The *Oxford English Dictionary* also testifies that 'solicit' was used in legal contexts in the English Renaissance.[6] Thus the term, intensified by other legal language that ensues, alerts readers, especially those trained in oratory as Daniel's and Shakespeare's original audiences were, to the connections between Rosamond's behavior and judicial situations. As John Kerrigan demonstrates, many complaints play on legal discourse;[7] we will encounter similar legal language, freighted with similar demands, throughout Shakespeare's poem. Hence we ask for the first of many times if Daniel's narrator – and his readers – are judge or defense attorney or some uneasy amalgamation, again a blurring of roles. That legal language also encourages us to read Rosamond's story, as we will read its analogue in 'A Lover's Complaint', in terms of the second part of judicial orations, the *narratio*, or narrative of the putative facts of the case. Some rhetoricians, such as the anonymous author of the *Rhetorica ad Herennium*, devote considerable attention to how a skilful lawyer could transform the *narratio* from an objective account of facts to a recital twisted to benefit the client. Arguably this is one version of what Rosamond is doing as her own lawyer and encouraging the narrator and reader to do as well. 'Sollicit' (33) could also carry with it connotations of disturbing or unsettling someone, and its other meanings indicate why Rosamond's entreaty is indeed troubling for both the narrator and the non-diegetic reader.

Rosamond's invitation then moves to the phrase, 'To forme my case' (35), in effect partly an invitation to compose the *narratio* and other parts of her case. Thus 'forme' begins to transfer some agency to the listener who is also now our narrator and is being urged to become Rosamond's; Rosamond is inviting him not merely to repeat what he has heard but to shape it, to reword it, an invitation complicated by the fact that 'case' can suggest both objective truth and potentially

[3] Carlson and Clark, 'Hearers and Speech Acts'.

[4] Other types of connection between Daniel and Shakespeare are acutely traced in Colin Burrow, 'Introduction', in William Shakespeare, *The Complete Sonnets and Poems* (Oxford, 2002), esp. 111–12.

[5] I cite Samuel Daniel, *'Poems' and 'A Defence of Ryme'*, ed. Arthur Colby Sprague (Chicago, 1930).

[6] *OED*, s.v. 'solicit'. This, like subsequent citations, is to the first edition.

[7] John Kerrigan, 'Introduction', *Motives of Woe: Shakespeare and 'Female Complaint'; A Critical Anthology* (Oxford, 1991), 28–9. He also draws attention here to the penitential sense of 'case'.

dubious legal representation.[8] The tension between the two in the word enacts cultural tensions about the reliability of a female speaker, another issue that will recur in Shakespeare's poem. 'Forme' (35) may also signal that he is putting it into a particular form, a species or genre, significant because Daniel's text, like Shakespeare's poem and many other complaints, is certainly a meta-complaint, and both those narratives explore the complicity of not only audiences but also literary types. These resonances, then, remind us that, in taking a task, the narrator is also taking and making a case, changing from potentially dispassionate observer to partisan pleader.

A word that not coincidentally appears in other poems in the same genre – in 'The Complaint of Elstred', for example, Thomas Lodge uses it and its cognates no fewer than three times, and it also recurs in 'A Lover's Complaint' – 'register' (35) suggests a kind of permanence in telling tension with the evanescence of that 'wofull Song' (34). In particular, as John Kerrigan points out, it could refer to one route towards permanence, putting something into print, an allusion that activates comparable associations with publishing in 'case' and 'forme' (35).[9] Again like 'case', 'register' (35) also on occasion may have some suggestion of reliability – one registers a birth, a fact. Thus the term not only intensifies the questions about judgement and responsibility raised by 'case' (35) but also prefigures the problems of closural certainty that we will shortly encounter in Shakespeare's text. And these issues, like so many others in Daniel's and in Shakespeare's poems, are gendered: a male is registrar for a female speaker, forming a case as he forms a fetus in many classical and early modern medical theories . . . and yet the poem implies that he is being seduced into the role of seducing others.

All these complexities are intensified by the final words in the thirty-fifth line. 'My wrong' can suggest the wrong done to Delia or the one she has done – or even the one she is doing in the act of inviting the narrator to join her in telling the story. Indeed, that wrong is itself registered in yet another meaning of the phrase, the possibility that the narrator will himself be the register of her wrong, that his body or the body of his text will inscribe it, so that this legal case in a sense becomes a case of an infectious disease. In short, within just three lines we confront the two movements we will trace throughout Daniel's and Shakespeare's complaints: the shift back and forth between the roles of speaker and listener and the one between complicity and neutrality.

'*Delia* may happe to deygne to read our story' (43), we ourselves read a stanza later.[10] Notice how the shift from the trochaic opening to the series of monosyllabic iambs – 'may happe to deygne to read' – slows down the line, suggesting deliberation rather than the pressure apparent in the extraordinary pronoun 'our'.[11] Daniel's speaker now is registering a wrong both in and to his own text, for invitation has become interpellation. Initially ratified listener, then invited participant in forming the story, the narrator, and possibly the reader, is now victim of, as well as potentially victimizer through, the tale. Or, to put it another way, the narrator is now at once its animator, its co-author, and, as the pronoun 'our' implies, its co-owner. Colin Powell insisted about Iraq, 'If you break it you own it'; here Daniel in effect says about stories, 'If you make it, you own it.'

On another level, however, a male poet is engaged in deflecting onto Rosamond and hence re-gendering his own guilt for telling the tale, one of many instances of deflected and re-gendered responsibility in the poem. Later, for example,

---

8 *OED*, s.v. 'case'.

9 Kerrigan, *Motives of Woe*, 166.

10 Compare Elizabeth Harris Sagaser's points about how *Delia* conflates the woman's beauty and the poet's song ('Sporting the While: Carpe Diem and the Cruel Fair in Samuel Daniel's Delia and The Complaint of Rosamond', *Exemplaria*, 10 (1988), esp. 156–7). Sagaser's acute observation that the poem is 'about being seen and being read' (161) is also germane to my argument.

11 Wendy Wall also analyses this pronoun but from a perspective very different from mine, arguing that the identification it creates stems from the fact that both Rosamond and Daniel seek Delia's sympathy and that Rosamond's problems deflect Daniel's (*The Imprint of Gender: Authorship and Publication in the English Renaissance* (Ithaca, 1993), pp. 255–6).

Rosamond will blame another woman for contributing to her seduction. Whatever other links one posits between this poem and the sonnets that precede it, might not their author be reacting misogynistically against the adulation of a woman enjoined by his sortie into Petrarchism, reacting against, so to speak, the problems Daniel faces in the lionizing den?

The volatile shifts in agency and authorship that we have traced throughout the text are mimed as well in the conditions of production for this poem, though a thorough analysis of that process necessarily requires a separate article.[12] Whether or not we accept the theory, promulgated by Katherine Duncan-Jones and John Kerrigan, that Daniel's volume helps to establish a widely imitated 'Delian structure' in which all texts are closely connected, it is indisputable that Daniel himself wished to link his sonnets and complaint: within the latter poem Rosamond alludes specifically to Delia and the speaker to his experiences as a sonneteer.[13] Yet because of the apparent interventions of printer and publisher, his volume itself gives mixed and inconclusive signals about the relationship of its texts, and those markers vary from one edition to another and among variants published in the same year in ways that are unlikely to accord to the author's wishes. Thus, for example, in the 1592 edition STC 6243.2 the complaint is not introduced with a half-title page, an absence that facilitates relating it to the preceding texts. In the same year, however, the same printer and publisher brought out a version (STC 6243.3) that distinguishes the sonnets and 'The Complaint of Rosamond' through the addition of such a page; the complaint is further set off by the use of a large capital, lacking in the ode and in the first sonnet. Given Daniel's obvious interest in connecting his sonnets and complaint, it is more likely though not certain that the printer added the half-title page to use up a blank sheet or that the publisher did so, probably hoping that the separate half-title would make readers think they were getting more for their money. Hence if printer and publisher were originally among the ratified listeners and animators, in an important sense they become rival authors. In short, then, materially as well as linguistically Daniel's text raises the two questions we will explore in Shakespeare's: how and why are the positions of speaker and listener so fluid? and how and why are the boundaries between and among cooperation, collaboration and cooption so porous?

## III

In 'A Lover's Complaint', a woman tellingly described as a 'fickle maid' (5) recounts the story of her seduction – a betrayal that involved the tales her lover told her – only to admit that she might make the same mistake again.[14] Even this condensed overview immediately gestures toward the significance of audiences in Shakespeare's 'A Lover's Complaint', and that issue has not been overlooked by critics: witness in particular cogent though brief observations by Colin Burrow and Katharine A. Craik.[15] Many previous studies, however, focus on a specific type of auditory position (thus, for example, Craik's article and an essay by Paul D. Stegner read the auditors in the poem in terms of the act of confession) and hence treat glancingly, if at all, the questions about shifting roles and their ethical dimensions that I address here.[16]

---

12 For a more thorough treatment of this issue see my forthcoming essay, provisionally entitled 'Shakespeare's Sonnets and "A Lover's Complaint": A Poststructuralist Reexamination of "the Delian Structure"', in *The Blackwell Companion to Shakespeare's Sonnets*, ed. Michael Schoenfeldt.

13 On 'the Delian structure', see Katherine Duncan-Jones, 'Introduction', in William Shakespeare, *Shakespeare's Sonnets*, ed. Katherine Duncan-Jones, The Arden Shakespeare (London, 1997), esp. pp. 88–92; John Kerrigan, 'Introduction', in William Shakespeare, *The Sonnets* and *A Lover's Complaint*, ed. John Kerrigan (Harmondsworth, 1986), esp. pp. 13–15.

14 All citations from Shakespeare are to *The Riverside Shakespeare*, ed. G. Blakemore Evans, 2nd edn (Boston, 1997).

15 Katharine A. Craik, 'Shakespeare's *A Lover's Complaint* and Early Modern Criminal Confession', *Shakespeare Quarterly*, 53 (2002), esp. 440, 443, 446; Colin Burrow, *Collected Sonnets and Poems*, esp. 5. I thank Craik for sharing her work prior to publication.

16 An exception is Craik's brief but important observation that in confessional situations both the diegetic and non-diegetic listener may be implicated (443).

Even – or especially – in the initial stanzas, 'A Lover's Complaint' draws attention to the varied and fluid roles an auditor may assume:

> From off a hill whose concave womb reworded
> A plaintful story from a sist'ring vale,
> My spirits t' attend this double voice accorded,
> And down I laid to list the sad-tun'd tale.
>
> (1–4)

So rapidly do characters change positionalities in the opening of the poem, as well as subsequently, that place comes to resemble its apparent opposite, the indeterminacies and fluidities of space.[17] Thus we soon discover that that 'sad-tun'd tale' (4) is overheard both by our narrator, who is an eavesdropper in the sense defined by the discourse analysts, and by a 'reverend man' (57).[18] Initially an eavesdropper himself, the latter becomes a ratified listener in that, encouraged by him to explain her grief, the so-called 'fickle maid' (5) tells him about her seduction, adding that the love tokens she is destroying are presents that her seducer received from other women and gave her. Certain of these gifts involve both a material object and some verbal gloss ('posie[s]' [45], for example, were inscriptions in rings), thus signalling the connection between material and epistemological ownership that is very relevant to the relationships between speakers and auditors throughout the poem.

The opening stanzas thus introduce several different types of listening. In an initial strophe that, as Wendy Wall and others point out, focuses on doubleness, the word 'reworded' (1) packs double meanings central to the story and to the position of auditors in particular: it can suggest unchanged, passive repetition or variation, thus recalling the ambiguities in Daniel's intriguing phrase, 'forme my case' (35).[19] To what extent, the term 'reworded' invites us to ask, does repeating a story involve independence and autonomy, to what extent collaboration and mutual cooperation, to what extent passive submission to its original teller? The physical posture of our narrator may well suggest his own passivity, an implication supported if we attend to Colin Burrow's suggestion that 'accorded' (3) may imply agreement.[20] Yet that recumbent figure is obviously himself a narrator, and he shapes the story by characterizing its teller as 'fickle' (5), a term whose early modern meanings could range from 'changeable' to 'inconstant' to 'deceitful'. And when, shortly afterwards, the reverend man elicits the story, he assumes not only the position of confessor, but also that of judge, an analogue suggested as well by the legal language as evident in this poem as in Daniel's.

Such questions are raised with particular intensity in the ensuing stanzas, when the woman begins to tell her tale. They are posed above all in the ways characters shift from the role of auditor to speaker – movements mimed by the shifts in ownership and meaning of material objects – or from receiver to dispenser of goods. That is, the maid repeats what her seducer has told her, thus moving from audience to animator of his story, and that story in turn involves his quoting what his lovers have supposedly told him.[21] Thus the seducer pretends to animate what he might better be described as appropriating or even misrepresenting.

Similarly, objects that previous lovers have given to him are passed to the so-called fickle maid as a passive recipient, who then assumes the more active role of destroying them. Hence the shifts in the positions of subjects and in the possession of objects suggested by the maid's tale raise the same questions about property and ownership signalled in the poem by metaphors related to the ownership

---

[17] Many critics have discussed the distinction between these categories. See, e.g., Yi-Fu Tuan, *Space and Place: The Perspective of Experience* (Minneapolis, 1977), Introduction.

[18] Paul Edmondson and Stanley Wells also note the presence of varied and echoing voices in the opening of the poem, arguing persuasively that this impels the reader to investigate multiple perspectives (*Shakespeare's Sonnets* (Oxford, 2004), pp. 108–9). I am grateful to the authors for allowing me to see their work prior to publication.

[19] Wall, *Imprint of Gender*, 259–60.

[20] Burrow, *Collected Sonnets and Poems*, 695.

[21] A number of critics have discussed ventriloquized utterances in early modern texts other than this one, though often from perspectives quite different from mine. See, e.g., the Lacanian analysis in Jonathan Goldberg, 'Shakespearean Inscriptions: The Voicing of Power', in his book *Shakespeare's Hand* (Minneapolis, 2003).

of land. As Christopher Warley acutely observes, the narrator represents her autonomy in terms of control over real property.[22] To his and other analyses we should add that this physical appropriation and transfer of ownership is accompanied by an appropriation and transfer of meaning: sonnets, locks of hair and so on that apparently signified other women's devotion to him are re-presented as signs of the seducer's putative love for our fickle maid and then reinterpreted by her as signs of his treachery. These processes of changing meaning are played against the apparently stable signification initially associated with the objects: it is telling that a number of them have some sort of verbal signal that apparently establishes their significance, so that these despoiling spoils include posies, or rings with inscriptions, and 'deep-brain'd sonnets' (209). Jonathan Gil Harris has recently argued that contemporary materialist critics need to look at objects diachronically, not synchronically, and there is no better evidence of his contentions than this poem.[23]

These changes in the subject positions of the characters, and the parallel changes in ownership, ontology and signification of objects, carry with them many implications for the central issues about author and audience that this chapter explores. First, the shifts in question play the possibility of a stable, closural meaning against fluid signification, with stability ostensibly represented by the posy or inscription on that symbol of closure and wholeness a ring.[24] Owning meaning is related to owning material objects. This is, I suggest, precisely the pattern writ large when the text as a whole contrasts the exemplarity associated with the complaint and with the history of the 'reverend man' (57) against the explicit refusal of didactic exemplarity in a stanza to which we will return shortly, lines 155–61.[25] Such doubts about the suasive force of examples thus render the poem both a meta- and an anti-complaint.

These troubled and troubling doubts about didacticism and its agents exemplarity and stable closure are enacted in the rime royal stanza form. Also deployed in *The Rape of Lucrece*, this strophe, *ababbcc*, is used to very different ends in this instance. Including as it does not one but two couplets, it offers double opportunities for sententious generalizations, as George Gascoigne implies when writing about the stanza.[26] The fifth line, a kind of bridge, also has the potentiality to stand apart and hence house sententiae itself. In *The Rape of Lucrece*, these sections of the stanza are often devoted to moral axioms, in 'A Lover's Complaint' less frequently. Moreover, in 'A Lover's Complaint', the irony that sometimes undercuts the humanistic sayings in *Lucrece* regularly takes centre stage. Not only does Shakespeare generally avoid moral truisms here, demonstrating the distrust of sententiousness writ large in the rejection of exemplarity; when he does include them he does so in a way that shows their dangers. For example, at one point he proffers a textbook instance of exemplarity in a stanza discussing its limits:

> But ah, who ever shunn'd by precedent
> The destin'd ill she must herself assay,
> Or forc'd examples 'gainst her own content
> To put the by-past perils in her way?
> (155–8)

On the other hand, with its characteristic commitment to paradox, the poem also undercuts its own undercutting of exemplarity by attributing cognate reservations about it to the seducer himself: 'When thou impressest, what are precepts worth / Of stale example?' (267–8). Thus a didactic and potentially paternalistic model for the relationship between speaker and hearer is repeatedly evoked, then challenged.

---

[22] Christopher Warley, 'Lyric and Property in Shakespeare's *A Lover's Complaint*', a paper delivered at the 2001 meeting of the Renaissance Society of America; I am grateful to the author for sharing his work prior to publication.

[23] Jonathan Gil Harris, 'Shakespeare's Hair: Staging the Object of Material Culture', *Shakespeare Quarterly*, 52 (2001), 479–91.

[24] These processes are further complicated, however, by the fact that, as Kerrigan points out (*Motives of Woe*, 46), we never actually learn what the tokens in question say.

[25] On the problems of exemplarity, cf. Burrow, 'Introduction', 144–5.

[26] George Gascoigne, *Certayne Notes of Instruction*, in George Gascoigne, *A Hundreth Sundrie Flowres*, ed. G. W. Pigman III (Oxford, 2000), p. 460.

In destroying the objects used to seduce her, the lady is at once acknowledging the power invested in them by the seducer and redefining them as symbols of her apparent independence and repentance, only to qualify her autonomy in her final remarks about her propensity to be seduced again. Having played the part of audience to her lover, in casting away the possessions he gave her in some sense she is destroying as well her own role as object and becoming speaker and subject, bravely appropriating his words just as she reassigns meanings to the goods he has given her. Yet from another perspective she is merely an animator repeating his seductive words, in this way anticipating her admission that she might once again yield to those words.

Thus the issues about subject positions and material objects raised by the woman's initial speech extend the alternative and shifting roles for audience suggested by the opening of the poem. At one pole of the spectrum, an audience can passively receive rhetoric, much as the prone narrator 'attend[s]' (3) the story and the lady initially receives rings with the original speaker's explanatory motto assigned. At the other pole, it can appropriate stories and objects, assigning its own meanings, inscribing its own posies. But the text explores troubling implications in these roles – for instance, is that passivity in fact a type of approval? when is exculpation involved?[27] And it demonstrates how and why these two apparently opposite roles can be further complicated, modulated and on occasion combined – changes that, as we have seen, are enacted through and represented by shifts in the ownership of material goods and in the control over the verbal glosses associated with them.

Such issues are then extended in some intriguing passages in which the maid proceeds to quote the seducer, who in turn quotes or claims to quote what his previous lovers said to him. These narrative techniques are emphasized and thematized by a few passages that announce that someone's sentiments have been expressed by someone else. Thus, in one of the most intriguing lines in the poem, we hear that observers 'dialogu'd for [the seducer] what he would say' (132), in so doing becoming his animators. The verb 'dialogu'd' stresses the doubleness that so often becomes duplicity elsewhere in this poem. And that term itself enacts another type of doubleness in that when listeners take the role of speaker yet lose autonomy in doing so, dialogue is prevented. Yet the hint that the role of animator necessarily involves subservience is further complicated when we realize that the seducer has himself been the animator of words that the previous lovers putatively authored, coopting them for his own ends when he quotes, or apparently quotes, what earlier lovers said to him. The blurrings of subjectivity here and elsewhere in the poem are enacted visually by the early modern practice of not using quotation marks to distinguish the words of different speakers.[28]

Another way the seducer attempts to control his audience is the inverse of 'dialogu'd for him what he would say' (132) and the sibling of his quoting the words of earlier lovers. If those women apparently anticipate what he would say, more duplicitously but no less effectively he pretends to know not only what they have said but also what they would say:

> Now all these hearts that do on mine depend,
> Feeling it break, with bleeding groans they pine,
> And supplicant their sighs to you extend
> To leave the batt'ry that you make 'gainst mine,
> Lending soft audience to my sweet design.
>
> (274–8)

In these lines the man reverses the rivalry he has earlier established in a quite extraordinary way, claiming that previous lovers actually favour this new relationship. But if competition is turned on its head, so too, once again, are the positionalities of the participants. His battery against his current target is represented as hers against him, a common re-gendering of guilt in love poetry, as we have

[27] On exculpatory agendas in the poem, see Ilona Bell, 'Shakespeare's Exculpatory Complaint', in *Suffering Ecstasy*, ed. Shirley Sharon-Zisser, forthcoming.

[28] Among the other critics who have noted the enfolding of one speech within another are James Schiffer ( '"Honey words": *A Lover's Complaint* and the Fine Art of Seduction', in Zisser, ed., *Suffering Ecstasy*) and Kerrigan; the latter also comments on the absence of quotation marks in early modern editions (*Motives*, 45).

already observed. And the audience of earlier victims is represented as according, speaking in one voice with the seducer; they are bystanders who become speakers and authors themselves through their sighs. Or, to put it another way, they are ostensibly given voice and agency, but the speaker appropriates both, much as he appropriates their gifts for his new conquest. In other words, when these previous lovers apparently switch from the subject position of bystander to that of participant, what is in fact involved is yet another seduction of the earlier lovers and yet another replication of their status as soft and malleable objects themselves.

Alerted to shifting positions in these ways, we may notice too that the referent of a phrase in the final line I quoted, 'Lending soft audience' (278), is tellingly ambiguous. It might seem at first to refer to the previous lovers who lend audience as they lend support; but as we read on we see that it apparently alludes to the fickle maid, describing what she will do when she leaves her battery. This doubleness, syntactically collapsing as it does the earlier women and the 'fickle maid' (5), aptly figures and prefigures the way she will shortly join their ranks as yet another victim.

We are now in a position to summarize what 'A Lover's Complaint' demonstrates about the relationships among several versions of the audience's position and several versions of speaker's. First, those roles, those places, are not stable but malleable and variable, not least because of the propensity of speakers to crossdress as listeners, and vice versa. And the changes in their positions do not have a simple and consistent effect on the balances of both power and authority. On the one hand, a skilled rhetorician can enlist an audience: having 'accorded' (3) to his or her own 'sad-tun'd tale' (4), its members in effect become ventriloquized speakers. Among the ways one can do so is by turning others into complicitous reciters of one's own tale, as Rosamond and the seducer here do. Yet on the other hand, Shakespeare's text also stresses the power and agency an audience may achieve. The repetition of someone else's tale, for example, can also be a rewording that appropriates and changes meaning.

## IV

What are the broader implications of Shakespeare's observations about audiences both for our study of his texts and for our lives within and outside the classroom? Given the complexity of many of the issues, they will necessarily be approached here suggestively, not exhaustively, or, to put it another way, sketched in as invitations for future work. First, while Colin Burrow's insistence that Shakespeare's non-dramatic poems should not be valued as mere glosses on his plays is no less sound than significant, studying 'A Lover's Complaint' does alert us to the recurrence of the issues it raises in many other texts.[29] Shakespeare's preoccupation with complicity has been traced, largely in his plays, by a critic no less prominent and perspicuous than Harry Berger, and more recently John Gillies has also offered powerful insights in an as yet unpublished paper; but the question is by no means exhausted.[30] Indeed, the significance of this issue for treatments of politics in his canon is flagged by his decision to refer to participants in plots as 'complices' five times and 'accomplices' once, a telling usage given how many other, less fraught terms – 'companions', 'fellows', even 'confederates', and so on – might have been used instead.[31] Much as the decision to open several plays on parental deaths signals Shakespeare's abiding preoccupation with that issue, so too the plotting on which *Othello* and *Henry V* open indicates their author's interest in the bonds it involves.

Shakespeare's plays also explore a specific question about the relationship between cooption and autonomy that we encountered in both his own and Daniel's complaint: does repeating someone else's

---

[29] For a powerful if perhaps overstated revisionist argument about the status of the non-dramatic poems in relation to the plays, see Burrow, *Complete Sonnets and Poems*, esp. 5.

[30] Harry Berger, Jr, *Making Trifles of Terrors: Redistributing Complicities in Shakespeare*, ed. Peter Erickson (Stanford, 1997); John Gillies, 'Shakespearean Theatre and Complicity', presented at Ohio Shakespeare Association Conference, November 2002 and University of Wisconsin, April 2003.

[31] Marvin Spevack, *The Harvard Concordance to Shakespeare* (Hildesheim, 1973), s.v. 'accomplices', 'complices'.

story result in independence or contagion or some admixture of both? That dilemma recurs in dramatic passages as diverse as Henry V's St Crispian Day speech and Desdemona's willow song. And if we interpret the repetition of someone's story as a version of learning her language or repeating a few of her words, we can recognize that the dynamics involved in Katherine's English lesson or Prospero's insistence that Ariel summarize Sycorax's curriculum vitae are too complex merely to be labelled as domination, though that element and the gendering it implies in the first instance are certainly prominent.

The issues we have been tracing are relevant not only to specific plays but also to theatrical practices.[32] 'A Lover's Complaint', as we have observed, repeatedly involves the incorporation of one speaker's words in the discourse of another. Hence might we not find in this poem oblique commentaries on the often conflictual collaborations that characterize Elizabethan and Jacobean theatre, whether among audience, printer and playwright or between and among playwrights? Might we not find connections between the jig as a form of appropriation and the versions of that appropriation we have been exploring?[33] The best if not the only jig-maker of Shakespeare's company, Will Kemp, may have antagonized his fellow players by, literally and otherwise, choreographing new steps and a new tempo for a play that had apparently ended, much as the locale and the meanings of the love tokens in 'A Lover's Complaint' are moved around by successive owners.

In addition, the issues about audience in 'A Lover's Complaint' arguably shape and are in turn shaped by Shakespeare's explorations of the soliloquy. The debate about the extent to which soliloquies are addressed to the audience – or, to put it another way, the question of whether non-diegetic listeners are ratified listeners, eavesdroppers or bystanders – is a fraught one in drama criticism. Positions range from Wolfgang Clemen's assertion that Shakespearian soliloquies were commonly though not universally addressed to the audience to James Hirsch's recent claim that monologues of that type largely died out in the sixteenth century. In any event, many recent directors have elected to establish the audience's intimate and intense involvement as addressees – and have frequently done so in circumstances where that involvement necessarily entails complicity. Witness, for example, Steven Pimlott's Royal Shakespeare Company production of *Richard II* in 2000, where Bolingbroke demanded that theatrical listeners share in his connivances. Four years later, in the production of *King Lear* Bill Alexander directed for the same company, Edmund invited and arguably elicited complicity from his theatrical auditors by directing his mockery of 'A credulous father' (1.2.179) to them and by informing them of his decision to betray that parent. Similarly, in *1 Henry IV* when Hal famously announces 'herein will I imitate the sun' (1.2.197), the import and impact of his words change if we consider the possibility that he is speaking to, not merely in the presence of, the theatrical audience. If so, he is rehearsing on – and, significantly, with – us the ruses he will later try on a broader public, forming his case and inviting the theatrical audience to register his wrong.

We could also profitably work further on how the issues raised in my often anticlosural essay illuminate the closural gestures in Shakespeare's plays, for at those junctures the erosion of the boundary between actor and audience frequently also involves the types of ethical erosion we have been tracing. Rosalind's reference to kissing the men in the audience invites them to participate in the sexually transgressive implications of her crossdressing – an invitation immediately qualified and in part contained by the last and most intriguing of the conditionals in the play, 'If I were a woman' (Epilogue, 18). When the Epilogue to *2 Henry IV* playfully suggests that the audience's disapproval could kill Falstaff, it thus compels us either to identify with or condemn the king's rejection of him, each of which from some perspectives implicates us. An analogue to the moral complexities of such epilogues is, of

[32] Compare Gillies's argument that complicity is both transmitted and thematized at the level of performance ('Shakespearean Theatre and Complicity').

[33] I thank my student Daniel Gibbons for this observation.

course, the conclusion of Jonson's *Alchemist*, where Face famously asks for the audience's endorsement, thus attempting yet again to transform leaden disapproval into golden approbation.

But the relationship between cooperation and cooption is no less significant in Shakespeare's nondramatic texts than the plays. Lucrece fears that she is in some way responsible for the rape – might St Augustine's attribution of guilt to the victim of that crime, which lies behind some of Lucrece's guilt, rank among the many factors that intensified Shakespeare's own interest in such issues? 'A Lover's Complaint', as we have seen, represents not only complicity but its relationship to changing positionalities, and that connection also recurs throughout its author's sonnets. Sonnet 138, which opens 'When my love swears that she is made of truth, / I do believe her, though I know she lies', stages the ways we can begin to believe the lies we tell. In so doing, this text, like 'A Lover's Complaint', draws attention to the interactions involved in that process – shifts between naivety and duplicity and between victim and victimizer are both its preoccupation and its praxis. But the most intriguing analysis in the sonnets of how the act of justifying shifts subject positions and creates moral ambiguities – and, indeed, one of the most intriguing sonnets for other reasons – is the thirty-fifth poem in the sequence.

> No more be griev'd at that which thou hast done:
> Roses have thorns, and silver fountains mud,
> Clouds and eclipses stain both moon and sun,
> And loathsome canker lives in sweetest bud.
> All men make faults, and even I in this,
> Authorizing thy trespass with compare,
> Myself corrupting, salving thy amiss,
> Excusing thy sins more than thy sins are;
> For to thy sensual fault I bring in sense –
> Thy adverse party is thy advocate –
> And 'gainst myself a lawful plea commence.
> Such civil war is in my love and hate,
> That I an accessary needs must be
> To that sweet thief which sourly robs from me.

Intimately related in its preoccupations to 'A Lover's Complaint', this text demonstrates how the process of offering excuses merges the role of accused and accuser, defendant, judge and lawyer. Miming those erosions formally, the sonnet ends on a passage that prosodically merges quatrain and couplet: 'Such civil war is in my love and hate, / That I an accessary needs must be / To that sweet thief which sourly robs from me' (12–14). Notice, too, that in the way they both reach towards and resist the closural certainties of an epigrammatic couplet these final three lines recall the rejection of exemplarity in 'A Lover's Complaint'.

My analyses of the positionalities of audience and speaker in that poem also have implications for the workings of narrative and lyric. Whereas the aims of narrative are often enumerated as building a city, gaining knowledge, possessing a lover's body, solving a riddle and so on, I suggest that encouraging listeners to become speakers who repeat the tale may be a no less central agenda, and one that often tropes the others.[34] One might say that breeding versions of one's own story and blocking alternative stories is a form of building the city and gaining possession of the body of the text.[35] As for lyric, 'A Lover's Complaint', as we have seen, both enacts and interrogates something analogous to lyric voiceability – that is, the widespread though problematical theory that, as Helen Vendler puts it, 'One is to utter [the words of lyric] as one's own words, not the words of another'.[36] 'A Lover's Complaint', like Daniel's 'Complaint of Rosamond', incorporates repeated invitations to such utterances and chronicles the dangers of responding positively to them. These warnings urge us to consider whether, *pace* Vendler and many others, voiceability is not necessarily the normative relationship of a reader to an early modern

---

34 One of the most useful analyses of the 'ends' of narrative appears in Peter Brooks, *Reading for the Plot: Design and Intention in Narrative* (New York, 1984), esp. ch 1.

35 For a fuller application of this argument to 'A Lover's Complaint', see my forthcoming article, '"The tip of his seducing tongue": Authorizers in *Henry V, A Lover's Complaint*, and *Othello*', in Zisser, ed., *Suffering Ecstasy*.

36 Helen Vendler, *The Art of Shakespeare's Sonnets* (Cambridge, MA., 1997), p. 18.

poem.[37] 'A Lover's Complaint' also comments on lyric by demonstrating the ease with which love stories can be borrowed and changed, thus drawing attention to the alienability of lyrics from their original authors and meanings.

The volatility of subject positions and the lability of ethical positions that I have been tracing have many implications not only for Shakespeare's lyrics and plays but also for theatres in broader senses. My arguments invite us to think further about how both power and authority work in the relationship between speaker and listener in venues ranging from a familial dinner table conversation to a political news conference. A very different type of interrogation and a very different type of theatre, that of a war, is, sadly, all too relevant as well: as I was drafting the original version of this essay, a recurrent defense offered by those present at the torture of prisoners in Iraq, a defense troped by the disturbed and disturbing use of photography, was 'I was only an observer, an audience.'

My explorations of the relationships among audiences and auditors also have numerous consequences for our pedagogical practices. Again borrowing the terminology of the discourse analysts, we might fruitfully rethink our lecturing techniques in terms of their categories – to what extent, in what ways, for what reasons, are we establishing our students as ratified listeners, or as eavesdroppers, or as bystanders? And when we reword a comment a student has made in order to integrate it into a discussion class, what are the benefits and what are the dangers? Because this act can indubitably be valuable for all parties, we often hone our skills at it without thoroughly examining its ambiguities and complexities. To begin with, the student in question, other members of the class and the teacher may each categorize the act in significantly different ways. As teachers, we could profitably acknowledge that it is multivalent. In particular, as animators we show respect for the student's ideas; yet in adapting them we, no less than Daniel's publisher and printer, risk becoming rival authors who coopt and distort meaning.

The poems explored above anatomize cognate risks and rewards. In a passage shortly after the one discussed near the opening of this essay, Daniel's Rosamond refers to her beauty as a 'Syren' (120). Like 'The Complaint of Rosamond', 'A Lover's Complaint' enacts and examines the siren song of language, demonstrating how it can seduce its listeners into changing course and changing place from audience to auditor, from judge to advocate, from observer to participant and even to perpetrator.

---

37 Compare William Waters's argument that the second-person pronouns in many lyrics offer an alternative to voiceability (*Poetry's Touch: On Lyric Address* (Ithaca, 2003), esp. pp. 14–15. I also discuss alternatives to and complications in identificatory voiceability in my recently completed manuscript, *The Challenges of Orpheus: Lyric in Early Modern England and Other Cultures*.

# 'ARMED AT POINT EXACTLY': THE GHOST IN *HAMLET*

R. A. FOAKES

## I

The ghost of Hamlet's father has received some notable attention recently, especially in two commentaries on the play. One is Stephen Greenblatt's *Hamlet in Purgatory* (2001), which is concerned with the resonances of the ghost's apparent claim to have come from purgatory, and the way contradictory interpretations of what happens in a play in which a 'young man from Wittenberg, with a distinctly Protestant temperament, is haunted by a distinctly Catholic ghost'.[1] The other is in the chapter devoted to 'ghosts and garments' in *Renaissance Clothing and the Materials of Memory* by Ann Rosalind Jones and Peter Stallybrass (2000). Here the emphasis is on what the authors see as the 'gross materiality' of renaissance stage ghosts, a materiality inescapable in the ways in which they were clothed. The ghost in *Hamlet*, they argue, has become an embarrassment since the eighteenth century, and 'Ridicule, rather than fear, has been the usual lot of Hamlet's ghost.'[2] It is worth pursuing further the question not considered by Greenblatt and touched on but not adequately considered by Jones and Stallybrass: why is this ghost, uniquely among the more than sixty stage ghosts in the drama of the period, clad in armour?

In the opening scene of the play the sceptical Horatio has to acknowledge seeing a ghost that appears in

> that fair and warlike form
> In which the majesty of buried Denmark
> Did sometimes march. (1.1.50–2)[3]

The ghost is twice described, by Barnardo at 1.1.53 and Marcellus at 1.1.68, as stalking, or moving stealthily, which is how ghosts were commonly perceived, but this ghost's stalk is unusual in being 'martial', which is appropriate, for it appears to Horatio in the 'very armour' he wore when fighting the 'sledded Polacks' (1.1.63). The ghost is seen as a 'portentous figure' (1.1.112), armed as if to connect the present threat of an invasion by young Fortinbras from Norway with old Hamlet's defeat in single combat of his father. The ghost disappears, perhaps aided by a little stage fog, since Marcellus says it 'faded on the crowing of the cock' (1.1.162). When Horatio reports to Hamlet what has happened, he reaffirms what was said earlier: the ghost, like old Hamlet,

> Armed at point exactly, cap-à-pie,
> Appears before them, and with solemn march
> Goes slow and stately by them. (1.2.200–2)

Hamlet questions Horatio and his companions as if specifically to confirm that the ghost was in full armour:

HAMLET Armed, say you?
ALL Armed, my lord.
HAMLET From top to toe?
ALL My lord, from head to foot.

[1] *Hamlet in Purgatory* (Princeton, 2001), p. 240.

[2] *Renaissance Clothing and the Materials of Memory* (Cambridge, 2000), pp. 246, 248.

[3] All quotations are from Harold Jenkins's edition for the Arden 2nd series (London, 1982).

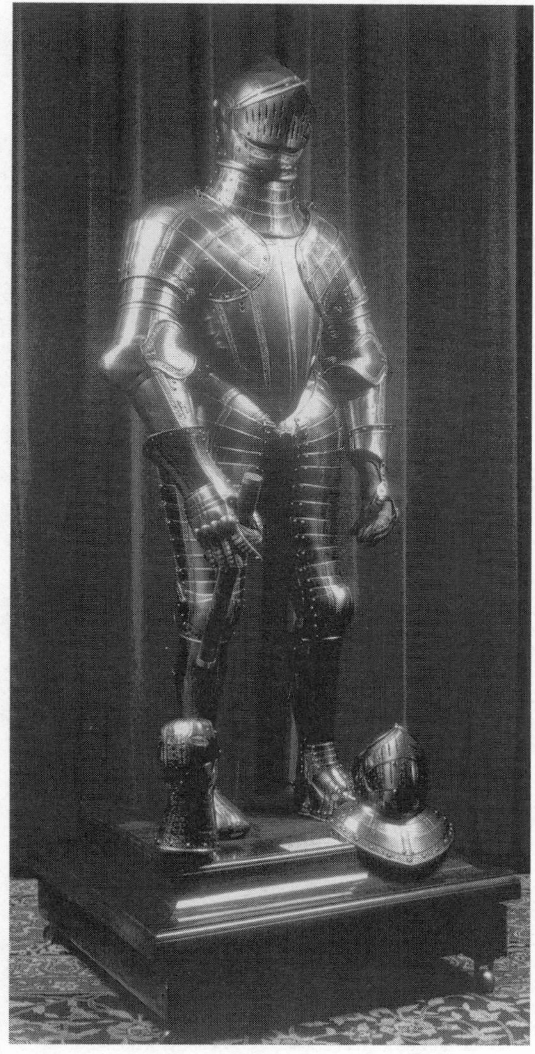

1 A 'cap-a-pie' armour of 'complete steel' made for Sir Henry Lee at about 1587

Then when eventually Hamlet confronts the ghost, he asks why this, 'dead corse, again in complete steel' returns to visit the earth.

Shakespeare thus takes much trouble to insist that the ghost is costumed in full armour. Horatio says he is armed 'at point', or properly in every detail, 'cap-à-pie'.[4] This term, commonly glossed in editions as equivalent to 'from head to foot', was properly used to describe a kind of heavy armour that encased the whole body, and was intended for use on horseback. Such armour could still be assembled for tilting in the 1580s, when Sir Henry Lee, the Queen's champion, had a suit made. This particular armour has survived (illustration 1). Sir Henry was born in 1532, and, as a cousin of Sir William Cecil, later Lord Burghley, gained access to the court and also to the favour of the Earl of Leicester.[5] He travelled in Europe, reporting to Cecil and Leicester and apparently yearning for military activity. In 1570 or thereabouts he established at Oxford what became an annual tilt to celebrate Elizabeth's accession day on 17 November, presenting himself as her champion. The tilt was transferred to Westminster in 1581, when Lee ran against Sir Philip Sidney. Lee resigned from his office as Queen's champion in 1590, pleading age, some years after she had made him in 1580 Master of the Royal Armouries, an important office during a period when the country was frequently at war. Lee thus, like old Hamlet, may be seen as outmoded by the end of the century. The armour he had made in 1587–8, apparently in case he could serve against the Spanish Armada, is technically a heavy field armour, such as might be worn by fully-armed cavalry. It seems, however, that while full body armour continued to be made in London until the late seventeenth century, its main use was ceremonial, for tilting on horseback. By the end of the sixteenth century such armour was obsolete in battle.

[4] The earliest example of the term in the *OED* is from Berners translation of Froissart, 1523, but it was in use much earlier and appears, for instance, in the description of the pageants staged to welcome Katherine of Aragon in 1501. See *The Receipt of Lady Catherine*, ed. Gordon Kipling (Early English Text Society, Oxford, 1990), p. 16.

[5] E. K. Chambers, *Sir Henry Lee An Elizabethan Portrait* (Oxford, 1936), pp. 31–4; see also Ian Eaves, 'The Greenwich Armour and Locking-Gauntlet of Sir Henry Lee in the Collection of the Worshipful Company of Armourers and Brasiers', *Journal of the Arms and Armour Society*, 16 (1998), 133–64. On 'Chivalric Ritual and Tournaments', see also *Elizabeth, The Exhibition at the National Maritime Museum*, ed. Susan Doran (London, 2003), pp. 91–7.

During the sixteenth century the practice of warfare changed radically, as the use of various kinds of portable guns became common. 'The day of the heavily armoured cavalryman, a feudal knight or nobleman' with his lance peaked around 1450 and was pretty much over by the sixteenth century, as they were no match for pikemen. The first mention of a pike as a weapon is recorded by the *OED* in 1511. By 1520 guns could slaughter pikemen, and by 1590 the Dutch army had two handguns for every pike.[6] The heavy harquebus, which had to be mounted on a tripod or something similar, was well established by the 1550s. The lighter caliver, which needed no rest, was in service by 1570, as was the pistol, which could be used 'by nobles and gentlemen to skirmish on horseback'.[7] By the late 1580s infantry were being armed with muskets. The common use of handguns helped to make heavy body armour redundant, since men needed to have arms and legs free and mobile for loading and firing.

If this is how an outline story might be presented now, writers on war and arms during the period did not see so clear a picture. During the later sixteenth century, and especially in the 1590s, a good number of books on the art of war were published. Many were principally concerned with the ordering of armies and battle tactics in relation to the need for 'practical expertise in leadership'.[8] At this time England was involved in campaigns against the Spanish in France and the Low Countries, and against the Irish, who were believed to be conspiring with Spain. Add the sense of being under threat of a Spanish invasion, and the proliferation of handbooks of instruction in the conduct of war becomes understandable. Most of these treatises deal at some point with arms and armour, and a number of writers take sides in a debate whether archers or men armed with guns were to be preferred in battle. This debate seems to have been initiated by Sir John Smythe in his *Certain Discourses Military* (1590), in which he laments that men of war in England extol the use of guns, and calls for a return to the longbow. Smythe was born in 1531, and his old-fashioned views were rejected by writers like Humphry Barwick, who replied in 1591 claiming that professional soldiers always prefer a gun. This debate reflected a larger traditionalist resistance to modern weapons and nostalgia for the past. Most tracts on war appeal to precedent, and cite Greek and Roman authorities and biblical precedents for the conduct of war.[9] Some of these works show a lingering nostalgia for older weapons and for the use of armour. So *Instructions for the Warres* (1589), translated by Paul Ive from a French treatise by Raimond de Fourquevaux published in 1548, begins from the Roman army and recommends that soldiers should wear armour, for 'although that Harness be too weak to resist ordnance or Harquebushes; notwithstanding, it dooth defend a man from the stroke of Pike, Halberd, and Sword, Cross-bow, Longbow, and from stones' (p. 98).

The nostalgia for armour was connected with its symbolic function as associated with 'the constitution of the aristocrat and the honour of a gentleman',[10] a function exemplified in the adventures of armed knights in Spenser's *Faerie Queene* as well as in Queen Elizabeth's birthday tilts. Armour also could be seen as embodying the stiffness of masculinity; remove it and the masculine body 'risks being spilled into the formlessness that is associated with the feminine'.[11] As late as 1597

6 See Andrew Cunningham and Ole Peter Grell, *The Four Horsemen of the Apocalypse. Religion, War, Famine and Death in Reformation Europe* (Cambridge, 2000), pp. 114–18. The change is registered in the shift from chivalry, the medieval term suggesting knightly prowess, to cavalry, mere horse soldiers in the sixteenth century.

7 Nina Taunton, *1590s Drama and Militarism* (Aldershot, 2001), p. 8.

8 Taunton, *1590s Drama*, pp. 133–4.

9 As, for example, do Matthew Sutcliffe in *The Practice, Proceedings, and Laws of Arms* (1593), who is fond of citing Livy on the wars of Scipio and Hannibal, and Barnabe Rich, *Alarm to England, foreshadowing what perils are procured where the people live without regard of martial law* (1578), who finds war 'wonderfully extolled in innumerable places of holy scripture' (A4r). Shakespeare gently mocks the absurdity of appealing to ancient classical precedents in the figure of Captain Fluellen in *Henry V*, whose ideas are drawn from the wars of Pompey and Alexander the Great.

10 Taunton, *1590s Drama*, p. 137.

11 Taunton, *1590s Drama*, p. 141.

2 Soldier armed with a caliver. From Jacob de Gheyn, *The Exercise of Armes for Caliveres, Muskettes, and Pikes* (The Hague, 1607, reprinted 1971)

3 Soldier armed with a pike

Sir Edward Hoby, in his translation of *Theorique and Practise of War* by Bernardino de Mendoza, acknowledges that victories at this time were won by artillery, muskets and harquebuses (p. 109), yet still recommends maintaining heavy cavalry armed with lances merely because all nations have 'used many ages to make their horsemen carry them' (p. 55). The nostalgia for armour and ancient weapons is counterbalanced by those who pleaded, like Robert Barret in *Theorike and Practise of Modern Wars* (1598), that 'we must accommodate ourselves to the now used weapons', the pike, the harquebus and the musket. His argument is presented as a debate between a Gentleman and a Captain, the Gentleman representing those who say soldiers should follow the practice of our ancestors who won battles with bows and arrows, the Captain observing that wars are much changed since 'fiery weapons' were invented (pp. 2–3). Barret starts by referring to the Spanish Armada of 1588 and the likelihood that Spain will attack again. Pikemen were expected to wear a headpiece and light armour covering trunk and thighs; musketeers, like argolotiers, or light cavalry mounting calivers, might dispense with armour, as shown in the illustrations (illustrations 2–4) to Jacob de Gheyn's *The Exercise of Arms* (1607). This book, printed in English as well as Dutch, represents 'the right manner and fashion of the arminge' of the guard of Maurits, Prince of Orange. It is in three unpaged sections, illustrating in detail instructions on the use of calivers, muskets and pikes. The handler of the caliver wears a light helmet to cover his head but not his face; the musketeer is depicted as having no armour at all; and the pikeman is shown with a light helmet and with a cuirass covering the

4 Soldier armed with a musket

front of his body, but not his arms or legs.[12] By 1642 Donald Lupton, in his *A Warre-like Treatise of the Pike . . . with the praise of the Musquet and Halfe-Pike* notes that 'Buffe-coats came so much in request, because they are so easy and comely, and (if good) as fit for defence as common Corslets' (p. 42).

In his account of a voyage undertaken in 1593 Sir Richard Hawkins described an encounter with hostile Spanish ships and famously observed, with reference to the accuracy of the enemy musketeers:

> I had great preparation of armours as well of proof and of light corselets, yet not a man would wear them, but esteemed a pot of wine a better defence than armour of proof.[13]

His men refused not only heavy armour 'of proof', proved or tested against weapons and maybe bullets, but light body armour or corselets made of steel; they no doubt felt safer being mobile with the chance of dodging enemy fire. Body armour gave way to the use by pikemen of a breast-plate or cuirass and light helmet to protect the most vital parts of the body, or simply a stout buff or leather coat.

Full body armour could be very heavy, and a complete helmet alone might weigh up to twenty pounds. How, then, was the ghost in *Hamlet* costumed? In his *Dictionary of Shakespeare's Military Language*, Charles Edelman comments on the various references to armour in the plays, noting a number of instances where the text implies that players are wearing armour, as when King Philip of France complains, 'With burden of our armour here we sweat' (*King John*, 2.1.92). Richard III, Antony and Macbeth have armour, and in *The Two Noble Kinsmen*, 3.6, Palomon and Arcite put on 'heavy' (3.6.56) armour in view of the audience.[14] Edelman is convinced, on the basis of such references, that 'The Globe players must have had many of them [i.e., suits of armour] hanging in the tiring house to wear in battle scenes.' All the characters associated with body armour appear in plays that are ostensibly set in what was for Shakespeare's audience the past, usually a distant past. The ghost in *Hamlet* is 'monumentalized'[15] in armour that endures, and recalls the effigies of knights who, from medieval times, and still to some extent in Shakespeare's age, liked to be represented with some hints of armour on their tombs, and perhaps with a trophy, sword and helmet hung above, such as Laertes laments were lacking in the 'obscure funeral' of Polonius (4.5.210). Stage

---

12 Jacob de Gheyn, *The Exercise of Armes, or Wapenhandelinghe* (The Hague, 1607; reprinted by de Tijdstroom, Lochem and McGraw-Hill, 1971). The work was dedicated to 'those that love the Exercise of Armes', and was printed with 'the privilege of the King of France'.

13 Sir Richard Hawkins, *Observations* (1622), ed. James D. Williamson (London, 1935), p. 148.

14 Edelman, *Shakespeare's Military Language A Dictionary*. Athlone Shakespeare Dictionary Series. (London and New Brunswick, 2000), pp. 20–24.

15 Ann Rosalind Jones and Peter Stallybrass, *Renaissance Clothing and the Materials of Memory* (Cambridge, 2000), pp. 250–1. In Kenneth Branagh's film of the play (1997) the ghost is first seen as a statue in armour coming to life.

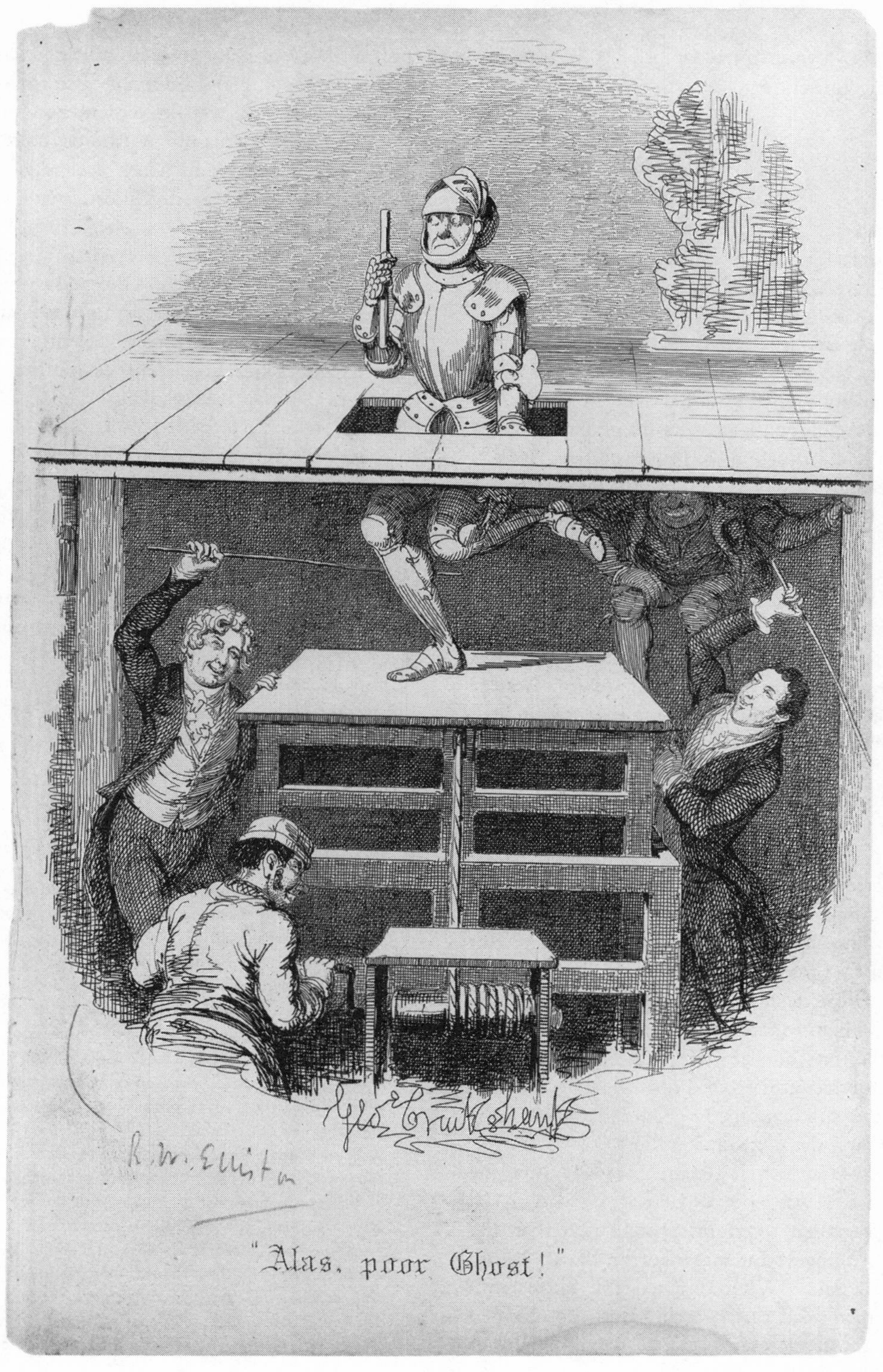


5 George Cruikshank, cartoon entitled 'Alas, poor Ghost!' (1849), as reprinted in George Raymond, *The Life and Enterprises of Robert Elliston* (1857), facing p. 116

armour, however contrived, no doubt appeared reasonably authentic.

## II

According to Ann Rosalind Jones and Peter Stallybrass, the ghost first appeared on stage 'at the historical point at which ghosts themselves become increasingly implausible, at least to an educated élite', so that 'to believe in them at all it seems necessary to assert their immateriality, their invisibility'.[16] They claim that the very materiality of the ghost in traditional armour made him by the late eighteenth century an embarrassment, a figure to be mocked as absurd; hence, 'it is as laughter increasingly threatens the ghost that he starts to be staged not in armor but in some form of "spirit drapery"'.[17] The works of Shakespeare, and especially *Hamlet*, his best-known play, provided endless material for burlesque and caricature in the late eighteenth and nineteenth centuries, and certainly the clumsy winching of the ghost through a trapdoor might raise laughter. George Cruikshank's well-known cartoon (illustration 5) in fact was based on a practical joke played by Robert Elliston and a friend on a fellow-actor who was descending to solemn music through a trapdoor. They 'applied their sticks sharply and rapidly to the thinly clad calves of his legs' making him dance and look foolish.[18] The play being performed was not identified, and it was Cruikshank who turned the figure into Shakespeare's Ghost in armour. But was it in fact materiality that gradually made the ghost an embarrassment or the costume of armour? In fact William Macready's 1849 production at the Haymarket was one of many that continued until the twentieth century to costume the ghost in what looked like full armour, in accordance with stage tradition and the text (illustration 6).

It seems that when theatres opened after the Restoration it was Thomas Betterton, who played Hamlet between 1663 and 1709, rather than the ghost who conveyed a sense of terror. Barton Booth reportedly said, 'When I acted the ghost with Betterton, instead of my awing him, he terrified me.'[19] Commentators on David Garrick's famous portrayal of Hamlet, first seen in 1742, were struck by his convincing embodiment of terror when he saw the ghost. A well-known mezzotint after a lost painting by Benjamin Wilson portrays Garrick with his legs apart and hands extended as when he was confronted by the ghost, who is significantly not included (illustration 7). Even Partridge in Henry Fielding's *Tom Jones* (1750), sceptical at first, because he knew that 'Ghosts don't appear in such Dresses as that', that is, armour, was overcome by fear, so that he 'fell into so violent a Trembling that his Knees knocked against each other'. He was frightened by Garrick playing Hamlet, 'the same Passions which succeeded each other in *Hamlet*, succeeding likewise in him'.[20] This kind of reaction is confirmed by Georg Lichtenberg's detailed account of Garrick's performance as making the whole audience 'terror-struck' into silence. The actor playing Hamlet, rather than the ghost, conveyed a sense of terror to the audience. Later interpreters of Hamlet could achieve a similar effect, according to William Winter, who said that when Edwin Booth played Hamlet, from 1864 onwards, 'the weird and awful atmosphere of the ghost-scenes was preserved by the actor's transfiguration into tremulous suspense and horror'.[21]

---

16 Jones and Stallybrass, *Renaissance Clothing*, p. 248.

17 Jones and Stallybrass, *Renaissance Clothing*, p. 246.

18 See George Raymond, *The Life and Enterprises of Robert William Elliston Comedian* (London, 1857), p. 117. In *Shakespeare and the Actors* (Cambridge, Mass., 1948), A. C. Sprague reports a comment made in 1884 by John Foster Kirk that until recently the ghost had traditionally descended through a trapdoor in Act 1 of *Hamlet*, but in Act 3 Hamlet sees him make his exit through a 'portal' or door.

19 Thomas Davies, *Dramatic Miscellanies* (1784), III, 31–2, cited in A. C. Sprague, *Shakespearian Players and Performance* (Cambridge, Mass, 1953), p. 12.

20 Fielding, *Tom Jones*, Book XVI, chapter 5.

21 William Winter, *The Life and Art of Edwin Booth* (New York 1893), p. 172. As always reactions vary according to the focus of different members of the audience. If the reviewers generally kept their eyes on Booth in his 1870 production, there was at least one commentator who attended to the ghost and was not impressed: 'In all respects it was a model ghost, stepping out like a pedestrian, holding its mace over its left shoulder in statuesque dignity, vocalizing with all Mr. Walker's music of intonation, strong in the traditional dolefulness on

6 William Macready as Hamlet encountering a ghost in armour (1849). Engraving by Hollis from a painting by Reid

By 1810 it could be said of *Hamlet* the play, 'from its being so frequently before the public, so very generally read, and so continually quoted, it is, more than any other, calculated to give to burlesque its full effect', and, the writer might have added, to caricature also.[22] By the middle of the nineteenth century the ghost in armour, like many other well-known figures in Shakespeare's plays, could be parodied in matter for a joke. Jones and Stallybrass can point to Mr Wopsle's amateur staging of *Hamlet* in *Great Expectations*, chapter 31, in which the ghost is played by an actor with a cough and a manuscript attached to his truncheon to remind him of lines he had forgotten; the 'terrors' of this ghost were

one note'. This comment, by 'Nym Crinkle' in the *Dispatch*, January 1870, is cited by Charles H. Shattuck in *The Hamlet of Edwin Booth* (Urbana, 1969), p. 86. The illustration of this scene (illustration 8) by Thomas Glessing shows the ghost carrying a short truncheon, but not holding a mace or anything over his shoulder.

22 Citing John Poole, preface to his *Hamlet Travesties* in *Nineteenth-Century Shakespeare Burlesques*, selected with an introduction by Stanley Wells (Wilmington, Delaware, 1978), p. 6; see also Jonathan Bate, *Shakespearean Constitutions:*

7 David Garrick's gesture on seeing the ghost, a mezzotint by James McArdell (1754) from a lost painting by Benjamin Wilson

'received derisively'. What such examples show, I suspect, is that it was not the ghost as such but the figure in armour, especially when sinking or rising through a trap, that became an embarrassment as ideas of a natural style of acting changed, and technological advances in staging, in lighting, in the use of shadows and gauzes, in the ability to create a sense of transparency or mystery, made possible the representation of a spectre or phantasm in place of an actor constrained by a rigid suit of armour. Such constraint might have anticipated Henri Bergson's perception of the comic as partaking 'rather of the unsprightly than of the unsightly, of *rigidness* rather than of *ugliness*', as when the human body 'reminds us of a mere machine'.[23] It seems likely that as armour fell quite out of use and phantasmic or transparent ghosts could be created on stage, the business of stimulating terror was transferred from the actor playing Hamlet to the stage effects associated with the ghost.

The ghost continued to be played in simulated armour, though often with drapery or a cloak covering much of his body, as in Edwin Booth's version in 1870, in which the ghost was clad in what looked like chain-mail (illustration 8). Some later productions also have retained a ghost in armour, for example Max Reinhardt's 1909 Berlin production, and the 1934 production at the New Theatre in London, in which John Gielgud played Hamlet and William Devlin the ghost.[24] Since the nineteenth century, productions have more generally aimed at relieving the actor playing Hamlet of establishing a sense of terror for the audience by creating a supernatural aura for the ghost by the use of phosphorescence, masks, mists, shadows, green or blue luminosities, and unearthly sounds. The ghost 'has been a moving shaft of light', it has seemed to be transparent, 'it has been a wraith of smoke or mist, an eerie glimmer, a vapor, a silky cloud'.[25] The image of the ghost in armour has long been pretty much abandoned in productions. The ghost may show a hint of some military connection, a glint of metal in a collar, belt or helmet, but as played by actors at the present time his body is usually covered by a coat or cloak. However, it would seem that 'All these non-bodily images may enhance the quality of the supernatural, but they may fail the horror and humanity Shakespeare designed.'[26] The problem, I think, is not that ghosts have become 'increasingly implausible' (as Jones and Stallybrass assert),

*Politics, Theatre, Criticism 1730–1830* (Oxford, 1989), and Alan R. Young, *Hamlet and the Visual Arts 1709–1900* (Newark, 2002); chapter 5 of this book is concerned with travesties of the play.

[23] Henri Bergson, 'Laughter', in Wylie Sypher, ed., *Comedy* (New York, 1956), p. 79. The early nineteenth century was a great age of caricature and cartoon, and Shakespeare's plays, especially *Hamlet*, were cited again and again in prints commenting on the excesses of politicians and of actors and the stage.

[24] See *Hamlet through the Ages. A Pictorial Record from 1709*, compiled by Raymond Mander and Joe Mitchenson (London, 1952).

[25] Marvin Rosenberg, *The Masks of Hamlet* (Cranbury, N.J., London, and Mississauga, Ontario, 1992), p. 21.

[26] Rosenberg, *Masks of Hamlet*, pp. 21–2.

8 Edwin Booth as Hamlet in Act 1, Scene 4, as Horatio and Marcellus try to restrain him from following the ghost

but rather that there is no way of recapturing the double nature of the ghost.

The materiality of the ghost is built into Shakespeare's play, since he has to lecture his son, and at the point where he begins his long critique of Gertrude and his account of the murder, he, so to speak, returns to life as a father explaining himself to his son. By the time of Garrick's *Hamlet* Barton Booth as the ghost entered with 'noiseless tread',[27] and Lichtenberg reports that a later ghost, Bransby, 'looked, in truth, very fine, clad from head to foot in armour, for which a suit of steel-blue satin did duty'.[28] Armour, or imitation armour, in this case chain-mail, was still used in Edwin Booth's staging of the play, though Hamlet was brilliantly lit as if by moonlight, while the ghost remained shadowed. Spectral innovations since the nineteenth century have tended to create an immense gap between old Hamlet the ghost and old Hamlet the father. It seems to me that the most moving ghosts in recent productions have emphasized materiality rather than the supernatural, and have presented the ghost as like other characters.[29] If the play is staged in neutral or modern dress, the ghost may simply

[27] Davies, *Dramatic Miscellanies*, III, 32.

[28] *Lichtenberg's Visits to England*, p. 11.

[29] In his *Hamlet* (Shakespeare in Performance. Manchester and New York, 1995), Anthony Dawson remarks, 'Of the various strategies that have been attempted, the least successful, I think, are those that shy away from a solid spectre to eerie lighting effects or amplified spooky voices with no material presence whatever. What is frightening about the ghost for those who see him is precisely that he is *there*, even though they know he is dead' (p. 127).

wear a military uniform, as in Steven Pimlott's production for the Royal Shakespeare Theatre in 2001, or a business suit, as in Michael Almereyda's film, 2000. The most harrowing representation I have seen was that by Paul Scofield in Franco Zeffirelli's film version (1990). This ghost was played not as a warrior, but as a suffering, bareheaded figure in a rich gown, sitting, rising on 'methinks I scent the morning air', and holding out his hands to the son he cannot touch. It seems we can have materiality or the supernatural, but not both convincingly at the same time, whereas Shakespeare could, I believe, assume that his audience would find both plausible in the staging of the play. In his production for the Royal Shakespeare Theatre in 2004 Michael Boyd chose the supernatural, the ghost appearing as an emaciated, bent, ghastly figure dragging an immense sword that rattled like a chain as he passed slowly through the audience. The effect was startling, but gained at the expense of omitting the numerous references to armour in the text, and sacrificing an important dimension of the play.

### III

The ghost is seen by Horatio and Marcellus in the opening scene as a portent in relation to a potential war between Denmark and Norway that never takes place, but his armour marks both the ghost's association with an old ethos based on violence, and also his cultural distance from young Hamlet, the student from Wittenberg. Hamlet idealizes his father as a warrior hero, and mythologizes him as a classical deity. At the Globe did such a ghost wear real or phantasmal armour? Since the ghost in *Hamlet* is unique in this respect, it is impossible to be sure; but he speaks as a king and father, and so becomes substantial, an actor, a human being. A full armour, head to foot, being made of metal, would make a considerable noise. A stage direction in *The Two Noble Kinsmen*, 5.1, calls for a sound effect, 'there is heard clanging of armour'. Did the ghost in *Hamlet* wear a real armour and make a sound on stage? The effect could have been striking, as when the ghost of Marley shakes his chains with a 'dismal and appalling noise' in *A Christmas Carol* (1843); Dickens begins his tale of Scrooge with a reference to the ghost in *Hamlet*, noting that what makes the ghost remarkable is our conviction that old Hamlet, like Marley, is dead. If indeed real armour was used, or even if the ghost had some kind of property armour, and, as Horatio says, wore also a helmet with the 'beaver'[30] or face-guard up so that his grizzled beard could be seen, then it is no wonder that his progress on stage was 'slow and stately' (1.2.202). An armour of 'complete steel' was suitable for heavy cavalry or tilting on horseback, but the text makes it clear that the ghost marches on stage. If he was costumed in armour, he would presumably have been not at all what an audience used to ghosts represented in burial garb, a white sheet, or sometimes day clothes, would have expected, for his costume is unique, and in many ways this ghost is 'radically different from any ghost that preceded or followed it in the drama of the English Renaissance'.[31] At the Globe this was an innovatory ghost, and may well have startled an audience that shared Burbage's display of terror. When the ghost begins to speak to Hamlet, he sounds more and more like a somewhat tedious father giving his son a moral lecture not about war or even about revenge after his first outburst, but about lust, poison and murder. Directors of the play have tried all kinds of ways of presenting him, and have found the shift awkward here as the ghost changes from a stately warrior figure to a troubled father.

Why then did Shakespeare invent this armoured ghost, and is anything lost if he does not appear as a marshal with 'an eye like Mars to threaten and command', wearing a helmet and carrying the

[30] The word 'beaver' derives from old French 'bavière', or child's bib, and properly covered the chin, not the upper part of the face, but by Shakespeare's time a single face-guard had replaced the separate chin-guard and eye-guard or visor, and Horatio must refer to this in saying the ghost 'wore his beaver up'; see Edelman, *Shakespeare's Military Language*, pp. 45–7.

[31] According to Eleanor Prosser, *Hamlet and Revenge* (Stanford, 1967, 1971), p. 264. See also Stanley Wells, 'Staging Shakespeare's Ghosts', in *The Arts of Performance in Elizabethan and Early Stuart Drama*, ed. Murray Biggs (Edinburgh, 1991), pp. 50–69.

truncheon that was an attribute of the god of war? I think the best answer may be that the obsolete militarism of the ghost enabled the dramatist to embody a range of conflicting values that establish the main parameters of the action. In the first place, his archaic costume associated him with a past that seemed distant and representative of outmoded habits of thought and action. Shakespeare needed someone to certify that the ghost indeed appeared in the image of old Hamlet, and uses Horatio for this purpose, who is too young to have known the old king when he settled an international quarrel by challenging old Fortinbras to single combat. In the present dispensation of Claudius, we have already seen him in 1.2 dealing with a similar problem by negotiation and diplomacy. Although Claudius has very recently taken over the rule of Denmark from old Hamlet, it is as if the change marks a transition from medieval to modern ways of handling affairs. The ghost also seems distanced in time by his claim to come from some kind of Purgatory, as

> for the day confined to fast in fires,
> Till the foul crimes done in my days of nature
> Are burned and purged away. (1.5.11–13)

These lines no doubt invited the audience to recall the Catholic doctrine of Purgatory, though an armed apparition is odd, for souls in purgatory might be expected to return by taking a phantasmal body only in order to ask the living for help through prayers or masses to relieve them of their torments.[32] Old Hamlet is a very solid ghost, and asks for revenge, not for prayers.

In writing the play Shakespeare had Virgil's *Aeneid* in mind, as is seen in the First Player's speech based on the story of Dido and Aeneas in 2.2; so he may well have been thinking here also of the classical idea of purgation by fire of evil deeds, referred to in the *Aeneid*, VI.742.[33] The ghost also may be related to the Senecan stage ghosts that called for revenge in plays familiar to many in Shakespeare's audience, like *The Spanish Tragedy*. The ghost carries a truncheon, which was associated with the authority of Mars as God of War: Troilus invokes this image when eager to fight with Diomedes; nothing can hold him back,

> Not fate, obedience, nor the hand of Mars
> Beck'ning with fiery truncheon my retire.
> (5.3.54–5)

Hamlet has already shown in his first soliloquy that he associates his father with classical deities (Hyperion, the sun-god) and heroes (Hercules; 1.2.140, 153), so that the ghost may be seen as related at once both to ancient classical and to old Christian frames of reference. The Catholic associations emerge again when the ghost complains that when he was murdered by Claudius he was deprived of the last rites, 'Unhouseled, disappointed, unanealed'. It is significant that Hamlet sees the ghost as belonging to a different world from his own, not only in his heroic or godlike stature, but also in religious terms. Hamlet has been a student at Wittenberg, where Martin Luther had initiated the Reformation, and, in contrast to the ghost, speaks as a Protestant. He assumes the ghost comes from heaven or hell (1.4.41; 1.5.92), and later suspects, in a conventional Protestant fashion, that it may be a devil.[34]

---

[32] See Mary Yardley, 'The Catholic Position in the Ghost Controversy of the Sixteenth Century', in John Dover Wilson's edition of Lewes Lavater, *Of Ghosts and Spirits Walking by Night* (1572; Oxford, for the Shakespeare Association, 1929), pp. 240–1; and Roland Mushat Frye, *The Renaissance Hamlet Issues and Responses in 1600* (Princeton, 1984), pp. 11–29. Stephen Greenblatt has made much of the afterlife of Purgatory in the play, while recognising the problem created by a ghost who calls for vengeance; he does not ask why the ghost appears in armour: see his *Hamlet in Purgatory* (Princeton, 2001), especially pp. 235–40. His account should be compared with Alexander Welsh's rejection of scholarly investigations of religious beliefs as little value in relation to ghosts in *Hamlet in his Modern Guises* (Princeton, 2001), 28–36: 'In a play or fiction, ghosts are among the easiest characters to put to use because they are not bound to be plausible in ways that other characters may be' (p. 36). On the peculiar nature of the ghost in *Hamlet* in relation to other Elizabethan stage ghosts, see also E. Pearlman, 'Shakespeare at Work: The Invention of the ghost', in *Hamlet New Critical Essays*, ed. Arthur Kinney (London and New York, 2002), pp. 71–84.

[33] See the note by Harold Jenkins in his edition of the play (Arden Series 2; London and New York, 1982), pp. 453–4.

[34] As Harold Jenkins points out in his edition, p. 483.

In other words, Hamlet belongs to a Protestant present, the ghost to a Catholic past.[35] The opening of the play established for the audiences at the Globe an immediate connection with their present time, with its image of nervous sentries on guard, watching for a possible invasion. This scene was performed between 1599 and 1604 against a backdrop of national mobilization 'of the sort renewed in London in the summers of 1599 and 1601', when there were invasion scares, uprisings in Ireland, and also fighting in the Netherlands – a play on the victory at Turnhout in 1597 was staged in October 1599, with actors representing the English generals Sir Francis Vere and Sir Robert Sidney, while the ongoing Siege of Ostend (1601–4) produced a stream of news pamphlets.[36] The sentinels on guard at Elsinore were, I think, costumed in contemporary military costume; the text gives no indication, but Marcellus offers to strike at the ghost with his 'partisan', a kind of spear with a 'tapering, two-edged, triangular-shaped blade' introduced in the early sixteenth century, first recorded in the *OED* in 1556, and still in use in Shakespeare's age.[37] Claudius likes to celebrate, as did the Danish court in Shakespeare's time,[38] by firing cannon (1.2.126; first recorded in 1525), and has a royal guard of Swiss soldiers or 'Switzers' (4.5.97, first recorded 1591), mercenaries much 'employed in Shakespeare's time', who might be confused with the guard of the Kings of Denmark, because the bright colours of their uniforms were similar.[39] Hamlet famously hopes to see Claudius 'Hoist with his own petard', a device using gunpowder to breach a wall or blow down a gate, first recorded in 1598, and he fights Laertes with a rapier, first recorded in 1553. According to Osric, Laertes bets he can beat Hamlet, staking six rapiers with their hangers, a term first recorded in 1598, and also six poniards, first recorded 1588. These dates are not important except in so far as they place Claudius, Hamlet and the sentries in Shakespeare's own time, a time of partisans, guns and rapiers, and mark their temporal distance from the world of old Hamlet.

In Shakespeare's age many people believed, with Lewis Lavater and others, that spirits could take bodily form and speak, and we can assume that the ghost in *Hamlet* was taken seriously by audiences at the Globe, and served an important function in the play. Hamlet idealizes his father as a warrior hero and mythologizes him as a classical deity; hence the enormous authority the ghost has for the prince when he begins to speak. The figure in full armour, whether clanking or simulated, is also an image from an older age and a different culture. It is a ghost from Purgatory that does not seek the help of the living to ease its torments, but instead calls for revenge. Only when the ghost goes on to moralize about the lust of Claudius and Gertrude, and to describe how the murder took place, does he suddenly close the gap in time and become Hamlet's father to the life, whose funeral Horatio hoped to witness. As the play continues, however, Hamlet associates the death of his father with the slaughter of Priam in calling for a speech from the Player, and later links old Hamlet with Hyperion, Jove, Mars and Mercury. Yet he also accepts the Protestant position that the devil might appear in the guise of a dead man, and that what men 'imagine they see or hear, proceedeth either of melancholia, weakness of the senses, fear, or of some other perturbation'.[40]

> The spirit that I have seen
> May be a devil, and the devil hath power
> T'assume a pleasing shape, yea, and perhaps,
> Out of my weakness and my melancholy,
> As he is very potent with such spirits,
> Abuses me to damn me. (2.2.594–9)

---

35 Stephen Greenblatt's comment that in the play 'a young man from Wittenberg, with a distinctly Protestant temperament, is haunted by a distinctly Catholic ghost' (*Hamlet in Purgatory*, p. 240) does not relate this contrast to images from the past and present in the action.

36 See Nick de Somogyi, *Shakespeare's Theatre of War* (Aldershot, 1998), pp. 225–35, and, for the play on the fight at Turnhout, G. B. Harrison, *The Elizabethan Journals* (2 vols., New York, 1965), 2, 122.

37 Edelman, *Shakespeare's Military Language*, p. 247.

38 Jenkins, *Hamlet*, p. 447.

39 Edelman, *Shakespeare's Military Language*, p. 352.

40 Lavater, ed. Dover Wilson, pp. 9, 234–5.

The ghost is thus a very complex figure, who marks the distance between ancient and modern in his armour and in his heroic classical associations, and marks the distance between Catholic and Protestant in his association with Purgatory and last rites. Yet he almost closes that gap when he speaks as a murdered father, and shows a puritanical obsession with sex and lust, an obsession Hamlet also reveals in the closet scene with his mother. The ghost appears again in this scene, where it is observed only by Hamlet, and not by his mother. Eighteenth-century representations of the ghost in this scene show him in the same armour he wore in Act 1, but this was, of course, before the identification in 1823 of the first printed text, the 1603 Quarto of the play. Most modern productions that bring the ghost on stage ignore the demand for armour 'head to foot' in Act 1, and he may appear in Act 3 in a brocade gown (Franco Zeffirelli's film, 1990), cloaked and bareheaded (Kevin Kline's TV version, 1990), dressed in a suit (John Barton, Royal Shakespeare Theatre, 1980), or cowled and cloaked like a monk (Kenneth Branagh's film, 1997).

Sometimes in modern productions of this scene the ghost remains offstage or off the screen as a figment of Hamlet's imagination. Sometimes directors have introduced the ghost here in a dressing-gown, following the stage direction in the first Quarto of 1603, 'Enter the ghost in his night gowne'. This direction in a garbled and unsatisfactory text may show what a touring company did, but has no authority and is not present in the full text of the second Quarto. Q1 also changes Hamlet's greeting of the ghost:

(Q1) Do you not come your tardy son to chide
That I thus long have let revenge slip by?

(Q2) Do you not come your tardy son to chide
That, laps'd in time and passion, lets go by
Th'important acting of your dread command?
O say.

The difference is significant, for Q2 shows it would be appropriate if the ghost again appeared in archaic armour, as a figure embodying that 'dread command'. As the ghost makes his exit, Hamlet says 'Look how it steals away. / My father in his habit as he lived' (3.4.135–6). What was his 'habit' here? I think he may well have costumed again as a soldier in what looked like armour, with 'an eye like Mars to threaten and command', the 'fair and warlike form' seen by Horatio. According to Hamlet, the ghost leaves the stage through 'the portal', presumably a stage door, not a trapdoor, and he may have entered in the same way in this scene, a very material ghost, in 'slow and stately' march, not seen or heard by his mother, and anticipating the arrival of another warrior, Fortinbras.

The entry in 4.4. calls for Fortinbras to march 'with his Army over the stage' on his way to smite the Poles much as old Hamlet had done. In some ways this warrior prince resembles old Hamlet. Are these Norwegian soldiers in armour here? I think they most likely appeared as modern soldiers, not in armour, but carrying pikes or guns. When Fortinbras arrives at the end of the play he treats the dead Hamlet as a soldier, who is carried off to 'The soldier's music and the rite of war' as the order is given, 'Go, bid the soldiers shoot'. Fortinbras may in some ways be a reincarnation of old Hamlet, but he belongs to the new age of guns and, visually, also to the new era of diplomacy, since he comes on with the English ambassadors. The play's final irony, of course, is that only in death is Hamlet at last, as it were, absorbed into the ideal of the warrior hero represented for him by his father, and sent off for a burial with full military honours. The final stage direction in the Folio text calls for a 'peal of ordnance' to be heard, so that the sound of cannon firing, which marked the drinking bouts of Claudius (1.4.6 and 5.2.271–5) now, more appropriately, provides the 'soldier's music and the rite of war' (5.2.404) that accompany the body of Hamlet as it is carried off at the end.

# WRITING ABOUT MOTIVE: ISABELLA, THE DUKE AND MORAL AUTHORITY

ANNA KAMARALLI

What more disruptive theatrical figure is it possible to conceive than a heroine with no interest in romance? In *Measure for Measure* Isabella's refusal to be bartered and, perhaps more importantly, her absolute refusal to treat men as if they are the most important thing in the world, is so outrageously radical that every means available has been employed to deflect, reduce, neutralize or trivialize the threat she poses. When Penny Gay discerns, in Barry Kyle's production, 'the *force majeure* which declares that men's experience is important and meaningful, women's merely the product of hysteria and ignorance about the real world',[1] her observation is applicable far beyond this single example, and could be summing up the majority of interpretations of Isabella, both critical and performative. It has been argued that this quality is inherent in the text: 'Isabella, for all her importance in the play, is defined theatrically by the men around her for the men in the audience.'[2] At some level this may be inevitable, given that Isabella is not a woman, but rather a fictitious construct from a male-dominated literary period. She exists, however, in some sublimely rich and eloquent exchanges of language that pose difficult ethical questions, and productions can choose to use these in a way that curtails her more challenging aspects or in a way that celebrates them.

Certainly, no other of Shakespeare's characters has prompted such widely varied responses, with critics tending either to praise or condemn immoderately. These contrasting approaches have shared a tendency to frame their arguments around a question of Isabella's motives, as if she were a fully formed human being, whose motivation can be determined and judged. If such a system of almost psychoanalytical (and openly anachronistic) character analysis is employed, are there possible readings that are less limiting to her character than those that, in the words of Jacqueline Rose, 'alternatively revered and accused her in such a way that her sexual identity has become the site on which dissatisfaction with the play, and disagreement about the play, have turned'?[3] The text supports the inference that Isabella makes independent decisions based on a rational moral code, and yet interpreters have frequently wound themselves into all sorts of deductive contortions in order to maintain that her motives are more personal, and that she is in need of rescue by the benevolent hand of the patriarch.

Isabella is not a typical romantic heroine, even within the comparatively serious style of the tragicomedy. Her concerns are in no way to do with love or marriage; they are much bigger. Life, death, the soul and redemption are her preoccupations; the nature of truth, seeming and being is her focal point. The only indication in the text of her having feelings for a man is that she loves her brother

[1] Penny Gay, *As She Likes It: Shakespeare's Unruly Women* (London, 1994), p. 136.

[2] Kathleen McLuskie, 'The Patriarchal Bard', in *Political Shakespeare*, ed. Jonathan Dollimore and Alan Sinfield (Manchester, 1985), pp. 88–108; p. 96.

[3] Jacqueline Rose, 'Sexuality in the Reading of Shakespeare: *Hamlet* and *Measure for Measure*', in *Alternative Shakespeares*, ed. John Drakakis (London, 1985), pp. 95–118; p. 103.

Claudio very much – 'I something do excuse the thing I hate / For his advantage that I dearly love' (2.4.120–1). At the conclusion of the play, the Duke proposes marriage to her twice, and each time Shakespeare gives her no scripted response. The remarkable openness of a character who is constantly speaking *with* feeling, but hardly ever *about* it provides an unparalleled opportunity for directors and actors to find their own sense of the relationships in the play.

Isabella is neither the instigator nor the concluder of the action but the pivot around which it turns. Marcia Riefer speaks of Isabella's 'powerlessness', because she does not control the direction of the plot in the way of many of Shakespeare's more comic heroines:

> Those heroines who have not actually been in control of the comic action have at least participated in it more actively than Isabella ever does. In *A Midsummer Night's Dream*, for instance, Helena and Hermia, while admittedly acting within Oberon's master plot, still take the initiative in pursuing their loves, which is certainly not true of Isabella.[4]

This seems, though, to be less powerlessness than a different kind of power. Helena and Hermia, along with virtually every other of Shakespeare's women, from Rosalind to Lady Macbeth, have been focused on 'pursuing their loves'. That is, whatever their independence of action, their object is, perpetually and indivisibly, a man. That this is 'certainly not true of Isabella' means, not that she is powerless, but that she does not measure her goals in the same terms as these others. Those interpretations of Isabella that focus on whether or not she is attracted to Angelo, or falls in love with the Duke, or is unnatural in not doing either, show an attempt to limit a woman's sphere of action to her relationships, and leave the men to work on life's larger issues. Isabella may not invent the direction of the plot, but at each turning point in the play its direction hangs on her yes or no. If that yes or no choice comes out of a moral code, rather than personal inclination, she has indeed usurped a power usually reserved for men.

*Measure for Measure* is based on an ancient narrative theme usually referred to as the 'monstrous ransom'.[5] Broadly speaking, this is a scenario where a woman is offered a deal whereby she can save a loved one from execution by agreeing to have sex with the judge of the case. The earliest version is attributed to St Augustine, but more direct sources of Shakespeare's play are Cinthio and Whetstone, who wrote a *novella* and a play on the theme. These sources are mainly useful in making clear which elements of *Measure for Measure* Shakespeare invented himself. While Cinthio and Whetstone both make use of the corrupt judge, each has the equivalent of Isabella succumb to the demand of the equivalent of Angelo, and then marry him, not the equivalent of the Duke. With the introduction of the refusal, the bed trick and the heroine as a novice nun, Shakespeare has gone to a tremendous amount of trouble to divert the story from its original simple path where a woman's wrongs could be redressed by marrying her to her abuser. In Cinthio, the Emperor marries Epitia to Iuriste, and her subsequent plea for him to be spared is based on her fear that it will reflect badly on her if she allows her husband to be executed without intervening for him. Whetstone's slightly less believable version has Cassandra, upon becoming Promos's wife, plead for him out of newfound loving devotion. In a colossal act of missing the point, Tillyard cites this change as a flaw in Shakespeare's version, saying of Isabella that 'Not having become Angelo's wife, she has no reason to recommend him to mercy as well as to justice'.[6] This change, however, is what turns the play from a story about social credit into a story about the power of mercy. Removing the heroine's concern over the appropriate behaviour for a wife makes her action one of pure principle.

---

[4] Marcia Riefer, '"Instruments of Some More Mightier Member": The Constriction of Female Power in *Measure for Measure*', *Shakespeare Quarterly*, 35 (1984), 157–69; p. 158.

[5] This phrase was coined by Mary Lascelles, *Shakespeare's 'Measure for Measure'* (London, 1953).

[6] E. M. W. Tillyard, *Shakespeare's Problem Plays* (London, 1950), p. 132.

Isabella's motivation for refusing Angelo's demand has been argued at length, but almost always seems to end up focussed on aspects of her sexuality. Most bluntly, Anne Barton wrote in a programme note for John Barton's 1970 production that 'Isabella's purity conceals an hysterical fear of sex.'[7] Barton was writing, however, in relation to a specific production, and her assessment of Isabella's motives is rendered problematic by the features of this production. Ralph Berry quotes Anne Barton's note, calling it the 'vital perspective' on Isabella, immediately following with 'and the conclusion leaves Isabella alone on stage, unresponsive to the Duke's overtures'.[8] John Barton's production concluded with the Duke and his entourage exiting, leaving Isabella behind to contemplate the marriage proposal he had just made, but such a scenario does not occur in isolation. Isabella was played by Estelle Kohler: young, pretty, with flowing blonde hair. Sebastian Shaw's Duke was old, bespectacled and bordering on incompetent. Berry's implication that this Isabella would need an hysterical fear of sex to be hesitant about marrying this Duke is only a more extreme version of Barton's belief that this is the only possible reason she would have to reject Angelo. Both make an assumption that a sexual rebuttal from a woman should be interpreted as a character flaw in her.

Sexual repression as the explanation for Isabella's decision is echoed by both conservative and feminist critics, including G. Wilson Knight ('Her sex inhibitions have been horribly shown her as they are, naked'),[9] Anne Barton ('afflicted with an irrational terror of sex'),[10] Edward Bond ('a vicious sex hysteric'),[11] David McCandless ('Isabella's beating fantasy enacts an atonement for Oedipal guilt, for incestuous desire of the forbidden father-figure, Angelo')[12] and Janet Adelman ('Isabella is forced to confront her sexual origins . . . The panic engendered by this incipient recognition is voiced in the hysteria with which she responds to Angelo and later to Claudio').[13] Underlying this perspective is an assumption that principle is an inadequate reason for Isabella to preserve her chastity; that there must be some other, concealed motive. Also that a person would need to be sexually inhibited to react negatively to the idea of being sexually abused. Vivian Thomas's discussion of the same issue is especially disturbing. He writes: 'Of course, this seeming callousness in large part reflects Isabella's fear of sexual violation. Her repressed sexuality is suggested in her interview with Angelo.'[14] It is the immediate juxtaposition of these two sentences that is alarming. If Isabella is afraid of sexual violation, it is not an irrational fear but because Angelo has told her that he plans to sexually violate her. Linking her 'fear of sexual violation' with 'repressed sexuality' implies either that Angelo forcing sex on Isabella would not be a violation, or that sexual violation is not something that it is reasonable to fear. The speech that Thomas quotes as demonstrating Isabella's repressed sexuality goes as follows:

> As much for my poor brother as myself.
> That is, were I under the terms of death,
> Th'impression of keen whips I'd wear as rubies,
> And strip myself to death as to a bed
> That longing have been sick for, ere I'd yield
> My body up to shame. (2.4.99–104)

These lines certainly seem infused with sexuality but it is hardly repressed. It seems instead to be very consciously expressed. Given Angelo's inability to express his sexuality at all at this point in the play (as he drops hints, but tries to avoid stating what he wants from her), Isabella's use of such

---

7 Anne Barton, Programme notes for production directed by John Barton (RSC, 1970).

8 Ralph Berry, *Changing Styles in Shakespeare* (London, 1981), p. 41.

9 G. Wilson Knight, *The Wheel of Fire* (London, 1930), p. 92.

10 Anne Barton, Introduction to *Measure for Measure*, in *The Riverside Shakespeare*, Vol. 1, ed. G. Blakemore Evans (Boston, 1974), pp. 545–9; p. 546.

11 Edward Bond, Programme notes for production directed by Keith Hack (RSC, 1974).

12 David McCandless, *Gender and Performance in Shakespeare's Problem Comedies* (Indianapolis, 1997), p. 106.

13 Janet Adelman, *Suffocating Mothers: Fantasies of Maternal Origin in Shakespeare's Plays, 'Hamlet' to 'The Tempest'* (New York, 1992), p. 96.

14 Vivian Thomas, *The Moral Universe of Shakespeare's Problem Plays* (London, 1987), p. 177.

sensual language could be read as a challenge to his repression, or a way of differentiating herself from it. It seems unlikely that someone who uses words as dextrously as Isabella does in her encounters with Angelo could be unaware of the resonances of her language in this speech. She repeatedly reflects Angelo's words back to him: 'Your brother is a forfeit of the law' becomes 'Why, all the souls that were, were forfeit once' (2.2.73 and 75); 'Maiden, no remedy' becomes 'Found out the remedy' (2.2.49 and 77); 'you are ignorant' becomes 'Let me be ignorant' (2.4.74 and 76); and so 'lay down the treasures of your body' becomes 'Th'impression of keen whips I'd wear as rubies' (2.4.96 and 101). The imagery can be firmly located in the extensive tradition of virgin-martyr literature, where martyrdom was the ultimate passionate act, putting love of God before love of the world.

Lisa Jardine also refers to Isabella's 'obsessive fear of her own sexuality', and identifies the intersection of this with virgin-martyr literature, seeing her as having failed the test that such a literature implies: 'The expectations concerning saintly virgins whose virtue is assaulted are used to undermine Isabella's position during the crucial scenes in which she allows her brother to go to his death rather than submit to Angelo.'[15] Jardine's logic, however, is confused. She claims that 'Claudio is right: the deed "becomes a virtue" in the tradition of *The Golden Legend*',[16] but her depiction of Isabella's relationship to that tale is that:

> Were Isabella a female saint of *The Golden Legend* (or one of the many romance female heroes who escape dishonour at the hands of a lord, like Greene's Cratyna), she would flee in disguise and do interminable servile penance for the lust she has aroused. Or she would stand firm and submit to torture, ending only with her death and martyrdom . . . Shakespeare's Isabella is belittled by the stereotypes to whom she so flagrantly refuses to match up. Her stature is diminished, her virtue is placed in question.[17]

It is clear from this description that none of these virtuous females actually did submit to their tormentor, as she implies Isabella should have. They all '*escape*' dishonour, even if only through martyrdom, and Isabella has quite firmly declared her willingness to take that course, were it permitted to her. Contrary to Jardine's deduction about Shakespeare's treatment of his character, Isabella is presented as very much the heir to such women, but one who is willing to take her independence and strength of character even further than they, by refusing to play the role of guilty party to someone else's behaviour, and in being vindicated in her decision by the play's conclusion. Jardine exemplifies the paradox that has dogged Isabella's choice: most critics concede that she could not possibly say yes to Angelo, but they nevertheless cannot forgive her for saying no. Some of this censure undoubtedly comes from discomfort with the manner in which she responds to the situation. Those who feel she is not upset enough at the prospect of her brother's death are not as far removed as one might think from those who call her hysterical. The problem is that she does not react in a 'womanly' way, with weeping, grieving and piteousness, but instead usurps a male privilege – anger.

A combination of modern secular sympathy and the principles of new historicism has produced a series of readings that have in various ways diminished the value of Isabella's vocation and principles. In his influential introduction to the Arden edition, J. W. Lever quotes the sixteenth-century writer William Tyndale on 'Lucrece as a martyr to pagan chastity: "She sought her owne glory in her chastite and not gods . . ." A real-life Isabella, despising Claudio for his unwillingness to sacrifice himself for his sister's "glory", would surely have received scant sympathy from Shakespeare's contemporaries.'[18] 'Glory' is Tyndale's term; Isabella uses no such self-aggrandizing words. Having brought into the argument the prospect of a 'real-life Isabella',

---

[15] Lisa Jardine, *Still Harping on Daughters: Women and Drama in the Age of Shakespeare* (Brighton, 1983), pp. 190–1.

[16] Jardine, *Still Harping*, p. 191. Claudio's full line is 'What sin you do to save a brother's life, / Nature dispenses with the deed so far / That it becomes a virtue' (3.1.135–7).

[17] Jardine, *Still Harping*, p. 191.

[18] J. W. Lever, Introduction to the Arden *Measure for Measure* (London, 1965), pp. lxxx–lxxxi.

it would be only fair for Lever to pursue this idea to its conclusion. The world of *Measure for Measure* is full of reminders of the real-life consequences of sex. Jokes about syphilis abound, and both Juliet and Kate Keepdown have suffered because of illegitimate pregnancy, the former imprisoned, the latter forced into prostitution.[19] Isabella shows herself aware of these consequences when she says, 'I had rather my brother die by the law than my son should be unlawfully born' (3.1.191–3). Lever's real-life Isabella can fully expect the result of her sacrifice for her brother to be public shame, condemnation, ostracism and possible destitution.

Mark Taylor combines a similar discussion of historic conditions with a psychological approach, and attributes Isabella's decision on Angelo to be an aspect of her sense of vocation, which he reads as a search for a father figure:

> The young girl Isabella lost a father and some time thereafter made plans to join the sisters of St Clare . . . Her desire for greater discipline in this life of withdrawal invites the hypothesis that she understands the sisterhood as filling the role of her lost father . . . The world can scarcely be more threatening than to a young girl who has lost her parents, and removal from the world's power can scarcely be more absolute (short of suicide) than in the form of retreat into a convent.[20]

Taylor thinks he is putting himself in Isabella's place, and envisions the world as something from which she would want to be rescued, and the Duke as appearing to her as a knight in shining armour. In reality, he is speaking much more from the point of view of the Duke, imagining how he would like Isabella to feel. His sense of her situation both over-reads the material in the text and inadequately historicizes the social context in operation for any girl of this period. A European girl in the seventeenth century was legally always under the control of a man: her father, then her husband, or in their absence her brother or son. The only place in the world she could go to avoid being under the direct control of a man was a convent, and yet Taylor finds a way to see her decision to enter one as an expression of her desire to be under the control of a man. He diminishes her choice, and by doing so neutralizes the threat she poses if she is genuinely not interested in men.

A different tactic to similar ends is the emphasis on Isabella's 'fear'; not only Barton's 'hysterical fear of sex', Jardine's 'obsessive fear of her own sexuality', and Thomas's 'fear of sexual violation', but also Rossiter's 'scared souls are small souls; and as she leaves Angelo, Isabella's soul is scared'.[21] Isabella has just confronted and defied the most powerful man in Vienna. In any other context this would be seen as an action requiring tremendous personal grit and courage. To suggest that this was an act that demonstrates fear rather than courage is again to diminish the character without justification. Isabella as fearful rather than courageous was the impression given to several reviewers by Nunn's production: 'Isabella may have gone into a nunnery because she fears the obscure perils of sensuality'[22] and 'the chaste Isabella, who regards sex with loathing and fear'.[23] Jeremy Kingston also speaks of her 'abhorrence of sex, with or without a wedding beforehand'.[24] These impressions are of a specific performance, and in that performance, 'David Haig's Angelo hurls the unfortunate novice on to

[19] Kate Keepdown's predicament is not explained in detail, but Lucio admits to the Duke that he is the father of her child. Had she already been a prostitute when Lucio had sex with her, there would be no way for him to know this for sure. It is most likely that she has had to resort to prostitution to support herself and the child after Lucio's refusal to do so. If this is extrapolating too far, it certainly happened all the time in Lever's 'real life'.

[20] Mark Taylor, 'Farther Privileges: Conflict and Change in *Measure for Measure*', *Philological Quarterly*, 73 (1994), 169–93; p. 181. It would be interesting to hear what a nun's response would be to the implication that following her spiritual calling is an action little short of suicide.

[21] A. P. Rossiter, *Angel With Horns and Other Shakespeare Lectures*, ed. Graham Storey (London, 1961), p. 160.

[22] John Peter, *Sunday Times*, 22 September 1991.

[23] Charles Spencer, *Daily Telegraph*, 20 September 1991. Spencer's is probably the most extraordinary of these reviews, as he thought Skinner 'heartrendingly suggests some buried trauma' that results in her 'ugly, fist-flying tantrum' with Claudio. Attributing Isabella's distress to a mysterious 'buried trauma' raises the question of where Spencer had been during Act 2.

[24] Jeremy Kingston, *Times*, 20 September 1991.

a chaise-longue with a view to rape.'[25] That these men could watch the kind of scene that Billington describes here and infer from it that Isabella has a fear of all sexual contact, suggests that concerns about aberrant sexuality might be better directed toward the reviewer than the character.

To counterbalance these examples, some feminist critics have examined the historical circumstances surrounding Isabella's decisions, first to enter a convent and second to refuse Angelo, and drawn very different conclusions. In direct opposition to Lever, Alison Findlay has theorized that, when the play was first performed, 'since many women had direct experience of persecution in more or less extreme forms, in their families, Isabella's image of martyrdom could have been a collective experience, shared by female spectators'.[26] Discerning the way in which 'in Vienna, mercantile sexuality and holy chastity exist in each other's sinews',[27] Findlay can see many legitimate reasons why a woman like Isabella might want to enter a convent, and draws detailed parallels with contemporary figures such as Mary Ward, who began in Isabella's order, the poor Clares, but went on to set up her own order that promoted venturing into the community to preach and do good works, challenging the idea of entering a convent as an act of retreat. Alice Arnott Oppen details the legal power of men over women in Shakespeare's period, and looks at some medieval nuns such as Hrotsvit, Hildegarde and Heloise, who used the convent as a base from which to pursue their writing on theology, philosophy and their own emotions.[28] Poonam Trivedi also discusses Mary Ward, and the way the dissolution of the monasteries curtailed opportunities for girls who sought independence from the rule of men. Like Jardine, Trivedi has historicized Isabella's position within virgin-martyr mythology but discerned in it support rather than criticism for Isabella's position. By examining the history of the cult of virginity in Renaissance Europe, she demonstrates what a vast body of literature sanctioned and approved of a woman's valuing of her virginity above all other considerations. She also points out the many ways that the story follows the traditional pattern of a virgin-martyr tale, including the elements of ritual public humiliation deemed necessary as a guard against pride.[29]

A number of critics believe there is a change between the Isabella of the first half of the play and the second. It is usually seen as primarily a change from coldness to warmth or harshness to charity, and its origin attributed to the wise and guiding hand of the Duke.[30] This is a reflection of the critical preoccupation with what is proper, or attractive, behaviour for a woman, and the denial of a personal journey for Isabella that is unrelated to male guidance. A change can be read in her character that originates much more in her exchange with Angelo, and is primarily about a concern with seeming, shifting to a concern with being. This is seen in her first presentation of Claudio's case to Angelo, when she begins with an awkward preamble that effectively says to Angelo, 'don't think that I'm the sort of person who approves of this kind of thing'. She initiates her position with:

> There is a vice that most I do abhor,
> And most desire should meet the blow of justice,
> For which I would not plead, but that I must;
> For which I must not plead, but that I am
> At war 'twixt will and will not. (2.2.29–33)

Not the sort of thing that would make Claudio feel encouraged, could he hear his advocate, but her motives may simply be to impress on Angelo that her request should not be dismissed as coming from someone who regards such matters lightly. This is a woman who feels it is important that

---

25 Michael Billington, *Guardian*, 20 September 1991.

26 Alison Findlay, *A Feminist Perspective on Renaissance Drama* (London, 1999), p. 38.

27 Findlay, *Feminist Perspective*, p. 35.

28 Alice Arnott Oppen, *Shakespeare: Listening to the Women* (Henley Beach, 2000).

29 Poonam Trivedi, 'Shakespeare's Problem Plays and Problem Women: Feminist Contexts' (unpublished doctoral thesis, University of Birmingham, 1988).

30 These include those as recent as Taylor (1994); Stephen Marx, *Shakespeare and the Bible* (Oxford, 2000); Peter Lake, 'Ministers, Magistrates and the Production of 'Order' in *Measure for Measure*', *Shakespeare Survey 54* (2001), pp. 165–181.

people not get the wrong impression of her. The coolness of her initial overtures has not gone unnoticed by critics, who have censured her for not showing greater enthusiasm for the task of saving her brother.[31] The reality of her position in this scene allows for other reasons beside callousness for her hesitancy. She has not met Angelo before, but knows that he is, at present, the highest authority in Vienna, and may also be aware of his reputation as 'a man of stricture and firm abstinence' (1.3.12). As a novice without public status, her position as a supplicant in the Viennese court could not help but be intimidating. Isabella's willingness to accept Angelo's judgement on her brother at first can be understood if she is someone who values appearance. As far as she knows, authority is wise and just, and Angelo is the very personification of authority. Here is a man who is clearly virtuous, noble and authoritative; how could he be wrong? The turnaround happens, very precisely, on her line 'Seeming, seeming!' (2.4.150), when she finally accepts that Angelo is serious about his proposition, and it is suddenly made obvious to her that appearance is meaningless. The man who appeared virtuous, just and righteous is none of these things, so she can no longer rely on appearance as a guide to truth. She fails at first to understand Angelo's insinuations, because that would involve seeing beyond the surface meaning of his statements, something she has not yet learned that there is any need to do. The unadorned, repeated word 'seeming' demonstrates the shock of someone who is discovering 'seeming' for the first time. The pivot of Isabella's character is this line. This change from faith in the appearance of right to faith only in the reality of right is much less appealing to most critics, as it comes spontaneously from Isabella herself, and cannot be cast as something she is deliberately led to by a man who knows what is best for her.

Inextricably tied in with Isabella's path is that of the Duke. Decisions about performing the role of the Duke will have a marked effect on the status and function of all the characters in this play, and will inevitably influence the presentation of Isabella. Is he Christ-like allegorical figure, storybook hero, or something more ambivalent? Wharton makes the point that the Duke's actions in Act 5 make sense if we take it that his motivation is to appear publicly powerful.[32] It might also be useful to observe that such a display of power makes best structural sense when taken in contrast to his rejection of it at the beginning of the play. His concluding actions show a significant change in the character from avoiding to accepting his responsibility to be a public leader. The Duke and Isabella have parallel but inverted journeys: she from a reliance on appearance as a guide to virtue to a realisation that it is what you know to be true that matters, not what people think; he from a belief that what matters is doing the right thing to a realisation that there are times when you have to show that the right thing is being done. In a reading that prioritizes the issue of seeming versus being, the Duke, in counterpoint to Isabella, begins by thinking that appearance is unimportant, and has shaped his rule accordingly. When he hears from Lucio that his quiet acts of charity can be made to seem surreptitious and guilty – 'The Duke yet would have dark deeds darkly answered' (3.1.435–6) – he is forced into the acceptance that to be a good ruler you have an obligation to appearance. This could provide a motivation for the long and complicated dénouement, when the Duke fully accepts his responsibilities for the first time. In the final scene, as Isabella demonstrates that she no longer sets store by what people think of her, the Duke demonstrates that he is now prepared to make an effort to shape what people think of him. Perhaps this puts them on a too uncomfortably even footing for the patriarchal order to accept as, in most criticism, the justice versus mercy issues seem to have completely subsumed the seeming versus being theme in the play.[33]

31 For example, Marx, *Shakespeare and the Bible*, p. 84.

32 T. F. Wharton, *The Critics Debate: Measure for Measure* (London, 1989).

33 Rossiter is exceptional in discussing the latter aspect explicitly ('All the problem plays are profoundly concerned with seeming and being', p. 127), but immediately goes on to incorporate this idea into a broader one about 'maskedness' without examining the point further.

The idea of seeming versus being is one that recurs many times in Shakespeare. *Hamlet* probably comes closest to rivalling *Measure for Measure* in the prominence of this theme, and yet the word 'seem' and its variations occur even more often in *Measure* than in *Hamlet*, a much longer play.[34] *Measure* is unique in describing a class of people by their ability to seem, when the Duke says of his leaving Angelo with the power of the State in his hands, 'Hence shall we see / If power change purpose, what our seemers be' (1.3.53–4). All the major characters 'seem' in some way at some key point. The Duke seems to be a friar. Angelo seems honourable. Claudio seems to be dead. Isabella seems to give in to Angelo, and Mariana seems to be Isabella. Isabella, Angelo and the Duke all reflect at key points on seeming and its conflict with truth. Isabella in her 'Seeming, seeming!', but also in the final scene: 'but let your reason serve / To make the truth appear where it seems hid, / And hide the false seems true' (5.1.65–7). The Duke also muses 'That we were all as some would seem to be – / From our faults, as faults from seeming free!' (3.1.306–7). Director Rex Cramphorn made use of this theme, and its tension with the matters of justice and mercy in his four Australian productions, but particularly in his Adelaide production of 1985, which was deliberately performed in repertory with *Hamlet*, with strategically planned doublings.[35] Adrian Noble, two years earlier, had also touched on this area when he 'directed the play as an indictment of mankind's self-deception'.[36] The production opened with the Duke standing in front of a full-length mirror, watching himself as servants dressed him in his robes of office. As the play progressed, however, the Duke began to adopt the position of comic hero, and this thematic concern seemed to evaporate from the production.

The lines that indicate Isabella's initial concern with how people see her set up a dramatic contrast with the Isabella of the final scene, who deliberately leads the whole of Vienna to believe the wrong thing about her, when she falsely confesses to fornication with Angelo. She does seem to have changed a great deal, in becoming someone who knows that it is the truth of who you really are that matters, not the appearance after all. This can also adequately explain why she is able to subscribe to the bed trick. Right will be done, even though it appears that wrong is being done. Submitting to the Duke's suggestion in this way is therefore different from submitting to Angelo and Claudio's requests, which would actually be doing wrong, not just appearing to do wrong.

It is significant that in Isabella's soliloquy that concludes this scene, the famous line 'More than our brother is our chastity' (2.4.185) is a change by Shakespeare from Cinthio and Whetstone's word 'honour'.[37] Cinthio's heroine, Epitia, is primarily concerned with the way the world will see her. It should be noted that honour is a 'seeming' word, a public word: it is possible to be corrupt and evil and still be honoured. Chastity is a word of actuality: if you are not chaste, you are not chaste, whether or not the world knows about it. The *Oxford English Dictionary* gives the meaning of chastity as 'purity from unlawful sexual intercourse; continence', with examples quoted from the fourteenth century to the eighteenth, and no mention of reputation in any of the definitions; and of honour (among others, which take up two full pages) as '(of a woman) chastity, purity, as a virtue of the highest consideration; reputation for this virtue, good name', with quotations from the fourteenth to the nineteenth centuries.[38] So it is possible to have honour by reputation for chastity, but the chastity itself only by fact.

This line of Isabella's soliloquy has received completely disproportionate critical attention, to the

---

[34] Twenty-two instances in *Measure*, twenty in *Hamlet*. *Oxford Concordances* (Oxford, 1973).

[35] Mark Minchinton, 'Experiments in Shakespeare: Rex Cramphorn and *Measure for Measure*, 1973–88', in *O Brave New World, Two Centuries of Shakespeare on the Australian Stage*, ed. John Golder and Richard Madelaine (Sydney, 2001), pp. 200–8; pp. 205–6.

[36] Carol Rutter, *Clamorous Voices: Shakespeare's Women Today* (London, 1988), p. 42.

[37] Cinthio and Whetstone's versions are detailed in the Appendices of the Arden edition.

[38] *Oxford English Dictionary*, 1972 edition (Oxford).

neglect of the rest of the passage. Rossiter, for example, spends two pages weighing up the 'difficulties' of this line, without seeking the answer in its context.[39] McLuskie, too, criticizes the speech as 'a pale affair', because it 'deals only in the abstract opposition of chastity against her brother's life'.[40] These arguments, and those of the critics fixated on repression or fear as Isabella's chief motivator, highlight an ongoing difficulty in coming to grips with critical thought regarding *Measure for Measure*, that is, that Angelo's proposed bargain is hardly ever discussed in terms of being an act of corruption. There has scarcely been a published tabling of the idea that even in a world where no value at all is placed on chastity or virginity, giving Angelo what he asks might still be wrong. Angelo is not asking Isabella for a date, he is asking her for a bribe. Is it ever acceptable to bribe a judge? Seeking explanations for Isabella's choice in a character flaw linked to a pathological sexuality ignores the nature of Angelo's proposal as not being merely about sex, but about corruption, bribery and violence.

When Juliet Stevenson was performing the role, she began by assuming that this well-known speech was about chastity, as that is the way it had always been described. However, upon closely examining the passage in order to determine how to perform it, she found that

> 'More than our brother is our chastity' is neither the premise of the speech, nor its conclusion. The soliloquy starts somewhere else and finishes somewhere else. And what happens first in the speech teaches you how to speak the difficult line. And it also, I think, tells you that the speech is not about chastity, it's about anarchy . . . by saying 'yes' to Angelo, Isabella would be committing herself to chaos. It's not her chastity that's at stake, it's order.[41]

It is quite true that the speech does not begin with the matter of chastity at all:

> To whom should I complain? Did I tell this,
> Who would believe me? O perilous mouths,
> That bear in them one and the self-same tongue
> Either of condemnation or approof,
> Bidding the law make curtsey to their will,
> Hooking both right and wrong to th'appetite,
> To follow as it draws! I'll to my brother.
> (2.4.171–7)

The first seven lines are about the horror of a situation where the person with the power to judge a case is corrupt. They are about the helplessness of the private individual in the face of governmental hypocrisy. Isabella is so far from being preoccupied with the matter of chastity that, in a seventeen-line soliloquy, only four lines are actually about the assault on her virtue.

The intricate sequence of ideas in this speech suggests a character possessed of a complex intellectual life, but one that has not always reached the stage. It has been noted that Peter Brook's 1950 production was cut in a way that removed the Duke's ambiguity.[42] What has generally escaped comment is his similar 'cleaning up' of Isabella. In the central 'plot' scene, where the Duke suggests the bed trick to her, Brook pared down Barbara Jefford's lines to the bare bones of what was necessary for the scene to function. The most telling excised lines were: 'I am now going to resolve him. I had rather my brother die by the law than my son should be unlawfully born' (3.1.191–3); 'I have spirit to do anything that appears not foul in the truth of my spirit' (3.1.207–9); 'What a merit were it in death to take this poor maid from the world! What corruption in this life that it will let this man live!' (3.1.233–5).[43] In other words, anything that suggests Isabella's complex moral stance was cut, including any lines suggesting her tendency to be enamoured of death; but taken with it is any sense of her articulateness, her intellect and her individuality. She became a simple heroine in the guiding hands of the hero.

This production reflects one of the most popular interpretations of the final act of the play: that the Duke wishes to effect a 'transformation' in Isabella, rescuing her from coldness and

[39] Rossiter, *Angel with Horns*, pp. 159–60.

[40] McLuskie, 'The Patriarchal Bard', p. 97.

[41] Rutter, *Clamorous Voices*, p. 51.

[42] Herbert S. Weil, 'The Options of the Audience: Theory and Practice in Peter Brook's *Measure for Measure*', *Shakespeare Survey 25* (1972), pp. 27–35.

[43] Promptbook: Brook production, 1950. Held by the Shakespeare Centre Library.

teaching her humanity and charity.[44] Many critics see Isabella's plea for Angelo to be spared from execution as something the Duke is trying to make her do. Frye thinks that 'as soon as she makes this speech we understand that this is really what the whole of the second half of the play has been about. The primary end and aim of everything the Duke is doing is to get that speech out of her.'[45] The completely speculative nature of this interpretation has not been acknowledged. There is in fact not one single line that indicates that the Duke is seeking to change Isabella, or that she has been changed at the end. A transformation in Shakespeare is usually flagged ('thou hast tamed a curst shrew', *The Taming of the Shrew*, 5.2.193), but there is no similar comment on Isabella. The Duke speaks to the audience, and shares his plans as much as any of Shakespeare's characters, and yet he does not mention what these critics take to be the central motif of the final act. The fact that his lines in the final scene actively discourage Isabella from adding her plea to that of Angelo's betrothed, Mariana, is read as ingenious reverse psychology. Stephen Marx is typical: 'The Duke refuses [Mariana's plea], secretly playing devil's advocate' – and he concludes: 'But the play audience has been shown a secret still hidden from everyone else in Vienna. They have seen how the inner light which [Isabella] now casts was kindled by the Duke.'[46] We know from what the Duke has said that he is planning to put Angelo through something rigorous and unpleasant in the final act ('By cold gradation and well balanced form, / We shall proceed with Angelo' (4.3.96–7)), but the text gives no indication that he is subjecting Isabella to the same kind of process, only that he is letting her believe that Claudio is dead in order 'To make her heavenly comforts of despair / When it is least expected' (4.3.107–8).

Isabella's plea for Angelo is both a culmination and an interpretation of the relationship of all the major characters as constructed by the preceding action. Although both Isabella and Angelo recede from centre stage in the second half of the play, as the Duke begins controlling the action, they still have one more crucial, albeit less intimate, moment together. Isabella responds to the Duke's order for Angelo's execution, with a plea that he be spared:

> Most bounteous sir,
> Look, if it please you, on this man condemned
> As if my brother lived. I partly think
> A due sincerity governed his deeds,
> Till he did look on me. Since it is so,
> Let him not die. (5.1.440–5)

The moment when Isabella kneels to plead for her enemy is the play's true climax.

Brook recognized this, and gave Jefford a very famous direction. He instructed her to pause before kneeling 'until she felt the audience could take it no longer'.[47] This created a superb moment of dramatic tension, as those onstage and in the auditorium alike held their breath to see what she would do. However, what makes a fine dramatic moment is not necessarily that which makes the best textual sense. The Duke has given the order for action. He has already said 'Away with him' twice and his last line before Isabella's is 'He dies for Claudio's death' (5.1.408 and 439), so there seems little cause for everyone on the stage to be standing stock still, instead of carrying out the clearly issued order. While the dramatic pause may appear to empower Isabella, by having the whole cast hanging on the move she is about to make, the same thing does ensure that, when she makes her plea, it looks unquestionably the result of the Duke's initiative rather than her own. A reading that emphasizes

[44] This theory is central, for example, to the interpretations of: E. M. W. Tillyard (1950); Harold C. Goddard, *The Meaning of Shakespeare Volume II* (Chicago, 1951); Bertrand Evans, *Shakespeare's Comedies* (Oxford, 1960); A. P. Rossiter (1961); J. W. Lever (1965); Robert Grams Hunter, *Shakespeare and the Comedy of Forgiveness* (New York, 1965); Darryl J. Gless, *Measure for Measure, the Law and the Convent* (Princeton, 1979); Northrop Frye, *The Myth of Deliverance* (Toronto, 1983); Vivian Thomas (1987); Ronald R. MacDonald, '*Measure for Measure*: The Flesh Made Word', *Studies in English Literature*, 30 (1990), 265–81; Mark Taylor (1994); Stephen Marx (2000).

[45] Frye, *Myth of Deliverance*, p. 29.

[46] Marx, *Shakespeare and the Bible*, p. 98. See also Bertrand Evans, *Shakespeare's Comedies*, p. 218.

[47] Peter Brook, *The Empty Space* (London, 1968), p. 89.

Isabella's autonomy of action, and may be more appropriate to the dynamic arising directly from the lines in the scene, would cast Isabella's 'Most bounteous sir' as interrupting the Duke's control of the flow of action, rather than serving it. The line scansion supports this reading, rather than one involving a pause. 'Most bounteous sir' is not a short line, it is the second half of a split line, making an even pentameter, and therefore implying a quickly picked-up cue:

DUKE He dies for Claudio's death.
ISABELLA Most bounteous sir:
(5.1.440)

Adrian Noble's 1983 production, despite Juliet Stevenson's portrayal of an independent and fiercely intelligent Isabella, was another that rested on the idea that her plea is the main goal of the Duke in the last act. Daniel Massey recalls his performance of this scene:

> The struggle to bring Isabella to her knees was quite literally exhausting. Juliet was wonderful here. In essence, of course, it was a battle of wills. Significantly, he is tougher and harsher with Isabella. Instinctively he knows that he must push her to the limit. He knows her well now, her passion, her stubbornness, above all her sense of justice. I remember that when she finally sank to her knees I gave in to an almost trance-like state.[48]

Massey does not seem to have given due weight to considering what sort of man this would make the Duke: a man whose chief goal is to bring to her knees the woman he wishes to marry. Beyond that, on closer examination, the idea of a battle of wills is difficult to make sense of. How did Isabella and the Duke end up on opposite sides in this scenario? If they are struggling against each other at this point, and the Duke wants Isabella to kneel, that means Isabella wants *not* to kneel, which means by kneeling she loses the battle. Once again, an action that seems very clearly a win for a strong and independent-minded woman is somehow talked around into a loss for a woman dependent on a man to show her the way.

It was George Geckle, in 1971, who first and most comprehensively examined and refuted the transformation interpretation by looking at the responses of the other characters, particularly the Duke, to Isabella's words: 'Does the Duke, generally acknowledged as the ultimate authority in the play, chastise Isabella for a lack of charity? He does not.'[49] Geckle's thorough analysis seems to have gone either unread or ignored by numerous subsequent critics, though none have put forward a direct refutation of his argument. These critics usually resort to begging the question: presenting Isabella's lines to Claudio as their evidence, with the implication that the argument that she is unsympathetic at this point has already been made. The assumption is that the person who says 'more than our brother is our chastity' and 'I'll pray a thousand prayers for thy death, / No word to save thee' (3.1.147–8) could not be the same person who makes the plea for Angelo's life. In fact, there is no inconsistency if speaking of a person who operates firstly, and before anything else, out of principle. Nick Enright's 1985 production presented Isabella in this way, as someone who operated according to the same moral framework from beginning to end. Susan Lyons, who played Isabella, feels that the character's strongest desire is always to live a life guided by principle and a meaningful ethical code. It was this code that made her reject Angelo's bargain and Claudio's begging when her feelings wanted her to give in and save her brother, and the same code that made her ask for Angelo's life to be spared, whether or not her personal desire was to see him punished.[50]

An alternative reading is that the Duke's goal is the shaming and redemption of Angelo, rather than Isabella, as a public demonstration of his own wisdom and authority. This would certainly be a play for power, as Wharton suggests, but it does not rely on the reading that his earlier reluctance

---

48 Daniel Massey, 'The Duke in *Measure for Measure*', in *Players of Shakespeare 2*, ed. Robert Smallwood and Russell Jackson (Cambridge, 1988), pp. 13–31; p. 29.

49 George Geckle, 'Shakespeare's Isabella', *Shakespeare Quarterly*, 22 (1971), 163–8; p. 167.

50 In interview with the author: Nick Enright, 15 August 2002; Susan Lyons, 25 November 2002.

to embrace power and its trappings is insincere. It shows a final acceptance of the responsibilities he had been avoiding. Working within this scenario, he would need to withhold from Isabella the fact of Claudio's escape because Angelo's redemption is dependent on his suffering the guilt of his action and the threat of his own execution, a charade that cannot be maintained if it is known that Claudio did not die. What he does not take into account is the fact that Isabella can go further than he in enacting the principle of mercy. When he says, 'He dies for Claudio's death', he thinks that he will bring Angelo to the block, then reveal Claudio, pardon Angelo and he will have effected a perfect God-like act of redemption and forgiveness. When Isabella kneels to plead for Angelo, it takes him completely by surprise and produces his rather clumsy rejection of her plea ('Your suit's unprofitable. Stand up, I say' (5.1.452)), because it did not figure in his plans. It is, however, the one thing that finally humbles him; hence his last-minute proposal. Like the 'transformation' theory, this one does rest on a sense of character as a coherent psychological entity that is not appropriate under all circumstances, but it does show how much interpreting what is happening in this story is shaped by personal values. There have been performances of the play that have functioned out of this contrasting position, one being John Bell's in 1972. For his very cynical Duke Isabella's plea 'came as a complete surprise'. But he also said, of his direction of Anna Volska in the role: 'Given the person she is, there was nothing else she *could* do.'[51] Also in Nicholas Hytner's 1987 production 'Isabella's plea was an astonishing, unlooked-for event.'[52]

Shakespeare's more apparent changes from his sources to the sequence of events at this point in the play had the flow-on effect of creating other more subtle, but more profound, changes. Interpretations, both literary and performative, that construct Isabella's plea as something she is led to by the Duke minimize its disruptiveness, but also diminish its power and beauty. The choices made on this issue will demonstrate a production's priorities. If a production is centred on the Duke as everybody's redeemer, Isabella's independence of thought and action will appear curtailed, and a production that wishes to maximize Isabella's power will need to show her act of mercy as self-generated. The latter will also shift the emphasis away from the intricacies of the plot, and toward thematic questions of personal ethics, arguably creating a more powerful humanist statement.

Readings of *Measure for Measure* that centre on the idea that Isabella learns about mercy from the Duke are perhaps weakest in their neglect of an important moment in Isabella's first exchange with Angelo that is too specifically constructed to be accidental. When she first pleads for Claudio's life to Angelo, she says:

> I would to heaven I had your potency,
> And you were Isabel! Should it then be thus?
> No; I would tell what 'twere to be a judge,
> And what a prisoner. (2.2.69–72)

When she says this, the likelihood of that scenario ever coming to pass seems non-existent. Then in the last scene Shakespeare sets up a situation where this is precisely what occurs. The fact that Isabella does exactly what she said she would do at the start of the play should not be treated as incidental. The moment when Isabella kneels down in front of everyone and says 'Let him not die' can become on stage a distillation of everything that is most moving and profound in this play, an image of the possibility of transcending vengeance through an unshakeable belief in something greater.

---

[51] In interview with the author: John Bell, 17 June 2002.

[52] Roger Allam, 'The Duke in *Measure for Measure*', in *Players of Shakespeare 3*, ed. Robert Smallwood and Russell Jackson (Cambridge, 1988), pp. 21–41; p. 38.

# WRITING PERFORMANCE: HOW TO ELEGIZE ELIZABETHAN ACTORS

TOBIAS DÖRING

In the second act of *Hamlet*, after the First Player has delivered his passionate speech of death and mourning, Hamlet says in praise of him that stage-players are 'the abstracts and brief chronicles of the time. After your death you were better have a bad epitaph than their ill report while you live' (2.2.505).[1] Professional players are here described in terms of cultural memory. Their work does for contemporaries what epitaphs do for posterity: they shape a person's image and show it to the world. The point was not lost on antitheatricalists either. In his *Anatomy of Abuses* (1583), Philip Stubbes railed against players as 'painted sepulchres'.[2] His emphasis lies clearly on 'painted', as a sign of professional hypocrisy, echoing Christ's words according to St Matthew (23.27). Nevertheless, it is telling that Stubbes's comment, just like Hamlet's, serves to associate actors with tombs, monuments and posthumous remains. What does remain, however, of an actor's art? If theatre performers generally take part in cultural commemorations, we might conversely ask what memorials or abstracts have been written for them after their own deaths. Plays in performance are strictly temporary acts, a mere two-hours' traffic on the stage. So how can a brief chronicle, an elegy or epitaph ever give us an account of any actor's true achievement?

The question involves larger issues, concerning the critical interface between stage and page as well as the poetic conventions here employed. Elegies and epitaphs are forms of commemorative writing produced to testify to a person's social standing. Distinguished mainly by their brevity, epitaphs are described by George Puttenham as giving a 'report of the dead persons estate and degree'.[3] The very fact that a memorial verse has been composed for a deceased individual signals his or her considerable status even if, due to practical requirements, the actual poem is very short. According to generic example, all epitaphs must say 'much in little'.[4] Elegies, by contrast, are long ceremonial poems, in Puttenham's terms 'Poeticall mournings in verse'.[5] Based on classical models, they give expression not only to personal grief but often suggest patterns of communal and ritual mourning. In this sense, Dennis Kay explains, many funeral elegies express 'both the inevitability of mortality and the capacity of art to depict it', while they set out to accommodate twinned yet contrary impulses: 'to lament and to comprehend a meaning in death'.[6] So how can they lament or comprehend an actor's death and offer some depiction of its meaning?

---

[1] Shakespearian texts are cited according to *The Norton Shakespeare*, based on the Oxford Edition, eds. Stephen Greenblatt, Walter Cohen, Jean E. Howard, Katharine Eisaman Maus (New York, 1997).

[2] Glynne Wickham, Herbert Berry, William Ingram, eds., *English Professional Theatre, 1530–1660* (Cambridge, 2000), p. 166.

[3] George Puttenham, *The Art of English Poesy* (London, 1589), p. 45

[4] Joshua Scodel, *The English Poetic Epitaph: Commemoration and Conflict from Jonson to Wordsworth* (Ithaca, 1991), p. 50.

[5] Puttenham, *English Poesy*, p. 39.

[6] Dennis Kay, *Melodious Tears: The English Funeral Elegy from Spenser to Milton* (Oxford, 1990), p. 12.

Memorializing actors in a literary form means to write performance, i.e. to face the problem of how written testimony can be given to a fleeting art. An actor's public standing or 'degree' fully derives from the actor's performative capacities on stage, which commemorative poems must try to record. For this reason, all such elegies contend with the prevailing notions that have shaped critical thinking about the claims of textual products in relation to theatrical productions. This is a famously contested field. As W. B. Worthen argues, what is at stake in all negotiations between textuality and performativity are questions of authority, questions still at work in many present-day debates: 'While the theatre is often described as licentious, promiscuous, innovative, imaginative, or merely haphazard in its representation of texts, to think of performance as conveying authorized meanings of any kind, especially meanings authenticated in and by the text, is, finally, to tame the unruly ways of the stage.'[7] So, if any writer tries to offer a description of such innovative, imaginative or unruly stage work – a description authorized or authenticated by a particular performance – he or she may quickly reach the limits of what words can do. When the rich experience of performance is rendered by means of verbal signs, immediacy yields to mediation and is turned into cultural representation. This is, in many popular accounts, a story of inevitable loss.

In fact, these issues have long been noted. Their awareness goes back at least to the generation of Jacobean writers who, like Thomas Heywood, first looked at Elizabethan theatre in retrospect, trying to record and keep its power for posterity. For them, commemorative writing was the only way to solve a pressing problem: how can readers be enabled, through the medium of language, to imagine what spectators once experienced in the playhouse? The great early modern actors were to be remembered for their professional achievements. So what words, what images, what literary devices are available so as to conjure, or to capture, the peculiar quality of bygone play-acting? In this paper, I would like to approach these questions with a reading of some Jacobean poems composed in memory of late representatives of the Shakespearian stage. The funeral elegy is crucial in this context because it is situated at the interface of performative and literary traditions. If its project is, according to Kay, to fit appropriate words to a particular occasion, it must always find some ways to particularize cultural memories and so express the uniqueness of the person mourned: 'And, as with the sermon, no matter how many practices and conventions and clichés accumulated, the funeral elegy was essentially a form without a form, a performance in which a high value was attached to individuality (of speaker as much as subject), invention, and improvisation, a genre defined by its occasion.'[8] So how does this genre rise to the occasion of commemorating pure performers?

In Peter Sacks's terms,[9] the 'work' of elegy is part of the cultural work of mourning which it records, performs and, in successful cases, eventually concludes. To this end, elegies like epitaphs employ a set of literary conventions, figural devices which serve to represent or symbolically reproduce the person passed away. Among these devices, the central trope is prosopopeia, the rhetorical figure endowing the text with a face and voice and thus promising to restore the persona – literally, the mask – of the deceased as a speaking subject. This is the main device which elegies employ to answer the imperative just noted: to give value to the individuality of their chosen subject. But when actors, i.e. professional maskers, are concerned, such a device comes up against dramatic problems.

'So great was the fame of this Roscius, and so good his estimation, that learned Cato made a question whether Cicero could write better than Roscius could speak and act.'[10] What Heywood here reports in *An Apology for Actors* (1612), formed a topos in theatrical debates and suggests that an actor's fame can indeed outlive the moment of his live appearance. Heywood refers to Roscius, a

7 W. B. Worthen, *Shakespeare and the Authority of Performance* (Cambridge, 1997), p. 3.

8 Kay, *Melodious Tears*, p. 5.

9 Peter M. Sacks, *The English Elegy: Studies in the Genre from Spenser to Yeats* (Baltimore, 1985).

10 Wickham *et al.*, *Professional Theatre*, p. 176.

Roman actor whose powers soon became proverbial. This classical example is then applied to 'our English actors', even those of an earlier, Elizabethan generation – William Knell, John Bentley, Tobias Mills, Robert Wilson – whom Heywood actually never saw on stage. And yet, he cites the 'report of many judicial auditors' to claim that 'their performance of many parts have been so absolute that it were a kind of sin to drown their worths in Lethe, and not to commit their (almost forgotten) names to eternity'.[11] His claim chimes in with the title character of Philip Massinger's *The Roman Actor* (1626), who proudly boasts: 'Our aim is glory, and to leave our names/ To aftertimes.'[12] And yet, such claims and tributes rather demonstrate the difficulty in elegizing actors and eternalizing their glorious names. For even while Heywood says their memories be green, his own conscious campaign for cultural remembrance implies how fast they actually wither. His report of Cato's praise for Roscius now backfires: the great Roman stage-player may well have been more powerful than the great Roman orator, but Cicero is sure to survive through his writing. Roscius, by contrast, can only 'speak and act' as long as he lives; aftertimes others must speak for him.

Actors, therefore, cannot lay claim to the Horatian topos that their true monument lies in their work because their work is, by its very nature, evanescent. Instead, their elegists must find some verbal means to ban the essence of performance and give to transient playing a local habitation and a name. It is this effort that I would like to trace in some of the poetical obituaries from the period, first commenting on fools and jesters before considering two prominent tragedians. The texts available[13] comprise diverse poems on a dozen actors, some of them by well-known poets, dramatists or fellow-actors – like Rowley's elegy on Hugh Attwell or Middleton's quatrain on Burbage – but most of them anonymous and only later published in printed collections. My selection and discussion of five texts should provide a working basis to explore the larger issues raised above, as they challenge us to rethink critical negotiations between performativity and textuality. Rather than assuming a stable opposition between the claims of page and stage, I argue, we should acknowledge their productive complications: performative acts in the texts of mourning manifestly demonstrate how to do things with poetic words. In addition, my subsequent readings hope to show how theatre performers put elegy's conventions to the test: the poems cannot easily come to terms with the players' paradoxical relation to death and dying, the cultural meanings of which they seem to disown.

Among the names commemorated in *An Apology for Actors*, Heywood singles out two famous clowns: 'Here I must needs remember Tarlton, in his time gracious with the Queen his sovereign, and in the people's general applause, whom succeeded Will Kemp, as well in the favour of her Majesty as in the opinion and good thoughts of the general audience.'[14] His comments provide striking evidence that even the comedians' dancing, singing, drumming or juggling, surely the most performance-based and least literary aspect of the theatre, can survive its moment of production and be enshrined in cultural memory. In his 1618 collection *Remaines after Death*, Richard Braithwaite indeed cites a proper epitaph for William Kempe, who died in 1608 or 1609:

> Welcome from Norwich, Kempe: all joy to see
> Thy safe returne moriscoed lustily!
> But out alass! how soone's thy morice done!
> When pipe and taber all thy friends be gone,
> And leave thee now to dance the second part
> With feeble nature, not with nimble art:
> Then all thy triumphs fraught with strains of mirth,
> Shall be cag'd up within a chest of earth.
> Shall be? they are: Thou'st danc'd thee out of breath,
> And now must take thy parting dance with Death.[15]

---

[11] Wickham *et al.*, *Professional Theatre*, p. 176.

[12] *The Selected Plays of Philip Massinger*, ed. Colin Gibson (Cambridge, 1978), 1.1.31–2.

[13] My main source for all of them is Edward Nungezer, *A Dictionary of Actors and of Other Persons Associated with the Public Representation of Plays in England before 1642* (New Haven, Oxford, 1929).

[14] Wickham *et al.*, *Professional Theatre*, p. 176.

[15] Nungezer, *Dictionary*, p. 222.

Not surprisingly, these anonymous lines focus on the clown's most famous feat, his morris dance from London to Norwich in 1600, a month-long performance by which, literally, he made the world his stage and at the same time, as he punned, danced himself 'out of the world'.[16] Leaving the Globe Theatre behind, whose shareholder he had become, Kempe freed himself from the apparent routines of the mirth industry, henceforth performing the jigs and triumphs recalled in this poem freelance and in public. Phrased in a traditional apostrophe to the deceased, the epitaph wavers between putting him to rest and still watching him perform. Kempe is welcomed 'from' Norwich in progress to 'the second part' of his performance and yet he has been immobilized: 'cag'd vp within a chest of earth'. Simulating a performative gesture, the poetic speaker even corrects himself in the last but one line to emphasize that Kempe has indeed danced himself 'out of breath'. The phrase is ambiguous and might perhaps read like a distant echo of one of Kempe's most celebrated stage appearances as Peter, servant to the Nurse in *Romeo and Juliet*, who had breath enough to explain that she was out of breath (2.4.30–32). But the central point remains: in memorializing this great comic player, the epitaph claims both that his performance now is 'done' and that it continues. Rather than on the traditional Dance of Death, the final focus here lies on Kempe's dance *with* death: it seems as if the clown, like a skeleton in motley, has charmed even grim mortality.

Robert Armin, too, who succeeded Kempe and died in 1615, was claimed to be immortal. In a commemorative verse, printed in John Davies's *Scourge of Folly*, the anonymous poetic mourner begins with a series of false starts:

> Armine, what shall I say of thee, but this,
> Thou art a foole and knaue? Both? fie, I misse;
> And wrong thee much, sith thou in deede art neither,
> Although in shew, thou playest both together.[17]

He then falls back on the familiar *theatrum mundi* topos ('this earthly stage'), trying to find adequate words with which to capture and commemorate the multiple and contradictory roles this performer had assumed in his long career. And again, the final lines insist that death has no power to end his career: even in 'the tyring-house of earth', Armin is observed to play his part to undying praise:

> So thou, in sport, the happiest men dost schoole –
> To do as thou dost, – wisely play the foole.

To be sure, such claims to immortality are commonplace in the repertoire of any elegist or eulogist. But when Kempe or Armin are concerned, the topos is remarkable because as fools their impact lies entirely with the here and now of their performance. It lives in the 'jigging veins' and improvised responses and other 'such conceits as clownage keeps in pay' (as the Prologue to Marlowe's *Tamburlaine* has it), which were not only criticized by serious-minded literati but which principally escape written fixity. And yet their afterlife is well attested.

Laudatory views and memories of Elizabethan clowns were frequently supported by the veritable cult which developed around Richard Tarlton, the Queen's favourite entertainer, who died in 1588 and was commemorated widely and wildly in all sorts of popular domains. Posthumously hailed for generations after, even by adverse observers of the stage like Edmund Howes, as the 'wonder of his time',[18] Tarlton's name and image circulated in many forms and cultural productions. Whether in pub signs or in broadsheet ballads, in costumes like his russet coat or instruments like his pipe, his acts and art lived on – not least in younger clowns like Armin, whom he had himself promoted. A commemorative verse of twenty lines, added to his picture, placed Tarlton above the entire company of jesters:

> The partie nowe is gone
> And closlie clad in claye;
> Of all the jesters in the lande
> He bare the praise awaie.[19]

---

16 Nungezer, *Dictionary*, p. 219.

17 Nungezer, *Dictionary*, p. 20.

18 Wickham *et al.*, *Professional Theatre*, p. 208.

19 Nungezer, *Dictionary*, p. 355.

But these words also imply that the revels now are ended, finally borne away with him 'who merry many made / when he appeared in sight'. Out of sight, however, the immortal master jester has – like all the rest – just turned to clay.

In this way, this obscure little poem about Tarlton chimes in with the most famous elegiac tribute to a jester in the culture of Elizabethan theatre, Hamlet's meditation on what he takes to be Yorick's skull and what contemporary spectators may well have taken to involve specific memories of Tarlton:[20]

> a fellow of infinite jest, of most excellent fancy. He hath borne me on his back a thousand times; and now, how abhorred my imagination is! My gorge rises at it. Here hung those lips that I have kissed I know not how oft. Where be your gibes now, your gambols, your songs, your flashes of merriment that were wont to set the table on a roar? Not one now to mock your own grinning? Quite chop-fallen! Now get you to my lady's chamber and tell her, let her paint an inch thick, to this favour she must come. Make her laugh at that. (5.1.171–80)

This powerful *memento mori*, a theatrical confrontation with the effects of death, centrally concerns our chief question: how to commemorate a pure performer in the rhetoric of mourning. Hamlet's speech employs the *ubi sunt* topos ('Where be your gibes now', etc.). But the familiar device barely covers and controls his gut reaction, which he notes with shocking immediacy: 'My gorge rises at it.' His following apostrophes structure a list of anecdotal moments that he remembers of the jester's jokes, culminating in his challenge to continue joking even with the face of death. A clown, this seems to say, cannot be remembered and mourned other than by laughter: a physical, if fleeting, tribute to his power of performance and the most appropriate response by the bereaved when they momentarily re-light his flash of merriment.

But laughter as a mode of mourning involves acute ironies – not least because the audience still remembers Hamlet's earlier censure of the same kind of clowning and hilarity which he now so wistfully recalls. Fools, he told the players in his instructions in act three, should be strictly supervised lest they overstep the boundaries of drama: 'And let those that play your clowns speak no more than is set down for them' (3.2.34–5). In Hamlet's reformed theatre, it was the dangerous excess of improvised performance, especially the corporeality of laughter with its tendency to transgress the textual framework of a play, which had to be tamed in more decorous forms of acting. The difference between Hamlet's theatre and the fools' may best be summarized by saying that Hamlet *re*-presents what the clowns *presented*. However, with his mournful musing about Tarlton, Yorick and their company, he now evokes the loss of laughter to mark the realities of death. As in the Jacobean epitaphs and poems, the great clowns' physical performance is abstracted into mere verbal signs. Historically, Robert Weimann argues, professional fools 'were relatively unconcerned with the symbolic, let alone iconographic, dimensions of their actions'.[21] And yet it is precisely this dimension – the symbolic, iconographic, emblematic shaping of cultural memory – that elegists, epitaph writers and other obituarists like Hamlet are concerned with when they turn the life's work and live work of the famous fools into brief chronicles and writing.

In this way, the cultural work of mourning does not just immortalize the clowns, but also immobilizes their memory as their most characteristic acts, the feats of unscripted performance, are consigned to some literary form. However, two points should be added to this preliminary account. First, clowns and jester were *relatively*, not *fully*, unconcerned with the symbolic. Many of them did indeed leave a considerable amount of written traces, documents and textual versions of their art – *Kemps Nine daies wonder*, Armin's and Tarlton's plays or the many pamphlets published in his name – which link them to the cultural domains of print and literature and which, in the cases mentioned, formed a

---

[20] For the likelihood of Tarlton memories in Hamlet's Yorick speech, see Nungezer, *Dictionary*, p. 355, and Alan and Veronica Palmer, *Who's Who in Shakespeare's England* (London, 2000), p. 248.

[21] Robert Weimann, *Author's Pen and Actor's Voice: Playing and Writing in Shakespeare's Theatre* (Cambridge, 2000), p. 22.

basis for their epitaphs and elegies. Second, there is an important difference between on-stage meditations such as Hamlet's about the bygone lives of players and their scripted versions published in print or engraved on tombstones. Unlike printed poems of mourning, the dramatic recollection is a memorial in kind. For all its acute sense of absence and abhorrence at the emptiness of Yorick's skull, Hamlet's commemoration is still contiguous with the late performer's presence simply because it is itself placed on a stage, enacted by a player and part of a theatrical event. In the theatre, the performances of mourning for a clown just as for an emperor find an appropriate place. The graveyard of Elsinore is a place of memory and oblivion, a site of monumental record as of levelling[22] – just like the playhouse is a space where memorials for the dead are both erected and erased, because it presents kings and clowns alike. Earlier in the play, in response to the ghost's command, Hamlet vowed that 'memory' still 'holds a seat' in the 'distracted globe' of his own head (1.5.96–97), thus vowing the work of the Globe theatre to cultural memory too. But with the ghostly recollection of the clowns, we are reminded that the theatre is the seat for all sorts of distractions.

Thus, my discussion so far has exemplified some of the issues raised at the beginning. But what is more, all such commemorative poems, as negotiations between textuality and performance, should be seen to involve acute questions of cultural authority. Whatever statements about public memory and mourning are made in elegies or epitaphs, they rest on prior statements about the force of language and the power of rhetorical devices to subject the complexities of lived experience to lasting memory with a few lines or words. Comic players are not the only challenge to this power. For different reasons, but with similar effects, tragedians also pose a problem when poets try to fix their image for posterity in writing. The two outstanding examples of this cultural conflict are Edward Alleyn and Richard Burbage, whose celebrity status occasioned some of the most challenging – and challenged – memorial poems of the period.

Ben Jonson's well-known tribute to Alleyn, to begin with, serves to illustrate the anxious self-positioning of a poet vis-à-vis a stage performer:

To Edward Alleyn

If Rome so great, and in her wisest age,
Feared not to boast the glories of her stage,
As skilful Roscius and grave Aesop, men
Yet crowned with honours as with riches then,
Who had no less a trumpet of their name
Than Cicero, whose every breath was fame:
How can so great example die in me,
That, Alleyn, I should pause to publish thee?
Who both their graces in thyself hast more
Out-stripped, than they did all that went before;
And present worth in all dost so contract,
As other speak, but thou dost act.
Wear this renown. 'Tis just that who did give
So many poets life, by one should live.[23]

This, surely, is a remarkable poetic homage. The text is loaded with a wealth of literary references, conspicuous echoes of Horace and Cicero, recruited to confirm the standing of the current writer – perhaps rather than his subject – as the administrator of classical heritage. Rome 'feared not', we learn, to write in praise of actors. But even as the poem thus tries consciously to place itself into a great tradition, we get a sense of its self-conscious fear that, doing so, it risks compromising itself through consorting with performance. For this reason, exactly half the text is spent in offering justification for writing it in the first place, and more than half the text offers us views of or about its writer rather than its avowed addressee. Syntactically, twelve of the fourteen lines consist of a central question: 'should I', the poet, 'pause to publish thee', the player? The answer is never actually spelled out. Instead, it is implied in the last two lines, which proceed to give Alleyn his due only by taking it from him. That this actor gave 'so many poets life' is here predicated on the present poet's power, a gesture of bestowing grace which only

[22] See Michael Neill, *Issues of Death: Mortality and Identity in English Renaissance Tragedy* (Oxford, 1997), p. 234.

[23] Ben Jonson, *Poems*, ed. Ian Donaldson (Oxford, 1975), p. 46.

the victorious can call 'just'. Alleyn may have 'outstripped' predecessors like 'skilful Roscius' or others who 'went before' him. Still, he has now come before a more skilful master who does not 'pause' to strip him of his popular standing by replacing stage arts with the hierarchy of literary values. The poet as self-commissioned life-giver can also, by implication, take it back.

But this poet takes even more. Jonson, literally, takes on performance. The proverbial contrast between 'speak' and 'act', to which he alludes in line twelve, is used to emphasize Alleyn's performative force and, at the same time, to adopt it. With its barely hidden sense of rivalry and its privileging of literary authorship, 'To Edward Alleyn' itself sets out to perform an act – though not primarily the one announced with its title. In the reading I suggest, Jonson's poetic tribute to Alleyn speaks praise while doing damage to this great tragedian, relegating him to a position of 'present worth' fully controlled by a writer's lasting worth and his own broad historical perspective. Nothing could better sum up this performative contradiction than the central line: 'How can so great example die in me', the poet asks a full ten years *before* Alleyn actually died.[24] Published among the 'Epigrammes' of Jonson's 1616 Folio, the poem in fact concerns a *living* artist. Neither elegy nor epitaph, it simply borrows from classic examples of commemorative writing to emulate their gestures and endow the persona, who features on the title page as 'The Author B. I.', with cultural authority. Alleyn had indeed retired from the theatre as player but continued to be patron of stage arts. With Jonson's pre-emptive epitaph, however, he must enter a pantheon of historical and textual figures – a move which might be dubbed the literary death of an actor. At any rate, this peculiar commemorative poem illustrates Jonson's well-attested anti-theatricalism[25] and falls squarely into the larger project of this stage writer's eventual self-invention as a literary author. The 1616 Folio edition of his *Works* – not *Plays*, as a contemporary epigram was quick to point out with some glee[26] – has been studied in this way. According to Douglas Brooks, his Folio undertook a pioneering act of publication that produced a textual hybrid 'wherein the epigrams and poems mark the spot at which untypically authorial play-texts have been grafted on to typically inauthorial masque texts and other similarly inauthorial pieces'. In sum, these complex dynamics between 'the book's two bodies' also drive the hybrid gestures noted in the poem.[27]

By way of comparison, I would now like to consider a poetic tribute occasioned by the death of Richard Burbage, to pursue the ways in which performative potentials can also be channelled or adopted in elegiac writing. Burbage died, appropriately enough, in Lent 1619, a mere eleven days after Queen Anne. Popular displays of grief for her were soon eclipsed by public acts of mourning for the tragic player. Several epitaphs and commemorative poems to him are preserved and they are surely better remembered than any for his Queen. Given the still uncertain social status of theatre entrepreneurs and artists like the Burbages, this point is already quite remarkable. But the imagery of 'eclipse' was actually employed in some of the poems. Middleton published a four-liner suggesting that this actor's death had led to 'a visible eclipse of playing', thus also suggesting Burbage's status as, literally, a star.[28] The best-known text on him, however, is a long, anonymous funeral elegy

---

24 Alleyn eventually died in 1626, a decade after the publication of the Epigram. While it was not entirely uncommon for Jonson to commemorate a living person in his work, the wording and idiom in which he does so here employs obituary rhetoric and clearly pre-empts funeral elegies.

25 See Jonas Barish, *The Anti-Theatrical Prejudice* (Berkeley, 1981), pp. 132–55.

26 '*To Mr. Ben Johnson demanding the reason / Why he call'd his playes works.* / Pray tell me Ben, where doth the mystery lurke, / What others call a play you call a worke', quoted in Douglas A. Brooks, *From Playhouse to Printing House: Drama and Authorship in Early Modern England* (Cambridge, 2000), p. 136.

27 Brooks, *From Playhouse to Printing House*, pp. 112–13.

28 'Astronomers and star-gazers this year / Write but of four eclipses; five appear, / Death interposing Burbage; and their staying / Hath made a visible eclipse of playing', Nungezer, *Dictionary*, p. 73.

surviving in three, slightly different versions.[29] Its relevance for my argument merits extensive quotation and some commentary, in several instalments:

Some skilful Limner helpe me, if not soe
Some sadd Tragedian helpe t'expres my woe
But oh he's gone, that could both best; both Lime
And Act my greife; and tis for only him
That I inuoake this strange Assistance to itt
And on the point inuoake himselfe to doe itt,
For none butt Tully, Tullyes praise can tell,
And as he could, no man could act soe well.
This part of sorrow for him, no man drawe,
Soe trewly to the life, this Mapp of woee
That greifes trew picture, which his loss hath bred
Hee's gone and with him what a world are dead.
Which he reuiu'd, to be reuiued soe,
No more young Hamlett, ould Heironymoe,
Kind Leer, the Greued Moore, and more beside,
That liued in him; have now for ever dy'de,
Oft haue I seene him, leap into the Graue
Suiting the person, which he seem'd to haue
Of a sadd Louer, with soe true an Eye
That theer I would haue sworne, he meant to dye,
Oft haue I seene him, play this part in ieast,
Soe liuly, that Spectators, and the rest
Of his sad Crew, whilst he but seem'd to bleed,
Amazed, thought euen then hee dyed in deed,
O lett not me be checkt, and I shall sweare
Euen yett, it is a false report I heare,
And thinke that he, that did soe truly faine
Is still but Dead in iest, to liue againe,
But now this part, he Acts, not playes, tis knowne
Other he plaide, but Acted hath his owne

The elegy opens with a call for help, suggesting the inadequacy of the present elegist and – conventionally enough – requesting support from a more competent authority. But the understatement here is not just used as a *captatio benevolentiae*, to mark a writer's modesty. We soon realize that the deceased himself is invoked, not just to console the bereaved but to show them how to express their deepest grief. The late actor was especially famous for his art of dying, a feat which he performed so frequently and so convincingly that his own death now, somehow, seems not good enough to be true. When it comes to elegizing a tragedian, this is the key issue we must face.

Comic players, I argued, raise a problem for the poetics of mourning because they never stay in the given frame of literary representation. Their performative power constantly overflows the written parts and transgresses the fictional identity scripted for them. Tragic players, on the other hand, present the opposite problem. There are always too many and too memorable scripted parts for them to live by – Hamlet, Hieronimo, Lear, Othello and more – so that there is an excess of roles in which they have lived and, even more problematically, in which they have come to death. Burbage's elegist himself makes this point: 'Oft have I seene him play this part in jest'. How can we know the player from the play? The highest praise for early modern tragic actors was to say they died well,[30] a bravura act of stage performance often written out in death scenes of extraordinary length and verbal profusion. It was the powerful enactment of Talbot's death that Thomas Nash recalled from *Henry VI* and praised for the abundant tears it drew a thousand times.[31] But while such frequent repetition does not seem to rob stage death of its impact on spectators, it complicates their responses to actual bereavement, as witnessed in this case. The poet tries to capture the crucial difference he must come to terms with in the opposition between 'playing' and 'acting' death. Yet neither of these terms can free itself from theatrical associations nor resolve 'the ambiguity of stage corpses'.[32] A powerful player, John Earle

[29] Nungezer, *Dictionary*, pp. 74–6. The elegy survives in 82, 86 or 124 lines. The two shorter versions are generally taken to be genuine, whereas the long version attributes to Burbage several parts in plays which belonged to other companies. For a more detailed discussion of this point, see Clement Mansfield Ingleby, *Shakespeare, the Man and the Book* (London, 1877), p. 180.

[30] See Meredith Ann Skura, *Shakespeare the Actor and the Purposes of Playing* (Chicago, 1993), p. 214.

[31] See Thomas Nash, *Pierce Penniless his Supplication to the Devil*, ed. Stanley Wells (London, 1964), pp. 64–5.

[32] Drew Milne, 'What Becomes of the Broken-Hearted: *King Lear* and the Dissociation of Sensibility', *Shakespeare Survey* 55 (Cambridge, 2002), p. 57.

wrote in 1628, can 'challenge any Cato, for it has been his practice to die bravely'.[33] To make not just an art of dying but a practice, though, sets up a troubling model for any actual attempts at mourning. Therefore, this poetic lament for Richard Burbage is haunted throughout by the expectation that this great griever and great dier will, like Falstaff at Shrewsbury, rise up once more and leave the killing fields behind.

As what, or who, then can the tragedian be mourned?

> Englands great Roscious, for what Roscious,
> Was unto Roome, that Burbadg was to us.
> How did his speech become him, and his pace,
> Suite with his speech, and euery action grace
> Them both alike, whilst not a woord did fall,
> Without just weight, to ballast itt with all,
> Hadst thou but spoake to death, and us'd thy power
> Of thy Inchaunting toung, att that first hower
> Of his assualt, he had Lett fall his Dart
> And quite been Charmed, by thy all Charming Art.
> This he well knew, and to preuent this wronge
> He therefore first mede seisure on his tounge,
> Then on the rest, 'twas easy by degrees
> The slender Iuy tops the smallest trees

These lines begin to fix his memory in the time-honoured Roscius topos. Yet the consolation so achieved does not last long. As soon as the poem asks what Burbage 'was to us', the mode of classical distancing gives way to a disquieting sense of presence and immediacy, which culminates in evoking his final scene: Death and the Actor. This fatal encounter is imagined here to have been charged with combative and performative power. The emphasis on Burbage's 'enchanting tongue' refers once more to his stage appearance when audiences were so charmed by the strange magic of his passionate delivery that, unlike Death, they fell under his spell. In terms of praise, this point repeats what otherwise was often used in terms of criticism or abuse against the playhouse. Anti-theatricalists routinely pointed out the dubious powers of seduction and, even more, the dangerous charms by which players transformed themselves in whatever shape they pleased. 'He is but a shifting companion', John Cocke wrote in *The Character of a Common Player* (1615), 'for he lives effectually by putting on, and putting off'.[34] Yet how, we must ask, can a shape-shifter like this ever die? In what form and guise should he be mourned and by what face remembered? 'Was this the face that launch'd a thousand ships?' Faustus's question is the most intense – and most intensely re-enacted – moment of metatheatrical reflection in the early modern theatre, and it sums up this institution's paradoxical engagement with the dead: a place of necromantic power and illusion, theatre lives by constantly putting on death and, yet again, putting it off. Richard Burbage certainly had a face, kept for posterity in a portrait picture. But he lent it to so many others that, for contemporaries, it launched a thousand other memories. Whenever a great actor dies, Thomas Overbury remarked in 1615, a host of familiar figures dies with him because 'we cannot be persuaded any man can do his parts like him'.[35] But, ultimately, such profusion threatens not only to make him faceless. It also undermines the poet's project to compose an elegy and, by means of prosopopeia, give him a face and voice.

These threats are registered when the present writer turns to his own art:

> Poets whose glory whilome twas to heare
> Your lines so well exprest, henceforth forbeare,
> And write no more, or if you doe let' t bee
> In Commike sceans, since Tragick parts you see,
> Dy all with him; nay rather sluce your eyes
> And hence forth write nought els but Tragedyes,
> Or Dirges, or sad Ellegies or those
> Mournfull Laments that nott accord with prose,
> Blurr all your Leaus with blotts, that all you writt
> May be but one sadd black, and open it
> Draw Marble lines that may outlast ye sunn
> And stand like Trophyes, when the world is done
> Turne all your inke to blood, your pens to speares
> To pearce and wound the hearers harts and Eares,
> Enrag'd, write stabbing Lines that euery woord
> May be as apt for murther as a swoord

[33] Wickham *et al.*, *English Professional Theatre*, p. 187.
[34] Wickham *et al.*, *Professional Theatre*, p. 180.
[35] Wickham *et al.*, *Professional Theatre*, p. 181.

That no man may suruiue after this fact
Of ruthless death, eyther to heare or Act

The exhortations issued here all contradict each other. Poets are first called upon to write no more, then to write only comedies, then tragedies, then elegies, then to produce nothing but black blots, then to use their pens for physical injuries in order to draw blood. On the one hand, these conflicting injunctions are self-referential hints at the present poet's efforts to find appropriate words and modes of mourning. On the other hand, they indicate nothing so much as their final futility: short of actually killing oneself, they suggest, nothing could ever be an adequate response to this loss. We note that in this context the conventional contrast between words and deeds is once more activated. To use pens for spears, as recommended, imagines the use of actual violence against the violent force of death, instead of framing or taming it in the symbolic practices of language. The point recalls the cruel, self-inflicted ending that one of Burbage's most celebrated tragic heroes suffered, Kyd's Hieronimo, when he killed himself with the pen-knife. Even to blur all leaves with blots, the other option proposed here, is not really less violent. It also involves a radical rejection of verbal means and, ultimately, a negation of linguistic power and convention. As the speech act of a writer lost for words, the black blot on the page aspires to a condition of direct, immediate communication and non-symbolic mediation. While such immediacy of presentation might be expected in the body acts of theatre performance, at least by some members of the audience, to writers this is principally denied. Their literary acts are necessarily conventional and symbolic.

This dilemma explains why, in the next section of the elegy, the poet turns to the theatre and calls on its professionals to stage more adequate performances of mourning:

And you his sad Compannions to whome Lent
Becomes more Lenton by this Accident,
Hence forth your wauing flagg, no more hang out
Play now no more att all, when round aboute
Wee looke and miss the Atlas of your spheare
What comfort haue we (thinke you) to bee theer
And how can you delight in playing, when
Such mourning soe affecteth other men,
Or if you will still putt' t out lett it weere
No more light cullors, but death liuery there
Hang all your house with black, the Ewe it bears
With Iseckls of euer melting teares,
And if you euer chance to play agen
May nought but Tragedyes afflict your sceane

With Burbage as its mighty support lost, the Globe theatre is shaken. But other than earlier assumed, it now turns out that the stage cannot provide a better place for mourning anyway. Although it commands various non-verbal means of grief, like colours, tears and physical gestures, its readiness to employ them for all sorts of spectacles casts doubt on any serious use. 'Hang all your house with black': this instruction echoes Bedford's oft-performed opening speech in *I Henry VI*. The heavens hung with black are therefore too familiar and too routinized a sight in the playhouse to mark the present sad occasion. And yet, there is a sense in which precisely the on-going routine of tragic stage performance offers a lasting and perhaps the only consolation for us when mourning a tragedian. Players, this elegy ultimately implies, always survive through and by other players' playing. Hamlet or Hieronimo, Lear or Othello may provisionally die with their impersonator's death, but they *as well as he* are soon recovered with new impersonations. Though Overbury remarked, as just quoted, that audiences are not easily 'persuaded' that any other man can do such parts, this is entirely a matter of persuasion. The rhetorical emphasis suggests that it only needs another powerful performance by a succeeding actor to persuade the bereaved that the essential part lives on or lives again.

Some of the material traces preserved from the culture of theatre professionals support this reading. When Augustine Phillips, one of the less famous members of Burbage's company, died in 1605, he bequeathed some money to his friends and colleagues: his 'fellow William Shakespeare', for instance, was to receive a 30*s* piece in gold, Robert Armin 20*s* in gold. But some valuable and more interesting things were thoughtfully handed down to others: 'Item: I give to Samuel Gilburne, my late apprentice, the sum of 40*s*, and my mouse-coloured velvet hose, and a white taffeta doublet, a black taffeta suit, my purple cloak, sword and dagger, and my bass viol. I give to James Sands, my apprentice, the sum of 40s, and a cittern, and a bandore, and a lute'.[36] When the dying master thus provides his young apprentices with material objects which must have been part of his stage-craft, he also establishes a continuity of stage performance, endorsed by the material identity of instruments, clothes or costumes. Endowed with some of the same props and clothes as their predecessor the new actors warrant that memory traces of the old remain. Players may be shape-shifters, but the shapes they assume basically stay the same as these are shifted from one generation to the next. As Jones and Stallybrass have argued in their study of Renaissance clothing, costumes often seemed to have absorbed actors' identities.[37] Therefore, the act to pass on his clothes, along with musical instruments, when an actor passes away, shows the materials of memory and manifests the resilience of performance – a cultural continuity which death can only momentarily interrupt. In a closely related sense, a Restoration poet was to write a generation after Burbage in praise of his most glorious successor: 'Such even the nicest critics must allow/ Burbage was once; and such Charles Hart is now.'[38] The player is dead – long live the player.

In this view, theatrical performance emerges as a process continuously encoding and recoding wider social practices, hence also offering a cultural model for engaging with the ruptures of bereavement. As such, it further suggests grounds to rethink the poetics of mourning in terms of their performative utterances. Before returning to this point in my conclusion, I wish to briefly note the ending of the elegy for Burbage:

> And thou deare Earth that must enshrine that dust
> By Heauen now committed to thy trust
> Keepe itt as pretious as ye richest Mine
> That Lyes intomb'd, in that rich womb of thine,
> That after times may know that much lou'd mould
> From other dust, and cherrish it as gould,
> On it be laide some soft but lasting stone
> With this short Epitaph endorst thereon
>   That euery Eye may reade, and reading weepe
>   Tis Englands Roscious, Burbadg that I keepe.

The ending is conventional enough. Referring to some 'lasting stone', the speaker hopes for a distinctive and remaining mark, a form of symbolization which, according to Sacks's account of elegiac conventions,[39] must generally provide the cover for a preceding lack, when the work of mourning is to be completed. Dust keeps no distinctions, so the only way to 'keep' England's Roscius lies in transforming the current acts of mourning for him into public memory and memory into cultural signification.

Against the background of these readings, we can now review the larger issues about writing and performance, which they exemplify and help to complicate. As textual products of a literary culture, early modern English elegies are part of a tradition which they commemorate, continue and, in some cases, redraw. It is part of this tradition that they construct the voice and presence of a mourner who struggles to express his grief and so presents himself as spokesman for the wider community of the bereaved. The various apostrophes, the false starts or the twists and turns of argument that have been noted in Burbage's or Armin's elegies all contribute to this poetic strategy: a self-conscious dramatic act to perform loss and lament in writing. In this sense, elegies can principally be understood to present words as gestures in performance. As the examples cited show, they emulate the effects of embodied language. With their residual ceremonial character, their invocations, their sense of passionate

[36] Wickham *et al.*, *Professional Theatre*, pp. 198–99.

[37] Ann Rosalind Jones, Peter Stallybrass, *Renaissance Clothing and the Materials of Memory* (Cambridge, 2000), p. 177.

[38] Nungezer, *Dictionary*, p. 79. Tiffany Stern makes the same point about John Lowen and Joseph Taylor as heirs to Burbage's parts, *Making Shakespeare: From Stage to Page* (London, New York, 2004), p. 72.

[39] Sacks, *English Elegy*, p. 18.

involvement and bewilderment often taking us from rage to resolution, elegies emerge as a poetic genre in which saying things appears to be a way of doing them.

By means of such complex verbal acts, the wound of bereavement is both addressed and dressed. 'When death inflicts wounds on our consciousness', David Shaw explains, 'elegists often turn descriptions of these wounds into performances that are self-therapeutic and cathartic'.[40] In fact, Puttenham already characterized the genre in such terms, drawing a medical analogy: 'as the *Paracelsians*, who cure *similia similibus*, making one dolour to expell another, and in this case, one short sorrowing the remedie of a long and grieuous sorrow'.[41] The funeral elegy, then, seems to work by the same principles of cathartic suffering and performance as does tragic drama. So when it sets out to address cultural wounds which are themselves dramatic and theatrical in nature, resulting from the death of actors, it engages rivalries within the powers of performance. Such rivalries also emerge with the construction of particular commemorative forms in which the late actors are to be enshrined but by which the current writers, too, can find – and perhaps seek – commemoration. As Kay points out[42] and as Jonson's ambiguous tribute to Alleyn exemplifies, elegy constitutes a space in which writers also make themselves their own subject. A mourner gains both authority and prominence in the act of public mourning.

How to elegize Elizabethan actors, therefore, involves a promise as much as a problem. On the one hand, theatre professionals appear to have a close affinity with the performative procedure of elegiac writing. And yet it is this very closeness, their multitude of roles and acts which, on the other hand, makes them so challenging a subject for commemorative verse. Central elegiac devices and generic gestures like prosopopeia fail, as we have seen, when they are used to address clowns or tragic actors, Proteus figures who elude the monumentalizing grasp of memorial language. Most attempts to do so mean either too much or too little. Above all, they cannot come to terms with the players' own professional performances of dying, celebrated stage acts that suggest their strange affinity to and, at the same time, their resilience against death.

All this might show, in Worthen's sense,[43] that performance is a mode of production, not merely a mode of enunciation. It is for this reason, I suggest, that theatrical performance retains its own peculiar reality and cannot readily be framed in common terms of affirmation or negation, truth or falsehood, life or death. This central point has best been formulated by the anthropologist Johannes Fabian: 'If "to be or not to be" is the question, then "to be and not to be" – to me the most succinct conception of performance – might be the answer'.[44] To me, this answer also gives the most succinct conception of how to elegize Elizabethan actors when they are dead and yet continue to live in their parts: to be and not to be remembered in posthumous writing just as in posthumous performance. The examples here discussed have all illustrated this double aspect, but none of them so strikingly as another epitaph for Burbage which was printed in the 1674 edition of Camden's *Remaines Concerning Britain*. It simply reads: 'Exit Burbage'.[45] Here, the briefest phrase captures both the painful and the playful aspect, so that we find both the ending as well as the continuance of this tragedian's performance acted out.

---

[40] W. David Shaw, *Elegy and Paradox: Texting the Conventions* (Baltimore, 1994), p. 8.

[41] Puttenham, *English Poesy*, p. 39.

[42] Kay, *Melodious Tears*, p. 8.

[43] Worthen, *Shakespeare and the Authority of Performance*, p. 24.

[44] Johannes Fabian, 'Theatre and Anthropology, Theatricality and Culture', in *The Performance Studies Reader*, ed. Henry Bial (London, New York, 2004), p. 179.

[45] Nungezer, *Dictionary*, p. 73.

# ELIZABETH MONTAGU: 'SHAKESPEAR'S POOR LITTLE CRITICK'?

FIONA RITCHIE

The publication of Elizabeth Montagu's *Essay on the Writings and Genius of Shakespear* in 1769 coincided with the zenith of eighteenth-century bardolatry. It is generally acknowledged that this was the era in which Shakespeare's central place in British literary culture was established. The eighteenth century saw a huge expansion of scholarly interest in the dramatist, opening up a significant new site for literary debate. In addition to the various critical editions of Shakespeare's works by men of letters such as Rowe, Pope, Theobald, Hanmer and Warburton, numerous essays, commentaries and critical monographs sought to explain and elucidate Shakespeare for the current age. Even works on wider subjects such as poetic theory (Charles Gildon's 1718 *The Complete Art of Poetry*) or theories of genius (William Duff's 1767 *An Essay on Original Genius*) increasingly turned to Shakespeare to illustrate their precepts. This new scholarship had the effect of establishing Shakespeare's literary value as on a par with that of the classical authors; indeed, he became known as the English Homer. Shakespeare's position as Britain's national poet and cultural hero was also confirmed in other ways, such as by the erection of a statue in Poets' Corner, Westminster Abbey in 1741. The culmination of this cultural canonisation came, as Michael Dobson has convincingly argued, with David Garrick's Stratford Jubilee of 1769.[1]

The establishment of Shakespeare's place in the literary canon offered an important opening to women. By the eighteenth century, women were increasingly involved and acknowledged in literature but they were still mainly confined to acceptable feminine genres and to imaginative rather than critical writing. Women had previously been excluded from criticism and scholarship, largely because until this time works in the ancient languages had received the greatest degree of critical attention and women for the most part lacked a classical education. Although there were some notable female classical scholars such as Anne Dacier and Elizabeth Carter, women were generally not taught classics simply because the professions in which such knowledge was necessary were not open to them. Furthermore, many Latin and Greek texts were considered improper reading material for the female sex. Women writers such as Montagu were able to use the growth of Shakespeare studies as an opportunity to become literary critics since the fact that they often lacked a classical education was in this instance not a barrier to entering the literary sphere: women could take their place as critics and scholars by writing about Shakespeare. Montagu's *Essay on the Writings and Genius of Shakespear* thus represents a significant

I am indebted to Robin Dix and Elizabeth Eger for their help with this article and to the AHRB for their financial assistance. The title's quotation is taken from Elizabeth Montagu's letter to Edward Montagu, 10 and 11 September 1769 in *Bluestocking Feminism: Writings of the Bluestocking Circle, Volume 1: Elizabeth Montagu*, ed. Elizabeth Eger, gen. ed. Gary Kelly (London, 1999), pp. 189–90. Subsequent references to Montagu's *An Essay on the Writings and Genius of Shakespear* and her letters are taken from this edition and occur parenthetically in the text.

1 Michael Dobson, *The Making of the National Poet: Shakespeare, Adaptation and Authorship, 1660–1769* (Oxford, 1992).

attempt by a woman writer to enter the previously male domain of literary criticism.

As well as the establishment of Shakespeare's role as British national poet, the eighteenth century also saw a reconsideration of British national identity. Indeed, there was often a degree of overlap between these two fields: Shakespeare was invoked in debates on nationalism and used as a tool to construct national identity. The eighteenth century was of course a time of substantial anti-French sentiment; thus it is unsurprising that Britain began to define itself in stark contrast and opposition to everything French. In this period it was widely believed that Britain's ruling classes were leading the country into French-style extravagance and unmanliness, erasing the country's virile Elizabethan character in the process. This view was espoused by John Brown in his 1757 *Estimate of the Manners and Principles of the Times*, where he claimed that 'the ruling Character of the present Times is that of a vain, luxurious, and selfish EFFEMINACY', the archetype of which was undoubtedly the manners of the French.[2] Shakespeare was often invoked both in order to counter the perceived pernicious influence of the French and as a way of defining the British character as 'natural'. This can be seen, for example, in Mark Akenside's 'The Remonstrance of Shakespeare: Supposed to Have Been Spoken at the Theatre Royal, While the French Comedians Were Acting by Subscription. MDCCXLIX', where 'Shakespeare' states that unlike the French dramatists he has not attempted to attract the audience 'with wretched bribes to luxury and vice' but that the aim of his drama was 'freedom, virtue, glory'.[3]

This use of Shakespeare also carried over into the field of literary criticism. At a time when there was great tension between the two nations, remarks which denigrated British history, literature or culture caused particular outrage. The full title of Montagu's essay reveals its agenda: *An Essay on the Writings and Genius of Shakespear, Compared with the Greek and French Dramatic Poets. With Some Remarks Upon the Misrepresentations of Mons. de Voltaire.* Montagu sets out her reasons for writing the *Essay* in her introduction: 'I will own I was incited to this undertaking by great admiration of his [Shakespeare's] genius, and still greater indignation at the treatment he had received from a French wit' (p. 6). Montagu emphasizes Shakespeare's perceived naturalness, describing him as a 'heaven-born genius' who 'has a right of appeal to nature herself' (p. 3). Unlike the works of the French dramatists, his plays are irregular but they are to be regarded as natural wonders of which England should be proud:

> Will not an intelligent spectator admire the prodigious structures of Stone-Henge, because he does not know by what law of mechanics they were raised? Like them, our author's works will remain for ever the greatest monuments of the amazing force of nature, which we ought to view as we do other prodigies, with an attention to, and admiration of their stupendous parts, and proud irregularity of greatness. (pp. 4–5)

Shakespeare's naturalness is, of course, used as a riposte to Voltaire and the French stage is criticized for its 'declamations' and 'rhetorical flourishes' (p. 12), unnecessary 'theatrical decorations' (p. 14) and excessive use of the artifice of rhyme, which renders 'many plays . . . little more than poems rehearsed' (p. 14). The *Essay* uses Shakespeare in the context of nationalistic debate: Montagu identifies 'our countryman' Shakespeare as Britain's principal dramatist and by stressing his native purity in the face of French extravagance and ornamentation, British national identity is simultaneously defined as natural, honest and unaffected.

Montagu's emphasis on Shakespeare's naturalness also serves to construct him as an unlearned genius. The idea of Shakespeare as a wild and uneducated poet was undoubtedly exaggerated by eighteenth-century critics to serve their own ends, not only to excuse Shakespeare's 'barbarism' but also to bolster their own aesthetic theories. Milton's portrait of 'sweetest Shakespeare fancy's child / warbl[ing] his native wood-notes wild' was seized on by theorists

---

[2] [John Brown], *An Estimate of the Manners and Principles of the Times*, 7th edn (London, 1757), p. 67, p. 135.

[3] In *The Poetical Works of Mark Akenside*, ed. Robin Dix (Madison, NJ, 1996), pp. 308–10 (line 42, line 44).

of genius such as William Duff since if genius did not depend on learning, this supported the contention that genius was innate.[4] But in praising the fact that despite his 'untutored mind' Shakespeare 'rose so much above the age and circumstances in which he was born' (p. 7), Montagu claims Shakespeare as an example to women.[5] Montagu's arguments in support of Shakespeare, therefore, can also be read as arguments in support of women's activity in the literary sphere: women may be unlearned but it does not mean that they are unable to produce something significant. Thus Montagu not only claims a place as a Shakespeare critic but also uses Shakespeare to justify her entry into the world of scholarship, at the same time producing an impressive piece of criticism and demonstrating her considerable learning.

Ultimately, it has been for her attack on Voltaire and French drama that Montagu's work on Shakespeare has come to be valued: although there were other works in the Voltaire–Shakespeare controversy, Montagu offers more arguments against Voltaire than any other critic of her time. Indeed, she was commemorated by Garrick as a warlike patriot, taking on 'the Gallic God of literary War':

> Out rush'd a Female to protect the Bard,
> Snatch'd up her Spear, and for the fight prepar'd:
> Attack'd the Vet'ran, pierc'd his Sev'n-fold Shield,
> And drove him wounded, fainting from the field.[6]

However, although the nationalistic agenda of the *Essay* is undoubtedly important, I believe that there is considerably more to Montagu's work on Shakespeare that is of interest and that has been neglected.[7]

As well as praising Shakespeare and criticising French drama, Montagu also advances her own theory of poetics. For Montagu, the principal aim of drama is to provide moral instruction: she claims that 'the first endeavour of the poet should be to touch the heart, the next to mend it' (p. 15). The action on the stage should move us to virtuous behaviour and here Shakespeare's ability to give 'an air of reality to every thing' (p. 8) is emphasized:

> The business of the drama is to excite sympathy; and its effect on the spectator depends on such a justness of imitation, as shall cause, to a certain degree, the same passions and affections, as if what was exhibited was real. (p. 12)

Johnson had also recognized and praised what Montagu calls Shakespeare's 'justness of imitation', proclaiming him 'the poet of nature; the poet that holds up to his readers a faithful mirror of manners and of life'.[8] This concept of Shakespeare as the 'poet of nature' (in contrast to Jonson, who was seen as the 'poet of art') was begun by the introductory pages to the First Folio of 1623 where Heminge and Condell call him 'a happy imitator of nature'. Montagu's and Johnson's emphasis on Shakespeare's naturalness, then, was not new but it was fundamental to the eighteenth-century conception of the dramatist and indeed had become a commonplace. But as well as allowing Montagu to retaliate against Voltaire's denigration of Shakespeare's barbaric and irregular plays by constructing

---

[4] John Milton, 'L'Allegro', in *John Milton*, eds. Stephen Orgel and Jonathan Goldberg, Oxford Authors (Oxford, 1991), pp. 22–5 (lines 133–34). William Duff, *An Essay on Original Genius* (London, 1767).

[5] Similarly, Aphra Behn had earlier asserted that Shakespeare's lack of learning allowed women dramatists an affinity with him in her Preface to *The Dutch Lover* (1673).

[6] David Garrick, 'The Dream', in *Women Reading Shakespeare, 1660–1900: An Anthology of Criticism*, ed. Ann Thompson and Sasha Roberts (Manchester, 1997), pp. 22–23 (line 7, lines 10–13).

[7] There have been two recent discussions of the *Essay*: Elizabeth Eger, '"Out Rushed a Female to Protect the Bard": The Bluestocking Defense of Shakespeare', *Huntington Library Quarterly*, 65 (2002), 127–51, and Judith Hawley, 'Shakespearean Sensibilities: Women Writers Reading Shakespeare, 1753–1808', *Shakespearean Continuities: Essays in Honour of E. A. J. Honigmann*, eds. John Batchelor, Tom Cain, and Claire Lamont (Basingstoke and New York, 1997), pp. 290–304. The former concentrates on Montagu's championing of the vernacular; the latter questions how groundbreaking eighteenth-century criticism of Shakespeare by women actually was.

[8] *The Yale Edition of the Works of Samuel Johnson*, 16 vols. (New Haven, CT, 1958–90), vol. 7, p. 62. Subsequent references to Johnson's works are taken from this edition and occur in parentheses in the text.

his works as natural rather than affected, the truth to life that Montagu sees so extensively in Shakespeare's works also means that his plays are, in her view, particularly able to fulfil the moral function of drama and the poet is thus to be regarded as 'one of the greatest moral philosophers that ever lived' (p. 21).

On the point of the moral instruction offered by Shakespeare's work Montagu differs from Johnson, who notably claimed that Shakespeare was 'so much more careful to please than to instruct, that he seems to write without any moral purpose' (vol. 7, p. 71). Although he concedes that 'from his writings indeed a system of social duty may be selected, for he that thinks reasonably must think morally', Johnson is uneasy about the need for the reader to actively construct Shakespeare's morality. Both critics take pleasure in mimesis but Johnson is aware that poetic justice is not often evident in the real world: the good may suffer and the bad prosper. He believes that moral instruction can only come from seeing the good rewarded and the bad punished; truth to life cannot, therefore, lead to moral edification. The death of Cordelia is Johnson's supreme example of Shakespeare depicting the world as it is rather than following the rules of poetic justice:

> A play in which the wicked prosper, and the virtuous miscarry, may doubtless be good, because it is a just representation of the common events of human life: but since all reasonable beings naturally love justice, I cannot easily be persuaded, that the observation of justice makes a play worse; or, that if other excellencies are equal, the audience will not always rise better pleased from the final triumph of persecuted virtue. (vol. 8, p. 704)

Montagu, however, has a simpler faith in the moral tendency of the world and celebrates 'justness of imitation' as she trusts it will have a positive moral effect on the spectator and will enable drama to achieve its object of 'the instruction of mankind, in religion, morals, philosophy, *&c*' (p. 9).

While there are many significant differences in their thought, including their view of the moral function of drama, the received opinion of Montagu's Shakespeare criticism is that it is limited by its adherence to the taste of the age and largely derived from Johnson, a view expounded by nineteenth- and early twentieth-century critics and recently taken up and endorsed by Brian Vickers and Jonathan Bate, among others.[9] Where Montagu's and Johnsons's thoughts concur, it is often on points that were commonplaces of eighteenth-century Shakespeare criticism, such as the distaste for Shakespeare's puns, or 'quibbles', so the use of similar language is understandable and even inevitable. The nature of eighteenth-century literary culture is also important here; Johnson and Montagu knew one another and doubtless attended literary salons together at which ideas on Shakespeare were discussed. While Johnson's Preface appeared before Montagu's *Essay*, her letters prove that she had formulated many of the precepts expressed in the work several years before she began to write it.[10] Although it has been accorded a pre-eminent place in Shakespeare criticism of the period, scholars have claimed that Johnson's Preface itself is derivative: it relies on established critical conventions and shares similarities in structure and in the choice of topics addressed to the writings of earlier critics.

Montagu clearly uses her criticism in the *Essay* to consider and engage with Johnson's ideas and the work seems to have been designed in part as a response to Johnson's Preface. Montagu felt that Johnson had not devoted sufficient attention to 'the dramatick genius of Shakespear' and set out in her *Essay* to give a fuller account of 'the dramatick art', as she explained in a letter to her friend Elizabeth Carter: 'I think the Theatrical entertainments capable of conveying so much instruction, & of exciting such sentiments in the people, that if I am glad he left the task to my unable hand, I dare hardly own

[9] Brian Vickers, *Shakespeare: The Critical Heritage*, 6 vols. (London, 1979), vol. 5, p. 328. Jonathan Bate, *Shakespeare and the English Romantic Imagination* (Oxford, 1986), p. 14.

[10] See for example her letter to George Lyttelton of 10 October 1760 in Eger, *Bluestocking Feminism*, pp. 157–61. Montagu corresponded with some of the most important thinkers of her day, including George Lyttelton, Adam Smith, Hugh Blair and Henry Home, Lord Kames, frequently discussing weighty intellectual issues in her letters.

it to myself' (21 October 1766, p. 173). From the outset of her essay, Montagu carves out her own unique space in the field of Shakespeare criticism; she clarifies that she will not 'entertain the vain presumption of attempting to correct any passages of this celebrated author' but will instead undertake 'a thorough enquiry into the genius of our great English classic' (p. 1). Since there was no precedent for a woman emending the text of Shakespeare this was perhaps unsurprising but her letter to Carter reveals that she saw herself as undertaking something more significant than mere editing. Her language demonstrates that she saw deficiencies in Johnson's treatment of Shakespeare which she believed she herself could remedy and suggests that she was deliberately setting herself up in competition with the eighteenth century's most celebrated man of letters: she considered Johnson's work on Shakespeare to be limited because he had concentrated primarily on 'the piddling trade of verbal criticism' and wrote that 'it has been lucky for my amusement, but unfortunate for the publick, that he did not consider his author in a more extensive view'.[11]

Johnson's focus on textual emendation and explanation ties him very much to the page. Montagu, on the other hand, constantly takes the dramatic nature of Shakespeare's works into account; she seems always to visualize the characters and their actions and is fully aware that drama is a distinct literary genre with 'a manner so different from any other kind of poetical imitation' (p. 9). She is conscious of 'the powerful agency of living words, joined to moving things, when still narration yields the place to animated action' (p. 10). Montagu praises the efforts of Shakespeare's editors in the *Essay* but the terms in which she does so reveal her preference for stage over page: the editors have enabled Shakespeare's spirit 'to come forth and to animate his characters, as often as Mr. Garrick, who acts with the same inspiration with which he wrote, assumes them on the stage' (p. 6). The *Essay* sets out to address Shakespeare's audience as well as his readers and in this sense could be said to be more inclusive than the works of the Shakespeare editors. Clearly Montagu's approach to Shakespeare criticism is decidedly and deliberately different from that of Johnson.

Johnson apparently held a low opinion of Montagu's *Essay*; his comments on the work are often quoted and may be partly responsible for its subsequent marginalization. Although he declared he had 'not read it at all', he claimed that

> when I take up the end of a web, and find it packthread, I do not expect, by looking further, to find embroidery. . . . there is no real criticism in it: none shewing the beauty of thought, as formed on the workings of the human heart.[12]

Boswell, who reports this view of the work, goes on to assert that although

> the admirers of the Essay may be offended at the slighting manner in which Johnson spoke of it . . . let it be remembered, that he gave his honest opinion unbiased by any prejudice, or any proud jealousy of a woman intruding herself into the chair of criticism.

Arguably, jealousy is precisely what Johnson's reaction to the *Essay* does demonstrate, along with his dissatisfaction at having to share his position as Shakespeare's most eminent critic with a woman.[13] Boswell in fact admired the *Essay* and realized that the work was of a different nature from textual emendation and elucidation, 'which alone Dr Johnson would allow to be "real criticism"'. In fact, the work was extremely successful: the first run of a thousand copies sold out rapidly, it went through seven editions and was translated into French and Italian. Its denigration of French drama and patriotic defence of Shakespeare meant that the *Essay* was bound to be a popular piece of criticism, and one also wonders whether a work in praise

---

11 21 October 1766 in Eger, *Bluestocking Feminism*, p. 173.

12 James Boswell, *Life of Johnson*, ed. R. W. Chapman, introd. Pat Rogers, The World's Classics (Oxford, 1980), pp. 413–14.

13 The competitive nature of the relationship between Montagu and Johnson is dealt with thoroughly in Norma Clarke, *Dr Johnson's Women* (London, 2000). Elizabeth Eger notes that Montagu's decision to align herself with the figures of the Scottish Enlightenment such as Blair, Smith and Kames was a deliberate move to distance herself from Johnson, whilst still participating in intellectual and cultural tradition (p. lxxiii).

of Shakespeare published in the year of Garrick's Jubilee could fail.

Nevertheless, writing about Shakespeare was a potential minefield for a woman. Unlike more feminine genres such as poetry or the novel, criticism necessitated judgement and learning, rather than just imagination. A connection was still made between learned women and sexual laxity, thus a woman who flaunted her learning by disseminating her writing had to take great pains to assert the inviolability of her chastity and morality at all times. In addition to this, one of the eighteenth century's most profound anxieties about Shakespeare's works was their perceived impropriety, which also caused difficulties for the female critic. Thus women had to employ certain strategies to make it acceptable for them to write on the 'improper' Shakespeare.

Like many of her contemporaries, Montagu is concerned with the historical context of Shakespeare's work: she is interested in the effects the cultural climate of Elizabethan and Jacobean England may have had on the dramatist. Indeed, it is the historicizing of Shakespeare which provides Montagu with her main defence of the poet: Shakespeare's barbarism should be excused, she argues, because he 'wrote at a time when learning was tinctured with pedantry; wit was unpolished, and mirth ill-bred' thus 'by contagion, or from complaisance to the taste of the public, Shakespear falls sometimes into the fashionable mode of writing' (p. 4). If aspects of Shakespeare's work do not please the eighteenth-century spectator, this can be attributed to the evolution of society to a greater level of aesthetic sophistication:

> He wrote to please an untaught people, guided wholly by their feelings, and to those feelings he applied, and they are often touched by circumstances that have not dignity and splendor enough to please the eye accustomed to the specious miracles of ostentatious art, and the nice selection of refined judgement. (p. 108)

Although this view was extremely common in the period, the emphasis on placing Shakespeare in his historical context is used to great effect in the *Essay*; in historicizing Shakespeare, Montagu does not condone his barbarism or impropriety but simply distances herself from it, thus distancing herself from possible criticism of a woman researching and writing on the more indecorous aspects of Shakespeare. Montagu's decision to focus on the dramatic nature of Shakespeare's work rather than undertake any form of textual emendation or explication is key here as it enables her to avoid dealing directly with the main source of Shakespeare's bawdiness: his language.

Eighteenth-century Shakespeare editors were part of this historicizing tendency in their attempts to set Shakespeare in his context and to recover lost meanings from obscurity in order to elucidate his works for a different cultural climate. But although it attempted to make Shakespeare more accessible for the current age, this trend in editing was in some way self-defeating as the editors' explanatory notes simply made the text bigger and more unwieldy. This was a particular problem for those without a classical education, that is, the vast majority of women, since only the texts of the classical authors had been published with critical apparatus before this time. Montagu's *Essay* could be seen as a reaction against the increasingly unmanageable eighteenth-century editions since it has the merit of being both a scholarly and accessible contribution to the field of Shakespeare studies. Montagu's brand of historicizing works very much to her advantage as a female critic by allowing her to distance herself from any problematic elements in Shakespeare and to concentrate on the elements of Shakespeare which she particularly enjoys.

Another danger for the female critic was the hostility that flaunting her learning might provoke. The *Essay* clearly shows Montagu's high level of knowledge; she repeatedly demonstrates that her French is better than Voltaire's English through her criticism of his translations and commentaries and the work also relies on a deep understanding of Greek drama (which she read in English, French and Italian translations). In a letter to her father, Montagu reveals herself to be fully aware of the objections that could be levelled at her authorship of the *Essay*:

In the first place, there is in general a prejudice against female Authors especially if they invade those regions of literature which the Men are desirous to reserve to themselves . . . Mr. Pope our great Poet, the Bishop of Gloucester our Great Critick, & Dr Johnson our great Scholar having already given their criticism upon Shakespear, there was a degree of presumption in pretending to meddle with a subject they had already treated tolerably well, sure to incur their envy if I succeded, their contempt if I did not. Then for a weak & unknown Champion to throw down the gauntlett of defiance in the very teeth of Voltaire appear'd too daring . . . I was obliged to enter seriously into the nature of Dramatick purposes, & the character of the best dramatick writings, & by sometimes differing from the Code of the great Legislator in Poeticks, Aristotle, I was afraid the Learned would reject my opinions, the unlearned yawn over my pages, so that I was very doubtfull of the general success of my work.

('To Matthew Robinson', 10 September 1769, pp. 185–8)

Montagu's work was originally published anonymously and her name did not appear on the title page until the fourth edition of 1777. Naturally the vast majority of readers simply assumed the *Essay* had been written by a man: Montagu commented in a letter 'they talk of him [the author] till they make me feel whether I have not a beard on my chin' ('To George Lyttelton', 4 June 1769, pp. 184–5). But as a prominent member of the Bluestocking circle with links to the famous literary figures of the day, Montagu could not entirely avoid suspicion; indeed it appears she had been widely identified as the work's author as early as December 1769. As has been noted, the *Essay* was extremely well received and Montagu seems to have been happy to be recognized as the author once the work's success had been established. It is significant, though, that she was willing to let readers believe the *Essay* was written by a man until she was sure of its favourable reception; she clearly acknowledged the resentment that female critics could encounter.

Montagu's greatest contribution to Shakespearian scholarship has so far not been acknowledged or explored by critics: her treatment of the history plays as a distinct and special genre. Shortly after the work appeared, Hugh Blair, one of the leading figures of the Scottish Enlightenment, singled out her treatment of the histories as the major achievement of the *Essay*:

I am particularly pleased with what you have said, on the Historical Drama. I was always at a loss before what to think of these pieces of Shakespear. You have placed them in a light that is New & Just; and have defended them, entirely to my Satisfaction, on the most rational principles of Criticism.[14]

Montagu excuses the irregular aspects of the history plays by historicizing them:

our author by following minutely the chronicles of the times had embarrassed his drama's [*sic*] with too great a number of persons and events. The hurley-burley of these plays recommended them to a rude and illiterate audience, who, as he says, loved a noise of targets.

(p. 26)

She praises Shakespeare's ability to create such great works 'from those aukward originals our old chronicles' (p. 32) and recognizes that the histories are neither comedies nor tragedies but a separate kind of play which cannot be judged by classical standards: 'being of an original kind and peculiar construction [they] cannot come within any rules which are prior to their existence' (p. 20). Johnson had made a similar remark in his Preface and used this as a way of dismissing the history plays from consideration in his attempt to defend Shakespeare against the charge of violation of the unities, stating briefly that they need only observe the unity of action (vol. 7, p. 75). In contrast, Montagu uses her observation on the unique character of the history play as a way into an extended discussion of the genre. The full ramification of the 1623 First Folio's division of Shakespeare's plays into comedies, tragedies and histories had yet to be fully investigated. In 1765 Thomas Percy had noted in his *Reliques of Ancient English Poetry* that the genre of the history play demanded greater exploration by literary critics but this had not yet been undertaken.

[14] Letter to Montagu, 3 June 1769, quoted in Eger, p. lxxii.

For Montagu the history plays are best able to fulfil the moral function of drama as they are particularly natural. In other types of drama moral reflections 'teaze the spectator, whose mind is intent upon, and impatient for the catastrophe' but in the history play when Shakespeare

> introduces a general maxim, it seems forced from him by the occasion. As it arises out of the action, it loses itself again in it, and remains not, as in other writers, an ambitious ornament glittering alone, but is so connected as to be an useful passage very naturally united with the story. (p. 22)

The English history plays move us to virtuous behaviour: 'The poet collects, as it were, into a focus those truths, which lie scattered in the diffuse volume of the historian, and kindles the flame of virtue, while he shews the miseries and calamities of vice' (p. 20). In fact, their ability to do so is enhanced by the fact that the history plays are of clear relevance to the audience, both in Shakespeare's time and in Montagu's, since the events and characters depicted are taken directly from life:

> The common interests of humanity make us attentive to every story that has an air of reality, but we are more affected if we know it to be true; and the interest is still heightened if we have any relation to the persons concerned. (p. 21)

However, truth itself is not sufficient unless it is expressed poetically: 'the force and lustre of poetical language join with the weight and authority of history, to impress the moral lesson on the heart' (p. 20).

Montagu's celebration of Shakespeare's histories is certainly in part motivated by the nationalistic aims of her work. The history plays are obviously significant in this respect for they help to construct British national identity by depicting the people and events of British history. Furthermore, her praise of the histories denotes a denigration of French drama for continuing to follow classical models and plots, which she implies are inferior in providing moral instruction:

> The catastrophe of these plays is not derived from a vain and idle fable . . . nor is a man represented entangled in the web of fate. Our noble countryman Percy, engages us much more than Achilles, or any Grecian hero. The people for whose use these public entertainments should be chiefly intended, know the battle of Shrewsbury to be a fact: they are informed of what has passed on the banks of the Severn; all that happened on the shore of the Scamander has to them the appearance of a fiction. (pp. 20–1)

Today this unquestioning belief that Shakespeare was representing what actually happened doubtless seems more than a little naïve. In fact, however, the *Essay*'s discussion of Shakespeare's histories is subtle and perceptive, exploring the significance of Shakespeare's use of the genre for the first time. Montagu notes that 'the nature of the historical play gave scope to the extensive talents of Shakespear. He had an uncommon felicity in painting manners and developing characters, which he could employ with peculiar grace and propriety' in this particular genre. She is also particularly sensitive to the power of the strength of the dramatist's characterization which

> must have engaged the attention of the spectator, and assisted in that delusion of his imagination from whence his sympathies with the story must arise. We are affected by the catastrophe of a stranger, we lament the destiny of an Œdipus, and the misfortunes of a Hecuba; but the little peculiarities of character touch us only where we have some nearer affinity to the person than the common relation of humanity; nor unless we are particularly acquainted with the original character, can these distinguishing marks have the merit of heightening the resemblance and animating the portrait. (p. 21)

Montagu also offers convincing explanations as to why the English history plays should be better able than classical drama to effect moral improvement on an English audience. She singles out the unique nature of their form:

> The various interests and characters in these historical plays, and the mixture of the comic, weaken the operations of pity and terror, but introduce various opportunities of conveying moral instruction, as occasion is given to a variety of reflections and observations, more useful in common life than those drawn from the conditions of kings and heroes, and persons greatly superior to us by nature or fortune. (p. 23)

Montagu sees the 'mingled drama' as particularly able to offer moral instruction because it replicates life more accurately and she sees this mixture of tragic and comic elements as particularly characteristic of Shakespeare's history plays.[15] She commends the fact that in these plays he 'broke down the barriers that had before confined the dramatic writers to the regions of comedy, or tragedy' and 'perceived the fertility of the subjects that lay between the two extreams' (p. 24). For Montagu, paramount in the histories' ability to offer a moral lesson is the relevance of their subject matter: 'As the misfortunes of nations as well as of individuals often arise from their peculiar dispositions, customs, prejudices, and vices, these homeborn dramas are excellently calculated to correct them' (p. 21). She is clearly aware that the genre can convey particularly effectively the self-knowledge that it is drama's primary function to provide.

Appreciation of Shakespeare's histories was not shared by all; John Upton, for example, saw little merit in the Gothic, by which he means specifically English, non-classical, elements of Shakespeare, commenting that 'Shakespeare never writes so below himself, as when he keeps closest to our most authentic chronicles.'[16] Montagu's decision to focus on the histories (she dedicates a chapter to the nature of the historical drama and a chapter each to the two parts of *Henry IV*) is a clever move, bearing in mind her position as a female critic.[17] If, as I have suggested, women writers were under pressure to emphasize their morality, it was surely shrewd of Montagu to concentrate on the genre she saw as having a particularly strong moral effect.

The fact that the histories focus on male characters and give relatively little attention to the relationships between the sexes is, I believe, an advantage to Montagu here. In her discussion of *1 Henry IV* she finds it relatively easy to justify one of the play's more morally problematic issues: the relationship between Hal and Falstaff:

> The Prince seems always diverted, rather than seduced by Falstaffe; he despises his vices while he is entertained by his humour: and though Falstaffe is for a while a stain upon his character, yet it is of a kind with those colours, which are used for a disguise in sport, being of such a nature as are easily washed out, without leaving any bad tincture. And we see Henry, as soon as he is called to the high and serious duties of a King, come forth at once with unblemished majesty. The disposition of the hero is made to pierce through the idle frolics of the boy, throughout the whole play; for his reformation is not effected in the last scene of the last act, as is usual in our comedies, but is prepared from the very beginning of the play. (p. 39)

But when she comes to the female characters, moral justification becomes more difficult. Whereas Mistress Quickly is excused because she 'helps to compleat the character of Falstaffe', Doll Tearsheet is dismissed as downright immoral:

> There are delicacies of decorum in one age unknown to another age, but whatever is immoral is equally blameable in all ages, and every approach to obscenity is an offence for which wit cannot atone, nor the barbarity or the corruption of the times excuse. (p. 47)

The vehemence of this response suggests Montagu's awareness of the fine line she is treading in attempting to vindicate plays that not all critics perceived as completely morally acceptable. Here even the impulse to historicize is not sufficient to excuse the immorality of this particular female character.

The reason for this seems to me to be that while there are elements of bawdy humour in the relationships between the male characters, Montagu

---

15 Johnson saw the mixture of tragic and comic elements in all Shakespeare's plays, not just the histories, and granted that tragicomedy was able to offer instruction (vol. 7, p. 67). However, in *The Rambler* 156 (1751) he expressed anxiety about the mixture of the tragic and the comic: 'the effects even of Shakespeare's poetry might have been yet greater, had he not counter-acted himself; and we might have been more interested in the distresses of his heroes had we not been so frequently diverted by the jokes of his buffoons' (vol. 5, p. 69).

16 John Upton, *Critical Observations on Shakespeare* (London, 1746), p. 40.

17 The other chapters deal with the nature of drama in general, the 'Præternatural Beings', *Macbeth, Julius Caesar* and Corneille's *Cinna.*

can pass over these more easily than the improper elements of the relationships between the male and female characters, which have a more sexual basis. While the female critic can profess not to understand aspects of male behaviour since knowledge of this falls outside her sphere of experience, she would be expected to condemn any aspect of a female character's behaviour which could conceivably be perceived as improper. Nevertheless, writing about the history plays presents far fewer problems for a female critic than writing about a play that deals more explicitly with gender relations (such as *Measure for Measure*, for example). Writing on the history plays is not only original, it also allows Montagu to sidestep censure as a female critic.

I do not wish to suggest that Montagu's interest in morality is solely a pose to defend her reputation. Indeed, that her belief that a play should have an improving effect on the audience was fervently held can be seen from her outrage at the lack of moral purpose in Corneille's *Cinna*: 'What is there in all this that can move either pity or terror? In what is it moral, in what is it interesting, where is it pathetic?' (p. 92). Furthermore, Montagu's praise of Shakespeare is not unconditional: 'Nature and sentiment will pronounce our Shakespeare a mighty genius; judgement and taste will confess that as a writer he is far from being faultless' (p. 8). But I believe that bearing in mind that Montagu herself was aware of the potential hostility that female critics faced, focusing on morality is beneficial to her in helping to deflect potential criticism. Neither, however, is Montagu simply a dry and didactic moralist. Her interest and delight in drama is evident throughout the *Essay* and she is often profoundly moved by Shakespeare's characters: for example, she refers not once but three times in the *Essay* to the moment where Macbeth is unable to say 'Amen'. For Montagu, Shakespeare's portrayal of character was central to his ability as a dramatist: 'In delineating characters he must be allowed far to surpass all dramatic writers, and even Homer himself' (pp. 7–8). She admired Shakespeare's ability to transform himself into the people he represents: she comments that

> Shakespear seems to have had the art of the Dervise in the Arabian tales, who could throw his soul into the body of another man, and be at once possessed of his sentiments, adopt his passions, and rise to all the functions and feelings of his situation. (p. 13)[18]

Montagu is impressed by Shakespeare's characterization in the history plays: 'the character of Henry IV is perfectly agreeable to that given him by historians' and Shakespeare's king unites 'the affectionate Father, the offended King, the provident Politician, and the conscious Usurper' (pp. 35–6). She clearly appreciates the ambiguous response Shakespeare's characters provoke and sees this as crucial to his ability to move the audience: although he is a rebel, Percy 'is still an object of admiration and wonder to every beholder' because he is portrayed so convincingly: 'his misdemeanours rise so naturally out of his temper, and that temper is so noble, that we are almost as much interested for him as for a more virtuous character' (p. 34). Similarly, although she acknowledges that the character of Falstaff is problematic, 'we must certainly admire it, and own it to be perfectly original' (p. 40). Although there may be a critical tendency to see Montagu's response to the plays as simplistically moralistic, in her appreciation of Shakespeare's characters, who often unite both good and bad in the same person, she demonstrates her sensitivity to the effects of the drama and her profound critical appreciation. Her response to character also shows Montagu's view of drama's morality to be more complex than it first appears: she recognizes that it is not sufficient to simply portray virtuous people performing virtuous actions, only by seeing the conflict between good and evil that naturally occurs in everyone can the audience truly be moved.

Critics seem to have found Montagu's insistence on Shakespeare's morality dull and uninspiring without considering how problematic the issue

[18] Montagu's praise of Shakespeare's ability to transform himself, Proteus-like, into the characters he creates and thus make them believable was not new. See Margaret Cavendish's comments in *CCXI. Sociable Letters, Written by the Thrice Noble, Illustrious, and Excellent Princess, the Lady Marchioness of Newcastle* (London, 1664), pp. 244–8.

of propriety was for women (particularly women writers) in the eighteenth century. However, the *Essay*'s exploration of the moral instruction offered by Shakespeare's works is more complex than has previously been realized. Montagu's emphasis on the importance of characterisation clearly shows that her work occupies a crucial place in a wider critical tradition. From the middle of the eighteenth century, the dramatist's ability to evoke an emotional response came to be valued more than observance of classical rules or unities and particular emphasis was given to the role of characters in exciting our sympathies. The *Essay* puts Montagu at the forefront of this movement away from reliance on neoclassical rules and toward an increasing acceptance and appreciation of subjectivity in criticism. This is important since the increased interest in individual response to literature was subsequently to play a significant part in the evolution of the sentimental novel and in the development of Romantic aesthetics. Her gender doubtless meant that she faced more obstacles than many of her male peers but Montagu's engagement with trends in eighteenth-century literary criticism demonstrates that women critics were beginning to break down the barriers which had previously prevented their involvement and acceptance in the literary sphere; in fact, Montagu made a significant contribution to the field of Shakespeare studies and played a crucial role in the development of eighteenth-century criticism. Montagu's evaluation of Shakespeare is anything but derivative and her analysis of the genre of the history play is a strikingly original contribution to Shakespearian criticism. Hugh Blair wrote that

> of all the commentators on Shakespear who have hitherto appeared, you are by far the Best; . . . you have done him more real justice, & have entered more into his spirit & character than any of the Writers who have attempted to delineate him.[19]

Montagu recognized the importance of Shakespeare's power to arouse our sympathies as central to his genius and, as Blair notes, this acknowledgement of the power of sympathy permeates Montagu's evaluation of Shakespeare and is the key to the success of her work on 'our great English classic'.

---

[19] Letter to Montagu, 3 June 1769, quoted in Eger, *Bluestocking Feminism*, p. lxxii.

# REWRITING LEAR'S UNTENDER DAUGHTER: FANNY PRICE AS A REGENCY CORDELIA IN JANE AUSTEN'S *MANSFIELD PARK*

CLARA CALVO

## I

Narrative revisions of *King Lear* in the twentieth century, unlike rewritings of other Shakespearian plays, are not numerous, but there are at least two novels that can claim a link with Shakespeare's tragedy of filial ingratitude: Jane Smiley's *A Thousand Acres* (1991) and Angela Carter's *Wise Children* (1991).[1] Smiley's novel is a feminist adaptation in modern dress; Carter's postmodern farce has its *King Lear* allegiances diluted in a richer broth of Shakespearian appropriation. Smiley adopts plot, characters and thematic content from *King Lear*, but alters the narrative's point of view. Carter, rejecting a direct appropriation of plot and narrative thread, retains some Shakespearian characters and the themes of ingratitude and father–daughter relations.

Over a century before Smiley or Carter found inspiration in *King Lear*, a Romantic English novelist saw the advantages of rewriting the Shakespearian adaptation of a popular tale about a father and his three daughters. As a rewriting of *King Lear*, Jane Austen's *Mansfield Park* (1814) has more in common with Carter's than with Smiley's, since the author mostly rejects the storyline but retains themes and characters.[2] Carter, however, rewrites the Shakespearian tragedy to produce a farce and Austen turns *King Lear* into a tragicomedy. In spite of their differences, they all decentre the Lear figure and rewrite Cordelia, divesting her of any trace of her

[1] Jane Smiley, *A Thousand Acres* (New York, 1991); Angela Carter, *Wise Children* (London, 1991). For the literary life of *King Lear* after Shakespeare see *Shakespeare Survey* 55 (Cambridge, 2002).

[2] The intertextual debt *Mansfield Park* bears to *King Lear* has been noticed by H. R. Harris, 'Jane Austen's Venture into Tragedy,' *Contemporary Review* 272 (1998), 314–18 and Susan Allen Ford '"Intimate by Instinct": *Mansfield Park* and the Comedy of *King Lear*,' *Persuasions* 24 (2002), 177–97. Harris pinpoints parallelisms between Shakespeare's tragedy and Austen's novel and sees *Mansfield Park* as Austen's reading of *King Lear* through Dr Johnson's eyes. Ford shows how the relationship between Sir Thomas and Fanny echoes that of Lear and Cordelia, particularly as constructed by Nahum Tate's adaptation, contemporary productions and eighteenth-century engravings and paintings. Ford's work has greatly stimulated my own thinking and I am much indebted to her for a copy of her essay before it appeared in print. John Wiltshire, *Recreating Jane Austen* (Cambridge, 2001), pp. 58–76, is rather dismissive, suggesting that 'plots being finite, and human relations being fairly constant' (p. 150), one can spot connections between Shakespeare's plays and Austen's novels everywhere. If this is so, it is difficult to explain why the parallelisms between *Mansfield Park* and *King Lear* have not been much discussed before. In relegating to an endnote the evidence which suggests that *Mansfield Park* is a rewriting of Shakespeare's tragedy, Wiltshire seems to be aware that it counters his argument. Richard Proudfoot, in 'Some Lears', *Shakespeare Survey* 55, pp. 139–52, has examined the influence of a scene from *King Lear* (2.4) on a dialogue between Mr and Mrs John Dashwood in *Sense and Sensibility* (Vol. 1, Chapter 2), thus proving Austen's intimate knowledge of this play. Isobel Armstrong, in *Jane Austen: Mansfield Park* (Harmondsworth, 1988), pp. 62–65, sees, in the mock wedding between Rosalind and Orlando in the Forest of Arden,

nineteenth-century attributes, her meek, angelic and suffering nature and her heroic and virtuous disposition.[3]

Angela Carter's revision of *King Lear* is the most radical rewriting of the three and reshapes Shakespeare's tragedy almost beyond recognition, although it never stops being concerned with one of its central topics, father–daughter relations. Like Smiley, Carter removes her Lear figure, famous Shakespearian actor Sir Ranulph Hazard, from the narrative's centre, which is taken over by his illegitimate daughters Dora and Nora, and, like Austen, chooses to focalize her narrative through Cordelia's eyes. Carter's resistance of Shakespearian authority often takes the shape of complicating, doubling, adding chaos and confusion to the Shakespearian raw material and instead of one tragic Cordelia, Carter produces twin Cordelias who seem to stem from the mature comedies or the late plays rather than from *King Lear*. Dora and Nora Chance, who do not bear their father's surname, have experienced since their birth the fate Cordelia meets after the division of the kingdoms when her father addresses her as 'thou my sometime daughter'. Dora and Nora are, like Cordelia, rejected by their father, who does not acknowledge them, either in public or private, as his natural daughters. Dora's absence of anger or spite for this and her unflagging desire to obtain her father's love and recognition turn her into a twentieth-century Cockney Cordelia.

In *A Thousand Acres*, Smiley's Cordelia (Caroline Cook) is far from being the model daughter she thinks she is. A selfish lawyer who has abandoned the family's rural environment for the big city (Des Moines), she cannot understand the needs or feelings of her elder sisters, trapped in the patriarchal structures of Midwest farming. Her siding with her father in his madness is presented as blind ignorance of reality rather than love. Smiley's narrator makes it impossible to sympathize with this modern Cordelia who gets out of the division of the farm because her interests are already elsewhere. Smiley's Goneril (Ginny Cook), instead, is rewritten as a caring, sensitive, balanced woman whose thoughts the reader is invited to share. If Ginny is forced to parapet herself behind solitude, it is due to the aggressive, oppressive, restrictive environment of her Midwest farming family. Smiley's reshaping of *King Lear* turns a hateful character into an appealing woman the reader cannot help liking. If Smiley's reshaping of *King Lear* challenges the received view of Goneril as monster of ingratitude, Austen's *Mansfield Park* rests on a subtle rewriting of Cordelia who is constantly pushed to take a centre-stage role. The playful author of the *Juvenilia*, who delights in literary parody, could easily reinvent Lear's youngest daughter. Austen's Cordelia (Fanny Price) is no longer presented as the paragon of virtues the reader is invited to admire. Shakespeare's Cordelia is replaced with a heroine few readers can warm to.

## II

Fanny Price has often been found priggish, passive, naive and hard to like.[4] After the publication of *Mansfield Park*, Austen amused herself recording reactions to her novel from family and friends and Chapman included these 'Opinions of *Mansfield Park*' in his edition of Austen's *Minor Works*.[5] Although we are assured that in Austen's immediate social circle Fanny was liked and thought to be very natural, not all of Austen's relatives were fond

---

a source of inspiration for the scene in which Maria Bertram and Rushworth stand together in front of the altar during the visit to Sotherton chapel. Marianne Novy, in *Engaging with Shakespeare: Responses of George Eliot and Other Women Novelists* (Iowa City, 1998), pp. 22–32, and Claire Tomalin, in *Jane Austen: A Life* (London, 1997), pp. 229, 329–30, also discuss, albeit briefly, Shakespearian appropriation in Austen's novels.

[3] Janet Bottoms, in '"Look on Her, Look": The Apotheosis of Cordelia,' *Shakespeare Survey* 55, pp. 106–13, has shown how nineteenth century narratives about Cordelia rewrote her 'story', turning her into a model for dutiful daughters and a heroine for young girls to emulate.

[4] This is a widespread critical view, but there have been attempts at vindicating Fanny's character. See, for instance, Susan Moore, 'The Heroine of *Mansfield Park*', *English Studies* 63 (1982), 139–144.

[5] Jane Austen, *Minor Works*, ed. R. W. Chapman (London, 1954), pp. 431–5. Subsequent page references are given in parenthesis in the text.

of her creation. Austen's mother 'Thought Fanny insipid' (*MW*, p. 432), her nephew George Knight 'disliked her' (*MW*, p. 431) and her niece Anna Lefroy 'could not bear Fanny' (*MW*, p. 431). Mr J. Plumptre made two objections, one of them being 'the want of some character more striking & interesting to the generality of Readers, than Fanny was likely to be' (*MW*, p. 434).

Lionel Trilling's harsh verdict on Fanny ('Nobody, I believe, has ever found it possible to like the heroine of *Mansfield Park*') probably encodes what most readers feel about her today – she is far too 'overtly virtuous' for the contemporary reader to like her.[6] Claudia Johnson has noted that both Janeites and non-Janeites have complained of 'the incapacity of it [*Mansfield Park*] and its little heroine to delight us'.[7] Many will also agree with Tony Tanner, who thinks that 'Nobody falls in love with Fanny Price', and with Kingsley Amis, who finds Fanny 'a monster of complacency and pride' who dominates the novel 'under a cloak of cringing self-abasement'.[8] Feminist critics in particular have been put off by her silences, her passivity and her aversion to action. For Marylea Meyersohn, Fanny is 'a center of nonenergy'.[9] Nina Auerbach finds *Mansfield Park* 'unlikeable' and its heroine 'particularly unaccommodating' and thinks that the 'silent, stubborn Fanny Price appeals less than any of Austen's heroines' and that readers 'shy away from her as a character'.[10] As a heroine, Margaret Kirkham points out, Fanny 'has proved . . . troublesome to critics'.[11]

For Auerbach, Fanny Price is also 'a relentlessly uncomfortable figure'.[12] Auerbach attributes this anxiety – what we 'ought' to feel about Fanny – to her similarity to Romantic heroes, including Byron's Child Harold, Coleridge's Ancient Mariner and Shelley's Frankenstein, and equates her passivity to Hamlet's refusal to act. The vision of Hamlet as 'Shakespeare's supreme anti-actor and counteractor' is a creation of Romantic drama criticism.[13] Hazlitt and Coleridge spotted the problematic nature of some Shakespearian characters, characters such as Malvolio and Hamlet who are not keen to act and are nevertheless forced to play a part they do not feel comfortable in. If Coleridge conceived Hamlet as 'a paragon of nonactivity' and 'a character too pure to act,' Austen recreated in Fanny Price the 'Romantic fascination with Hamlet as a modern type'.[14]

Imaginative as Auerbach's view of Fanny as a female Hamlet is, Cordelia is no doubt the Shakespearian character who lies behind the heroine of *Mansfield Park*. Even Wiltshire, who thinks that 'if Austen does indeed have some affinity with Shakespeare it is in vain to establish this through allusions and other signs of conscious remembering',[15] admits that 'Fanny is surely a shadowy reworking of Cordelia, the virginal right-thinking heroine who opposes the will, and braves the fury, of the patriarch, and is banished from his domain to Portsmouth, just as Cordelia is banished to France'.[16] If Fanny is not really Sir Thomas Bertram's daughter, she nevertheless becomes his daughter-in-law when she marries Edmund. At the end, Sir Thomas's affection for Fanny closely resembles Lear's feelings for Cordelia in Act 4:

---

[6] Lionel Trilling, '*Mansfield Park*', *The Opposing Self* (New York, 1955). Reprinted in *Jane Austen: A Collection of Critical Essays*, ed. Ian Watt (Englewood Cliffs, N J, 1963), pp. 124–40. Both quotations taken from p. 128.

[7] Claudia L. Johnson, *Jane Austen: Women, Politics and the Novel* (Chicago, 1988), p. 94.

[8] Tony Tanner, *Jane Austen* (London, 1986), p. 143; Kingsley Amis, 'What Became of Jane Austen?', *The Spectator*, no. 6745 (October 4, 1957), 339–40. Reprinted in Watt, *Jane Austen: A Collection of Critical Essays*, pp. 141–4 (p. 144).

[9] Marylea Meyersohn, 'What Fanny Knew: A Quiet Auditor of the Whole', in *Jane Austen: New Perspectives*, (*Women and Literature* NS 3) ed. Janet Todd (New York, 1983), pp. 224–30, p. 224.

[10] Nina Auerbach, 'Jane Austen's Dangerous Charm: Feeling as One Ought about Fanny Price,' in Todd, *Jane Austen: New Perspectives*, pp. 208–23, (pp. 208–9).

[11] Margaret Kirkham, 'Feminist Irony and the Priceless heroine of *Mansfield Park*,' in Todd, *Jane Austen: New Perspectives*, pp. 231–47.

[12] Auerbach, 'Jane Austen's Dangerous Charm', p. 218.

[13] Auerbach, 'Jane Austen's Dangerous Charm', p. 214.

[14] Auerbach, 'Jane Austen's Dangerous Charm', p. 214.

[15] Wiltshire, *Recreating Jane Austen*, p. 62.

[16] Wiltshire, *Recreating Jane Austen*, pp. 150–1.

> Fanny was indeed the daughter that he wanted. His charitable kindness had been rearing a prime comfort for himself. His liberality had a rich repayment, and the general goodness of his intentions by her, deserved it. He might have made her childhood happier; but it had been an error of judgement only which had given him the appearance of harshness, and deprived him of her early love; and now, on really knowing each other, their mutual attachment became very strong.[17]

Shakespeare's Cordelia, in fact, permeates Fanny's character at deeper levels than plot and incident. Fanny's most irritating traits of character, her passivity and silences, can be better understood if they are read as a rewriting of Cordelia's famous line: 'What shall Cordelia do? Love and be silent' (Q 1.57); 'What shall Cordelia speak? Love and be silent' (F 1.1. 62). Love Edmund and be silent is in fact what Fanny does in *Mansfield Park*. Meyersohn describes Fanny in terms that would suit a description of Lear's youngest daughter: 'a heroine in flight from speech', 'a Cinderella', 'patient, voiceless, controlling emotion before others, a quiet centre of duty';[18] 'strangled by speech,' 'unable to speak', 'she will not talk', 'ventures speech to no avail', 'colors and says nothing', 'forced into speech as a last resort against evil'.[19] Fanny overcomes her laconic disposition only when she 'says "no" to males who wish to force her into morally indefensible acts' and so does Cordelia.[20] For Cordelia, this occurs at the opening of the play, during the division of the kingdom scene, and her effort in overcoming her aversion to speak earns her a loss of dowry and her banishment from the realm. For Fanny, this takes place in the first chapter of volume III, when she both rejects Crawford's marriage offer and resists Sir Thomas's attempt to make her change her mind. As happens to Cordelia, Fanny's speaking exertion – 'She could say no more; her breath was almost gone' (*MP*, p. 315) – is to no avail: her words fail to extricate her from what is regarded as sheer ingratitude and she is banished from the comforts and elegance of Mansfield Park.

Although Fanny herself does not see her trip to Portsmouth in the company of her beloved brother William as punishment for not providing the dutiful and expected answer, Sir Thomas clearly regards her trip as penalty rather than treat, or as a correctional measure at least. He wants her to be 'heartily sick of home before her visit ended' and he hopes that 'a little abstinence from the elegancies and luxuries of Mansfield Park, would bring her mind into a sober state, and incline her to a juster estimate of the value of that home of greater permanence, and equal comfort, of which she had the offer' (*MP*, p. 369). The point is further conveyed to the reader by a long paragraph in which the narrator's voice continues its focalization through indirect thought. The metaphorical discourse of illness present in Kent's ironic speech when he attempts to make Lear revoke Cordelia's banishment ('Kill thy physician, and thy fee bestow / Upon the foul disease', 1.1.162–3) is parallelled in Sir Thomas's train of thought:

> It was a medicinal project upon his niece's understanding, which he must consider as at present diseased. A residence of eight or nine years in the abode of wealth and plenty had a little disordered her powers of comparing and judging. Her Father's house would, in all probability, teach her the value of a good income; and he trusted that she would be the wiser and happier woman all her life, for the experiment he had devised. (*MP*, p. 369)

Fanny Price is sent to Portsmouth, as Cordelia is sent into banishment, for not complying with the patriarchal order, for failing to provide the appropriate answer which, as daughter, is expected of her. The exchange between Lear and Cordelia in the division of the kingdom scene (1.1) reverberates in the dialogue between Fanny and Sir Thomas after Crawford's proposal (*MP*, Vol. III, Ch. 1). Like Cordelia, Fanny is repeatedly invited by Sir Thomas to mend her speech a little, but she refuses to:

---

[17] Jane Austen, *Mansfield Park*, ed. R. W. Chapman, 3rd edn, (London, 1934), p. 472. Subsequent page references are given in parenthesis in the text.

[18] Meyersohn, 'What Fanny Knew', p. 226.

[19] Meyersohn, 'What Fanny Knew', p. 227.

[20] Meyersohn, 'What Fanny Knew', p. 227.

> 'Am I to understand,' said Sir Thomas, after a few moments silence, 'that you mean to *refuse* Mr. Crawford?'
>
> 'Yes, Sir.'
>
> 'Refuse him?'
>
> 'Yes, Sir.'
>
> 'Refuse Mr. Crawford! Upon what plea? For what reason?'
>
> 'I – I cannot like him, Sir, well enough to marry him.'
>
> (*MP*, p. 315)

If Cordelia is accused of being 'So young and so untender' (F 1.1.106), Fanny is accused of 'ingratitude': 'But, Fanny, if your heart can acquit you of *ingratitude* –' (*MP*, p. 319). Cordelia has her sisters set up as a model for her ('What can you say to draw a third more opulent / than your sisters? Speak' F 1.1.85–6), and Fanny is set against her cousins, who are presented to her as examples of daughterly obedience and duty: 'And I should have been very much surprised had either of my daughters, on receiving a proposal of marriage at any time, . . . and without paying my opinion or my regard the compliment of any consultation, put a decided negative on it . . . I should have thought it a gross violation of duty and respect' (*MP*, p. 319). If Cordelia's silence is read as untenderness, Fanny's rejection of a convenient suitor who can offer her a desirable establishment is also read as lack of gratitude toward a loving uncle who has provided for her, educated her and raised her above her station as daughter of an impoverished Lieutenant of Marines.

Chastity is another trait Fanny shares with Cordelia – chastity is, in both *Mansfield Park* and *King Lear*, symbolically linked to silence. Unlike Cordelia, who is silent and single at the onset of the play, Goneril and Regan are articulated, married and sexually charged, and so are Maria and Julia Bertram, both of whom are 'out', as opposed to Fanny, who Mary Crawford concludes must not be 'out' because 'she says so little' (*MP*, p. 48). Fanny is a spoil-sport who can ruin family ceremonies and entertainments, such as the performance of private theatricals. Fanny does not welcome the play and is reluctant to take a part in it, claiming she cannot act. Cordelia also refuses to act and fails to deliver a suitable speech at the division of the kingdom ceremony: 'Unhappy that I am, I cannot heave / My heart into my mouth' (F 1.1.91–2). If Fanny can be said to be 'a killjoy, a blighter of ceremonies and divider of families',[21] the same can be said of Cordelia.

Fanny's silences are counterbalanced by her ability to see what others do not see, particularly Edmund and Sir Thomas. Seeing – like silence, Nature, gratitude and self-knowledge – is one of the thematic strands which *Mansfield Park* shares with *King Lear*.[22] When alluding to Henry Crawford's flirting with both Maria and Julia, Fanny says 'I was quiet, but I was not blind. I could not but see that Mr Crawford allowed himself ingallantries which did mean nothing' (*MP*, p. 363). In taking her leave of her sisters, Cordelia shows she does not share his father's 'blindness' in judging their characters:

> Ye jewels of our father, with washed eyes
> Cordelia leaves you. I know you what you are
> And like a sister am most loath to call
> Your faults as they are named (F 1.1. 258–61).

The symbolic discourse on blindness that permeates *King Lear* – real blindness for Gloucester, symbolic for Lear – is echoed in *Mansfield Park* through numerous references to 'seeing' and 'not seeing'. Sir Thomas shares Lear's symbolic blindness when he deludes himself in his judgement of Henry Crawford's character – unlike Fanny, he does not see through the acting and promotes the marriage of his niece with the man that will bring havoc to his household by eloping with his eldest daughter *after* her marriage to Mr Rushworth. Edmund also fails to see, or rather persuades himself he does not see what he sees, the true nature of Mary Crawford.

Fanny's ability to see, like Cordelia's, detaches her not only from Sir Thomas or Edmund but even from Maria Bertram, whose blindness in admitting that the return of his father in November will make her marriage to Rushworth inevitable stems from a decided unwillingness to see:

---

21 Auerbach, 'Jane Austen's Dangerous Charm', p. 211.

22 Ford, 'Intimate by Instinct', p. 178.

It was a gloomy prospect, and all that she could do was to throw a mist over it, and hope when the mist cleared away, she should see something else. It would hardly be *early* in November, there were generally delays, a bad passage or *something*; that favouring *something* which every body who shuts their eyes while they look, or their understandings while they reason, feels the comfort of.

(*MP*, p. 107)

Throwing a mist over what they choose not to see is a common disease in the Mansfield household. Only Fanny seems to have escaped the infection. Sir Thomas, with his severity and lack of an affectionate disposition, is responsible, like Lear, for encouraging the growth of this canker.

Fanny's silences are often noticed by the narrator or by other characters in *Mansfield Park*. Like Cordelia, she is often laconic when a response is expected of her; like Cordelia, she is often found enigmatic:

'I do not quite know what to make of Miss Fanny. I do not understand her. I could not tell what she would be at yesterday. What is her character? – Is she solemn? – Is she queer? – Is she prudish? Why did she draw back and look so grave at me? I could hardly get her to speak.'

(*MP*, p. 230)

Her silence is often a measure of her disapproval of Henry Crawford's behaviour, just as Cordelia's laconic answer in the division of the kingdom is the result of her disapproval of her sisters' protestations of daughterly love and dutiful obedience. Fanny, however, is not just a cloned Cordelia. Ford points out that Austen's 'most radical revision' is to foreground Shakespeare's marginal Cordelia.[23] Austen resists the authority of the Bard further and divests her own Cordelia of the most singular trait of Shakespeare's character: her allegiance to truth, her display of sincerity. Cordelia's punishment descends from her greatest virtue since she is rejected for being sincere: 'So young, my lord, and true' (F 1.1.107). No one could say to Fanny, as Lear says to Cordelia, 'Thy truth then be thy dower' (F 1.1.108). Fanny does not incur in untruths but she can be duplicitous and insincere, at least on one occasion. In her interview with Sir Thomas in the East Room, after rejecting Mr Crawford, she hides from him the ultimate reason why she will not accept his offer of marriage – her love for Sir Thomas's own son. She has no need to lie, since Sir Thomas never puts the question directly, but she is close enough to duplicity: 'She would rather die than own the truth, and she hoped by a little reflection to fortify herself beyond betraying it' (*MP*, p. 317).

Fanny's concealment of her love for Edmund makes her different from other heroines who are also put to a truth test that doubles as a love test. In *The True Chronicle History of King Leir* (published 1605, in existence 1594 or earlier), Leir announces that Cordella has sworn she will only marry a man she loves ('My youngest daughter, fayre *Cordella*, vows / No liking to a Monarch, unlesse love allowes' 1.1.61–2).[24] Leir then devises a love test which is also a truth test; if Cordella really loves him more than her sisters, she will accept the husband he has in mind for her: 'Even as she doth protest she loves me best, / Ile say, Then, daughter, graunt me one request, / To shew thou lovest me as thy sisters do, / Accept a husband, whom myself will woo' (1.1.84–7). Sir Thomas Bertram's pressure on Fanny to accept Crawford can also be read as a love test. Cordelia in *King Lear* and Amelia in Elizabeth Inchbald's *Lovers' Vows* (1798) flaunt their sincerity, the first when asked how much she loves her father, the second when examined by her father about how much she likes the Count for a husband:

BARON . . . I will ask you a few questions on this subject; but be sure to answer me honestly – Speak truth.
AMELIA I never told an untruth in my life.
BARON Nor ever *conceal* the truth from me, I command you.
AMELIA [*Earnestly*] Indeed, my lord, I never will.

(*Lovers' Vows*, 2.2, p. 495)[25]

---

[23] Ford, 'Intimate by Instinct', p. 182. Ford also notes here that Tate's adaptation almost doubled the number of Cordelia's lines: 115 in F, 89 in Q and 210 plus a 26 line epilogue in Tate.

[24] *The True Chronicle Historie of King Leir*, in *Narrative and Dramatic Sources of Shakespeare*, ed. Geoffrey Bullough, Vol. 7 (London, 1961), pp. 337–402.

[25] *Lovers' Vows*, Elizabeth Inchbald's adaptation of a German play by August von Kotzebue (1791), is the play chosen for the amateur theatricals in Mansfield Park. Reprinted in Austen, *Mansfield Park*, ed. R. W. Chapman, pp. 481–536.

'Pictures of perfection as you know make me sick & wicked', Jane Austen once declared.[26] Inchbald's Amelia, with her protestations of sincerity in this scene, must have made her very sick indeed and the playful pleasure of inversion may be behind Fanny's economy with the truth in her interview with Sir Thomas. Fanny's silence in this occasion is incriminating – since she conceals the truth from Sir Bertram – and clashes with nineteenth-century visions of Cordelia as a saint-like sample of female virtues who 'repays his [Lear's] cruelty with loyalty'.[27] Fanny's hidden motivation in her conversation with Edmund about Mary Crawford (*MP*, Vol. I, Ch. 7) could be equally analysed in terms of her duplicitous nature, since behind the appearance of an objective, detached, unimpassioned analysis of Mary's behaviour, the attentive reader – or the reader who rereads – may discover Fanny's ulterior motives – to present Mary's character in an unbecoming light to Edmund's eyes. It is a scene which has a certain Shakespearian ring – it is a sort of trial of Mary Crawford in her absence, recalling the mock trial of Goneril and Regan in *King Lear*.

## II

Filial ingratitude was a topically relevant theme while Austen was writing *Mansfield Park* (1811–13), since George III's second fit of illness in 1810 brought back 'the spectre of the libertine Prince destroying his father's political house'.[28] The Prince Regent and Tom Bertram, as Roger Sales has shown, have much in common: a fondness for gambling and the theatre and an eagerness for stepping into their father's shoes. Sales has also shown how the identification of the estate and the state was common practice in the political literature of the Regency. Readers could encounter this metonymy in *The Morning Post* and it was also deployed in Edmund Burke's *Reflections on the Revolution in France* and in the writings of Mary Wollstonecraft; both conservatives and radicals made connections between the estate or the family and the state.[29] Seeing in *Mansfield Park* a microcosm that depicts how the heir (Tom/The Prince Regent) threatens to bring disaster to the estate/state with the help of dandies (Henry Crawford/Brummel, the Whigs) means reading the novel along the lines of daily life, political commentary and contemporary political works.

On 10 January 1809, Jane Austen wrote to her sister Cassandra: 'The Regency seems to have been heard of only here, my most political Correspondents make no mention of it. Unlucky, that I should have wasted so much reflection on the subject!'[30] After reminding the reader that, in this letter to Cassandra, Austen reveals that she was more than accidentally interested in politics and suggesting that *Mansfield Park* can be regarded as a Condition-of-England novel that 'debates topical issues such as the conduct of the war and the Regency Crisis',[31] Sales produces a critical pirouette and seems to be wanting to have his scholarly cake and eat it critically. On the one hand, *Mansfield Park* gives a representation of the Regency crisis but the novel is not 'a self-consciously camouflaged script'.[32] On the other, the widespread identification of estate and state in the period suggests that *Mansfield Park* could be read 'as a reasonably open, if not a transparent, one'.[33] However, Sales argues, since Leigh Hunt and Cobbett were imprisoned for criticizing the Regent, it has to be assumed that 'There were certainly pressures on Austen not to produce a representation of a regency crisis.'[34] The only way out of this scholarly/critical loop is to conclude that 'an author's intentions do not always provide a reliable guide to what is eventually produced'.[35] Austen, in other words, was clever in spite of herself. This

---

26 Letter to Fanny Knight, 23–5 March 1817. *Jane Austen's Letters*, ed. Deirdre Le Faye, 3rd edn (Oxford, 1997), p. 335.

27 Bottoms, '"Look on Her"', p. 111.

28 Roger Sales, *Jane Austen and the Representations of Regency England* (London, 1994), p. 57.

29 Sales, *Representations*, pp. 88–9.

30 Letter to Cassandra, 10–11 January 1809, *Letters*, p. 163. See Sales's comments on this letter in *Representations*, p. 56.

31 Sales, *Representations*, p. 88. Brian Southam also reads *Mansfield Park* as a Condition-of-England novel in *Jane Austen and the Navy* (London, 2000), p. 181.

32 Sales, *Representations*, p. 93.

33 Sales, *Representations*, p. 93.

34 Sales, *Representations*, p. 93.

35 Sales, *Representations*, p. 93.

conclusion divests Austen of authority (both in the sense of control over the creative process and over its meanings) suggesting that she produced a representation of the Regency crisis without being aware of what she was doing.

Regarding *Mansfield Park* as a rewriting of *King Lear* that explores the condition of the estate as a metonymy for the condition of England, necessarily turns it into one of the few Romantic works of either criticism or fiction to make a connection between Lear's tragedy and contemporary politics. Political interpretations of *King Lear* sprout, as Foakes has suggested, after 1960, and point to an evident change in the play's reception.[36] Before 1960, 'the reception of King Lear has to do for the most part with an evasion of political issues' and this critical tide did not begin to turn until 'a period of political change . . . affected the mood of people in Britain and the United States'.[37] It was not until the 1960s that *King Lear* began to be read as a play about the dangers of absolute power.

In the Restoration, though, *King Lear* was topically appropriated by Nahum Tate in his 1681 adaptation, *The History of King Lear*.[38] Nancy Klein Maguire has argued convincingly that 'Tate's *Lear* was part of the Tory counter-propaganda campaign', as it 'could easily and safely comment on the 1678–83 Exclusion Crisis'.[39] Maguire attributes to the topicality of Tate's adaptation its 'immediate success'.[40] Michael Dobson has also shown that Tate's Shakespearian adaptations (*Richard II*, *King Lear* and *Coriolanus*) were 'conditioned by royalist politics'.[41] Tate's Lear was 'produced just when Whig demands for the legitimization of Monmouth were reaching their climax', and it can be regarded as 'a timely alteration of a Shakespeare play about British history' – one of its major alterations being to show on stage how 'a bastard's rebellion is crushed and the legitimate monarch triumphantly restored'.[42] Dobson also argues convincingly that the pre-eminence given to the love interest and the final marriage between Cordelia and Edgar in both the adaptation and its preface is a smoke screen to disguise its topicality. For Dobson, the reasons behind Tate's rewriting of *King Lear* 'have far more to do with contemporary politics than with contemporary literary criticism' as he is more bent on supporting Charles II and the anti-Whig faction than in endorsing neoclassical decorum – even if he 'resorts to "apolitical" domestic pathos at crucial moments'.[43]

Like Tate, Austen is writing her appropriation of *King Lear* at a time of political and dynastic crisis, when Whigs and Tories are using a monarch's right to rule for the self-fashioning of their own identities as emergent political parties and for securing power and influence in court and Parliament. Tate's adaptation of *King Lear* was the only version of the play known to theatregoers in Austen's lifetime and it is Tate's *Lear* that Elizabeth Inchbald included in her *British Theatre*.[44] In her preface to the play, Inchbald equates James II's fate with Lear's, both abandoned by their daughters, the second pelted by a storm and the first by his 'merciless subjects'.[45] Susan Ford has meticulously dissected the traces of Tate's *Lear* in *Mansfield Park* and she exposes how Austen both benefits from her predecessor and distances herself from it.[46] Austen's appropriation of *King Lear* is more deeply topical than Tate's and more ambivalent too. Austen's rewriting of *King Lear* turns the Shakespearian tragedy into a novel

---

36 R. A. Foakes, *Hamlet versus Lear: Cultural Politics and Shakespeare's Art* (Cambridge, 1993), pp. 3–6.

37 Foakes, *Hamlet versus Lear*, p. 45; p. 4.

38 Nahum Tate, *The History of King Lear* (1681), reprinted in *Adaptations of Shakespeare: A Critical Anthology of Plays from the Seventeenth Century to the Present*, eds. Daniel Fischlin and Mark Fortier (London, 2000), pp. 68–96.

39 Nancy Klein Maguire, 'Nahum Tate's *King Lear*: "the king's blest restoration"', in *The Appropriation of Shakespeare: Post-Renaissance Reconstructions of the Works and the Myth*, ed. Jean I. Marsden (New York, 1991), pp. 29–42, p. 30. On the 'ideological demands' that Tate's Lear 'transitionally satisfied', see Peter Womack, 'Secularizing *King Lear*: Shakespeare, Tate and the Sacred,' *Shakespeare Survey 55*, pp. 96–105.

40 Maguire, 'Nahum Tate's *King Lear*', p. 39.

41 Michael Dobson, *The Making of the National Poet: Shakespeare Adaptation and Authorship, 1660–1769* (Oxford, 1992), p. 80.

42 Dobson, *The Making of the National Poet*, p. 81.

43 Dobson, *The Making of the National Poet*, pp. 83–4.

44 *The British Theatre* (London, 1806–9).

45 Inchbald's preface is reproduced in Jonathan Bate, *The Romantics on Shakespeare* (London, 1992), p. 381.

46 Ford, 'Intimate by Instinct', *passim*.

that foregrounds the threats the new generation poses to the estate and the state. In Tate's adaptation, the topicality and the political message are disguised and pushed to the margins by the apolitical domestic plot line. Austen's rewriting makes a political play of *King Lear* by politicizing the domestic and turning the Cordelia–Edgar love interest into an element of the political since Fanny and Edmund, the most deserving characters, do not inherit their father's estate. In *Mansfield Park*, the rebel son is not crushed – although he is reformed and abandons his former friends, paralleling the Prince Regent's betrayal of the Whigs and reward of their support with ingratitude during the Regency.

Nahum Tate's political reading of the play suggests that Austen had models to see how *King Lear* could be politically appropriated. Recent studies have shown that Austen had a considerable knowledge of Restoration and eighteenth-century drama, both as literary text and theatrical performance, and that she used it liberally for her own narrative purposes.[47] Penny Gay and Paula Byrne have both shown how Austen manages dialogue, character and plot in theatrical ways, developing character through dialogue and managing entrances and exits. Gay has noticed how Austen gave Julia Bertram a 'fine dramatic entry, which brings down the curtain on volume I of *Mansfield Park*'[48] and Byrne has shown the theatrical tempo of the iron gate scene at Sotherton, when Fanny seated on a bench watches other characters as they enter, have a dialogue and exit.[49] Austen's representation of a Regency Crisis in *Mansfield Park* could be, to some extent, a conscious one, inspired by her familiarity with dramatic techniques of her time. The stage has always been eager to appropriate the literary text for topical allusion, particularly so in times of political crisis. If Tate's adaptation could be seen as topical in 1681, it could probably be seen as topical at the turn of the nineteenth century, when the Prince Regent, aided by the Whigs' thirst for power and office, was staging a dandy's rebellion against his royal father.

Austen may or may not have constructed her representation of the Regency Crisis in *Mansfield Park* with the intention of conveying a political message – the author's intention is not what is at stake here. Rather, it is her narrative art and the raw material her creative imagination availed itself of. It seems unlikely that a pen fit for literary parody since childhood, surrounded by an exceptional literary-minded family able to spot and relish her ability to mock and make fun of human weaknesses, would ignore the parallelisms between Mansfield Park and Regency England's political house, between Tom's love for comedy, gambling and moving the furniture and the Prince Regent's tastes, between the power crisis generated by George III's illness and Sir Thomas's absence, between the witty, elegant and wordly Crawford's sway over the Bertrams and Brummel's over the Prince. Byrne has suggested that in *Mansfield Park* Austen revives the interest in drama and contemporary theatre that emerged in her juvenile parodies of well-known dramatic types and situations.[50] The 'prejudiced historian' who wrote the *History of England* was sensitive to heirs who are eager to grab the crown before their fathers' death – a description that equally suits Prince Hal, the future George IV and Tom Bertram.[51] Austen's dislike of the Prince Regent is known – when she was invited to dedicate her next novel to him, she did so, but in a somehow reluctant manner. She paid a visit to Carlton House

---

47 See Penny Gay, *Jane Austen and the Theatre* (Cambridge, 2002) and Paula Byrne, *Jane Austen and the Theatre* (London, 2002).

48 Gay, *Austen and the Theatre*, p. 98.

49 Byrne, *Austen and the Theatre*, pp. 181–3. Tomalin, in *Jane Austen*, p. 329, has noticed a parallelism between this scene in which young couples chase each other in a garden and *A Midsummer Night's Dream*.

50 Paula Byrne '"We Must Descend a Little": *Mansfield Park* and the Comic Theatre', *Women's Writing* 5 (1998), 91–102, (p. 93).

51 In 1791, when she was only sixteen, Jane Austen wrote a parody of Oliver Goldsmiths's *History of England* (1771) that she entitled *The History of England from the reign of Henry the 4th to the death of Charles the 1st, by a partial, prejudiced, and ignorant historian*. Of Henry IV, she wrote: 'he did not live for ever, but falling ill, his son the Prince of Wales came and took away the crown; whereupon the king made a long speech, for which I must refer the Reader to Shakespear's Plays' (Jane Austen, *The History of England: A Facsimile*, ed. Deirdre Le Faye (London, 1993), p. 3).

after the publication and dedication of *Emma* and was relieved not to have been asked to meet the Prince himself. His dissipation and drunkenness were not the only traits of character to put her off; her criticism of his improper behaviour toward his wife, Princess Caroline, is recorded in her letters.[52] Austen's resistance to Shakespearian authority in refusing to present a Sir Thomas affected by madness, like Tate's love plot involving Cordelia and Edgar, functions as a smoke screen, protecting *Mansfield Park* from being taken for transparent political satire. Austen never makes it explicit that *Mansfield Park* is a rewriting of *King Lear* and probably had no wish to turn her novel into an explicit political tract – yet it is hard to believe she wrote *Mansfield Park* unaware of the common ground shared by Shakespeare's tragedy, the Regency crisis and her own novel. It is equally hard to believe that being aware she did not consciously strengthen the parallelisms, if only for the relish of members of her family circle. Her creatively imaginative way of letting both topicality and her literary predecessors have a hand in the construction of her novels seems characteristic of her craft of fiction.

Austen's rewriting of *King Lear* in *Mansfield Park* as a Condition-of-England novel may have been inspired then, like so many other features in its narrative fabric, by her familiarity with and enjoyment of contemporary theatre, including Tate's *Lear*. Her reading of *King Lear* as a political play both aligns her with and distances her from the Romantic reception of Shakespeare's tragedy. Unlike *Hamlet*, a play which in the nineteenth century was resonant with political connotations, *King Lear* did not possess a political dimension for the Romantics. Hazlitt, Keats and Shelley were among the first to claim for *King Lear* a distinguished place at the top of the Shakespearian canon and helped to counteract Dr Johnson's endorsement of the happy ending in Tate's version, but 'in the final years of the reign of George III, it was perhaps inevitable that the Romantic critics should avoid political issues and concentrate on the personal relations of Cordelia and Lear'.[53] Lamb saw the play's strength in promoting an identification between critic/reader and Lear ('while we read it, we see not Lear, but we are Lear').[54] Hazlitt, who saw the political implications of *Coriolanus* or *Hamlet*, was mostly interested in *King Lear* as a play describing strong passions and Foakes gives the same source for Keats's attraction to the play.[55] As Foakes concludes: 'The Romantics located the tragedy within the mind of Lear, and tended to reduce the external action to a domestic drama centred on the old King's quarrel with his daughters.'[56]

The appropriation of *King Lear* as point of departure for *Mansfield Park* problematizes Austen's relation to the Romantics. There has been a shift in Austen studies from considering Austen an author who remained in the Augustan literary past and ignored the Romantic revolution to a reading of Jane Austen as a Romantic.[57] *Persuasion*, her last finished novel, has been often pointed at to prove that Austen's pen underwent a change of sensibility favourable to the Romantic imagination, but traces of Austen's interest and communion with the Romantic mind can be detected in *Mansfield Park* too. Fanny's sympathies for Romantic poets and Romantic landscapes are revealed by the transparencies decorating the lower panes of a window in her private space, the East Room, 'where Tintern Abbey held its station between a cave in Italy, and a moonlight lake in Cumberland' (*MP*, p. 152). Austen's interest in the tragedy of Lear and his daughters in her most 'serious' novel places her in line with Lamb, Hazlitt, Keats, Shelley and

---

52 'She [Princess Caroline] would have been respectable if the Prince had behaved only tolerably by her at first.' Letter to Martha Lloyd, 16 February, 1813, *Letters*, p. 208. Sales comments on this letter in *Representations*, pp. 68–9.

53 Foakes, *Hamlet versus Lear*, p. 45.

54 Quoted in Foakes, *Hamlet versus Lear*, p. 45.

55 Foakes, *Hamlet versus Lear*, p. 46.

56 Foakes, *Hamlet versus Lear*, p. 47.

57 See Clara Tuite, *Romantic Austen: Sexual Politics and the Literary Canon* (Cambridge, 2002). See also Anne K. Mellor, *Romanticism and Gender* (London, 1993) and 'British Romanticism, Gender, and Three Women Artists,' in *The Consumption of Culture 1600–1800: Image, Object, Text*, ed. Ann Bermingham and John Brewer (London, 1995).

Coleridge, all of whom were fascinated by *King Lear*. For Hazlitt, this is 'the best of all Shakespear's plays' and Coleridge thought it contained the best of *Macbeth* and *Hamlet* since it 'combines length with rapidity'.[58] Coleridge's interest in the figure of Edmund, whom he compared to Napoleon,[59] explains Austen's interest in the predicament of a Regency gentleman's second son suffering from the ills of primogeniture (Edmund Bertram) and in the figure of the ambivalent villain – exactly what Henry Crawford turns out to be in the end.

Austen has, in fact, developed Shakespeare's Edmund by splitting him into two contrasting characters. Henry Crawford has inherited the villain-like nature of Gloucester's son and his flirtation with both Maria and Julia Bertram parallels Edmund's sexual involvement with Goneril and Regan. Edmund Bertram shares with Shakespeare's Edmund his condition as second brother to an elder brother who will inherit the family estate. Through the character of Edmund, *Mansfield Park* owes to *As You Like It* a little more than a mock wedding. Like Orlando's, Edmund Bertram's future depends on his elder brother, since Tom's debts have reduced Edmund's share of the Bertrams' fortune. Ordination, one of the novel's central themes, is a study of the place of a brother in Regency England. Though Henry Crawford may be the Richard III vice-like figure he is most of the time, as Penny Gay has noticed,[60] he is partly redeemed in the reader's eyes through his sincere love for Fanny Price and his suffering for it when he has Mrs. Rushworth's character to compare with hers. Coleridge's Napoleon and Austen's contrast between Edmund Bertram and Henry Crawford enable a reading of Shakespeare's Edmund as something more complex than a simply satanic figure.

Austen, however, detaches herself from Romantic readings of *King Lear* in three respects: her politicization of the play through the metonymic dimension of the family site as Regency England, her reading of the division of the kingdom as a story about property, inheritance and primogeniture and her blemished, imperfect Cordelia. Foakes has noted that even if Hazlitt and Coleridge had reservations about Cordelia, particularly regarding her behaviour at the division of the kingdoms scene, Romantic critics on the whole 'tended to foster the idealization of Cordelia'.[61] In this respect, Austen is at variance with most Romantic criticism of Shakespeare's plays. She nevertheless retains the redemptive power associated with Cordelia, since Sir Thomas's mistakes in the education of his eldest daughters, although they cause him suffering and force him to go through a process of self-discovery, do not lead to insanity and despair but to the gift of a loving daughter-in-law. Whether the politicization of *Mansfield Park* as a representation of the Regency crisis is regarded as intentional or not on Austen's part, her recreation of Lear as the stern but rational Sir Thomas is carried out against a background of potential threats to the social order. Austen's contribution to Shakespearian criticism is a Romantic reading of *King Lear* which presents the errors of the owner/ruler of the estate as accountable for precipitating social disaster and economic disorder.

If Cordelia explains Fanny Price, *Mansfield Park* helps to explain *King Lear*. Austen's contribution to the criticism of Shakespeare's tragedy lies in having drawn attention to the play as a fresco depicting a state crisis with contemporary resonances and a domestic crisis about property and inheritance, not merely a tragedy about father–daughter relations or about the predicament of a single human being who has to face the consequences of his own errors and hope for redemption or suffer despair. Her critical contribution can also be found in her problematizing the character of Cordelia, who in *Mansfield Park* is no longer Mrs Jameson's 'celestial visitant', the saint-like daughter set up as a model for young ladies,[62] but an occasionally duplicitous

[58] Bate, *The Romantics on Shakespeare*, pp. 394, 385.

[59] See Foakes, *Hamlet versus Lear*, p. 46.

[60] Gay, *Austen and the Theatre*, pp. 99–102.

[61] Foakes, *Hamlet versus Lear*, p. 47.

[62] Anna Jameson, *Characteristics of Women, Moral, Political and Historical* (1833), reissued as *Shakespeare's Heroines* (London, 1897), p. 204. Quoted in Foakes, *Hamlet versus Lear*, p. 47.

young woman who can use her silences in her own self-interest, even if she does so in the name of a sincere attachment to her cousin Edmund and to elude the pressures of patriarchal society. Jane Smiley's Ginny Cook has made it possible to look at Goneril not as a virago but as a woman with motives to act as she does[63] and Jane Austen's Fanny Price redraws the contours of Cordelia who becomes more of a woman and less of an angel.

[63] Smiley's Ginny has had, no doubt, predecessors. Shakespeare's text implicitly makes a case for Goneril and Peter Brook's 1962 RSC production explicitly staged Lear's rage as an act of violence that left behind a battlefield of tables and benches overturned with food and drink spilled on the floor. Brook's performance certainly gave Goneril reasons to curtail her father's train. Gamini Salgado thought Brook may have been inspired by Granville-Barker's Preface to *King Lear* ('What a good case Goneril makes for herself') as his 1962 production was 'notable for the lengths to which it went to justify Goneril and Reagan' (*King Lear: Text and Performance* (Basingstoke, 1984), p. 68).

Research for this article has been made possible by Research Project BFF 2002–02019, financed by the former Spanish Ministry of Science and Technology and the current Ministry of Education and Science.

# THE PREQUEL AS PALINODE: MARY COWDEN CLARKE'S *GIRLHOOD OF SHAKESPEARE'S HEROINES*

SARAH ANNES BROWN

The principal task of the prequel is to return to the imagined origins of a well-known text's events and characters. This curious exercise – an excavation of a text's hypothetical history – might be compared with a Freudian case study: the present can only fully be understood with reference to a reconstituted past. The successful prequel, I would argue, is an essentially subversive form. A sequel can interest and surprise us without making us view the original in a different way, simply by introducing further characters and incidents, or by moving on to the next generation. A successful sequel can be an imitation or pastiche of the original, such as the sequels that have been written to many popular mainstream novels.[1] But in a prequel, where the end of the story is already known, this freedom simply to expand is lacking, and some kind of disjuncture between the original and the new text is probably required. A prequel's readers don't want simply to be told what they know already; rather they want to be offered a new way into the old text. This desire in the reader for a twist or surprise is fully satisfied by Jane Smiley in *A Thousand Acres* (though, strictly speaking, this is an imaginative updating of *King Lear* with prequel elements rather than a pure prequel – much of the action corresponds to that of Shakespeare's play itself).[2] The key to this family's dysfunctional dynamic lies in its incestuous secrets – Larry Cook abused his two elder daughters after his wife's death, though not his youngest, Caroline. Although Smiley does not set out to prove in any crude way that *King Lear* itself is a play about incest, neither does she want us to see her interpretation as wild, anachronistic speculation. In an interview published by *The Atlantic Online* in 1998 she explains:

> I'm not saying that Shakespeare ever thought of Lear as an incest perpetrator. I am saying that some people think there's a kind of coded reference to incest in this group of folkloric stories, and that therefore you could plausibly attribute the older sisters' deep, deep anger to abuse that they had undergone.[3]

Another significant prequel is John Updike's *Gertrude and Claudius* (London, 2000). Updike's novel excavates, not simply the early life of Gertrude, but also the play's textual history. Its three sections all use different names for the principals, mirroring the same variations in *Hamlet* and its two main sources, earlier versions of the story by Saxo Grammaticus and Belleforest. This literary self-consciousness seems typically modern, as does Updike's sympathetic focus on Gertrude as a pawn of dynastic ambitions, whose own needs and interests are routinely ignored. The action of the novel stops just before the familiar events of *Hamlet* itself unfold, inviting us to return to the play with fresh eyes. Chronologically, the end of Updike's novel and the beginning of Shakespeare's play may

---

I would like to acknowledge Professor Neil Rhodes's help in the preparation of this article.

[1] Of course this is not to say that prequels have the monopoly on edginess. Emma Tennant's *Emma in Love* (London, 1998) builds on a (possible) hint at a lesbian attraction between Emma and Harriet Smith to create a far more unequivocal sexual charge between Emma and a French emigrée.

[2] Jane Smiley, *A Thousand Acres* (London, 1992).

[3] *The Atlantic Online*, 28.5.1998.

dovetail neatly, but in most other respects – tone, characterization and genre – the later text is clearly going against the grain of the original.

The qualities identifiable in Smiley and Updike – their literary self-consciousness, their interest in sexual politics, their readiness to view Shakespeare's text through the lens of their own era's preoccupations – seem characteristically modern. Mary Cowden Clarke's intentions in writing prequels to fifteen of Shakespeare's best-known plays, as articulated in her preface to *The Girlhood of Shakespeare's Heroines*, form an apparently telling contrast. She subordinates her stories to Shakespeare, presenting him as the fixed trunk around which she entwines the *Girlhood* as a compliant vine:

> The aim has been to invent such adventures as might be supposed to color the future lives; to place the heroines in such situations as should naturally lead up to, and account for, the known conclusion of their subsequent confirmed character and after-fate; in short, to invest each story with consistent and *appropriate* interest.[4]

But Mary Cowden Clarke's meek words seem disingenuous once we have read the tales themselves. Nina Auerbach rightly acknowledges the imaginative power of Cowden Clarke when she asserts that 'More completely even than Jameson, Clarke frees the heroines from the boundaries of their plays, endowing them with rich lives of their own whose autonomy is impinged on by neither Shakespeare nor the man his play will make them love.'[5] However part of the strength of *The Girlhood* lies in the way it *does* make us think about both Shakespeare and his heroes. Only in the gap between text and intertext does the full subversive force of her championing of women and resentment of male-dominated society emerge; she repeatedly engages in antagonistic struggle with Shakespeare's male characters, even with Shakespeare himself. Although she invokes shared certainties about Shakespeare's characters and plots – 'the known conclusion of their subsequent confirmed character and after-fate' – his plays have stimulated fierce debates, and Cowden Clarke's prequels are partisans rather than neutral witnesses. Two features of her work in particular might be said to typify this combative approach. One is her interest in male sexual delinquency: libertinism, incest and even child abuse are all dangers her heroines must avoid. The other is her use of doubles – frequently faulty male characters of her own invention who seem to throw the good qualities of the original Shakespearian heroes into relief, but who in fact may undermine them.[6]

Cowden Clarke's radical revision of Shakespeare has, I think, been underestimated even by readers who admire her work. Ann Thompson and Sasha Roberts, for example, in their appreciative account of her contribution to Shakespeare criticism, assert that

> Mary did not, however, always take what might be described as a 'progressive' stance on the representation of women in Shakespeare . . . Portia's complete happiness is to be found not in the legal profession but in marriage, and Katherine the Shrew discovers that it is 'not altogether painful' to be 'mastered' by . . . 'strong, manly arms'[7]

---

[4] Mary Cowden Clarke, *The Girlhood of Shakespeare's Heroines* (London, 1850–1), vol. 1, p. iv.

[5] Nina Auerbach, *Woman and the Demon: The Life of a Victorian Myth* (Cambridge, Mass., 1982), p. 212.

[6] Cowden Clarke's boldness may be reflected in some of the changes effected by Sabilla Novello when she prepared a condensed edition of *The Girlhood* in 1879. She omits or greatly weakens several of the most striking passages and episodes discussed below, including Katherine's masochistic pleasure at being constrained, Portia's study of law and her uncle's comments on women's capacity, Lady Capulet's jealous preoccupation with young girls, the intimations of child abuse in 'Olivia: The Lady of Illyria', and the evidence of Orsino's culpable neglect of the custody case in the same tale.

Cowden Clarke's distrust of Shakespeare's heroes is hinted at in the heroines she singles out for praise in 'Shakespeare as the Girl's Friend', an essay she wrote for *The Girl's Own Paper*. Much of this piece is devoted to praising the constancy of his women – Hero, Julia, Mariana, Hermione and Imogen – at the expense of their unsteady lovers. (Mary Cowden Clarke, 'Shakespeare as the Girl's Friend', *Shakespeariana*, 4 (1887), 355–69).

[7] Ann Thompson and Sasha Roberts, 'Mary Cowden Clarke: Marriage, Gender and the Victorian Woman Critic of Shakespeare' in *Victorian Shakespeare Volume Two: Literature and Culture*, eds. Gail Marshall and Adrian Poole (London, 2003), pp. 170–89. I am very grateful to the authors and to Gail Marshall for letting me see an advance copy of this chapter.

But in both these prequels (though they are complex enough to bear different interpretations) the *telos* of a 'happy' marriage, though predetermined by Shakespeare, is problematized in advance, as it were, by Cowden Clarke. 'The Shrew and the Demure' is one of *The Girlhood*'s most compelling narratives. Katherine may enjoy being 'mastered' but this enjoyment, it is implied, is unhealthy, even perverse, and can be traced back to her convent girlhood. Here the wonderfully sinister, smiling Abbess immediately identifies Katherine as a troublemaker: '"Tie that little vixen's hands behind her," said the lady Abbess in a bland voice to one or two of the nuns who stood nearest' (II.122). When she is later tied up once again, this time by a teasing boy, it is, I think, by no means clear that her surprised enjoyment of the experience is presented in a wholly positive light:

> As the strong, manly arms hold her firmly, constrained there to abide his will, she feels her spirit as well as her body give way, and own itself vanquished. One of the most singular features of this new state of feeling, is, that the sense of defeat, for the first time in her life, is not altogether painful. As her woman's frame involuntarily yields to his masculine strength – as her feebler limbs bend beneath his will, and submit to his power, there is an inexplicable acquiescence, an absence of resentment and resistance, altogether unwonted, and surprising to herself. (II.164–5)

There is something cool, almost forensic, about the way Katherine's experience is described, a precision in the build up of clauses which is judicious rather than dramatic or breathless. There is no sense that the narrator is caught up in the heroine's excitement. Cowden Clarke simultaneously follows and interrogates the romantic template of the masterful man to whom the heroine yields with delight.

Neither is the other example of a happy marriage cited by Thompson and Roberts, that of Portia and Bassanio, entirely straightforward. Certainly Cowden Clarke's penchant for playing up the strengths of Shakespeare's female characters while pouncing on any possible flaws in his men is well displayed in 'The Heiress of Belmont'. While watching *The Merchant of Venice* we may admire Portia's skill as a lawyer, but tend to accept her self-assured grasp of the complex issues as little more than a dramatic device. But Mary Cowden Clarke enhances the value of Portia's legal success by presenting it within a more realistic, more novelistic context.[8] We learn that Portia's triumph is the result of a sustained course of study made with her lawyer uncle, Bellario. Despite the tale's Renaissance setting, this episode would be quite at home in a Victorian novel. Bellario warns her that women can never become lawyers:

> In the exercise of their discernment, they will frequently triumph too early in the discovery of an advantage; and it is the part of a clever lawyer not to betray his own strength and his adversary's weakness too soon. To skilfully treasure up each point successively gained, and by a tardy unmasking of your own plan of action, to lead your opponent on to other and more sure committals of himself, is more consonant with the operation of a man's mind, than suited to the eager, impulsive nature of woman. (I.52)

No real argument is proffered either by Portia or the narrator to counter Bellario's judgement on women. He is a sympathetic character, no obvious straw man like Tom Tulliver, and we might think Cowden Clarke agreed with him that Portia should only use her expertise in law to manage her own estate. Yet the wording of Bellario's objection to female lawyers actually obviates the need for Cowden Clarke to deny its validity – any reader who remembers the play can immediately import Portia's conduct of Antonio's defence into her reading of 'The Heiress of Belmont' and realize just how mistaken Bellario is. When defending Antonio she deploys precisely those 'masculine' tactics her uncle claims women lack.[9] So for the full impact of the story to be felt we must read novella and play side by side. In Clarke Portia's training is never put to the test; without the new context provided by Clarke the true significance of

---

8 The Victorian reception of Portia is discussed by Julie Hankey, 'Victorian Portias: Shakespeare's Borderline Heroine', *Shakespeare Quarterly*, 45 (1994), 426–48.

9 Cf Hankey, 'Victorian Portias', pp. 442–3.

Portia's legal role in *The Merchant of Venice* may be overlooked. Although we cannot infer that Clarke actually thought women should enter the legal profession, the fact that cogent objections to such a step are voiced and implicitly disproved draws more attention to Portia's mastery of a difficult branch of study, supposedly beyond female wit, than if Bellario had never checked her ambition. Testimony to Portia's vulnerability to Victorian opprobrium is offered by the author's husband, Charles Cowden Clarke:

> There is a class of my own sex who never fail to manifest an uneasiness, if not a jealousy, when they perceive a woman verging toward the manly prerogative; and with such, the part that Shakespeare has assigned to Portia in the trial scene would induce this prejudice against her.[10]

And we may compare the judgement of Anna Jameson on Portia's character:

> A woman constituted like Portia, and placed in this age and in the actual state of society, would find society armed against her; and instead of being like Portia, a gracious, happy, beloved, and loving creature, would be a victim, immolated in fire to that multitudinous Moloch termed opinion.[11]

We may infer that by drawing attention to Portia's intellectual abilities Mary Cowden Clarke risked alienating at least a portion of her readership.

It is significant that Mary Cowden Clarke elevates her heroine's intelligence at the expense of a male authority figure's judgement. Patriarchy is interrogated elsewhere in the novella, and the role of Portia's father Guido is particularly open to criticism. If her learning becomes more impressive within the context of Victorian realism, the will of her father takes on a far more sinister and oppressive character when divorced from its fairy-tale setting. Even in *The Merchant of Venice* the casket scheme is not above criticism. Portia is inclined to resent the restriction on her choice – 'Is it not hard, Nerissa, that I cannot choose one, nor refuse none?' (1.2.25–6) – and the happy ending may be marred if we remain unconvinced that Bassanio is a worthy suitor.

When we first meet Portia's father, Guido, he is an attractive and generous youth, devoted to his friend Bellario whose sister he later marries. But that sense of women as objects of exchange between men – whether they strengthen or weaken male friendship – which is so apparent in the homosocial world of *The Merchant of Venice*, is uneasily present too in the opening of 'The Heiress of Belmont'. First thinking that Bellario's sister – also called Portia – is his wife Guido rejoices that the couple are safely married; if still single her beauty might have effected a troubling barrier between him and his friend. She is perceived as a spur to treachery as much as an object of love. And when he finally proposes to her, though she is present, it is to her brother that he appeals: 'We must not part! We will never leave Belmont! Give her to me, Bellario! Give me your sister for my wife!' (1.30).

As he grows older Guido's judgement becomes more and more faulty. One episode in particular places his casket scheme in an unfavourable light and puts the reader on guard against Bassanio. Although the suitor Guido approves for Portia, the libertine Marquis of Montferrat, is ostensibly contrasted with Bassanio, the two are nonetheless companions, and we learn that Montferrat has succeeded in encouraging Bassanio to squander his possessions. The narrator condemns Montferrat's love of show – a fault which, we may recollect from the play, is shared by Bassanio, who borrows money from Antonio in order to make a good – and misleading – impression on Portia. It is his discovery that he has been mistaken about Montferrat which makes Guido so distrustful of judgement in general, not just his own, and subsequently prompts him to leave his daughter's fate to chance. His decision ironically takes no account of the fact that neither Portia nor Nerissa had ever been taken in by Montferrat. He deprives her of

10 Charles Cowden Clarke, *Shakespeare-Characters: Chiefly Those Subordinate* (London, 1863), p. 401.

11 Anna Jameson, *Shakespeare's Heroines: Characters of Women Moral, Poetical and Historical* (London, 1832 repr. 1897), pp. 53–4.

the right to choose when her own judgement has never been at fault. The casket scheme is explicitly described by the narrator as 'a scheme as eccentric in its aim, as his former exercise of judgement had been hasty and defective' (71). Pressure is put on Portia by her dying father to agree to the will, and we learn that Bellario 'secretly doubt[s]' (84) its wisdom. Thus Portia's eventual 'happy' fate is, Cowden Clarke suggests, more the result of luck than judgement – the test is stripped of the glamour of authority it accrues in Shakespeare's more fairy-tale vision of Belmont. Furthermore, because Bassanio is tainted by association with Montferrat, we are encouraged to focus on Shakespeare's ambivalent presentation of his 'hero' and on the ambiguities of the play's conclusion.

Because *The Girlhood* shares so many characteristics with the Victorian novel the reader might compare the eccentric will of Portia's father with the insulting codicil appended to his will by Casaubon in *Middlemarch*. Although a chance and remote connection it is significant that in other plays by Shakespeare – *The Tempest* and *Pericles* for example – excessive control over a daughter's sexuality may be linked with the father's submerged incestuous desire for her. Indeed Mark Taylor notes the common connection between a father setting riddles to test suitors and father/daughter incest.[12] By reviving Portia's dead father in her prequel, this latent possibility is realized by Cowden Clarke. In the interview quoted above, Jane Smiley explained her interpretation of *King Lear* with reference to 'a kind of coded reference to incest in this group of folkloric stories', and it would seem that Cowden Clarke may have been similarly alert to such codes. In her prequel, as in *The Winter's Tale* and *Pericles*, the potential for incest is strengthened by a long period of separation between father and daughter. Overcome with sorrow after his wife's death Guido leaves his daughter in Bellario's care. His first reaction to a fleeting glimpse of Portia is full of significance: 'That fair creature whom you led to the terrace, then, was – Gracious heaven! I have seen her! My child! I fancied that fair being by your side was your own, your wife! A second such delusion! And are you indeed destined to bestow upon me a second Portia?' (I.57). Thus the spectre of possible incestuous feelings between Portia and both her uncle and father is invoked, particularly as the reference to 'a second such delusion' reminds us that he made precisely the same mistake when he first glimpsed his own wife, Bellario's sister Portia. Guido's feelings for his daughter become still stronger and more oppressive, if not absolutely inappropriate: 'In his craving wish to behold her unceasingly, to enjoy her presence exclusively, he would fain have engrossed her thoughts as she absorbed his, and he almost jealously beheld her eyes, her words, her attention directed to any other object but himself' (I.58). The force of 'jealously' is strengthened rather than softened by 'almost' because the qualification seems to acknowledge jealousy's inappropriate, sexual aspect. And when he knows that his feelings are returned, the language used seems more suited to romantic than filial love:

> He could not doubt the interpretation of the joy that played in her smiles when she saw him approach, the eagerness that impelled her toward him, the beaming eyes that met his in soft response, or the warmth with which his paternal caresses were welcomed, and returned by her filial ones. (I.59)

Although Guido's anxiety may be explained by his long absence from home this is still a strange account of the feelings between father and daughter. The difficulty he experiences in interpreting 'joy' and 'eagerness' is striking. Surely such emotions *always* betoken affection; the father's trepidation can best be explained if we imagine him wondering whether he has grounds for hoping that her love is sexual. Although incest is not an overt presence in 'The Heiress of Belmont' and may not have been consciously considered by the author, her introduction of certain typical incest motifs into the prequel to a play which already featured a riddle

[12] 'This means, not that there is any necessary coalescence of incest and riddles, but that the two will often conjoin to create an atmosphere in which the unspeakable is made manifest' (Mark Taylor, *Shakespeare's Darker Purpose: A Question of Incest* (New York, 1982), p. 71).

test is suggestive, particularly in the light of other intimations of incest in *The Girlhood*. In 'The Magnifico's Child', for example, Gratiano experiences a textbook case of incestuous attraction following separation[13] when he first sees his niece Desdemona as an adult: 'Who has not felt this inexpressible, yet invincible attraction toward some object of the kind, at some time or other?' (I.344).

Some critics have detected a shadow of daughter/father incest lying behind *Romeo and Juliet*. Jane Ford, for example, finds significance in the Capulets' anxiety to marry Juliet off at a very young age:

> Although her father is at first disposed to let her postpone any action until she is sixteen, he agrees to allow Count Paris to woo her and ultimately seems caught up in that frantic haste to get the daughter safely married off that characterizes other father/daughter plots – especially Shakespeare's. This dramatizes the father's necessity for a resolution of his own incestuous impulses through immediate marriage.[14]

Cowden Clarke's own response to the play, which focuses on the youth of Lady Capulet rather than on Juliet herself, suggests a similarly edgy take on the Capulet household. Whereas Ford describes a father suffering from incestuous anxieties, Cowden Clarke, not unnaturally, locates anxiety in the mother. We learn that Lady Capulet was the daughter of a friend and contemporary of Capulet's, and that it was the dying wish of her father that she should marry his old friend. Capulet has a reputation for gallantry, and Lady Capulet's jealous fears are quickly awakened if she sees him paying particular attention to any pretty girl. The first is Giacinta, with whom she incorrectly believes her husband is in love. When she dies suddenly Lady Capulet is secretly gratified: 'A sense of security, of triumph, took possession of her, as she looked again upon the marble stillness of those features, whose beaming expression of fond happiness had once caused her such misery' (II.371). Immediately she learns that her fears were misplaced, for a young man suddenly appears at her funeral and stabs himself, falling on her corpse. The couple were betrothed secretly and 'were borne together to one tomb, and side by side rested in death' (II.372). This apparently gratuitous anticipation of Juliet's fate gains more importance in the context of later events. It is significant that Capulet was Giacinta's guardian, for the next object of Lady Capulet's jealousy, Leonilda, is the daughter of old friends of her husband. Thus she and both of her two 'rivals' stand in a quasi-daughterly relation to Capulet, established not only through his much greater age but, more importantly, through a network of social connections which bind him to the parents of all three girls. Although Capulet's friendships with both rivals are quite innocent, circumstances conspire to suggest otherwise – and these circumstances, while still unresolved, arouse some suspicion in the reader also. The result is to suggest that Capulet is attracted to daughter surrogates, while ostensibly denying that this is the case.

Even though Juliet is still only a little child, concrete connections are made between her and the adult rivals in addition to the prolepsis of Giacinta's fate. Maddened by jealousy Lady Capulet prepares a gift of poisoned gloves for Leonilda. She is then horrified to see her daughter playing with a similar pair – but these turn out to be undoctored. Although Lady Capulet is presented as a doting mother the narrative reminds us that a fourth 'daughter figure' might emerge to threaten Lady Capulet's peace of mind, Juliet herself.

Although she throws away the gloves, later she is tempted to employ an assassin to despatch Leonilda. Capulet is distraught to learn of her death, mourning 'a flower! a very blossom!' (400) anticipating his grief at Juliet's own eventual death: 'Death lies on her like an untimely frost / Upon the sweetest flower of all the field' (4.4.55–6). Eventually it turns out that heart disease, and not the assassin, killed Leonilda. This uncertainty as to whether her death was unnatural or natural again suggests a resemblance to Juliet who appears to die naturally (when

[13] Jane Ford, *Patriarchy and Incest from Shakespeare to Joyce* (Gainesville, 1998), p. 8.

[14] Ford, *Patriarchy and Incest*, p. 39.

only drugged) before dying unnaturally, through suicide.

Although in neither play nor novella is father/daughter incest presented in thought or deed it nevertheless hovers in the gap between the two, fuelled by such odd repetitions and coincidences which contrive to connect Lady Capulet's jealousy of girls who share her daughterly connection with Capulet with the eventual death of her own daughter. Here as elsewhere, returning to Shakespeare after reading Cowden Clarke provides further food for thought. Jane Ford identifies 'incestuous implications . . . in her father's violent reaction'[15] to Juliet's reluctance to marry Paris, but Lady Capulet's reaction seems at least as intemperate. She explains to her husband: 'Ay, sir, but she will none, she gives you thanks. / I would the fool were married to her grave!' (3.5.139–40). At some level Juliet's fate could be perceived as the secret wish of her insecure mother. Even Lady Capulet's ill-tempered exchange with her husband on the eve of Juliet's planned wedding becomes strangely suggestive. The nurse teases him for being a 'cot-quean' (4.4.6) because he is so interested in all the domestic arrangements:

CAPULET No, not a whit. What, I have watched ere now
All night for lesser cause, and ne'er been sick.
CAPULET'S WIFE Ay, you have been a mouse-hunt in your time,
But I will watch you from such watching now.
*Exeunt Capulet's Wife and Nurse.*
CAPULET A jealous hood, a jealous hood! (4.4.9–13)

In the light of Cowden Clarke's contribution to our 'knowledge' of the Capulet household there seems a strange slippage between Lord Capulet's allusion to 'watching' – overseeing the welfare of his household and daughter – and Lady Capulet's immediate allusion to woman-chasing. 'I will watch you from such watching now' seems less a wifely appeal to him to stop fussing than a covert warning that Juliet will soon be out of his reach. Such tiny details may have little (or no) resonance when Shakespeare is read in isolation, but form an important part of Cowden Clarke's own project, which sometimes seems to be to transform rather than complement our understanding of Shakespeare.

Suggestions of incest can also be detected in 'Olivia: The Lady of Illyria', although these are overshadowed by fears that a child might be sexually abused by a family friend. In *Twelfth Night* Olivia is still mourning the loss of her brother and in her own tale Mary Cowden Clarke sets out to explain why his death had such an impact on her. Sometimes the way Clarke picks up on details from the plays and works them into her prequels can be heavy-handed, but here it is interesting to see how she creates a story of Olivia's girlhood which accounts for her response to both Orsino and Viola.

In the prequel Olivia's brother is called Cynthio, a fair and delicate boy who is in love with their adopted sister Astrella, a beautiful foundling. However she is attracted toward a villainous knight called Dorfaux who first meets the family while they are still children. Although critics have acknowledged Cowden Clarke's interest in child abuse, they note that the phenomenon is described so cagily that her girl readers very probably wouldn't understand what was being described.[16] This is true, but although Cowden Clarke obviously couldn't be any more explicit, the lack of explicitness is arguably a very effective way of conveying the impact of such encounters on her heroines, themselves very innocent. This is how she describes Olivia's response to Dorfaux pushing her in a swing: 'He continued for some time swinging Olivia, the two other children looking on. Once or twice they spoke to her; but Olivia seemed distracted from attending to them by something or other; uneasy, and unable to answer them' (III.122). She gets off the swing and 'freed herself from his arms as quickly

[15] Ford, *Patriarchy and Incest*, p. 39.

[16] See George C. Gross, 'Mary Cowden Clarke, "The Girlhood of Shakespeare's Heroines" and the Sex Education of Victorian Women', *Victorian Studies*, 16 (1972), 37–58. Cicely Palser Havely also notes the attack on double sexual standards and plea for sexual honesty in 'The Votaress', Cowden Clarke's prequel to *Measure for Measure* ('Saying the Unspeakable: Mary Cowden Clarke and *Measure for Measure*', *Durham University Journal*, 56 (1995), 233–42.

as she could, and walked away to a seat somewhat apart' (III.122). The effect of this very understated method of describing her experience seems less prudish than suggestive of Olivia's bewilderment, of her inability to articulate what happened. George C. Gross writes of Cowden Clarke 'She was also aware of the dangers from monstrous men which may beset small girls as well as their blooming elder sisters.'[17] He adds that there is no biographical evidence for any personal knowledge of such matters. However it may be significant that Mary Cowden Clarke's husband Charles Cowden Clarke – who was only six years younger than her father – was a friend of the Novello family and first met Mary when she was seven.[18] (Without accusing Cowden Clarke of any sexual impropriety, it seems possible that knowing her future husband as an adult when she was a little child might have made Mary more sensitive to the possibility of such liaisons, even at a time when intergenerational marriages were more accepted. Certainly we might conjecture that Charles Cowden Clarke, like Capulet, would have had friends with daughters the same age as his wife.)

Some years later Dorfaux returns and experiences a more normal attraction to the adult Astrella. However his principal motive for marrying her is financial, and Mary Cowden Clarke's vigorous attack on male control of women's property clearly reflects the realities of nineteenth-century life more urgently than those of the Renaissance. (In some ways she anticipates Wilkie Collins's *The Woman in White*, written some ten years later. Dorfaux's superficial politeness, his barely concealed impatience with his wife and her family, and his mercenary schemes align him with Collins's dastardly Sir Percival Glyde.) Another topic much debated at the time was child custody. Until 1839 a woman had no rights to custody if she separated from her husband.[19] The dying Astrella charges Olivia and Cynthio to look after her daughter: 'Should her father's caprice ever claim her as his child, promise me that you will refuse. He is no meet parent – no fit protector, guide, for childhood – for girlhood!' (III.179). One wonders whether she remembers his sexual interest in her and Olivia when they were children. But perhaps she simply fears his bad example, just as Helen Huntingdon fears the effect her husband's drunkenness will have on her little boy in the contemporary *Tenant of Wildfell Hall*.

The presentation of Dorfaux is quite bold and racy, and suggests at least a reforming if not a revolutionary feminist spirit. This aspect of the tale could clearly be grasped even by someone with no knowledge of Shakespeare. But only a reader who knew *Twelfth Night* would be in a position to understand the more subtle subversion at work in this sensational tale. Dorfaux is entirely Cowden Clarke's own invention. In a sense his very awfulness is almost reassuring – he could be perceived as the exception rather than the rule. In some ways her very brief introduction of the character of Orsino, Olivia's admirer of *Twelfth Night*, is far more unsettling. He is first introduced when Dorfaux tries to assert his rights over Astrella's child, and goes to the Duke for help. Orsino doesn't care for him, and decides to look into the matter himself, thus paving the way for his first meeting with Olivia. Crucially, he allows his love for her to jeopardize his handling of the case: 'He contrived that it should be protracted, and judgement deferred, as long as might be; trusting that these silent attentions might win him a way to her liking, ere he risked a declaration of his sentiments' (III.185). No comment is offered on his procedure, but its effects are devastating: Dorfaux kidnaps the child, whom he allows to fall from his horse to her death.[20] Such

[17] George C. Gross, 'Mary Cowden Clarke', p. 44.

[18] An account of their marriage can be found in Richard D. Altick, *The Cowden Clarkes* (London 1948).

[19] Alan Chedzoy, *A Scandalous Woman: The Story of Caroline Norton* (London, 1992) p. 179.

[20] An interesting comparison is Caroline Norton's account of her marriage; this was written in 1854, but deals with events which took place in the 1830s and 1840s. (Useful extracts can be found in Harriet Devine Jump, *Women's Writing of the Victorian Period 1837–1901, an Anthology* (Edinburgh, 1999), pp. 77–88.) One of her sons died following a fall from horseback while in the charge of her estranged husband. The remote setting of Cowden Clarke's tales would not have diminished their power as testimonies to the wrongs suffered by nineteenth-century women at the hands of men, and a legal system which favoured men.

a striking integration of a pressing contemporary concern into a response to Shakespeare has no real parallel in Updike or even in Smiley's updated *Lear*, powerful though it is. A better comparison is provided by Tim Supple's recent film of *Twelfth Night*, shown on Channel 4, in which Viola and Sebastian are reinvented as Asian asylum seekers.

It is hardly surprising that this trauma, and her experience of Dorfaux both as adult and child, should make Olivia wary of men. Even Orsino, presented in an apparently positive light, is implicated indirectly in the child's death because of his procrastination in making a judgement. Earlier we saw how a strikingly faulty invented character – Montferrat – appeared to function as a clue to the more subtle faults of the Shakespearian hero, Bassanio. The same could be said of Dorfaux. By introducing Orsino into the narrative, by implicating him, however unwittingly, in Dorfaux's behaviour, Cowden Clarke alienates the reader from the play's 'hero'.

These traumatic experiences have a profound psychological effect on Olivia. George C. Gross, talking of Cynthio's love for his foster sister Astrella, observes that this is 'about as close as Mary Cowden Clarke could come to the popular Romantic theme of incest'.[21] But Olivia's feelings for her blood brother Cynthio could be seen as more simply and literally incestuous. She tells him that she looks for a lover more delicate and graceful than Orsino: 'I could describe to thee precisely the sort of being, to whom, methinks, I could give my whole heart, were it not that instead of painting thee a picture, thou wouldst say I but held up a mirror before thee' (III.194–5). Olivia's hints at attraction echo Viola's heartfelt though stifled attempts to express her feelings to Orsino in *Twelfth Night* (2.4.21–8). Attention is drawn to Olivia's expressions of love by the excessive anxiety she manifests before speaking her mind: 'Dared I speak frankly to you, Cynthio mine, – dared I tell you all that is in my heart' (III.194). Cynthio then protests that Olivia might as well fall in love with a girl as with a girlish youth like himself. She replies enthusiastically: 'Could a girl look like the glorious creature I see before me . . . I should sooner be bewitched into losing my heart to such a semblance, than to the substantial proportions, and giant bulk of my lord duke' (III.195). Incest shades into lesbianism, laying the ground, of course, for her passion for Viola. It is the Duke's masculinity which repels Olivia, reminding her of men's power to oppress and injure women. Her preference for an effeminate youth, even for a girl, is therefore made tolerably convincing, psychologically. Thus does Mary Cowden Clarke take what appear to be givens of the play's plot, strategies for furthering the action – namely Olivia's dislike of Orsino and her attraction to Viola – and give them a new significance. Both these character traits reflect the suffering she and her family have met with at the hands of a patriarchal society. Whereas in *Twelfth Night* it is possible to say that Olivia falls in love with Viola in spite of her sex, Cowden Clarke suggests that her feminine appearance lies at the root of the attraction. It does not simply anticipate her more 'appropriate' attraction to Viola's twin, Sebastian – rather, her marriage with Sebastian is only brought about because of his similarity to a girl. Again, it is vital to read tale and play as a unit – in isolation Olivia's words to her brother read like an adolescent's knee-jerk reaction to very recent events. Read alone, *Twelfth Night*'s presentation of Olivia's exasperation at Orsino's suit and favour of Viola lack special significance. But if we read them together we must interpret both her dislike of Orsino and her attraction to Viola as the twin results of events which have given her a lasting distaste for conventionally masculine men, events whose impact is still felt seven years later. (Again, if we think forward to twentieth-century responses to canonical texts, we might draw a parallel between the way Cowden Clarke gives an emphatic significance to same-sex attraction, rather than choosing to read Olivia's interest in Viola as simply comic or innocent, with Emma Tennant's decision to develop Emma's lesbian potential.)

In 'The Peerless', the prequel to *Cymbeline*, Mary Cowden Clarke treats Posthumus as sceptically

[21] George C. Gross, 'Mary Cowden Clarke', p. 52.

as Bassanio and Orsino. Yet again it is a hidden scepticism, only recognizable if we are alert to her allusive strategies – the same techniques of repetition and prolepsis used in 'The White Dove of Verona'. Imogen's mother Guendolen is a Griselda-like figure, poor but virtuous and entirely obedient to her husband Cymbeline who is presented in a most unattractive light: 'While he exalted her outwardly, he subjugated her the more entirely in herself; and while he idolized her beauty, he played the despot with her nature. He took advantage of her timidity; practised on her meekness; and tyrannized over her passive spirit' (III.412). Lack of trust is his most abiding fault; when he accuses his loyal servant Belarius of treachery the wronged man takes revenge by abducting the King's two sons. Later Cymbeline is convinced by a scheming lord, Mempricius, that his own wife has wronged him, and she and Imogen are banished to a remote dwelling. Guendolen dies saving Cymbeline from a raging lion and Imogen is taken back into favour. Posthumus is the Queen's champion, yet despite his apparently positive characterization he is problematized by the tale. The King's readiness to condemn his wife clearly foreshadows Shakespeare's own presentation of the similarly credulous Posthumus. The resemblance to Shakespeare's story is heightened by the deathbed confession of Mempricius who, like Iachimo, repents his treachery. There is another odd and ostensibly tedious anticipation of the play when Posthumus is imprisoned by the wicked queen, escapes from a dungeon and finds his way unwittingly into Imogen's apartments. Here we get a description where almost every detail mirrors Iachimo's later intrusion into her bedchamber (2.2.11–24). This repetition functions as an 'Alexandrian footnote'[22] – the reference to 'memory' functions outside as well as within the fiction of the text, for we too remember this description:

> And as he gazed, something that he had heard of the particulars of these costly fittings, smote upon his memory . . . There were the rich silken hangings of Tyre, wrought in silver, with the story of that Egyptian queen who had lately filled the world with her fame of witchery; the golden-fretted roof; the marble-sculptured chimney, with its figures so life-like moulded in grace and beauty, of Dian and her attendant nymphs; the silver andirons on the hearth . . . (III.499)

These odd repetitions of Shakespeare perhaps have more point than is first apparent. On the surface Posthumus is an attractive figure in 'The Peerless'. But the effect of the King's treatment of Imogen's mother, presented as entirely unreasonable, might make us reflect that Posthumus behaves even worse – he orders that his wife be killed, not merely cast off. And by making him anticipate the voyeuristic role of Iachimo, however innocently, the narrative seems to work to implicate Posthumus in Iachimo's villainy, perhaps to imply that we can't just blame Iachimo – Posthumus should have had more trust in his wife, particularly, of course, as he knows how Imogen's mother was similarly wronged.

It seems that, because Posthumus is the play's 'hero', the husband of the Shakespearian heroine whom the Victorians thought most perfect,[23] his faults must be glossed over. Yet a substratum of the narrative refuses to forgive Posthumus, and associates him with the much more obviously unattractive Cymbeline and Iachimo. Anna Jameson's opinion of Posthumus provides an interesting comparison – typically slippery, her praise of Posthumus sows seeds for doubt.

> Neither does it appear to me that Posthumus is unworthy of Imogen, or only interesting on Imogen's account. His character, like those of all the other persons in the drama, is kept subordinate to hers; but this could not be otherwise, for she is the proper subject, the heroine of the poem. Everything is done to ennoble Posthumus and justify her love for him, and though we certainly approve him more for her sake than for his own, we are early prepared to view him with Imogen's eyes, and not only excuse, but sympathise in her admiration . . .[24]
>
> (*Shakespeare's Heroines*, 186)

[22] 'Certain allusions are so constructed as to carry a kind of built-in commentary, a kind of reflexive annotation, which underlines or intensifies their demand to be interpreted *as* allusions' (Stephen Hinds, *Allusion and Intertext: Dynamics of Appropriation in Roman Poetry* (Cambridge, 1997), p. 1).

[23] See for example Anna Jameson, *Shakespeare's Heroines*, p. 181.

[24] Anna Jameson, *Shakespeare's Heroines*, p. 186.

The tacit assumption of dissent, the hint that Shakespeare has had to resort to special pleading, and the ambiguous force of words such as *early* and *excuse*, betray Jameson's own lack of affection for Posthumus.

Doubt is cast on the character of a far more celebrated Shakespearian hero in 'The Rose of Elsinore'.[25] Little Ophelia's peasant foster brother Ulf's oafish persecution of her when a mere child affords some unpleasantly lurid moments. But it is Ophelia's more indirect brush with a very different exploiter of women – a handsome seducer from court called Eric – which tells us most about Cowden Clarke's relationship with Shakespeare. Eric, like Dorfaux, is of course her own invention, another non-Shakespearian villainous male who is introduced to make a point about the difficulties facing women in a patriarchal society. Although the Shakespearian hero appears to be exonerated from such blame, he, like Orsino and Posthumus, is subtly implicated in the more obvious male villain's wrongdoing.

Eric is introduced to the story while little Ophelia is living with her peasant foster family in the country. She and her foster sister Jutha discover him in the forest as he rests after hunting. Jutha is immediately attracted by his handsome appearance.

> 'Sure, a prince – no less; such a prince as they tell of in the wondrous tales I have heard. How passing beautiful he is! . . . Look at this brave stranger. See how bright and handsome his clothing. Look what a goodly beauteous face he hath! He is as glorious to behold, as the king's son, who had a fairy for his godmother!' (II.201–2)

Though a nobleman, Eric is not in fact of royal blood. But Jutha's naive assurance that he is a prince serves to connect the unidentified youth with Hamlet himself. There is perhaps another Alexandrian footnote here – we, like Jutha, have heard tales about Danish princes! Perhaps more significant than Jutha's assurance that he is royal is the echo in her artless apostrophe of Hamlet's famous speech: 'What a piece of work is a man! How noble in reason, how infinite in faculty, in form and moving how express and admirable, in action how like an angel, in apprehension how like a god!' (2.2.303–7). In the light of these implicit parallels between Eric and Hamlet it is significant that the former seduces Jutha thoughtlessly, abandoning her when she becomes pregnant. Her death in childhood has a painful impact on the young Ophelia which is revived when she later meets Eric again at court. Now he is the professed admirer of her friend Thyra, who is abandoned like Jutha, and commits suicide in her despair. The adventures of Eric may seem repetitive, but gain importance as part of a sequence which will only be completed in *Hamlet* itself, but which is foreshadowed toward the end of the story. Ophelia suffers from brain fever and has a prophetic dream in which she sees first Jutha, then Thyra, and then a strange white figure whom she cannot identify, all dead. The last woman is clearly her later self, and by associating her with Jutha and Thyra Cowden Clarke seems to imply that Ophelia was a victim of men, that she was in fact later seduced by Hamlet, even though, when he appears on the margins of Cowden Clarke's text, it is as an apparently attractive and kind young man.[26]

We have already seen how Updike brings Shakespeare's sources into play in *Gertrude and Claudius*; he draws on them for names and some plot details. It is possible that Cowden Clarke, a Shakespeare scholar as well as a creative writer, also knew of these earlier versions of Hamlet's story. In Saxo's narrative Hamlet feigns idiocy, rather than madness, and his own foster-sister is offered to him (Ophelia-like) as a sexual temptation. Perhaps by clouding Ophelia's early years with memories of a sexually predatory, half-witted, foster-brother Cowden Clarke (like Updike) is excavating the history of Hamlet as a story as well as the origins of Ophelia's mental state. And if we are (counter-intuitively)

---

25 This tale is discussed by Elaine Showalter, 'Representing Ophelia: Women, Madness, and the Responsibilities of Feminist Criticism' in *Shakespeare and Tragedy*, ed. John Drakakis (London, 1992), pp. 288–9.

26 Ophelia's purity was not beyond question, as Grace Latham's defence of her character in 'O Poor Ophelia' reveals (Ann Thompson and Sasha Roberts, *Women Reading Shakespeare 1660–1900* (Manchester, 1997), pp. 165–8).

intended to make any connection between the predatory Ulf and Hamlet, such a link strengthens the text's tacit criticism of the prince.

It is significant that Ophelia's prophetic vision is brought to her by the ghost of old Hamlet, as though her own personal, domestic and very feminine sorrow deserves a supernatural messenger every bit as much as Hamlet's tragic destiny. (In her prequel to *Macbeth* Cowden Clarke provides Lady Macbeth with a vision of her future fate comparable to her husband's encounter with the witches.) Jessica Slights observes of Cowden Clarke: 'her project is to use the Shakespearian canon in order to construct an argument for change by giving voice to women who have been silenced by male history'.[27] And in its own way Mary Cowden Clarke's re-vision of Shakespeare is as significant and legitimate – and as subversive – as more fashionable responses to his plays, such as Jane Smiley's *A Thousand Acres* and Updike's *Gertrude and Claudius*, where Shakespeare's marginalized heroines are similarly moved centre stage.

---

[27] Slights, Jessica, 'Historical Shakespeare: Anna Jameson and Womanliness', *English Studies in Canada*, 19 (1993), pp. 387–400, p. 388.

# SHAKESPEARE AMONG THE WORKERS

ANDREW MURPHY

> The day has arisen, when this Shakspeare will visit you; in your verdant homes he will soon be with you. In the meantime, seek him in the nearest library, he will not mock your poverty; if you cannot afford him in a morocco case, he will not despise a paper cover. Yes, I have faith, that in a few more years, the spread of Education and Science will break down the barriers that Bigotry, Prejudice, and Conventionalism have been studiously building up in years past, and patching, again and again, as the breezes of knowledge have weakened them. They are now going down with a fell crash; Progression examined them, and pronounced them rotten . . . For such an age was Shakspeare specially ordained. Try him; you will find him
>
> ONE ENTIRE AND PERFECT CHRYSOLITE[1]

So Christopher Thomson writes in his *Autobiography of an Artisan*, published in 1847. Thomson was born in the dying days of the eighteenth century, on Christmas day, 1799. Over the course of the new century, Shakespeare's appeal would broaden considerably to take in a new, popular readership, and Thomson brings together here some of the key elements which contributed to this development. During the course of the century, the educational franchise expanded, carrying literacy downwards into the poorest sectors of society and creating new generations of readers. At the same time, books became ever cheaper and more plentiful, so that this emergent class of readers could in time afford to become book buyers.[2] Many of these readers found their way to Shakespeare and they were able, as Thomson suggests, to buy the playwright's works in cheap paper covered editions, even if they could not afford them in elegant leather bindings. For the first time, then, Shakespeare began to have a significant working-class readership – even among those whom Thomson styles the 'factory-workers, whose right to earn a scanty supply in ten short hours, in [a] miasmatic atmosphere, is questioned by brassy capitalists'.[3] This new readership embraced the playwright's work with a passionate enthusiasm – Thomson himself tells us that 'Many a time have I felt my soul light up with pure and holy fire at the altar of our Shakespeare.'[4] The aim of this article will be to track the process whereby these new readers were able to find their way to Shakespeare; to map some of their responses to his work (and the political value it had for some readers); and to give brief consideration to the question of why this expanded readership ultimately

---

This article is based on a paper delivered at the International Shakespeare Conference in Stratford in July 2004. I am very grateful to Russell Jackson and John Jowett for their invitation to speak at the conference; to Peter Holland for suggesting that I submit the paper for consideration at *Shakespeare Survey*; and to the many conference delegates who made very helpful suggestions for strengthening the piece.

1 Christopher Thomson, *The Autobiography of an Artisan* (London, 1847), p. 294.

2 For a useful account of street bookselling in working class districts, see The Journeyman Engineer [Thomas Wright], *The Great Unwashed* (London, 1868; reprint edition New York, 1970), pp. 225–33.

3 Thomson, *Autobiography*, p. 292.

4 Thomson, *Autobiography*, p. 101.

began to contract as the century drew to a close.[5]

The growth in educational provision is the cornerstone of Shakespeare's new readership in the nineteenth century. The culture of popular education in England and Wales began to shift significantly from the closing years of the eighteenth century.[6] In 1785, for example, the Sunday School Society was founded and, by 1838, some 1,548,890 children were enrolled in the Sunday school system.[7] The standard of teaching being provided in the few hours per week that students attended these establishments was often rather indifferent at best, but the fundamental aim of the programme was to teach children the basics of reading and understanding the Bible and, outside the classroom, the skills learned in this process could, of course, always be turned to other, less religiously orientated, ends. Joseph Barker, a Yorkshire weaver born in 1806, observed in his autobiography that 'Almost the only opportunity I had of learning anything . . . was by attending the Sunday-school. When we had work, we had not time to go to school; and when we had not work, we had nothing with which to pay school wages, so that Sunday-school was our only resource.'[8] Likewise, the weaver poet Samuel Bamford, writing of the period running up to 1815, observed in his *Passages in the Life of a Radical* that 'the Sunday Schools of the preceding thirty years, had produced many working men of sufficient talent to become readers, writers, and speakers in the village meetings for parliamentary reform'.[9]

The Sunday schools were supplemented by dame schools and other small-scale local arrangements. Here, again, standards varied enormously. The Committee of the Manchester Statistical Society, reporting on educational provision in Manchester, Liverpool, Salford and Bury in the 1830s, observed of dame schools that 'they are generally in a most deplorable condition: the greater part of them are kept by females; but some by old men, whose only qualification for this employment seems to be their unfitness for any other'.[10] Mary Smith, born in 1822 in Cropredy, Oxfordshire, recalled of her local teacher, Dame Garner that 'No smile was ever seen to illuminate her stern countenance, from the time of our arrival at school, to the time we made our curtsies and hurried out of it' and she concluded bitterly that 'For long years Englishwomen's souls were almost as sorely crippled and cramped by the devices of the school room, as the Chinese women's feet by their shoes.'[11] Charles Shaw, a potter and Methodist preacher born ten years later than Smith, by contrast remembered both his Sunday school and his local dame school more fondly. Of the former he observed: 'To speak of the benefit it has been to this nation would be a joy, and all I could say would fail to tell the measure of its beneficence and inspiration, especially to the children of the poor in those days.' Of his dame school teacher 'old Betty', he notes: 'She was, perhaps, above the average of her class who taught the children of England in those days for a mere pittance, when our rulers were squandering the resources of the nation in

[5] This article is, in a sense, a companion piece to my 'Shakespeare Goes to School: Educational Stationers', *Analytical & Enumerative Bibliography*, n.s. 12 (2002), 241–63. In that article I sought to trace some of the history of the incorporation of Shakespeare into the English educational system over the course of the nineteenth century.

[6] The discussion of educational developments in this article refers only to the systems which were established in England and Wales in this period. Scotland and Ireland had (and have) wholly separate educational regimes.

[7] Anon, 'Schools for the Industrious Classes; Or, the Present State of Education among the Working People of England', in Central Society of Education *Papers*, vol. 2 (London, 1838), p. 345.

[8] John Thomas Barker, ed., *The Life of Joseph Barker. Written by Himself* (London, 1880), pp. 34–5.

[9] Samuel Bamford, *Passages in the Life of a Radical*, included in W. H. Chaloner (ed.), *The Autobiography of Samuel Bamford* (London, 1967), vol. II, pp. 7–8. The Central Society of Education took a rather more soberly pessimistic view, noting that the possibility 'that Sunday school instruction alone is generally efficient for teaching the art of reading . . . may be reasonably doubted', *Papers*, vol. 2, p. 349.

[10] Quoted in Editor, 'Analysis of the Reports of the Committee of the Manchester Statistical Society on the State of Education in the Boroughs of Manchester, Liverpool, Salford, and Bury' in Central Society of Education *Papers*, vol. 1 (London, 1837), p. 295.

[11] Mary Smith, *The Autobiography of Mary Smith, Schoolmistress and Nonconformist* (London, 1892), pp. 7, 32.

less useful ways, and were blind to the wisdom of educating the children of the country'.[12]

From the early decades of the nineteenth century, the dame schools came gradually to be supplemented by the much more highly organized local schools established throughout England and Wales by the dissenting British and Foreign School Society (founded in 1807) and the rival orthodox Anglican National Society (founded four years later).[13] W. E. Adams, born, like Charles Shaw, in 1832, noted that local education in his native Cheltenham was provided by a National Society school, later supplemented by a rival Wesleyan establishment, and he observes of the National Society that it 'rendered unmistakable service to a past generation' of poor children.[14] In 1813, the two religious societies had, between them, established 230 schools serving in excess of 40,000 students. By 1830, these numbers had risen to 3,670 schools, serving some 346,000 students.[15]

As in the case of the dame schools, the quality of education offered in these establishments was often less than adequate – not least, of course, because of the monitorial system of teaching which both societies employed and, indeed, claimed to have invented. However, the broader point to be made here is that all of these educational initiatives, taken together, served to provide at least the basic elements of literacy to the children of the poorest sectors of society. And, equipped with these tools, a significant number of working class readers were ultimately able to comprehend and appreciate writers such as Bunyan, Defoe, Milton and Shakespeare when, at a later point in life, they began to encounter their work.[16] Many of these readers themselves became writers, charting the trajectory of their own lives in a new tradition of working-class autobiography. It is through this writing that we can in some measure trace their responses to their Shakespearian encounters.

The process of finding Shakespeare was often something of a haphazard affair for this new class of readers. For Joseph Arch, born in Barford in Warwickshire in 1826 and destined to become a trade union activist, the Shakespearian encounter was an entirely natural one, as his native village was 'situated on a bend of willow-fringed Avon', a place which 'William Shakespeare may have seen, and even entered'. Arch's mother 'was a great admirer of Shakespeare. She used to talk about him very often, and she was well versed in his works. She would read bits aloud to me of an evening and tell me tales from the plays.'[17] By contrast, Mary Smith, who we have already encountered as an unhappy dame school pupil, struggled as a reader in a home where her mother was sceptical and suspicious of her daughter's enthusiasm for books. 'My poor mother', she tells us, 'looked upon reading, even when I was a little child, as a species of idleness; very well for Sundays or evenings, when baby was asleep and I was not wanted for anything else'. Her father was, however, a touch more sympathetic, and one day, Smith notes, he came home

> saying he had been at a sale, and had bought a lot of old books. They were duly brought, and laid down on the floor; a lot of tattered books of all descriptions; novels, histories, poems, plays (including some of Shakespeare's). He had surely thought of his little girl, who was so fond of books, for he was too busy to look them over.

It was from this first chance encounter with Shakespeare, Smith observes, that she 'learned to love classical poetry'. The books themselves were quickly consigned to the attic, but Smith raided the tattered library on a regular basis. 'Often and often', she writes, 'on wet evenings, or on Saturday afternoons, when released from household work, I

---

12 [Charles Shaw], *When I was a Child by an Old Potter* (London, 1903, reprinted in facsimile Firle, Sussex, 1977), pp. 7, 5.

13 For a general account of developments in education in this period, see W. B. Stephens, *Education in Britain, 1750–1914* (Basingstoke, 1998).

14 William Edwin Adams, *Memoirs of a Social Atom*, 2 vols. (London, 1903), I, p. 74.

15 R. K. Webb, *The British Working-Class Reader, 1790–1848: Literacy and Social Tension* (London, 1955), p. 17.

16 *Pilgrim's Progress, Robinson Crusoe, Paradise Lost*, the Bible and Shakespeare are among the works most frequently cited as early serious reading by working-class biographers from this period.

17 Joseph Arch, *The Autobiography of Joseph Arch*, ed. John Gerald O'Leary (London, 1966; originally published in 1898, under the title *Joseph Arch: The Story of his Life*), pp. 19, 22.

would creep quietly up to the attic where the books were kept.'[18]

For John Brown, a shoemaker, soldier, sailor and sometime actor, it was a senior journeyman colleague who brought him to Shakespeare. They shared lodgings together and the older man offered him access to a small collection of books, which they read together in the evenings. 'This was the first time I ever had an opportunity of reading Shakspeare', Brown writes. 'The book opened at that beautiful speech on Mercy, put into the mouth of "Portia" in the *Merchant of Venice*. Never before had my senses been so completely captivated. I could have read all night.' Later his colleague asks him to read some of *Hamlet* to him: 'I complied at once, and derived unspeakable delight from that marvellous creation of the immortal bard. . . . I read over and over again, the soliloquy, "To be or not to be," &c., until I had committed it to memory.'[19]

Brown's experience of a sympathetic and nurturing workmate contrasts sharply with that of W. E. Adams, who discovered Shakespeare in the mid-1840s, through a penny-a-play series, which he considered a 'cheap treasure'. 'I was a poor errand boy at the time', he writes, and when out on his errands he 'used to steal odd moments to read my penny Shakspeare.' However, one day,

> another lad – a bit of a rogue I knew – asked to look at the play I was reading. Out of pure devilment (for he couldn't read himself) he refused to return it. I followed him through many streets, thinking he was playing a joke, and imploring him to give me back my precious property. But I never saw the little book again. To this day the remembrance of grief and mortification is as vivid as ever. The scene, the book, the thief – all are clearer now than greater events of yesterday.[20]

Later in the century, the basket-maker Thomas Okey secured an even greater Shakespearian bargain than Adams had done, but suffered similar resistance to his reading habits. Okey picked up a copy of John Dicks's collected edition of Shakespeare, which he characterizes as 'a marvellous feast of cheap publishing'. Dicks's text was issued in 1867 and it cost just a shilling, garnering sales of some 700,000 copies, making it one of the most commercially successful editions of the century.[21] 'To read in secret', Okey writes, 'I encamped to the washhouse' and he recalls being discovered there by his grandfather, as he pored over the Dicks's volume. 'Ah Tom,' his grandfather exclaims 'sternly reproachful', '*that*'ll never bring you bread and cheese!'[22]

The senior Okey was perhaps right in some respects: reading the works of a long-dead playwright was often of little enough value in a working-class world where the business of getting through life could be a constant struggle. Certainly, many working class readers were frustrated by the disjunction between the intellectual world they longed fully to inhabit and the everyday world where they were forced to earn, as Okey puts it, their 'bread and cheese'. The solitary activity of reading could also serve, as we have seen, to cut off the reader from his or her own immediate community. Adams, in his revealingly titled autobiography, *Memoirs of a Social Atom*, indicates the break he felt compelled to make with his established friends within the local community:

> One Sunday afternoon the usual call was made for a ramble in the fields. Word was sent to the callers that their old companion was not going to join them. I heard from an upper room, not without a certain amount of tremor, their exclamations of surprise. They wandered off into the fields in one direction; I, with a new companion, wandered off into the fields in another. My new companion was Young's 'Night Thoughts.' The old companions were never joined again.[23]

---

18 Smith, *Autobiography*, pp. 26, 39, 40.

19 John Brown, *Sixty Years' Gleanings from Life's Harvest. A Genuine Autobiography* (New York, 1859), pp. 35, 41.

20 Adams, *Memoirs*, I, p. 11.

21 For further information on Dicks's edition, see my *Shakespeare in Print: A History and Chronology of Shakespeare Publishing* (Cambridge, 2003), pp. 177–8.

22 Thomas Okey, *A Basketful of Memories: An Autobiographical Sketch* (London, 1930), p. 18; in a footnote, Okey observes: 'As a fact it led in later years to a much more varied diet.' J. R. Clynes had a similar experience with a mill foreman who caught him reading *Paradise Lost* during working hours: '"Books!" he exclaimed contemptuously. "What the 'ell dost tha want wi' books? Books'll never buy thee britches!" ' J. R. Clynes, *Memoirs: 1860–1924* (London, 1937), p. 45.

23 Adams, *Memoirs*, I, pp. 108–9.

Joseph Arch, too, felt that reading and education brought with it a certain sense of alienation – in his case from his own spouse, of whom he ruefully observes that she 'was a good, clean wife, and a good mother; she looked after my father well; she was always attending to her home and to her family; but she was no companion to me in my aspirations'.[24]

There were, then, many within the working-class community who could not see the practical point of reading Shakespeare, and some working-class readers themselves felt that reading served to disjoin them from their own community and inculcated in them a sense of isolation and alienation. At the same time, however, for many working-class readers part of the value of reading Shakespeare was precisely that he served as a kind of intellectual and spiritual ally in the various campaigns for political change and reform that were waged across much of the century. Shakespeare was available to be recruited to these campaigns in part because of the way in which he was frequently configured within nineteenth century culture. When many in the period thought of Shakespeare's life, they summoned up not 'William Shakespeare, Gent.', with his newly minted coat-of-arms and his comfortable Stratford retirement, but rather a Shakespeare who was imagined as emerging from humble origins – a man of the people who made his mark in the world by virtue of his native talents and hard work. Thus Mary Smith observes, in the context of visiting the Shakespeare memorial at Westminster Abbey, 'Our noblest Shakespere was a poor man's child.'[25] Likewise, in an address 'to the workmen and operatives of the United Kingdom', the Working Men's Committee who undertook to celebrate the 1864 tercentenary in London observed of Shakespeare that 'He sprang from the class to which you belong, yet is the counsellor of dignitaries and rulers – the same to-day as he was two centuries and a half ago, and as he will be a thousand years hence.'[26] During an anti-religious phase of his career, the Leicester radical Thomas Cooper jointly celebrated Jesus and Shakespeare as native geniuses, united in their humble origins, and he asks:

> Was it more wonderful that that young man of Nazareth, that despised carpenter's son, should be born with an organisation to discern moral beauty, and be girt up to proclaim love, and pity, and mercy, and goodness, even to the death – than that Shakspeare, with all his capacity for fathoming and depicting the human heart, and for universal creation, should be born in a woolstapler's shop?[27]

For Cooper, then, Shakespeare and Jesus are from common stock and it is from their imagined origins among the lower artisanal elements of society that they draw their true power.

Cooper is the best example of a working class twining together of Shakespearian and radical political concerns. Born in 1805, he was, as a teenager, apprenticed to a shoemaker who had spent some time in London and who spoke to him of his visits to the theatre to see Shakespeare performed by the likes of Kemble and Siddons. 'All this', Cooper observes, 'directed me to a more intelligent reading of Shakpeare.'[28] For much of the first stretch of his life Cooper was an ambitious political activist, considering the greatest honour imaginable to be the struggle 'to win the social and political rights of millions'.[29] He led a break-away group from the local chartist organization, ultimately aiming to assert his authority over the movement regionally, if not nationally. He named his local faction 'The Shaksperean Association of Leicester Chartists' and jointly they composed and produced a volume entitled the *Shakespearean Chartist Hymn Book*. The 'Shakespearian' tag, in both instances, was fortuitous, in that the meeting place the group used was the 'Shaksperian Room' of the local Leicester Amphitheatre. But the resonances certainly pleased

---

24 Arch, *Autobiography*, p. 36.

25 Smith, *Autobiography*, p. 176.

26 A copy of this address is included in file ER1/107 at the Stratford Records Office.

27 Thomas Cooper, *The Life of Thomas Cooper* (Leicester, 1971; originally published London, 1872), p. 363, quoting from his own article in *Reasoner* vol. iii, p. 507.

28 Cooper, *Life*, p. 43.

29 Cooper, *Life*, p. 147

Cooper, who observed that 'The wondrous knowledge of the heart unfolded by Shakspeare, made me shrink into insignificance; while the sweetness, the marvellous power of expression and grandeur of his poetry seemed to transport me, at times, out of the vulgar world of circumstances in which I lived bodily.'[30]

Cooper's chartists met two or three times a week in the Shakesperian Room and he lectured to them on political, historical and literary topics, including the works of Shakespeare. In giving his lectures, Cooper drew upon an extraordinary autodidactic programme that he had mapped out for himself in his early twenties. At this point in his life, Cooper set himself the task of memorizing seven complete Shakespeare plays, while simultaneously attempting to learn Latin, Greek, Hebrew and French – at the same time he was also, for good measure, attempting to memorize *Paradise Lost* in its entirety.[31] This relentless, not to say obsessive, programme of self-education led, perhaps predictably, to a physical and mental collapse, but not before Cooper had, indeed, managed to get at least all of *Hamlet* by heart. He put his knowledge to good use when, some years later, he was charged with inciting a riot in the Potteries and, to raise funds for his defence, he staged a production of *Hamlet* in his native Leicester, taking the lead role himself. His theatrical ventures notwithstanding, Cooper still went to prison, where he continued his studies and composed an extended epic poem in Spenserian stanzas, entitled *The Purgatory of Suicides*. Toward the end of his stint as a prisoner, an anonymous benefactor offered to pay for him to attend Cambridge, on the sole condition that he agree to give up his political activities. Cooper declined but, in fact, much of the latter part of his life was dedicated to itinerant lecturing and preaching (he had by this time regained a more orthodox sense of religious belief). His teachings often included, as he tells us in his autobiography, lectures on 'the Genius of Shakespeare'.

For Cooper, then, Shakespeare was a source of intellectual sustenance and, in the early part of his life, the playwright's works also had real purchase for his sense of political mission. Cooper was certainly not the only active campaigner in this extended period for whom Shakespeare had genuine political force. Later in the century, Robert Smillie (1857–1940), miner, union activist and founder-member of the Independent Labour party, found a real sense of liberation in discovering Shakespeare. He tells us that he 'read and re-read the great plays. It was a new and enchanting world. Those tragedies and comedies, to an ardent young mind which had hitherto been "cribb'd, cabin'd, and confin'd," caught and held in the iron clutch of the industrial machine, were a sheer revelation'. Knowledge of the plays, he indicates, often served a useful purpose when he was campaigning: 'such was the glamour the poet held for me in [my] early days, that, blest with a very retentive memory, I can quote, if need be, freely and extensively from the best passages of his works, and a Shakespearean quotation has often stood me in good stead when I lacked words of my own'.[32]

Moving a little further on in the century, we find that Smillie's fellow Labour activist, J. R. Clynes (1869–1949), who worked in the textile industry and who eventually became Home Secretary, also felt himself to be deeply indebted to Shakespeare. For Clynes, reading the playwright was, in itself, something of a political education. Most of his reading was done at the Oldham Equitable Co-operative Society's library. 'I remember', he says, 'my discovery of *Julius Caesar*, and how the realisation came suddenly to me that it was a mighty political drama, not just an entertainment'. Through reading Shakespeare in the 'drab reading-room' of the library, he observes, 'history became

[30] Cooper, *Life*, p. 64.

[31] Cooper was not the only autodidact to attempt an absurdly ambitious programme of memorization. The miner-poet Joseph Skipsey set himself the task of memorizing the Bible in its entirety. His biographer, Robert Spence Watson, notes that 'Fortunately, before he had got very far with the painful and somewhat unnecessary task, some good friend discovered what he was about and succeeded in persuading him from going any further with its commitment to memory.' Robert Spence Watson, *Joseph Skipsey: His Life and Work* (London, 1909), p. 20.

[32] Robert Smillie, *My Life for Labour* (London, 1924), p. 50.

real to me, and its characters changed from dusty puppets into men and women, fanatics and patriots, many of whom had died for their beliefs'. Like Smillie and Cooper, Clynes was able, when necessary, to turn his knowledge of Shakespeare to solid practical ends. At one point in his career as a trade union official, he was asked to negotiate with a man he characterizes as 'a particularly dogged employer of the old school'. Clynes takes up the story:

> With considerable persistence I succeeded in obtaining an interview with him. I quoted a line from *Much Ado About Nothing*, and he stared in astonishment. Then we plunged into a discussion about Shakespeare's comedies, which lasted us till luncheon was announced.
>
> Hearing the butler's voice, he started and dragged out a big gold watch.
>
> 'Tut, tut! I'd no idea the time had gone so quickly,' he said. 'You'll stay to lunch, of course!'
>
> Over the fish we commenced a new argument about Shakespeare's value as a historian and, later, my host queried a remark of mine that I knew certain scenes from some of the historical plays off by heart. So, when the coffee cups had been removed, I declaimed the whole of one longish scene from *Julius Caesar* to him.
>
> After that, I tactfully led back the conversation to the subject of the strike. It was speedily settled, and that night I was able to convey to the men the good news that the concessions for which they had decided to fight were granted.[33]

What we witness in this particular story is less the programmatic deployment of Shakespeare for political ends than the ability of the Shakespeare text to serve as a common ground on which representatives of two distinct strata within society can meet and negotiate, both culturally and in more pragmatic, quotidian terms. The story indicates the extent to which Shakespeare had, over the course of the century, become a common cultural property. It would be wrong, of course, to suggest that this position had been achieved exclusively by the wider dissemination of printed texts and their consumption by a readership which extended gradually downward to encompass an expanding working-class element. As scholars such as Richard Foulkes and Richard Schoch have indicated, theatre – both in its orthodox and its burlesque traditions – also played an important role in broadening Shakespeare's appeal in this period, and we should perhaps note here John Clare's famous comment that the 'common people' know 'the name of Shakspeare as a great play writer, because they have seen him nominated as such in the bills of strolling-players, who make shift with barns for theatres'.[34] It does seem clear, however, that the expansion of a working class readership was certainly an important factor in establishing Shakespeare's central position within a populist cultural field in the nineteenth century.

If it is accepted that Shakespeare had a broad-based appeal in this period, it also seems clear that the cross-class appreciation of the playwright's work began to break down somewhere around the turn of the century. Thus Jonathan Rose observes that 'If Shakespeare still had a proletarian following in the nineteenth century, it melted away in the twentieth.'[35] The reasons for this decline are complex. I have related the rise in Shakespeare's popularity among a working class readership specifically to the gradual expansion of educational provision among the poor from the close of the eighteenth century through the early to middle decades of the nineteenth century. It is tempting to tie the decline in Shakespeare's broad-based popularity to the changes in educational culture which occurred as the century progressed. The history of educational provision across this entire period is one of increased formalization, as the system was brought more and more within the remit of government control. By 1862, with increasing amounts of public money going to subsidise the church schools, the government introduced a system of 'payment

---

33 Clynes, *Memoirs*, p. 49, 80–1.

34 See Richard Foulkes, *Performing Shakespeare in the Age of Empire* (Cambridge, 2002) and Richard Schoch, *Not Shakespeare: Bardolatry and Burlesque in the Nineteenth Century* (Cambridge, 2002). John Clare, 'Popularity in Authorship', *European Magazine*, Nov. 1825, reprinted in J. W. and Anne Tibble (eds.), *The Prose of John Clare* (London, 1951), p. 256.

35 Jonathan Rose, *The Intellectual Life of the British Working Classes* (New Haven, 2002), p. 124.

by results'. The system enforced a testing regime which, as John Burnett has observed, had the effect of 'turning the teacher into a grant-earning instructor rather than an educator'. As Burnett explains,

> The effects on children were to emphasize mechanical drilling of the three Rs, to restrict the curriculum, and, often, to vitiate relationships between teachers and pupils since teachers had little choice but to try to earn the maximum grant – by threat, by punishment, even by bringing sick children into school on examination day if they were likely to win points.[36]

At the beginning of the next decade, the 1870 Education Act sought to plug the gaps in the provision offered by the church schools and effectively for the first time established a government-regulated national school system. Having been born in the year before the act was passed J. R. Clynes was among the very first batch of students to go through the reconfigured system and his experience of the new educational regime was certainly not positive. He writes of 'the everlasting pressure that education seemed to exert to prevent me from thinking for myself' and he recalled 'the drudgery of repeating one passage [of poetry] or another till it became a mere meaningless chant'.[37]

It would be possible to envisage an argument suggesting that, as part of this ongoing process of standardizing education and making it amenable to regimes of testing and assessment, the dead hand of formalized, examination-orientated education fell on Shakespeare, killing off any possibility of his sustaining his broad-based audience. This is effectively the argument which Rose makes when he observes that 'a bureaucratized system of compulsory education reduced Shakespeare to tedious classroom drill'.[38] The facts, however, do not seem quite to square with this view. John Roach has described public examinations as 'one of the great discoveries of nineteenth-century Englishmen' and it is certainly true to say that Shakespeare was folded into what could be a numbing culture of formal examinations from a relatively early date.[39] From the late 1850s, both Oxford and Cambridge became involved in administering exams to secondary school students and Shakespeare was included in the syllabus of these exams pretty much from the first. However, the relevance of the Oxford and Cambridge exams specifically to working-class students is difficult to establish. Such students were much more likely to have been confined to the basic elements of assessment imposed by the 'payment by results' scheme, which ran through to 1897. Shakespeare only became an explicit, formal part of this assessment regime in 1882, when students in Standard VI were required to be able to 'read a passage from one of Shakespeare's historical plays or from some other standard author, or from a history of England'. But there are a couple of additional points that need to be made here. Standards V and VI equated roughly to students in the age bracket of ten years or older. But this was, effectively, the threshold age at which children could opt to leave school (or, more to the point, perhaps, it was the age at which parents could withdraw their children from education so that they could be placed in employment). School attendance up to age ten had been made compulsory in 1876 and the age was not raised to eleven until 1893, rising again to twelve in 1899. It is, then, by no means certain quite how many working-class students would have found themselves encountering an assessment requirement specifically in Shakespeare in this period. This is borne out by examination statistics. In 1882, of the 3,500,000 children who were presented at the annual inspection, only 1.9 per cent entered and passed at Standard VI – the standard which required an ability to read from Shakespeare or another canonical author. Throughout the 1880s an average of no more than four Standard VI passes per year were being achieved in each inspected institution.[40]

---

[36] John Burnett, ed., *Destiny Obscure: Autobiographies of Childhood, Education and Family from the 1820s to the 1920s* (London, 1982), p. 150.

[37] Clynes, *Memoirs*, p. 31.

[38] Rose, *Intellectual*, p. 124.

[39] John Roach, *Public Examinations in England, 1850–1900* (Cambridge, 1971), p. 3.

[40] See David Vincent, *Literacy and Popular Culture, England 1750–1914* (Cambridge, 1989), pp. 90–1.

Drawing on these facts we might argue that, in a sense, it was not what we might call Shakespearian 'square-bashing' that drove children away from the playwright. The decline in Shakespeare's mass reading audience would seem to have something more to do with the changes in intellectual culture effected by the new educational regime. W. E. Adams was a life-long political activist, who lived to see the broadening of both the electoral franchise and the educational franchise. He was deeply disillusioned with the latter, observing that 'Nothing is more disappointing to early reformers than the comparatively little benefit that has accrued to society from the millions of money that have been spent and that are being spent on School boards and Board Schools.'[41] Adams himself belonged to one of those earlier nineteenth century generations for whom a small amount of basic education paved the way to greater things. Successor generations at the latter end of the century received more in the way of education but, paradoxically perhaps, it was of a kind that was less likely to spur them on to greater intellectual achievements. Thus, tracking the history of working class autobiography in the nineteenth century, Burnett observes that these 'writings demonstrate a contrast between the struggles and sacrifices of highly motivated individuals for education and self-improvement in the earlier part of the century and the more passive acceptance of the majority when schooling became compulsory after 1876'.[42]

There is another factor here, which has been identified by David Vincent in *Literacy and Popular Culture*, and that is the fact that, from the closing decades of the nineteenth century, elevated levels of working class literacy were beginning to be served by new sets of publishing materials. Vincent argues that

> Football, and in particular, gambling on racing, which became the great passions of the male urban working class during the last quarter of the nineteenth century, were quintessential products of the era of mass communication. . . . From the 1880s football and horseracing exploited and in turn sustained popular sporting journalism in the form of supplements to Saturday papers, extensive coverage in the cheap Sundays, and nationally circulating weeklies. The new sports needed the speedy dissemination of their time-tables and results, and the press required the rapidly improving transport and telegraph systems. What brought them together was the enlarged reading public, attuned to the discipline and regularity of organised sport, and prepared to participate in it through the medium of the printed word.[43]

My intention here is not to suggest that the decline in Shakespeare's broad popularity can be attributed simplistically to the rise of professional football, horseracing and other sports, but Vincent's argument does have a certain force and logic to it. If working-class readers in the latter end of the nineteenth century found themselves diverted towards alternative forms of reading matter, then the effect was to create a cultural split, whereby Shakespeare was likely to drift from the mainstream to what would become a newly constituted realm of elite culture. (And it might be noted here in passing that it is precisely at this time that Shakespeare is starting to move into higher education.[44]) At the same time, of course, as Richard Foulkes has indicated, developments in the theatre were running in a parallel direction. Foulkes charts the decline of a populist theatrical Shakespeare within roughly the same timeframe, tying it to a late nineteenth century division between traditionalists and progressives. He argues that

---

41 Adams, *Memoirs*, II, p. 584.

42 Burnett, *Destiny*, p. 168.

43 Vincent, *Literacy*, p. 190.

44 To take just a couple of simple illustrative examples: it is in this period that the editing of Shakespeare moves from the realm of the gentleman scholar to that of professional academics, starting with the significantly named 'Cambridge' edition of 1863–6; it is also in this period that the first chairs in English literature are established at English universities – Henry Morley, who edited all of Shakespeare's plays for Cassell's National Library, was appointed to a lectureship in English at King's College, London in 1857, becoming Professor of English at University College, London nine years later and simultaneously occupying a chair in English at Queen's College, London from 1878. On the Cambridge edition, see *Shakespeare in Print*, pp. 202–6; on Morley, see Henry Shaen Solly, *Life of Henry Morley* (London, 1898).

> Shakespeare traditionalists, working on commercial lines, had basically served public taste, though often giving it a nudge and a jolt in the process. Since their production methods were costly they necessarily sought to attract large and socially diverse audiences for long runs. The progressives, opting for simpler staging, set their sights on the more discerning playgoers, who could appreciate the artistic merit of what they saw.

The ultimate effect of this, Foulkes concludes, was that Shakespeare became 'an unapproachable icon, associated with high culture and erudition rather than the fount of popular entertainment'.[45]

What we witness, then, at the end of the century, is the emergence of a distinct split between an elite and a popular culture, with working-class readers and theatregoers increasingly failing to find their way to Shakespeare. Lawrence Levine traces the emergence of a similar schism at a broader level within the context of nineteenth-century American culture. For Levine, the crucial mechanism of this split is the progressive suppression of the communal response to culture in favour of the constrained and controlled response of the isolated individual. As he observes, the 'desire of the promoters of the new high culture [was] to convert audiences into a collection of people reacting *individually* rather than collectively'.[46] In studying developments in British politics in the nineteenth century, James Vernon has made what might be seen as an interestingly analogous argument. The nineteenth century was, of course, the great era of reform and many tangible political advances had been made by the reformists by the latter half of the century. Vernon has argued, however, that these advances were made at a price that has rarely been recognized. Where politics had been a communal affair before the great reformist advances, it increasingly became privatized in the wake of those advances. Thus, Vernon argues, 'Far from representing a triumphant march towards the model parliamentary democracy, nineteenth-century English politics witnessed the gradual and uneven closure of the public political sphere. In short, the invention of democracy in England turned upon a broadly liberal conception of politics as private, individualistic, and rational.' The emblematic instance of this for Vernon is the secret ballot, which brought to an end the carnivalesque communal ritual of the traditional hustings and associated public political events. Thus he argues that

> the introduction of the secret ballot in 1872 transformed the cultural poetics of elections. The public nomination, which had been the occasion on which the disenfranchised exercised most influence, was legislated out of existence and replaced by written nominations to the returning officer. The provision of a greater number of indoor polling booths also assured the dispersal of any potential crowd of people thereby reducing the risks of intimidation and disorder. In short, many of the electoral events which had previously afforded the disenfranchised their most powerful role were eroded or abolished.[47]

Vernon concludes that the effect of the Ballot Act was to secure 'the closing down of the public political sphere by officials who sought to replace the public and collective experience with an increasingly private and individual . . . one'.[48] So, just as Levine charts a privatization of culture, Vernon charts a privatization of politics.[49]

---

45 Foulkes, *Performing*, p. 206.

46 Lawrence W. Levine, *Highbrow/Lowbrow: The Emergence of Cultural Hierarchy in America* (Cambridge, MA, 1988), p. 195.

47 James Vernon, *Politics and the People: A Study of English Political Culture, c. 1815–1867* (Cambridge, 1993), pp. 160, 157–8.

48 Vernon, *Politics and the People*, p. 158. In fact the full quotation here reads 'to replace the public and collective experience with an increasingly private and individual *male* one' (my emphasis). A serious gap in this present article is the neglect of any consideration of the issue of gender and of how culture and politics played themselves out differently for men and for women. In terms of the immediate evidential bases of this present study, the issue of gender difference is difficult to access, given that the working-class autobiography is, in this period, overwhelmingly a male form (of the 136 autobiographies listed for the period 1790–1850 by David Vincent in *Bread, Knowledge and Freedom: A Study of Nineteenth-Century Working Class Autobiography* (London, 1981), only six are identifiably by women writers, and only two of these are book-length works). Further work on this issue is, however, clearly needed.

49 A neat illustration of the ongoing process of compartmentalization and social fragmentation is provided by the Bolton union organizer Alice Foley who, early in the twentieth century, as she called from door to door pursuing her union

Coming back again finally to Shakespeare, we can say that, by the beginning of the twentieth century, his popular audience had begun to fall away, as his text, both as read and as performed, had begun to drift into the space of elite culture. At the same time, as the enjoyment of such culture became a private affair, his work began also to drift out of the sphere of a public politics that was itself also becoming increasingly privatized. So if Shakespeare was deprived of a popular audience he was also, we might say, increasingly deprived of the kind of political purchase that he held for many nineteenth-century working-class readers.

These shifts are, of course, never wholly decisive: any attempt to map strong chronological breaks on to cultural history are inevitably vulnerable to the evidence of counter-instances. And counter-instances there certainly are: Jonathan Rose himself notes the case of Nancy Sharman (b. 1925), who

> recalled that her mother, a Southampton charwoman, had no time to read until during her last illness, at age fifty-four. Then she devoured the complete works of Shakespeare, and 'mentioned pointedly to me that if anything should happen to her, she wished to donate the cornea of her eyes to enable some other unfortunate to read'.[50]

Jenny Lee, a Labour MP born in Fife in 1904, who became Britain's first Arts minister under Harold Wilson, recalled receiving a complete works of Shakespeare from her coalminer father for her tenth birthday – an experience which had real resonance for her husband, Aneurin Bevan (founding father of the British welfare state).[51]

Such counter-evidence notwithstanding, it seems clearly to be the case that, after about 1900, a combination of educational, cultural and political shifts led to Shakespeare falling away from a truly central position within the general field of popular culture and the realm of progressivist popular politics. Certainly, as the new century advanced, Thomas Cooper – autodidact Shakespeare lover and Shakespearian political activist – began increasingly to look like a curiously anomalous figure.

---

duties, found herself increasingly confronted with the new technology of the 'yale lock', then replacing the traditional simple door latch: 'I recall quite vividly standing on doorsteps and gazing at those curious brass key-holes, feeling somewhat rebuffed, but not impatient, for I was aware that the simple gadget afforded a measure of needed privacy to its inmates. All the same, in an odd way, I regretted this element of human separation that had begun to dim, or quench, the warm, close intimacy of the street community of childhood days.' Alice Foley, *A Bolton Childhood* (Manchester, 1973; reissued Bolton, 1990), p. 77.

50 Rose, *Intellectual*, p. 5.

51 A conversation with Lee recalled by Sir John Drummond in an interview on *Cultural State*, programme 3 ('Ministers of Taste'), BBC Radio 4, 20 September 2004.

# VIRGINIA WOOLF READS SHAKESPEARE: OR, HER SILENCE ON MASTER WILLIAM

JULIA BRIGGS

If [the] number 18 [bus] still runs, let us take it, when the owling time is at hand, down to London Bridge. There is a curious smell in this part of the world, of hops, it may be; & also a curious confraternity . . . The gulls are swooping; & some small boys paddle in the pebbles. Above the sky is huddled & crowded with purple streamers . . . because it was here that the Globe stood.[1]

Near the end of her life, probably in January 1941, Virginia Woolf tried once again to make her way to the Globe theatre, to net Shakespeare in a web of words; yet even before she began, she experienced a sense of defeat:

One reason why Shakespeare is still read is simply the inadequacy of Shakespearian criticism . . . it is always autobiographical criticism. It is a commonplace to say that every critic finds his own features in Shakespeare. His variety is such that every one can find scattered here or there the development of some one of his own attributes. The critic then accents what he is responsive to, and so composes his own meaning, in Shakespeares words . . . But there always remains something further . . . that lures the reader. And it is this quality that finally eludes us, gives him his perpetual vitality, he excites perpetual curiosity. . . . One reading always supercedes another. Thus the truest account of reading Shakespeare would be not to write a book with beginning middle and end; but to collect notes, without trying to make them consistent.[2]

Which is largely what she did.

In this unrevised paragraph from an unwritten book, to be entitled 'Reading at Random', or perhaps 'Turning the Page', Woolf represents Shakespeare as at once mirror and mystery. She attempts to stalk her elusive subject through a series of drafts, but the essay devoted to Shakespeare continued to elude her. She felt defeated by the weight of what had already been said, as she had admitted fifteen years earlier in her essay 'On Being Ill', which argues that the recklessness of illness is essential to break down the barriers between Shakespeare and the reader:

his fame intimidates and bores . . . Shakespeare is getting flyblown; a paternal government might well forbid writing about him, as they put his monument at Stratford beyond the reach of scribbling fingers. With all this buzz of criticism about, one may hazard one's conjectures privately, make one's notes in the margin, but, knowing that someone has said it before, or said it better, the zest is gone.[3]

---

[1] Transcribed from Woolf's notes by Brenda R. Silver, in '"Anon" and "The Reader": Virginia Woolf's Last Essays', *Twentieth Century Literature*, 25 (1979), 434 (with my minor expansions). As Silver points out, Woolf did indeed visit London on 13 January 1941, probably the same times as she made this note. She 'went to London Bridge' and 'looked at the river; very misty; some tufts of smoke, perhaps from burning houses'. Her diary entry (for 'Wednesday 15 January' 1941) mourns for the destruction of London in the Blitz, and reflects on the death of James Joyce at Zurich, also on 13 January. On Woolf's readings of Shakespeare, see Alice Fox's chapter in *Virginia Woolf and the Literature of the English Renaissance* (Oxford, 1990), pp. 94–158; Christine Froula, 'Virginia Woolf as Shakespeare's Sister: Chapters in a Woman Writer's Autobiography', in Marianne Novy, ed., *Women's Re-Visions of Shakespeare* (Urbana, 1990), pp. 123–42.

[2] Brenda Silver, '"Anon" and "The Reader"', pp. 431–2.

[3] 'On Being Ill', Virginia Woolf, *Collected Essays*, vol. 4, ed. Leonard Woolf (London, 1967), p. 200; his note, that the essay was first published in 1930 (as a Hogarth Press pamphlet),

Woolf's difficulties with Shakespeare were deeply rooted, going back to her childhood where Shakespeare had been part of the literary world inhabited by her elder brother and her father. Leslie Stephen was a professional literary biographer and a founding editor of the *Dictionary of National Biography*, though it was his co-editor, Sidney Lee, who contributed the life of Shakespeare (Lee's massive two-volume life grew out of that initial research).[4] As a young woman, Virginia Stephen had felt daunted by all those 'lives of great men'; her response anticipates that of the feminist Julia Hedge, who, in *Jacob's Room*, sits beneath the dome of the British Museum Reading Room reading the names of authors written around it in gold letters – Shakespeare's, of course, among them: 'the names of great men which remind us – "Oh damn," said Julia Hedge, "why didn't they leave room for an Eliot or a Brontë?"'[5]

Woolf began work on 'Reading at Random' in the autumn of 1940, as she was writing the unfinished memoir now known as 'A Sketch of the Past'. There, she recalled her initial difficulties with Shakespeare and how she and her older brother Thoby had disagreed about the plays:

> A play was antipathetic. How did they begin? With some dull speech; about a hundred miles from anything that interested me. I opened [*Twelfth Night*] to prove this; I opened at 'If music be the food of love, play on . . .' I was downed that time. That was, I had to admit, a good beginning.[6]

Their letters continue the debate. Virginia read *Cymbeline* (then very much admired, in the wake of Swinburne's enthusiasm), finding herself as exasperated by the characters as she was entranced by their language:

> Why aren't they more human? Imogen and Posthumous and Cymbeline – I find them beyond me – Is this my feminine weakness in the upper region? But really they might have been cut out with a pair of scissors – as far as mere humanity goes – Of course they talk divinely. I have spotted the best lines in the play – almost in any play I should think – Imogen says – Think that you are upon a rock, and now throw me again! And Posthumous answers – Hang there like fruit, my Soul, till the tree die. Now if that doesn't send a shiver down your spine, even if you are in the middle of cold grouse and coffee – you are no true Shakespearian![7]

Was Shakespeare too difficult for women to understand? Woolf's complex, and at times uneasy relationship with Shakespeare is reflected in a series of divagations, rejections and rediscoveries that closely parallels her retrospective relationship with her Victorian parents, and what they stood for – a simpler, more ideal and more romantic vision of the world than she normally allowed herself, an outlook that risked becoming 'sentimental'. *To the Lighthouse* is the novel that depicts her parents and herself as a child, a novel she feared might also be regarded as 'Sentimental? Victorian?'[8] In a scene at the end of the first part, 'The Window', Mr and

---

overlooks its earliest publication in T. S. Eliot's *New Criterion* for January 1926 – see Andrew McNeillie's note to the earlier text in his *Essays of Virginia Woolf*, vol. 4: 1925–8 (London, 1994), p. 327 (though I have cited the later version).

[4] For Sidney Lee's biographies of Shakespeare, see Samuel Schoenbaum, *Shakespeare's Lives* (Oxford, 1970), pp. 506–26, and for Virginia Stephen's response to Lee's life of Shakespeare, see her letter to Thoby Stephen, [May 1903], *The Flight of the Mind: The Letters of Virginia Woolf*, vol. 1, 1888–1912, ed. Nigel Nicolson (London, 1975), p. 77.

[5] *Jacob's Room*, 1922, ed. Sue Roe (London, 1992), p. 91, and see also p. 94, where the stones of the British Museum are bones covering 'Plato's brain and Shakespeare's'. These stones are protected by the Museum's night-watchmen, while 'the woman in the mews . . . cries all night long, "Let me in! Let me in!"'

[6] 'A Sketch of the Past', in Virginia Woolf, *Moments of Being: Unpublished Autobiographical Writings*, ed. Jeanne Schulkind (London, 1976), p. 139. This section of the text is dated 'October 12th 1940' and the first notes for 'Reading at Random' are dated 18 September 1940 – Silver, p. 356 (I have preferred the earlier version to that given in the revised edition of 1985).

[7] To Thoby Stephen, 5 Nov (1901), *Letters*, vol. 1, pp. 45–6; *Cymbeline*, 5.6.264–5 – in *Jacob's Room* (partly based on Thoby Stephen) Jacob's friend Cruttendon quotes this line as one of '"the three greatest things that were ever written in the whole of literature"', p. 110. The opening words of Fidele's dirge from the same play, 'Fear no more the heat of the sun', become a repeated refrain in *Mrs Dalloway*, where they comment on the death of the young.

[8] [Sunday 5 September 1926], *The Diary of Virginia Woolf*, vol. 3, 1925–30, ed. Anne Olivier Bell (London, 1980), p. 107.

Mrs Ramsay (portraits of Leslie and Julia Stephen, as Woolf readily admitted), sit together at the end of the day, each with a book in hand. Mr Ramsay is reading from Scott's novel *The Antiquary*. Mrs Ramsay is reading sonnet 98, – 'From you have I been absent in the spring':

> [she] raised her head . . . She was climbing up those branches, this way and that, laying hands on one flower and then another.
>
> Nor praise the deep vermilion in the rose,
>
> she read, and so reading she was ascending, she felt, on to the top, on to the summit. How satisfying! How restful! All the odds and ends of the day stuck to this magnet; her mind felt swept, felt clean. And then there it was, suddenly entire shaped in her hands, beautiful and reasonable, clear and complete, the essence sucked out of life and held rounded here – the sonnet.[9]

Their different reading experiences are subtly gendered: Mr Ramsay is reading prose, and participating vicariously in a masculine world of action – the drowning of Steenie – while Mrs Ramsay reads poetry as if climbing through the branches of the text, and enjoys a world of feeling – perhaps of feminine feeling? – exemplified by the Shakespeare sonnet. As Jane Marcus suggests in her subtle analysis of this scene, 'Mr Ramsay reads to find himself, Mrs Ramsay to lose herself.'[10]

This is a moment of brief but perfect poise and harmony, yet Shakespeare could have a very different significance for women, and indeed does so in a passage from the first draft of this novel. It occurs during the early stages of the family dinner party (near the end of 'The Window'), but was excluded from the final version (whereas the account of Mrs Ramsay reading sonnet 98 was added at a late stage and did not appear in the manuscript version). In this draft sequence, Shakespeare is absorbed into the misogyny of Charles Tansley, whose assertion 'Women can't write, women can't paint' threatens the painter Lily Briscoe, undermining her confidence when she most needs it. Her reaction takes the form of a soliloquy:

> Why, then, did one mind what [Charles Tansley] said, Lily Briscoe wondered. – insignificant as he was! O it's Shakespeare, she corrected herself – as a forgetful person entering Regent's Park, & seeing the Park keeper was coming toward her menacingly; might exclaim Oh of course I remember dogs must be on a lead! So Lily Briscoe remembered that every man has Shakespeare & women have not. What then could she say? inferior as she was; & was it not much easier to be inferior after all? – That is the whole secret of art, she thought to herself. To care for the thing: not for oneself: what does it matter whether I succeed or not?[11]

Here Shakespeare is cast as an official policing the park of literature. The imagery of Lily's soliloquy anticipates those scenes early in *A Room of One's Own* where the narrator is ordered off the college lawn by a Beadle and out of the Wren Library by a librarian because she is an outsider and a woman. Misogyny such as Charles Tansley's was the irritant that prompted Woolf to write *A Room*, where his sentence 'Women can't write, women can't paint' is translated into the assertion of an unidentified old gentleman, 'Cats do not go to heaven. Women cannot write the plays of Shakespeare'.[12]

These two episodes from *To the Lighthouse* point in opposite directions: Mrs Ramsay's reading of sonnet 98 suggests that Shakespeare supremely expressed the life of feeling and imagination that Woolf associated with her mother and herself, while Lily Briscoe's thoughts link Shakespeare with a territory exclusive to men, a parade ground for the masculine intellect. Was writing about

---

9 *To the Lighthouse* (1927), ed. Stella McNichol, intro. Hermione Lee (London, 1992), p. 131.

10 'Still Practice, A/Wrested Alphabet: Towards a Feminist Aesthetic', *Art & Anger: Reading Like A Woman* (Columbus, 1988), p. 246. The figure of a primeval 'woman in a tree' reappears in *Women & Fiction: the Manuscript Versions of 'A Room of One's Own'*, ed. S. P. Rosenbaum (Oxford, 1992), pp. 143, 144.

11 *To the Lighthouse: The Original Holograph Draft*, ed. Susan Dick (London, 1983), p. 136 (slightly simplified from Dick's transcript). Woolf originally wrote 'Hyde Park', and then altered it to 'Regents Park', perhaps, as Michael Dobson has suggested, because there were open-air performances of Shakespeare in Regents Park from as early as 1900.

12 *To the Lighthouse*, p. 94; *A Room of One's Own* (1929), with *Three Guineas*, ed. Michele Barrett (London, 1993), p. 42.

Shakespeare a form of trespassing, for Woolf? Taking up *Romeo and Juliet* as a young woman, she had wondered 'Who shall say anything of [it]? Do I dare?'[13] Is this the reason she never formally wrote about Shakespeare?

By the beginning of the twentieth century, the difficulties of doing so were almost as daunting as they are today: Shakespearian scholarship had become the 'Shakespeare industry', reflected in the mass and solidity, the monumental character of Sidney Lee's two-volume *Life*, while productions of the plays tended to be richly costumed, elaborately set, and often suggested Royal Academy paintings in their attention to physical (and naturalistic) detail. During the nineteenth century, scenes from Shakespeare had become particularly popular as subjects for paintings, so much so, indeed, that Katherine Mansfield in a moment of exasperation, exclaimed of Gertrude's curious account of Ophelia's death (so visually detailed, but so difficult to explain plausibly), 'Dear Shakespeare has been to the Royal Academy . . . for his picture'.[14]

The modernist project of demythologizing Shakespeare has continued to the present day, with occasional interruptions or backlashes, moments when a more dignified or a more patriotic version was called for. Oppressed by ancestral voices (amongst which Shakespeare's was the most pervasive), modernism had to confront the too familiar words, to rework the 'orts, scraps and fragments'[15] it had inherited. The process of interrogating those echoes was already under way when Virginia Woolf began writing. The ninth chapter of Joyce's *Ulysses*, the 'Scylla and Charybdis' chapter, is set in the National Library of Dublin, the repository of so many English words. Here the so-called Quaker librarian, Lyster, and his assistant, Mr Best, listen as Stephen Dedalus propounds his theories on Shakespeare, and argue with him about Wilde's *Portrait of Mr W. H.*, and the relative merits of Shakespeare's recent biographers, George Brandes, Frank Harris and, of course, Sir Sidney Lee. But before Stephen unveils his mystery, he evokes a little local colour:

> It is this hour of a day in mid June . . . The flag is up on the playhouse by the bankside. The bear Sackerson growls in the pit near it, Paris garden. Canvasclimbers who sailed with Drake chew their sausages among the groundlings.[16]

Stephen Dedalus rejects the romantic identification of Shakespeare with Hamlet, arguing that when Shakespeare wrote the play, he was too old to identify with the young prince just back from university. Associating the physical and metaphysical modes of begetting makes Shakespeare simultaneously the author of *Hamlet*, and the father of Hamnet, his real-life son. According to a long theatrical tradition, Shakespeare plays Hamlet's father's ghost,[17] a role that enables him to warn both his real and fictional sons against their mothers' infidelities. Through the figure of Stephen Dedalus, Joyce thus confronted Shakespeare as rival poet and ghostly (fore)father, while endowing him with his own methods of composition, for Joyce had drawn upon the narrative of his own life for 'Stephen Hero', and later, for *Portrait of the Artist as a Young Man* and *Ulysses*. Stephen's disquisition on Shakespeare's biography is thus self-reflexive. It is also retrospective in one sense, since (though he does not know it) Stephen is about to step down in favour of the more universal figure of Leopold Bloom

---

13 Cited by Alice Fox from Woolf's Holograph Reading Notes, Jan. 1909–March 1911, at the back of the holograph draft of *Night and Day*, in the Berg Collection of the New York Public Library, *Virginia Woolf and the Literature of the English Renaissance*, p. 98,

14 *The Critical Writings of Katherine Mansfield*, ed. Clare Hanson (Basingstoke, 1987), p. 120 (and see pp. 118–19 for Mansfield's hilarious account of her response to *All's Well that Ends Well*). Mansfield probably had John Millais's famous painting of Ophelia in mind.

15 Woolf uses this phrase in *Between the Acts* (1941), ed. Gillian Beer (London, 1992), p. 111 (and echoed on pp. 112 twice, 114 and 127), recalling 'The fractions of her faith, orts of her love, / The fragments, scraps, the bits and greasy relics, / Of her o'ereaten faith', *Troilus and Cressida*, 5.2.161–3.

16 *Ulysses*, ed. Hans Walter Gabler (London, 1986), p. 154, lines 154–7.

17 It derives from Nicholas Rowe's 'Account' of Shakespeare introducing his edition of the *Works* (1709), vol. 1, p. vi.

who materializes at the Library, at the end of the chapter.

While Joyce thus covertly acknowledged the autobiographical nature of his fiction, he also insisted upon the artist's necessary distance from his material – he must be god-like and stand back from his work, paring his fingernails.[18] T. S. Eliot declared that 'the more perfect the artist, the more completely separate in him will be the man who suffers and the mind which creates'.[19] The ninth chapter of *Ulysses* was published in the *Little Review* in May 1919. When Eliot reviewed J. M. Robertson's book *The Problem of Hamlet* for the *Athenaeum* in September of the same year, he recalled the debate in the National Library as he argued that Shakespeare's problem in *Hamlet* was that he had become too personally involved, had failed to establish the necessary artistic distance, to find what Eliot termed 'the objective correlative' for his emotions, with the result that the play was 'most certainly an artistic failure'.[20]

If *Hamlet* posed one sort of problem, *Henry V* created another: before the First World War, Henry V was widely regarded as the epitome of an English gentleman, though one Irish gentleman, W. B. Yeats, protested that he occasioned 'the admiration . . . that schoolboys have for the sailor or soldier hero of a romance in some boys' paper', and contrasted him unfavourably with Richard II, a version of the Yeatsian dreamer ('I cannot believe that Shakespeare looked on his Richard II with any but sympathetic eyes').[21] The disillusion brought by the War led to a new and very different interpretation of Henry V – as a callous hypocrite – from the poet and critic Gerald Gould.[22] For Virginia Woolf in her earliest novel *The Voyage Out* (begun in 1907, and completed in 1913, though not published until 1915), *Henry V* was still a touchstone for patriotism and Englishness. In this novel, Clarissa Dalloway and her husband Richard, a Tory MP, make their first appearance as absurd and sentimental imperialists, satirized for their chauvinism. At the end of the fourth chapter, as the sinister shape of the 'Dreadnought' battleship comes into sight, Clarissa squeezes the heroine's hand, demanding '"Aren't you glad to be English!"'[23]

Earlier, Mr Grice, the ship's steward, shows Clarissa his collection of sea creatures, while reciting in

> an emphatic nasal voice:
> Full fathom five thy father lies,
> 'A grand fellow, Shakespeare,' he said . . .
> Clarissa was so glad to hear him say so.
> 'Which is your favourite play? I wonder if it's the same as mine?'
> '*Henry the Fifth*,' said Mr Grice.
> 'Joy!' cried Clarissa, 'It is!'
> *Hamlet* was what you might call too introspective for Mr Grice, the sonnets too passionate; Henry the Fifth was to him the model of an English gentleman.[24]

As if to counterbalance this note of satire in her first novel, Shakespeare figures quite differently in Woolf's second novel, *Night and Day* (1919), where he is comfortably assimilated into the eccentric and feminine world of Mrs Hilbery, mother of the heroine, who sees her daughter as Rosalind, and herself as a Shakespearian fool:[25]

> Beginning with a perfectly frivolous jest, Mrs Hilbery had evolved a theory that Anne Hathaway had a way, among other things, of writing Shakespeare's sonnets, . . . she had come half to believe in her joke, which was, she said, at least as good as other people's facts . . . She had a plan . . . for visiting Shakespeare's tomb.[26]

---

18 'The artist, like the God of the creation, remains within or behind or beyond or above his handiwork, invisible, refined out of existence, indifferent, paring his fingernails', *A Portrait of the Artist as a Young Man* (1916), ed. Hans Walter Gabler (New York, 1993), p. 242, lines 1467–9.

19 'Tradition and the Individual Talent', *The Sacred Wood: Essays on Poetry and Criticism* (1920; London, 1976), p. 54.

20 'Hamlet and his Problems', *The Sacred Wood*, pp. 100–1, 98.

21 'At Stratford-on-Avon' (1901), W. B. Yeats, *Selected Criticism and Prose*, ed. A. N. Jeffares (London, 1980), pp. 99, 100.

22 Gerald Gould, 'A New Reading of *Henry V*', *The English Review*, 29 (1919), pp. 42–55; reprinted in '*Henry V*', *a Casebook*, ed. Michael Quinn (London, 1969), pp. 81–94.

23 *The Voyage Out* (1915), ed. Jane Wheare (London, 1992), p. 60.

24 *The Voyage Out*, p. 46.

25 *Night and Day* (1919), ed. Julia Briggs (London: Penguin, 1992), p. 260 (and see also, p. 146).

26 *Night and Day*, pp. 258–9.

Mrs Hilbery's jest (like Mrs Hilbery herself) was inspired by Anny Thackeray Ritchie, daughter of the great Victorian novelist, and elder sister of Leslie Stephen's first wife. 'Aunt Anny' was her father's biographer, and a novelist in her own right. When Samuel Butler was working on *Shakespeare's Sonnets Reconsidered* (1899), she had asked him 'O, Mr Butler, I hope you think they were written by Anne Hathaway to Shakespeare?' Her joke was in part an allusion to Butler's previous book, *The Author of the Odyssey* (1897), which had argued that the great Greek epic had been written by a woman (Butler, apparently, was not amused).[27]

In Woolf's novel, Mrs Hilbery sets off for Shakespeare's tomb, 'the heart of the civilized world','with a passion that would not have been unseemly in a pilgrim to a sacred shrine'. It seems that she is planning to dig up the tomb in search of the buried manuscripts of Anne Hathaway's sonnets – a scheme that threatens 'the safety of the heart of civilisation', through its challenge to the myth of the supreme male author.[28] At the novel's climax, Mrs Hilbery returns from Stratford weighed down by branches of laurel and garlands of spring flowers : '"From Shakespeare's tomb!" exclaimed Mrs Hilbery, dropping the entire mass upon the floor, with a gesture that seemed to indicate an act of dedication'.[29]

'Old gentlemen' were not slow to inform Mrs Woolf that leaves and flowers do not grow on Shakespeare's grave, but she refused to alter it – the scene was artistically right, if not precisely 'true to the facts'.

Gender complicated Woolf's response to Shakespeare, as did his appropriation for patriotic propaganda, and while the beauty of Shakespeare's language and the beauty of Shakespeare's landscapes always held a strong appeal for her, she was well aware that they could be exploited for unwelcome political ends. An uneasy blend of amusement and embarrassment is evident in a letter she wrote to Raymond Mortimer in the spring of 1926, when she and Leonard visited Cranbourne Chase for a short holiday. Here, they had found the woods carpeted with violets, and the cuckoo singing overhead. 'We stole off and were divinely happy for five days at Iwerne Minster, in a country, at a moment, which really made one almost ashamed of England being so English; and carpeting the woods, and putting cuckoos on trees, and doing exactly what Shakespeare says'[30] (she was thinking of the spring song at the end of *Love's Labour's Lost*). As the national poet, Shakespeare was also the poet of the English landscape. For Richard Jefferies, Shakespeare 'carries, as it were, armfuls of violets and scatters roses and golden wheat across his pages, which are simply fields written with human life'.[31]

During the First World War, Shakespeare had been invoked as a source of patriotic sentiments by a number of critics (as he would be again in the Second World War), among them, the Merton Professor of English Literature, Sir Walter Raleigh. Although he had taught her friend Lytton Strachey (who remembered him with affection), Woolf herself had felt revolted by Raleigh's enthusiasm for the War – '[w]hen the guns fired in August 1914 no one saluted them more rapturously than the Professor of English Literature at Oxford'.[32] Her dislike was intensified by reading his published letters for review during her visit to Cranbourne

---

[27] Desmond MacCarthy relates this anecdote in his Foreword to *Thackeray's Daughter: Some Recollections*, eds., Hester Thackeray Fuller, V. Hammersley (Dublin, 1951), p. 7. Butler's *Shakespeare's Sonnets Reconsidered* had been inspired by Wilde's *Portrait of Mr W. H.* (1889), which argued that the sonnets were written for a boy actor, Willie Hughes (or Hewes). Butler sought through contemporary records, and discovered a sea-cook of that name; in his account, Shakespeare loves the sailor but is betrayed by his coarseness.

[28] *Night and Day*, p. 364 (in *Women & Fiction*, Woolf would imagine an Amazonian tribe whose 'chief poetess, the poet Maya Hina [may be] the superior of Shakespeare', p. 55).

[29] *Night and Day*, p. 408.

[30] 27 April 1926, *Congenial Spirits: The Selected Letters of Virginia Woolf*, ed. Joanne Trautmann Banks (London, 1989), p. 207.

[31] *Jefferies' England*, ed. S. J. Looker (London: Constable, 1937), p. 256, cited by Peter Brooker and Peter Widdowson, 'A Literature for England', in *Englishness: Politics and Culture 1880–1920*, ed. Robert Colls and Philip Dodd (London, 1986), p. 131.

[32] 'A Professor of Life', *Vogue*, early May 1926, reprinted in *The Essays of Virginia Woolf*, vol. 4, 1925–8, ed. Andrew McNeillie (London, 1994), p. 346 ( McNeillie's notes provide further details of her indignation with Raleigh).

Chase. The same letter to Mortimer complains of 'that beast Walter Raleigh who fills my soul with loathing'. Her most recent novel *Mrs Dalloway* (1925) had alluded pointedly to the exploitation of Shakespeare to attract young men into the army (efforts in which Raleigh had been implicated). Septimus Warren Smith 'was one of the first to volunteer. He went to France to save an England which consisted almost entirely of Shakespeare's plays and Miss Isabel Pole in a green dress walking in a square'[33] (Miss Isabel Pole was his adult education tutor). Small wonder that with so many conflicting feelings – her pleasure in the spring woods, her disgust with Sir Walter Raleigh – she felt 'almost ashamed of England being so English' – it was, of course, a joke, a joke that exposes, (as jokes are inclined to), underlying tensions and self-divisions.

When Septimus Warren Smith returned shell-shocked from the War, his disillusion coloured his reading of Shakespeare. He saw '[h]ow Shakespeare loathed humanity – the putting on of clothes, the getting of children, the sordidity of the mouth and the belly! This was now revealed to Septimus; the message hidden in the beauty of words'.[34] *Mrs Dalloway* is, of course, the novel in which Clarissa and Richard Dalloway reappear, but now their 'Kensington' conventions and high Tory politics have been displaced onto more minor characters such as Hugh Whitbread, a stuffy official at 'the Palace', and Lady Bruton, who has somehow absorbed Shakespeare instinctively: her 'love for "this isle of men, this dear dear land" was in her blood (without having read Shakespeare)'.[35]

Woolf did not actually visit Stratford and Shakespeare's tomb until May 1934, when she and Leonard were motoring back from their first (and only) visit to Ireland, a visit that, given Ireland's recent troubled history, must have prompted thoughts about nationalism and its effects. She liked the town of Stratford, finding it surprisingly unspoiled, and imagined the spirit of Shakespeare close at hand, in the mulberry tree at New Place, where '[a]ll the flowers were out in Sh[akespea]re's garden . . . He is serenely absent-present; both at once; radiating round one; yes; in the flowers, in the old hall, in the garden; but never to be pinned down . . . there was no impediment of fame, but his genius flowed out of him, & is still there, in Stratford'.[36] If Shakespeare's spirit, hovered, an Ariel unconfined, around his birthplace, the aura of the national poet also imbued his native county: in January 1941, when the war was at its darkest, Woolf told her friend Ethel Smyth that London was her 'only patriotism: save one vision, in Warwickshire one spring when we were driving back from Ireland and I saw a stallion being led, under the may and the beeches, along a grass ride; and I thought that is England'.[37]

Woolf deeply distrusted patriotism and nationalism, believing they fomented wars; such feelings were particularly ill-suited to women living in a patriarchy, whose stake in society was significantly different from that of men. And just as gender affected or inflected her sense of patriotism, so it could not be kept entirely separate from her response to Shakespeare even though (as we have seen), she also read him as a writer who spoke directly to women through his insight into the inner life. Such conflicting responses waited to be reconciled.

From an early stage, no doubt encouraged by the *zeitgeist* and her friendships with Rupert Brooke and T. S. Eliot, Woolf had read widely among Shakespeare's contemporaries, writing essays on Elizabethan drama ('Notes on an Elizabethan Play'), as well as on Gabriel Harvey (in 'The Strange Elizabethans'), Sidney, Spenser, Donne, and more than once on Hakluyt, whom she had loved since

---

33 *Mrs Dalloway* (1925), ed. Stella McNichol, intro. Elaine Showalter (London, 1992), p. 94.

34 *Mrs Dalloway*, p. 97.

35 *Mrs Dalloway*, p. 198. The allusion is to John of Gaunt's speech, 'This royal throne of kings' (*Richard II* 2.1.40 ff., esp. 45, 57), a 'locus classicus' for patriotic sentiment (we are told on p. 115 that Lady Bruton 'never read a word of poetry herself'). For Richard Dalloway's youthful response to the Sonnets in this novel, see below, n. 43.

36 (Wednesday 9 May 1934), *The Diary of Virginia Woolf*, vol. 4 1931–5, ed. Anne Olivier Bell (London, 1982), p. 219–20.

37 12 Jan. 1941, '*Leave the Letters Till We're Dead: The Letters of Virginia Woolf*, vol. 6, 1936–41, ed. Nigel Nicolson, p. 460.

childhood. Yet there is no single essay devoted to Shakespeare, not, it seems, from any lack of enthusiasm on her part, nor from any shortage of invitations on the part of others – a letter to David Garnett politely thanks him for inviting her to do so, adding, by way of explanation, 'I have a kind of feeling that unless one is possessed of the truth, or is a garrulous old busybody, from America, one ought to hold one's tongue. So I will. I mean I wont. Send it [an unidentified book on Shakespeare] to Logan [Pearsall Smith] is what I mean, and take my blessing'.[38]

The closest she came to doing so was a review of Tyrone Guthrie's production of *Twelfth Night* at the Old Vic in September 1933, a piece written reluctantly and from a sense of duty, since Lydia Lopokova (now Lydia Keynes) was playing Olivia, in an attempt to convert her career as a dancer to that of an actress.[39] Woolf carefully avoided direct comment on Lopokova's performance by taking up the old debate on the difference between a play read and a play acted (Dr Johnson had claimed that '[a] play read affects the mind like a play acted'). The shortcomings of Lopokova's performance could thus be represented as resulting from the inevitable difference between a private reading and a public performance. Her review is so carefully worded that, at first glance, one might mistake it for praise.

One reason Woolf never wrote directly about Shakespeare was that for her, fiction usually came first and theory afterwards, and in dealing with controversial topics (such as sex or Shakespeare – or even both together), 'one cannot hope to tell the truth. One can only show how one came to hold whatever opinion one does hold . . . Fiction here is likely to contain more truth than fact'.[40] Yet the fiction which might have been expected from its title and historical moment to portray Shakespeare only does so obliquely: *Orlando: A Biography* begins as the story of a young man in love with a girl dressed as a boy, the story of a hero run mad for love (behind Shakespeare's choice of 'Orlando' as the name of the third son of Sir Rowland de Bois lay Ariosto's epic, *Orlando Furioso* – Orlando maddened).[41]

*Orlando* can be read as an act of homage to Woolf's androgynous aristocratic friend Vita Sackville-West or even to Shakespeare, the dramatist whose comedies celebrate the possibilities of gender change and fluidity, yet if so both 'begetters' are notable for their absence, though they are never very far off. But if Shakespeare is absent, or very nearly so, his dark shadow, the Salieri to his Amadeus, is present in the character of Nick Greene, almost (if not quite) the rival playwright and pamphleteer Robert Greene. For Nick Greene in Woolf's novel, the writing of the modern age – of any modern age – is to be deplored. The envious Greene becomes Orlando's treacherous pensioner, his overweaning protégé.[42]

At the heart of Woolf's novel lies the identity of Orlando with Woolf's beloved Vita, and the unspoken (because at that time unspeakable) history of their friendship (Radclyffe Hall's novel of lesbian love, *The Well of Loneliness*, was prosecuted in November 1928, a month after *Orlando*'s publication). With this open secret at its heart, the text makes great play with disguise and concealment, with masks and masquing. In an episode later abandoned, Greene gives Orlando a letter he just happens to have on him – it is 'Shakespeares own account of his relations with that Mr W. H. & the dark Lady written by him with great fulness &

[38] Sunday [10 December 1933], '*The Sickle Side of the Moon: The Letters of Virginia Woolf*, vol. 5, 1932–5, ed. Nigel Nicolson (London, 1979), p. 257.

[39] '*Twelfth Night* at the Old Vic', *New Statesman & Nation*, 30 September 1933, pp. 385–6, reprinted in *Collected Essays*, vol. 1, ed. Leonard Woolf (London, 1966), pp. 28–31. Woolf referred to it as 'Lydia's extortion' in *Diary*, vol. 4 (Saturday 23 September (1933), p. 179), and see her letter to Quentin Bell, Tuesday 19 September 1933, *Letters*, vol. 4, p. 227.

[40] *A Room of One's Own* (1929), with *Three Guineas*, ed. Michele Barrett (London, 1993), p. 4.

[41] As Woolf indirectly acknowledged in a passage cut from the published text that records the contents of Orlando's library as 'Petrarch; Bocaccio; Ariosto;' – see *Orlando: The Holograph Draft*, ed. S. N. Clarke (London, 1993), p. 145.

[42] He is also the contemporary critic Edmund Gosse, as Vita told her husband Harold Nicolson in a letter of 11 October 1928, – see Victoria Glendinning, *Vita: The Life of V. Sackville-West* (New York, 1983), p. 202.

spirit.' But instead of relating its contents, the narrator consigns it to the fire, on the grounds that 'when Truth and modesty conflict (as they so often do) who can doubt which should prevail? . . . No one of British blood will censure us for the course we took; & as for the rest, their opinions on a matter of this sort, scarcely matter.' Thus, an officious – and properly 'British' – propriety deprives the reader of a possible solution to the most notorious of all literary mysteries.[43]

Greene was not the only Elizabethan pamphleteer to figure in *Orlando*: Thomas Dekker's 'The Great Frost or Cold Doings in London, except it be at the Lottery' provided Woolf with an unforgettable vision of London and the River Thames in the grip of the Great Frost of 1608, – which parallels the frozen passion that grips Orlando. For those brief weeks, it possesses him, as he and Sasha sweep and swoop over the ice. As it thaws, her love melts, carrying Sasha back to Muscovy and Orlando into the frenzy of grief that links him to Ariosto's hero (a frenzy anticipated by seeing a performance of *Othello* on the ice[44]).

Orlando – both the character and the novel – are haunted by a mysterious figure glimpsed when Queen Elizabeth visits Orlando's great house, a house never named, just as this figure is never named (his identity is confined to the liminal column of the index).[45] Glancing into the housekeeper's sitting-room as he passes, Orlando catches sight of 'a rather fat, rather shabby man' in a dirty ruff, holding a pen in his hand. He 'seemed in the act of rolling some thought up and down, to and fro in his mind till it gathered shape or momentum to his liking. His eyes, globed and clouded like some green stone of curious texture, were fixed. He did not see Orlando . . . the man turned his pen in his fingers . . . and gazed and mused; and then, very quickly, wrote half-a-dozen lines and looked up.' His vision haunts Orlando for the rest of his/her life,[46] perhaps as it had haunted Woolf herself, for ten years earlier, in the first short story she wrote for the Hogarth Press, she imagined just such a figure sitting in an arm-chair and gazing into the fire (as she herself is doing), while '[a] shower of ideas fell perpetually from some very high Heaven down through his mind. He leant his forehead on his hand, and people, looking in through the open door –' (as Orlando would later do).[47] Woolf's next novel, *The Waves*, is similarly haunted by a vision of an unidentified writer – the lady of Elvedon, who 'sits between the two long windows, writing'.[48]

To discover the nature of the relationship between the stranger in Mrs Stewkley's parlour and his female equivalent, the absent figure of Vita or Orlando herself, we must turn to Woolf's next book, her polemic, *A Room of One's Own*, a book unexpectedly twinned with *Orlando* in terms of theme and construction. Where *Orlando* had dramatized the difficulties encountered by the woman artist, *A Room of One's Own* theorizes them, and it is here that Woolf finally confronts the old gentleman's assertion that 'Cats do not go to heaven. Women cannot write the plays of Shakespeare.'[49] Woolf's work up to this point had in various ways been asking 'To whom does Shakespeare belong? To men or to women?' The conclusion she reached lies in the unexpected connection she now found between the two absent presences of *Orlando*. Orlando – like Vita (or Shakespeare), was a poet, and as a poet, s/he was marked out by the quality that also characterizes Vita and Shakespeare – that is, a refusal to be pinned down, to be

43 *Orlando: The Holograph Draft*, p. 72 – the theme of homosexual desire gives the sonnets a special relevance to *Orlando*; see also *Mrs Dalloway*, where the young Richard at Bourton 'got on his hind legs and said that no decent man ought to read Shakespeare's sonnets because it was like listening at keyholes (besides, the relationship was not one that he approved)', p. 82.

44 *Orlando* (1928), ed. Brenda Lyons, intro. Sandra Gilbert (London, 1993), pp. 40–1.

45 *Orlando*, p. 230.

46 *Orlando*, p. 16, and see also pp. 56, 116–17, 215–16, 226.

47 'The Mark on the Wall', *The Complete Shorter Fiction of Virginia Woolf*, ed. Susan Dick (London, 1989), p. 85.

48 *The Waves* (1931), ed. Kate Flint (London, 1992), p. 11 (memories of her return at pp. 18, 93, 147, 164, 185, 191, 196, 206).

49 *A Room of One's Own*, p. 42 (though cats 'have, he added, souls of a sort').

confined, and in particular to be confined to a single gender role. Shakespeare, like Vita, and like Orlando, is androgynous. Coleridge, greatest of all Shakespearian critics, had observed that 'a great mind is androgynous'.[50] Here lay the explanation for Shakespeare's plenitude: 'If ever a human being got his work expressed completely, it was Shakespeare. If ever a mind was incandescent, unimpeded . . . it was Shakespeare's mind.'[51] '[Coleridge] meant, perhaps, that the androgynous mind is resonant and porous; that it transmits emotion without impediment; that it is naturally creative, incandescent and undivided. In fact, one goes back to Shakespeare's mind as the type of the androgynous, of the man–womanly mind.'[52] Shakespeare, in other words, is Orlando's ideal/ized double (as Nick Greene is Shakespeare's darker shadow).

But Woolf hadn't quite finished with the old gentleman, the cats that don't go to heaven and the women who cannot write Shakespeare's plays. Unexpectedly, she now agrees that the old gentleman was 'right at least in this; it would have been impossible, completely and entirely, for any woman to have written the plays of Shakespeare in the age of Shakespeare', an age when women had little status and no history, for 'nothing is known about women before the eighteenth century'.[53] This explains why Orlando cannot become a woman until then, and her first incarnation must inevitably be as a man. Now, in an act of imaginative resistance, Woolf invents another double for Orlando (and perhaps for Shakespeare too) in the form of Shakespeare's imaginary sister Judith who aspires to become a playwright. Her history is not so much a blank as a series of disasters, – and that echo of Viola in *Twelfth Night* is deliberate, since the invention of Judith Shakespeare as a kind of extension of her more famous brother echoes Shakespeare's own invention in *Twelfth Night*, when he transforms the androgynous Viola/Cesario into the heavenly twins, Viola and Sebastian, in order to untie the play's love-knot.

Judith Shakespeare flees from her parental home at Stratford to London and the playhouses, hoping to become an actress and a writer. There, she is inevitably seduced by the odious Nick Greene (familiar from *Orlando*), and finds herself pregnant. She, for 'who shall measure the heat and violence of the poet's heart when caught and tangled in a woman's body? – killed herself one winter's night and lies buried at some cross-roads where the omnibuses now stop outside the Elephant and Castle'.[54] Judith Shakespeare's dark fate no doubt precluded her from figuring in the essentially comic narrative of *Orlando*, though her close connections with that novel and its hero are reflected in the structural similarities between the two books. Judith Shakespeare appears and dies at the heart of chapter 3 of *A Room*, at a point closely corresponding to Orlando's sex-change at Constantinople, in chapter 3 of the earlier novel. Judith Shakespeare is thus Orlando's sixteenth-century female self, frustrated and finally destroyed by the patriarchal culture of her time. But even now, Woolf hasn't quite finished with her – she must undergo a further transformation. Though 'despised and rejected' in her first incarnation, 'the dead poet who was Shakespeare's sister will put on the body which she has so often laid down'; 'she will be born',[55] she will come again, and women must wait and work for her second coming.

The invention of Shakespeare's sister suggests a fundamental difference between Woolf and Joyce in their responses to the complex balance of threat and inspiration that Shakespeare constituted for

[50] *A Room of One's Own*, p. 88 (see Coleridge's *Table Talk*, 1 September 1832).

[51] *A Room of One's Own*, p. 52 – these sentences may be Woolf's response to Eliot's critique of *Hamlet*.

[52] *A Room of One's Own*, p. 89.

[53] *A Room of One's Own*, p. 42. We now know that Woolf's assumption was wrong, but in making it, she urged her young women listeners to go out and find out more about women's history – our knowledge is in part the result of their having followed her instructions.

[54] *A Room of One's Own*, p. 44 (the crossroads are conveniently close to the Old Vic, with its long tradition of Shakespearian performance).

[55] *A Room of One's Own*, pp. 102–3.

each of them. Though both responded through fiction, they did so in diametrically opposed ways, and along contrasting axes. The 'Scylla and Charybdis' chapter begins with Lyster talking of Goethe as 'a great brother poet',[56] yet Joyce read his relationship with Shakespeare in terms of father and son, on what is essentially a 'vertical' axis. Shakespeare plays the ghost that haunts his son, and Stephen identifies with young Hamlet. Though Stephen tosses in an argument about Shakespeare's brothers, Gilbert and the more sinister Edmund and Richard,[57] it is the impact of his father that predominates, while old Hamlet is obscurely linked with Simon Dedalus, another primal story-teller, according to the opening lines of *Portrait of the Artist*. The ghost of old Hamlet suggests the Oedipal anxieties involved in resisting a father's influence, for Freud has also made a contribution to Joyce's reading. And if the tensions between father and son determine Stephen's relationship with Shakespeare, it is further complicated by nationality, so that his language is and is not Shakespeare's.[58]

While Joyce's relationship with Shakespeare is problematized by race and nationality, Woolf's is complicated by gender – 'Women cannot write the plays of Shakespeare', so is there any point in trying? Unlike that of Joyce, Woolf's relationship to Shakespeare lies along a horizontal, rather than a vertical axis: despite her own writing father, she sees herself not as Shakespeare's daughter but his sister. Unlike Eliot, she refuses to be fazed by the problems of Hamlet. 'If you find *Hamlet* difficult, ask him to tea. He is a highbrow. Ask Ophelia to meet him. She is a lowbrow. Talk to them as you talk to me.'[59] Shakespeare is Judith's older brother – and this was also true of her personal experience, since Shakespeare had played a key role in her relationship with her older brother Thoby, who died young in 1906 and whose death is mourned in *Jacob's Room* and *The Waves*. Thoby had 'consumed Shakespeare, . . . had possessed himself of it'. It was 'his other world' – and Woolf echoed Hamlet's epitaph, 'Had he been put on, he would have proved most royally.'[60] Her arguments with him had had a further function, for they created a bond between them that had excluded Vanessa, Virginia's sister and beloved rival, from their conversation. Thus Shakespeare, for Virginia, was, from the beginning, bound up with sibling love and rivalry within the family.

So though in one sense, Woolf never wrote about Shakespeare, in another sense she never stopped writing about him, and he continued to hover 'serenely absent-present', as she had sensed at Stratford, until the end of her life. *The Waves*, partly inspired by sonnet 60, 'Like as the waves make toward the pebbled shore', and written as a series of dramatic soliloquies to an epic form and on an epic scale, is arguably Woolf's most Shakespearian work, but Shakespearian imagery and language run through her later novels. In the final section of *The Years*, North opens an unidentified book at random and reads '"The scene is a rocky island in the middle of the sea"' – a Victorian stage direction, it seems, for Act 1 Scene 2 of *The Tempest*,[61] and Shakespeare's 'last' play dominates Woolf's final novel, *Between the Acts*. Here Prospero is transformed into the stout middle-aged lesbian, Miss La Trobe (meaning 'finder' or 'inventor'), the artist as magician, yet, like Prospero, troubled and marginalized, presiding uneasily over a pageant that itself includes a scene from an imaginary Elizabethan play. As *The Tempest* does, *Between the Acts* adopts a unified time scheme and setting, and Woolf quietly acknowledges her debt at several points: 'Isa had done with her bills. Sitting in the shell of the room, she watched the pageant fade. The flowers flashed before they faded. She watched them flash.'[62]

---

56 *Ulysses*, p. 151, line 3 (Lyster refers to 'those priceless pages of *Wilhelm Meister*').

57 *Ulysses*, pp. 171–4.

58 In chapter 5 of *A Portrait* Stephen discusses the English language with the (English) dean, and thinks 'that the man to whom he was speaking was a countryman of Ben Jonson', p. 216, lines 551–2.

59 'Middlebrow' (written late October 1932), *Collected Essays*, vol. 2., ed. Leonard Woolf (London, 1966), p. 201.

60 'A Sketch of the Past', *Moments of Being*, ed. Jeanne Schulkind (London, 1985), pp. 138–9.

61 *The Years* (1937), ed. Jeri Johnson (London, 1998), p. 253.

62 *Between the Acts*, p. 128.

As always, Woolf's echo brings something new to her allusion, transforming and reactivating its words. If Woolf never wrote the essay on Shakespeare that we might have looked for, scattered throughout her writings, – her novels and essays, but in particular her diaries – a portrait of Shakespeare emerges – '[s]omewhere, everywhere, now hidden, now apparent in whatever is written down',[63] the result of a serious reading of one great writer by another. And, as one might have suspected, that reading is often formalist in its emphasis, exploring how it is that Shakespeare achieves his effects and wondering what might be learned from his example. In particular, as Woolf was working on the huge, and (as she felt) inchoate material that eventually became *The Years*, she wondered at the extraordinary ease with which Shakespeare apparently jumped from one mood and level of experience to another, from scenes of simple action to scenes of great inwardness – especially when she herself was finding it difficult to make such transitions.[64]

At other times, she abandons herself to an 'O altitudo!' as in this passage from her diary, written during the writing of *The Waves*:

I read Shakespeare *directly* I have finished writing, when my mind is agape & red & hot. Then it is astonishing. I never yet knew how amazing his stretch & speed & word coining power is, until I felt it utterly outpace & outrace my own, seeming to start equal & then I see him draw ahead & do things I could not in my wildest tumult & utmost press of mind imagine. Even the less known & worser plays are written at a speed that is quicker than anybody else's quickest; & the words drop so fast one can't pick them up. Look at this, Upon a gather'd lily almost wither'd (that is a pure accident: I happen to light on it.) Evidently the pliancy of his mind was so complete that he could furbish out any train of thought; &, relaxing lets fall a shower of such unregarded flowers. Why then should anyone else attempt to write. This is not 'writing' at all. Indeed, I could say that Sh[akespea]re surpasses literature altogether, if I knew what I meant.[65]

---

[63] Written of Sir Thomas Browne in 'Reading', *Collected Essays*, vol. 2, p. 29.

[64] See, for example, *Diary*, vol. 4, Thursday 17 April [1934], p. 207 – 'An idea about Sh[akespea]re . . . This is working out my theory of the different levels in writing, & how to combine them'.

[65] *Diary*, vol. 3, Sunday 13 April (1930), pp. 300–1. As a note points out, the quotation's from *Titus Andronicus*, 3.1.114, and the phrase 'my wildest tumult and utmost press of mind' deliberately echoes a favourite Shakespearian formula.

# SHAKESPEARE AND THE INVENTION OF THE EPIC THEATRE: WORKING WITH BRECHT

CHARLES EDELMAN

In David Lodge's novel *Small World*, the Irish scholar Perse McGarricle is unable to get his thesis about Shakespeare's influence on T. S. Eliot published, until having had a few drinks at a conference, he asserts that it is about 'the influence of Eliot on Shakespeare', explaining

> We can't avoid reading Shakespeare through the lens of T. S. Eliot's poetry. I mean, who can read Hamlet today without thinking of 'Prufrock'? Who can hear the speeches of Ferdinand in *The Tempest* without being reminded of 'The Fire Sermon' section of *The Waste Land*?[1]

In building on McGarricle's ground-breaking study, I hope to show that another great twentieth century poet and dramatist, Bertolt Brecht, had an even more profound influence on Shakespeare. Indeed, in writing the two parts of *Henry IV*, Shakespeare was the inventor of what Brecht and his colleague Erwin Piscator later called the 'epic theatre'.

I am far from the first to see Shakespeare as an epic dramatist, and the work of another distinguished critic – one who actually exists – needs to be acknowledged. In his delightful review of Harold Bloom's *Shakespeare: The Invention of the Human* for *The New Statesman*, Terence Hawkes writes:

> The concern of the so-called 'history plays', as well as of most of the others, is as much with public as with private matters: with politics, economic and social structure, the world of governance and power, and the stresses and strains inherent in the construction of the project called 'Great Britain'. They constitute what Brecht called 'epic' drama: its function to confront its audience with the 'outer' public world and to probe the insistent demands that that makes on any 'inner' private counterpart.[2]

## 'IT IS A KIND OF HISTORY'

(*The Taming of the Shrew*, Ind.2.136)

From neo-classicists such as Dr Johnson, who regards Prince Hal as 'the hero of both the comick and tragick part' to modern commentators such as David Scott Kastan, who expertly analyzes the interrelationship of the 'comic' and 'historical' scenes of *1 Henry IV*, critics have generally seen a mixing of genres as a key element of the structure of the *Henry IV* plays.[3] While undoubtedly justified, this view has its limitations: anyone who has acted in these plays would know that not all audiences agree on what is meant to be funny and what is meant to be serious. However, there is another structural pattern, one that can take us more deeply into how the plays operate: rather than alternating between the comic and the historical, they move between the past and the present.

Amongst the many faults Dr Johnson ascribes to Shakespeare is a lack of any clear sense of historical difference:

> He had no regard to distinction of time or place, but gives to one age or nation, without scruple, the customs,

1 David Lodge, *Small World* (London, 1984), p. 52.

2 *New Statesman*, 12 March 1999.

3 Samuel Johnson, *Johnson on Shakespeare*, ed. Arthur Sherbo (New Haven, 1968), p. 523; David Scott Kastan, ed., The Arden Shakespeare. King Henry IV, Part 1 (London, 2002), pp. 7–17.

institutions, and opinions of another, at the expence not only of likelihood, but of possibility. These faults Pope has endeavoured, with more zeal than judgement, to transfer to his imagined interpolators. We need not wonder to find Hector quoting Aristotle, when we see the loves of Theseus and Hippolyta combined with the Gothick mythology of fairies. Shakespeare, indeed, was not the only violator of chronology, for in the same age Sidney, who wanted not the advantages of learning, has, in his Arcadia, confounded the pastoral with the feudal times, the days of innocence, quiet and security, with those of turbulence, violence and adventure.[4]

Johnson finds another example of Shakespeare's violation of chronology in *1 Henry IV*: Hal's characterization of Douglas as 'he that rides at high speed and with his pistol kills a sparrow flying' (2.5.348–9). He comments,

> Shakespeare never has any care to preserve the manners of the time. 'Pistols' were not known in the age of Henry.[5]

Given that the events of *1* and *2 Henry IV* occur only two hundred years before the time of the plays' production, the anachronisms are not as obvious as we find in the Roman plays, such as Cassius observing that 'the clock hath stricken three' in *Julius Caesar* (2.1.192), but Johnson could have cited many others. Not only is there frequent mention of pistols, along with a *character* named Pistol, over a century before the wheel-lock pistol was known in Europe,[6] but what is Falstaff doing drinking sack?

Aside from explicit reference to actual events or people, anachronisms generally occur by reference to political, social, legal or religious institutions, inventions and other forms of technology, games and sports, articles of clothing, musical instruments and so on. One must be wary, however, of assuming that because something is given its modern, that is, Elizabethan, name, it cannot stand for something that existed earlier. It is no use insisting that Shakespeare should have written *Richard II* in Middle English.

In her *Stages of History*, Phyllis Rackin offers a fascinating overview of how the critical response to Shakespeare's use of anachronism has varied at different times, and goes on to note that 'anachronisms can disrupt the historical context to create direct confrontations between the past and the present . . . especially in conjunction with metadramatic allusions, [they] can also produce a kind of alienation effect'.[7]

But is Douglas's pistol an anachronism? Contrary to Dr Johnson, I would argue that in *1* and *2 Henry IV*, Shakespeare has *every* care to preserve the manners of the time, since that time is not exclusively the early fifteenth century of Henry IV and Hotspur: much of each play is set in Shakespeare's own time.

The *Henry IV* plays are written in two periods, and they are carefully divided. The episodes drawn from Holinshed and other chronicle sources are clearly and accurately set in the early 1400s, while those involving Falstaff and his gang provide a rare Shakespearian view into Shakespeare's own times – except for the brief Sly induction to *The Taming of the Shrew*, 'Shakespeare's England', so far as we are able to visit it in his plays, is 'Falstaff's England', in *1* and *2 Henry IV* and *The Merry Wives of Windsor*.

In all of *1* and *2 Henry IV*, there is only one clear intrusion from the early modern period into the late medieval world of the King and the Percies. When Prince Hal assures his brothers that they have nothing to fear from him, he compares himself with Sultan Murad III, who came to power in 1574:

> This is the English not the Turkish court;
> Not Amurath an Amurath succeeds,
> But Harry Harry. (*2 Henry IV* 5.2.47–9)

Otherwise, the past is shown with a clear sense of difference from the present.

Hotspur's account of the 'certain lord, neat and trimly dressed' (*1 Henry IV*, 1.3.32) who

---

[4] Johnson, p. 72.

[5] Johnson, p. 470.

[6] See Charles Edelman, *Shakespeare's Military Language: A Dictionary* (London, 2000), pp. 261 and 2. An impressive wheel-lock at the Art Institute of Chicago is dated 1589.

[7] Phyllis Rackin, *Stages of History: Shakespeare's English Chronicles* (London, 1990), p. 94.

> . . .'twixt his finger and his thumb he held
> A pouncet-box, which ever and anon
> He gave his nose and took 't away again –
> Who therewith angry, when it next came there
> Took it in snuff – and still he smiled and talked
> (1.3.37–40)

is usually considered to be a satire on the Elizabethan gentleman, which of course it is, but there is nothing in it that could not apply equally to 1402, the year of the Battle of Homildon. We think of taking snuff as being inextricably associated with tobacco but, as David Bevington notes in the Oxford edition, the snuffing of 'various roots, barks, [and] leaves'[8] is far older. Indeed, in Bartholomaeus Anglicus's *De Proprietatibus Rerum* (*c.* 1250), known to us chiefly through Trevisa's translation, we are advised that if cumin is 'ywette in vynegre and first yparched and yblowe into the nosethirls, it maketh a man snese'.[9]

Although *OED*'s first recorded use of 'pouncet box' is this very passage, aromatic powders, whose chief uses must have been in the kitchen and for perfuming clothes, had to be kept in something, and we are in danger of thinking that, because there was no distinct name for an article, that article did not exist. In a will dated 1413, one Agnes, widow of Geoffrey Creke, bequeathed such an engraved silver powder box to her daughter.[10]

As for the use of 'parmacity [spermaceti] for an inward bruise', although the famous alchemist George Ripley, in *The Compound of Alchymy* (written 1471), has nothing to say about that specific ailment, he does recommend

> For grosse humors be purged by sweate kindely,
> Use Diacameron then confect with perfect golde
> Hermidocles for watry humors good I holde,
> Use spericon perforat with milke of tincturiall,
> And Sperma Ceti with red wine, and when you wax olde,
> And Goats milke sod with wine nourisheth moysture radicall.[11]

The certain lord's claim that

> but for these vile guns
> He would himself have been a soldier
> (1.3.62–3)

also invites comment, since guns were not, in fact, used at Homildon. That was because early fifteenth century cannon was too heavy to be an effective field weapon; Henry IV made full use of gunpowder artillery when besieging the Percies at Berwick, Alnwick and Warkworth in 1405.[12]

## BUT ONE HALFPENNYWORTH OF BREAD TO THIS INTOLERABLE DEAL OF SACK!

(*1 Henry IV* 2.5.533–4)

Things are different in Falstaff's London and Shallow's Gloucestershire, where Falstaff can extol the virtues of 'a good sherry-sack' (*2 Henry IV* 4.2.93), having already sold his soul 'on Good Friday last, for a cup of Madeira and a cold capon's leg' (*1 Henry IV* 1.2.114–15). As many commentators have noted, neither wine was imported in large quantities until Tudor times – indeed *1 Henry IV* is *OED*'s earliest citation for both Madeira and the 'anchovies' that Falstaff enjoys with more sack 'after supper' (2.5.541).[13]

If the two periods are kept separate, how does Prince Hal fit in to this great scheme of things? His ability to move freely, from one time to the other and back again, is another reason the character is, as Dr Johnson says, 'great, original, and just'.[14]

This inter-relationship of past and present is what I believe gives the *Henry IV* plays much of their

---

8 David Bevington, ed., *Henry IV, Part 1* (Oxford, 1987), p. 146.

9 Bartholomaeus Anglicus, *On the Properties of Things: John Trevisa's translation of Bartholomaeus Anglicus De proprietatibus rerum*, ed. M. C. Seymour *et al.*, vol. 2 (Oxford, 1975), p. 932.

10 C. C. Olson and M. M. Crow, ed., *Chaucer's World* (New York, 1948), p. 342.

11 George Ripley, *The Compound of Alchymy* (London, 1591), sig. M1r. Ripley is mentioned in Jonson's *The Alchemist*.

12 Edelman, pp. 28–30.

13 Margery Kirkbride James, *Studies in the Medieval Wine Trade*, ed. E. M. Veale (Oxford, 1971), p. 29; Tim Unwin, *Wine and the Vine: Historical Geography of Viticulture and the Wine Trade* (London, 1991), pp. 221, 223 and 245. The word 'sack' is spoken 21 times in *1 Henry IV* and 11 times in *2 Henry IV*.

14 Johnson, p. 523.

power – a key feature of epic theatre, as in Robert Corrigan's description:

> Brecht dispenses with linear form of beginning, middle, end, and instead has a constantly shifting series of episodes. The dramatic recesses of history never do end, they only move on to the next episode.[15]

In the same manner, *1* and *2 Henry IV* move through time and place without restriction. While a linear narrative is not dispensed with completely, Shakespeare's interweaving of past and present is reminiscent of *Galileo* and *Mother Courage*, where many episodes are a parody of what the audience has just seen.

We are often on the lookout for 'metadrama', and it is impossible to encounter much performance criticism without reading of what 'draws an audience in' compared with what 'distances it'. The vagueness of these terms, in that those using them often accept the realistic, proscenium arch theatre as the norm from which to depart, has rendered them problematic – to speak of 'distancing' an audience privileges realism as being somehow more proper to the art of drama. Whatever one's opinion on this matter, not much reading is required to learn that one critic's empathy is another's *verfremdungseffekt*, one's metadrama is another's drama. When considering the alienation effect, we should remind ourselves that for Brecht, there was something to be alienated from. All of the well-known techniques used to various degrees by Meyerhold, Piscator, Erich Engel and Brecht, devices, as John Willett observes, 'to show everything in a fresh and unfamiliar light, so that the spectator is brought to look critically even at what he has so far taken for granted',[16] are just not necessary on the non-illusionistic, Elizabethan platform stage.

Brecht's influence on Shakespeare is not limited to matters of dramatic construction. *1* and *2 Henry IV* are also prime examples of how politics inform the epic theatre, and here we must allow equal credit to Brecht's colleague Erwin Piscator, who preferred the term 'political theatre' to 'epic'. These terms are very imprecise because the people who used them were always applying them in new ways, but I follow John Willett in saying that for Piscator, 'epic' had to do with dramaturgy, while 'political' had to do with subject matter.[17]

In discussing the plays' political nature, I am not referring to Lily B. Campbell's demonstration of the parallels between the Percies' rebellion in the plays and that of 1569. Campbell is precisely correct but, in order to make that the texts' main concern, she completely removes Falstaff from them, saying that his scenes are 'a series of comic interludes' that 'interrupt the continuity' of the two *Henry IV* plays.[18] True, except that in *2 Henry IV*, the 'interludes' comprise two-thirds of the play.

A constant theme of *Henry IV* criticism, and rightly so, is the derivation, one might say, the ancestry of Falstaff: the Vice figure, Miles Gloriosus, the Lord of Misrule, the historical Sir John Oldcastle. Deserving of more emphasis is that from the moment Falstaff gives up his vocation, as he calls it, of thief and receives his 'charge of foot' (*1 Henry IV* 2.5.548), he is a character with no antecedent except real life. The sequences in which he leads his soldiers to Shrewsbury in *Part One* and recruits them for the Yorkshire conflict in *Part Two*, inform these plays with some of the most biting political comment in the history of English drama, worthy of Piscator's *Rowdy Red Revue* or his adaptation of *The Good Soldier Schweyk*.

Falstaff as the murderously corrupt military officer would have been instantly recognizable to anyone in the original audience, especially anyone who had fought in Ireland, Normandy or the Low Countries – although there would not have been too many still alive to see the play. He accepts a bribe from any able-bodied man who can buy his way out of serving, fills his ranks by conniving with the Justices to empty out the prisons and then deliberately sends his soldiers to their deaths

---

15 Robert Corrigan, *The Theatre in Search of a Fix* (New York, 1973), p. 222.

16 John Willett, *The Theatre of Bertolt Brecht* (London, 1959), p. 179.

17 Willett, *The Theatre of Erwin Piscator: Half a Century of Politics in the Theatre* (London, 1978), pp. 107–8.

18 Lily B. Campbell, *Shakespeare's Histories: Mirrors of Elizabethan Policy* (London, 1947), p. 213.

so that he can pocket their pay. In so doing, he enacts what had become a national outrage. A few years before Falstaff coined the term 'food for powder', Sir John Smythe's *Certain Discourses Military* was published and immediately suppressed; Smythe charges Elizabeth's captains with every one of Falstaff's abuses, along with a few more, including lodging the men in a disease-ridden area to finish off those who did not fall to enemy bullets.[19]

Smythe was not alone in calling attention to these abuses. The State and Privy Council Papers are a seemingly endless list of such complaints, and one report, sent from Ireland in December of 1596, is of particular interest to Shakespearians. Its subject is Sir Thomas North, whose translation of Plutarch's *Lives of the Noble Grecians and Romans* was the main source for the Roman plays.

> Of all the captains in Ireland, Sir Thomas North hath from the beginning kept a most miserable, unfurnished, naked, and hungerstarven band. Many of his solders died wretchedly and woefully at Dublin; some whose feet and legs rotted off for want of shoes, and albeit these poor souls were left thus at random, uncared for and unrelieved, yet were their names still retained in the muster-roll. And no doubt pay will be duly demanded in England; but great justice it were that the same should be suspended, even as the solders in their extremities were rejected.[20]

One of the rare and honourable exceptions was another Sir Thomas, Sir Thomas Digges, who served as muster master to the astoundingly incompetent Leicester in the Low Countries campaign of 1586. Digges tried to see the soldiers properly paid and fed, and sent scathing reports back to London similar to the one about Sir Thomas North just cited. As a result, his fellow officers ostracized him and got him recalled to London – Digges never received his own back pay of £1000. He was the father of Leonard, author of 'To the Memory of the Deceased Author Master W. Shakespeare'.[21]

*Part Two*, with the great muster scene at Justice Shallow's Gloucestershire farm, is also rife with contemporary politics. As I have noted elsewhere,[22] Shakespeare places this scene in the late 1590s with almost total precision: Silence remarks that his cousin Shallow was at Clements Inn 'fifty-five year ago' (3.2.207) – if we accept a date of 1598 for *2 Henry IV*, Shallow was at the Inns of Court in 1543, when he could very well have been 'Sir Dagonet in Arthur's show' (3.2.277–8), a reference to Prince Arthur's Knights, the archery society established by Henry VIII in memory of his elder brother. Indeed, he could even have seen Falstaff 'break Scoggin's head' (3.2.29) – Scoggin went on to become Edward VI's jester.[23]

Interestingly, Shallow's reminiscence of old Double includes the play's single intrusion of the late medieval into the modern, i.e. Elizabethan, world: 'A shot a fine shoot. John o' Gaunt loved him well, and betted much money on his head' (3.2.43–4). As to why Falstaff is in Gloucestershire when he is supposed to be on his way to fight the Percies in Yorkshire, the answer is that Mouldy, Wart, Feeble and company are not being mustered for Yorkshire at all, they are headed for Ireland. No county was more called upon for Irish troops than was Gloucestershire, and in no county was the level of corruption and literally murderous incompetence greater, especially in the last few years of Elizabeth's reign.[24] Furthermore, the terrible suffering caused by the poor harvests and consequent rise in grain prices at the time can also be connected to Shallow's real-life counterparts. Shallow informs Davy that he should 'sow the headland' with 'red wheat' (5.1.12–13). On September 8,

---

[19] Sir John Smythe, *Certain Discourses Military, in Original Letters of Eminent Literary Men of the Sixteenth Seventeenth and Eighteenth Centuries*, ed. Henry Ellis (London, 1843), pp. 49–51.

[20] *Calendar of State Papers Relating to Ireland of the Reigns of Henry VIII, Edward VI, Mary, and Elizabeth: 1596–7*, p. 115. See also Harold H. Davis, 'The Military Career of Thomas North', *Huntington Library Quarterly* 12 (1948–9), 315–321.

[21] See Henry J. Webb, 'The Mathematical and Military Works of Thomas Digges, with an Account of his Life', *Modern Language Quarterly* 6 (1945), 389–400; C. G. Cruickshank, *Elizabeth's Army*, 2nd edn (Oxford, 1966), pp. 137–9.

[22] Edelman, pp. 27–8.

[23] Giorgio Melchiori, ed., *The Second Part of King Henry IV* (Cambridge, 1989), p. 120.

[24] See, in particular, *Acts of the Privy Council*, 42 v., ed. J. R. Dasent (Nendeln, 1974), 24: 81, 82, 257–8; 26: 240–1, 277–8, 30: 20–1, 160–1, 552.

1596, the Privy Council wrote to the Justices of Gloucestershire and demanded to know why they had not carried out their orders to provide famine relief:

Yf the orders which we have prescribed and published of late were as they ought to be dulie put in execucion, though it had pleased God at this tyme to visitt this land with verie extraordinary scarcetie and dearth, yet nether the want nor the complaint of the poore people would be so great as it is. But when the Justices of Peace (and indeede we thincke diverse of the Justices more in fault than any others) whose dutie is to reforme those abuses are themselves aucthors and maynteyners of the same, no mervaile though the poor people fynde no remedy nor our orders take effect, But that which is neglected by some we must comitt unto others that are of better conscience to see reformed, and therefore we do by theis our letters againe most earnestly pray and require you to cause our aforesayd orders for reformacion of markettes to be put in practize and dulie observed.[25]

Specifically, the Council is referring to 'two speciall inconveniences . . . as causes of this dearth in that countrie: the immoderate quantity of mault made even by some of the Justices of Peace themselves and the transporting of corne by the river of Severn'.[26]

So in this time of extreme deprivation, Justice Shallow, when he was not mustering troops for Ireland, was selling his grain to the local breweries, or exporting it to the continent at inflated prices to supply the army sutlers.[27]

## 'UNHAPPY THE LAND THAT NEEDS A HERO.'

Brecht, *Life of Galileo*

Brecht's apparent hand in *1* and *2 Henry IV* does not end with this mixing of past and a very political present for, in nearly every respect, Falstaff is the epitome of the Brechtian hero.

In April of 2000, Michael Billington reviewed Nancy Meckler's production of *Mother Courage* in London, a week after seeing the RSC *1 Henry IV* at Stratford:

I was constantly reminded of the parallels between the two works. Brecht consciously used the structure of the Shakespearian chronicle-play as a model. Allowing for differences of class and gender, there are striking similarities between Falstaff and Mother Courage. Both are cynical realists who see war as a source of profit. Falstaff cries 'God be thanked for these rebels' and proceeds to make money out of his Lazarus-like recruits. Courage frets during peace and tells her daughter, 'there's life in this war, isn't there?'. Both characters also take a ruthlessly pragmatic view of honour. 'What is honour?' asks Falstaff. 'A word.' Similarly Courage cries: 'Honour! What's that? One battle we lost, I got a big white horse out of it.'[28]

The connection of Courage, with her philosophy, and Galileo, with his gluttony, to Falstaff might seem too obvious even to mention, but one important person seems to have been completely unaware of it: Bertolt Brecht.

Along with adapting some of Shakespeare's plays, and one by Marlowe, Brecht was an enthusiastic reader of Shakespeare all his life, usually in German translation. Later, when he was in Los Angeles and trying to improve his English, his 'plan for the day', as he recorded in his *Journals*, was to read 'half a page of Shakespeare' and a crime novel.[29] It is generally true that Brecht, as Billington notes, used the Elizabethan chronicle play as a model, but more via Büchner than directly, and after a lot of searching I have been able to find only one reference to Falstaff in Brecht's own writings on the theatre, a rather confused analysis of the rejection in *2 Henry IV*:

Since only what is contradictory is really alive, classical works always have dialectic elements, at least for dialecticians. But even in such obviously dialectic scenes as that in which Falstaff is rebuked by the newly crowned Henry – when the man who has just, with general

[25] *Acts*, 26:152–3.

[26] *Acts*, 26: 153.

[27] Interestingly, the Stratford records of 1598 list one William Shakespeare amongst the chief malt-holders there, but according to Schoenbaum his holding of ten quarters was average and does not seem to represent illegal hoarding (S. Schoenbaum, *William Shakespeare: A Documentary Life* (Oxford, 1975), p. 178).

[28] *Guardian*, 29 April 2000.

[29] Brecht, *Journals: 1934–55*, trans. Hugh Rorrison, ed. John Willett (London, 1993), p. 327.

consent, been rejected as a scoundrel suddenly enjoys general sympathy – the dialectic is not of a kind that would offer lessons with regard to social reality.[30]

Brecht is more or less correct, as he also notes in his *Journals*, in thinking Shakespeare's plays were the product of 'the working methods of a collective', especially if we define the word as does Christopher Hampton in his play, *Tales from Hollywood*: 'a theatre collective is a group of actors and technicians who, after frank, exhaustive, and democratic discussion of any given topic, will then decide to do exactly what Brecht wants'.[31] Yet Brecht seems extraordinarily wrong when writing

Plays like Shakespeare's histories, dramatizations of chapters of chronicles, always seem closest to reality. There's no 'idea' in them, no concern to shape a plot, scarcely any topicality. All you get is an illumination of established facts with occasional corrections on the lines of 'any other way is almost unthinkable'.[32]

This hardly accounts for the existence of a Falstaff, who is completely topical, and is a walking visual aid to finding some 'other way'.

Courage tells the sergeant,

They call me Courage . . . because when I saw ruin staring me in the face I drove out of Riga through cannon fire with fifty loaves of bread in my wagon. They were getting moldy, it was high time, I had no choice.[33]

and in a brilliant essay on the play, Eric Bentley asks

Did those who gave her the name intend a joke against an obvious coward? Or did they think she was driven by heroic valor when in fact she was impelled by sheer necessity? Either way, her act is utterly devoid of the moral quality imputed. Whether in cowardice or in down-to-earth realism, her stance is Falstaffian. What is courage? A word.[34]

Falstaff's 'stance' is perhaps best evoked when he says, just before the battle of Shrewsbury, 'What is that "honour"? Air. A trim reckoning! Who hath it? He that died o' Wednesday' (5.1.135–6). The words of this great 'catechism' (5.1.140) and Sir John's other speeches on honour are perhaps not so important in themselves as to whom they are addressed. He is often seen as the corrupter of Prince Hal, but Hal is not on stage when Falstaff delivers them: a major factor in establishing his Brecht hero credentials is that he is the only person in the *Henry IV* plays to address us directly, simultaneously a character in the action and someone who stands aside and comments upon it, urging our complicity or at least our understanding.[35]

Well, if Percy be alive, I'll pierce him. If he do come in my way, so; if he do not, if I come in his willingly, let him make a carbonado of me. I like not such grinning honour as Sir Walter hath. Give me life, which if I can save, so; if not, honour comes unlooked for, and there's an end. (*1 Henry IV* 5.3.56–61).

Surely, no more eloquent a statement of the Brecht hero's attitude to life has ever been uttered, except perhaps for the one voiced by Falstaff's comrade in arms, Schweyk, who offers identical sentiments on the subject:

great men are always unpopular with the common people. The masses don't understand them, they think all those things are unnecessary, even heroism. The little man doesn't give a shit about a great era. All he wants do to is drop into the bar now and then and eat goulash for supper.[36]

---

30 Brecht, *Schriften zum Theater*, 7 v. (Frankfurt, 1963–4), 7: 298. My thanks to Werner Habicht for providing me with a translation.

31 Brecht, *Journals*, p. 115; Christopher Hampton, *Tales from Hollywood* (London, 1983), p. 79.

32 Brecht, *Journals*, p. 167

33 Brecht, *Mother Courage and Her Children*, trans. Ralph Manheim, in *Collected Plays*, v. 5 (New York, 1972), p. 137.

34 Eric Bentley, *Theatre of War* (New York, 1972), p. 166.

35 When I gave an earlier version of this paper at the 2004 International Shakespeare Conference, several people challenged this point, arguing that Hal's 'I know you all' speech (*1 Henry IV* 1.2.192–215) is also addressed to the audience. I believe Hal is 'thinking aloud' to himself in this speech.

36 Brecht, *Schweyk in the Second World War*, trans. Max Knight and Joseph Fabry, in *Collected Plays*, vol. 7 (New York, 1975), p. 75.

# DRAMATIZING THE DRAMATIST

PETER HOLLAND

Here are eight events in Shakespeare's life and afterlife of which many readers of this article will be unaware:

(1) At the Kenilworth entertainments Leicester introduced to Queen Elizabeth 'a lad / From Stratford-upon-Avon near this place / Beyond his years precocious'.[1] Elizabeth quizzed young Shakespeare and her own protégé Francis Bacon about poetry and philosophy at length and both the boys were carried high in triumph.

(2) Arriving in London from Stratford, Shakespeare saved Southampton from serious injury or death by grabbing the bridle of the aristocrat's horse as it was about to throw its mount into the river. Southampton rewarded him with a ring and his patronage, announcing 'What nobler exercise for wealth than this – . . . to foster Genius.'[2]

(3) But Shakespeare also applied to Raleigh for a place on the Virginia expedition that established the Roanoke colony in 1587. Raleigh had heard Shakespeare praised by Sir Philip Sidney as someone who had 'the gift of words' when he had listened to Shakespeare 'reciting ballads' at the Mermaid Tavern. Raleigh advised the young man to 'cherish that gift' rather than travel to America.[3]

(4) Shakespeare and Marlowe fought in Deptford over Mary Fitton with whom both were in love. By accident, as Marlowe lunged at Shakespeare, 'his arm [was] knocked up, striking his own forehead' and Marlowe fell dead.[4]

(5) John Manningham's account of the occasion when Shakespeare had sex with a citizen in Burbage's place with the retort 'that William the Conqueror was before Richard the Third' was inaccurate. Shakespeare had actually forestalled Lord Wilson from wooing the actress Clarence with the line 'Richard III comes too late. William the Conqueror commands the fortress.'[5]

(6) 'Tomorrow and tomorrow and tomorrow' was written in response to Burbage's demand for a soliloquy for Macbeth mourning Lady Macbeth. Burbage had proposed that it should begin 'O dearest chuck, it is unkind indeed / To leave me in the midst of my sore need.'[6]

(7) Shakespeare's last words were 'When that I was and a little tiny boy . . . *In manus tuas*

[1] Tresham D.Gregg, *Queen Elizabeth, or The Origin of Shakespeare* (London, 1872), p. 109.

[2] Charles A. Somerset, *Shakspeare's Early Days* (Cumberland's British Theatre, London, n.d.), p. 38.

[3] Paul Green, *The Lost Colony*, ed. Laurence G. Avery (Chapel Hill, NC, 2001), p. 55.

[4] Clemence Dane, *Will Shakespeare. An Invention in Four Acts* (London, 1921), p. 94.

[5] Alexandre Duval, *Shakespeare Amoureaux* (1804), translated by Richard Penn Smith as 'Shakespeare in Love' in Richard Penn Smith, *The Sentinel and Other Plays*, ed. Ralph H.Ware and H. W. Schoenberger (*America's Lost Plays*, vol.13; Princeton, NJ, 1941), p. 114.

[6] Maurice Baring, 'The Rehearsal' in *Diminutive Dramas* (London, 1911), p. 70.

*Domine*'[7] or they were 'We have heard . . . the chimes . . . at midnight, Master . . . Shallow, Dickon: Shallow!'[8] or they were 'Was anything done?'[9]

(8) Shakespeare's ghost has walked on a number of occasions, the most memorable being his appearance to the new owner of the birthplace in the mid-nineteenth century when he was accompanied by a number of his characters, including Othello who carried a banjo and was 'dressed partly as an Ethiopian Serenader'.[10]

My concern is with plays in which Shakespeare appears as a character and this article acts as a preface or prequel to Jill Levenson's in this volume: to divide the topic between us, we agreed that I would look at plays across the three centuries up to the 1970s while she got all the interesting ones. I should also make clear that this is a field for which some useful charting was done by Maurice O'Sullivan and which Michael Dobson and Nicola Watson have tilled brilliantly, especially in works where Shakespeare encounters Queen Elizabeth, while Paul Franssen knows more about it than the rest of us put together.[11]

My examples so far have traversed a wide range of dramatic forms and a broad historical spread. Shakespeare, you will not be surprised to read, has figured as a character in many plays, acted, unacted and unactable. The meeting with Elizabeth at Kenilworth comes from *Queen Elizabeth or the Origin of Shakespeare, A Drama in Five Acts after the Elizabethan Model* by the Reverend Tresham D. Gregg, chaplain of St Nicholas Within in Dublin, published in 1872, one of a group of appalling and totally unactable plays Gregg wrote in this style (and which bear scant relation to any Elizabethan model I can recognize). The play's purpose, through its mad and maddening form, is to keep England and Ireland true to Protestantism, a difficult quest for an Anglican chaplain in a predominantly Roman Catholic community. But the consequences of such an achievement would have been considerable, for, as Shakespeare announces in the epilogue,

> Be true to HIM . . .
> And Shakespeare after Shakespeare you will see.
> Poor Shakespeare, then! I sha'nt [*sic*] be any wonder
> When Him you make your own, who makes the
> thunder. (p. 126)

For Gregg, Shakespeare is God's sign of his approval of the Protestant cause. But, whatever its significances, the play can stand here for the lunatic extremes of such drama.

Shakespeare saved Southampton in Charles Somerset's *Shakspeare's Early Days* (1829), probably the first English play with Shakespeare as the leading character and a work which marked, for Somerset's contemporaries, a crucial transition: 'The present age, so fertile in inventions, has exhibited Shakspeare in *propriâ persona* on the scene where he

---

7 Conal O'Riordan (Norreys Connell), *Shakespeare's End and Other Irish Plays* (London, 1912), p. 166.

8 Wilfrid Blair, *The Death of Shakespeare* (Oxford, 1916), p. 24.

9 Edward Bond, *Bingo* (London, 1974), p. 50.

10 J. Stirling Coyne, *This House to be Sold* (London, n.d.), p. 10.

11 See Maurice J. O'Sullivan, ed., *Shakespeare's Other Lives: An Anthology of Fictional Depictions of the Bard* (Jefferson, NC, 1997) – Sullivan's introduction was first published as 'Shakespeare's Other Lives', *Shakespeare Quarterly*, 38 (1987), 133–53; Michael Dobson, *The Making of the National Poet* (Oxford, 1992); Michael Dobson and Nicola Watson, *England's Elizabeth* (Oxford, 2002); Paul Franssen, 'Portraits of Mr W. S.: The Myth of Sweet Master Shakespeare in Asimov, Wilde, and Burgess' in A. J.Hoenselaars, ed., *Reclamations of Shakespeare* (Amsterdam, 1994), pp. 139–50 and 'The Bard, the Bible, and the Desert Island' in Paul Franssen and Ton Hoenselaars, eds., *The Author as Character; Representing Historical Writers in Western Literature* (Madison, WI, 1999), pp. 106–17 and 'The Bard and Ireland: Shakespeare's Protestantism as Politics in Disguise' *Shakespeare Survey 54* (Cambridge, 2001), pp. 71–9. There is a very substantial list of texts with Shakespeare as a character in the appendices to Berit Bettina Schubert, *[Enter SHAKESPEARE.]: Der Dramatiker als Figur in modernen Drama* (Frankfurt am Main, 2003. Münchener Universitätsschriften, Band 27), pp. 305–22 (my thanks to Sonja Fielitz for providing me with a copy). But there are other texts still to be tabulated: Professor Alexander Bartoshevich mentioned to me a Russian play, *A Man of Stratford*, by Samuel Alyoshin staged by the Moscow Maly Theatre in 1955/6 and later filmed for television, in which Shakespeare's lover disguises herself as a man and joins the Lord Chamberlain's Men in order to be near Shakespeare.

was *once* illustrated in all his glory.'[12] This movement, as it were, from Betterton to Barnum, as if the exhibition of the playwright is zoological, was also part of a deliberate historicism in the sets, generating 'a rich antiquarian treat . . . The illusion was perfect', all a source of pride in the perfection of early-19th century theatre.[13] It was reasonably successful in production at the Theatre Royal, Covent Garden, with Charles Kemble in the role for, as the play's editor announced, 'to whom could *The Immortal* be assigned with greater propriety, than to this superb actor and accomplished gentleman?'[14] The collocation of actor and gentleman resonates back into the play itself where Shakespeare is sustainedly and heroically genteel. For the saving of Southampton is Somerset's deliberate use and transformation of a Shakespeare legend, his note at this moment announcing 'It is thus that I have endeavoured to adhere to the tradition that Shakespeare held horses at the Globe Theatre – yet giving it a more honourable interpretation.'[15] I use it as a rare example of a Shakespeare play that reached the professional stage but also an example of the common genus of Shakespeare gentrified.

Shakespeare has not been going to America almost every year since 1935 when Paul Green's *The Lost Colony: A Symphonic Drama of American History* was first performed by local amateurs at Roanoke as it has been every year since, though, for a while after 1946, the Shakespeare episode was cut from the text.[16] Shakespeare's incorporation in the narrative as a kind of moment of alternative history could function as an epitome of cultural anxiety – What if Shakespeare had been American? What if America had been the cause of Shakespeare's death, like the rest of those colonists, and the plays stayed unwritten? – one that is unnecessary post-war and can be more confidently renegotiated by the 1950s.

Shakespeare is partly responsible for the death of Marlowe, who is insistently and energetically heterosexual in almost all these plays, in Clemence Dane's *Will Shakespeare: An Invention in Four Acts* (1921), a West End success with Claude Rains as Marlowe. Fitton was drama's most frequent candidate for Dark Lady in the period, as in the two rival plays of 1910, Frank Harris's *Shakespeare and his Love* and Shaw's brilliant *The Dark Lady of the Sonnets*, or in Rubinstein and Bax's *Shakespeare*, published the same year as Dane's play in 1921. Yet Dane, more completely than any other dramatist interested in Shakespeare in lust, sets Fitton against Anne, here turned into Solveig from Ibsen's *Peer Gynt*, often only an unseen voice, waiting, endlessly waiting, for Shakespeare's return to Stratford. The negotiation between Stratford and London, between family and fate, is central to many – and many of the best – of these plays.

The confusingly named actress Clarence (properly, of course, with French pronunciation) is in Alexandre Duval's *Shakespeare Amoureaux* of 1804, a play in which Anne Shakespeare is conveniently ignored so that Shakespeare could be amorously but not unfaithfully shown in love in appropriately French romantic style, without the bawdy details of Manningham. Its first translation into English, by a Philadelphian lawyer Richard Penn Smith, named it 'Shakespeare in Love' and the line from Clarence to Viola de Lesseps is a short one. But it was also translated and adapted into Spanish as *Shakespeare Enamorado* by Ventura de la Vega in 1828 at a time when Shakespeare's plays were little known and largely unperformed.[17]

---

[12] Somerset, *Shakspeare's Early Days*, p. 8.

[13] Somerset, *Shakspeare's Early Days*, p. 8.

[14] Somerset, *Shakspeare's Early Days*, p. 8. Samuel Schoenbaum, who praised the play as 'the century's most successful biographical drama on the Shakespearian theme', uncharacteristically confused Charles Kemble with his father as the actor here (*Shakespeare's Lives* (Oxford, 1970), p. 367).

[15] Somerset, *Shakspeare's Early Days*, p. 38.

[16] Avery is not entirely clear for how long the episode was dropped; see Paul Green, *The Lost Colony*, pp. 21–2.

[17] On this adaptation see Keith Gregor, 'Shakespeare as a Character on the Spanish Stage: A Metaphysics of Bardic Presence' in A.Luis Pujante and Ton Hoenselaars, eds., *Four Hundred Years of Shakespeare in Europe* (Newark, NJ, 2003), pp. 43–53. Gregor discusses a number of other Spanish plays in which Shakespeare appears as a character. My thanks to Clara Calvo for drawing my attention to this article and for letting me read her paper 'Shakespeare, Napoleon and Juan de Grimaldi: Cultural Politics and French Troops in Spain' (forthcoming).

My sources so far have only inadvertently been comic. Maurice Baring's superbly funny sketch 'The Rehearsal' was one of his 'diminutive dramas', originally written for *The Morning Post* and collected in 1911 – note, by the way, the flurry of Shakespeare-in-drama activity between 1910 and 1916 that the accumulation of dates is indicating. Shakespeare as the put-upon writer is a common comic trope in the genre, like the one in David Magee's 'What's in a Name?' produced at the Bohemian Club in 1961 (and note here a sign of the frequent link between Shakespeare sketches and private performances) who wants to begin Hamlet's soliloquy in his hilarious comedy *Hamlet* 'Shall it be thusly or shall it not be thusly' until the 'Re-write Man' hired by Burbage, 'a Madison Avenue-type Tudor, snappy of brim and brain',[18] turns the line into the familiar one, turns the play into a tragedy and turns out to be Francis Bacon, the incidence of whose presence in Shakespeare comedies is extraordinarily high – I recommend, for example, Samuel Cox's *Shakespeare Converted into Bacon* (1899) or George Moore's *The Making of an Immortal* (1927) as examples of the Bacon-meets-Shakespeare trope.

Shakespeare died piously as a Catholic in Norreys Connell's *Shakespeare's End* (1912), in which he is, as Connell wrote to Joseph Conrad, nothing more than a convenient device to focus the play's central argument, the contrast between an English seaman (a symbol of the imperial exploitation of workers as army) and an Irish priest (a symbol both of nation and religion as opposition to that empire).[19] He died smilingly correcting Burbage's quotation in Wilfrid Blair's piously adoring tercentenary 'Chronicle Play in Two Scenes' *The Death of Shakespeare* (1916) and he died despairingly and suicidally, lamenting the ineffectiveness of his plays in changing the inequities of capitalist society, in Edward Bond's similarly bardolatrous *Bingo* (1973).

Finally, but chronologically earliest, Shakespeare's ghost seems to have been appearing on stage for 130 years before he would be manifested in living form, especially as prologue to adaptations of his own plays, from the prologue to Dryden's *Troilus and Cressida* (1679), through joint appearances with, appropriately enough, Dryden's ghost in both Bevil Higgons's prologue to Granville's *The Jew of Venice* (1701) and Elizabeth Boyd's *Don Sancho* (1739),[20] to the childhood drama by Richard Cumberland, 'Shakspeare in the Shades' of which Cumberland was embarrassed but not so embarrassed that he did not include large segments of it in his memoirs.[21] As in Cumberland's play, Shakespeare was again accompanied by his characters, but now including Othello as minstrel, in a 'musical extravaganza' performed at the Adelphi in 1847 in response to the recent sale of the Shakespeare Birthplace, with the title *This House to Be Sold; (The Property of the late William Shakespeare.) Inquire Within*, written by the wonderfully-named J.Stirling Coyne.

My presentation of the texts that constitute this kind of writing of Shakespeare, these dramatizings of the dramatist, has been a consciously arbitrary construction of two overlaying but contradictory sequences. In part my purpose in this paper is to question the kinds of narrative that our critical sequences construct, to place precisely as having been constructed and imposed those structures which, in areas of our work far away from plays-with-Shakespeare-as-a-character, we use as mechanisms for that writing. I am, implicitly throughout this article, wondering what kinds of organization would aptly reflect these materials: generic, biographical, political, chronological, aesthetic, auspices of (non)production, alphabetical. The materials pose their own problems of taxonomies, a multi-dimensional tabulation of possible mappings, ones which O'Sullivan's, the only attempt so far, covers inadequately because incoherently. He moves from intended audience (his

[18] David Magee, 'What's in a Name?' in Loyall McLaren, David Dodge and David Magee, *Shakespeare in Bohemia: Three Plays* (New York, 1961), pp. 63 and 61.

[19] Connell, *Shakespeare's End*, p. 15.

[20] See Dobson, *The Making of the National Poet*, pp. 151–3, 159–61.

[21] Richard Cumberland, *Memoirs*, ed. Henry Flanders (1856), pp. 35–9. The *Memoirs* were first published in 1806. See also *Garrick in the Shades* (London, 1779), pp. 24–6 for a report of an encounter with Shakespeare's spirit.

category of 'Cygnets', works intended for children) to how evidence is treated ('Daytrippers'), from content ('Domestics' showing Shakespeare at home and 'Players' showing him in the theatre) to contemporary, from the 'Obsessed' to the aesthetic judgement implicit in his category of the 'Wits'.[22] My structure so far has, of course, been deliberately self-conscious, ironically aware of these two kinds of sequencing with which and on which it plays: my initial organization across the narrative of Shakespeare's life, biography as chronology; and a growing chronology that has been articulated implicitly by the steady drip of dates, something that would then reveal the spread and notional interconnection of the materials. If the former's history is individualistic (the necessary irreducibility of Shakespeare's life and the kinds of restrictions that the mythified life still contains), the latter might suggest a genre and tradition that would be a falsification of the cultural presences these texts occupy. On the one hand, Shakespeare's life is malleable into dramatic structure; on the other the forms that that manoeuvred existence take are strikingly disjunct in their historical moments. The apparent narratives are no narratives at all.

Let me pursue the second of these threads for a moment. There are of course moments that interconnect because of the local histories that generate them: the three direct addresses of the first decade of the 17th century that use Shakespeare's ghost, Gildon's epilogue to his *Measure for Measure* (1700), Higgons's prologue to Granville's *The Jew of Venice* (1701) and John Dennis's 1707 prologue for a revival of *Julius Caesar*[23] clearly speak of and to each other in that sequence. Frank Harris published his Mary Fitton play, *Shakespeare and His Love*, with a preface furious about the imminent production of Shaw's *The Dark Lady of the Sonnets*, a play which Harris is sure uses Harris's theories, though 'I have not yet read or seen Mr Shaw's play.'[24] Shaw's preface has, then, to negotiate with Harris's anger in return, something Shaw brilliantly and wittily does.[25] That others in the succeeding years, like Clemence Dane or Rubinstein and Bax, made use of the Mary Fitton theory says little about the continuing potency of Harris's play (which, rejected by Beerbohm Tree and Granville Barker, was unperformed) or Shaw's deliberately ephemeral sketch as part of the campaign for a National Theatre, and says rather more about the dramatic attractiveness of a theory that had, through much of the 1920s, sufficient academic respectability to be usable as an underpinning for a series of Shakespeare inventions that each sought adequately to balance the scholarly acceptability of their materials against the theatrical viability of the results. Rubinstein and Bax's play, for instance, appeared with a beautifully begrudging preface by the scholar A. W. Pollard, clearly annoyed that he had rather enjoyed the play and prepared to admit only that '[the] talk in this play very seldom jars'.[26] The structure of the play was heavily dependent on the kinds of periodization of Shakespeare's life that Dowden had made popular rather earlier, so that the play's five acts pivot on a sequence beginning with the tyro playwright wanting to have *Love's Labour's Lost* performed, moving through *Romeo, Hamlet* and *Timon* to, inevitably in this Dowden-defined process, the peacefulness of *The Tempest*. Rubinstein later indicated their necessary awareness of Harris's 'best-selling fantasy' *The Man Shakespeare*, along with A. C. Bradley, but not of Harris's play.[27] Shakespeare criticism, not any supposed genre of Shakespeare dramas, is the textual and cultural context. The dramatic context was, as Pollard astutely noted, the impact of John Drinkwater's long-running play at the Lyric Hammersmith, *Abraham Lincoln*, in 1919, a success which spawned a flood of chronicle plays, including many on early modern figures, like

22 O'Sullivan, *Shakespeare's Other Lives*, pp. 2–24.

23 John Dennis, 'Prologue to the Subscribers for *Julius Caesar*' in *A Collection and Selection of English Prologues and Epilogues*, 4 vols. (London, 1779), vol. 3, pp. 1–2.

24 Frank Harris, *Shakespeare and His Love* (London, 1910), p. x.

25 See Bernard Shaw, *Collected Plays with Their Prefaces* (New York, 1972), vol. 4, pp. 269–304.

26 H. F. Rubinstein and Clifford Bax, *Shakespeare* (Boston, 1921), unpaginated Prefatory Note.

27 On the influence of Dowden and the others on the play, see H. F. Rubinstein, *Unearthly Gentleman* (London, 1965), pp. 7–9.

Shakespeare, providing a form of escapist costume-drama masquerading as serious history play.[28] Rubinstein's later trilogy of privately performed Shakespeare plays, *Unearthly Gentleman* (1964, one of the surprisingly few Shakespeare dramas for the quatercentenary), is written through the lenses of other Shakespeare criticism, not as a rethinking of his earlier play. Hence, too, when Paul Franssen juxtaposes Tresham Gregg's *Queen Elizabeth* with Norreys Connell's *Shakespeare's End*, rightly seeing them as contrasting signs of how the cultural and political presence of Shakespeare in Ireland is articulated in terms of nation and religion, he is also implicitly aware that Connell has almost certainly no knowledge of Gregg's bizarre play.[29]

The recurrence of particular devices in these plays constitutes a continual reinvention of the wheel, of the kind convenient for breaking butterflies. Take these examples of Shakespeare and the fairies. In 1789 the young Ludwig Tieck wrote a dramatic fragment, *Die Sommernacht*, in which the boy Shakespeare, lost in the wood, falls asleep. Enter Oberon and Titania who, after debate, bless the child:

> Oh sing, as none before thee ever sung,
> As never mortal after thee shall sing! –
> Shine thou, thy happy country's richest gem –
> Live thou, delight of ages yet to come . . .[30]

Shakespeare awakes, transformed as much as Bottom by his dream:

> How wondrous fair this world! Each pulse, each breath,
> Each fibre of my body, thrills with joy!
> Whither? Ah whither? I am rapt! Am lost![31]

And the fragment thankfully ends.

Potently influential on Tieck though the fragment may have been,[32] it remained unpublished until 1851 when Tieck's affection for the piece allowed Eduard von Bülow to persuade Tieck to allow him to publish it. It cannot, then, have had any effect on Charles Somerset who, in *Shakspeare's Early Days* in 1829, over twenty years earlier, has Shakespeare fall asleep in 'An extensive and beautifully romantic landscape, on the banks of the River Avon' where 'all nature appears decked out in her gayest holiday attire'. Oberon and Titania appear and bless him: 'The son of Genius, who now slumbers there, / Hath from his youth been our especial care'.[33] They produce a vision of Shakespeare's future characters, after which Shakespeare wakes, remembers his vision, and recalls:

> As they, in goodly numbers,
> Pass'd me in my golden slumbers,
> Methought I heard them all exclaim
> "In Oberon and Titania's name!
> Shakspeare, arise to deathless fame!"
> (p. 17)

After which he 'stands wrapt in thought'.

The trope continues. Young Will Shakespeare encounters Oberon and Titania in Dan Totheroh's *Master Will*, 'A Play for Children about Young Will Shakespeare' (1957), and, most famously for recent studies of Shakespeare in popular culture, in the comic-strip narrative, 'A Midsummer Night's Dream', first published in *Sandman* in 1990.[34]

These examples are not sequence but accident and, as such, constitute a recurrent cultural questioning of the means of comprehending Shakespeare's talents. If Tieck's play is the demonstration of Shakespeare as 'fancy's child', these dramatic representations of Shakespeare as blessed writer are an explicit demonstration of the cultural reluctance, across a long period of time and a number of countries, to be prepared to accept the

---

[28] On the impact of Drinkwater's play, see, for example, Allardyce Nicoll, *English Drama 1900–1930: The Beginnings of the Modern Period* (Cambridge, 1973), pp. 409–10.

[29] See Franssen, 'The Bard and Ireland', pp. 71–9.

[30] Ludwig Tieck, *Die Sommernacht*, translated by Mary C.Rumsey as *The Midsummer Night* (London, 1854), pp. 28–9. For Tieck's play see *Schriften 1789–1794* (= *Schriften*, vol.1) (Frankfurt am Main, 1991), pp. 11–25. I am grateful to Carmen Wong for preparing a translation of Tieck's play for me.

[31] Tieck, *The Midsummer Night*, p. 35.

[32] See, for example, Roger Paulin, *Ludwig Tieck: A Literary Biography* (Oxford, 1985), pp. 239–41.

[33] Somerset, *Shakspeare's Early Days*, pp. 15–16.

[34] See Neil Gaiman, 'A Midsummer Night's Dream', in *The Sandman Library III: Dream Country* (New York, 1995).

ways Shakespeare actually wrote. While the plays recurrently show Shakespeare writing, not one of them shows Shakespeare reading. Just as *Shakespeare in Love* cannot contemplate a Shakespeare who reads Arthur Brooke's *The Tragical History of Romeus and Juliet* or who writes with the book open on the desk in front of him but only a writer who invents narrative, and who writes so sequentially that he does not know the end of the play until he is some way into rehearsal, so these plays often seek to identify the natural – that is, Stratford – sources for the plays.

Sometimes this is achieved with genuine wit. Lieutenant-Colonel Hamley, later Major-General Sir Edward Bruce Hamley, author of *The Operations of War* (1867) and a regular contributor to *Blackwood's Edinburgh Magazine* on matters military and imperial, also published there in 1873 a short play called *Shakespeare's Funeral* in which Michael Drayton and Young Raleigh, son of Sir Walter, arrive at the Falcon in Stratford on April 25th 1616, as the Hostess sends Kit Sly on an errand, only to hear the sad news that they have come too late and Shakespeare is no more. As they pay their respects and stay for the funeral, Drayton also uses the opportunity to show Raleigh various townspeople: Sir Thomas Lucy (defined as the source of Shallow), his nephew Master Thynne (= Slender), Master Sherlock the money-lender (Hamley here anticipating Stephen Orgel's recent argument for the English origins of Shylock),[35] Shakespeare's old family servant Adam (who turns up in at least one other play, E. Hamilton Gruner's cavalcade *With Golden Quill*),[36] the New Place maidservant Cicely Hacket (from the Induction to *The Taming of the Shrew*), and the eight locals whom Shakespeare has carefully nominated to bear his coffin: Hugh Bardolph and Corporal Nym, John Rugby and James Gurney, Thomas Wart and Kit Sly, Snug the Joiner and Nick Bottom.[37] Imagination is localized and source-study is simply a matter of observation.

Hamley debunks the cultural anxiety that seeks to explain Shakespeare's working methods in ways less prosaic than reading and less troubling than imagination and genius. The search for the dramatically realized Shakespeare is also a quest for a normalized Shakespeare, caught, often, between duty to Anne and the children and the lure of fame and fortune in London, a dilemma to which Sir Thomas Lucy's response to the poaching provides a convenient means of dramatic resolution. The antithesis is present in a powerful play by a decent playwright like William Gibson's *A Cry of Players* (1969)[38] or one as weak as William Saward's *William Shakespeare* of 1907[39] or one as intentionally funny as Richard Garnett's excellent *William Shakespeare, Pedagogue and Poacher* (1905). The essential dramatic structure was glimpsed by Washington Irving in Paris in October 1823:

> Thursday 23 – fine weather – rise at 1/2 past 6 Oclock – dressing think of subject for play – Shakespeare as young man. Seen with Ann Hathaway – her song – Scene with roistering companions – at night – Deer stalking – seizure by trusty old huntsman – prisoner Keepers lodge
>
> Examination before country squire –
> his assurance – fury of squire
> *Act 3*. Shakespeare absconding –
>
> Adieu to Ann Hathaway who resolves to follow him – Beautiful Scene – Adieu to Stratford – bells at distance chime midnight – Dream – scenes of his plays pass before his mind – His own figure in temple of fame – wakes – feels the impulse – determines to make for London[40]

---

35 See Stephen Orgel, 'Shylock's Tribe' in Tom Clayton *et al.*, eds., *Shakespeare and the Mediterranean* (Newark, NJ, 2004), pp. 38–53 (pp. 43–4).

36 E. Hamilton Gruner, *With Golden Quill* (Stratford-on-Avon, 1936); Adam is the New Place gardener in Act 3, mourning his kind master, pp. 179–80.

37 Sir E. B.Hamley, 'Shakespeare's Funeral', *Blackwood's Edinburgh Magazine* vol. 103 (April 1873), pp. 379–406.

38 William Gibson, *A Cry of Players* (New York, 1969). The copyright date of 1946 suggests the play was written considerably earlier, though it was first performed in 1968.

39 William T. Saward, *William Shakespeare* (London, 1907). The dedication to 'My friend Herbert Beerbohm Tree the most versatile actor of his day' did not secure a production.

40 Stanley T. Williams, ed., *Journal of Washington Irving (1823–1824)* (Cambridge, Mass., 1931), pp. 57–8. In essence the materials for this (probably never written) play are present in 'Stratford-on-Avon' in *The Sketch Book of Geoffrey Crayon, Gent.* (ed. Haskell Springer, *The Complete Works of Washington Irving*, vol. 8 (Boston, 1978), pp. 209–24).

Irving was too good a writer to turn these morning musings into labour but it is the model that, all unknowingly, numerous other dramatists adopted. I seem to have read Washington Irving's play over and over again, as if the legends constructed in the spaces of the evidence for Shakespeare's biography almost naturally fell into this dramatic template.

There is an overwhelming emphasis in the genre (or do these plays explode and deny the conceptualization of genre itself which I offer in the word?) on the young Shakespeare in Stratford, a young man who is frequently deep in playwriting: even the youngest of them, Dan Totheroh's Master Will Shakespeare, aged eleven, has been made by his schoolmaster to wear a dunce's cap home for writing a play when he should have been studying Latin.[41] A Stratford Shakespeare is also a non-working Shakespeare, someone separate from the business economics of the theatre. But he is also the Shakespeare about to become Shakespeare, the man who will be Shakespeare but is not Shakespeare yet. The implicit Shakespeare is the comprehensible Shakespeare in this cultural modelling, the child father to the man, the genius waiting to be discovered, not created – and hence the frequency with which the plays end with Queen Elizabeth publicly recognizing England's bard.

Of course, many of the plays present Shakespeares who are anything but normal, turned instead into representations of ideals of human behaviour, repositories of morality and honour. The pompously sanctimonious Shakespeare of David Adee's 'Bacon and Shakespeare. A Study', published in 1896 in, of all things, *The United Service*, an American *Monthly Review of Military and Naval Affairs*, arrives first on stage to find poor Ben Jonson harried by the bailiffs; he pays the debt of £29 and then apologises: 'Thy pardon for officiousness. Each one's affairs are sacred to himself'.[42] Even this Shakespeare's conversations with Bacon, with whom he collaborates, are deferentially smug: 'The sayings of the Promus which thou gav'st me are plentifully grafted on the dialogue with such historic coloring as thou hast kindly recommended. My stagecraft, mingled with thy weight of learning, should endow almost any work with popular approval' (p. 525). And there are Shakespeares whose normality is at an extreme distance from anything usually recognizable, like the oafish, illiterate William Shaxper of William Leigh's *Clipt Wings*, a Baconian's attempt at drama, published in 1930 with a preface by the improbably-named Henry Wellington Wack. *Clipt Wings* is the close rival to Tresham Gregg's *Queen Elizabeth* for the title of looniest Shakespeare play: Michael Dobson and Nicola Watson summarise the plot fairly fully[43] but I should mention that Bacon is Queen Elizabeth's son, she is murdered by Cecil because she will not name Cecil as her heir, while Shaxper is murdered by Jonson and Drayton to keep the Baconian authorship secret.[44]

Drama as the representation of conspiracy is effective: *Clipt Wings* is surprisingly readable, almost stageable. I suggested earlier that the mythified life of Shakespeare is malleable and Leigh's play shows it more malleable than most. But all write across the spaces of the biography, filling in the blanks with the drama, turning evidence and its limitations – particularly what the audience might be expected to know of that evidence – into the gap where the play can be written, where the novelized *vie romancée* can become drama. I take it that Duval's audience for *Shakespeare Amoureaux* would not know why Shakespeare should not have written roles for actresses. If Charles Somerset's Shakespeare arrives in London with *Hamlet* already complete and conveniently to hand when he saves Southampton, then Somerset can justify it by a note that 'The chronological order of Shakspeare's plays, being by no means clearly established, I considered myself at liberty to select which I pleased as our

41 Totheroh, *Master Will Shakespeare*, p. 10.

42 David Graham Adee, 'Bacon and Shakespeare. A Study', *The United Service* n.s., 15 (1896), 512–36 and 16 (1896), 48–66 (here, p. 520).

43 Dobson and Watson, *England's Elizabeth*, p. 136.

44 Another candidate in this category is Denton J. Snider's interminable *The Shakespeariad: A Dramatic Epos* (St Louis, MO., 1916), over 450 pages of bizarre conversations between Shakespeare and his characters, many taking place in Shakespearopolis, 'the city of the magic isle'.

bard's supposed first production.'[45] If it is inconceivable in Greek tragedy to contemplate an Oedipus who has not killed his father and had sex with his mother, if there is, in the narrative structures of myth, an irreducible core, then Shakespeare's biography constitutes a similarly limited field of play. The search for the dramatists is then for the moments of pivot, like the journey to London, which will accomplish drama, while also needing there to be continuities across that transition. Leigh's Shaxper is in London only to escape his wife and the bailiffs. No other dramatic Shakespeare has such a limited reason for the trip. Whether or not Shakespeare became a member of the Queen's Men is not an issue; most of these plays need a Shakespeare already fascinated by players. The narratives of these dramas provide curious intersections with the aims of our scholarship, ones that might intrigue or make us nervous: the antedating of the plays, for instance, is of a piece with a Shakespeare who carries *Hamlet* with him while tending horses at the theatre; the Shakespeare who joins travelling players, be it the Queen's Men in some biographies or the Earl of Leicester's in Gibson's *A Cry of Players*, answers to the same need, a Shakespeare already predisposed to become player-poet, a coherence and single-mindedness that has no space for a radical career-change, only a geographical manoeuvre.

The most striking of all refusals, though, is the complete absence of King James. If Shakespeare in these plays is remarkably likely to be favoured by Good Queen Bess – and numerous of these plays show different marks of that recognition of England's greatest son by England's favourite monarch, as Dobson and Watson have documented superbly – Shakespeare never has any contact with her successor. If Elizabeth's court is nostalgically dramatic, James's is apparently perfectly antitheatrical. For all the frequency with which the King's Men performed Shakespeare plays at James's court, no one seems to have thought it worth dramatizing such a moment, an absence that continues through the later works that Jill Levenson considers.

Edward Bond's *Bingo*, the most familiar – and unquestionably the best – of all the plays I have been using, is, as Bond's introduction makes clear, working within the same conceptual framework for the modelling of Shakespeare biography as drama, particularly the fascination with the hypothesized retired Shakespeare, the man who stopped writing, the writer looking back, the exhausted or tranquil figure, like the hero of Charles Lawrence's *The Hour of Prospero* (1927), whose plays 'Othello and Hamlet – they drained the life from him . . . They aged him', as Judith says, and who is finally reconciled with Ann [*sic*] when she listens to Prospero on dreams and finally realizes the value of poetry: 'I have done you wrong, husband. I have done you wrong. You – wrote that?'[46] Precisely the absence of evidence creates the space – and, after all, there is no firm evidence that Shakespeare did retire to Stratford and good evidence for his continuing presence in London. But, just as Gordon McMullan has been showing us why we constructed the concept of late Shakespeare,[47] so we have needed the concept of the retired Shakespeare, ever since Rowe's creation of Shakespeare as the gentleman among gentlemen in Stratford.

Bond makes changes to the historical evidence but 'I made all these changes for dramatic convenience' (p. vi). The play works with 'the material historical facts so far as they're known' and from that it is based on 'the psychological truth so far as I know it' (p. vii) – or, at least, this becomes sequential if we are generous enough to accept that Bond constructs the psychology from history rather than constructing the politics of his history from assumptions of psychology. In any case, for Bond biography has political

---

[45] Somerset, *Shakspeare's Early Days*, p. 41.

[46] C. E. Lawrence, *The Hour of Prospero* (London, 1927), pp. 14, 35. Lawrence frequently seems to want to use the play pompously to correct popular misconceptions about Shakespeare, e.g. Shakespeare's explanation that 'The manuscripts, with the prompter's script, and much else, are not my property' (p. 25).

[47] See, e.g., Gordon McMullan, '"The technique of it is mature": inventing the late plays in print and in performance' in Peter Holland and Stephen Orgel, eds., *Performance to Print in Shakespeare's England* (Basingstoke: Palgrave Macmillan, forthcoming).

function as drama, not a historiographical truth. Almost alone among these writers, he is prepared to state that: 'I'm not really interested in Shakespeare's true biography in the way a historian might be' (p. vii). The absence of Susanna from the play is not essentially different from Christopher Brooke Bradshaw's invention in *Shakespeare and Company* (1845) of Eleanor, Susanna and Katharine, 'Assumed Sisters of Shakespeare' as the cast-list calls them, for whose romantically appropriate marriages he is responsible.[48] Bradshaw's sympathetic representation of Katharine's match, Simeon de Castro, a young and rich Portuguese Jew, becomes, in this context, as strong a political statement about religious tolerance in mid-nineteenth-century England as Bond's exploration of the writer and capitalism is for the late-twentieth-century nation. Bond plays with and on the Shakespeare legends, like the fatal drinking bout with Jonson, and his Shakespeare is no more or less the pretext for the play's argument than, say, Tresham Gregg's or Norreys Connell's.

It is precisely with the dramatists' conception of the cultural needs to which these dramas answer that I want to end. For some, the drama is a response to a specific kind of Shakespeare event. Charles Williams's *A Myth of Shakespeare* (1929) was written for a Shakespeare festival at the request of A. C. Ward, providing a means of stringing together some scenes from the plays with, Williams writes, 'no thesis of Shakespeare's life, character, or genius, except that he was a born poet and working dramatist' – again that assumption that poets are born, never made.[49] For others, the fascination with the life behind the works, something of which Rowe was fully aware, is irresistible and the plays become a means of negotiating the limitations of historical evidence while contributing to the cult. Henry Curling, author of *The Merry Wags of Warwickshire* (1854), is eloquent in this regard:

> The attempt to embody a portion even of the scanty materials actually existing of Shakspere's biography, in a dramatic form, will doubtless appear to most minds a presumptuous undertaking. The author . . . is quite sensible of this objection; but . . . he submits for the indulgent consideration of other worshippers at the shrine of England's *greatest light* whether the very scantiness of our knowledge of the man, apart from his vocation of actor-poet, does not in some degree justify this mode of depicting his character.[50]

But there is also the most dangerous of all aims: to become Shakespeare in the act of writing about Shakespeare. Humblingly bad though most of these plays are, they seem often to be driven by an awareness that the activity is itself Shakespearian. H. F. Rubinstein, for instance, prefaces his later trilogy with the comment: 'Writing plays about Shakespeare may seem to be an unprofitable pastime, but it is one way of approaching biographical problems, and happens to be Shakespeare's way, which is a recommendation.'[51] To write a play about Shakespeare might be to be infused with Shakespeare's talents.

Only two of my playwrights know that that is not the case. Norreys Connell, with all the advantages of the stance oppositional to England, uses Shakespeare as an enabling device:

> As for Shakespeare, I have pressed him in my service for the reason that the author of *Everyman* enlisted Adonai; because the mere name facilitates the treatment of the fable . . . As Shakespeare found Cæsar of use to keep the wind away, so do I find Shakespeare.[52]

Above all, there is Shaw's awareness, in his last grappling with Shakespeare, his tiny masterpiece the puppet play *Shakes Versus Shav* (1949), 'in all actuarial probability . . . my last play and the climax of my eminence, such as it is', that writing about Shakespeare is really the same as writing about

48 Christopher Brooke Bradshaw, *Shakespeare and Company* (London, 1845), sig. [A]2b.

49 Charles Williams, *A Myth of Shakespeare* (Oxford, 1929), p. 7.

50 Henry Curling, *The Merry Wags of Warwickshire* (London, 1854), unpaginated preface. Compare, for this sense of worship, Frank Harris's comment on his *Shakespeare and His Love*: 'It suffers from an extraordinary, and perhaps extravagant, piety . . . It seemed to me that no one had the right to treat the life-story, the soul-tragedy of a Shakespeare as the mere stuff of a play. Within the limits of the truth, however, I did my best' (pp. xiii–xiv).

51 Rubinstein, *Unearthly Gentleman*, p. 7.

52 Connell, *Journey's End*, pp. 14–15.

Shaw: 'Enough too for my feeling that the real Shakespear might have been myself, and for the shallow mistaking of it for mere professional jealousy'.[53] Shav's last lines in the play might have been voiced by every one of the dramatists who dramatized Shakespeare:

Peace, jealous Bard:
We both are mortal. For a moment suffer
My glimmering light to shine.
*A light appears between them.*

And Shakes's response, with the unanswerable authoritative power of self-quotation, is the one that all these dramatists actually received:

SHAKES Out, out, brief candle! [*He puffs it out*].
*Darkness. The play ends.* (p. 477).

[53] Bernard Shaw, *Collected Plays with Their Prefaces* (New York, 1972), vol. 7, pp. 469, 471.

# SHAKESPEARE IN DRAMA SINCE 1990: VANISHING ACT

JILL L. LEVENSON

## I

My topic isolates a small part of the vast subject Shakespeare and modern drama, the title of my latest project. When Virginia Woolf confronted a similarly challenging subject, 'women and fiction', for an address at Cambridge University in 1928, she 'sat down on the banks of a river and began to wonder what the words meant'.[1] I found this eminent example reassuring and tried the same exercise – indoors. With time a few conclusions emerged which led me to notice a group of plays since 1990 using materials from Shakespeare's life. A brief review of the exercise will follow the logic that situates these dramatic texts.

In the process of wondering what the words meant, the analogy of a map proved helpful, starting with definitions of the title's co-ordinates. The name 'Shakespeare,' with its wide array of meanings, now signifies the historical person, his texts, and attitudes toward both. By comparison, the term 'modern drama' has narrower limits. Specialists set its chronology between 1850 and the present, starting with plays created by important dramatists of the nineteenth century who lived into the twentieth century.[2] Consequently, 'modern drama' refers primarily to dramatic texts of the period, extant or not, rather than productions or theatre history; but the distinction can blur when the staging of a well-known script like *Hamlet* appears extreme enough to constitute a new play.

As co-ordinates, Shakespeare and modern drama chart vast, complex and unpredictable terrain. The topography extends, more or less, into every continent; and it covers a period over 150 years long. Substantial evidence, such as published scripts and theatre reviews, indicates that it contains hundreds of modern plays related to Shakespeare. Should our calculations include ephemeral productions, the kinds performed by amateur groups and local theatre festivals, the number might increase to thousands. Not surprisingly, this difficult territory remains largely unexplored.

The size of this topic poses a challenge, and other factors complicate a straightforward investigation. For example, the chronological trajectory varies from year to year and culture to culture: Shakespeare and modern drama converge at different times for irregular durations in the infinite number of communities that constitute the modern world. Wherever we look, the ground constantly shifts; it lacks an overall pattern. This incoherence not only complicates the topic but energizes it, opening new views of both Shakespeare and modern drama. Whatever compass directs the inquiry, exploration leads to discovery and discovery adds impetus to the pursuit. In short, the dynamics between Shakespeare and modern drama both invites and resists formulation. During the years since 1990, the most evident challenges of this subject have continued to be its scope and its refusal to stand still.

[1] *A Room of One's Own / Three Guineas*, ed. Michèle Barrett (London, 1993), p. 3.

[2] By 'specialists' I mean the editors and contributors to the international quarterly journal *Modern Drama*, published since 1958, and Myron Matlaw, who compiled *Modern World Drama: An Encyclopedia* (New York, 1972).

There have been other continuities. From the beginning – that is, Ibsen, Strindberg, Chekhov, Shaw – playwrights acknowledged Shakespeare as a model and expressed their ambivalence toward his authority. That kind of ambiguous response would become a constant in the plays and commentary of later dramatists who rewrote Shakespeare's texts or his biography. Modern playwrights have criticized what they conceive as either Shakespeare's aesthetic or his politics. Their mixed feelings, determined by the temperament and self-consciousness of each artist, have found expression in a range of styles from subtle parody to undisguised insults.

Certain kinds of modern dramatic appropriations span the whole period: plays which rewrite Shakespeare's biography or his dramatic texts. Others have become especially prominent since the 1960s, when a major change took place, an increasing politicization in modern dramatic treatments of Shakespeare in response to pressing contemporary issues. At least two examples come to mind immediately: postcolonial rewritings of *The Tempest* in particular and women's rewritings of Shakespeare in general.

Like other components of the topic Shakespeare and modern drama, modern plays deriving from Shakespeare's life form part of a larger narrative with a complex history. They belong to biography, which chronicles individual lives with varying ratios of fact to fiction. More specifically, the modern plays belong to the category of biographies centred on authors, usually famous canonical writers. Although data for a life of Shakespeare remains famously sparse, Shakespearian biography retains a sizeable share of this category, and biographers have created many Shakespeares. Jorge Luis Borges, thinking about the way Shakespeare expresses himself through his dramatic characters, reaches a conclusion which applies beyond his theory: 'No one was ever so many men as that man.'[3]

Modern plays make use of the many Shakespeares, adjusting models that originated well before the modern era in relationships with famous contemporaries such as Ben Jonson and Queen Elizabeth. They also adapt material from broader developments in Shakespearian biography, including the authorship controversy and biographies which looked to the renowned works for information about the illustrious life. Occasionally they assimilate conventions from earlier fictional accounts.

While Shakespeare's life engaged an assortment of biographers since the Restoration and eighteenth century, it also attracted writers of drama and prose fiction. Of course, biographies had mixed legend with documents from the very beginning, but the genres Samuel Schoenbaum calls 'honest fictions' created more imaginative and contemporary versions of the national poet.[4] Shakespeare appeared as prologue or epilogue to adaptations of his plays at least as early as 1679, when he introduced John Dryden's *Troilus and Cressida, or Truth Found Too Late* in the figure of a royal ghost resembling Hamlet's father. By the 1730s he had secured the position of 'a monitory ghost' who endorsed the appropriations.[5] The first novel to present Shakespeare as a character, *Memoirs of the Shakespear's Head in Covent-Garden: By the Ghost of Shakespear* (published 1755), allows him to comment as a moralist on a sequence of scandalous episodes which unfold at a tavern in Georgian London.[6] In the early nineteenth century, the character of Shakespeare would become prominent in novels and plays.

The 1970 edition of *Shakespeare's Lives* contains a section on 'Plays and Novels' which concentrates on the first half of the nineteenth century (pp. 365–80); and Schoenbaum's overview of the twentieth century offers additional examples. From these references and other evidence, it seems that the period from the mid-nineteenth century to the present has witnessed a steady flow of dramas which

---

3 'Everything and Nothing' (1961), quoted in *Shakespeare's Other Lives: An Anthology of Fictional Depictions of the Bard*, ed. Maurice J. O'Sullivan, Jr (Jefferson, NC, 1997), p. 202.

4 *Shakespeare's Lives*, published first in 1970, was revised and updated for reissue in 1991 (Oxford). The phrase 'honest fictions' appears on p. 365 of the earlier edition.

5 Michael Dobson, *The Making of the National Poet: Shakespeare, Adaptation and Authorship, 1660–1769* (Oxford, 1992), p. 101.

6 Dobson, *The Making of the National Poet*, pp. 211–12.

rely on Shakespeare's life for source material. Several dozen plays span the decades, clustering in the first three decades of the twentieth century, the 1970s (a smaller group), and the years since 1990. Although many remain obscure, some claim authorship by George Sand, George Bernard Shaw, and playwrights notable since the 1960s. At first glance prose fictions, from short stories to three-volume novels, appear to outnumber dramas by almost two to one. But the calculations for plays are unavoidably rough, because so many elude any kind of formal record. Inevitably statistics miss ephemeral productions, unpublished scripts presented in limited runs or temporary venues. Yet performances in local theatre festivals alone – a Shakespeare-figure appeared in a minimum of three at the 2002 Toronto Fringe Theatre Festival – suggest that Shakespeare's life has informed a vast array of modern dramas.

Plays between 1850 and the early twenty-first century adapt all of the biographical traditions that originated in the Restoration and became more elaborate throughout the nineteenth century. As a result legends attached to Shakespeare's early life, such as poaching deer from Sir Thomas Lucy or looking after horses outside a London theatre, make their ways into the modern dramas. Different phases of Shakespeare's reputation, his public or private links with contemporaries, contenders for authorship, and his canon as biographical data bank, all surface in theatrical texts since 1850. Now and then modern plays echo earlier dramatic conventions, as Tom Stoppard does in *Dogg's Hamlet, Cahoot's Macbeth* (first performed 1979) when Shakespeare delivers a prologue composed from quotations of *Hamlet*: 'Cat will mew, and Dogg will have his day!'[7]

In a statement cited more than once, Schoenbaum observes 'that biography tends towards oblique self-portraiture' (pp. viii–ix). Certainly modern biographical plays often explore questions about the dramatists' own art through their portrayals of Shakespeare. But dramas since 1990 tend to diminish the Shakespeare-figure in various ways, reducing the possibilities for such analysis. The rest of this paper will ask how and why.

## II

The figure of Shakespeare as bard or icon had been transformed in modern drama before 1990, taking a secondary role and sometimes no role at all. For instance, Snoo Wilson (b. 1948) makes Shakespeare part of an Elizabethan group portrait in *More Light* (1987), a play for the fringe Bush Theatre in London.[8] The cast list states that '[t]he part of Shakespeare is played by a woman' (p. 124), indicating the kinds of liberties that the script will take with Shakespearian biography. But Shakespearian biography remains secondary to the surrealistic action, set in an English heaven, where Queen Elizabeth and a handful of other Renaissance figures try to save philosopher Giordano Bruno from the wrath of the Pope. Shakespeare enters almost half-way through the first of two acts in this full-length play, and s/he remains present for much of the rest. In Wilson's erratic narrative, typical of his style, Shakespeare provides one more unstable point of reference, writing *Love's Labour's Lost* and *The Merry Wives of Windsor* '*at a white cube of a desk*' (p. 143) or interacting with the others.

Wilson's title may refer to Shakespeare obliquely as author of *Love's Labour's Lost*, with reference to a line in the last act: 'We need more light to find your meaning out' (5.2.21). By contrast, the production called *Shakespeare's Memory* (1976) makes a direct allusion and a pun. Peter Stein (b. 1937), the great German director, and his company, the Schaubühne, played on the English title to mean both 'the thing remembered' and 'the faculty of memory'. Yet Shakespeare never appeared in this performance-event, two full evenings long. The

7 Tom Stoppard, *Plays One* (London, 1996), p. 164.

8 Seven of the eight plays discussed in this section have been published. The following pages will cite these texts in order: Snoo Wilson, *More Light*, in Snoo Wilson, *Plays:1* (London, 1999); Peter Lackner, 'Stein's Path to Shakespeare', *The Drama Review* 21 (1977), pp. 79–102; Peter Whelan, *The School of Night* (London, 1992), and *The Herbal Bed* (London, 1996); Frank McGuinness, *Mutabilitie* (London, 1997); Timothy Findley, *Elizabeth Rex* (Winnipeg, Man., 2000); David Williamson, *Dead White Males*, in *Contemporary Australian Plays*, ed. Russell Vandenbroucke (London, 2001), pp. 105–98.

project had an aesthetic and social agenda beyond personal history: scenes from Shakespeare's plays concluded a re-creation of Shakespeare's world – from its arts to its sciences – to present the drama as part of the culture. In this production the historical Shakespeare, behind the scenes, functioned as the absent presence intended to make the performance cohere.

Since 1990 a series of plays have adapted Shakespeare's life by comparable strategies, often viewing the character as part of an ensemble, distant or virtually absent. Their titles refer to the historical figure elliptically, if at all; they signal the subordination of his role to other characters and issues. In these dramas, which run the gamut from tragedy to history to comedy, the identity and influence of Shakespeare emerge through his relationships. The figures with whom he engages, known or fictional, take his measure not only in his own age but in ours.

Peter Whelan (b. 1931) has created two versions of Shakespeare in dramas performed initially by the Royal Shakespeare Company at The Other Place in Stratford-upon-Avon. Although *The School of Night* (1992) centres on the death of Marlowe, it offers the modern playwright's more complex portrayal of Shakespeare. Whelan acknowledges the works of Calvin Hoffman as his inspiration (see 'Cast of Characters'), locating the play's origins in the theory that friends in high places faked Marlowe's death to save his life and published his works in Shakespeare's name. At the end of *The School of Night* this scheme goes awry when the death of Marlowe does take place. Meanwhile Whelan invents a mysterious Shakespeare whose motivations are difficult to fathom. During action which unfolds between summer 1592 and spring 1593, the character appears in eight of the play's eleven scenes under an assumed name, 'Tom Stone'; yet his real name and identity become serious concerns for Marlowe soon after Shakespeare enters.

MARLOWE Why tell us your name was Stone?
STONE . . . It's my stage name. I shortened a name I once used as a pamphleteer . . . 'Touchstone' . . . 'the test of truth'. (p. 33)

In a dramatic thriller about Elizabethan espionage, everyone wants to know Shakespeare's background: 'Whose man is he? Why is he here?' (p. 36). Whelan provides no satisfactory answers to these questions, sketching a Shakespeare whose reasons for collaborating with Marlowe never become totally clear. But Marlowe has a deep insight into Tom Stone/Shakespeare, perceiving signs of a double:

> Whenever Touch looks at you, have you noticed . . . you feel you're being watched from another quarter. He smiles, but the other doesn't. His familiar. His fetch. His other self. Now which is Tom? (p. 43)

*The School of Night* captures not only the elusiveness but also the power of Shakespeare, who finally overwhelms his brilliant contemporary. Just before the death scene Marlowe responds to Stone '*in terror*', 'He's swallowed me!' (pp. 88–9). At last the specific questions posed by the play turn into a larger interrogation about the identity of Shakespeare, the writer with the vague biography whose canon and reputation have subordinated those of many other artists over the course of four centuries.

Whelan sets *The Herbal Bed* (1996) during the summer of 1613, almost three years before Shakespeare's death; and he centres the plot on Shakespeare's eldest daughter, Susanna Hall, married to physician John Hall. In this case he has shaped the two-act play from documented events, a public accusation that Susanna committed adultery and her successful defence in consistory court. As the drama builds to a suspenseful trial scene, the ailing Shakespeare remains off-stage; but the set and dialogue of the six scenes remind the audience of his proximity, both literal and figurative. Most of the action takes place in the Halls' garden, around the corner from New Place, where young Elizabeth Hall goes to visit her doting grandfather. Using the resources of the garden, Susanna tries to find remedies for Shakespeare's illness. This attempt and the love affair provoking the accusation generate the kinds of moral conflicts that agitated Jacobean culture as well as Shakespeare's later plays.

Within the charged atmosphere specific references to Shakespeare enhance a sense of his immediacy until the last scene, when the Halls prepare to receive him at their home. By now the audience know that Susanna has been seeking relief for Shakespeare's symptoms of gonorrhoea, and that she shares with her father his unusual capacities for both emotional warmth and dissemblance. Her closing speech makes the connections explicit:

> He was a liar, too. Must have lied to my mother every time he came home. Yet when he was with us . . . we were so warm! (p. 123)

As the play ends the audience listen to the sounds of Shakespeare's conveyance into the house, but they never see him or hear his voice. Whelan's second Shakespeare, elusive in new ways, functions as more of an immanence than a consuming force. His influence pervades not only his own world but that of the modern dramatist.

Irish playwright Frank McGuinness (b. 1953) imagines Shakespeare's effect on a different historical era in another country. Set in late sixteenth-century Ireland, *Mutabilitie* (1997) refers in its title and theme to the poetry of Edmund Spenser, the other major poetic figure in this play. It invents a meeting between Shakespeare and Spenser in Ireland during the English settlement of Munster, when Irish rebels burned Spenser's residence, Kilcolman Castle in County Cork. To begin with, it is a new kind of history play for Ireland in the late twentieth century, combining fact with myth and fantasy to re-view issues of English colonization as they apply to recent events in Northern Ireland. Despite continuities, McGuinness's account of the two sides is never monochromatic: it blends their weaknesses and strengths in distinctive portrayals, sharing the blame for violence. *Mutabilitie* premièred at the Royal National Theatre in London.

Into his original formulation McGuinness introduces the figure of Shakespeare, represented by the play as a poet who deals in the constants of human nature. The Irish File, a female character identified in the cast list as 'a bard', has prophesied that Shakespeare will arrive to save her people:

> A man will come amongst us. He will be from a river. The water shall save him. The river shall reveal him. He shall speak our stories. (p. 16)

File has envisioned a mythical figure, but the Shakespeare she meets disappoints her. More down-to-earth than timeless, he describes himself as '[a]nother crooked sixpence in a crooked house among men as crooked as myself' (p. 93). Face to face with him as the play closes, File struggles to understand his significance when she asks, 'Do you not exist? Did you ever exist?', and he replies, 'I do exist but not as you imagined' (p. 93).

According to this depiction, Shakespeare is and is not a desideratum for Irish art, an ambiguous model difficult to comprehend or adapt. While he wrote *Mutabilitie*, McGuinness explained his characterization of Shakespeare in the Foreword to a book about Shakespeare and Ireland.[9] His efforts to decipher Shakespeare's life began in frustration: 'I don't know who this writer is. I don't know what is his country' (p. xi). Teaching the plays in Maynooth, a centre of Catholic learning, McGuinness wanted to believe in Shakespeare as a Catholic dissident; but he decided he was wrong, 'sentimentalizing' the English paragon, and this angered him.

> In my anger I decided to create Shakespeare [in] a play, . . . He would come to Ireland and be confronted by an Irishwoman. The fight would be to the death, and she would win it. She didn't. She was a wise woman. Full of learning, full of revenge, against him and her tribe. But he belonged to no tribe. In every scene that he appeared in, he changed character and colour. He left as quickly as he arrived, his entrance always being an exit. . . . I've accepted that's his way: he's a bolter. (pp. xi–xii)

A composite of biographical bits and pieces – son to a Warwickshire family, married man, father to two daughters and to a son whose death haunts him – this Shakespeare intrudes on McGuinness's play as he seems to have intruded on the playwright's consciousness as an artist and intellectual.

Canadian writer Timothy Findley (1930–2002) created a less demanding Shakespeare for *Elizabeth Rex* (2000), a play launched at the Stratford Festival of Canada in Ontario. Interweaving the histories

---

9 *Shakespeare and Ireland: History, Politics, Culture*, ed. Mark Thornton Burnett and Ramona Wray (Basingstoke, 1997), pp. xi–xii.

of the Elizabethan period and its theatre, most of this drama occurs on the night of Shrove Tuesday, 1601. Findley takes as his starting-point the fact that Queen Elizabeth asked Shakespeare's company to perform for her on the eve of an execution: her former favourite, Robert Devereux, second earl of Essex, condemned to death for his doomed rebellion earlier in February. According to the dramatic fiction Shakespeare's company and the Queen spend that night together 'in the white-washed interior of a barn' (p. 12), confined by a curfew, after a performance of *Much Ado About Nothing*. Shakespeare delivers much of the Prologue to Findley's play, his speech fixing the date as the eve of his death, 22 April 1616; he recalls events in 1601 and sets them in place as a flashback. Then he appears in all eighteen scenes of the two acts, speaking in every one but Act 2, Scenes 2 and 7.

Despite his presentness, however, Shakespeare has little impact on the dynamic confrontation at the heart of the drama between Queen Elizabeth and Ned Lowenscroft, the intense actor dying of syphilis who played Beatrice. As the first act ends, the Queen challenges Ned: 'I will strike a bargain with you. If you will teach me how to be a woman . . . I will teach you how to be a man' (p. 50). During the remaining scenes he tries to elicit emotion from her, and she attempts to make him admit the circumstances which have led to his crisis. Shakespeare stays on the periphery while others relate love-stories. From beginning to end he takes notes, reads Plutarch and writes *Antony and Cleopatra*. The more vivid characters engage him in dialogue now and then, questioning the autobiographical content of the Sonnets or commenting on the accuracy of the history plays; but Shakespeare, unforthcoming, responds equivocally and lacks passion. In *Elizabeth Rex* Findley seems to use the character of Shakespeare as a guide through the historical fiction, allowing less familiar persons and events to grow more accessible by association. Perhaps the development of this play at Canada's main site for Shakespearian performances inhibited the modern dramatist, who does not permit his character to become deeply involved in a fervent debate about love and sexuality.

By contrast two other modern dramas, a satire and a parody, position Shakespeare at the centre of debates. David Williamson (b. 1942), a very successful playwright in his native Australia, wrote *Dead White Males* (1995) in reaction to an academic paper which he considered incomprehensible: a young male lecturer talking about deconstruction and post-structuralism had mystified an audience of writers (p. 107). Retaliating, Williamson organized his dramatic action as an updated morality play or psychomachia, good forces contending with bad in a typical human mind. The hypocritical Dr. Grant Swain represents literary theory in most of its recent manifestations, especially feminism and disputes about gender. On the other side Shakespeare stands for liberal humanism in its broadest sense, or timeless and general truths. Between these two figures three university students make efforts to find their ways, in particular the protagonist Angela Judd. Finally Angela quits Swain's class, although she still has a few reservations about Shakespeare. Williamson's experience dramatizing the academy (*The Department* (1975)) and dialectic (*The Perfectionist* (1982); *Emerald City* (1987)) has resulted in an amusing if not subtle examination of theoretical issues in *Dead White Males*.

Not surprisingly the Shakespeare-figure is one-dimensional and comic, although Williamson describes him as 'the Shakespeare Angela needs in order to make sense of her life' (p. 108). Because Angela needs Shakespeare again and again, he continues to pop up and into the twenty-eight scenes like a caricature rather than a character. He materializes immediately in the opening moments as he appears to Angela in her room, where a man (later identified as Swain) shoots him dead and 'ANGELA *is left staring at the body*' (p. 111). Nevertheless he reappears in the sixth scene, when Angela amazes him with news about his fame ('In all the world's history *I* am of such import?' (p. 125)) and prevents Swain from shooting a second time. As *Dead White Males* proceeds, Shakespeare and his plays become more implicated in the action. For instance Angela and her friend Melissa give tutorial papers on *As You Like It* and *The Taming of the Shrew*, disagreeing about Shakespeare as an agent for patriarchal ideology. Later allusions to both comedies and to *King Lear* support Shakespeare's point of view, especially performance of the marriage-and-reconciliation scene from the end of *As You Like It* which concludes the first of Williamson's two acts. A coda to this performance demonstrates the modern playwright's strategy.

SHAKESPEARE A fantastical, magical, diversion from the tepid weariness of sordid reality. A statement of hope.

SWAIN (*drawing his pistol*) For four centuries we've suffered this insidious shit! Enough!

ANGELA *intervenes, placing herself angrily between the two men.*

ANGELA No!

SWAIN *reluctantly pockets his pistol . . .*

ANGELA *looks from one to the other. She cannot choose. She clicks her fingers and Shakespeare then Swain disappear.* (p. 150)

This is not the only time Angela makes Shakespeare disappear by snapping her fingers, a gesture which empowers her while reducing him to a magical trick or light-switch.

If Williamson ridicules academic debate in a cheerful satiric play, Amy Freed (b. late 1950s) enacts the dispute over Shakespeare's authorship in a parody. *The Beard of Avon* (2001), which opened in Costa Mesa, California and quickly travelled to other cities in North America, refers to Shakespeare as a 'beard' or front man for another writer, Edward de Vere, seventeenth earl of Oxford, an aristocrat who wants to remain anonymous in the world of the Elizabethan stage. Set in 1583, the action moves from Stratford to London and back as the country bumpkin Shakespeare grows more adept in revising Oxford's plays to make them saleable. Freed dispenses with accurate chronology and biographical data, producing a swift run of scenes composed from information about Tudor personalities, references to Shakespeare's works and allusions to twentieth and twenty-first-century media. A boisterous *tour de force, The Beard of Avon* makes Will Shakspere (Freed's spelling for the cast-list) a clever man of the theatre with practical skills. 'I see a . . . hunchback', Oxford tells him at one point, 'you flesh it out'. In her programme notes Freed suggests that her play addresses important subjects. 'On the surface, it's a spoof or parody about authorship issues, but on a deeper level it's about what makes a writer like Shakespeare. Is it talent? Is it access? Can you do it by genius alone?' In performance, however, the surface of the play tends to obscure its depths, as Shakspere and eighteen other characters interact busily through dialogue or effects which adjust *Blackadder* and *Shakespeare in Love* to the Elizabethan age.

## III

The six plays discussed here form part of a larger group: my net lacks capacity to gather and hold all the biographical plays that have appeared since 1990. Obviously it has missed ephemera from the various fringes (like *Shakespeare's World Cup* (2002) and *Shakespeare's Gladiator Games* (2003), dramatic sporting events which happen annually in Toronto); and it has not caught plays which had limited runs at alternative theatres (like Blair Fell's *Naked Will*, performed at P. S. 122 in New York, August 1999) or plays which have been similarly inaccessible (for instance, Naomi Claire Wallace's *Madman Shakespeare* (2001) and William Dorian's *A Rose by Any Other Name* (2001)). Moreover, it was not set to pick up examples written for highly specialized audiences, such as Claudia Leaf's *Radical Will: A Dramatization of Shakespeare's Life and Work for Reluctant Students* (published 1997).[10]

---

[10] At the 2004 International Shakespeare Conference, where this paper was originally presented in a shorter version, several colleagues added to the list of plays I had missed. Fortunately for me, the examples diminish Shakespeare in one way or another, relegating him to positions in a cynical prologue (Peter Barnes, *Jubilee* (London, 2001)), as a victim of social injustice (David Rudkin, *Will's Way* (Shipston-on-Stour, 1993)), or on the very perimeter of the action (Peter Whelan, *Shakespeare Country* (London, 1993); Reg Mitchell, *The Quiney Affair* (Stratford-upon-Avon, 2001) and *Hallmarks or Doctor Hall's Dilemma* (Stratford-upon-Avon, 2001)). In particular, I owe thanks to Paul Edmondson of

These six plays, written for adult audiences and performed in professional (often mainstream) venues, may not represent all trends in dramas using Shakespeare's biography, but they represent some. In the first place, they come from English-speaking countries. If other nations have experimented with Shakespeare's texts since 1990 – from Brazil to China to Nigeria – they have not found his life as engaging. The gap may be cultural in a very specific sense, the result of another trend in life-writing. In the second place, that is, the six plays exploit current interest in biography, particularly literary biography, in English-speaking countries. They adapt the genre to different degrees and with different intents, whether following one life or several. In addition, they exploit current interest in appropriations of Shakespeare by popular culture. Such interests had existed earlier, of course, but they reached a peak in the 1990s.

During April 1993 two conferences on literary biography were held in Europe, one at the University of Newcastle-upon-Tyne and the other at Schloss Hofen on Lake Constance. John Batchelor, who edited a volume of essays in 1995, mostly from the Newcastle conference, opens his volume with a recent quotation from Terry Eagleton: 'there would seem no end to the peculiar English mania for the Individual Life'.[11] 'The present buoyancy of literary biography' (p. 9) becomes a major theme of the volume; and the Englishness of the phenomenon is emphasized by a German academic, Jürgen Schlaeger:

> If you will allow me to make one more personal observation I should like to describe an impression which I always have when I am in England. Wherever you go, wherever you are, faces stare up or down at you as if crying: 'Look at me! Look at what I have done! And what have *you* done?' . . . For me the country oozes biography from every pore. You will now understand why for a person with my non-English sensibilities a visit to the National Portrait Gallery is traumatic. The existence of such an institution is in itself a strong indicator of a personality-centred culture.[12]

What Schlaeger says about England can probably be extended without too much distortion to other English-speaking countries.

Further, what critics say about the conservatism of the form bears on analysis of the latest plays drawing material from Shakespeare's life. Eagleton states that the subject-matter of biography determines its form: 'The structure of biography is biology: even the most wayward of geniuses have to get themselves born and educated, fight with their parents, fall in love and die'.[13] Catherine Peters calls the genre 'a traditional, rather old-fashioned form'[14]; and Schlaeger places it in relation to theory:

> Compared with the images of our culture which post-modernism projects, biography is, in spite of its inter-textual construction, fundamentally reactionary, conservative, perpetually accommodating new models of man, new theories of the inner self, into a personality-oriented cultural mainstream, thus always helping to defuse their subversive potential. (p. 63)

In the same volume Park Honan writes about Shakespearian biography in connection to the New Historicism, concluding that Shakespeare data outstripped Shakespeare biography at the moment and that new biographical forms were needed.[15] He made that claim eight years before Katherine Duncan-Jones published *Ungentle Shakespeare* (London, 2001), trying 'to bring Shakespeare down from the lofty isolation to which he has been customarily elevated, and to show him as a man among men' (p. x). Since 1990 plays incorporating Shakespeare's life have continued to use the

the Shakespeare Birthplace Trust and to Sonja Fielitz, University of Munich, who forwarded a copy of Berit Bettina Schubert's *[Enter SHAKESPEARE.] Der Dramatiker als Figur im modernen Drama* (Frankfurt am Main, 2003).

[11] *The Art of Literary Biography* (Oxford, 1995), p. 1.

[12] 'Biography: Cult as Culture', in Batchelor, *The Art of Literary Biography*, pp. 63–64.

[13] Quoted in Batchelor, *The Art of Literary Biography*, p. 3.

[14] 'Secondary Lives: Biography in Context', in Batchelor, *The Art of Literary Biography*, p. 44.

[15] 'Jane Austen, Matthew Arnold, Shakespeare: The Problem of the *Opus*', pp. 187–99.

old forms, sequential narratives with minor variations, and at the same time they have often brought Shakespeare down from lofty isolation.

While life-writing flourished in particular cultures as the century turned, Shakespeare thrived everywhere in popular culture. Douglas Lanier enumerates '[m]ovies, television, radio, pulp fiction, musicals, pop music, children's books, advertisements, comic books, toys, computer games, pornography: nearly every imaginable category of contemporary pop culture features examples of Shakespearian allusion or adaptation'.[16] In 2002 he describes Shakespeare's image as 'currently hip', 'the creation in large part of the Shakespeare film boom of the 1990s' (p. 3). Unlike literary biography, popular culture gets a major charge from post-modernism, experimenting with its most well-known qualities and techniques from indeterminacy and irony to collage or pastiche. A number of contemporary presentations of Shakespeare incline to demystify him, sometimes to a vulgar level below 'a man among men' (Lanier, p. 116).

Peter Whelan lines up publicly with the literary biographers. Just before *The Herbal Bed* opened, he attended a writers' conference run by David Edgar on the theme 'Reality Time', that is, the way fact balances imagination in the work of many modern playwrights. In an interview he explained how he applied the idea to Shakespeare, looking in the texts for clues to the life and in the life for clues to the artist's creativity.[17] Clearly this process got under way before he wrote *The School of Night*, which includes a play within a play as well as allusions to *Venus and Adonis*, the Sonnets, and more than half a dozen scripts from *Henry VI* to *Othello*. At the centre of Whelan's drama, Marlowe and Shakespeare debate the purpose of writers and writing after the performance of the inner play, a *commedia*:

STONE . . . if the actors devise the play where is the unique vision of the mind that every play must have? Unique is one. I. Me. Singular. Not the many.

MARLOWE Surely you can't mean the author's purpose.

STONE Not my purpose . . . My mind's purpose. . . . One is that which I create. The other is created for me. One I know. The other . . . never. (p. 59)

When he composed *The Herbal Bed*, Whelan reworked scenes from *All's Well That Ends Well* and *Romeo and Juliet*, and he echoed lines from several other plays. Michael Attenborough, director of the first production, cut the most unsubtle passage about *All's Well* from 1.3, as Susanna expresses Whelan's belief (stated in the interview) that 'Helena is Susanna':

SUSANNA . . . I wanted to be Helena . . . she's a character of my father's . . . the daughter of a doctor who's died. She cures the king of France with a cure she's inherited. And, for me, she becomes the doctor . . .

RAFE You see yourself in her?

SUSANNA I do . . . and I don't. I'm drawn to her inner passion. Oh . . . that's another thing. She loves a man who everyone will say she shouldn't love . . . (p. 50)

In a review of this production Juliet Fleming wrote, perhaps unkindly, that Whelan '[leaves] us to wonder in whom [he] sees himself'. At the end of her critique she says: 'If the play does not cohere into a serious analysis of anything, that is a reflection both of the strength of its parts, and of the influence that, for good or bad, Shakespeare still casts over British theatre'.[18] Whelan himself supports her conclusion in his interview: '(Nice to slip myself in beside the greats. Working alongside Shakespeare at the Royal Shakespeare Company can give a playwright a complex. Bit like being in Madonna's chorus line.)' The reference to Madonna comes as close as Whelan gets to noticing popular culture in his thinking. But his methods, articulated in conversation and the two plays, reveal

---

16 *Shakespeare and Modern Popular Culture* (Oxford, 2002), p. 3.

17 'Characters under Study', *Times Educational Supplement*, 10.5.96.

18 'Flowers for the Furnace', *Times Literary Supplement*, 14.6.96.

how he inflects historical data with Shakespeare's art to invent theatrical biography, emulating what he considered Shakespeare's technique in his own playwriting. As traditional narratives, both Whelan texts are absorbing; as theoretical speculations on Shakespeare's aesthetic and effect (or Marlowe's for that matter), they are intermittently revealing. At his best, Whelan conveys an elusive Shakespeare, gifted and influential: a figure recognizable from the least speculative modern biographies. Whether on the stage or in the wings, this Shakespeare is rarely forthcoming.

Frank McGuinness, preoccupied by Shakespeare's identity despite himself, does not seek out correspondences between the life and art, although he invents at least one (Sonnet 87 becomes a eulogy for dead Hamnet in 4.2) and uses others which have become familiar (for example, William casts a spell as if he were Prospero). If he avoids issues of Shakespeare's subjectivity, however, he deliberately set out to subvert his concept of Shakespeare's dramatic form. In an interview after *Mutabilitie* appeared at the National, McGuinness explained his intention 'to construct an Elizabethan or Shakespearian five-act play, sticking as closely as possible to the rules and regulations of that form and then to undermine and disband them'.[19] He treats Shakespearian dramaturgy as imitable in these remarks, an easy deconstruction, but his play's representation of William gives a different impression, another display of the tensions between the modern playwright and his early modern exemplar.

Like Whelan, McGuinness generates Shakespeare from biographical data and allusions to the verse and plays. At various points several characters, including William himself, describe his past – family, schooling, sexual preferences, work in the theatre ('BEN [. . .] He's strung together a fair few plots and he does know how to polish up a speech.' (p. 36)) – and almost all of them quote from his works. In 4.3, the stabbing to death of Richard re-enacts the assassination scene in *Julius Caesar*. At the centre of *Mutabilitie*, as at the centre of *The School of Night*, Shakespeare debates with another poet, Edmund Spenser, the purpose of his art:

> WILLIAM I know how to lie intelligently, to lie beautifully. I have taken this knowledge and placed it on a stage. I have written in the vernacular so that all who see and hear must first understand and afterwards embrace the doctrine of plays, and thereby be led, knowingly, to what salvation is contained therein. I have paraded before the people those thoughts, those images, those words, those hearts, those minds, that until the time of the reformation lay concealed in the corrupt cloisters and confined courts of kings – let those see who would see, hear who would hear. (p. 52)

Admitting Shakespeare to his historical fantasy, another sequential narrative, McGuinness creates a figure of contradictions admired for his intellect by Spenser, mocked by his fellow men of the theatre, and disappointing to File. Yet his works underpin McGuinness's play, even as his temperament and inspiration escape it. Finally the authenticity of McGuinness's William resides in his evasiveness: he fails to add up as the sum of his parts, and in that failure he demonstrates the modern playwright's struggle to see Shakespeare whole.

Timothy Findley creates a few parallels between Shakespeare's life and art: for instance, *Antony and Cleopatra* corresponds to the romance of Queen Elizabeth at the heart of the play. But genuine biography is scarce through *Elizabeth Rex*. In the Prologue Will quickly surveys his life and anticipates accounts of his death. During the straightforward narrative he writes his observations of the events and his readings in a notebook, Findley's only comment on the source of Shakespeare's invention. At the same time Findley's play is thick with allusions to Shakespeare's canon, with five, six, ten echoes in a scene; 2.9 centres on a play within a play; and 2.10 incorporates features of a romantic-comic ending.

Kate Taylor, reviewer for the *Globe and Mail*, responded to the composite as '[t]his secretive Will': 'when it comes to Shakespeare, Findley

[19] *Studies: An Irish Quarterly Review* 87 (1998), p. 272.

hesitates. [Peter] Hutt makes the man wry and repressed, and the character seems to remain as closed to the actor as he is to the audience'.[20] This character remains closed to his author as well, an artistic temperament marginalized in the dramatic narrative as Findley borrows from his works. In *Elizabeth Rex* the disjunction between the Shakespeare-figure and his art allows Findley to diminish his model while skipping the acknowledgements, almost as if he were trying to block Shakespeare out.

In the two comic treatments of Shakespeare, David Williamson and Amy Freed also diminish their subject, but they state acknowledgements clearly, even clamorously. Williamson, known for his comedies of manners, makes Shakespeare part of a narrative more like a sitcom or soap opera. As a component of twentieth-century university experience, and a commentator on male/female relationships universally, this Shakespeare coexists with Jean-Claude Van Damme and Madonna:

ANGELA Then why is [Shakespeare] the most famous person in the Earth's history?

SWAIN Why is Madonna currently the second most famous? Madonna used the metaphor and rhetoric of body language to suggest that she is the sexiest person alive, Shakespeare uses the metaphor and rhetoric of language to suggest that he is the wisest person who ever lived.

(p. 127)

Williamson juxtaposes Shakespeare and popular culture in a play which nails its points with elaborate references to Shakespearian drama. In effect, he produces his own idiosyncratic appropriation.

Freed also produces a signature appropriation: *The Beard of Avon* follows a series of her earlier plays which target literary figures from Poe and Dickens to Plath and Sexton. According to the artistic producer in Toronto, who advertises the performance as 'our merry romp', 'Freed seizes the legend by the beard, kicks him off his pedestal and shows the genius for a man.'[21] The modern playwright, intrigued not only by the authorship controversy but also by the paucity of information about Shakespeare's life, fills out what she considers a mystery with a steady infusion of anachronisms. Life and works, supplemented by allusions to film, television, and contemporary music, turn into an animated pastiche. Among other things, Freed's composition allows her to glance at Shakespeare's role in popular culture and, as Will puts it in the second half of the play, Shakespeare as a brand name.

Lanier suggests that Shakespeare has been recast 'as a viable commercial property' by films in the 1990s (p. 124), but the brand name has graced many products during the modern era. In drama the Shakespeare-figure, present or absent, has defined not only merry romps but also a variety of plays with serious objectives. In British amateur theatre, he appears in quite a few scripts, usually an example of moral superiority.[22] On the professional stage he centres a small number of political dramas, such as Clemence Dane's *Will Shakespeare* (1921), an early feminist construct of Shakespeare as the creation of three important women, or Edward Bond's *Bingo* (1974), the disparaging portrayal of Shakespeare as an artist lacking social conscience. In *Shakespeare's Memory* his very absence focuses the play, a void representing Stein's fear of producing Shakespeare. 'We approached Shakespeare as we would a great continent', he admitted, 'and perhaps our navigational means were not quite adequate.'[23] 'We do this evening so that our audience can experience Shakespeare's world with the actor – not to convince ourselves that we can do Shakespeare. We don't know how to do Shakespeare.'[24]

Other literary artists have been especially popular on the British stage over the past four decades, often voicing the playwrights' political views in scripts

20 'Delicious Performances Abound in New Findley Play', *The Globe and Mail*, 1.7.00.

21 Programme notes, Sept./Nov. 2002.

22 See Heinz Kosok, 'Making Short Work of the Bard: Shakespeare's Character and Shakespearian Characters in British Amateur Theatre', in *Historicizing / Contemporizing Shakespeare: Essays in Honour of Rudolf Böhm*, ed. Christoph Bode and Wolfgang Klooss (Trier, 2000), pp. 159–83.

23 Quoted in Michael Patterson, *Peter Stein: Germany's Leading Theatre Director* (Cambridge, 1981), p. 132.

24 Lackner, 'Stein's Path to Shakespeare', p. 98.

by Bond, Stoppard, Brenton, Bolt and Edgar. These artists, present or absent, have also had significant impact on a variety of plays. According to Christopher Innes, 'the Romantic poets [are] the most numerous of all writer-figures in British drama'.[25] In 1975 Bond dispatched John Clare to the periphery of *The Fool* to make him a political spokesman. Stoppard's *Arcadia*, which circles around the absent Byron, brilliantly explores the impossibility of recovering either the individual life or the Romanticism it supposedly represents.

Stoppard's play, premièred in 1993, banishes its literary figure to concentrate on both the processes of writing in general and the problems of life-writing in particular. Like other modern plays it demonstrates that distancing or subordination of a writer's part need not diminish the writer. But plays since 1990 which include Shakespeare seem to have that effect. Adopting familiar approaches to the life, they demystify the artist without any other compelling purposes. They do express the modern dramatists' curiosity about Shakespeare, the great continent, with a range of intensities, but they do not venture far. Perhaps more than the Romantics, Shakespeare encapsulates a dilemma identified by Malcolm Bradbury in 1988: 'So this is how we live in two ages at once: the age of the author studied, pursued, celebrated and hyped, and the age of the author denied and eliminated, airbrushed from the world of writing'.[26] In recent plays deriving from Shakespeare's life, at least, dramatists incline toward denial.

---

[25] 'Elemental, My Dear Clare: The Case of the Missing Poet', in *Biofictions: The Rewriting of Romantic Lives in Contemporary Fiction and Drama*, ed. Martin Middeke and Werner Huber (Rochester, NY, and Woodbridge, Suffolk, 1999), p. 190.

[26] See 'The Telling Life: Some Thoughts on Literary Biography', in *The Troubled Face of Biography*, ed. Eric Homberger and John Charmley (London, 1988), pp. 134–5.

# WRITING ABOUT [SHAKESPEARIAN] PERFORMANCE

MICHAEL DOBSON

I should apologize first of all for starting this chapter thus in the first person and for returning to it so often in what follows, but this consideration of the special problems involved in writing about present-day Shakespeare productions in relation to the texts they use is in part a purely personal reflection on my own experiences to date of reviewing Shakespeare for this journal. All I'm going to do is give a very cursory and simplistic description of a body of recent criticism, which has been concerned above all with how performances exceed texts; then I'm going to describe some particular ways in which the openings of two recent productions did indeed supplement and overflow their respective texts; and then I'm going to consider how best one might harness the criticism to deal satisfactorily with both productions.

My title puts the word 'Shakespearian' in square brackets; I don't much like titles with brackets in them as a rule, but these have in effect been inserted for me by a major current in contemporary performance criticism, one that has usefully problematized the status of the Shakespearian text in relation to the ever-proliferating range of modern performances given in its name. According to this school of criticism, perhaps most fully represented by the work of W. B. Worthen, most extant academic accounts of Shakespeare on the stage have tended to belittle and misunderstand the very nature of performance by representing Shakespearian productions primarily or even exclusively as interpretations of Shakespearian texts. Actors and directors have been written about as though they were just academic critics who have simply chosen a different medium through which to offer 'readings' of plays, plays which somehow remain unproblematically self-identical over time however multiply embodied in print and on the stage. In reality, however, such critics point out, the live event can never be a mere belated gloss to the First Folio; not only will any performance's provision of bodies and voices inescapably exceed any cues or implications we may wish to attribute to the text, but the production's main effects and meanings may be far better described and explained in relation to the other present-day modes and examples of performance, of artistic reproduction and indeed of behaviour with which the performance will inevitably share conventions and assumptions. What we need above all to do is to approach contemporary treatments of the plays on their own performative terms, as if performance criticism weren't a poor relation of Shakespearian editing but actually confronted Shakespearian productions as examples of present-day theatre and indeed cultural politics in their own right. The logical extension of this idea is that it would be better if we were to describe any given production of, say, *The Tempest* without spending any of our time referring 'back' to its script or discussing how this company seemed to understand that script. But whatever procedure we follow, we are urged to ditch the comfortable notion that everything done in the name of Shakespeare can be contained as one more expression of his literary authority, in favour of a less blinkered appreciation of both the aesthetics and the sociology of such theatrical events as happen to feature his name on their posters. It would be better, really, if we could write about Shakespeare in the theatre while mentioning Shakespeare as little as possible; this misleadingly implied *auteur* (to use a term helpfully borrowed from antique film criticism by Courtney Lehmann) at very least needs to be put into square brackets while we pay attention to what is really being communicated, shared, enacted or enforced by an event which we only travesty by describing it as if it were just some sort of three-hour footnote to an Arden introduction.

I am more than happy with this line of argument, I should say; certainly I go to the theatre in order to get away from Arden introductions rather than to meet them there, however determined the programme-notes department of the RSC may be to frustrate me in this respect. The approach I've described has done much to invigorate the field of performance studies over the last decade, but I do want to spend some of this chapter offering my own small set of caveats and qualifications. The principal one of these is purely self-interested: namely, much as I might enjoy writing about post-modern performance in general – the category within which live Shakespeare currently happens and outside which it can't be understood – I actually want to go on writing about Shakespearian performance (or [Shakespearian] performance) in particular. This, incidentally, seems to be a desire shared even by the most vigorous present-day opponents of the idea that Shakespearian performance is all about Shakespeare, who, despite their keen awareness of the misleading comforts of the false category 'Shakespeare', continue to produce books called things like *Shakespeare and the Authority of Performance, Shakespeare and the Force of Modern Performance, The Shakespeare Trade, The Shakespeare Effect*, and so on. These are very good books, I should say, and I wish I'd written any or all of them, but another thing about them which for my own particular reasons I find unhelpful is a tendency to choose examples from the range of contemporary live Shakespeares which fit the perspective I've outlined above comparatively easily. It's not all that difficult to suggest the inadequacy or irrelevance of any simple notion of what Shakespeare's text may mean or may be made to mean in performance if the performance you're writing about is a *Timon of Athens* staged in six different languages using a chain-saw, a video loop of the 5th Airborne Division and four stuffed pandas, a show which has been mounted by a group who above all wanted to put on a show in six different languages using a chain-saw, a video loop of the 5th Airborne Division and four stuffed pandas but who recognized that they stood a better chance of attracting a subsidy and an audience if they nominally based it on *Timon of Athens*. It's even easier if you're writing about something still weirder, namely the sort of Shakespearian performances that go on at Shakespeare's Globe. Nor is it too difficult to apply this particular critical paradigm when one is in fact not describing performances at all but interpreting the textual traces of performances. Worthen's *Shakespeare and the Authority of Performance*, for example, is self-confessedly a book purely about the ways in which other people have written about Shakespearian performance, but a surprising percentage even of performance criticism that deals with specific productions is in fact concerned with performances the critics have only heard about at second or third hand. Many performance critics actually spend a fair amount of their time, as I do, dabbling in a disowned sub-discipline known as 'theatre history', engaged in much the same business of reconstructing and explicating past cultural events from surviving documentary evidence as any literary historian. Robert Shaughnessy's excellent *The Shakespeare Effect*, for example, is 'A History of Twentieth Century Performance', and it only gets around to offering an eye-witness account of a production in its last chapter; sure enough it's an avant-garde production, *Five Day Lear* by the Sheffield group Forced Entertainment. It sounds like a terrific show, but from my own selfish perspective Shaughnessy's account of it doesn't immediately assist me in the work I have in hand.

Let me at last admit what the work is to which I would like to be able to harness this school of criticism, work which in its turn seems to demand the qualification of some of this school's claims. My problem is that I not only want to go on writing about Shakespearian performances in particular, present-day ones as well as ones I didn't see, but I want to go on writing about mainstream Shakespearian performances. Among the tasks currently before me are two which demand that I write about a range of present-day live performances of Shakespeare, and many of those performances, however complex, bizarre or intellectually demanding I regularly find them, are of kinds sometimes dismissed as 'conventional' – as if once something had been identified as working with the expectations and codes of a substantial number of people, we could let ourselves off having to think about it. One task is the composition of the annual account of Shakespearian productions in this country which I've now been contributing to this journal since volume 54. Now even at the most pragmatic level, it wouldn't be that easy to produce an account of all one year's major revivals of plays by Shakespeare for *Shakespeare Survey* without mentioning Shakespeare: I could try it, but I suspect that the results would resemble one of those tedious riddles with which the Anglo-Saxons are supposed to have whiled away the Dark Ages. I'm reluctant, likewise, to attempt to describe the year's Shakespeare productions solely in terms of their deliberately- or inadvertently-deployed modes of post-modern performance, if only because my sense of that category has by now been fatally warped by the experience of having for the past five years seen on average a Shakespeare every ten days and not much else. Constraints of time, energy and resilience being what they are, this Atkins diet of blank verse has been qualified by sadly few new plays; it has been mitigated instead, with whatever further distorting effect on my sense of what normal present-day performance is really like, primarily by modes favoured by other members of my family, namely grand opera, Peking opera, at least four pantomimes and a school nativity every Christmas, and a surprising proportion of ice-dance. Beyond the requirements of *Shakespeare Survey*, my other task is the research for a book about non-professional Shakespearian performance, which is in large part a work of cultural history but which will inevitably involve the description and analysis of some present-day productions. Hence this summer I'm seeing professional and amateur Shakespeare in about equal quantities, both unnaturally large, and I have to write about both, with or without treating their various procedures as so many belated explications of or improvisations around Shakespeare's texts.

I'll try to deal more adequately with the intellectual problems this involves later on; meanwhile let me at last turn to my two examples. I'm going to look at the openings of two recent productions, and especially at what their respective audiences were given before they heard any of Shakespeare's lines. I'm interested particularly in the extent to which these 'preludes', if that isn't too misleading a term for describing what were important parts of the shows proper, did and didn't assume that these audiences were going to understand what they saw and heard as emanating from the script's author.

The first production takes place in a roofed, carpeted, insulated theatre, but after we have heard a taped warning to switch off our mobile telephones and digital watches and the house lights begin to dim, we find ourselves outdoors. The gauzes towards the rear of the stage carry a suggestion of leaves; some of the yellow-and-green-toned lights are shining through filters that create shadows like dappled shade in autumn on the surface of the stage; and the theatre's elaborate digital sound system is relaying birdsong. Very soon, even before the house-lights have finished dimming, those discreetly-concealed speakers are also relaying music, played live by a small ensemble almost invisible on a balcony to the right of the stage. It is courtly and sombre, dominated by a 'cello, and its semi-pastiche of Purcell's string fantasias suggests that this opulently-simulated space must be an aristocratic park. Hence when a single mature female figure arrives on the stage, wearing a black dress of a Jacobean design with a high white ruff, our first assumption is that she must be its mistress. This hypothesis, however, is not what is uppermost in our response to her entrance, which is instead compounded of two affecting shocks. One is a well-nigh physical surprise, as this is a very abrupt entrance: she is half-running toward us, breaking the decorous codes implied by her clothes, clearly under the pressure of some strong emotion. Given that she appears to be in mourning, this emotion is presumably grief, and given the way in which she keeps looking intently at what appears to be a wedding ring on one of her fingers, this is presumably grief for a dead husband. The other shock, as she pauses to collect herself, glancing huntedly behind her as if toward an offstage pursuer, is one of intense familiarity: it feels suddenly that we are in the presence not just of a grief-stricken woman but of a grief-stricken member of our own families. The auditorium instantaneously warms into a state of heightened and concerned attention, and it is as if on the strength of this wave of collective feeling that she is able to reassume her correct, controlled social persona just in time to be caught up with on the stage by a group of other characters, also in Jacobean mourning clothes. She turns apologetically toward the oldest of them, a man of her rank who clearly enjoys the status of an old family friend, in order to explain and excuse this temporary lapse into unsociability, and for the first time that evening the audience encounter in person once more and perhaps for the last time the rich, confiding, unmistakable voice they would probably have paid double to hear: 'In delivering my son from me I bury a second husband'. The performer is of course Dame Judi Dench, playing the Countess of Roussillon in Gregory Doran's RSC production of *All's Well That Ends Well*, which opened at the Swan in Stratford in early November 2003 and closed at the Gielgud in London in early May 2004. Many readers of this journal, I fear, must have missed it. Tough. I'm sorry, but that's one of the tricky and faintly disreputable problems with performance criticism; the writer was there and the reader generally wasn't; the work of art against which you might want to double-check my interpretation or even my description was vanishing forever even as I was seeing it. Unlike reading, performance is irredeemably parochial; no matter how celebrated the performer or the company, it remains confined to a particular assembly of people at a specific time and place.

Many in that audience in November definitely knew that the opening stage direction in the text of *All's Well That Ends Well* doesn't specify a solo entry for the Countess in advance of the rest of her household; and very few can have imagined that Shakespeare wrote the role specifically as a vehicle for Dame Judi, though a great many clearly felt that he obviously would have done if he'd had the chance. That this performance should exceed what traces we have of Shakespeare's notion of *All's Well* by using a female performer in the midst of some highly mimetic lighting and sound effects was unremarkable enough; what was more striking was the way in which the stature of this particular performer, her presence over time in the minds and lives of that audience, both mandated and vindicated this small initial piece of adaptation. Though I have myself tried to miss as little of her work as possible, I did miss seeing Judi Dench as Juliet – unfortunately I couldn't get up to the Old Vic at all that season, as I was too busy being born. To my eternal regret I was still going to bed too early for evening shows when she was cast as Viola, and in the event I only caught up with Dench's theatre work when she was playing Lady Macbeth – a role in which, even allowing for the fact that I was very impressionable at the time, she was amply impressive enough for me to resolve to watch her as often as possible thereafter. But many people in the opening night audience of *All's Well* at the Swan had clearly been admirers from the very earliest phase of Dench's career, before even that wonderful episode of the police series *Z-Cars* in which she was the juvenile delinquent who spat all over Brian Blessed, and what the opening gambit of Doran's *All's Well* achieved perfectly was to harness and acknowledge their emotions toward the actress herself as a sort of induction to the play. In all our minds was the consciousness that, thanks to the special exception to the normal realist rules against cross-age casting that is habitually made in favour of experienced popular actresses, this would almost certainly be the last Shakespearian role Dame Judi would ever play on stage. Despite the fact that the Countess, with a son who hasn't yet attained his majority, was probably imagined by Shakespeare as no older than forty (certainly younger than Gertrude, a part played this same year as a winsome ingenue at the

Old Vic, by Imogen Stubbs), this is conventionally the last role in the canon a major Shakespearian actress ever plays, and this play is often revived solely to enable her to do so. Dame Edith Evans played the Countess in her last Stratford season in 1959; Dame Peggy Ashcroft played it in hers in 1981. To last in the profession long enough to get cast as the Countess at all, you have to be very good; and just as successful corporate accountants, because their work deals in large sums of money, get very rich, so successful actresses, because their work deals in the feelings of large roomfuls of people, get very much loved. Dame Judi Dench's last live performance in a Shakespearian role, regardless of which role it was or how she played it, was inevitably going to be one of those occasions of national mourning which the English do so well, partaking slightly of the mood of the Queen Mother's funeral or the last scheduled flight of the Concorde. To this extent Doran's show couldn't really fail to be both memorable and moving – quite apart from the fact that by this stage in her career Judi Dench can probably manage to produce a pretty reasonable performance with only a minimum of directorial assistance. But that opening trick – of having her enter alone for what amounted to a momentary wordless soliloquy before the other characters specified in the text's opening direction could reach the stage – did more than allow her to remind us unexpectedly soon of how good she is at expressing finely variegated shades of sorrow and stoicism. Her initially overwrought and then visibly composed initial appearance suggested that she was fleeing to the stage – to us – in search at once of privacy and of comfort. We were thus granted an intimate relationship to her which trumped her relations with any of the characters who subsequently arrived on the stage (a relationship which risked trumping our relations to them too: in this play, the character granted the privilege of the first solo encounter with the audience is usually Helena). It was a relationship, furthermore, which she apparently needed to get her into and through the script of the play at all. Anticipating an audience who had arrived at the theatre sorrowful about the imminent departure of Judi Dench from the Shakespearian stage, that stage immediately mirrored that feeling back to us in the person of a Dench-as-Countess who was herself in mourning and who, moreover, could just about be comforted in private by us. If this performance looked inevitably like a live seventeenth-century recapitulation of Dench's cinematic performance as a grieving Queen Victoria, then this time it was we who were cast as John Brown. Before a word of the script had been spoken, as if behind its back, an odd and affecting contract of mutual consolation had been signed.

One of this contract's terms, however, was that we were all to pretend that Dench's valedictory performance was completely subordinate to the play, and we signalled our acceptance of this condition by conscientiously not clapping. For perhaps the first two thirds of Dame Judi's career, giving a long-serving actress an elaborate entrance of her own and a pause before her first line meant only one thing: here's the star you've paid to see, reassure her that she's still famous by applauding now. Doran's handling of the beginning of *All's Well* was to that extent pure old-style West End (actually, so was his handling of much of the middle and the end of it too). But Dame Judi is a Shakespearian actress, not just a West End one, and this production wasn't supposed to be just show-business, subject to having its cast take bows at the expense of the script, and so we tacitly, unclappingly, welcomed Dench as a sharer of Shakespeare's authority, willing to assume that however her presence might overshadow the comparatively minor role in which she had been cast, her performance would not violate that authority's limits. The production tempted us to be vulgar enough to greet her with applause, and then congratulated us on saving it all up for the curtain call. In the meantime, the usual house rules applied.

There's a great deal more that might be said about this opening, needless to say, but I'm going to postpone any further discussion of this show for the moment and turn instead to the opening of a different production, where a different sense of what it was in the performances and their circumstances that might exceed the Shakespearian text prevailed. This time we genuinely are outdoors from the very beginning, in a real garden to which we could not normally have obtained admission at any other time. It is one of the only evenings this English July when anyone would want to be outdoors, and despite a faint odour of insecticide that suggests that the temporary auditorium has been subjected to a pre-emptive spraying before our arrival, the local mosquitoes are delighted. A raked bank of seating with a central aisle slopes down to face a floodlit area of exquisitely-manicured lawn, beyond which lie a herbaceous border and a high wall; this grassy acting area is bounded to our left by the walls and windows of a building which, though familiar, is only habitually seen from this particular angle by a small and select group of people. The building is the Divinity School, part of what is now the Bodleian Library; we are in the Fellows' Garden of Exeter College, Oxford, now temporarily a theatre over which the dome of the Radcliffe Camera, beyond back-stage left, looms like an architectural balloon. Although all the seats cost the same amount of money, the audience this first night, which isn't a capacity one by any means, is divided into two distinct constituencies. The rows of seats nearest the acting area are occupied by what their stoical anoraks declare to be local people, some in old and middle-aged couples, some in extended family groups; clearly long-familiar with this venue from other summers, they pad their plastic seats with the blankets they have brought with them for this purpose, and tuck away thermos-flasks of hot tea by which they hope to survive the long and increasingly chilly second half. The raised banks of benches further back, however, are primarily occupied by foreign summer-school students, temporary residents of this and other Oxford colleges during the lucrative summer months; they haven't had block-bookings made on their behalf, but have just drifted along in small groups, alerted to this particular instance of local culture by the posters which are at present advertising this and at least three other outdoor Shakespeares within a half-mile radius. When the advertised starting time of seven-thirty arrives, a man in casual clothes, who has hitherto been helping with front-of-house duties, walks around the side of the seating and onto the lawn. His entrance produces a ripple of recognition in the front rows, since like Judi Dench he too is an almost legendary figure – although I must admit that I only know this from having just read his bio in the programme:

> Gerard's directing portfolio is almost legendary, with *Twelfth Night* in New College Gardens (2000) and *The Mysteries* at the Old Fire Station (2002) . . . he has also directed *The Comedy of Errors, The Taming of the Shrew, Hamlet* (three times), *Julius Caesar, Macbeth, The Merry Wives of Windsor, Much Ado About Nothing, Richard III* and *Romeo and Juliet.* He now trains candidates for their audition pieces for drama schools . . .

This is Gerard Gould, the production's director, taking the opportunity to address his public before the play proper gets under way. 'Ladies and gentlemen', he announces, 'before we begin, I would just like to remind you to switch off all mobile telephones, and the flashes on your cameras, and also those bits on some cameras that go bleep. Right. Now, welcome to Venice. Over here – ' (he points to the right-hand side of the acting area, where three small pedestal tables are draped mysteriously in green) ' – is the beautiful resort of Belmont, rich, courtly and palatial. Whereas over here – ' (he indicates the left-hand side of the lawn, beyond which three curious small awnings have been erected along a railing) 'is the crowded city of Venice, and just back there are the docks, where traders and merchants throng, making deals. Good. We hope you'll enjoy the show.' The light applause which greets his bowing exit converts, even as he disappears around the side of the auditorium, into a welcome for the entire cast of the play who, to a taped flourish of early music, simultaneously emerge from behind the audience onto the lawn from both sides and begin energetically miming conversations with one another in artfully dispersed groups all over it. As I also know from the programme, this production has enjoyed the services of two wardrobe mistresses and a wardrobe assistant, and they have clearly all been extremely busy dressing a company of eighteen in a range of elaborate approximations to the shapes and textiles of Renaissance Venice. The visual impact of this unscripted ensemble opening is almost overwhelming. Whereas before our field of vision was wholly occupied with soothing natural greens, it is now a mass of vibrant yellows, golds, reds, blues, greys, mauves and purples, striped, embroidered, beribboned, veiled, flocked, trimmed. The extraordinary thing is that even on individual performers nearly every visible scrap of miscellaneous fabric clashes hideously with every other: the whole stage picture is rather like a sudden random rendezvous between the chorus of a light opera and all the least favourite curtains of one's childhood, and the more I look the more it occurs to me that perhaps that is just what it is. But even so, I find that I am still clapping; and so is everyone else. It's another instance of a director's old-school West End instincts mandating the postponement of the Shakespearian text. Just as polite London audiences used to be given a moment between the raising of the curtain and the first actor's first entrance in which to applaud the set, so this audience has carefully been given an opportunity to applaud the production's costumes, which have so far taken precedence over Shakespeare's script. But after a few disbelieving seconds of automatic clapping, this hallucinatory Venice of velvet and lurex is already fading like some Lewis Carroll nightmare. Still chatting vigorously and silently, different groups of bonnets and tights and tunics are leaving the lawn and, as the taped viols fade down only three figures remain, on the left-hand side of the lawn, safely away from the three green tables. One is a tall thin man in a predominantly black costume which may well have appeared in all three of Gerard Gould's interpretations of *Hamlet*; another is a squarish figure whose short legs, protruding from beneath a brown and burgundy mini-tunic, are clad in off-puce tights, and whose large head is made the more disproportionate by a heavy blue hat complete with dangling purple scarf; and the third, for the time being, is partly obscured behind the first. But as the man in black begins for the first time to speak audibly – 'In sooth, I know not why I am so sad', he intones, looking soulfully above our heads – his other interlocutor steps fully into view for the first time. Once more, strangely, and quite irrelevantly to the nominal content of Shakespeare's text, I find myself consoled by the excessiveness of a live Shakespearian performance: for even then and there I know that, whatever disasters may befall me in life, I will from now on always be able to comfort myself with this thought: *at least I don't have to wear the costume issued to Salerio in the 2004 Oxford Theatre Guild production of The Merchant of Venice.*

Now as no one knew better than Shakespeare, it is very easy to be snide at the expense of non-professional performers, and before I go any further I should say that many of the performances in this *Merchant of Venice*, from a blandly evaluative standpoint, weren't bad at all; in fact the Portia made considerably more sense of her role than did the last two I've seen in the professional theatre. This show's Launcelot Gobbo wasn't any more or less embarrassingly unfunny than the Lavache in Doran's *All's Well That Ends Well*; and to damn with equally faint praise, its Jessica was no less nuanced than was Doran's Diana. Purely because I'm writing, as usual, for a readership familiar with the RSC and probably not well acquainted with the Oxford Theatre Guild, I've said more about the sociology and the venue when describing the latter, but what I've described as being the case about the audience in Exeter Fellows Garden in any case closely parallels how things are in Stratford: there's a loyal core of solid middle-class habituees which is effectively subsidized by a large proportion of tourists and students. Despite the fact that one of these shows 'welcomes Accenture as [its] Global High Performance Business Partner' while the other 'acknowledges the invaluable help of the 8th Oxford Scout Group', what these productions have in common is probably more obvious and more important than what divides them. Both take the first available opportunity to assert the authority of the director, who has choreographed an initial entry which we couldn't have anticipated from the text alone, offering us a glimpse of his vision of Shakespeare's Rousillon or Shakespeare's Venice before any of the actors can get to work speaking any lines. In fact both directors even ensure that their own voices are heard before those of anyone in their respective casts, since the taped announcement in the

Swan warning you to switch off your mobile was pre-recorded by Gregory Doran just as the comparable announcement in the garden was made in person by Gerard Gould. Both productions invoke Shakespeare in a context of domestic and international cultural tourism, at sites associated with a picture-postcard view of the real old England. Above all, and in harmony with this last point, both productions choose to play their respective texts using costumes, props and incidental music which are all supposed to match, and which in both instances are supposed to imitate the appearance of Shakespeare's own time. The RSC may have a more accomplished and better-resourced wardrobe department than does the OTG, and their actors may be better at wearing their handiwork as though they were clothes, but both companies are engaged in treating Shakespeare as costume drama.

It's pretty clear what follows from this, from the point of view of the kind of criticism I was describing earlier. The main thing I ought to do with both shows is offer a critical explication relating their chosen theatrical language to the aesthetic codes of Merchant-Ivory films and nineteenth-century historical novels, and going on to discuss their implication in a heritage industry which perpetually invokes a notion of history only in such a way as to erase the conflicts of which that history is composed. I should be attending closely to the ways in which the actors in each production had been encouraged to feel that their principal task while on stage was fully to inhabit the discourses of realism, simulating clearly-motivated natural behaviour which is all nonetheless subordinated to the disciplinary practices embodied by the director; and in so far as I should be mentioning the Shakespearian text at all, I should be commenting on how both shows used their scripts only as pretexts for theatrical spectacles that were really all about comfort and reassurance. The words, I should point out, were secondary to the *mise-en-scène*, never allowed to challenge the assumptions which all the technical resources of both shows did their best to confirm; all was subordinated cosily to the rules of what remains one of the most powerful conservative genres of our time. This is all perfectly fair, and as far as it goes absolutely right; these were two very cosy pieces of work. Gould's *Merchant of Venice* politely refrained from so much as hinting that the play's depictions of anti-Semitism might have any direct application to the present-day world; Doran's *All's Well That Ends Well*, perversely, did much the same thing for class, depicting a world in which social distinctions were really a problem only in Bertram's head. Helena never really looked very daunted by the gulf between herself and the young Count; in reality the Rousillon household was so merrily egalitarian that the Countess herself participated in the jolly forcible bathing of Lavache. Gould's *Merchant* offered a children's picture-book image of sixteenth-century Venice, Doran's *All's Well* a National Trust reconstruction of Renaissance France. Both shows were formally and ideologically highly conservative.

The trouble with simply treating both productions as insidious purveyors of comforting illusions, though, and what continues to give me pause about this approach, is that it implies that such attempts to play Shakespeare's scripts as blandly escapist costume drama and nothing but blandly escapist costume drama continuously succeed. My own experience, however, suggests that this is not the case; in practice, not only does performance exceed the text but it usually exceeds the conscious aims and aesthetics of the production as well, and occasions on which a director genuinely manages to make a Shakespeare play as homogenous and dull as his or her own ideas about it may be are in practice mercifully rare. For one thing, certain performers simply won't be flattened down into the realist picture. I've already discussed the ways in which Judi Dench threatened to dwarf the Countess and one way in which Doran dealt with this, but one of the other great delights of Doran's *All's Well* was the constant, alienating juxtaposition between Jamie Glover's Bertram and Guy Henry's Parolles. Glover gave the perfect realist performance, simulating real awkward behaviour for all he was worth, speaking even his asides as if completely confident that he just was Bertram and was not, repeat not, in a play. But that's never the way with Guy Henry, whose performances are fascinating partly because they always leave you wondering whether he is an extremely brilliant actor or a very cunningly bad one; whatever the generic or theatrical context, he exudes a strangely gripping embarrassed self-consciousness that we can only partly read as belonging solely to the role; like his unusual height, it is nearly always in excess of the dramatic situations in which his character may be placed, and he is far more at home – in so far as he ever can be – in soliloquy, dealing directly with us in ways which have no parallel in the canons of the BBC classic serial (despite Andrew Davies' recent flirtations with direct address to the camera). This sort of effect is achieved even more frequently in amateur productions, where it is even less likely to seem under the tyrannical control of a director or a particular set of theatrical conventions. The very costumes which were supposed to make Gould's *Merchant* so seamlessly Merchant-Ivory in practice foregrounded the shocking physicality of an occasion on which we were permitted to stare for three hours at the bodies of complete strangers who weren't even insulated from the normal implications of our gaze by membership of the theatrical caste. The trial scene was as shocking as I've ever seen it, and not primarily because the man who played the Duke had the nerve to try to upstage 'The quality of mercy' by nodding sagely and taking notes with a huge quill pen while Portia was speaking. When Antonio removed his shirt in anticipation of Shylock's knife, we were genuinely in the presence of someone else's frail, vulnerable flesh, and the social reality of this was too transgressive to be read as contained by a framework of illusionistic realism. As performance criticism never tires of pointing out, watching performances of Shakespeare isn't like reading critical essays; you are there for three hours or more, it's usually quite comfortable, the actors are speaking some pretty odd and interesting lines even if they are only interested in translating them into immediate objectives, and you can think about it all, in any number of ways above and beyond those which this particular performance is trying to encourage. Even taken on their own chosen terms, live productions tease and challenge and occasionally baffle audiences with such a range and succession of interpretative possibilities that the summary description 'this one was a conservative costume drama' can never be fully adequate; at moments even in the most resolute example of the genre, the historical clothes at which we are looking won't be the simulated externals of a past society but will just be fancy dress, worn in the present by people. The range of dramatic conventions within which Shakespeare worked haven't comfortably fitted the theatrical conventions of any period subsequent to his own, if they even fitted that, though different aspects of the plays have come into focus at different points over time: and one result of this is that inside every Gregory Doran or Gerard Gould production, thank goodness, there is a Brecht or an Artaud or a Garrick or a Brook one struggling with intermittent levels of audibility to get out. If it is true that performance by its very nature exceeds the Shakespearian text, as we are now acknowledging, then we still need to acknowledge that the Shakespearian text exceeds any given performance. So far from staying put around the figure of the author, the position of those square brackets remains endlessly negotiable.

# SHAKESPEARE AND THE PROSPECT OF PRESENTISM

EWAN FERNIE

This essay argues for the crucial importance of Shakespeare *now*. It reflects on presentism: a strategy of interpreting texts in relation to current affairs which challenges the dominant fashion of reading Shakespeare historically. Where new historicism emphasizes historical difference, presentism proceeds by reading the literature of the past in terms of what most 'ringingly chimes' with 'the modern world'.[1] This does not of course compel a choice between antiquarian irrelevance and self-repeating complacency. As we shall see, established new historicism is a complex practice and so – already – is presentism. But a deliberate synthesis of presentism's commitment to 'the now' and historicism's orientation to what is 'other' might reveal a way forward: an alternative presentism focused on, and concerned to maximize, the difference literature makes to the present. With respect to new historicism, the singularity of literature includes but also exceeds historical difference.[2] *Hamlet* stands apart from its conditions of production. It also stands provocatively apart in the present. In his remarkable meditation on the play, Jacques Derrida characterizes 'a masterpiece' in terms of endless uncanny and effective otherness:

> A masterpiece always moves, by definition, in the manner of a ghost. The thing haunts, for example, it causes, it inhabits without residing, without ever confining itself to the numerous versions of this passage, 'The time is out of joint'.[3]

This is the sort of challenging presence I want to put into presentism. Like Shakespeare's ghost, *Hamlet* breaches and disrupts successive presents. The times are thrown into a process of dialectical self-questioning which might result in an alternative future. 1980s deconstruction argued identity is determined by difference rather than presence. But we need a new concept of presence if we are to appreciate the immediacy and power of Shakespeare. Drawing on the burgeoning literature of presentism, George Steiner, Jean-Luc Nancy and Stanley Cavell, this essay begins to provide one. Briefly to exemplify the kind of presentism I have in mind, I argue at the end that *Hamlet*'s singular dramatization of spiritualized violence compels us to confront the defining issue of our present: terrorism.[4] I also contend that the freedom and originality of Shakespeare are better grounds than have

I'm grateful to Hugh Grady, Terence Hawkes and Kiernan Ryan for their expert help with this essay. I'm also indebted to Evelyn Gajowski, David Ruiter, Roger Starling and – as ever – Deanna Fernie. And I'd like to thank Eric S. Mallin, who has helpfully corresponded with me about presentism since his SAA seminar where I first tried my hand at it, and Simon Palfrey, for vigorous discussions of Shakespeare in the present and of *Hamlet*.

1 Terence Hawkes, *Shakespeare in the Present* (London and New York, 2002), p. 22.

2 See Derek Attridge, *The Singularity of Literature* (London and New York, 2004).

3 Jacques Derrida, *Specters of Marx: The State of the Debt, the Work of Mourning, and the New International*, trans. Peggy Kamuf (London and New York, 1994), p. 18.

4 For a longer reading of *Hamlet* that develops in a somewhat different direction, see 'The Last Act: Presentism, Spirituality and the Politics of *Hamlet*', in *Spiritual Shakespeares*, ed. Ewan Fernie (London and New York, 2005), pp. 186–211.

been offered in recent criticism for radical hopes of a transformed future.

### PRESENTING THE PRESENT

According to Helen Moore writing in the *TLS*, 'Presentism is the new kid on the Shakespearean block.'[5] Having argued the case for 'presentism' since *The Modernist Shakespeare* (1991), Hugh Grady explains in his most recent book, 'I borrow and redefine this term from the field of history and the philosophy of history, where it is a pejorative designating a naïve view of the past as homogeneous with the present.'[6] Within Shakespeare and Renaissance studies, the word 'presentism', where it is employed at all, has also tended to be used pejoratively: Jean E. Howard used the term in this negative fashion (after the historian Dominick LaCapra) in her influential consideration of new historicism in 1986, and David Scott Kastan has more recently done so in *Shakespeare After Theory* (1999).[7] 'However', Grady contends, 'so dominant have historicist premises become in Shakespeare studies that we need a positive term for that necessary form of historical perception which understands that *any* view of the past is formed within discourses of the present.' In spite of the negative associations attaching to 'presentism', it is adopted by Grady, he says, 'for want of a better' term.[8]

Grady's pioneering work demonstrates that critically reflecting on the beginnings of modernity may help to negotiate its end. In *Shakespeare's Universal Wolf* (1996), Grady argues that the Bard criticized the incipient devastation of communal life by the 'purposeless purposiveness' of science and capitalism at the onset of the modern era.[9] A conviction of the priority of the present enables him to defy the chronology of the plays and read with a view to intervening in the present. Having treated *Troilus and Cressida, Othello* and *King Lear* as attacks on the increasing mechanization of culture, Grady ends his book by holding up *As You Like It* 'as a kind of photographic negative of reification', 'a utopian projection of imagined alternatives to an increasingly reified social reality' – a beacon of postmodern hope.[10]

An even more unabashed engagement with the present is evinced by Terence Hawkes's *Shakespeare in the Present* (2002). Hawkes's readings of Shakespeare's texts offer not so much 'the methodical exposition of a thesis' as a series of performances which, dancing balletically between past and present, defy paraphrase even while they each land a polemical punch.[11] Hawkes reads *Hamlet*, for example, through the extraordinary story of Mauriz Leon Reiss, a Jewish actor who defied the death camps to endorse Shakespeare's play for the Allied censors as suitable for the moral reformation of fallen Berlin. In light of the history of the twentieth century, 'the passive sweet William of romantic legend' should, according to Hawkes, be supplanted by 'the intervening, directing, policing Old Bill appropriate to a harsher reality'.[12] Another central argument of *Shakespeare in the Present* is that, after 'devolution' and the establishment of Welsh, Scottish and Northern Irish parliaments in 1999, 'the "Great Britain" project, chronicled and

5 Helen Moore 'Present and Correct', *Times Literary Supplement*, August 15 2003, p. 22.

6 Hugh Grady, *The Modernist Shakespeare: Critical Texts in a Material World* (Oxford, 1991); *Shakespeare, Machiavelli and Montaigne: Power and Subjectivity from Richard II to Hamlet* (Oxford, 2002), p. 1, n. 1.

7 Jean E. Howard, 'The New Historicism in Renaissance Studies', in *New Historicism and Renaissance Drama*, ed. Richard Wilson and Richard Dutton (London and New York, 1992), p. 26; David Scott Kastan, *Shakespeare after Theory* (London and New York, 1999), p. 17. Margreta de Grazia criticized presentism for collapsing historical difference in a 2004 SAA session in New Orleans titled 'Missing Links: Historicism, Presentism and the Limits of the Modern'. For a detailed printed critique of presentism, see Robin Headlam Wells, 'Historicism and "Presentism" in Early Modern Studies', *The Cambridge Quarterly*, 29 (2000), 37–60 and *Shakespeare on Masculinity* (Cambridge, 2000). See also Edward Pechter, 'What's Wrong with Literature?', *Textual Practice*, 17 (2003), 505–26. For more positive overviews, see Moore and Marshall Brown, 'Literature in Time', *Modern Language Quarterly*, 65 (2004), 1–5.

8 Grady, *Shakespeare, Machiavelli and Montaigne*, p. 1, n. 1.

9 Hugh Grady, *Shakespeare's Universal Wolf: Studies in Early Modern Reification* (Oxford, 1996), p. 33.

10 Grady, *Shakespeare's Universal Wolf*, p. 56.

11 Hawkes, *Shakespeare in the Present*, p. 1.

12 Hawkes, *Shakespeare in the Present*, p. 82.

reinforced throughout Shakespeare's plays', is 'now thoroughly suffused with different levels and intensities of irony', as Hawkes's readings of *Henry IV* and *Cymbeline* in the contexts of this recent history bear out.[13] Such irony, Hawkes intimates, ought to nail the imperial project in its coffin for good.

One further, more developed example will give a better idea of Hawkes in action. Hawkes observes that Kenneth Grahame's model for Rat in *The Wind in The Willows* was supposedly Frederick James Furnivall, founder of the New Shakspere Society, which was devoted to sorting Shakespeare's messy corpus out by means of 'scientific' textuality. He asks,

> Is it possible that 'Ratty' and his friends, with their quaint public-school slang, their cosy plying of hamper, toast and teapot, their unhesitating contempt for the poorly spoken, property-invading, red-eyed scavengers, the weasels, might offer a useful purchase on the essence of New Shakspere-ism? Are they the lighter side of a cruder project whereby Shakespeare's cruel and savage England itself contracts into a comfy theme park, thronged by the outrageous and endearing, but surrounded by a wild wood peopled by foreign weasly creatures?[14]

Once he has proposed this link between the decorum of Victorian Shakespeare scholarship and English class prejudice and xenophobia, Hawkes recalls that 'for years the Royal Shakespeare Theatre at Stratford put on annual, and hugely successful dramatizations of *The Wind in the Willows*'.[15] He then subverts the political project implicit in this and, he suggests, much Shakespeare teaching in schools – that of shaping the subjectivity of children – by reverting to the uncontainable Mr Toad, and his similarly disruptive Shakespearian antetypes, 'Sir Toby Belch, Sir John Falstaff and Bully Bottom'.[16] Recalling his signature blast on the horn of his newfangled motor car – 'O bliss! O poop-poop!' – Hawkes further associates Toad with jazz, in particular with Duke Ellington's Shakespearian *Such Sweet Thunder* and 'Sonnet to *Hank Cinq*'. For Hawkes, the concept of 'playing' brings jazz improvization together with the unscripted, extra-verbal and spontaneous dimension of Shakespeare's plays, in a serious challenge not just to the language-centred rationalism of Victorian textual scholarship but to the symbolic order itself.[17]

While they remain highly compatible and complementary, particularly in their dissenting politics, Hawkes's and Grady's respective versions of presentism are also different. Grady's definition and practice of presentism are essentially historical, enabled by his crucial recognitions that the past can be seen only from the perspective of the present and that Shakespeare's position at one end of modernity is structurally similar to our own equally transitional situation at the other. Hawkes's presentism is more performative: an assertion and demonstration of the immediate freedom and energy of the critical act.

Both Grady and Hawkes play up presentism's challenge to new historicism, but I shall argue in the next section that the conditioning of the past by the present is also a long-standing and increasingly urgent issue within new-historicist theory and practice. Pertinent to new historicism as well as to those looking for an alternative, presentism should be on the agenda of literary criticism as such.

## THE NEW IN NEW HISTORICISM

After a quarter of a century of new historicism, it is time to bring Shakespeare blinking into the present. New historicism has often recognized that the past is conditioned by the present, but it typically disavows this knowledge as an obstacle to experiencing historical difference and distance. Insistently anti-essentialist, new historicism stresses the alterity of the past. It reads literature in terms of past time in order to recover and reveal its 'embeddedness' and foreignness. But if reality is thoroughly historical and changing, and there is no vantage point outside history, then the difference of the past is ultimately inconceivable and unreachable, because

[13] Hawkes, *Shakespeare in the Present*, pp. 62, 4.
[14] Hawkes, *Shakespeare in the Present*, p. 122.
[15] Hawkes, *Shakespeare in the Present*, p. 123.
[16] Hawkes, *Shakespeare in the Present*, p. 107.
[17] Hawkes, *Shakespeare in the Present*, pp. 107, 126.

it will always be filtered through the difference of the present. Benedetto Croce takes this so far as to see all history as 'history of the present'.[18]

In *Renaissance Self-Fashioning* (1980) – the book which established the critical ascendancy of new historicism – Stephen Greenblatt accepts 'the impossibility of fully reconstructing and re-entering the culture of the sixteenth century, of leaving behind one's own situation'. He admits that 'it is everywhere evident in this book that the questions I ask of my material are shaped by the questions I ask of myself'.[19] According to Graham Holderness, new historicism recognizes history 'only as a contemporary activity of narrating or representing the past'.[20] Jeffrey Cox and Larry Reynolds concur that new historicism 'rejects the idea of "History" as a directly accessible, unitary past, and substitutes for it the conception of "histories", an ongoing series of human constructions'.[21] In the view of John Parker, moreover, precisely what distinguishes new from old historicism is the realization that 'literature's context obeys no clear boundaries and includes, along with all the exotic anecdotes culled from obscure sources, the present'.[22]

In addition to recognizing the general impact of the present on the past, new historicism has often reflected on its own historical situation. In *Shakespeare's Universal Wolf*, Hugh Grady suggests that the acknowledgement of 'the inescapable reality of cultural and historical difference' should logically entail a self-reflexive recognition of the historicity of new historicism and its historicizing procedures themselves.[23] But it often has. Richard Wilson's introduction to his and Richard Dutton's co-edited *New Historicism and Renaissance Drama* (1992) is concerned with 'historicising new historicism'.[24] Howard argues that 'the Renaissance, seen as the last refuge of preindustrial man, is of such interest to scholars of the postindustrial era because these scholars construe the period in terms reflecting their own sense of the exhilaration and the fearfulness of living inside a gap in history'.[25] Louis Adrian Montrose observes that new historicism might be 'compensation for the acceleration in the forgetting of history which seems to characterize an increasingly technocratic and future-oriented academy and society'. Elsewhere Montrose suggests that the new-historicist characterization of 'writing as a mode of *action*' might additionally compensate for a 'nagging sense of professional, institutional and political impotence' in the academy.[26] And, in *Practicing New Historicism*, Greenblatt and Catherine Gallagher write as follows about new historicism's opening up such novel subjects as race and gender for historical enquiry:

> It is hardly an accident that this broader vision of the field of cultural interpretation, which had been mooted for more than a century, first took hold in the United States in the late '60s and '70s. It reflected in its initial period the recent inclusion of groups that in many colleges and universities had hitherto been marginalized, half hidden, or even entirely excluded from the professional study of literature: Jews, African Americans, Hispanics, Asian Americans, and, most significantly from the point of view of the critical ferment, women.[27]

The present also impinges powerfully on new-historicist critical practice. Claire Colebrook observes that 'a feature of new historicist criticism' is 'the *recognition* of new historicism's own theory

---

18 Benedetto Croce, *History as the Story of Liberty*, trans. Sylvia Spriggs (London, 1941), p. 19.

19 Stephen Greenblatt, *Renaissance Self-Fashioning: from More to Shakespeare* (Chicago and London, 1980), p. 5.

20 Graham Holderness, *Shakespeare Recycled: The Making of Historical Drama* (Hemel Hempstead, 1992), p. 2.

21 Jeffrey N. Cox and Larry J. Reynolds, eds., *New Historical Literary Study: Essays on Reproducing Texts, Representing History* (Princeton, 1993), p. 1.

22 John Parker, 'The Promise of History', *Shakespeare Studies*, 30 (2002), 43–6; p. 44.

23 Grady, *Shakespeare's Universal Wolf*, p. 24.

24 Richard Wilson, 'Introduction: Historicising New Historicism', in *New Historicism and Renaissance Drama*, pp. 1–19.

25 Howard, 'The New Historicism in Renaissance Studies', p. 22.

26 Louis Adrian Montrose, 'Renaissance Literary Studies and the Subject of History', *English Literary Renaissance* 16 (1986), 5–13; p. 11 and 'The Elizabethan Subject and the Spenserian Text', in *Literary Theory/ Renaissance Texts*, ed. Patricia Parker and David Quint (Baltimore, 1986), p. 332.

27 Catherine Gallagher and Stephen Greenblatt, *Practicing New Historicism* (Chicago and London, 2000), p. 11.

in the texts it studies'. 'There are certain critical motifs at work in new historicism', she writes, 'which the critic frequently sees as already thematized by Renaissance texts themselves'.[28] In *Renaissance Self-Fashioning*, it is impossible to distinguish the meaning of the texts Greenblatt surveys from his seemingly Foucauldian, twentieth-century theory of power. The Renaissance texts being examined seem to produce the theory at the same time as they are reproduced by it; historicism and presentism are oddly at one. Colebrook also notes that '[t]he choice of the Renaissance as one of new historicism's privileged domains of examination is significant here. If the Renaissance is the beginning of both capitalism and modernity, then any critical reading of the Renaissance will also be a critique (and recognition) of the present'.[29] A major indication of the part an embryonic historical presentism plays in new-historicist criticism is the widespread replacement of the historical label 'Renaissance' by 'early modern'. Implicit in this refiguration of the period is not only the assumption that it is in our time-zone, but also that it occupies a structurally comparable position at one end of that epoch to ours at the other. This exactly parallels Grady's assumption of the same continuity from early modern, to modern, to postmodern.

Grady's key insights – into the conditioning of the past by the present, and the structural relation between the beginning and the end of modernity – are, therefore, both echoed in new historicism; but, whereas they provide the inspiration for Grady's critical project, in new historicism they tend to be hurriedly repressed. Notwithstanding his admission in *Renaissance Self-Fashioning* that his work is influenced by the present, Greenblatt goes on to assert that his chapters are dictated by the historically 'specific situation of the author or text'.[30] As Grady suggests, 'consciousness of the present is allowed to dissolve into a familiar historical reconstruction which appears to recover the truth of the past unproblematically'.[31] In fact, as we have seen, Greenblatt's methods bring historicism and presentism together by 'discovering' twentieth-century theory in Renaissance texts, but it is definitely the present rather than the past which is denied and elided as he apparently transports us back in time. Peter Erickson agrees that new historicism 'regards the present as an influence to be neutralized, or escaped'.[32]

As Ivo Kamps admits, the new-historicist critic's task 'is . . . a difficult and paradoxical one: to study a distant past that is shrouded in/by the present'.[33] Leonard Tennenhouse understands this task 'as something akin to wriggling out of my cultural skin, much as someone might wriggle out of a particularly close-fitting turtleneck shirt'.[34] This seems to admit the impossibility of being really historical. Notice how strained the simile is. It's not only that it simply isn't so easy to slip out of one's cultural skin as it is to disengage oneself from even 'a particularly close-fitting turtleneck'; given the cardinal new-historicist belief that reality, and subjectivity in particular, is altogether historically determined, it has to be impossible. In the Routledge *Encyclopaedia of Literature and Criticism*, Don E. Wayne finds new historicists typically guilty of using a smokescreen of 'often ingenious and agile rhetoric . . . to avoid articulating . . . the cultural economy of their relation to the past', but Tennenhouse, stuck and struggling in his cultural turtleneck, makes plain the continuing problem for historicism of the conditioning of history by the present.[35]

Of course, many historicist works, particularly in their introductions and conclusions, do verge on and even declare a subdued presentism. In a passage

[28] Claire Colebrook, *New Literary Histories: New Historicism and Contemporary Criticism* (Manchester and New York, 1997), p. 200.

[29] Colebrook, *New Literary Histories*, p. 200.

[30] Greenblatt, *Renaissance Self-Fashioning*, p. 8.

[31] Grady, *The Modernist Shakespeare*, pp. 229–30.

[32] Peter Erickson, 'Rewriting the Renaissance, Rewriting Ourselves', *Shakespeare Quarterly*, 38 (1987), 327–37; p. 335.

[33] Ivo Kamps, *Materialist Shakespeare: A History* (London and New York, 1995), p. 3.

[34] Leonard Tennenhouse, *Power on Display: The Politics of Shakespeare's Genres* (New York, 1986), p. 11.

[35] Don E. Wayne, 'New Historicism', in *Encyclopaedia of Literature and Criticism*, ed. Martin Coyle, Peter Garside, Malcolm Kelsall and John Peck (London and New York, 1990), p. 802.

which resonates with the brief reading of *Hamlet* at the end of this essay, Richard Wilson's *Secret Shakespeare* links early modern militant Catholicism to 'religious violence' before and after 9/11: 'For as I write this, on the site of Shakespeare's Gatehouse, the "Ring of Steel" around Blackfriars and the City, first erected to counter the Catholic IRA, is being reinforced, to seal the precinct even more securely from a world elsewhere'.[36] Erickson characterises responsibility toward the present as a salient feature of feminism as opposed to new historicism.[37] Works like Fran Dolan's *Dangerous Familiars: Representations of Domestic Crime in England, 1500–1700*, and the developing corpus of works on female agency, are powerfully motivated by continuing historical injustices to women.[38] But in the deceptively simple manoeuvre of promoting such responsibility toward the present above the historicist obligation to the past, presentism constitutes a major methodological departure.

Grady is convinced of the increasing exclusion of presentism by historicism in contemporary Shakespeare and Renaissance studies. In 2002, he reported, 'today in early modern literary studies, historicism, new or old, interwoven with feminism and psychoanalysis or not, has become virtually an unrivalled paradigm for professional writing. The turn to historicism has become taken for granted.'[39] But, as we have seen, the present is not so much done away with in new historicism as it is repressed. As what must be excluded from critical awareness in order to sustain historical contact, the present may be considered the unconscious which new historicism occasionally appeases and betrays. So desperately is it repressed in one of the most influential historicist interventions in recent years as to suggest imminent theoretical crisis. In *Shakespeare after Theory*, Kastan advocates 'a robust sense' of Shakespeare's historical 'particularity and contingency' which entails strenuously ignoring the fact that the present conditions the past, even though Kastan admits the 'situatedness of the critic . . . determines the questions that are asked of the past'.[40] The repression of the present here is intellectually unsustainable – all the more so since the spectacle of a prominent critic looking so fixedly backwards in an effort to ignore the present must itself be a compelling feature of the present.

The present is the stumbling-block in front of the past which historicism pretends to step round. But historicist critics also need this obstacle to sustain their own desire for history. We come close to the source of new-historicist motivation with these strange and famous words:

> I began with the desire to speak with the dead . . . If I never believed that the dead could hear me, and if I knew that the dead could not speak, I was nonetheless certain that I could recreate a conversation with them. Even when I came to understand that in my most intense moments of straining to listen all I could hear was my own voice, even then I did not abandon my desire. It was true that I could only hear my own voice, but my own voice was the voice of the dead . . .[41]

Greenblatt's desire, as it is expressed here, is premised on impossibility. If he could speak with the dead, then he wouldn't need to. It is the impossibility of Greenblatt's desire which provokes the weird improvisation he describes of a dialogue in which he takes his own voice firstly as his and then as the voice from the grave. This is a brilliant condensation of the procedure of historicism; Kastan is essentially doing the same in his comparable effacement of the present. It isn't quite a *reductio ad absurdum*, not so much because of the qualifications

[36] Richard Wilson, *Secret Shakespeare: Studies in Theatre, Religion and Resistance* (Manchester, 2004), p. 7.

[37] Erickson, 'Rewriting the Renaissance', p. 385.

[38] Frances E. Dolan, *Dangerous Familiars: Representations of Domestic Crime in England, 1500–1700* (Ithaca, 1994). For examples of work on female agency, see Kathryn Schwartz, '"Fearful Smile": Stealing the Breech in Shakespeare's Chronicle Plays', *Shakespeare Quarterly*, 49 (1998), 140–67; Barbara E. Bowen, 'The Rape of Jesus: Aemilia Lanyer's *Lucrece*', in *Marxist Shakespeares*, ed. Jean E. Howard and Scott Cutler Shershow (London and New York, 2001), pp. 104–28; and Clare McManus, *Women on the Renaissance Stage: Anna of Denmark and Female Masquing in the Stuart Court 1590–1619* (Manchester and New York, 2002).

[39] Grady, *Shakespeare, Machiavelli and Montaigne*, p. 1.

[40] Kastan, *Shakespeare after Theory*, p. 17.

[41] Stephen Greenblatt, *Shakespearian Negotiations: The Circulation of Social Energy in Renaissance England* (Berkeley and Los Angeles, 1988), p. 1.

Greenblatt goes on to make as because there is something impressive, even heroic, about new historicism's impossible yearning for historical contact. Indeed, Greenblatt's words echo Lacan's imperative, 'Do not give up on your desire!'[42] But Greenblatt's make-believe séance also involves the laboured repression and distortion of the truth of our severance from the past which we have observed in new historicism in general.

The present is the inassimilable element in new historicism, it is the obstacle to fulfilment which sustains its desire, and it is becoming increasingly impossible to disavow. A major reckoning with its place in literary criticism is essential to the continued credibility of Shakespeare studies.

## THE PRESENCE OF THE TEXT IN THE PRESENT

Grady's and Hawkes's presentism specializes in the very 'situatedness of the critic in the present' with which new historicism has struggled to cope. Grady resituates history in the present, and Hawkes privileges criticism as present action. But presentism is also in a position to engage with the presentness of the historical work of art. I propose that presentism should study the presence of the Shakespearian text in the present, with the notion of presence being partly reconceived, after post-structuralism, in terms of difference rather than essence. Shakespeare, in particular, is primarily a contemporary dramatist and writer, because he is currently taught, read and performed on a global scale unmatched by any other author. With respect to new historicism, this means that he is more embedded in our modern world than he ever was in the Renaissance. The historicist project of transporting the Bard back to an alien history, while it may (so far as this is possible) restore his work to 'the specific imaginative and material circumstances in which they were written and engaged', labours unhelpfully against the fact of their presence and embeddedness here and now.[43] But, *pace* Grady and Hawkes, I will contend that literature is in the present but at odds with it – decisively dissonant, rather than concordant, with 'the modern world'. This holds true for literature now and, in the case of Shakespeare, is only partly a function of age. The gap between Shakespeare's historical dimension and the present helps constitute literature as a present experience of historical difference but, insofar as it is singular and creative, the Shakespearian text is also irreducible to history. And the creativity of literature is a concrete revelation of the possibility of change.

Grady's technique of drawing an historical analogy between early and late modernity casts light on but also predetermines the meaning of Shakespeare's texts in the present. Hawkes's stress on what Shakespeare can be made to mean by present criticism obscures what the alien presence of the text in the present may signify or suggest to us by itself. The emphasis in new historicism on the alterity of the past warns against the homogenization of history, which is a major danger for presentism. But new historicism's backwards orientation prevents much recognition and analysis of the presentness of the historically alien text. Putting the presence into presentism matters if George Steiner is right that 'the eclipse of the humanities, in their primary sense and presentness, in today's culture and society, implicates that of the humane' and that

> [w]e flinch from the immediate pressures of mystery in poetic, in aesthetic acts of creation as we do from the realization of our diminished humanity, of all that is literally bestial in the murderousness and gadgetry of this age. The secondary is our narcotic. Like sleepwalkers, we are guarded by the numbing drone of the journalistic, of the theoretical, from the often harsh, imperious radiance of sheer presence.[44]

After 1980s deconstruction, 'presence' has been avoided as a suspect category that helped secure

---

[42] See especially Jacques Lacan, *The Ethics of Psychoanalysis 1959–1960; The Seminar of Jacques Lacan*, ed. Jacques Alain Miller, trans. Dennis Porter (London and New York, 1992).

[43] Kastan, *Shakespeare after Theory*, p. 17. Presentism is not necessarily restricted to the established canon: the effort in recent criticism to rehabilitate obscure, excluded and devalued writers (especially women) is itself an effort to make them present.

[44] George Steiner, *Real Presences: Is There Anything in What We Say?* (London and Boston, 1989), pp. 49–50.

the tyranny of transparently present truths and the present social order. This is probably why it hasn't been considered before in relation to presentism. But the demise of presence has blunted critical receptivity to the savour and immediacy of Shakespeare in particular and experience in general. Steiner's vocabulary of 'mystery' and 'the humane' is uncompromisingly traditional but his thought resonates more with current thinking when he writes, 'The meaning, the existential modes of art, music and literature are functional within the experience of our meeting with the other'.[45] This particularly brings to mind the poststructuralist ethics of Emmanuel Levinas and the later Jacques Derrida that has come to the forefront of critical debate since Steiner wrote *Real Presences* in 1989.[46]

We need a new concept of presence, and recent theory can help. In the work of Levinas, the face of the Other is the sublime exemplum of a new, more mysterious kind of presence, which is at once absolutely compelling and finally ungraspable. After Levinas, postmodern thought evokes presence in terms of difference rather than essence and substance. Precisely because it is irreducibly different, the Other remains demandingly present: it can't be blithely ignored or absorbed. Crucial to this theoretical refit of presence is Jean-Luc Nancy.[47] According to Nancy, presence is the core of experience. Consciousness is exposed to an open-ended series of presences, an ecstatic process of 'presencing' which Nancy thinks of as its continuous 'birth to presence'. In relation to the experience of early modern drama, Gary Taylor observes that presence is not absolute but relative to proximity and perspective.[48] Presence never becomes knowledge, however close we come. It is experienced as the powerful *imminence* of sense – ineffably beyond thought, which it nonetheless irresistibly solicits. Simultaneously with becoming suddenly, overwhelmingly present another person or a play of Shakespeare's becomes mysterious and intellectually engaging.

Steiner writes of aesthetic response: 'our endeavour at welcome, our questioning, will always take place *now* in the presentness of a presence'.[49] According to Nancy, art is the intellectual mode of presencing, whereas philosophy is a procedure of naming and explaining. The difference between art and philosophy 'is, quite simply, a question of knowing, in a voice, in a tone, in a writing, whether a thought is being born, or dying: opening sense, ex-posing it, or sealing it off (and wishing to impose it)'.[50] Thought called by presence to exceed itself; the vital transcendence of philosophy: these thinkers offer criticism a more exalted and creative sense of itself. But Steiner suggests 'we crave remission' from the shocking and commanding pressure of presence, which he conceives in terms of difference that 'enters into us' and 'makes us other'.[51] Current criticism typically fails even to acknowledge the work of art, side-stepping an encounter with its astringent otherness into 'the immunities of indirection'.[52]

Such inoculations have certainly been provided by contemporary Shakespeare and Renaissance criticism's turn toward context, which in practice means anything but the text – from 'preparing a pig for consumption in the Renaissance' to the tourist industry of Stratford-upon-Avon.[53] This

45 Steiner, *Real Presences*, p. 138.

46 Steiner wrote *Real Presences* partly contra deconstruction but, as I shall show, poststructuralist ethics can be creatively combined with his main arguments.

47 See especially Jean-Luc Nancy, *The Birth to Presence*, trans. Brian Holmes *et al.* (Stanford, 1993).

48 See Gary Taylor, 'Divine [ ]sences', *Shakespeare Survey 54*, (Cambridge, 2001), 13–30.

49 Steiner, *Real Presences*, p. 167. Steiner's thought resonates with Jacques Derrida, 'Hostipitality', in *Acts of Religion*, ed. Gil Andijar (London and New York, 2002), pp. 356–421.

50 Nancy, *The Birth to Presence*, p. 4.

51 Steiner, *Real Presences*, pp. 39, 188. Steiner's language resonates here with Levinas's account of how the subject is persecuted and held hostage by the Other. See, for instance, Emmanuel Levinas, *Ethics and Infinity: Conversations with Philippe Nemo*, trans. R. A. Cohen (Pittsburgh, 1985).

52 Steiner, *Real Presences*, p. 39.

53 The quotation is from Patricia Fumerton, 'Introduction: A New New Historicism', in Patricia Fumerton and Simon Hunt, eds., *Renaissance Culture and the Everyday* (Philadelphia, 1999), p. 1. For material on tourism in Stratford, see Barbara Hodgdon, *The Shakespeare Trade: Performances and Appropriations* (Philadelphia, 1998).

contextual framing and focus tames the text's challenging otherness. Steiner concludes: 'I sense that we shall not come to the facts of our unhousedness, of our eviction from a central humanity in the face of the tidal provocations of political barbarism and technocratic servitude, if we do not redefine, if we do not re-experience, the life of meaning in the text, in music, in art.'[54] For Steiner as for Nancy, the work of art is an epitome of presence. The intensity of aesthetic experience reveals the crucial structure of experience as being in the presence of a presence. If we fail in aesthetic response, we are liable to fail at ethics. And, if human being is self-transcending and relational, then we will fail to be or become ourselves.[55]

But, as Steiner's title suggests, 'real presences' nonetheless press powerfully against our critical exclusion zone. Although new historicism has distracted critics through its stress on historical context, Greenblatt has long sensed a presence, like a ghost, in the text, and has recently complained, echoing Steiner, 'It seems a bit absurd to bear witness to the mystery of *Hamlet*; but my profession has become so oddly diffident and even phobic about literary power, so suspicious and tense, that it risks losing sight of – or at least failing to articulate – the whole reason anyone bothers with the enterprise in the first place.' Greenblatt's particular susceptibility to the ghost of Hamlet's father resonates with Derrida's.[56] It is a reminder that Shakespeare's presence is built out of the range of human presences to which he lends dramatic life: not just the ghost but also Lear, Rosalind, Caliban, and so on. Shakespeare makes his own way into the present only inasmuch as his characters come alive here. Since the concept of presence links dramatic character and 'real' human being, presentism may point the way for a revivified character criticism, which explores how and with what effects Shakespeare's characters intrude into our time.

Even though it privileges the critical act, Hawkes's *Shakespeare in the Present* stresses the immediate, incarnate presence of drama. Plays are always bursting with energy physically to break into the present. At the centre of all drama 'there throbs a "live", unpredictable quality of immediacy' which seems 'to frame, manage and work with contingency, with unshaped "here and now" experience, making that a fundamental part of what they have to offer'.[57] Hawkes's reading of drama as improvisatory and interactive rather than mimetic completes an important shift already begun by new historicism's notion of literary and ideological representations as 'shaping fantasies' in an overall poetics of culture.[58] 'The essence of playing', Hawkes writes, 'lies in a symbiotic relationship neatly characterized by the metaphor of the [jazz] trumpeter. Adjustable, responsive, shifting position to "get an echo", it's far more concerned to interact with the material reality of the spectator's world than to impersonate a different "reality" on stage'.[59]

Hawkes's main example of such a rupture – 'when the play's own continuity appears to break down and it seems suddenly to leap out at us' – is the curious one of the mute but menacing proposition he discerns in *Hamlet* that Claudius is really Hamlet's father.[60] This notion of Shakespeare's play possessing an Iago-like power of insinuation represents it in terms of an almost-human ambivalent agency, adding extra density to Steiner's notion of works of art as real presences. Hawkes contrasts the physical immediacy and improvised character of a play in performance with its scripted

54 Steiner, *Real Presences*, pp. 49–50.

55 If recent thought has developed a new, theoretically defensible conception of the Other's presence, Slavoj Žižek has redescribed subjectivity as a 'traumatic excess' or difference which 'shines through' mere creatureliness. See, for instance, Slavoj Žižek, *On Belief* (London and New York, 2001). For Žižek, as for Alain Badiou in, for instance, *Ethics: An Essay on the Understanding of Evil*, trans. Peter Hallward (London and New York, 2001), the 'traumatic excess' which constitutes human being is expressed in both the Freudian 'death drive' and in any self-sacrificing idealistic project.

56 See Greenblatt, *Shakespearian Negotiations*, p. 1. The quotation is from Stephen Greenblatt, *Hamlet in Purgatory* (Princeton and Oxford, 2001), p. 4.

57 Hawkes, *Shakespeare in the Present*, p. 89.

58 See Louis Adrian Montrose, '"Shaping Fantasies": Figurations of Gender and Power in Elizabethan Culture', *Representations*, 2 (1983), 61–94.

59 Hawkes, *Shakespeare in the Present*, p. 111.

60 Hawkes, *Shakespeare in the Present*, pp. 137, 135–7.

fixity, bringing out the messy, excessive sensuality of drama by provocatively blurring the distinction between Shakespeare's plays and early modern bear-baiting. He comes closest to evoking a real presence when he writes of 'a figure [that] might be dimly seen gesturing at us' in or through Shakespearian drama.[61] In his contention that 'at work beneath the surface, there was always – and there remains – a just discernible, non-textual, perhaps non-discursive and even non-human dimension, which requires fully to be confronted in the twenty-first century', he is near to Steiner's suggestion that we are at an existentially and ethically damaging remove from what is other to our habitual, rational humanity.[62] To the phenomenological susceptibility to otherness of Nancy and Steiner, Hawkes adds his own post-Marxist materialism. He senses the presence of a Lacanian pre-symbolic Real in Shakespeare, a 'rough beast' that could throw down the unjust symbolic order insecurely resting on its back.[63]

An original encounter with Shakespeare's presence draws the critic into the present as such. Just waiting to spring into life, drama is 'explosive, propulsive'.[64] Far from containing that energy in historical contextualization, the critic's task is, in Hawkes's view, to play with it in a similarly creative and purposive contribution to the present.[65] There is an obvious but nonetheless compelling reason for favouring the present over the past: *it's happening now*. The present is where we live, and we still may intervene and alter it. It matters precisely that much more than history. The implicit positive corollary of new historicism's view of history as a process of difference is that we are always in a position to begin again. Relieved of new historicism's primary commitment to what is dead and gone, presentism is free to use the insights of new historicism as a pretext for immediate real change. Here is a criticism which, as Hawkes says, 'will not yearn to speak with the dead' but 'will aim, in the end, to talk to the living'.[66] With its emphasis on what is now happening, presentism is in a perfect position to recognize drama in its classical ontology as action and the present as the window of opportunity for its own creative contribution to history.

In the context of the disabling 'blanket coverage' of the present that is provided by contemporary world-wide news agencies and 'the media', Stanley Cavell suggests that Shakespeare's plays have a special capacity 'to make us practical, capable of acting'.[67] They demonstrate, in Cavell's view,

> that events are still specific, that guilt will alter or puff itself out of shape, in order to deny debt for the specific deed for which one is responsible, that the stakes of action and inaction are what they always were, that monsters of evil are only men, that the good in the world is what good men do, that at every moment there is a present passing me by and the reason it passes me by is the old reason, that I am not present to it.[68]

Perhaps new historicism seeks to escape the moral complexities of the present into the simpler atmosphere of another culture's absent and largely vanished past. The recognition that the compelling presence of a Shakespeare play might help us not only to acknowledge the Other but also to recover the power of decision by teaching 'there is a present passing me by and the reason it passes me by is the

61 Hawkes, *Shakespeare in the Present*, p. 125.

62 Hawkes, *Shakespeare in the Present*, p. 126.

63 Hawkes, *Shakespeare in the Present*, p. 126.

64 Hawkes, *Shakespeare in the Present*, p. 115.

65 Recognising the phenomenal presence of the work of art operates here as an induction into responsibility in the present in general. Of course, it would be unfair to regard new historicism as irresponsible. As we have seen from the quote from Greenblatt and Gallagher's *Practicing New Historicism* above, its frustrated presentist tendencies are strongly informed by sympathy for the oppressed and marginalized. Moreover, as I intimated in my remarks on Greenblatt's desire, new historicism's major project of communicating with an ultimately indeterminable, alien past resonates with the impossible passion for the unreachable other that is the defining feature of poststructuralist ethics.

66 Hawkes, *Shakespeare in the Present*, p. 4. Presentism is able to maintain the important ethical distinction between the living and the dead which Derrida struggles to make in *Specters of Marx* but which is recognized in the Gospels when Christ says starkly, 'Let the dead bury their dead' (Matthew 8:22, Luke 9:60).

67 Stanley Cavell, 'The Avoidance of Love: A Reading of *King Lear*', in *Must We Mean What We Say? A Book of Essays* (Cambridge, 1976), p. 118.

68 Cavell, 'The Avoidance of Love', pp. 118–19.

old reason, that I am not present to it' is a good reason to advocate presentism instead.

If presentism is the study of the presence of the text in the present, such study involves a recognition of being in the presence of the text: of being required to respond, of being responsible. That in itself it is an induction into action.

### TIME AND THE TEXT

Presentism relinquishes the fantasy of recovering the text's previous historical reality in favour of embracing its true historicity as a changing being in time. The charge typically levelled against presentism is that, by reflecting the present back at itself from an alien past, it dissolves historical difference. Since historical difference is one means of challenging the present, it follows that new historicism has an advantage over presentism as a form of oppositional thinking. But the kind of presentism I am putting forward has the potential to be more fully responsive to historical difference than new historicism typically is, and it also brings back into view the difference that the literary text makes to history.

The presence of the historical text in the present never simply mirrors and affirms the present. This is partly because the historical text brings into contemporary life its own alien history. Fredric Jameson observes that the literature of the past has drawn the historical Real 'into its own texture', and Greenblatt acknowledges 'the presence within the work of its social being'.[69] We don't need extra history to manifest the historicity of the text: even while it is being read or played in the present, the historical text is clearly historically other to the present, in manifold and unmissable details of its language and cultural logic. But presentism, I suggest, should attend more explicitly to the paradoxical presence of the historically alien text.

For presentism is more able than new historicism to profit from the subversive potential of historical difference which new historicism has impressively emphasized. Backward-looking criticism cannot discriminate what is subversive in the present. Subversion is thoroughly temporal. What is subversive remains so only as long as it threatens the dominant culture. Greenblatt admits, 'we find "subversive" in the past precisely those things that are *not* subversive to ourselves, that pose no threat to the order by which we live and allocate resources', which suggests that new historicism actually *prefers* to treat as subversive that which no longer retains any power to subvert. If this is true, new historicists have indeed shown that '[t]here is subversion, no end of subversion, only not for us'.[70] By contrast, because it is orientated toward what is happening now, presentism can only treat as subversive what remains subversive in the present. It follows that, in Jameson's words,

> the past will itself become an active agent . . . and will begin to come before us as a radically different form of life which rises up to call our own form of life into question and to pass judgement on us and through us on the social formation in which we exist. At that point the very dynamics of the historical tribunal are unexpectedly and dialectically reversed: it is not we who sit in judgement on the past, but rather the past . . . which judges us, imposing the painful knowledge of what we are not, what we are no longer, what we are not yet.[71]

To the extent that it pays heed to this dialectical presence of the historical text in the present, presentism could be the fulfilment of the 'ethos' that, in 1990, Wayne saw 'struggling to emerge' through new historicism. Wayne read the new-historicist deconstruction of identity in *Renaissance Self-Fashioning* and other seminal works as the precondition of, and as already tending toward, a post-modern ethics 'based on the acknowledgement of difference, but also on the principle of relationship'. He elaborated as follows: 'By understanding our relationship to the past as different but not disconnected, and by recognizing that our construction of

[69] See Kiernan Ryan, *Shakespeare*, 3rd edn (Basingstoke and New York, 2002), pp. 41, 24–5, 40.

[70] Stephen Greenblatt, 'Invisible Bullets', in *Shakespearian Negotiations*, pp. 39 and 65.

[71] Fredric Jameson, 'Marxism and Historicism', in *The Ideologies of Theory: Essays, 1971–1986*, Volume Two: *The Syntax of History* (London, 1988), p. 175. Quoted in Ryan, *Shakespeare*, p. 40.

the past is a function of our relation to the present, we can participate in producing alternatives to the present.'[72] Here an encounter with the alterity of the historical text engenders an awareness that the future will be different again, and Wayne begins to perceive that the past is at once importantly remote from us and ours to put to work in the process of transforming our lives. A more dialectical presentism is in a position to begin this work in earnest.

I am proposing a more complex relation between time and the text than currently obtains in critical discourse. In spite of their disagreements, Grady, Hawkes and the new historicists are all contextualising thinkers who relate the text to one context at a time or, in Grady's case, two matching contexts. Notwithstanding its acknowledgement that the past is conditioned by the present, new historicism, as we have seen, reads the text in relation to the past. Hawkes reads Shakespeare in relation to the present, and Grady reads him relatively to both the (early modern) past and the (late or post modern) present insofar as they are already related or the same. Recent studies in appropriation exemplify the same method of matching texts to single contexts by considering Shakespeare's plays in a linear series of contexts. I have suggested that the literary text is simultaneously in the present and of the past. What I now wish to emphasize is that the presence of the text in the present affords a limited phenomenological comprehension of past, present and future. This is not because the text transcends time, but because of its complex imbrication in history. Carrying its history into the present, it simultaneously foreshadows its different reception in times to come. As Kiernan Ryan writes,

> No matter how complete or cogent our interpretations may appear, and how faithfully they comply with the constraints of the texts, their blinkered standpoint in the present inevitably blinds them to all the other implications stored in the texts, waiting to be unpacked by critics, directors, and actors of the future, with other matters on their minds. To grasp a Shakespeare play as fully as possible at any point in time is to recognise that its gaze is bent on a vanishing point at which no reader or spectator can ever hope to arrive. Like the hat that the circus clown kicks out of reach every time he steps forward to pick it up, final comprehension of the play is indefinitely postponed by each act of interpretation.[73]

In sum, literature constitutes an experience of historicity beyond the scope of rear-view historicism, and the historical difference and intimations of the future this involves provisionalize the present.

That said, inasmuch as it cannot be reduced to historical causes and explanations, the literary text is not just historical, as Steiner's emphasis on its irreducible alterity suggests. J. Hillis Miller writes that 'what makes a literary text important, or literary, is what *exceeds* the social and historical determinants of a text'.[74] Slavoj Žižek asks:

> What if, however, what remains is *the remainder itself*, what Schelling called the 'indivisible remainder', that which STICKS OUT from the organic Whole, the excess which cannot be . . . integrated . . . so that, far from providing the harmonious total image of an epoch, poetry gives voice to that which an epoch was UNABLE to include in its narrative(s)?[75]

For these and other thinkers, a sense of the literary text as an unprecedented and not wholly explainable event is crucial to the experience of its presence here and now. In 'The Origin of the Work of Art', Heidegger writes of 'the bringing forth of a being such as never was before and never will come to be again'. He goes on:

> The more essentially the work opens itself, the more luminous becomes the uniqueness of the fact that it is rather than is not. The more essentially this thrust comes into the open region, the more strange and solitary the work becomes. In the bringing forth of the work there lies this offering 'that it be'.[76]

This acknowledgement of art as an advent within history of that which is not historical is thoroughly

---

72 Wayne, 'New Historicism', pp. 802–3.

73 Ryan, *Shakespeare*, p. 175.

74 J. Hillis Miller, *The Ethics of Reading: Kant, de Man, Eliot, Trollope, James and Benjamin* (New York, 1987), pp. 8–9.

75 Žižek, *On Belief*, p. 96.

76 Martin Heidegger, 'The Origin of the Work of Art', in *Basic Writings*, ed. David Farrell Kreel (London, 1977), p. 181.

at odds with prevailing concepts of the literary after new historicism. Here the strangeness of the work is much more than a by-product of historical difference. It is, we might say, the difference beyond historical difference. Literature is, as Miller says, 'genuinely productive and inaugural in its effects on history'.[77] Emerson's understanding of Shakespeare is relevant here. In 'The American Scholar', he describes the Bard in terms of 'savage unhandselled nature'.[78] A 'handsell' is 'a gift or present (expressive of good wishes) at the beginning of a new year, or on entering upon any new condition, situation, or circumstance' (*OED*). Shakespeare is 'unhandselled' because he is wildly beyond or ahead of convention, his art its own inauguration. Emerson reaches for a neologism in order to demonstrate that what Shakespeare has done cannot be formulated in existing terms.

If we put the historicity of literature, as I have described it above, together with this creative advent within history, we would have to say something like this: the presence of the historical text in the present involves the whole scope of time and yet is simultaneously an experience within time of that which exceeds temporal determination. On the one hand, the literary text absorbs history into itself and constitutes an experience of historicity. On the other, it confounds history as the manifestation of what is historically unprecedented within history. This conception of literature instructs us in the reality of historical time – to be in the audience of a performance of *Hamlet* is automatically to entertain, all at once, a sense of the past from which it originates, the present in which it is now being played, and the future to which it is already on its way. But the phenomenology of the literary text is also testimony to a thrilling potential for breaking out of history. Even the most diligent student of *Hamlet* after Greenblatt would be unable to explain it historically. As much as it is enabled by its historical conditions, Shakespeare's play also transforms them.

And it *retains* the power to draw our minds beyond what is thinkable – to lead thought beyond complacent presentism to a place where the future might be conceived. Remember Derrida's assertion that 'a masterpiece' moves through successive presents, throwing them productively out of joint, like Shakespeare's ghost. With respect to Derrida, Hamlet's god of 'rashness' (5.2.7) is a better figure than the ghost for the challenging otherness of literature. Though often sidestepped in recent criticism,[79] this strange god – 'a divinity that shapes our ends' (5.2.10), 'a special providence in the fall of a sparrow' (5.2.165–6) – brings us nearer to historical difference, confronting modern western secularism more than the ghost does with an outright spirituality beyond its purview. It is also more 'other' than Shakespeare's patriarchal revenant which, for all its uncanniness, is very much an emanation of the social status quo. As a god not of being and the beyond but of becoming and history, Hamlet's 'divinity' evokes the theology of the incarnation. As a 'special providence', it recalls the specifically Calvinist theology of 'predestination': Alan Sinfield points to parallels between Hamlet's phrasing and Calvin's in the *Institutes*.[80] But the pure violence of this fastidiously unspecified 'divinity' which Hamlet speaks of exclusively in contexts of hoisting friends with their own petard and agreeing to take part in a suspicious sword-fight that turns into an orgy of death is entirely subversive of Christian orthodoxy. Its opacity suggests otherness irreducible to any determinate content, let alone early modern Christianity. Hamlet's obscure deity manifests presence as Nancy describes it. Overwhelmingly significant and yet unknowable, it draws the Prince into a dreadfully thrilling, incalculable drama where the only way to respond is rashly. In an exact reversal of what we might expect, Hamlet's mystical experience turns him from a kind of conscientious objector into an activist who says, 'The readiness is all' (5.2.168).

---

77 Miller, *The Ethics of Reading*, p. 8–9.

78 Ralph Waldo Emerson, 'The American Scholar', in *Ralph Waldo Emerson: Selected Prose and Poetry*, ed. Reginald L. Cook, 2nd edn (New York, 1969), p. 48.

79 Notably, it makes little impact on *Hamlet in Purgatory*.

80 Alan Sinfield, *Faultlines: Cultural Materialism and the Politics of Dissident Reading* (Oxford, 1992), p. 226.

In our present, this can't but solicit the ubiquitous thought of terrorism. Sulayman Al-bassam's recent *The Al-Hamlet Summit* (2004) cast Hamlet as a diffident, Europeanized Arabic playboy. It brought *Hamlet* shockingly into the present when the Prince reappeared in the robes of Islamic fundamentalism.[81] Hamlet's passive, indifferent 'readiness' doesn't readily square with militant conviction or with the sort of premeditated violence that has terrorized the imagination of the West in recent years. But it does plunge ethical idealism into the flux and chance of history, abolishing a separate sphere of ethics. And it demonstrates how a pledge to the absolute can combine the violence of a specific commitment with the assurance of doing right. Hamlet cannot do justice in his own behalf, especially as he is the son of the victim. As Kant saw, justice must be performed in the name of transcendental objectivity.[82]

But what sort of justice is achieved at the end of *Hamlet*? Rough justice, certainly. Hamlet, as Sinfield writes, 'plays with Osric (this scene seems purposefully desultory), competes recklessly with Laertes, makes no plan against the king. The final killing occurs in a burst of passionate inspiration'.[83] Moreover, others besides Claudius – namely, Gertrude, whose guilt is disputable, and Laertes – are killed; and Polonius is slain already. And yet, the play has carefully prepared us for rough justice beyond human scope in Hamlet's testimony that 'a special providence' operates *exactly* through such 'rashness' and seemingly random contingency. Moreover, a kind of spirituality of rashness is inherent in the structure of *Hamlet*. A theatrical pun is at work in that Hamlet's act ends the last act of the play, and with the specific act expected with increasing intensity from the beginning. Hamlet's is a last or ultimate, an eschatological act, because it's performed in the name of the absolute, because it's the last thing he does and because it entails his own death.

*Hamlet* frighteningly teases us with the seductive appeal of violent rashness. The last act presents a strange experience, a transaction beyond representation and reason, by means of which a hero stirs, awakes and at last does what must be done. Moreover, the indiscriminate violence at the end of the play, which Hamlet contributes to and lets be, undoes the existing social order, potentially making way for a new one – although that potential is crudely blocked by the incoming throwback, Fortinbras. On the other hand, it remains possible that Hamlet's 'letting be' is really just letting go or giving in:[84] precisely the kind of pointless violence that revolted Hamlet when he advised the players previously. If Hamlet's action is hollow, that might intimate in our present that, far from being the passionate enemy of western culture, terrorism is the last gasp of an exhausted postmodernism without values, a form of careless killing: 'casual slaughters' (5.2.336). In any case, a presentist consideration of the play, that doesn't baulk at its uncompromising strangeness, might help us think through the present crisis.

Any work of literature that is really new manages both to encompass history and to change it. To read works by, say, Shakespeare, Dickens or Dickinson is to realize that they mark time in two very different ways. They do so firstly because the complex processes of past, present and future can be read off from the dialectical interplay between their origins and their changing reception. But they also mark time in that they have altered it as if from outside. Inasmuch as they maintain any vital force, they continue to do so. They can't be completely explained by history, but go on leaving their mark on it. Their 'radiance of sheer presence', to which Steiner testifies, is the enduring wonder and promise of

---

81 This reworking of *Hamlet* produced by Zaoum Theatre from an Arabic viewpoint and in a non-specific Arabic setting won a Fringe First Award at Edinburgh in 2002. It played at the Riverside Studios, London in 2004.

82 Kant writes, 'I ought never to act except in such a way that I could also will that my maxim should become a universal law' (Immanuel Kant, *Groundwork of the Metaphysics of Morals*, trans. Mary Gregor (Cambridge, 1997), p. 402).

83 Sinfield, *Faultlines*, p. 228.

84 Most editors have Hamlet say 'Let be', though he does not in the Folio text. See, for instance, *Hamlet*, ed. G. R. Hibbard (Oxford, 1987), 5.2.170.

originality itself. Hamlet moves beyond remembrance. Surely our task is in the end not to remember but to experience the play's originality? *Hamlet* seems to speak – as a distinct presence, from a unique standpoint – to the current situation. It may function again as a point of origin here, and in future presents.

In the power it cedes to art, this phenomenology of the presence of the text in the present might seem troublingly reminiscent of the escapist, even idolatrous excesses supposed to have preceded new historicism, but I would suggest that it is in fact powerfully exemplary for culture and politics in general. It is time, after new historicism, to recover the creativity and agency that blaze in the Shakespearian text as the promise of human possibility. Creativity is the best-known and most obvious face of art. How can we ignore it? To do so suggests, as Steiner says, a self-preserving recoil from the challenging otherness of literature – facilitated, I would add, by the scholasticism and detachment from experience of contemporary 'research culture'. But it may also be indicative of a sad abrogation of our own creative power and, in consequence, our responsibility for making something of our own lives and time. The art work is an act as Žižek has recently described it:

> On the one hand, an act is, as Kant and Schelling have put it, the point at which 'eternity intervenes in time', at which the enchainment of temporal causal succession is interrupted, at which 'something emerges-intervenes out of nothing', at which something takes place which cannot be explained away as the outcome/result of the preceding chain (to put it in Kant's terms, the act designates the direct intervention of the noumenal dimension into phenomenality; to put it in Schelling's terms, the act designates the moment at which the abyssal/atemporal principle of identity – 'I did it because I did it, for no particular reason' – momentarily suspends the reign of sufficient reason). On the other hand, the act is at the same time the moment of emergence of time in/from eternity: as Schelling put it, the act is the primordial decision/separation [*Ent-Scheidung*] that represses into an eternal past the deadlock of pure simultaneity . . . . In short, an act proper is the opening up of the timeless/'eternal' gesture of overcoming eternity, opening up the dimension of temporality/historicity.[85]

All this is richly and powerfully anticipated by *Hamlet*. It is clear that Hamlet's last act 'cannot be explained away as the outcome/result of the preceding chain', because it evades the paternal mandate which required it. Hamlet's act is explicitly clothed in a 'noumenal' dimension but, as much as it transcends history, it is simultaneously a decisive historical intervention which restarts history, both because it entails the killing of a king and because it initiates and crystallizes a metaphysical and creative conception of action in terms of a god of rashness.

As *Hamlet* suggests, rashness can have good as well as evil effects. Nancy proposes historicism 'presupposes that history has always already begun, and that therefore it always merely continues'.[86] What we get is the endless production of predictable effects; what we miss is the surprising effectivity of a particular beginning. As the pre-eminent and most vivid symbol and example of historical creativity, the work of art itself defies such history. It exemplifies instead Nancy's alternative vision of historical time as 'coming-into-presence':[87] a process by which *something happens* in and as history, something irreducible to historical causality. Is art a kind of rashness without physical violence: an unprecedented, incalculable act, a crazy wager on the future, and one which actually pays off, bringing something into being that is truly new and valuable? The god of rashness conveys the effective power of literature better than Old Hamlet's ghost because it is Hamlet's response to that strange god, not his father's furious spirit, that causes him to act. Just as Hamlet divorces himself from his traditional father, Shakespeare's play breaks away from the lost original Thomas Nashe and Thomas Lodge ridiculed.[88] To this extent, *Hamlet* is a monument

---

85 Slavoj Žižek, *The Fragile Absolute – or, Why is the Christian Legacy Worth Fighting For?* (London and New York, 2000), pp. 93–4.

86 Nancy, *The Birth to Presence*, p. 146.

87 Nancy, *The Birth to Presence*, p. 161.

88 See G. R. Hibbard's 'General Introduction' to *Hamlet*, pp. 12–13.

to its own god of rashness. Whatever we think of the Prince, the play's advent in the present encourages us to be rash too.

As Steiner writes, with echoes of both Sidney and Shakespeare, 'Deep inside every "art-act" lies the dream of an absolute leap out of nothingness, of the invention of an enunciatory shape so new, so singular to its begetter, that it would, literally, leave the previous world behind'.[89] In its achieved form, the text is already a new order. But a play does not only present an alternative world. In moving around and restructuring a group of antagonistic individuals, it jolts its audience into imagining that its own condition can be similarly reshaped. It is, therefore, a particularly effective vehicle for realizing social change. Shakespeare's comedies best exemplify this. But Hamlet's career has evacuated in advance the restored old world Fortinbras represents and suggested another way. In the words of the author of *The Hamlet Machine*, 'What I'm trying to describe is the point at which another vitality is created. Theatre has the task of asserting that vitality against the pressure and / or demand merely to reproduce reality. For it is at this point that theatre threatens reality, and this is surely its most important political function. . . . If art does not threaten reality, then it has no function'.[90]

Radicalism has neglected its best resource. The utopian longings to transform the present that are nurtured by much historicist criticism are weighed down by history itself.[91] In the current critical context, history has become the far horizon and sole explanatory hypothesis to the extent that conceiving of and accounting for resistance to history has become a notorious problem. I have touched already on Greenblatt's view that subversion is always contained. Cultural materialism evades this position by emphasizing that history is always fractured and divided.[92] The efforts of radical critics to wrest counter-histories from the history that prevailed are instructive but not very inspirational. They neglect the positive leap into a revolutionary alternative that is habitually performed by the subject matter of Shakespeare criticism itself. If we can make that leap more manifest in what we teach and write, it will encourage a praxis not of beleaguered resistance but of hope and vision.

---

89 Steiner, *Real Presences*, p. 202.

90 Heiner Müller, 'The Less You See the More You Describe', in *Theatremachine*, trans. and ed. Marc von Henning (London and Boston, 1995), p. xx.

91 For instance, the hope of a new, freer and more mobile sexuality declared by Valerie Traub towards the end of *The Renaissance of Lesbianism in Early Modern England* is effectively crushed in advance by her copious and minute specification of the 'phallogocentric' logic whereby sexual identity is welded to particular bodily parts and practices (Valerie Traub, *The Renaissance of Lesbianism in Early Modern England* (Cambridge, 2002), p. 228).

92 Sinfield, for instance, has found a way of combining the conviction of historical and cultural determinism with the possibility of resistance to history in the notion of 'subcultures' (Sinfield, *Faultlines*, pp. 35–48).

# WRITING SHAKESPEARE IN THE GLOBAL ECONOMY

MARK THORNTON BURNETT

Over the past long decade, Shakespeare on film has enjoyed a spectacular resurgence: beginning with Kenneth Branagh's *Henry V* (1989), the newly filmic face of Shakespeare has revealed itself in such diverse fare as Oliver Parker's *Othello* (1995), Richard Loncraine's *Richard III* (1995), Michael Hoffman's *A Midsummer Night's Dream* (1999), Julie Taymor's *Titus* (1999), Christine Edzard's *The Children's Midsummer Night's Dream* (2001) and, most recently, Peter Babakitis' *Henry V* (2004), and this partial list does not even mention the numerous spin-offs – such as John Madden's *Shakespeare in Love* (1998) and Kristian Levring's *The King is Alive* (2002) – which respectively reinvent *Romeo and Juliet* and *King Lear* for pre-and post-millennial audiences. In deploying modes of popular entertainment, editorial restlessness, action-oriented narratives, intertextual borrowings and self-conscious registers, the films display an acute responsiveness to the conventions and exigencies of the global Hollywood machine. Consequently, these and other film adaptations have shifted the conventional textual and theatrical axes of Shakespeare, granting him a fresh vernacular applicability and, in terms of the Bard's postmodern meanings, establishing the crucial importance of the screen. The multiplex, the video, the DVD player, the PC, the laptop – these are the spaces in which Shakespeare is now written and rewritten – with an unprecedented degree of accessibility and visibility.

Via his reanimation in the cinema, Shakespeare has been confirmed as a cultural property of global proportions. Directors and publicity play upon the Bard's ubiquitous geographical kudos, as when Kenneth Branagh describes his film version of *Much Ado About Nothing* (1993) as 'belonging to the world' or the poster for Baz Luhrmann's *William Shakespeare's 'Romeo + Juliet'* (1996) introduces the 'greatest love story the world has ever known'.[1] The very fact that Shakespeare has proved an accommodating friend to Hollywood filmmaking has been read as evidence of his universality and timelessness. 'As long as people are being born and having children, and falling in love and getting married, and dying, then Shakespeare is relevant', claims Michelle Pfeiffer (Titania in Michael Hoffman's 1999 production of *A Midsummer Night's Dream*).[2] Her observation, typical of those promoting Shakespeare in films of the past decade, reveals a devotion to a fantasy of the dramatist as both transcendent and transnational. His basis in normative sexuality notwithstanding, this is a poet and interpreter who, across history and across the globe, delivers the same messages in words that magically retain their communicative efficacity.

Interestingly, the depth and scale of cinematic claims for Shakespeare's universality run counter to the majority of recent critical understandings. Since at least the early 1980s, the trend has been to discredit essentialist notions such as those pedalled by Shakespeare film purveyors. Instead, attention has been paid to the ways in which individual

[1] Kenneth Branagh, *'Much Ado About Nothing' by William Shakespeare* (New York, 1993), p. x.

[2] Michael Hoffman, *William Shakespeare's 'A Midsummer Night's Dream'* (New York, 1999), p. 45.

nations romance Shakespeare, to the importance of different locally-inflected productions, and to the emergence of dissident voices that write the dramatist according to the pressures of discrete environments.[3] In these revisionist approaches, there is no mutually agreed Shakespeare, only competing 'Shakespeares' that jostle for prominence. In fact, so dominant is this trend that discussion of universality has mainly ceased, to be replaced by a discourse of endless Shakespearian versatility. Notably underscored is the capacity of the Bard to assume distinctive guises and the conviction that there is no agreed sense of his inherited values or ideological applications. Between cinema's universals and criticism's particulars, then, there is something of an impasse, with contemporary culture contemplating a Shakespeare who is free-floating, nationless, constant and homogeneous, and contemporary criticism judging him contextually tied, heterogeneous, intermittent and nationally specific.

Presented with these two apparently polarized positions, Shakespeare on film critics have tended to accommodate both in ways that have become predictable. While elaborating the universalizing effect of Shakespeare's film treatments, for example, critics simultaneously detail such cultural tendencies as necessarily politically retrograde and in thrall to globalizing structures.[4] A complementary preoccupation has demonstrated the ways in which the Shakespearian universal is transmuted into, and overtaken by, American culture and its concomitant global identity.[5] For both sets of critics, the Shakespearian local is largely irrelevant; rather, as cinematic myth, it is the Shakespearian universal that requires careful deconstruction.

This paper sees both cinematic and critical fields of operation as oversimplifying the complex niche occupied by Shakespeare in the global economy. Mediating between current perspectives, it explores film versions of *Hamlet* and *Macbeth* made over the course of the 1990s and beyond as instances of the ways in which a local reading, absence or situation complements and challenges a larger global picture. The local is not always to be found where one might conventionally expect to find it. Nonetheless, a comparative assessment of the films' preoccupations reveals the virtues of an approach which emphasizes the meaning of the local inside a mondial arrangement and which discovers the Shakespeare of modernity as a simultaneously local and global phenomenon.

Traditionally, *Macbeth* has been written as one of Shakespeare's most regionally-rooted plays. Yet in recent film realizations – Jeremy Freeston's cinematic 1996 version, Michael Bogdanov's 1997 Channel Four production and Gregory Doran's 2001 filmed Royal Shakespeare Company release – it is striking that an evacuation of distinctiveness, or a loss of regional signifiers of 'Scottishness', becomes apparent. The opening of Bogdanov's *Macbeth*, for example, plunges us into a quarry

3 Representative studies include Pascale Aebischer, Edward J. Esche and Nigel Wheale, eds, *Remaking Shakespeare: Performance Across Media, Genres and Cultures* (Basingstoke, 2003); Michael D. Bristol, *Shakespeare's America/America's Shakespeare* (London, 1990); John Russell Brown, *New Sites for Shakespeare: Theatre, the Audience and Asia* (London, 1999); Mark Thornton Burnett and Ramona Wray, eds, *Shakespeare and Ireland: History, Politics, Culture* (Basingstoke, 1997); Thomas Cartelli, *Repositioning Shakespeare: National Cultures, Postcolonial Appropriations* (London and New York, 1999); Michael Hattaway, Boika Sokolova and Derek Roper, eds., *Shakespeare in the New Europe* (Sheffield, 1994); David Johnson, *Shakespeare and South Africa* (Oxford, 1996); Dennis Kennedy, *Foreign Shakespeares: Contemporary Performance* (Cambridge, 1993); Francesca T. Royster, *Becoming Cleopatra: The Shifting Image of an Icon* (New York, 2003); Xiao Yang Zhang, ed., *Shakespeare in China: A Comparative Study of Two Traditions and Cultures* (Newark, 1996).

4 Richard Burt, 'Shakespeare, "Glo-cali-zation," Race, and the Small Screens of Post-Popular Culture', *Shakespeare, the Movie, II: Popularizing the plays on film, TV, video, and DVD*, ed. Richard Burt and Lynda E. Boose (London, 2003), pp. 14–36; Courtney Lehmann, *Shakespeare Remains: Theater to Film, Early Modern to Postmodern* (Ithaca, 2002), passim; Sarah Mayo, '"A Shakespeare for the People?": Negotiating the Popular in *Shakespeare in Love* and Michael Hoffman's *A Midsummer Night's Dream*', *Textual Practice*, 17.2 (2003), pp. 295–316.

5 Denise Albanese, 'The Shakespeare film and the Americanization of culture', *Marxist Shakespeares*, ed. Jean E. Howard and Scott Cutler Shershow (London, 2001), pp. 206–26; Curtis Breight, 'Elizabethan World Pictures', *Shakespeare and National Culture*, ed. John J. Joughin (Manchester, 1997), pp. 295–325; Linda Charnes, *Notorious Identity: Materializing the Subject in Shakespeare* (Cambridge, Mass., 1993), pp. 148–53.

masquerading as the 'blasted heath' in which dummies, burned-out cars and televisions litter the scene. It is a post-apocalyptic – or, in Susanne Greenhalgh's words, 'devastated' and 'shell-shocked' – moment characterized by ruination, decay and detritus; at the same time, the environment highlights a postmodern condition.[6] Not only do the dummies connote the imitation and the facsimile, so, too, do the televisions, since their screens reveal both the production's title and the battle action as it happens. In this sense, we are positioned not so much in the expanse of the 'noir western', as it has been argued, but rather, in the territory of Jean Baudrillard, which is 'the third order, no longer the order of the real, but of the hyperreal'.[7] Because a screen is privileged as the prime representational medium in this landscape seemingly recovering from a 'global catastrophe', we confront a further dimension of the postmodern – the extent to which war, in Slavoj Žižek's words, has been 'deprived of its substance' and replaced by 'the spectre of an "immaterial" war where the attack is invisible'.[8] The opening establishes both a tone and appearance of mondial homogeneity, and, indeed, there is little to choose between this 'Scottish' scene and other nuclear wastelands characteristic of recent Hollywood cinematic outings. Despite his film's entertainment of signifiers of Scotland elsewhere, Bogdanov here seems more committed to exploring the ways in which a national aesthetic is imperilled at the hands of technology, industrial excess and global conflict.

Bogdanov's prioritizing of homogeneity is a precondition for Gregory Doran's *Macbeth*, which goes further in its anatomization of an increasingly absent Scottish centre. Camera work in Doran's release is hand-held and giddy, while the editorial technique is impatient and telegraphic; as a result, one experiences *Macbeth* as a kind of documentary in which the Shakespearian play becomes difficult to separate out from other generic styles. The production's predilection for lurching tracking-shots and low-resolution lighting functions to evoke the Gulf Wars and sci-fi shows such as *The X-Files*. Clearly, an investment in introducing contemporary registers to *Macbeth* works to privilege the unexplained and the arena of international political warfare; an additional by-product, however, is that we come to inhabit a world with no firm dividing-lines: one modality is synonymous with the next. Filmed in the stark interior of the Roundhouse Theatre in London, whose only feature is a metal catwalk, this *Macbeth* gives no clue as to its imagined geographical anchorage and favours only narrative essentials. Lanterns, spotlights and torches focus upon silver buttons and militaristic garb, but no attempt is made to suggest affiliations: each major player is cut from the same cloth. A prevailing greyness means that the mindset of the individual is also the psychology of the collective. Antony Sher (Macbeth) writes that what was aimed for in the production was a sense of a 'modern world . . . you can't . . . identify. Everything . . . will be caked in soot, oil, grime, dried blood . . . and you can't say which war this is either: Flanders, Vietnam, Balkans?'[9] Global homogeneity, in short, is the production's interpretive template, and it is applied in such a way as to collapse temporal specificity and flatten national borders. Doran's *Macbeth* situates Scotland at its furthest remove, with the local being hollowed out and vacated.

In this version of *Macbeth* and others, no longer is the dramatist the guarantor of singular or distinctive values: rather, it is anonymity that is stressed and the notion that Shakespeare inhabits an essentially featureless cultural space. Such a suggestion is at work in intriguingly complementary ways in recent filmic *Hamlet*s, chief among which are Kenneth Branagh's lavish 1997 spectacle and Michael Almereyda's sombre 2000 cinematic outing. Notwithstanding their differences, these films also

[6] Susanne Greenhalgh, '"Alas poor country!": Documenting the Politics of Performance in Two British Television *Macbeth*s since the 1980s', *Remaking Shakespeare*, ed. Aebischer, Esche and Wheale, pp. 96, 105.

[7] Courtney Lehmann, 'Out Damned Scot: Dislocating *Macbeth* in transnational film and media culture', *Shakespeare, the Movie, II*, ed. Burt and Boose, p. 236; Jean Baudrillard, *Selected Writings*, ed. Mark Poster (Cambridge, 1988), p. 121.

[8] Slavoj Žižek, *Welcome to the Desert of the Real* (London, 2002), pp. 17, 37.

[9] Antony Sher, *Beside Myself* (London, 2001), p. 341.

9 Design sheet from Kenneth Branagh's *Hamlet*.

imply that the Shakespearian tragic register becomes comprehensible only inside a disindividuated schema. Design sheets in the Kenneth Branagh Archive at Queen's, Belfast, for instance, make clear that no one European nation is envisaged as the context for his nineteenth-century *Hamlet*; rather, a vaguely non-English setting is evoked in such a way as to allude simultaneously to various countries without any of them being specifically pinpointed.[10] Similarly, Almereyda's *Hamlet*, which takes a late twentieth-century millennial moment as its central conceit, seems at first to be marked by a comparable lack of particularity. His city scene is stamped with corporate facelessness, with a proliferation of brand names alerting us to a corresponding diminution of meaningful human interaction. Assemblages of concrete, collocations of rigid glass structures and,

[10] To judge from these forms of representation, Russia, in Branagh's *Hamlet*, contrary to some views, is but one suggested point of reference in a larger and more diffuse territorial whole. For criticism which sees an evocation of Russia and its revolutionary era as central to the film, see Samuel Crowl, *Shakespeare at the Cineplex: The Kenneth Branagh Era* (Athens, 2003), p. 142; Douglas Lanier, '"Art thou base, common, and popular?": The Cultural Politics of Kenneth Branagh's *Hamlet*', *Spectacular Shakespeare: Critical Theory and Popular Cinema*, ed. Courtney Lehmann and Lisa S. Starks (Madison, 2002), p. 158; Nina da Vinci Nichols, 'Branagh's *Hamlet* Redux', *Shakespeare Bulletin*, 15.3 (1997), 38–41; p. 38; Kenneth S. Rothwell, *A History of Shakespeare on Screen: A Century of Film and Television* (Cambridge, 1999), p. 257; Carol Chillington Rutter, *Enter the Body: Women and Representation on Shakespeare's Stage* (London, 2001), p. 52; Julie Sanders, 'The End of History and the Last Man: Kenneth Branagh's *Hamlet*', *Shakespeare, Film, Fin de Siècle*, ed. Mark Thornton Burnett and Ramona Wray (Basingstoke, 2000), pp. 154–6.

to cite Barbara Hodgdon, 'radiant, ephemeral surfaces' – all point up a generic environment recognizable only in its identikit familiarity.[11] For both Branagh and Almereyda's films of *Hamlet*, these nowhere landscapes are defined by self-absorption. Elsinore's political isolation is one of the most arresting aspects of the visual vocabulary of Branagh's *Hamlet*. White blinds are invariably shot as drawn; the gates of the castle always feature as closed; a 'watery wintry mist' envelops Denmark; and the mirrors that decorate the state hall stand as testimony to a court that looks inwards rather than outwards.[12] Because Elsinore in Almereyda's *Hamlet* is envisaged as a luxury hotel – the headquarters of Denmark Incorporated – the action clusters around a self-enclosed world, with the majority of the characters represented as living existences dictated to by the all-consuming insularity of global business. Like the landscape that produces it, the business is never specified – the logo both replaces and negates a finer sense of place.

Crucially, however, in Almereyda's *Hamlet*, the landscape that lacks identity is simultaneously discovered as New York. This representation is of a piece with films like Greg Lombardo's *Macbeth in Manhattan* (1999), which highlights theatrical rehearsals of *Macbeth* and the play's connections to the urban condition, and Kenneth Branagh's *Macbeth* in process, which centres on 'a global media empire . . . the murders take place on Wall Street'.[13] In writing New York as a soulless centre, the films avail themselves of one resonant strand of cinematic narrative – Martin Scorsese's *Taxi Driver* (1976), John Carpenter's *Escape from New York* (1981) and Mary Harron's *American Psycho* (2000) establish New York both as a metaphorical gaol and as a breeding ground for neuroses and acquisitiveness.

In line with such a trajectory, Almereyda's *Hamlet* and its counterpart *Macbeth*s privilege their unfeeling backdrops as keys to individually damaged psychologies. All three films draw upon New York's postmodern connections to melancholia and mental illness, with the horrendous realities of 9/11 bringing into tragic focus the sense of psychological affliction with which the city is coloured. Visual designs lend emphasis to inventively introspective investments, such as the scene in Doran's *Macbeth* where Lady Macbeth (Harriet Walter) is filmed upside-down and underwater as her voiceover reflects upon her husband's 'human-kindness', or when Hamlet (Ethan Hawke) watches a close-up of himself lamenting the fact that he has 'lost all [his] mirth'.[14] More often in these films, however, characterological particulars are represented as submerged beneath technology: Macbeth looks directly into the camera on accepting the title of Thane of Cawdor, but places his hand over the lens when speculating upon how he will the 'multitudinous seas incarnadine, / Making the green one red'.[15] Here, the filmic discovery of the self is both desired and denied – there is an acknowledgement of the gap between a needful public manifestation and a feared private revelation.

The idea that filmmaking/videomaking provides a means of writing a personal script is most fully encoded in Almereyda's *Hamlet*: his camera dwells repeatedly on Hamlet's *auteurial* eyes, alerting us to the ways in which, as Katherine Rowe states, he probes the 'strengths and limitations of different memory technologies'.[16] As the film understands it, Hamlet is dislocated in direct relation to the *faux* historical nature of his urban contexts. Imitative Chippendale markers on skyscrapers and ersatz architectural symbols in New York have resulted in a fragmentary landscape in which the inhabitant can only be isolated and angst-ridden. The protagonist is a cipher for Fredric Jameson's concept of the

[11] Barbara Hodgdon, 'Re-incarnations', *Remaking Shakespeare*, ed. Aebischer, Esche and Wheale, p. 200.

[12] Kenneth Branagh Archive [hereafter K. B. A.], Queen's University, Belfast, *'Hamlet' by William Shakespeare: Adapted for the Screen by Kenneth Branagh*, 1st draft screenplay (1995), p. 33.

[13] K. B. A., *Kenneth Branagh's The Shakespeare Film Company* (London, [2000]), unpaginated insert.

[14] *William Shakespeare's 'Hamlet': A Screenplay Adaptation by Michael Almereyda* (London, 2000), p. 55.

[15] Quotations from *Macbeth* are taken from William Shakespeare, *The Complete Works*, ed. Stanley Wells, Gary Taylor, John Jowett and William Montgomery (Oxford, 1986), 2.2.60–1.

[16] Katherine Rowe, '"Remember Me": Technologies of Memory in Michael Almereyda's *Hamlet*', *Shakespeare, the Movie, II*, ed. Burt and Boose, p. 43.

'human body' struggling 'to organize its immediate surroundings perceptually, and cognitively to map its position in a mappable external world'.[17] As an experimental filmmaker, Hamlet mobilizes a seemingly unconnected bricolage involving a greedy cartoon dragon, a dinosaur skeleton and a Da Vinci drawing. Within its own logic, the sequence posits a Hamlet who, caught in a 'time' that is 'out of joint', looks to the evolution or origin of things as a means of, in Douglas M. Lanier's words, creating 'an art of resistance' and contesting late capitalist modalities of consumption.[18]

Constructions of the past appear in different forms throughout Almereyda's film, but they invariably function to evoke counter-cultural possibilities. In contradistinction to the ubiquitous chrome and blank modernity of his surroundings, for example, Hamlet's room, with its baroque furniture and black and white photographs, appears as a dissident cell, a personal refuge. But most interesting is the film's summoning of Ireland as a multivalent trope betokening release, opportunity and hope. Just as Almereyda detects a withdrawal away from the global in the (Gothicized?) cultures of the central protagonists, so does he find in Ireland a potentially contestatory metaphor. The protagonist's connection with Ireland is initially suggested via the casting of Horatio (Carl Geary): his Dublin accent and dominant role work to formulate Ireland – not New York – as an exceptional landmass where loyalty, support and integrity are still valued. The corresponding linkage of the University of Wittenberg and the city of Dublin confirms Ireland as the repository of traditions of books and poetry, and implies Hamlet's preference for this latter territory (the film's opening point of view shot can only be that of a prince called home against his will). A map of Ireland adorns Hamlet's wall, its presence in the *mise-en-scène* continually pointing up a geographical entity that is at one and the same time inspirational and aspirational.

A complementary, but older, image of Ireland is summoned in Branagh's *Hamlet*. Co-existing with the European anywhere is a vivid sense of an Ireland drawn from eighteenth and nineteenth-century literary traditions and, particularly, the 'Irish Gothic'. Chiefly a vehicle of representation for the waning control of the Anglo-Irish ascendancy, 'Irish Gothic' privileges a beleaguered, besieged 'Big House', which points up, on the one hand, the exhausted and declining state of the landowning class and constitutional politics and, on the other hand, the potential and threat of revolutionary idealism and mob violence.[19] The genre's domestic elements centre upon cells, labyrinths

[17] Fredric Jameson, *Postmodernism, or, The Cultural Logic of Late Capitalism* (London, 1991), p. 44.

[18] Douglas M. Lanier, 'Shakescorp *Noir*', *Shakespeare Quarterly*, 53.2 (2002), 157–180; p. 172; Shakespeare, *Works*, 1.5.189.

[19] For useful discussions, see Seamus Deane, *Strange Country: Modernity and Nationhood in Irish Writing since 1790* (Oxford, 1997), pp. 21, 87–8, 91, 117–18, 166, 196; Vera Kreilkamp, *The Anglo-Irish Novel and the Big House* (New York, 1998), pp. 9–10, 21–3, 73, 96–7, 106–09, 119–20, 249–52; W. J. McCormack, *Dissolute Characters: Irish Literary History through Balzac, Sheridan Le Fanu, Yeats and Bowen* (Manchester, 1993), p. 101; W. J. McCormack, 'Irish Gothic and After', *The Field Day Anthology of Irish Writing*, ed. Seamus Deane, 5 vols (Derry, 1991–2002), vol. 2, pp. 831–54. Philippa Sheppard's otherwise very useful study ('The Castle of Elsinore: Gothic Aspects of Kenneth Branagh's *Hamlet*', *Shakespeare Bulletin*, 19.3 (2001), pp. 36–9) neglects to mention that the 'Gothic' is invariably nationally and locally differentiated.

That Ireland is remote from Branagh's own conception of shifting national borders in the nineteenth century is indicated in his remarks on the film's evocation of historical context: the 'emerald isle' does not feature in the field of reference. See K. B. A., *Commemorative Programme: William Shakespeare's 'Hamlet' directed by Kenneth Branagh* (Belfast, 1997), p. 4; K. B. A., *'Hamlet': Production Information* (1996), pp. 4, 10; Crowl, *Shakespeare at the Cineplex*, p. 151; Ramona Wray and Mark Thornton Burnett, 'From the Horse's Mouth: Branagh on the Bard', *Shakespeare, Film, Fin de Siècle*, ed. Burnett and Wray, pp. 170–1.

While Branagh has argued in interview that his film eschews the 'Gothic' (K. B. A., *Pamela Wallin: Live* (19 December 1996) and K. B. A., *Voices from the Smithsonian Associates: Kenneth Branagh* (21 December 1996)), it seems that what he primarily sought to avoid was a sense of prevailing cinematic gloom. Moreover, from another perspective, it is clear that, in the original conception of the film, there was to have been a greater reliance upon another strand of the 'Gothic', as indicated in the first screenplay's references to skulls, death-heads, maggots, falling trees and mutilated anatomies. See K. B. A., *'Hamlet' by William Shakespeare: Adapted for the Screen by Kenneth Branagh*, 1st draft screenplay (1995), pp. 44, 52, 86, 135, 187, 188.

and secret rooms; its familial preoccupations cluster around mad women, usurping uncles and genealogical catastrophe; and its material concerns extend to dispossession, conflagration and exile. Clearly, 'Irish Gothic' and Branagh's *Hamlet* are mutually reinforcing: Elsinore (Blenheim Palace) is visualized as a 'Big House' whose interior hides prisons and passageways, while the failure of the Danish royal family to take proper account of the world beyond is linked both to the ease with which Fortinbras and his 'modern mass-political movement' gains power (as evidenced in illustration 10's storyboard) *and* to the rapidity with which the line is extinguished.[20] Siobhán Kilfeather has argued that 'Irish Gothic' is mobilized 'as a response to modernization, a mode of registering loss and of suggesting that new forms of subjectivity are necessary to deal with the new forms of knowledge and power that are conquering past systems and beliefs'.[21] Judged in this light, Branagh's *Hamlet* becomes, via one version of Ireland, an instrument of nostalgia, a testament to memory, and a paean to politically mythologized heroes of contrasting religious persuasions.

In Almereyda's *Hamlet*, the notion of Ireland as the spiritual home of the Shakespearian hero is at one with Hamlet's more general predilection for revolutionary iconography. Juxtaposed alongside the map of Ireland are images of Che Guevara and Malcolm X, which suggests a student equation of figures and places marked by resistance. But Almereyda's glance toward Ireland is more intimately rooted. A split-screen shot establishes a parallel between the political persecution of the Irish nation and Hamlet's domestic experiences. For the upright, bullying Hamlet *père* replicates the geographical site occupied by England on the map, while a crouching, subordinate Hamlet *fils* imitates the shape and location of a subordinate Ireland. At once, this is a further indication of Hamlet's identification with the Irish subaltern; more broadly, the mediation of Old Hamlet via an abusive kind of global paternalism links British and American forms of empire. The consequences of the expansionist urge are discernible in the simultaneous shot of a TV monitor broadcasting burning images redolent of the internecine strife of Northern Ireland's 'troubles'. Such an elision of England and Old Hamlet bolsters Almereyda's unique writing of an aggressive ghost and a dysfunctional father–son relationship. This cartographical configuration notwithstanding, however, the ultimate location of Ireland is more slippery than that allowed by the film's liberationist ideology. The imagery of Ireland used, and the meanings generated, deny the complexities of sectarian conflict, reducing them to a simple colonial paradigm. Similarly, the messy history of partition is elided in the relationship between Horatio and Marcella. An alliance of north and south (Marcella's northern intonation is the counterpart to Horatio's Dublin vowels) suggests Ireland as a seamless ideological unity.[22] In fact, what is finally made visible through such a romanticization of Ireland is the nation's commodification in a global economy. Thus, while Hamlet gestures toward Irish models, so, too, does Claudius (Kyle MacLachlan): ensconced in his limousine, the CEO reaches out to touch a television image of Clinton, a highlight of whose presidency was the brokering of the Northern Irish peace agreement. As a site for social values remote from corporate capitalism, Almereyda's Ireland emerges both as a radical ideology and as an imagined idyll spectrally present in spite of current political realities.

The phenomenon of Ireland as spectre is fully realized in Kenneth Branagh's *Hamlet*. Old Hamlet (Brian Blessed) appears both as a species of the local and as a particular construction of Ireland. Not least because of his colossal proportions and association with quagmires, Old Hamlet evokes the Irish giants

20 See Lanier, '"Art thou base, common and popular?"', *Spectacular Shakespeare*, ed. Lehmann and Starks, p. 162.

21 Siobhán Kilfeather, 'The Gothic Novel', *The Cambridge Companion to the Irish Novel*, ed. John Wilson Foster (Cambridge, 2005), p. 98.

22 Almereyda is himself an active participant in the stereotypical construction of Ireland, remarking in interview that 'the entire cast is American except for a couple of Irish people thrown in for good luck'. See Ross Anthony, 'Interviews with Actor Ethan Hawke and Director Michael Almereyda of *Hamlet*' (http://www.rossanthony.com/interviews/hawke.shtml).

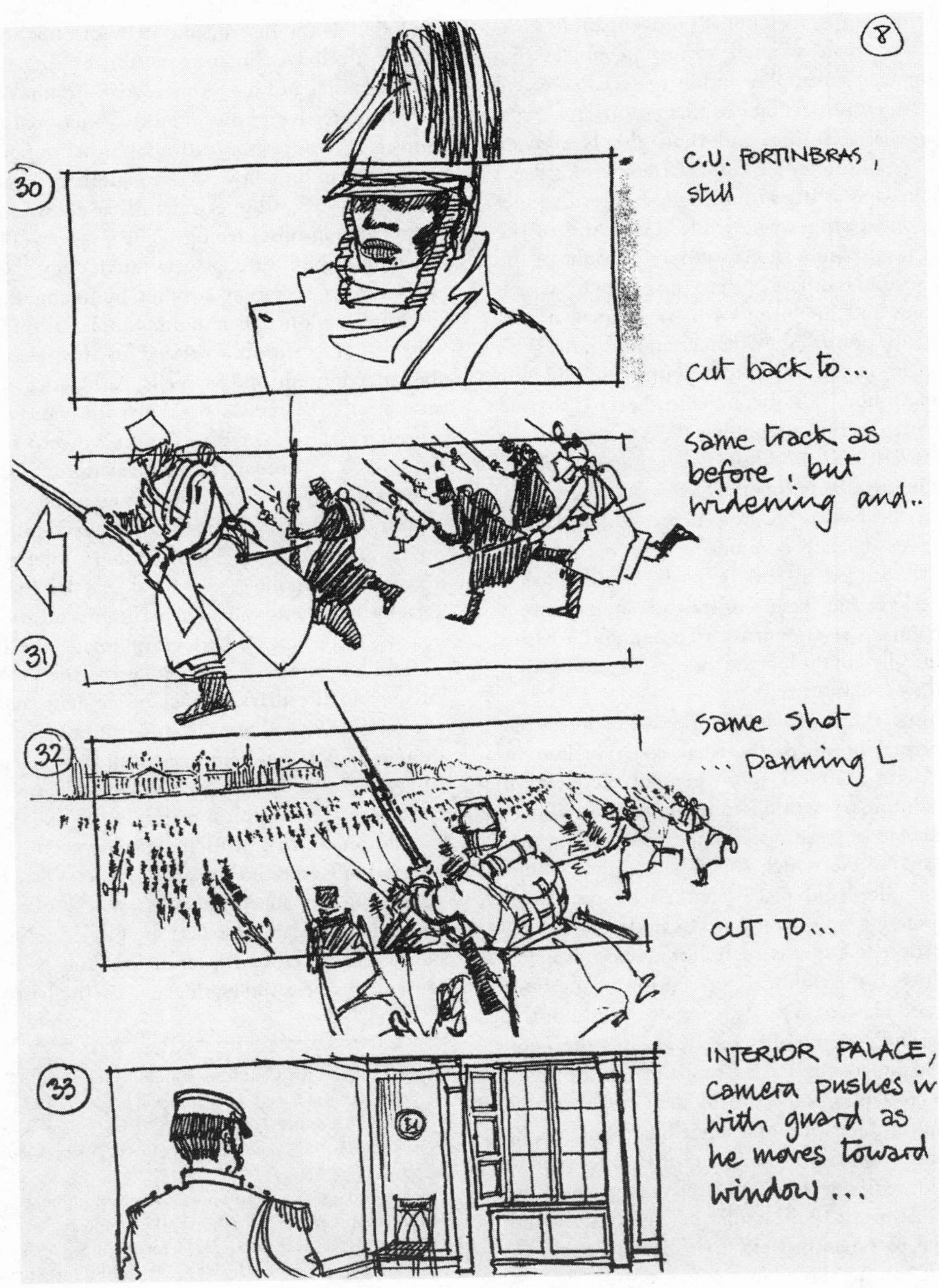
8
30
C.U. FORTINBRAS,
still
cut back to...
same track as
before, but
widening and..
31
32
same shot
... panning L
CUT TO...
33
INTERIOR PALACE,
camera pushes in
with guard as
he moves toward
window...

10 Storyboard for Kenneth Branagh's *Hamlet*.

of antiquity: among these, Brian Boru, a mythical giant Irish king, was the most celebrated. Yet, at the same time, in his sallow, pale manner and hollow, preternaturally blue-eyed appearance, Old Hamlet connects with historical Irish giants such as Corney Macgrath, who was exhibited in the eighteenth century and whose bones are still on display at Trinity College, Dublin.[23] Like Macgrath, Old Hamlet, in his posthumous manifestation, experiences exhibition, only in the form of a statue rather than a skeleton. Moreover, as ghost, Old Hamlet moves across a distinctively 'Irish Gothic' terrain, his presence in the film recalling the similar place occupied by spirits in the novels of, for instance, Sheridan Le Fanu and Bram Stoker, works where the undead walk to seek redress for past crimes of a specifically national inflection.[24]

Despite their apparently anonymous settings, then, uneasily haunting these filmic versions of *Hamlet* is an Irish spectre, one that assumes different shapes but that consistently connotes possibility and registers desire. In gathering up stereotypical national associations, both Branagh and Almereyda's *Hamlet*s chime with the recent filmic *Macbeth*s, which, from a comparable perspective, invest in the past, romance the regional and deploy visuals of place as ciphers of wish-fulfilment.

For instance, despite the claim that Freeston's *Macbeth* 'is set in eleventh-century Scotland', and notwithstanding its diegetic deployment of such regional markers as castles, indigenous accents and Celtic crosses, this is no historically 'authentic' creation.[25] Rather, the forms enlisted betray a romanticized and stereotypical imperative that accords with Fredric Jameson's description of the 'nostalgia film', a narrative that approaches 'the "past" through stylistic connotation, conveying "pastness" by the qualities of the image' and medievalism 'by the attributes of fashion'.[26] Bogdanov's *Macbeth* offers a similar case in point. Here, too, a version of Scotland is glimpsed in the tying together of traditional modalities and modes of virtue (Lady Macduff feeds her children porridge) and in the use of dress (characters appear as twentieth-century street fighters in combat gear with tartan detailing). Interestingly, these details of food and attire survive in the film's fabric only because of their nostalgic potential. The signifiers are periodic, pointing up the occasional quality of 'Scottishness' and the reduction of the 'national particular' to the status of a historical echo.

The notion that a nationless Shakespeare is mediated via a process of localization should not surprise us; as Darren O'Byrne states, 'the "global" is itself constructed through local practices'.[27] As synecdoches for the local, Ireland and Scotland become what is not global in the same moment as they constitute themselves as necessary components of the mondial make-up. Out of these filmic reworkings of *Hamlet* and *Macbeth* emerge Irelands and Scotlands that are metaphorical landscapes both local and global – 'glocal' – in orientation.[28]

The untenability of an unmediated regional frame of reference is encapsulated in the intertextual staging of the close of Freeston's *Macbeth*, which discovers tartan-clad warriors executing bloody charges and falling to their deaths upon sharpened stakes. At this point, the film assembles highlights from both Kenneth Branagh's *Henry V* (1989) and Mel Gibson's *Braveheart* (1995), highly successful productions which, backed by the US corporations of the Samuel Goldwyn Company and Paramount, made Shakespeare palatable to non-European audiences and indulged quasi-mythologized delineations of Scotland for American consumption. Both Shakespeare and Scotland can be seen as culturally acceptable only if filtered through global representational requirements.

---

23 Peter Somerville-Large, *Irish Eccentrics* (London, 1975), pp. 46–50.

24 See Victor Sage, 'Irish Gothic: C. R. Maturin and J. S. Le Fanu', *A Companion to the Gothic*, ed. David Punter (Oxford, 2000), pp. 81–93.

25 The quotation is taken from the film's video jacket.

26 Jameson, *Postmodernism*, p. 19.

27 Darren O'Byrne, 'Working-Class Culture: Local community and global conditions', *Living the Global City: Globalization as Local Process*, ed. John Earle (London, 1997), p. 73.

28 The phrase is Roland Robertson's in his 'Glocalization: Time-space and homogeneity-heterogeneity', *Global Modernities*, ed. Mike Featherstone, Scott Lash and Roland Robertson (London, 1995), pp. 23–44.

The Scottish-American connection comes under sustained scrutiny in one of the most recent *Macbeths* to be released. *Scotland, PA* (2001), directed by Billy Morrissette, features Scotland in a displaced incarnation. In the director's conception, the Gallic region has transatlantically shifted from Scotland (UK) to Scotland (Pennsylvania). Literalizing the movement traced by seventeenth-century Scottish *emigrés*, the film, via its title, underscores the Scottish origins of what emerges as a very American tale. The McBeths are white trash restaurant workers of the 1970s with ideas above their station; Norm Duncan is their sleepy, too trusting boss. Matching the more general voyage made by Shakespeare to the US, *Scotland, PA* translates the Renaissance text into modern parlance, with the Shakespearian script remaining at the level of textual allusion, verbal patterning and suggestive imagery.

One of the most consistent of these patterns is a rhetoric of prediction and futurity. Like the play, the dialogue of *Scotland, PA* gestures forwards. Typical are Norm Duncan's promise that 'Tonight, you two are going to witness history' and Joe McBeth's comment that 'Intercom' is 'the way of the future'. In the terms of the film, that 'history' and 'future' embrace the replacement of the family-run, independent restaurant with large-scale multinational franchises. What is suggested through *McBeth's* eatery, in fact, is not so much the prominence of 'Enron', as Courtney Lehmann has argued, as the emergence of McDonald's, the incorporated global industry *par excellence*.[29] Confirming this global corporation's inseparability from, in Anthony Giddens's words, 'Americanization' is *Scotland, PA*'s representation of McBeth's rise; as he goes from strength to strength, his diner becomes not only more homogenized but, crucially, more patriotic.[30] In documenting this process, the film clearly charts a movement away from Duncan's benevolent patriarchy and home-cut chips and toward a nutritionally empty landscape of corruption, jingoism and exploitation. The range of allusiveness in this film suggests both the richness of locality inside constructions of America and the unpredictability of the interaction between Shakespeare and the global economy. Even inside what might appear traditional modalities there is scope for both newly localized readings and resistant positions. But *Scotland, PA* is more subversive than even this allows. McDuff (Christopher Walken), who, in the play, defeats Macbeth and wins freedom for Scotland, is figured as a police lieutenant. Over the course of the film, however, and in part because of his exposure to the food business during his investigations, McDuff decides to downshift. The film's final montage of McDuff chomping upon a cigar-like carrot outside his new organic vegetarian restaurant completes his triumph over the McBeths and incarnates a new regime, one that counters both the global threat embodied in the big 'M' and the broader cultural phenomenon that George Ritzer has termed the 'McDonaldization of society'.[31]

*Scotland, PA*, then, does not only thematize McDonald's rise; it simultaneously glances forwards to its decline. In 2002, soon after the film's release, the McDonald's corporation reported its first major loss: share prices slumped; outlets closed; and health-oriented rivals successfully competed for customers.[32] The closing prominence accorded to McDuff's 'garden burger', as well as signalling an Almereyda-like counter-culture, encodes a meditation upon this more recent trajectory, upon the ways in which the global is invariably forced to adapt and co-opt. In this respect, the sequestered Americanism of the film's setting is purposeful, linked as it is to a sense of inwardness and to a historically particular illusion of invulnerability that, at least before 9/11, was actively entertained. *Scotland, PA* addresses but does not endorse fictions of self-sufficiency, the interpenetration of external influences, the dialogic condition of the global, and

---

29 Lehmann, 'Out Damned Scot', *Shakespeare, the Movie, II*, ed. Burt and Boose, p. 247.

30 Anthony Giddens, *Runaway World: How Globalization is Reshaping Our Lives* (London, 2002), p. xxi.

31 George Ritzer, *The McDonaldization of Society* (London, 2000).

32 See 'Big Mac Under Attack', BBC2 (15 July 2003); John Arlidge, 'The healthy option from Mr McHamburglar', *The Sunday Times: Business*, 28 March 2004, p. 10.

the ideological work that an applied sense of the local is able to perform.

'At bottom', writes Jacques Derrida, 'the spectre is the future', and the repositioned Scottish ghosts which historically anchor *Scotland, PA* – as well as the *Macbeth* play – certainly bear out this logic.[33] Similarly, it is possible to read the ghost of Ireland in Almereyda's *Hamlet* as also enjoying a prophetic role. This is confirmed in the film's penultimate shot of Augustus Saint-Gaudens's New York sculpture of General William Sherman. Accompanying the figure is the angel of Nike, triumphantly leading his horse forward. It is perfectly possible, of course, to read Fortinbras into the statue and to detect in Sherman's repression of the 'south' in order to save the 'north' a codified comment upon the bipolar structure of Ireland's political organization. Yet Fortinbras seems less forcefully evoked here than Hamlet who, via the statue, is situated in a historical idiom: the protagonist resolves his vexed relation with time and the metropolis. Moreover, because Saint-Gaudens was born in Dublin and, shortly before his death in 1907, was working on a huge figure of Charles Stewart Parnell, the suggestion is that Hamlet, akin to the sculptor, is being claimed by his national Irish forefathers and guided toward a culturally emancipated spiritual destiny. A passing shot of an airplane's jet trail reinforces the impression and works as an analogy for a soul-in-progress. Even this reading, however, is compromised by Nike, and not least because this classical goddess has been hijacked as a logo by the Nike Corporation, a global brand closely associated with third-world exploitation.[34] The question of Hamlet's ultimate destination is balanced in the final *montage* between both local and global scenarios, and any sense of resolution hinges upon this uneasy equipoise.

A material enactment of such cinematic 'glocalism' can be found in the 1997 European *première* of Branagh's *Hamlet*. Taking place in Belfast at the Waterfront Hall, the event explicitly figured Branagh as a homegrown talent who was introduced to the audience as 'your boy'.[35] However, audience expectation was dashed when the local hero appeared in ghostly form available only via a videotaped message. Simultaneously locally rooted (his continuing commitment to his Northern Irish birthplace is well documented) and overtly pledged to a mass market (global) Shakespeare, Branagh signifies the perennial artist who finds himself only when he has vacated his homeland. Notwithstanding the local sentiments espoused in Branagh's communication, the lure of the mondial stage had proved 'mettle more attractive'.[36] (He had commenced filming his role as an American detective for Robert Altman's *The Gingerbread Man* [1997]). Intriguingly, one of the main charities to benefit from the *première* was an organization founded in order to enable local thespians to pursue theatrical ventures outside Northern Ireland. Both encouraging a movement away from the local, and embracing its worth and particularity, the occasion exemplifies the 'conflicted . . . cultural politics' of a creative practitioner who aspires to local participation in the same moment as he is moulded by the global exigencies of the Hollywood movie machine.[37]

An alternative path for the Shakespearian filmmaker presents itself intriguingly in Stephen Cavanagh's *Hamlet*, (2005) which is set and filmed in Londonderry, Northern Ireland. To understand his *Hamlet* is to acknowledge the history of Derry and to recognize its origins as a contested English

---

[33] Jacques Derrida, *Spectres of Marx: The State of the Debt, the Work of Mourning, and the New International*, tr. Peggy Kamuf (New York, 1994), p. 39.

[34] See Robert Goldman and Stephen Papson, *Nike Culture: The Sign of the Swoosh* (London, 1998), passim. As a 'global power' company, Nike has itself been seen as a revealing symptom of the 'McDonaldization' process. See Steven Miles, 'McDonaldization and the Global Sports Store: Constructing Consumer Meanings in a Rationalized Society', *McDonaldization Revisited: Critical Essays on Consumer Culture*, ed. Mark Alfino, John S. Caputo and Robin Wynyard (Westport, 1998), p. 63.

[35] For Julie Christie's description, see Mark Thornton Burnett, 'The "very cunning of the scene": Kenneth Branagh's *Hamlet*', *Literature/Film Quarterly*, 25 (1997), 78–82; p. 82.

[36] Shakespeare, *Works*, 3.2.105.

[37] The phrase is Douglas Lanier's in '"Art thou base, common and popular?"', *Spectacular Shakespeare*, ed. Lehmann and Starks, p. 166.

plantation founded by the Corporation of London in 1613, its status, following the siege of 1688–9, as the saviour of Protestantism, its narratives of internecine Catholic/Protestant conflict, and its association with the Civil Rights movement, the 'Bloody Sunday' march of 30 January 1972, and the Saville enquiry.[38] Here, because of this setting, the spectres haunting previous film *Hamlet*s are granted a more complete embodiment. The use of English in a Northern Irish intonation, for example, allows the dissident accent of Marcella in Almereyda's *Hamlet* to be formulated as a type of universal: that linguistic sub-plot now becomes a major narrative. Similarly, the quasi-revolutionary sub-text of Almereyda is pushed to an extreme by Cavanagh and, in this respect, Derry is once again richly evocative. During the 1970s, part of the city was declared 'Free Derry', a Utopian Catholic enclave inside the 'occupied six counties'; judged alongside Almereyda's investments, the location signifies a material enactment of the idealized political space Hamlet is represented as striving towards.[39]

Lending Ireland the central role while still managing to accommodate the Shakespearian original, Cavanagh's film opens up new avenues for exploring the relationship between the Shakespearian local and the Shakespearian global. Global gestures are easily discerned: the narrative pace of the film is quick and compressed, and guns and cameras, the insignias of a Luhrmannesque Shakespeare, are given pride of place. Yet, at the same time, by translating *Hamlet* to Derry, the director explicitly draws upon the associations embedded in a locally-charged environment. Although overt 'political statements', to quote Cavanagh, are avoided, political images, in particular, are privileged, with Derry's seventeenth-century walls featuring prominently, as do torchlit soldiers and the Guildhall, seat of a fractured administration.[40] Such visual paraphernalia have a two-fold effect. On the one hand, they lend the film an acute historical suggestiveness, positing the siege of the city (in which the Protestant 'apprentice boys' of Derry famously held it against the Catholic James II) as an event whose mythological overtones are still being replayed. And current political pressures, which have a highly charged importance in Northern Ireland, are felt throughout, as in Hamlet's anxiety that his colleagues will 'reveal' his precious secret.[41] There is, as Cavanagh admits, a 'high security culture under Claudius' and the all too familiar presence of governmental surveillance.[42] On the other hand, the film's appeal to the eye brings the Shakespearian 'original' back to mind, making of Hamlet a type of apprentice and forging a bridge between Derry and Wittenberg, home of Protestant radicalism. Unlike the *Hamlet*s of Branagh and Almereyda, which concentrate respectively on nineteenth- and twentieth-century manifestations, Cavanagh's filmic writing addresses Shakespeare through a longer and more uneven timeframe of Ireland's political fortunes. Thus, while globalization dictates the film's typology and style, Cavanagh's subjects remain locked in a richly-determined local distinctiveness. As such, his *Hamlet* offers us a denser reading of the Irish 'heritage', suggesting that the local is at its most communicative only when it has absorbed its historical particularity.

Local distinctiveness can also blur interestingly into a confrontational exclusiveness. Whereas Almereyda and Branagh deploy the local to reduce the global, Cavanagh deploys the local to confront Shakespeare and his global status as transnational voice. Offering a verbal counterpoint to Branagh's notion of a cross-cultural Shakespearian tongue and granting the most famous speech its most local purchase, 'To be or not to be' is delivered in Irish. Such an innovative directorial undertaking is explained by Cavanagh as follows: 'Hamlet has the idea that

[38] See Jonathan Bardon, *A History of Ulster* (Belfast, 1992), pp. 128–30, 152–8, 687.

[39] Bardon, *Ulster*, p. 662.

[40] Interview between Mark Thornton Burnett and Stephen Cavanagh, 4 April 2003.

[41] Shakespeare, *Works*, 1.5.122.

[42] Interview between Mark Thornton Burnett and Stephen Cavanagh, 4 April 2003.

Claudius is listening and he doesn't want to be understood. He doesn't want his intentions to be transparent from what he says.' The use of hand-held camera work in this scene, as elsewhere, allows for a 'visceral' impression and makes a virtue of the linguistic decision, forcing us to be 'complicit in [Hamlet's] emotional life'.[43] More arrestingly, an Irish-speaking protagonist brings to mind the ways in which Irish has been used in Derry in opposition to British dominance and helps to formulate Hamlet's bifurcated identity in terms of the unresolved resonances of a disappearing national language. If nothing else, this moment posits the complex necessity of reading local practices alongside the mainstream activities of a multinational film industry.

Understood in relation to the realities of the global Hollywood machine, recent film treatments of *Hamlet* and *Macbeth* exemplify a trajectory that culminates simultaneously in anonymity and in a mediated manifestation of the local. In a period dominated by homogeneity of production values and market forces, the tragedies suggest that the local is never entirely expunged; rather, local concerns are always accommodated by, and in conversation with, global imperatives. Overlapping and multivalent, the local as an operative category is arguably at its most powerful when it discharges critical regional comment. Because of his transnational status, notions of Ireland and Scotland cluster around Shakespeare; moreover, versions of both 'ideoscapes' return, ghost-like, in such a way as to assert both the vibrancy of particularized constituencies and the importance of dissident positions.[44] It is a measure of the scope of the local that, in certain deployments, there is ironization and even interrogation of its global niche. Such a dialogue allows for Shakespearian meanings to be animated and transfigured via 'glocalization', with the dramatist's individual applications continuing to enjoy a salient late twentieth- and early twenty-first-century purchase. Despite current critical constructions, then, no clearly demarcated split between a universal and a particular Shakespeare can easily be maintained, since space for one exists inside the other, each playing a mutually constitutive role.

If Ireland and Scotland are ghosts, then so, too, is Shakespeare, a spectre that comes back from a past that, according to Jacques Derrida, 'never was and can never be lived in the originary or modified form of presence'.[45] It is a symptom of postmodernity that things come back – as parodies, allusions, echoes and fragments – and cinematic representations of Shakespeare betray notably valuable instances of this process. Yet, as this brief catalogue makes clear, the return is intermittently straightforward, consistently different. In this sense, Shakespeare's periodic place in the global economy accords with the 'growing disjunctures' and 'increasingly nonisomorphic paths' that some commentators have identified as among globalization's chief features.[46] Saskia Sassen's remark that the mondial system 'generates contradictory spaces characterized by . . . internal differentiation' is typical.[47] Certainly, *Macbeth* and *Hamlet* work in the cinema to suggest not that the local substitutes for authenticity but to point out that there is only ever romance and desire. Inside that arrangement, Ireland and Scotland figure, on the one hand, as utopian prospects. With Shakespeare as the facilitative instrument, versions of the Celtic hinterland discover the U.S. recollecting origins and projecting ideas of connection and identification otherwise compromised in the global landscape. The movement, however, is not one-way. A migratory phenomenon moving here and there according to present needs, representational developments

43 Interview between Mark Thornton Burnett and Stephen Cavanagh, 4 April 2003.

44 Arjun Appadurai, *Modernity at Large: Cultural Dimensions of Globalization* (Minneapolis, 1996), p. 35.

45 Jacques Derrida, *A Derrida Reader: Between the Blinds*, tr. Peggy Kamuf (New York and London, 1991), p. 42.

46 Appadurai, *Modernity*, p. 37.

47 Saskia Sassen, *Globalization and Its Discontents* (New York, 1998), p. xxxiv.

and modifications in the geographical ownership of power, Shakespeare demonstrates that, on the other hand, Scotland and Ireland can court America and that film is the means of accessing its values and interpretive registers. Thus, encompassing and complimenting its contestatory capacity, recent versions of the tragedies on screen point up the fact that the local ultimately performs as a vehicle of fantasy, suggesting through opposition what is unrealizable and self-consciously rewriting the Shakespearian past to meet contemporary energies and agendas.

# THE 'COMPLEXION' OF TWELFTH NIGHT

JANET CLARE

As a *fin-de-siècle* romantic comedy, *Twelfth Night* represents Shakespeare's final working of the genre. The play was written and performed at the cusp of the old Elizabethan courtly and romantic comedy and the new social and satirical comedy aggressively promoted by Jonson in his second 'humours' play and second Globe play, *Every Man Out of His Humour*. It could be argued that *Twelfth Night* already appeared dated when it was performed at the Globe in the wake of *Every Man Out* in 1601.[1] Yet that Shakespeare could hardly have been unaware of competing aesthetics and of an apparent shift in taste is evidenced in his experimentation with and dilution of both comedy in *Measure for Measure* and romance and the romantic in *Troilus and Cressida*.

The transitional nature of comedy at the turn of the century and the fierce debates about the nature and purpose of dramatic representation have been the focus of much scholarly and critical analysis. Opinions differ as to the complexion of the – now canonical – relationship between Shakespeare's romantic comedy and what was a radical new departure on the London stage, Jonson's 'comical satire'. Does *Twelfth Night* evince exhaustion with the genre? In *Twelfth Night* and the subsequent darker comedies, was Shakespeare readjusting to and accommodating satire within his preferred comic forms? Or, on the contrary, was he confidently reaffirming in *Twelfth Night* the tropes and dynamics of romantic comedy in opposition to rival forms? Recently, contrary to earlier examinations of what has become known as the 'poets' war', Jonson and Shakespeare, rather than Marston, Dekker and Jonson, have been seen as 'rival playwrights'. In this context intertextual links between Jonson's 'comical satires' and Shakespeare's later comedies have been examined.[2]

This chapter attempts to avoid reading *Twelfth Night* teleologically, that is, through the lens of the subsequent, more problematic comedies. Nor is it concerned with the alleged rivalry between Jonson and Shakespeare, reconstructed through oblique personation, jibes and innuendo in a sequence of

1 *Terminus ad quem* is the documented performance at Middle Temple in February 1602. It is usually thought that the play was written after the visit to court of Don Virginio Orsino, the Duke of Bracciano in January 1601. Leslie Hotson, *The First Night of Twelfth Night* (1955) proposed that the play was written as part of the entertainment of Virginio Orsino. It is unlikely that the play was written for either of these occasions since all plays were tested in the public playhouse before a commissioned performance. See Andrew Gurr, *The Shakespeare Company, 1594–1642* (Cambridge, 2004), p. 124.

2 See, for example, John Hollander, '*Twelfth Night* and the Morality of Indulgence', *Sewanee Review* 67 (1959), 220–38; Russ McDonald, *Shakespeare and Jonson/Jonson and Shakespeare* (Brighton, 1988); David Bevington, 'Shakespeare vs. Jonson on satire', *Proceedings of the World Shakespeare Congress*, ed. Clifford Leech and J. M. R. Margeson (Toronto, 1972), 107–122; Nancy S. Leonard, 'Shakespeare and Jonson Again: The Comic Forms', *Renaissance Drama*, 10 (1979), 45–69; Anne Barton, 'Jonson and Shakespeare', *Shakespeare, Man of the Theater*, ed. Kenneth Muir, Jay Halio and D. J. Palmer (Newark, 1983); James Shapiro, *Rival Playwrights: Marlowe, Jonson and Shakespeare* (New York, 1991), pp. 137–46; Ann Blake, '"Sportful Malice": Duping in the Comedies of Jonson and Shakespeare', *Jonson and Shakespeare*, ed. Ian Donaldson (Canberra, 1983), 119–34; and James Bednarz, *Shakespeare and the Poets' War* (New York and Chichester, 2001).

plays. Instead, I want to examine both Shakespeare's participation in the late Elizabethan controversy about the social implications of comedy and the theoretical underpinning of drama through a discussion of intertextuality in *Twelfth Night* and *Every Man Out of His Humour* that would have been apparent to the interpretative community of the Globe audience. The relationship between the two plays in the context of Inns of Court performance has been discussed in some detail by Henk Gras.[3] Gras has contended that *Twelfth Night* was written with performance at Middle Temple in mind and that this venue prompted a re-working of motifs found in *Every Man Out*. Jonson's play also had Inns of Court affiliations: it was dedicated to the Inns and possibly performed at Middle Temple during the 1599/1600 Christmas season.[4] I do not fundamentally disagree with Gras's view of Shakespeare as using conventions which Jonson held in contempt and turning Jonsonian materials inside out. However, attention to the auspices of the occasional performance displaces the importance of the Globe and public theatre audiences as the testing ground for contestatory representations of comedy. In the following discussion of specific, and what I see as antagonistic, textual inter-relationships, my emphasis is rather different from that of Gras. In its exuberant manipulation of romantic plot devices, *Twelfth Night* is the most self-consciously theatrical of Shakespeare's comedies. It is a play in which performance, actual and metaphorical, is central. Yet it is also a play in which theatrical illusion remains consistently intact. Part of my argument, then, is that it is in response to the very literariness of Jonson's satirical comedy that the play can be seen to assert its theatricality and performativity. At the same time it reaffirms and extends the generic conventions of romantic comedy.

In a recent investigation, the most thorough to date, of the Poetomachia of 1599 to 1602, James Bednarz has shifted the emphasis from the 'war of the theatres' to the 'poets' war'. In place of Alfred Harbage's persuasive and influential idea of a commercial rivalry between the public theatres on one hand and the private coterie theatres, on the other, Bednarz has argued instead that these years mark a struggle for poetic authority, a legitimation crisis in which Shakespeare was highly involved. Bednarz, however, shifts his analysis away from interpersonal conflicts and the personation of dramatists.[5] Against such personalized and to an extent anecdotal accounts of rivalries and animosities between Jonson, Marston and Dekker, in Bednarz's revision the 'poets' war' can be regarded as the 'most complex and thorough transaction of dramatic criticism in the English Renaissance', constituting a major debate on the nature and function of drama. In this debate Jonson and Shakespeare are the central protagonists, with Jonson defining himself through his drama in opposition to Shakespeare and Shakespeare shaping his own literary response in answering Jonson's criticism. It is in *Twelfth Night*, it will be argued here, that Shakespeare embeds his strongest reply to Jonson.

It is, of course, evident that the modes through which Jonson and Shakespeare articulated convictions about the forms and purposes of comedy are in themselves quite oppositional. Jonson's theories of comedy are superimposed and explicitly stated in paratextual material and by thinly disguised author figures such as Asper in *Every Man Out*, Crites in *Cynthia's Revels* and most explicitly Horace in *Poetaster*. Inductions, stage commentators, authorial spokesmen were at this stage of his career all part of Jonson's dramatic strategies to orientate his audience. Shakespeare's ideas of theatre and theories of drama are, on the other hand, as Pauline Kiernan has amply illustrated, built into the very

3 Henk Gras, '*Twelfth Night, Every Man Out of His Humour* and the Middle Temple Revels of 1597–98', *Modern Language Review*, 84 (1989), 545–64.

4 '*Twelfth Night, Every Man Out of His Humour* and the Middle Temple Revels of 1597–98', p. 552.

5 Josiah H. Penniman, *The War of the Theatres* (Boston, 1897) and R. S. Small, *The Stage-Quarrel between Ben Jonson and the So-Called Poetasters* (Breslau, 1899). Matthew Steggle, *Wars of the Theatres: The Poetics of Personation in the Age of Jonson* (Victoria, BC, 1998) develops this argument so that interpersonal conflicts reveal 'crucial intellectual and practical struggles over the nature and future of the drama' (p. 11).

forms and structures of the plays.[6] A 'defence of drama' inheres not in reiterated statements of dramatic mimesis, as in Jonson, but in the implication that fiction explores realities rather than imitates them. In consequence, as David Bevington has said, Shakespeare 'resists cataloguing of his own biases', displaying a 'lack of pretentiousness as a critic', and simply his 'attitudes are harder to pin down'[7] or, as Bednarz puts it, Jonson's comedy tends to be 'authoritarian and self promoting' while Shakespeare's is 'indeterminate, self-effacing and sceptical'.[8] However one glosses the modes of expression, it is possible to see how in specific works by Shakespeare and by Jonson the idea of the play, indeed, a theory of drama, and more specifically comedy, becomes a central preoccupation during the poets' war as different dramatic practices decisively emerge and are thrown into relief.

Such contestatory dialogue can be deciphered through the intertextuality of *Every Man Out of His Humour* and *Twelfth Night or What You Will*. *Every Man Out* (published in two editions in 1600) was one of the first plays to be performed at the newly constructed Globe in 1599. Shakespeare did not act in this play as he had done in the earlier 'humours' play, *Every Man in His Humour*, possibly because, as has been suggested by Katherine Duncan-Jones, he was keen to distance himself from an author who had recently killed a fellow actor, Gabriel Spencer.[9] As Duncan-Jones and others have noted, *Every Man Out* contains several ironic references to Shakespeare's plays, including *Romeo and Juliet* and the near contemporaneous *Julius Caesar* as well as a personalized jibe at Shakespeare's attempt to be upwardly mobile in his recent acquisition of a coat of arms. The would-be gentleman, the clownish Sogliardo, buys a coat of arms with the crest of 'a boar without a head, rampant' (3.1.220).

More significant here, however, is how one of the disquisitions on comedy in *Every Man Out* significantly prefigures and prompts a retaliation in the romantic structures and motifs of *Twelfth Night*. The loose construction of *Every Man Out* – essentially scenes in which various 'characters' configure and expose degrees of vanity and stupidity – is given a more formal framework by the device of the Chorus or 'Grex' which intersperses irregularly the 'action' of the play. Through the Chorus, comprising the 'author', Asper, and his two associates Cordatus and Mitis, Jonson repeatedly seeks to legitimate satiric comedy as against its implied rival, romantic comedy. The exchange of specific relevance here is one in which Mitis raises objections to this pattern of satiric self-exposure. Mitis's views are not to be taken too seriously: he is the last to be described in Jonson's resumé of characters which prefaces the play and in which he is briefly alluded to as 'a person of no action' and therefore he is 'afforded no character'.[10] His role is to anticipate disingenuously a general objection to contemporary satire that can then be confuted by Cordatus.

After a protracted scene in 'the middle aisle of Pauls' in which most of the characters at some point make an appearance, Mitis raises another objection. An audience, he argues, would prefer a different scenario from the discursive encounters they have just observed:

> the argument of his comedy might have been of some other nature, as of a duke to be in love with a countess, and that countess to be in love with the duke's son, and the son to love the lady's waiting maid: some such cross-wooing, with a clown to their servingman, better than to be thus near, and familiarly allied to the time.
>
> (3.1. 516–21)

Mitis's objection to the comedy on the grounds that it is 'familiarly allied to the time' prompts a vigorous defence of satire on the grounds of its social relevance. Cordatus implies that romantic comedy is *passé*; only an 'autumn judgement' could prefer the hackneyed formulae outlined by Mitis. Such romantic comedy has no classical precedent and no generic status. According to Cordatus the answer

---

6 Pauline Kiernan, *Shakespeare's Theory of Drama* (Cambridge, 1996), pp. 94–9.

7 'Shakespeare vs Jonson on Satire', p. 114.

8 *Shakespeare and the Poets' War*, p. 18.

9 Katherine Duncan-Jones, *Ungentle Shakespeare: Scenes from His Life* (London, 2001), p. 119.

10 References are taken from *Every Man Out of His Humour*, ed. Helen Ostovich (Manchester, 2002).

to 'Quid sit Comoedia?' can only be answered by a Ciceronian definition of comedy as an imitation of life, a mirror of manners, an image of truth; 'a thing throughout pleasant and ridiculous, and accommodated to the correction of manners'. Jonson's theory of comedy adapted from Minturno's *De Poeta* and Donatus's attribution to Cicero is thus legitimated by its Latin citation of Cicero while a competing aesthetic is ridiculed by a parodic summary of a romantic plot.

The preferred romance plot outlined by Mitis and vigorously rejected by Cordatus, while refracting mythic/archetypal structures of romantic comedy, does, as has not gone unnoticed, bear more than a passing resemblance to *Twelfth Night*, more so than any other of Shakespeare's early comedies which predate *Every Man Out*. Duke Orsino (as in the speech prefixes and stage directions, although 'count' in the dialogue) is in love with a countess who does not reciprocate his love, but falls in love with the count's servingman (one better than the count's son). From here, Shakespeare's play takes a slightly different turn, but in Viola's proxy wooing of Olivia and in the confusion of the identities of Viola and Sebastian, Shakespeare exploits the motif of cross-wooing. In Feste, there is, of course, a servingman who moves between two households, and who is also the clown. So close is the resemblance of facetious plot line to actual play in *Twelfth Night* that it has been suggested that *Twelfth Night* must have predated *Every Man Out*.[11] On circumstantial evidence of dating, this argument has been rejected, but there has been a slow recognition of the alternative possibility that Shakespeare quite deliberately and effectively re-appropriated what Jonson had held up to ridicule. Anne Barton, commenting on the above exchange in *Every Man Out*, interprets the line as if only an expression of character and refers simply to a 'wistful anticipation of *Twelfth Night*'.[12] James Bednarz takes this further and comments on *Twelfth Night* as a 'response' to comical satire in its revitalization of the ridiculous formula of cross-wooing.[13] Certainly, the point should be emphasized that nowhere are the different concepts of theatre held by Jonson and by Shakespeare more starkly exposed than in the dialogue of Mitis and Cordatus and in Shakespeare's subsequent composition of *Twelfth Night* with what could be seen as a self-reflexive flaunting of romantic absurdities and fantasies.

A simple comparison of Jonson's hackneyed plot outline and the dilemmas and errors that constitute *Twelfth Night* does not, of course, do justice to the playful boldness of Shakespeare's text. Jonson's parodic scenario produces comedy from the discrepancies in age and class of 'cross-wooing'. Shakespeare extends Jonson's 'cross-wooing' to cross-sexual wooing, thereby creating in romantic comedy a sexual ambivalence entirely absent in the conventions and formulae mocked by Jonson. Jonson evokes a chain of desire, whereas desire in *Twelfth Night* is circular: Orsino loves Olivia, Olivia loves Cesario/Viola, Viola loves Orsino. The plot hinges on Viola carrying a particular erotic charge as Orsino, as well as Olivia, love Cesario, as he believes, without desire. There is a lifting of the taboo as Orsino's erotic feelings are converted to heterosexual love and the taboo is kept in abeyance as Olivia's desire for Viola is supposedly aroused – and satisfied – by heterosexual love. Such an exploration of erotic desire and sexual ambiguity and the fantastic recourse to doubling in *Twelfth Night* mark a new departure in romantic comedy.

The innovatory exploitation of disguise and errors in the plot of *Twelfth Night* in response to Jonson's deprecatory references to romantic comedy is complemented by a conscious reworking in *Twelfth Night* of specific comic devices from *Every Man Out* for quite different dramatic ends. These appear to have received no commentary in any recent editions of the two plays. The first scene in *Every Man Out* re-presented in *Twelfth Night* is that of the ridiculous charade played out between the vainglorious knight, Puntarvolo, who according

[11] See E. A. J. Honigmann, *Shakespeare's Impact on His Contemporaries* (London, 1982), pp. 101–102.

[12] Anne Barton, *Ben Jonson: Dramatist* (Cambridge, 1984), p. 69.

[13] *Shakespeare and the Poets' War*, p. 179. Bednarz is, however, more concerned with the relationship of *Twelfth Night* and *Cynthia's Revels* and with *As You Like it* as a response to *Every Man Out*.

to Jonson's initial description of him is given to 'strange performances' and a gentlewoman, who serves his wife. Puntarvolo arrives at his own castle and questions the gentlewoman about himself and his lady. Later he enacts with his wife games of courtship 'as she were a stranger never encountered before'. When Puntarvolo has approached his castle he questions the 'gentlewoman':

PUNTARVOLO Tis a most sumptuous and stately edifice. What years is the knight, fair damsel?
GENTLEWOMAN Faith, much about your years, sir.
PUNTARVOLO What complexion or what stature bears he?
GENTLEWOMAN Of your stature, and very near upon your complexion.
PUNTARVOLO Mine is melancholy –
CARLO So is the dog's, just.
PUNTARVOLO – and doth argue constancy, chiefly in love. What are his endowments? Is he courteous? (2.1.227–36)

This absurd dialogue of self-gratification has been refashioned and inset into the one substantial scene in *Twelfth Night* between Viola and Orsino before the final scene of unmaskings and revelations and Orsino's rather cursory proposal to Viola that she should become her 'master's mistress'. Much depends, then, on the earlier scene to establish and effectively convey the feelings of both. Orsino is curious when Viola acknowledges that her eye 'hath strayed upon some favour that it loves' and, intimating his own desires, he questions her about her love:

ORSINO What kind of woman is't?
VIOLA Of your complexion.
ORSINO She is not worth thee then. What years, i'faith?
VIOLA About your years, my lord. (2.4.25–7)

The terse replies of both Viola and Orsino are ironically nuanced. The occasion offers Viola some emotional relief from the anguish of love: direct questioning enables her to release feelings which she has had to conceal and suppress and hitherto has only explored in soliloquy. Orsino not only intimates his own sublimated desire for Cesario/Viola – no woman could be worth Viola's love – but suggests also an unconscious recognition that he cannot be 'worth' the selfless devotion of Viola.

The verbal parallels between the scenes in the respective plays are sufficient to suggest that they cannot be accidental. Noting the verbal echo, Henk Gras comments only on the repetition of 'complexion' and concludes that Shakespeare must have relied here on Jonson.[14] But Shakespeare does much more than rely on Jonson. In the Gentlewoman's use of 'complexion', as is clear from Puntarvolo's definition of his own as 'melancholy', the term is confined within the limited psychology of humours character as famously outlined in *Every Man Out*. In the Induction to the play Asper, as Jonson's spokesman, had defined the four bodily humours as metaphorically applicable to character: 'As when some one peculiar quality / Doth so possess a man that it doth draw / All his affects, his spirits, and his powers / In their confluxions all to run one way.' Even this definition of character in terms of humour is undercut, as Carlo punctures Puntarvolo's self-regarding assessment of his melancholy humour by likening it to that of a dog. In *Twelfth Night* Viola's allusion to loving a 'woman' of Orsino's 'complexion' releases a whole range of possible signification relating to temperament, 'nature', character, disposition and mental constitution.[15] More than a mere verbal echo, Shakespeare's dramatic appropriation is extremely suggestive. In both *Twelfth Night* and *Every Man Out* characters have assumed and are acting out different roles. Shakespeare, however, subverts Jonson's depiction of role-playing. For Puntarvolo the role he enacts and the response he solicits from the gentlewoman are there for self-gratification; the gentlewoman and his wife collude in the fancy and there is no moment of self-recognition. In *Twelfth Night* the dialogue hints at Orsino's attraction to

[14] '*Twelfth Night, Every Man out of His Humour* and the Middle Temple Revels of 1597–98', p. 550.

[15] The use of 'complexion' elsewhere in *Twelfth Night* implies more limited meaning. See 2.3.152 and 2.5.25.

Viola and produces a poignant moment of self-revelation for her. An absurdly satiric moment in *Every Man Out* is transformed in *Twelfth Night* to relay the desires of romantic comedy.

The second intertextual relationship points to situational rather than verbal resonance and concerns the representation of a comic duel in the two plays.[16] In *Every Man Out*, arising from no specific cause, Fastidius Brisk, the affected clotheshorse of a courtier, recounts in great and deliberately tedious detail, an abortive duel with 'Signor Luculento'. 'Let the cause escape, sir' is his airy dismissal of what prompted the occasion, as he proceeds to describe various sartorial depredations before the two duellists 'lighting at the court gate both together, embraced and marched hand in hand up into the presence' (4.3.435–7). The scene is, of course, static, and the comedy arises from Brisk's preoccupation with his clothes and his mannered account of the lack of any real action. There is bathos in the way speech builds up to an event that will not happen.

In contrast, the arrested duel in *Twelfth Night*, which Sir Andrew Aguecheek is provoked into fighting with Viola, provides extensive stage business. From Aguecheek's challenge to Viola to Antonio's intervention to rescue the person he thinks is Sebastian, the abortive duel in *Twelfth Night* spills over several scenes, producing diverse comic effects, both verbal and visual. Sir Andrew, ignoring the conventional brief and modest formula of the challenge, issues a comically 'saucy' and verbose one. Sir Toby uses the occasion to milk Sir Andrew once again by promising him that he will intervene to buy off Viola in return for Aguecheek's horse. Anxiety prompts Viola's wry innuendo, 'Pray God defend me. A little thing would make me tell them how much I lack of a man' (3.4.293–4). Finally, as Antonio risks the threat of death in Orsino's territory by coming to the rescue of Viola, love and loyalty intervene in a scene structured as farce. The fairly stock device of a threatening, but unrealized duel thus renders considerable dramatic and theatrical capital. In contrast to Jonson's limited use of the device as yet another means to define the 'humour' of Fastidius Brisk, in *Twelfth Night* the episode has tonal and dramatic range, beginning in farce and ending on a serious note with Antonio's arrest and Viola's puzzled rejection of his friendship. These two contrasting episodes in the respective plays would seem to illustrate not only the quite distinctive elements of romantic and satiric comedy as Shakespeare subverts satire to reinforce a notion of the shifting relationships of romantic comedy, but also, in clear contrast to Jonson, the privileging of performance over textuality.

It has been argued none the less that *Twelfth Night* more than gestures towards the dominant satiric trends in the public and private theatres. There is some support for the play's accommodation of satire in what we know of its reception. Katherine Duncan-Jones has drawn attention to the fact that the last two years of Elizabeth's reign were a period when Shakespeare had no aristocratic patronage. She concludes that, without the need to gratify individual patrons, Shakespeare was preoccupied with attracting large audiences to the new Globe and was anxious above all to capture 'the lively Inns of Court market'.[17] Katherine Duncan-Jones does not suggest that *Twelfth Night* was written for the Inns of Court,[18] although as is very well known the play was produced at Middle Temple. The frequently quoted comment in the note book of John Manningham, a student of the Middle Temple, conveniently dates an occasional performance of *Twelfth Night* on 2 February 1602 and records something of the Templars' response:

> At our feast we had a play called 'Twelfth Night, or What you Will', much like the Comedy of Errors, or Menaechmi in Plautus, but most like and near to that in

[16] Anne Barton comments that in the encounter between Daw and La-Foole in *Epicoene*, Jonson was 'remembering' the mock combat between Viola and Aguecheek, *Ben Jonson*, p. 125. No reference is made to *Every Man Out*.

[17] *Ungentle Shakespeare*, pp. 135–6.

[18] Dover Wilson in the 1930 Cambridge edition suggested that the play was written with a performance at Middle Temple in mind. Henk Gras (p. 546) accepts that the play was written for the Middle Temple, but not only for that occasion.

Italian called Inganni. A good practice in it to make the steward believe his Lady widow was in love with him, by counterfeiting a letter as from his Lady in general terms, telling him what she liked best in him, and prescribing his gesture in smiling, his apparel, etc and then when he came to practise making him believe they took him to be mad.[19]

Manningham's account of the performance is of interest for what it omits and for what it gets wrong. Clearly what he – and we may assume other lawyers – responded to in the play was not its portrayal of romantic love and erotic desire, but the baiting and gulling of the would-be social climber, Olivia's steward Malvolio. The prolonged duping and persecution of Malvolio is an aspect of the play that, despite the character's blatant self-righteousness, often leaves modern audiences with feelings of unease. In the light of the work of Philip Finkelpearl on the literary milieu of the Inns of Court, Manningham's response, however, seems entirely predictable.[20] Spearheaded by writers like John Marston and Evarard Guilpin, dramatic and non-dramatic satire proliferated at the Inns. Manningham's selection of the more satirical rather than the romantic thrust of the play clearly reflects the literary taste of the Middle Temple audience. Indeed, such is Manningham's apparent disregard of the romantic entanglements and complexities of the plot that he associates Olivia's mourning with widowhood (possibly confusing it with either the source of Celia's grief in Marston's contemporaneous *What You Will* or Olivia's counterpart, Julina, in Barnaby Riche's *Apolonius and Silla*, the principal source for *Twelfth Night*) rather than the death of her brother. Manningham thus ignores the counterpoint with Viola's grief for the supposed loss of Sebastian. The closest he gets to the romantic element of the plot of *Twelfth Night* is in the comparison to the more farcical *Comedy of Errors*. We know from the early history of *Twelfth Night* that 'Malvolio' almost became in some circles a metonym for the play.[21] Yet, we have to allow that, as always, the constituency of an audience affects the meanings attached to a play. Conditioned by current satirical comedy as well as by the reading of verse satire, the Inns of Court audience found in the baiting of Malvolio what it easily recognized, elements of social satire. As was the practice in the public theatres, the play was no doubt cut for this particular performance. It is unlikely that any of the music or songs of *Twelfth Night* were lost since music was such an integral component at the principal feasts of the Inns (the stipends of the musicians being increased at such a time).[22] Indeed, the significant contribution of music to *Twelfth Night* and its integration into the plot might suggest an awareness of potential performance at that venue. I offer as an aside the conjecture that the version of the play which Manningham and fellow Templars saw in February 1602 was one in which scenes of cross-wooing and courtship may have been abridged thus giving greater prominence to subplot and bringing satire into sharper focus.

Certainly, in the 'comic' subplot to *Twelfth Night* Shakespeare seems not to have been uninfluenced by the 'characters' of satirical comedy. If there are satiric elements here, it is notable, however, how Shakespeare consistently turns Jonson's remorseless satire of exposure into a form of comedy where remorse is induced after laughter. As a knight and suitor to Olivia, Andrew Aguecheek, for example, has some of the ridiculous traits of Jonson's Puntarvolo. Like Puntarvolo, Aguecheek supposedly has a propensity for travel and a proficiency in languages that suggests a satirical allusion to the aristocratic grand tour. For all his illusions, Aguecheek is not, however, entirely an object of ridicule. There is some unease as we watch him being shamelessly exploited by Toby Belch and there is a trace of poignancy in his plaintive reply to

[19] *Diary of John Manningham, of the Middle Temple and of Bradbourne, Kent, Barrister-at-Law, 1602–1603*, ed. John Bruce (1868), p. 18.

[20] See Philip J. Finkelpearl, *John Marston of the Middle Temple* (Cambridge, Massachusetts, 1969).

[21] See Leonard Digges's dedicatory verse to *Poems: Written by William Shakespeare* (1640). Digges wrote: 'The Cockpit galleries, boxes, all are full / To hear Malvoglio[sic] that cross-gartered gull'.

[22] See William Dugdale, *The History and Antiquities of the Four Inns of Court* (London, 1780), p. 141.

Toby's boast that Maria adores him, 'I was adored once, too' (2.3.175).

It is, of course, in the duping of Malvolio that the influence of Jonson's comical satires has been most consistently detected. In discussing possible ways of portraying Malvolio, John Barton has commented that the danger with Malvolio is that he is 'basically a Jonsonian humours part' and that his part is in a different style from the rest of the play.[23] David Bevington has described the gulling of Malvolio as displaying 'fully the characteristics of Jonsonian satire' in that it resembles 'the manipulation of an exposure plot aimed at a socially ambitious hypocrite . . . [who is] laughed at scornfully by the audience, and is subjected to a ridiculous form of punishment befitting the nature of the offence'.[24] In formal outline the tricking of Malvolio does seem to correspond to the public exposure and humiliation of Jonson's characters driven by their dominant humours. Yet, as John Barton concedes, Malvolio can be 'played in many, many different ways' which could not be said of a Jonsonian 'humours character'. Later twentieth-century representations of Malvolio[25] have ranged from Ian Holm's self-made, middle-class Elizabethan in a production directed by Peter Hall (1966) to Antony Sher's tragic, demented figure in a production directed by Bill Alexander (1987). Donald Sinden's initial response to the part, 'I find him tragic' came close to that of Sher.[26] Sinden's exploration of the role exposed a whole range of moods from hauteur and offended dignity to ebullience and madness.

If in the treatment of Malvolio Shakespeare took his cue from the repetitive plot device of humiliation and exposure of *Every Man Out*, he did it with great imaginative freedom and the effects are far removed from the humours 'reformation' and social catharses of Jonson. For a start, the exposure and humiliation of Malvolio are not instigated by a self-righteous author figure, but by a morally dubious group of roisterers intent on petty revenge against a figure who has interrupted their drunken revels. In the success of the plot there lies for Maria the possibility of social advancement in marriage to Sir Toby. Rather than instigating the morally driven exposure of a social hypocrite or parasite, the deception of Malvolio is devised to provide 'pleasure'. A pleasure which is patently sadistic: 'We shall make him mad indeed', declares Fabian, and Toby Belch elaborates the stratagem: 'We'll have him in a dark room and bound. My niece is already in the belief that he's mad. We may carry it thus for our pleasure and his penance till our very pastime, tired out of breath, prompt us to have mercy on him' (3.4.133–7). Penance seems misplaced here. It has been argued that Malvolio's 'punishment' is all part of the ritual of comedy: the expulsion of a Lenten spirit from carnival.[27] Yet, if this is so, there are in the text traces of anxiety about the procedure. Even amongst its perpetrators there is a sense in which comic revenge gets out of hand; albeit motivated by self-interest and fear of Olivia's opprobrium, Toby Belch does later comment to Maria that he wishes they 'were well rid of this knavery'. And, of course, the trick culminates not in public exposure of a foolish character leading to metamorphosis, but in an angry figure making his final exit vowing revenge. The plot against Malvolio does not in fact follow a Jonsonian pattern at all; even to describe it in terms of exposure needs some qualification, since his pathetic fantasy of becoming 'Count Malvolio' is fuelled by Maria. In place of Jonson's stated intention in the Induction of *Every Man Out* 'to strip the ragged follies of the time', in *Twelfth Night* there is a strong sense that human folly, also a source of human vulnerability, is not easily eradicated and that theatre is an ineffectual medium for the purpose.

---

[23] See *Directors' Shakespeare: Approaches to Twelfth Night*, ed. Michael Billington (London, 1990), p. 81.

[24] 'Shakespeare vs Jonson on Satire', p. 120.

[25] See *Directors' Shakespeare*, pp. xx, xxvii.

[26] See 'Donald Sinden, Malvolio' in *Players of Shakespeare*, ed. Philip Brockbank (Cambridge, 1985), 41–67, p. 43.

[27] Notably expressed by C. L. Barber, *Shakespeare's Festive Comedy: A Study of Dramatic Form and its Relation to Social Custom* (Princeton, New Jersey, 1959), pp. 256–7. See also François Laroque, *Shakespeare's Festive World: Elizabethan Seasonal Entertainment and the Professional Stage*, trans. Janet Lloyd (Cambridge, 1991), pp. 227, 254–5.

The relationship between *Every Man Out* and *Twelfth Night* is one of intertextual antagonism. In its response to *Every Man Out*, there is in *Twelfth Night* a pronounced reworking of Jonsonian motifs which reaffirm both a festive and romantic ethos and an assertion of illusion over mimesis and performance over textuality. *Every Man Out* offers a mimetic theory of comedy with all the distortions of 'humours' satire, while *Twelfth Night* seems to be a deliberate reaffirmation of all that is 'far-fetched' and fantastic about romantic comedy. Perhaps, as he saw his company perform *Every Man Out* or read the text published immediate to the Globe production, Shakespeare took his cue from Mitis's sample plot and determined to subvert the parody. Fabian's oft-quoted comment 'If this were played upon a stage, now, I could condemn it as an improbable fiction' (3.4.125–6) is sometimes read as a reworking of the 'world as stage' conceit. But it is almost like a Jonsonian device, integrated into the text, as it anticipates and pre-empts criticism of the improbable nature of theatrical illusion celebrated in *Twelfth Night*. In its assertion of the unreality and improbability of dramatic illusion, the remark could serve as a riposte to Jonson.

While aspects of *Twelfth Night* have been interpreted as a response to humours comedy, it would seem from an examination of specific scenes that signs of deviation from 'comical satire' are far more marked than those of accommodation. The adaptation, or indeed the reclamation, in *Twelfth Night* of scenes and dialogue from Jonson's play, shorn of their satiric impulse, to convey moments of emotional and psychological insight instead draws attention to the limits of satire. Change and temporality are suggestively concomitant in *Twelfth Night* and set against the contrived purgation of humours, what Russ McDonald has described as acts of 'authorial prestidigitation'.[28] Indeed, in its insistence on a more complex complexion of character than that determined by the limited complexion of the humours and psychological fixation, *Twelfth Night* exposes all that is de-humanizing about comical satire. The linear plot of exposure in *Every Man Out* has been replaced by one that emphasizes instead a creative circular interplay. Even revenge, with its inherent linear dynamic, becomes, in Feste's apt metaphor for the play as a whole, part of the 'whirligig of time' (5.1.373).

The text of *Every Man Out*, published so immediate to production in 1600, contained, as Jonson declared on the title page 'more than hath been publicly spoken or acted' at the Globe (the declaration is somewhat superfluous since the text in its entirety is unstageworthy). Title page, typography of text, Theophrastian definitions of character, the 'presence' of the author, all maintain the play's textuality and literariness over production. The primacy of performance over text, theatricality over literariness in *Twelfth Night*, on the other hand, is attested by the simple fact that it was not available in print until the Folio. Seemingly composed in defiance of the current and persistent vogue for satire, the play brilliantly and boldly reappropriates the tropes of romantic comedy. *Twelfth Night* may represent a consummation of romantic comedy, but it does not evince an exhaustion with the genre. On the contrary, its tonal range and what has been described as its 'sheer kaleidoscopic range of moods'[29] suggest a greater assurance in the form. Whatever comic experimentation was to follow, *Twelfth Night* cannot be seen as a play that capitulates to the emergent and increasingly dominant satiric norms.

---

[28] *Shakespeare and Jonson / Jonson and Shakespeare*, p. 73.

[29] *Directors' Shakespeare*, p. ix.

# TRANSLATION AS APPROPRIATION: VASSILIS ROTAS, SHAKESPEARE AND MODERN GREEK

TINA KRONTIRIS

In the relatively recent conjoining of translation and cultural studies, the rendering of Shakespeare into various languages has received increasingly greater attention, especially since the publication of *European Shakespeares* (1993).[1] One result of the attention to this intercultural aspect of Shakespeare is the recognition that the translation of the English dramatist into non-English cultures has not always been a simple, ordinary event. Like the translation of the Bible in earlier centuries,[2] that of Shakespeare's corpus in more recent times has often been linked to wider national, linguistic, and aesthetic preoccupations or movements. In Hungary the first translation of the complete works of Shakespeare, carried out by eminent literary men of the nineteenth century and motivated by patriotism, took on the importance of 'a major force' in the cultural development of the country.[3] In Norway the English bard played a part in the revival of the native language and literature via the influence he exerted on the first major Norwegian poet, Henrik Wergeland.[4] In colonial South Africa he was used by the black-African translator Solomon Plaatje as a resource in the project for the preservation of a threatened Sechuana language and culture.[5] In communist Bulgaria he was deployed in a series of cultural activities designed to legitimize the soviet-type socialist regime.[6] The list of the purposes which Shakespeare has been called to serve outside his native England could go on. In this study I intend to discuss the case of Vassilis Rotas, who employed Shakespeare in promoting a particular form of modern Greek language and culture. In the process I hope to throw some light on the cultural–historical forces that influenced this translator, as well as on the relationship between appropriative translation and textual identity: to show how Rotas's purposeful choices affect the status of the Shakespearian text and its dramatic effectiveness.

In the course of the twentieth century there have been various attempts to render Shakespeare's plays into the Greek language, but there has been only one translation of the *Complete Works* of William Shakespeare, that by the writer and theatre man Vassilis Rotas. His translation is a work of historical

[1] Dirk Delabastita and Lieven D'Hulst, eds., *European Shakespeares: Translating Shakespeare in the Romantic Age* (Amsterdam, 1993). The tendency is now to try to incorporate research on translated Shakespeare into mainstream Shakespeare studies. Evidence of that is the recently published volume of essays edited by Ton Hoenselaars, *Shakespeare and the Language of Translation*, Arden Shakespeare Series (London, 2004).

[2] For example, Martin Luther's use of East Middle German in his rendering of the Scriptures contributed to the further establishment and standardization of this linguistic form – Jean Delisle and Judith Woodsworth, eds., *Translators through History* (Amsterdam, 1995), pp. 45–7.

[3] Thomas Mark, 'The First Hungarian Translation of Shakespeare's Complete Works', *Shakespeare Quarterly* 16 (Winter 1965), p. 110.

[4] Kristian Smidt, 'The Discovery of Shakespeare in Scandinavia' in *European Shakespeares*, p. 100.

[5] David Schalkwyk and Lerothodi Lapula, 'Solomon Plaatje, William Shakespeare, and the Translations of Culture', *Pretexts* 9 (July 2000), pp. 9–26.

[6] A. Shurbanov and B. Sokolova, 'Translating Shakespeare under Communism: Bulgaria and Beyond', in Hoenselaars, *Shakespeare and the Language of Translation*, pp. 82–97.

importance, not only because it made available the whole of Shakespeare's corpus to the Greek public, but also and mainly because it intended to exert an influence on the development of the Greek language and of the theatre. Born in 1889 of humble parents in the province of Corinthia, he was educated in Athens, where he pursued studies in philology at the University and attended theatre courses at the Odeon School of Drama.[7] After serving in various wars, he established the Popular Theatre of Athens,[8] an experimental type of stage that put up performances for unsophisticated audiences in a lower middle-class neighborhood of the capital. In the Theatre's magazine *Prosopa & Maskes* [Faces & Masks], published only once in June 1930, Rotas mentions three Shakespearian plays – *Othello, A Midsummer Night's Dream* and *The Comedy of Errors* – that were scheduled for performance, but there is no evidence that they were actually produced.

Rotas's major engagement with Shakespeare was in the field of translation.[9] The rendering of the English dramatist's works into modern Greek seems to have occupied him at various points of his life and over a long period of time – from 1928, when he translated *A Midsummer Night's Dream*, to 1974 when he finished his last play, *Henry IV Part 1*, along with the sonnets. Rotas tackled the majority of the plays after 1950, when he had retired from theatrical and political activity. In this later period he translated mainly for publication (he had a contract with Ikaros, an Athens publisher), and took the decision to translate the complete works only after he had rendered all but a few of the plays. In the years 1960–74 he collaborated with his companion, Voula Damianakou,[10] who in addition to helping in a number of translations also oversaw the publication of the last plays they rendered jointly.[11] But Rotas's seminal work was done earlier in the 1930s and 1940s, when he was very active in the theatre. During the 1930s he translated three Shakespeare plays – *Twelfth Night* (1932), *King Lear* (1933) and *Hamlet* (1937) – two of which were published shortly after they were completed (*Lear* in the periodical *Mousika Chronika* and *Hamlet* in book form). During the 1940s, when Rotas was engaged in his theatrical workshop and involved in the Resistance Movement against nazism, he translated three more plays – *Henry V* (1941), *Much Ado* (1946), and *Richard II* (1947).[12] By 1950, therefore,

---

7 For biographical information on Rotas as well as for discussions of his own writings see the following: Eleni Vassilopoulou, ed., *Vassilis Rotas, 1889–1977* (Athens, 1979); 'Vassilis Rotas: 25 chronia apo to thanato tou' [25 years from his death], in the magazine *Diavazo*, issue 434 (Athens, Nov. 2002), pp. 79–114; 'Vassilis Rotas, 1889–1977', in the magazine *Erevna*, number 13, issue 1 (Athens, Jan. 2001), entire issue; and 'Vassilis Rotas', in the literary magazine *Lexi*, issue 116 (Athens, July – August 1993), pp. 419–47.

8 This Theatre opened in 1932 and operated intermittently until 1948 (in the later years under the name Theatriko Spoudasterio [Theatrical Workshop]). For the conditions under which the Workshop was formed, see Vassilis Rotas, 'To Theatriko Spoudasterio', *Epitheorisi Tehnis* [Art Review] (Athens, 1987–8), pp. 306–9. For its contribution to popular theatre at large, see Dimitris Spathis, 'E gennisi tou democratikou theatrou sti synchroni Ellada' [the birth of democratic theatre in contemporary Greece], *Aeolika Grammata* 8 (May – August 1978), pp. 202–9.

9 The first and, to my knowledge, the only attempt to study Rotas's translations of the English dramatist was made by Panos Karagiorgos in his unpublished PhD thesis, *Greek Translations of Shakespeare*, Shakespeare Institute, University of Birmingham, 1979, pp. 146–59 and 242–7. Karagiorgos has more recently published a useful bibliography of Greek translations for each of Shakespeare's plays – see 'Bibliographia ton metafraseon sta ellinika ton theatrikon ergon tou Saixpir' in the magazine *Porphyras*, January–March 2001, pp. 673–96.

10 They worked together on over twelve plays, with Damianakou translating mainly from French and German versions, as her knowledge of English was limited. The plays that Rotas translated in collaboration with Damianakou have been considered inferior to the ones he rendered on his own.

11 Although the actual translation had finished in 1974, three years before Rotas's death, it was not until 1985 that the publication of all the plays had been completed. Voula Damianakou attributes this to the inconsistency of the publisher – Voula Damianakou, *Ouilliam Saixpir: korifea ekfrasi tou neoellinikou dramatikou logou* [William Shakespeare: the highest expression of modern Greek dramatic language] (Athens, 1994), p. 166.

12 Nearly all of the translations done by Rotas in the 1930s and 1940s were commissioned by the National Theatre, which held the lead in Shakespeare productions at that time. The translations of *A Midsummer Night's Dream* and *Twelfth Night* were published in a two-play volume in 1949, though the *Dream* had already appeared in the magazine *Ellinika Grammata* [Greek Letters] when it was first translated in 1928. The 1934 scheduled production of *King Lear*, for which the

Rotas had translated a total of seven plays, including the 1928 *Dream*. Though the number seems small in comparison to the later output, the groundwork was clearly laid in this earlier period. The elaborate comments and Introduction which surround his 1938 edition of *Hamlet*[13] show quite clearly that Rotas had formulated his translating theory and had acquired a thorough knowledge of Shakespeare and the Elizabethan period before 1940. Thus early on he had prepared the ground for his future translations.

Like many others, Rotas admired Shakespeare's craftsmanship and more specifically 'his descriptive power', 'the liveliness of his dialogue', 'his rich images and metaphors', 'his passionate and musical lyricism', 'his imposing tragic tone', 'his refreshing and witty jokes', 'the charming grace of his language'.[14] He tried in fact to imitate some of these characteristics in one of his own plays, *Kolokotronis*.[15] For Rotas Shakespeare was the Titan holding upon his shoulders the European Renaissance; he was the greatest modern dramatic poet, comparable only to the dramatists of Attic Greece.

Yet this high opinion was apparently not the only reason why Vassilis Rotas devoted so much of his energy and time to the Elizabethan poet. The translator saw in the rendering of Shakespearian verse an opportunity to enrich his national literature and to support both theatre and popular culture. For him the translation of great European drama was a patriotic act, to be distinguished from the time's general xenomania, the indiscriminate adoption of foreign styles and obeisant attitudes toward the 'protective' superpowers (England and France at that time). He drew a line between the culture of exploitation, as represented by Elgin and his descendants, and the culture of the great European civilization, as exemplified by Goethe, Schiller, Dante, Hugo, Shakespeare and others.[16] Translation of the foreign classics could enrich the modern Greek stage. It could provide it with a wider range of repertory and high quality plays, especially needful before 1940 when original, native drama was relatively simplistic and unable to meet the demands of the time.[17] Although Rotas always encouraged the staging of contemporary Greek drama, and in fact criticized the National Theatre for its exclusive emphasis on ancient Greek and foreign plays during the 1950s and 1960s, he could not conceive of quality theatre in Greece without the modern European classics. In the case of Shakespeare there were, of course, other translations available, but only of certain plays – nothing that could represent the Elizabethan poet entirely and responsibly. Even the great tragedies had been subject to misreading, bowdlerizing or arbitrary skipping. A skilful rendering of Shakespeare's works could thus enhance the national literature, for it would assimilate them in a way that would make this great poet a possession of the Greek people, an asset in their own language.

It is in fact the cause of language that ties this particular translator most strongly to Shakespeare. As I shall attempt to demonstrate in the following

---

translation was intended, did not take place because of the death of Fotos Politis, Director of the National Theatre at the time. The performance, with the same translation, took place on 21 October 1938. *Richard II* was apparently assigned to two translators, Rotas and Kartheos. The National Theatre decided to use the Kartheos translation for its 1947 production, directed by Rondiris. The Nazis occupied Greece shortly after the performance of *Henry V*, so the publication of the translation of this play was delayed until 1947.

13 All of Rotas's published translations include a brief introduction and some notes at the end. His 1938 edition of *Hamlet* is unique in the quality and quantity of the editorial apparatus it offers. Despite his disclaimer, Rotas apparently thought of his translation as the definitive Greek edition of *Hamlet*. For a description of this translation and the handling of the textual cruxes by Rotas, see Karagiorgos, *Greek Translations of Shakespeare*, pp. 146–59.

14 Vassilis Rotas, *Theatro kai Glossa* [Theatre and Language], Vol. B (Athens, 1986), p. 377. The translation here and throughout are my own.

15 Costas Georgousopoulos, 'V. Rotas kai to laiko theatro, piges tou: tragodia, Saixpir, Karagiozis' *Theatro* 57–58 (May – August 1977), pp. 83–90. (The article is on Rotas's popular drama and its sources: Greek tragedy, Shakespeare and Karagiozis.)

16 Voula Damianakou, *Ouilliam Saixpir*, p. 161.

17 Qualitatively speaking, the writing of original drama experiences a lapse between 1922 and 1940, both in relation to earlier samples and to international production – Theodoros Grammatas, *To Elliniko Theatro ston 20° Eona* [Greek Theatre in the twentieth century], vol. A (Athens, 2002), p. 174. Generally, modern Greek drama cannot claim the equivalent of a Seferis in poetry or a Kazatzakis in prose.

pages, he appropriated the famous Elizabethan poet to lend status to popular culture and its language. But before I go farther in the discussion of Rotas's engagement with language and popular culture, it would be useful to give a brief contextual account of the major linguistic debate in modern Greek history.

For nearly 100 years – from the publication of Yiannis Psiharis's *Journey* in 1888 to the definitive settlement of the language issue by law in 1976 – Greece was intensely preoccupied with the form of its national tongue. Would the official language be the same as that which its people spoke at home, within the family and the surrounding community, or would it be some other archaic form that, cleansed of its 'foreign' elements, could link the modern nation to its ancient past? This important question that was ultimately linked to the quest for national identity, constituted the basis of the on-going debate over *demotiki* and *katharevousa* or popular and purified Greek.[18] ('Demos' means the people, as in *demo*cracy; 'katharos' means clean or pure.) Generally speaking, those in favour of *katharevousa* turned their attention towards the past and especially toward the culture of Attic Greece, whereas those in favour of *demotiki* sought to cultivate the living language and the popular traditions as they had been formed through the centuries with influences from the east. The issue divided the Greek people sharply, while the debate waxed and waned especially before the middle of the century. In the 1910s and 1920s, when Rotas formed his ideas about language and theatre, it was going strong. In the aftermath of the social disturbance caused by specific attempts to translate the New Testament gospels as well as Aeschylus' *Oresteia* into *demotiki*, the Greek state determined (through a codicil included in the revised constitution of 1911) that *katharevousa* would be the official language of the nation.[19] During the three months that the issue was debated in the Revisional Parliament, disturbances occurred as a group of students, watching the proceedings from the people's boxes over the Parliament Room, clapped for the MP who spoke in favour of *demotiki*. The students were violently removed by the guards and jeered by the crowd that had gathered outside the Parliament building.[20] No action concerning the language issue went unnoticed. Events like the persecution of Alekos Delmouzos, a schoolmaster who was brought to trial in 1914 for his use of *demotiki* in the Volos Girls' School, fuelled the already heated discussions. Eventually, and especially after 1920, when the linguistic problem became the crux of educational reform, *katharevousa* was associated with political conservatism and *demotiki* with progressive ideas, as one tendency within the Demotic Movement was to subordinate the solution of the language question to the more permanent social problems.[21] Thus *demotiki* was linked to the fundamental principles of democracy and social justice.

Allying himself with the socialist tendency within the movement, Rotas sought to support demotic culture and its language. The idea of a neglected popular tradition that needed to be brought forward preoccupied Rotas continually and not solely at the theoretical level. He searched and uncovered old traditions, poems, popular fairy tales and songs, which he used in his staging of plays, seeking to feed them into the main stream. Rotas saw, with great regret, that in the social and demographic reality of his time the general tendency, lead by the urban elite, was to denigrate demotic culture through an identification with rusticity, crudeness and illiteracy. This socio-cultural (and essentially economic) problem was linked to the linguistic question. As mentioned earlier, many supporters of the Demotic Movement saw the language issue as part of a larger social change that needed to be effected in the country.

[18] The adjective *demotic*, as it will be used in this essay, will refer to the Greek native element, which has its roots in village life and folk culture. Thus *popular* and *demotic* are used synonymously.

[19] Emmanuel Kriaras, *Glossa mas: parelthon kai paron* [Our Language: Past and Present] (Thessaloniki, 1992), pp. 181–2.

[20] Kriaras, *Glossa mas*, p. 185. There is a strong possibility that the young Rotas was in this group, for a year earlier he appears among the founding members of the Students' Association, a collective devoted to the discussion of the popular language.

[21] Kriaras, *Glossa mas*, p. 189.

Rotas belonged to this group. His insistent attempts to identify Shakespeare with popular culture constitute an appropriation of the English poet for ideological purposes.

The translator perceived many popular elements in Shakespeare's plays. His description of his first experience with the English dramatist (watching a performance of *A Midsummer Night's Dream*) is very revealing about the angle from which he saw and read Shakespeare: '[t]he exaltation that my spirit felt at the work of Shakespeare was like a newly-felt joy . . . that brought to life in my mind the fairy tales and the songs that had charmed my childhood years, the dances and the funfairs I had seen, even the Karagiozis [theatre of the shadows] that I had myself played'.[22] What Rotas apparently saw in Shakespeare was a kind of archetypal folk tradition in which he recognized the forms of his native country. When he later came to translate Shakespeare he continued to read the plays of the English poet from the same perspective. Thus he saw popular elements everywhere: 'The whole of his work, from his earliest to his most mature', he stated, 'sails in the ocean of popular language, popular tradition, popular creation'.[23] His view of popular traditions inscribed in Shakespeare is not of course groundless. C. L. Barber was later to substantiate such a view in his well-known book *Shakespeare's Festive Comedy*, which places Shakespearian comic drama in the context of English popular games, entertainments and holiday rituals. But Rotas's persistence in reading Shakespeare from a specifically popular perspective shows his particular preoccupation, reflected also in the great regard he feels for the songs the dramatist intersperses in his plays. Considering these songs remnants of old traditions, he established parallels with Greek folk songs in the textual notes, and took special care to retain their meter and rhythm, even where this necessitates a freer translation.

By linking Shakespeare with popular tradition, Rotas established the context for the linguistic medium he would use – demotic Greek. In an article entitled 'My struggle with a Titan' (written around 1974 when he had just finished the translation of all the plays and poems) Rotas looked back and described the problems and difficulties he encountered in working with Shakespeare. By far the greatest problem he encountered was the choice of language. 'How am I going to transfer this unprecedented linguistic wealth', he asked, 'into a neglected language and, what's worse, unknown to the educated?'[24] Rotas had always held that 'the theatre cannot take any other language except the language of the people'.[25] But what does he mean by 'the people' (the Greek word *λαός*)? The concept, a central one in his writings, is more romantic than communist. Rotas clearly attributes great authority to 'the people', yet he sees them/it as a massive entity unmediated by party politics. He does not include everyone in 'the people', certainly not the educated elite whom he considers ignorant in matters pertaining to native tradition. In this frequently used, homogenizing term Rotas apparently conflates a number of lower social groups, all sharing a lack of sophistication and formal learning – villagers, dwellers of poor urban neighborhoods, plain people who have retained their origins. But in the phrase 'the language of the people', he specifically refers to the inhabitants of small towns and remote villages, to the 'forgotten and neglected' carriers of tradition. Regrettably, Rotas remarks, their language is not taught in any school.[26] The translator himself feels unprepared to handle the popular language he has decided to use in the translation:

> With the dead letters I had learned in the schools of poor Greece I could not even from a distance approach the work of the Titan of the Renaissance . . . Thus I returned to the language I had learned from my illiterate mother, to the songs, the legends and the proverbs of the Greek people, to the living expressions that I heard from their mouth.[27]

---

[22] Rotas, *Theatro kai Glossa*, vol. B, p. 456.

[23] Rotas, *Theatro kai Glossa*, vol. B, p. 459.

[24] Rotas, *Theatro kai Glossa*, vol. B, p. 459.

[25] Rotas, *Theatro kai Glossa*, vol. B, p. 462.

[26] Vassilis Rotas (trans.), *Saixpir Amlet, me prologo kai kritika sholia* [Shakespeare's *Hamlet*, with Prologue and Critical Comments] (Athens, 1938), p. 10.

[27] Vassilis Rotas, *Theatro kai Glossa*, vol. B, p. 461.

This means that Rotas rejected not only *katharevousa* but also current *demotiki* as a target language in translating Shakespeare. The return to his illiterate mother and to the legends of country folk signals his decision to synthesize a language that will enable him to bring out native Greek culture and inscribe Shakespeare in it. Indeed the translator constructs a particular linguistic idiom, which consists of various demotic forms (from oral and literary traditions), along with certain loan words and phrases from *katharevousa*. The use of his particular brand of *demotiki* often results in incongruity, semantic confusion and loss of poetic or dramatic effectiveness. Rotas is aware of this; yet his aim is as much to translate Shakespeare faithfully as to render familiar to a wider public the various unfamiliar forms of *demotiki*. I shall attempt to illustrate this with reference to his translation of *Macbeth* (published 1962). While any play could have served the purpose of my analysis, I have selected this one because it would seem least amenable to the translator's particular appropriation: it has a pronouncedly Scottish setting and a tight dramatic construction, none of which can be easily negotiated.

Rotas generally prefers linguistic forms from local dialects. For example, in translating Duncan's promise to Macbeth, 'I have begun to plant thee and will labour / To make thee full of growing' (1.4.28–9), he uses a regional verb form for 'full of growing' (which he interprets as 'cultivate'), when he can just as easily employ the standard form of the same verb.[28] He likewise favours words that show an eastern influence (like the Turkish-derived *bentenia* for 'battlements', p. 34, and *siritia* for 'streaks', p. 66). Sometimes he introduces rare or obsolete terms,[29] while occasionally he even coins new meanings from widely-known demotic words (as in the case of the noun *fileftis*, p. 38, which he derives from the verb *filevo*, meaning to treat someone).[30] In such instances neither meter nor meaning require the translator to resort to extreme forms. It seems that he aims simply to put these forms in circulation in order to render them familiar to the wider public. Their effect is to raise some eyebrows and occasionally to send the reader, if not the spectator, to the dictionary.

However, the use of rare, obsolete, dialectical or colloquial demotic forms is not always harmless. Such words influence the play's dramatic effect by estranging the audience at crucial points, while they also have an impact on the production of meaning. For example, in rendering Banquo's cry to his son: 'Fly, good Fleance, fly, fly, fly!/ Thou mayst revenge' (3.3.17–18), the translator uses for the word 'revenge' a Greek

[28] He uses *καλουργήσω* (p. 31), rather than the more common *καλλιεργήσω*, which has exactly the same meaning and yields the same number of syllables. Quotes from the translated text of *Macbeth* throughout this study will refer to the edition of Epikairotita (Athens, 1987) by page numbers. For the lexical analysis I have relied on the dictionary *Lexico tis Koinis Neoellinikis* (Thessaloniki, 1998). I have also benefited from discussions with the classical philologist Dimitris Lypourlis and the linguist Anna Symeonidis. I thank them both.

[29] Ross's consoling words to Siward in 5.11.10–11 – 'Your cause of sorrow / Must not be measured by his worth, for then / It hath no end' – are rendered as follows: 'Η αιτία/ του πόνου σου με την *αξιά* του δε μετριέται,/ *τι* αλλιώς θα' ναι άπειρος ο πόνος σου' (p. 117). *Αξιά*, meaning 'worth' and pronounced as a two-syllable word, is very rare, used only in certain regions of Greece, in place of the more standard tri-syllabic *αξία*. The conjunctive *τι*, meaning 'for' or 'because', is a highly learned choice, used by Kazantzakis and Kakridis in their translation of the *Iliad* but not present in current demotiki. Equally surprising is the use of obsolete expressions like 'ένα τέτοιο *'θελά χεράκωνα* όργανο' (p. 43) for 'such an instrument I was to use' (2.1.43) or 'όλα χαμένα δίχως *διάφορο*' (64) for 'Nought is had, all's spent' (3.2.4). The words 'θελά' (I was going to), *χεράκωνα* (from *χερακώνω*, I grasp firmly in my hands) and *διάφορο* (net gain) are entirely out of circulation in current demotic Greek. The same is true of the verb *ματιάζω* (matiazo), which is used by Rotas in the obsolete sense of 'point to' ('What concern they'= 'Και ποιον *ματιάζουν*', p. 98).

[30] He does something similar with the adjective *αψιά* [apsia], sharp, and the noun *ισάδα* [isada], straightness. The first (derived from αψύς [apsis], sharp-minded, normally refers to a human characteristic, but in this translation it is used to describe an object ('*αψιά* σαν το σπιρούνι του' = 'sharp as his spur', p. 36); the second, *ισάδα*, is customarily used only for surfaces, but here it is made to signify a virtue in character ('justice, verity, temp'rance' = 'δικαιοσύνη, *ισάδα*, εγκράτεια', p. 94).

equivalent (*gdikionome*)[31] that survives in some regional dialects and has passed into literature but is unknown to the wider population. The greatest part of the audience is likely to rely on context to make sense of Banquo's caring command, but the contextual meaning is 'fly to be saved or to escape', since young Fleance's life is in danger. The idea of revenge is thus lost. A similar problem is created by the use of *ouranos* as a synonym for heaven or paradise in the translation of the Porter's famous monologue in the second act.[32]

There are times when the translator deliberately chooses to demoticize certain parts of the play, to bring it closer to the popular culture, through an association with Greek history and the popular traditions. One such instance is the translation of Macbeth's defiant pronouncement, 'Blow wind, come wrack, / At least we'll die with harness on our back' (5.5.49–50). In Rotas's version the last line of this quote reads, 'I'll die an armed man.'[33] But for 'armed man' he uses the noun *armatolos*, whose specific historical connotations affect the play's meaning. Under the Ottoman Empire, which from the late fifteenth century to the early nineteenth occupied the greatest part of Greece, an armatolos was a Greek member of an irregular local police force (equivalent to the Venetian *armatore*), appointed by the Turkish pasha to keep the peace and provide security against resistance-criminals (known as *kleftes*), who were especially active in inaccessible, mountainous regions.[34] In the modern Greek consciousness the term *armatolos* conjures up the image of a man who persists in fighting, does not yield to the enemy, and dies armed. It seems at first an appropriate term to describe the adamant Macbeth, who refuses until the very end either to 'play the Roman fool' or to yield to his enemy. But the image of an Ottoman-Greek *armatolos* creates also wider reverberations (concentric circles of meaning) that, superimposed on the image of Scottish Macbeth, blur the character of the protagonist at a very crucial point in the drama. The question arises: if Rotas's Macbeth is an *armatolos*, who are his counterparts or opponents in the fighting – who are the *kleftes*? Historically, *kleftes* (meaning 'thieves') were rebellious, armed men, who used theft and looting as a means of resistance against the foreign occupier. But if anyone is a thief and a criminal in the play's Scotland it is the usurper himself – not Malcolm or Macduff. Thus while the term *armatolos* brings Macbeth closer to a Greek audience, it creates semantic problems because it suggests an inappropriate relationship to his opponents.

The most striking instance of the translator's attempt to link *Macbeth* with the Greek popular tradition is his use of the term *strigles* (singular, *strigla*) for the witches, in place of the more standard word *magisses* (singular, *magissa*). In Greek folklore, a *strigla* was an ugly, old woman, who possessed the power to transform herself and become

31 Banquo's words are rendered as follows: 'φεύγα, Φληνς, ω, φεύγα/ φεύγα να γδικιωθείς' (p. 67). The last word (*γδικιωθείς*), is derived from the ancient Greek verb *γδικιώνομαι*, which is rarely used.

32 In its singular form the noun *ouranos* usually means the sky. The plural form (*ouranoi*) is sometimes used, especially in a religious context, to signify heaven or the heavens (as in the well-known phrase,'η βασιλεία των ουρανών' = 'the kingdom of the heavens'). Following an oral tradition that survives in certain Greek villages, Rotas uses the singular *ouranos* to signify God or paradise. Thus in the Porter's monologue, where the speaker imagines a situation at the gate of hell (*kolasi*, in Greek), the line 'here's an equivocator . . . who committed treason enough for God's sake, yet could not equivocate to heaven' (2.3.7–8) is translated as 'έκανε κάμποσες προδοσιές για την αγάπη του Θεού κι όμως δεν κατάφερε με τη διγλωσσία του να πάει στον *ουρανό*' (p. 48). The semantic disjunction here occurs because the opposite of *kolasi* (hell) is *paradisos* (paradise), not *ouranos* (sky).

33 The entire passage is translated as follows: 'έλα, ο χαλασμός!/ τουλάχιστο ας πεθάνω σαν *αρματολός*' (p. 112).

34 The *armatoloi* enjoyed a large degree of independence and many privileges. They were very well-trained, dextrous, risky and fearless fighters, especially known for their resistance to hunger and physical hardship. Their opponents, the *kleftes*, were a match in strength and combat technique, so that the best of them were eventually recruited for the position of *armatolos* in exchange for many privileges. The battles between *armatoloi* and *kleftes* (usually at night) were long and persistent in the earlier years of the Ottoman occupation, but as time went on the two armed groups got closer to one another and provided the basis on which resistance against the Turks was organized – *Neoteron Egyclopedicon Lexicon 'Heliou'* [The New Encyclopaedic Dictionary of 'Helios'], vol. IV (Athens, 1975), pp. 498–9.

invisible. Through the practice of witchcraft, *strigles* were thought to cause destruction to people, especially to mothers lying in child-bed and to their unbaptised babies, whose blood they would suck till they died.[35] The word *magisses*, on the other hand, used in other modern Greek translations of *Macbeth*,[36] is a more neutral and widely known term, the equivalent of the English 'witch' (a woman who practices witchcraft). Rotas's choice affects the meaning of the play, as *strigles* emphasizes the evil-doing aspect of the witches, without suggesting prophetic powers. The nature of the witches in *Macbeth* is not a clear matter, of course, for the text creates uncertainty about their identity and even about their very existence (1.3.81–3). They seem to be nebulous, composite figures, possessing characteristics of the sexless demons, the stereotypical witch and the three fates. Although they cannot be placed in a definite category, their primary function in the play's narrative is to pronounce the prophecies which will enkindle Macbeth's ambition and imagination. Rotas's *strigles* do, of course, perform that function, but there is an overall incongruity produced between their function and the specific connotations attached to a *strigla* in folklore (an old woman who causes harm to newborns and their mothers). Furthermore, very few people in the audience would understand Rotas's reference to folk tradition, for the word *strigla* is in fact metaphorically used in current Greek to describe a vicious, wayward and verbally aggressive woman – a shrew.[37] Between dramatic or semantic efficiency and demotic education the translator chooses the second, thereby estranging the audience.

The estrangement created by Rotas's use of *demotiki* is occasionally compounded by the awkwardness resulting from his decision to remain faithful to Shakespeare's wording. We observe this in several instances, such as in the rendering of Macbeth's question to Banquo in 3.1.19, 'Ride you this afternoon?' and his exhortation a few lines later, 'Hie you to horse'. Horse-back riding is an activity whose translation into modern Greek presents problems. *Demotiki*, being the language of the common people, does not afford an expression for such aristocratic leisure activities. This is why other translators either paraphrase the lines or leave out altogether the idea of horse-riding. But Rotas uses a literal translation,[38] which creates awkwardness and semantic confusion. In one important instance, which concerns Macbeth's famous lines, 'upon this bank and shoal of time, / We'd jump the life to come' (1.7.6–7), literal rendering even produces an inappropriately comic effect.[39]

The awkwardness or semantic confusion that we frequently come across in Rotas's translation of Shakespeare is often the result of his attempt to render Shakespeare's style (syntactical density, internal rhyme, word play, etc.) in a verse form that becomes inflexible. Unlike English, which has many short words, Greek is a polysyllabic language and therefore unsuitable for the ten-syllable, five-beat line that Shakespeare employs. As a poet and a dramatist himself, Rotas is highly aware of this, but he does not opt for the most flexible equivalent in Greek verse, which would be the fifteen-syllable iambic line with four major stresses. He finds this verse form 'too striking, and hence inappropriate for dramatic verse, where rhythm cannot have the upper hand'.[40] He chooses instead the diversified but constricting choriambic trimeter (a

---

35 *Neoteron Egyclopedicon Lexicon 'Heliou'*, vol. XXI, p. 99.

36 See, for example, the translations of the play by G. Heimonas, E. Belies, and C. Pagoureli.

37 Shakespeare's *Taming of the Shrew* is usually translated in Greek as *το Ημέρωμα της Στρίγγλας* (To Imeroma tis Striglas).

38 'Θα βγεις το απόγεμα καβάλα' (58), and 'Βιάσου για καβάλα' (p. 58).

39 In Rotas's version these lines read as follows: 'σε τούτη την αχτή και ξέρα του καιρού,/ πηδάγαμε την άλλη ζωή' (in this shore and dryness of time we jumped the other life), p. 37. In English editions of Shakespeare, the clause 'We'd jump the life to come' is usually taken to mean 'we would risk afterlife' (jump=hazard). The translated line ('πηδάγαμε την άλλη ζωή') conveys no such meaning and becomes rather nonsensical. But this is not all. In colloquial Greek the verb *πηδάω* (jump) means, among other things, to jump a female, human or animal (i.e. fuck). Hence, in context, the Greek phrasing could yield a comic reading: if Duncan's murder had no further consequences, we'd fuck the afterlife.

40 Vassilis Rotas (trans.), *Saixpir Amlet, me prologo kai kritika sholia* [Shakespeare's Hamlet, with Prologue and Critical Comments], p. 201.

combination of trochaic and iambic rhythms in an eleven- to fourteen-syllable line with three major stresses), and this inevitably gets him into difficulty. For metrical reasons he sometimes inserts a pronoun, chooses unidiomatic expressions or employs convoluted syntax. Occasionally he even resorts to elliptical sentences, omitting articles of nouns to save a syllable.[41]

Rotas's handling of the play's resounding phrase 'of woman born' offers the best evidence of how his cumbersome metrical form and his professed fidelity to certain stylistic aspects of Shakespeare obstruct semantic and dramatic effectiveness. The phrase occurs for the first time when Macbeth meets the witches in the fourth act: 'for none of woman born/ Shall harm Macbeth' (4.1.96–7). Aiming to create a Greek equivalent for Shakespeare's internal rhyme ('none' – 'born'), Rotas renders this phrase as 'no woman's childbirth [*gynekas genna*] can harm you'.[42] Metrically the phrase works well, but semantically it fails because it takes the emphasis away from the man (not born of woman) and implies that what Macbeth would have to fear is a woman's childbirth – a weak and dramatically inoperative proposition. The translator picks up the Shakespearian meaning in 5.3.6–7, where he is more flexible with meter and not constrained by rhyme.[43] However, when the phrase recurs in Macbeth's scoff at the slain Young Siward in the fifth act, 'But swords I smile at, weapons laugh to scorn,/ Brandished by a man that's of a woman born'(5.7.13–14), he returns to the childbirth terms – 'I scorn spears held by men who are a woman's childbirth'.[44] In the Greek of this phrase he reproduces Shakespeare's rhyming couplet at the expense of meaning and dramatic effectiveness. He retains the semantic twisting in the last occurrence of the phrase in question, 'I bear a charmèd life, which must not yield / To one of woman born' (5.10.12–13), which he translates as, 'I have charms in my life and it cannot suffer from a woman's childbirth.'[45] Though he is in no need of rhyme at this point, the translator has no choice but to echo the same phrase (*gynekas genna* = woman's childbirth), for the last two instances occur very closely in time. The cost to dramatic effectiveness is greatest in this last instance, however, for the magic phrase is spoken seconds before Macduff reveals to Macbeth that he 'was from his mother's womb / Untimely ripped' (5.10.15–16). The semantic difference between 'born' and 'birth' turns out to be very significant indeed.

Thus the dramatic effectiveness of the translated text is compromised by Rotas's double-poised commitment to popular Greek and to Shakespeare's style. Yet in the final analysis it is not the metrical form but the *language* he uses throughout that gives his translations their particularity and historical significance. His construction of a vocabulary that goes back to the roots of demotic culture as well as his use of the folkloric term *strigles* for the witches never lets us forget that the translator is situating *Macbeth*, as indeed all of his Shakespeare, within the popular Greek tradition.

Rotas aimed at creating a lasting Shakespeare that would be assimilated into the national literature of his country and included in the major theatrical repertory. By translating the English poet into a particular form of modern Greek he apparently felt that he was advancing popular culture, illuminating the neglected aspects of its tradition. His commitment to *demotiki*, to popular theatre and to Shakespeare were all part of the same socialist and romantic ideal: the establishment of a more egalitarian society, the blurring of the dividing line between 'high' and 'low', city and country culture. How far did the appropriation of Shakespeare help Rotas achieve his goal? One way to answer

41 On pp. 30 and 112 of the translated text one can find examples of unidiomatic Greek and syntactical twisting. Here's an example where Rotas omits an article to save a syllable: 'να πνίξουν [τα] δάκρυα τον άνεμο', p. 38.

42 In Greek, 'γιατί καμιά/ γυναίκας γέννα δε μπορεί να βλάψει εσένα' (p. 83). Notice the internal rhyme in 'γέννα-εσένα'.

43 In this instance he correctly translates the phrase 'none of woman born' as 'κανείς ποτέ που να τον γέννησε γυναίκα', p. 106).

44 In Greek, 'περιφρονώ κοντάρια από άντρες κρατημένα / που 'ναι *γυναίκας γέννα*' (p. 114).

45 In Greek, 'έχω μάγια στη ζωή μου/ και δεν παθαίνει από *γυναίκας γέννα*' (p. 116).

this question is by assessing the impact of his translation.

Some, especially those who saw the use of a popular-poetic language as a form of political statement, stood in complete awe of Rotas's accomplishment. One of these writes:

> The quality and the magnitude of Rotas' translation is a work of life . . . Above all it stands irreconcilable [in its commitment] toward the popular language. No concession to the *katharevousa* (unless it is to be ironical toward it) . . . It uses a vocabulary which comes whole from the national, popular poetic language and from the simple and unsophisticated language of the common people.[46]

Others were more selective in what they praised. Yiannis Sideris, a committed demoticist and prominent theatre historian (who also carried out extensive research on Shakespeare in Greece)[47] found Rotas's rendering of the *Dream* 'unforced' and 'refreshing', but overall he discerned a problem in the colloquial *demotiki* Rotas uses, especially in the later translations:

> his tendency toward popular colloquiality, in words that a dramatic person cannot speak in accordance with common sense and his social psychology, is not yet dominant, but it is apparent; later [after the *Dream*] it will become more striking, so that his pages will lose their nobility . . . . [T]hese not so "noble" words we consider almost a negation of the Poet. On the contrary, we consider the translator's neologisms, especially in the later plays, welcome and necessary.[48]

A similar observation was made several years later by the dramatist and theatre critic Solon Makris, who commented on Rotas's tendency to homogenize the language spoken by socially unequal persons in Shakespeare's dramatic world: 'The poetic and replete translation of Vassilis Rotas suffers always from the scattered popularized and prosaic expressions . . . [which] are incongruous in the mouth of "noble" Shakespearean heroes'.[49]

Still others objected to Rotas's conversion of certain words from *katharevousa* into the popular tongue. Especially after 1970, when demotic Greek had become established through use and had acquired its own grammar and vocabulary, there was the danger of semantic confusion:

> The demoticization of expressions and words from *katharevousa* does not always yield the same meaning. For example, the verb 'prokatalavainei' is used in the sense of 'prokatalamvano', but 'katalavaino' in Demotic Greek means 'I understand', whereas 'katalamvano' means 'I conquer'.[50]

Despite specific objections, Rotas's translations were generally held in high esteem. When the entire project was finished, it was the only complete Shakespeare available to Greek speakers. The translator's broad knowledge of drama, combined with a unique blend of poetic skill, theatrical experience and self-taught English had produced plays that were relatively faithful to the original texts. They could serve readers as well as theatre directors, who sought a stageable Shakespeare. Rotas's translations, along with those of K. Kartheos, were the most widely used in the theatre for many years. Of the thirty Shakespeare productions recorded for the decade 1970–1980, about half used Rotas's texts.[51] But in the next decade this number dropped to a quarter. Indeed by the early eighties Rotas's work was deemed outdated and many theatres were subsequently forced to commission a translation in order to use a text that was closer to contemporary Greek. On 28 March 1986 Melina Merkouri, Minister of Culture in the Government of Andreas

---

46 Stathis Dromazos, 'Theatriki Kritiki' (performance criticism for *Timon of Athens*), in the newspaper *Kathemerini*, 18 August 1978, p. 6.

47 See the series of articles in the theatrical magazine *To Theatro*, vol. 13 (1964) to vol. 21 (1965).

48 Yiannis Sideris, 'O Saixpir stin Ellada III: fotismenoi kai steiroi metafrastes' [Shakespeare in Greece III: enlightened and sterile translators] in the magazine *To Theatro* 15 (1964), p. 28.

49 Solon Makris, 'To Theatro' (performance criticism of *King Lear*), in the periodical *Nea Estia* 103 (May 1978), p. 616.

50 A. Margaritis, newspaper *Ta Nea*, 21 February 1973, p. 4.

51 The 1970s mark the zenith of the popularity of Rotas's translations on the stage. In the 1950s out of the 21 recorded productions 6 use Rotas, 9 Kartheos and 6 other translators. In the 1960s the share of Rotas is about the same – of the 16 productions, 5 use Rotas, 4 Kartheos, and 7 other translators. After the Rotas boom in the seventies, the situation changes again in the 1980s when in 24 stage productions 6 use Rotas, 6 Kartheos, and 12 other (mostly new) translators.

Papandreou, announced her intention to sponsor a new translation of Shakespeare. 'The Ministry will ask poets and scholars', she said 'to reread the great Elizabethan and render him for the theatre and the public'.[52] Although the Ministry's intent was never put to practice, the announcement is indicative of the pressures that the Ministry was apparently receiving to establish a standard Greek translation of the English dramatist that would take the burden off having to re-translate every time a theatre company decided to stage a Shakespeare play. A new translation meant greater cost for the theatre company as well as for the Ministry, which had begun to subsidize many experimental and regional productions. Today, Rotas's translations are still printed, but most directors express unease about using a translation whose language sounds more and more removed. They have to hire free-lance translators or do the translation themselves, sometimes via French or German to avoid dealing with early-modern English.

Ironically, Rotas's attempt to inscribe the English poet in the heart of native Greek tradition proved inimical to his overall project of creating an enduring Shakespeare. The extreme linguistic elements which he used in order to educate the public in the varieties of demotic Greek were responsible for rendering his work outdated, even before he had finished translating it. Rotas was aware of the criticism of his work, but he was unable to respond to it positively. He attributed it to political disagreement or ignorance. Thus, referring to the critics, he states in the Prologue to his 1938 edition of *Hamlet*: 'Because they never observed nor cared to learn the language of the people, every time they read in literature or they hear in the theatre a word unknown to them instead of being glad and thanking the author, they get angry and criticize him'.[53] Some thirty-five years later (*c.* 1973) he expresses the same view: 'They wrote to me that often I make up words, because the words I used, those which the people use in their speech, are unknown to them. But theatre cannot take any other language except the language of the people, and it is this theatre that is the real judge of the language'.[54] Thus Rotas reiterates his socialist-romantic terminology without actually addressing the real issue posed by the critics. The 'language of the people', as we have seen, is derived from remote villages and neglected traditions, oral and literary. The theatre, which the translator here places in the position of a judge, had early on adopted *demotiki* as its language, yet in terms of audience constitution it was anything but homogeneous. The National Theatre, the biggest producer of Shakespeare and the sponsor of Rotas's earlier translations, could not be said to represent 'the people'. With its glamorous, highly aestheticized performances and its largely foreign repertoire, the national stage had discouraged wider attendance by the poor and the uneducated. Nor could the commercial theatres claim the kind of audience the translator implies. The only type of theatre in fact that could be the judge of Rotas's language was his own Popular Theatre back in the 1930s or the ideal theatre he envisioned in the 1950s (a 'holy place' where 'his majesty the people' came to see the performance without regard to social class).[55] He assumed, erroneously as it proves, that apart from the critics and the educated elite all others would understand the 'language of the people' or that they would not mind having a lesson in demotic Greek along with their Shakespeare. Rotas does not consider the possibility that dramatic language may be resistant to imposed forms, that the linguistic elements he is introducing might be of interest to a philologist but not to the wider public. By 1974 when Rotas translated his last play, 'the people' had changed and their language had taken its own course, as languages usually do. For though the legal settlement was delayed, modern

[52] Newspaper *Eleftherotypia*, 28 March 1986, p. 11.

[53] Vassilis Rotas (trans.), *Saixpir Amlet, me prologo kai kritika sholia*, p. 11.

[54] Rotas, *Theatro kai Glossa*, vol. B, p. 462.

[55] Rotas's ideal theatre, which combines practices from ancient Greece and Elizabethan England mixed with a communist ideology, is described in a series of articles written (mostly) between 1950 and 1957. It is a state-supported theatre marked by its imposing structure and its large size. Its function, according to Rotas, is to educate the people, to help shape their consciousness – *Theatro kai Glossa*, vol. B, pp. 559–68.

(demotic) Greek, as it is known today, had been largely shaped. Rotas does not reflect this change. Though there may be fluctuations in the quality of his translating work, he maintains more or less the same linguistic idiom throughout. To change the language midway through the complete works might of course prove awkward. But Rotas does not even drop the rare or obsolete forms. As a critic quoted above stated, Rotas was irreconcilable.

The reason for this adamant insistence on old and rare forms, I suggest, has to do less with Rotas's socio-linguistic perceptions than with his political views and his age. After 1950, many socialists felt embittered by the defeat of the communists in the Civil War and disillusioned by the country's inability to secure a lasting democracy. Sticking to ideas and forms that had been at stake in the past was a matter of personal pride and spiritual survival. For people like Rotas, who fought long and hard for these ideas, it was a matter of defending their entire life and ideological choices. To compose or translate literature in the more contemporary and, in the eyes of the old fighters, degenerate linguistic form, was tantamount to abnegation. As the member of a generation of ideologues that had survived the hardship of two world wars and civil strife, Rotas represents a long and turbulent segment of Greek cultural and political history, a period that spans from approximately 1910 to the mid 1970s. At the start of this period Greece was a poor and powerless nation, politically unstable, subject to foreign influence, and without a stable language that all its citizens could speak and be proud of. At the end of it, and specifically after 1974, the year that marks the fall of the military dictatorship, the country turned a page in its history, entering a new phase during which its profile changed rapidly in all aspects – linguistic, cultural, political, economic. Thus Rotas's death in 1977 stands symbolically at the closing of an era that was marked by the people's struggle for democracy, economic improvement, social justice and the development of a self-determined cultural identity. The translation and appropriation of Shakespeare by Vassilis Rotas can only be fully comprehended within the context of the agonistic forces of that era.

# HOW OLD WERE SHAKESPEARE'S BOY ACTORS?

DAVID KATHMAN

Female roles on the pre-Restoration English stage were played not by women but by boys dressed as women. This well-known fact has occasioned much comment in recent years by critics interested in the gender implications of boys playing women who sometimes disguised themselves as boys.[1] Many such critics have implicitly assumed that the 'boys' in question were pre-adolescent children, perhaps eight to twelve years old, whose ability to play the complex female roles of Shakespeare or Webster would be questionable. They have thus suggested that such roles must have been played by adult sharers, much as in modern all-male productions at Shakespeare's Globe and elsewhere.[2] From a psychosexual perspective, it makes an obvious difference whether Cleopatra was played by a ten-year-old child, a thirty-year-old man, or by a 'boy' of some intermediate age, such as seventeen.

Such discussions have tended to be short on hard evidence, often relying on subjective notions of what would or would not have been plausible for an Elizabethan playing company. It is often assumed that little or no documentary evidence survives about these boys, and that we must rely mostly on guesswork and speculation.[3] In fact, a substantial amount of documentary evidence does survive about pre-Restoration boy players, but much of it has remained buried in archives or scattered across various books and articles. When gathered and analysed, this evidence points to a consistent conclusion: until the early 1660s, female roles on the English stage (including the most demanding, complex parts) were played by adolescent boys, no younger than twelve and no older than twenty-one or twenty-two, with a median of around sixteen or seventeen. Many of these boys were legally apprenticed to adult players who were members of London livery companies such as the Grocers and Goldsmiths. Not coincidentally, the age range in which these boys are found playing women corresponds closely to the typical age range for London apprentices.[4]

This paper focuses on the evidence relating to specific actors known to have played specific female roles, a group which is larger than many people

1 See, for example, Michael Shapiro, *Gender in Play on the Shakespearean Stage: Boy Heroines & Female Pages* (Ann Arbor, 1994); Stephen Orgel, *Impersonations: The Performance of Gender in Shakespeare's England* (Cambridge, 1996), and Carol Chillington Rutter, *Enter the Body: Women and Representation on Shakespeare's Stage* (London and New York, 2001).

2 Such doubts have most notably been expressed by James Forse, *Art Imitates Business* (Bowling Green, Ohio, 1994), pp. 71–99; Carol Chillington Rutter, *Documents of the Rose Playhouse* (Manchester and New York, 1999), pp. 124–5, 224–5; and Marvin Rosenberg, 'The Myth of Shakespeare's Squeaking Boy Actor – Or Who Played Cleopatra?', *Shakespeare Bulletin* 19.2 (2001), 5–6. In opposition to these doubts, Joy Leslie Gibson's *Squeaking Cleopatras: The Elizabethan Boy Player* (2000) argues that female roles were written to accommodate the smaller lung capacity of boys, but Gibson provides no new documentary evidence.

3 For example, Forse asserts that 'there is no evidence regarding the recruitment of boys', whom he assumes must have been 'pre-pubescent' (78).

4 I discuss the relationship between livery companies and the professional stage in more detail in David Kathman, 'Grocers, Goldsmiths, and Drapers: Freemen and Apprentices in the Elizabethan Theatre', *Shakespeare Quarterly* 55 (2004), 1–49.

might think. In the ideal situation, we would have a cast list showing that a given actor played a given female role in a given production, and we would know both the date of the production and the actor's birthdate. Sometimes we can only approximate the date of a production; in other instances, we don't know the actor's exact birthdate, but we know that he was called a 'boy' or was an apprentice at the time. In theory, we might find a case where an actor played a female role at a time when he was known to be an adult sharer in the company but, with one doubtful exception, such cases do not exist. From the sixteenth century right up to the onset of actresses in the early 1660s, women were played by teenagers or young men no older than about twenty-one.

## BACKGROUND AND DEFINITIONS

The popular literature of the sixteenth and early seventeenth centuries contains many references to the practice of male actors playing women on stage. Such references occur often in anti-theatrical polemics and the responses to them. For example, in *Playes Confuted in fiue Actions* (1582), Stephen Gosson wrote that it is a lie 'In Stage Playes for a boy to put one the attyre, the gesture, the passions of a woman', and John Rainoldes wrote in *Th'overthrow of stage playes* (1599) that 'you should condemne all stage-playes, wherein young men are trained to play such wemen partes'.[5] Most notoriously, William Prynne referred repeatedly in his massive polemic *Histrio-Mastix* (1633) to 'Men-women actors' and 'our English Man-women monsters', but also condemned 'this very putting on of womans apparell on Boyes, to act a Play', and discussed whether it is 'more commendable for Boyes to act in womans attire', then to bring women-Actors on the stage to personate female parts'.[6] On the pro-theatrical side, Thomas Heywood in *An Apology for Actors* (1612) referred to 'our youths attired in the habit of women', and J. Cocke in *Satyrical Essayes Characters and Others* (1615) referred to a newly married actor who 'mistakes the Woman for the Boy in Womans attire'.[7] In her prose romance *The Countess of Montgomery's Urania* (1621) and its manuscript continuation, Lady Mary Wroth alluded to 'a delicate play-boy acte a louing womans part' and 'a play boy dressed gaudely up to shew a fond loving woemans part'.[8]

Such references are helpful, but they have led to some confusion because of differing perceptions of how old a 'boy' may be. As Richard Rastall has noted, many theatre historians have assumed that a 'boy' must refer to a male with an unbroken voice who has not yet reached puberty, and is thus no older than about fourteen; a 'man', in contrast, is assumed to be mature, adult and postpubertal.[9] This assumption is illustrated by Marvin Rosenberg's statement that he 'could not find a shred of evidence that a child played any of Shakespeare's great adult women'.[10] However, such an assumption is undercut by the references to female roles being played by 'men', 'young men' and 'youths', terms which are sometimes used interchangeably with 'boy' by the same author on the same page, as in Prynne's polemic cited above.

This issue can be partly resolved when we recognize that puberty, and thus the changing of boys' voices, could extend several years later in Shakespeare's time than it typically does today. There are numerous references to fourteen as the traditional starting age of puberty in boys; for example, *The Problemes of Aristotle* (1595) asks, 'Why

[5] Stephen Gosson, *Playes Confuted in fiue Actions* (London, 1582), p. 197; John Rainoldes, *Th'overthrow of Stage-Playes* (London, 1599), pp. 17–18.

[6] William Prynne, *Histrio-Mastix, The Players Scovrge, or Actors Tragedie* (London, 1633), pp. 187, 188, 212, 214. Rosenberg, 'Myth', p. 5, cites the first of these passages and gives the misleading impression that Prynne refers only to 'men-actors', but in fact he refers to 'boys' just as often, if not more so.

[7] Thomas Heywood, *An Apology for Actors* (London, 1612), C3v; John Stevens, *Satyrical Essayes Characters and Others* (London, 1615), p. 248.

[8] See Michael Shapiro, 'Lady Mary Wroth Describes a "Boy Actress"', *Medieval and Renaissance Drama in England*, 4 (1989), 187–94.

[9] Richard Rastall, 'Female Roles in All-Male Casts', *Medieval English Theatre* 7 (1985), 25–50, esp. pp. 25–6.

[10] Rosenberg, 'Myth', p. 5.

are boyes apt to chaunge their voyce about 14. yeares of age?', and *The Office of Christian Parents* (1616) says that childhood extends to age fourteen in boys and twelve in girls, 'because at that yeeres they beginne the flower of youth, preparing it selfe to the state of manhood or marriage'.[11] Yet there is also evidence that male puberty commonly lasted into the late teens. Henry Cuffe's *The Differences of the Ages of Man's Life* (1607) says that following infancy and boyhood comes 'our *budding* and *blossoming age*, when our cheekes and other hidden parts begin to be clothed with that mossie excrement of haire, which is prorogued vntill the eighteenth year'.[12] Citing the research of David Wulstan and others, Richard Rastall has argued independently that males in sixteenth-century Europe often did not reach puberty until age seventeen or eighteen. While some boys' voices undoubtedly started to break earlier than that, some boys probably retained the ability to sing or speak in a treble voice until the age of twenty.[13]

With this knowledge as background, in the following pages I will discuss every actor known to have played a female role for a professional adult company before 1642 – nearly fifty names in all. Because my focus is on the professional theatre, I will not deal systematically with amateur productions such as the medieval mystery plays put on by guild members. Though it is clear that female roles in such productions were played by male actors, evidence about these performers' ages is scarce, and the little evidence which does exist was ably collected and discussed twenty years ago by Meg Twycross.[14] I will also not examine university dramatic productions at Oxford and Cambridge, even though many cast lists survive. The student population at Oxbridge was all-male and fairly homogeneous in terms of age, so it is not too helpful for our purposes to know that women in university plays were played by teenage boys; essentially all the roles in these plays were played by teenage boys.[15]

Similarly, I will not deal in depth with the Elizabethan and Jacobean all-boy companies, even though they deserve a full treatment of their own. At the peak of the boy company vogue around the turn of the seventeenth century, the evidence suggests that the members of these companies were between ten and fourteen years old, somewhat younger than most of the 'boys' in the adult companies. When Henry Clifton complained in 1601 about his son Thomas being kidnapped to act for the Children of the Chapel by Nathaniel Giles and Henry Evans, he specified that the boy was thirteen years old.[16] Several of the other Chapel boys named in Clifton's complaint can be identified, and all were within a year or two of Clifton in age.

Specifically, John Chappell, 'a grammar school scholar of one Mr. Spyke's school near Cripplegate, London', was later admitted a scholar at Trinity College, Cambridge in 1605, suggesting that he was born around 1590 and about eleven years old

---

[11] *The Problemes of Aristotle, With Other Philosophers and Phisitions* (Edinburgh, 1595), C5v; *The Office of Christian Parents* (Cambridge, 1616), L1r. I am indebted to Lucy Munro for bringing these references to my attention, along with several others cited in this paragraph. See her *Children of the Queen's Revels: A Jacobean Theatre Repertory* (Cambridge, 2005), especially chapter 1.

[12] *The Differences of the Ages of Man's Life* (London, 1607), 13r–v.

[13] Rastall, 'Female Roles', pp. 28–9. See also David Wulstan, 'Vocal Colour in English Sixteenth-Century Polyphony', *Journal of the Plainsong and Medieval Music Society* 2 (1979), 19–60, esp. 25–7.

[14] Meg Twycross, '"Transvestism" in the Mystery Plays', *Medieval English Theatre* 5 (1983), 123–80.

[15] There were certainly some Oxbridge students in their twenties or older, and some of them performed in plays there. But Alan Nelson, editor of REED Cambridge and co-editor of REED Oxford, informs me that no female role at Oxbridge is known to have been played by anyone older than twenty-one or twenty-two, exactly as we find in the professional theatre.

[16] Glynne Wickham, William Ingram, and Herbert Berry (eds.), *English Professional Theatre, 1530–1660* (Cambridge, 2000), pp. 264–7, 510–1. Thomas Clifton went on to matriculate in 1606 as a fellow-commoner from both Trinity and King's Colleges, Cambridge, receive a BA from King's in 1609–10, and enter the Middle Temple in May 1609. His will was proved in 1621, when he was about thirty-four. See John Venn and J. A. Venn, *Alumni Cantabrigienses*, vol. 1 (Cambridge, 1922), p. 356.

in 1601. Chappell received several degrees at Cambridge, performed in academic plays there, and probably wrote a Latin comedy, *Susenbrotus*.[17] John Motteram, 'a grammar scholar in the free school at Westminster', was christened on 6 July 1589 at Addlethorpe, Lincolnshire, and thus was about twelve in 1601.[18] Salomon Pavy, 'apprentice to one Peerce', acted in Ben Jonson's *Cynthia's Revels* (1600) and *Poetaster* (1601), and Ben Jonson's famous epitaph on Pavy claims that 'years he number'd scarce thirteen / When fates turned cruel'. Actually, Pavy was about twelve when he acted in *Cynthia's Revels*, thirteen at the time of Clifton's complaint, and fourteen when he died. He was baptized at St Dunstan Stepney on 12 May 1588 as 'Salomon sonne of John Pavy baptized from the howse of Mrs Pelson at Milend', and was buried at St Mary Somerset on 25 July 1602 as 'Sollomon Pavy'.[19] Nathan Field, 'a scholar of a grammar school in London kept by one Mr. Mulcaster', was baptized on 17 October 1587, and thus was about thirteen and fourteen when he acted alongside Pavy in *Cynthia's Revels* and *Poetaster*. Field later became a famous actor with the King's Men and a playwright.[20]

## FEMALE ROLES IN TWO CAROLINE CAST-LISTS

The best way to illustrate the casting of female roles on the pre-Restoration professional stage will be to examine in detail two of the surviving cast lists from that era which specify who played women: *Holland's Leaguer* (performed in December 1631 by Prince Charles's Men) and *The Roman Actor* (performed in October 1626 by the King's Men). The actors named in these two cast lists illustrate the full range of ages we find for female roles, as well as the nature of the apprenticeship system which underlay the casting of teenage boys as women.

For our purposes, the cast list in the 1632 quarto of Shakerly Marmion's *Holland's Leaguer* comes close to the ideal situation alluded to earlier. This list specifies the actors who played each role, including female roles. We know when the play was first performed and when several of the actors playing female roles were born, allowing us to determine their ages when they played these roles. Best of all, we have explicit testimony from one of the actors in question, giving his age and explaining the circumstances under which he performed.

We know with unusual precision when *Holland's Leaguer* was first performed through the office book of Sir Henry Herbert, Master of the Revels from 1623 to 1673. Though the book itself is now lost, Edmond Malone (who had access to it) reported that 'the play of Holland's Leaguer was acted six days successively at Salisbury Court, in December, 1631, and yet Sir Henry Herbert received on account of the six representations but *one pound nineteen shillings*, in virtue of the *ninth* share which he possessed as one of the proprietors of that house'.[21] The play was entered in the Stationers' Register less than two months later, on 26 January 1632, and was printed that year in quarto with a title page saying it had been acted by Prince Charles's servants at Salisbury Court. The quarto also contained a cast list naming sixteen members of the company and specifying the roles they had played. Six of these are female roles. Robert Stratford played Triphoena, wife to Philautus; Richard Godwin played Faustina, sister to Philautus; John Wright played Millicent, daughter to Agurtes; Richard Fouch played Margery, her maid; Arthur Savill played Quartilla,

[17] John C. Coldewey and Brian F. Copenhaver, eds., *Pseudomagia; Euribates Pseudomagus; Susenbrotus, or Fortunia; Zelotypus*, Renaissance Latin Drama in England, Second Series, 14 (Hildesheim, Zurich, New York, 1991), pp. 12–19; John Venn and J. A. Venn, *Alumni Cantabrigienses*, Part I, vol. 1 (Cambridge, 1922), p. 324.

[18] Addlethorpe parish register, Lincolnshire Archives, Lincoln.

[19] St. Dunstan Stepney baptisms 1568–1608 (London Metropolitan Archives X024/066); St. Mary Somerset parish register 1558–1653 (Guildhall Library MS 5710/1), the latter also cited in Gerald Eades Bentley, 'A Good Name Lost: Ben Jonson's Lament for S. P.', *Times Literary Supplement*, 30 May 1942, p. 276.

[20] William Peery, *The Plays of Nathan Field* (Austin, 1950), p. 4.

[21] N. W. Bawcutt, ed., *The Control and Censorship of Caroline Drama: The Records of Sir Henry Herbert, Master of the Revels 1623–73* (Oxford, 1996), p. 174.

gentlewoman to Triphoena; and Samuell Mannery played a bawd.[22]

The first thing worth noting about these six is that none of them was a sharer in the company. The licence which created Prince Charles's Men on 7 December 1631 names ten members: Andrew Keyne (Cane), Ellis Worth, Josephe Moore, Mathew Smith, Richard Ffowler, William Browne, James Sneller, Thomas Bonde, Henry Gradwell and William Hall. In May 1632, all these men except Moore, plus Thomas Plumfield and George Stutville, were sworn Grooms of the Chamber in ordinary 'to attend the Prince his Highnes in y^e^ quality of players'.[23] Eight of these players (Cane, Worth, Smith, Fowler, Browne, Sneller, Bond and Gradwell) are included in the *Holland's Leaguer* cast list, but none played a female role.

Of the six who did play female roles, four (Mannery, Savill, Wright and Stratford) can be identified with a high degree of certainty. All four were teenagers in December 1631, and at least three of them were apprentices in London livery companies. As I have shown in detail elsewhere, many professional players and musicians were free of livery companies such as the Goldsmiths, and they often bound apprentices who were trained on the stage.[24] Samuel Mannery, for example, was bound on 1 August 1629 for a term of nine years to Thomas Goodwin, a professional musician who was free of the Farriers. Mannery married Mary Finch at St Giles in the Fields on 28 October 1638, three months after his apprenticeship ended, and was still acting the following year with the King and Queen's Young Company (Beeston's Boys) at the Cockpit. He was buried in St Giles in the Fields on 1 November 1648.[25] We do not know exactly when Mannery was born, but at the time of his binding in 1629 he cannot have been much younger than fourteen, the traditional lower age limit for apprentices in the London livery companies. Thus, he was probably around sixteen or seventeen when he appeared in *Holland's Leaguer*.

The ages of three of the other boys can be determined more precisely. As it turns out, all three have connections to Andrew Cane, who played Trimalchio alongside them in *Holland's Leaguer*, and who was also a freeman of the Goldsmiths' Company. Robert Stratford was the son of William Stratford, a player in the Prince's/Palsgrave's company; on 30 April 1624, William Stratford signed a bond along with Andrew Cane and four others to act together at the Fortune. Robert Stratford was baptized at St Giles Cripplegate on 6 April 1618, and was thus thirteen years old, going on fourteen, when he played Triphoena.[26] Arthur Savill was baptized at St James Clerkenwell on 27 February 1617, the son of Cordaile Savill, gentleman, and was apprenticed to Cane as a Goldsmith for eight years on 5 August 1631; he was thus a few months short of fifteen years old when he played Quartilla.[27] John Wright was apprenticed to Cane as a Goldsmith on 27 November 1629 for eight years as the son of John Wright of St Giles Cripplegate, baker. He gave his age as forty in a Chancery deposition on 1 February 1655; thus, when he played Millicent, he was about seventeen years old.[28]

---

22 Gerald Eades Bentley, *The Profession of Player in Shakespeare's Time* (Princeton, 1984), pp. 279–81.

23 N. W. Bawcutt, 'Documents of the Salisbury Court Theatre in the British Library', *Medieval and Renaissance Drama in England* 9 (1997), p. 182; G. E. Bentley, *The Jacobean and Caroline Stage*, vol. 1 (Oxford, 1941), pp. 302–3.

24 Kathman, 'Grocers, Goldsmiths, and Drapers'.

25 Farriers' Apprentice Bindings (Guildhall Library MS 5526/1), p. 74; Bentley, *Jacobean and Caroline Stage*, vol. 2, p. 506. Two of Goodwin's apprentices (John Yockney and William Young) eventually became royal musicians, and another (Marmaduke Wright) became a London city wait; all bound multiple apprentices in the Farriers. When Goodwin bound Wright, he promised to give him a treble viol or treble cornet at the end of his apprenticeship ((Guildhall Library MS 5526/1), p. 51).

26 Guildhall Library MS 6419/2. The normally thorough G. E. Bentley unaccountably missed this entry among others referring to William Stratford. Though Stratford is called 'yeoman' in the 1618 entry, he is called both 'yeoman' and 'player' in later entries.

27 William Ingram, 'Arthur Savill, Stage Player', *Theatre Notebook* 37 (1983), 21–2; Goldsmiths' Apprentice Book 1, f.294v.

28 Goldsmiths' Apprentice Book 1, f. 305r; Public Record Office C24/785/53 (plaintiff's depositions for De Caine v. Wintershall).

Wright later provided further details in the 1655 deposition cited above, part of a lawsuit over the same 1624 bond signed by Cane and William Stratford. Wright testified that it was the usual practice for the 'Masters & Chiefe Actors' of the London companies to bind 'boyes & youthes as Apprentices to themselfes or some others that were freemen of some trade or other', and that these boys acted in comedies and tragedies even though they were not technically apprenticed as actors. Wright further testified

> that hee himselfe was bound as an Apprentice to the said partie [Cane] for A Certaine number of yeares to Learne the trade of A Goldsmith, And hee sayeth that hee this Deponent Did vsually Acte & play partes in Comidyes & Tragedies in the tyme of his Apprenticeshipp and was afterwards made free of the Trade of A Goldsmith which the said partie vsed[29]

Wright was indeed freed as a Goldsmith, though not until 1646. As we will see below, quite a few other performers of female roles were formally apprenticed in livery companies. Those whose ages we can determine were between the ages of thirteen and sixteen at the time of binding and it seems reasonable to assume that the others were around the same age.

The *Holland's Leaguer* cast provides a valuable snapshot, but it leaves some important questions unanswered. We do not know any other specific roles played by any of these boys, including Wright, and thus we cannot be sure how long they remained in such roles. Fortunately, the cast list of *The Roman Actor* helps answer these questions. Not only can we determine the ages of most of the boys in the cast, but we can trace their later careers through other King's Men cast lists, providing a good picture of how boys' acting careers developed.

Philip Massinger's *The Roman Actor* was licensed for performance by the King's Men on 11 October 1626 and printed in quarto in 1629. As with *Holland's Leaguer*, sixteen actors and their roles are named in the quarto, but here only four of them correspond to female roles. These are John Tompson, who played Domitia, the wife of Aelius Lamia; John 'Hvnnieman' (Honeyman), who played Domitilla, cousin germane to Caesar; William Trigge, who played Julia, Titus's daughter; and Alexander Gough, who played Caenis, Vespatian's concubine.[30] As with the list from Prince Charles's Men, one thing we can tell right off the bat is that none of these four was a sharer in the King's Men. None of them are among the thirteen men listed in the company patent issued on 24 June 1625 after the accession of Charles I, nor are any of them among the fifteen men named in the livery allowance of 6 May 1629.[31]

However, we do have baptism dates for two of these performers, showing that they were comparable in age to the Prince Charles's boys we saw earlier. Alexander Gough was the son of Robert Gough, a minor player with the King's Men, and was baptized at St Saviour's Southwark on 7 August 1614; he was thus twelve years old when *The Roman Actor* was first performed.[32] John Honeyman was christened on 7 February 1613 at St Botolph Bishopsgate, the son of Richard Honeyman; he was thus thirteen years old in late 1626. If the printed cast list refers to a production later than the first one, Gough and Honeyman might have been as old as fifteen and sixteen when they played these roles.

Both of these boys can be traced with the King's Men in later years, and through these later cast lists we can trace their transition from female roles to male ones. In Lodowick Carlell's *The Deserving Favorite*, printed in 1629 and probably performed a year or two earlier, Honeyman played Clarinda, while Gough did not appear. In Massinger's *The Picture*, licensed on 8 June 1629 and printed the following year, Gough played Acanthe, a maid of honour, and Honeyman played Sophia, wife

[29] PRO C24/785/53. This transcription expands abbreviations and incorporates deletions and insertions into the text. I discuss the lawsuit in more detail in the paper cited above.

[30] Bentley, *Profession of Player*, pp. 250–1.

[31] Bentley, *Jacobean and Caroline Stage*, vol. 1, pp. 80–3.

[32] Bentley, *Jacobean and Caroline Stage*, vol. 2, pp. 446–7. He was most likely named after King's Man Alexander Cooke, who had been buried in the same parish six months before and had been an apprentice in the company alongside Robert Gough.

to Mathias. In John Clavell's *The Soddered Citizen* (*c.* 1630) we find Honeyman playing a male role for the first time, namely Sly the servant. Gough played a page, Fewtricks, in the same production. Thereafter, we find Honeyman only in minor male roles: the First Merchant in Massinger's *Believe As You List* (licensed 6 May 1631) and a young factor in Fletcher's *The Wild Goose-Chase* (1632). Gough, however, continued to play female roles: Eurinia in *Believe As You List* and Lillia-Bianca in *The Wild Goose-Chase*.[33] Thus, while Honeyman appears to have transitioned to minor male roles around age seventeen, Gough continued to play women until he was at least eighteen. We know of no further roles for either actor. Honeyman died in 1636 at the tender age of twenty-three, while Gough became a publisher during the Interregnum.

William Trigge appears between Honeyman and Gough in the cast list for *The Roman Actor*, playing Julia, Titus's daughter. Trigge had been apprenticed to John Heminges of the King's Men, who was free of the Grocers, on 20 December 1625 for a term of twelve years.[34] After his minor part in *The Roman Actor*, Trigge played other minor female roles in 1628–32 alongside Gough and Honeyman. He was Corsica, Sophia's woman, in *The Picture*; Modestina, an orphan, in *The Soddered Citizen*; Selina, daughter to Clephis, in *The Swisser*; and Rosalura, one of the 'Aerie Daughters of Nantolet', in *The Wild Goose-Chase*.[35]

Right in the middle of this period, in October 1630, Trigge's master John Heminges died. His apprenticeship contract passed to Heminges's eldest son and heir William, who had earned a BA and an MA at Christ Church, Oxford, but was now leading a profligate lifestyle which eventually landed him in the Marshalsea prison. William Heminges also inherited his father's shares in the Globe and Blackfriars playhouses, but John Shank testified several years later that William had nothing to do with running either theatre but merely collected the income.[36] These cannot have been ideal conditions for Trigge and, on 11 August 1631, he addressed a petition to the Mayor's Court of London asking to be released from his indenture of apprenticeship. In this petition, written on parchment in legal French, Trigge describes himself as the son of Randall Trigge of 'Morte flatte' (Mortlake?), Kent, clerk, and says that he had been apprenticed on 20 December 1625 to John Heminges, citizen and grocer, for a term of twelve years, 'pur appr[en]dre lart que le dite John hennings adonc vsait . . . l'arte d'une Stageplayer' ('to learn the art which the said John Heminges then used . . . the art of a stageplayer').[37] Here, as with John Wright, we have an apprentice explicitly testifying that he had been bound in a livery company in order to act.

Somewhat surprisingly, Trigge did not ask to be released from his indenture because his master had died; rather, he claimed that the indenture should be void because, at the time it was signed, he was only thirteen years old rather than the customary minimum of fourteen.[38] This was clearly a technicality, for it was not uncommon for boys younger than fourteen to be apprenticed; in fact, John Heminges himself had been only eleven when he was bound.[39] It seems probable that the

33 Bentley, *Profession of Player*, pp. 251–69, transcribes and discusses all these cast lists.

34 Guildhall Library MS 11571/11, f.139v.

35 Bentley, *Jacobean and Caroline Stage*, vol. 2, pp. 604–6.

36 G. C. Moore Smith, 'Introduction', *William Hemminge's Elegy on Randolph's Finger* (1923), pp. 1–9.

37 Corporation of London Record Office, Mayor's Court Original Bills, MC1–53, membrane 54. This record was cited inaccurately by Bentley (*Profession of Player*, p. 122), who does not mention the purpose of the petition and mistakenly says that it gives the date of Trigge's apprenticeship as 20 December 1626. The date given in the document is 'Le vnitiesm [sic] iour de december en l'an du reigne Seigneur Charles le Roy d'angleterre le premier' ('the twentieth day of December in the first year of the reign of lord Charles, King of England', i.e. 1625). I am grateful to James Sewell of the Corporation of London Record Office for helping me decipher parts of the petition.

38 He asserted 'que le dite vnitiesme iour de december il fuist dedans le age de quatorziesme ans c'esta scavoir de l'age de xiii ans et non plus pur quoy Lavant dite Indenture est void' ('that the said twentieth of December he was under the age of fourteen, that is to say, the age of xiii years and no more, for which reason the abovementioned indenture is void').

39 He was baptized in Drotwich, Worcestershire, on 25 November 1566, and apprenticed for nine years to James

real reason for the petition was that Trigge did not want to be bound to William Heminges. Whatever the reason, the petition was eventually successful; Heminges made four defaults by failing to appear before the Mayor's Court, and when he failed to appear on 20 and 21 June 1632, the court discharged Trigge from the residue of the term of his apprenticeship. Three weeks later, on 11 July 1632, William Trigge claimed his freedom in the Grocers by patrimony as the son of Robert Trigge, deceased.[40]

These records provide valuable information about Trigge's age, though not without some complications. If Trigge was under fourteen years old on 20 December 1625, as he claimed, then he must have been born after 20 December 1611. However, this would also mean that when he claimed his freedom in the Grocers he was a few months short of twenty-one, the normal minimum age for sons to claim freedom by patrimony. This is not a major problem, for such age requirements were not always strictly enforced in an age without birth certificates. There is a close parallel to Trigge in Anthony Munday, who was baptized on 13 October 1560 but convinced the Court of Orphans on 12 January 1581 that he was twenty-one in order to receive his portion from his deceased father's estate.[41] If Trigge was born roughly in the course of 1612, as his testimony implies, then he was between fourteen and seventeen when he played Julia in *The Roman Actor*, and around twenty when he played Rosalura in *The Wild Goose-Chase*.

Finally we come to the performer of the most important female role in *The Roman Actor*, namely John Thompson, who played Domitia. Thompson played women for the King's Men over a span of at least eight years, and possibly more. The 1679 Beaumont and Fletcher folio lists him in the cast of *The Pilgrim*, performed at court on New Year's Day 1622, though no role is given.[42] His earliest definite female role is the Cardinal's mistress in Webster's *Duchess of Malfi*, printed in 1623 and performed some time in the previous two or three years. On 3 December 1623, Sir Edward Dering paid *6s* to see a play, plus another *2s 6d* 'Given to little Thomsone there'.[43] Presumably this was John Thompson, and the appelation 'little' suggests that he was still quite young. In addition to the Cardinal's mistress in *Duchess* and Domitia in *The Roman Actor*, Thompson played numerous other important female roles: Cleonarda in *The Deserving Favorite* (*c.* 1628), Miniona in *The Soddered Citizen* (*c.* 1629), Queen Honoria in *The Picture* (1629), and finally Panopia, the King's sister, in *The Swisser* (1631).[44] He died in 1634.

We do not know exactly when or where Thompson was born (the name is exceedingly common), but he was apparently bound as an apprentice to King's Man John Shank, who was free of the Weavers. In the 'Sharers' Papers' of 1635, Shank wrote that he 'hath still of his owne purse supplyed the company for the service of his Ma$^{ty}$ w$^{th}$ boyes as Thomas Pollard, Iohn Thompson deceased (for whome Hee payd 40$^{li}$) yo$^{r}$ supplt hauing payd his part of 200$^{li}$ for other boyes since his coming to ye Company, Iohn Honiman, Thomas Holcome and diuerse others & at this time maintaines 3 more for the sayd service'.[45] Shank explicitly calls Thompson a 'boy', which presumably has the same meaning we have seen in other theatrical contexts, i.e. 'male teenager' and/or 'apprentice'.

Collins, Grocer, on 25 May 1578. J. M. Nosworthy, 'A Note on John Heminge', *The Library*, 5th Series, 3 (1949), 287–8; Guildhall Library MS 11571/6, f. 473v.

40 Guildhall Library MS 11571/11, f.406r. Robert Trigge had been freed as a Grocer in 1596. One might question whether this is the same William Trigge from the Mayor's Court petition, who claimed to be the son of Randall Trigge. Given the closeness of the dates, I am inclined to think that both records refer to the same William Trigge, and that Randall was a legal guardian, perhaps an uncle. Such discrepancies are not at all uncommon in the records of the time.

41 Mark Eccles, 'Anthony Munday', in *Studies in the English Renaissance Drama*, edited by Josephine Bennett, Oscar Cargill, and Vernon Hall, Jr (New York, 1959), pp. 95–105.

42 Bentley, *Jacobean and Caroline Stage*, vol. 3, p. 391.

43 James M. Gibson, ed., *Records of Early English Drama: Kent: Diocese of Canterbury*, vol. 2 (Toronto, 2002), p. 920.

44 Bentley, *Jacobean and Caroline Stage*, vol. 2, pp. 599–600.

45 Bentley, *Jacobean and Caroline Stage*, vol. 2, p. 566. The apprenticeship records of the Weavers are unfortunately lost for this period, or we might be able to confirm whether Pollard and/or Thompson was formally apprenticed to Shank in that company.

However, the eight-year span of Thompson's service in female roles suggests that he may have been in his very early twenties when he played the last of these. If so, he could have been around thirteen when Dering called him 'little', and sixteen when he played the demanding role of Domitia. The eight-year-plus span of Thompson's career playing women corresponds almost exactly to the range of ages we have just seen for these King's Men boys in female roles – from twelve years old (Gough) to twenty (Trigge).

Collectively, all this evidence demonstrates convincingly that female roles in the early Caroline period (1626–31) were played by teenage boys, no younger than twelve and no older than twenty-one. However, a sceptic might argue that it does not prove that women had always been played by boys of that age, as opposed to adult men or small children. While the evidence from other periods is generally not as explicit as what we have just seen, it is complete and consistent enough to make it clear that these Caroline casts were not an isolated phenomenon. In order to demonstrate this, the rest of this paper will systematically go through every person known to have played a specific female role on the English stage before the onset of actresses in the early 1660s, and will outline what is known about that person's age. This evidence ranges in time from the late sixteenth century to the Restoration, and it shows boys in their teens or very early twenties playing women throughout that whole time.

## EVIDENCE FROM ELIZABETHAN STAGE PLOTS

The earliest professional cast lists to pair actors with the roles they played date from the last few years of Queen Elizabeth's reign.[46] These lists derive from a handful of manuscript 'plots', or documents which were hung backstage at playhouses to help the actors keep track of the entrances and exits for each scene. Most of the seven surviving Elizabethan plots originated with the Lord Admiral's Men, the main company associated with Philip Henslowe during the period in question, and thus can often be co-ordinated with the information in Henslowe's Diary and related documents. This information shows that the main male roles in the plots were played by adults, usually sharers, but that female roles were invariably played by non-sharers who were sometimes explicitly identified as boys. Several of these 'boys' doubled youthful male roles, suggesting that they must have been teenagers or young men rather than prepubescent children.

Two of the plots, *The Dead Man's Fortune* and *2 Fortune's Tennis*, have little that is relevant for our purposes – each contains only a few actors' names, none of which clearly corresponds to a female role. One of the others, *Troilus and Cressida*, survives only in a fragment from a production in spring 1599, but this fragment does contain some relevant evidence. At one point Cressida enters with 'a waighting maid wth a light', and the actor playing the maid is given as 'mr Jones his boy'. Later Cressida enters with some beggars, who are identified as 'pigg, Stephen, mr Jones his boy & mutes'.[47] This boy was apparently attached to Richard Jones, one of the principal Admiral's Men, and was young enough to play a maid but old enough to play a beggar. We cannot identify him with certainty, but his name may have been James, for on 17 November 1599, about six months after the date of the plot, Henslowe lent 'mr Jonnes player' 40 shillings 'wch is boye Jemes feched'.[48]

Looking at the other surviving plots, we encounter similar evidence. *Frederick and Basilea* dates from June 1597, and identifies the actors for three female roles. The minor role of Athanasia was played by 'Griffen', who does not appear elsewhere

[46] There are earlier cast lists from academic plays performed at Oxford and Cambridge, but these are not relevant for our purposes because the actors were all university students. See Frederick S. Boas, *University Drama in the Tudor Age* (Oxford, 1914), and Alan Nelson, ed., *Records of Early English Drama: Cambridge* (Toronto, 1989), pp. 942–62.

[47] W. W. Greg, ed., *Henslowe Papers, Being Documents Supplementary to Henslowe's Diary* (London, 1907), p. 142.

[48] R. A. Foakes, ed., *Henslowe's Diary*, 2nd edn (Cambridge, 2002), p. 32. It is possible, but not likely, that Jones's boy was James Bristow, whom Henslowe bought from William Augustine as discussed below.

in the plots or in Henslowe's Diary. The similarly minor role of Leonora was played by 'Will', who Greg suggested was the 'little will Barne' who later appeared as a pygmy in *1 Tamar Cam*.[49] Whatever their precise identities, neither 'Griffen' nor 'Will' was a sharer in the company, or otherwise identifiable as an adult. The lead female role of Basilea was played by 'Dick', who is distinguished from a 'Black Dick' who played several minor male roles. At one point, Philipo and Basilea enter together, and the actors are identified as 'E Dutton his boye'. Since 'Dutton' is elsewhere identified as playing Philipo, 'his boye' must refer to the actor playing Basilea, i.e. 'Dick'.[50]

The plot for *The Battle of Alcazar*, dating to either 1598 or 1600, identifies an unusual number of boys, though only two of them played female roles.[51] 'Dab' and 'Harry' played young brothers of the Moor who later appear as ghosts, and Dab also played another child. Two moorish pages were played by 'mr Allens boy' and 'mr Townes boy'. While we can't be sure who these two were, pages were typically teenagers or young men rather than small children. The actor playing the lead female role of Calipolis is not identified, but the female roles of Abdula Rais and Ruben Arches were played by 'Dick Jubie' and 'Jeames' respectively. Dick Juby is probably the boy 'Dick' who had played Basilea in *Alcazar*, and in this play he also played the youthful courtier Christophero de Tavolo, a male role appropriate for an older teenager. James may be Richard Jones's boy who had played both female and male roles in *Troilus*, and in this production he also played a page. Thus, each of these actors played both female roles and youthful male roles in the same production, strongly suggesting that they were teenagers.

The final plot associated with the Admiral's Men is *1 Tamar Cam*, datable to 1602–3.[52] Here Dick Juby reappears but playing only male roles, namely the chorus and several smaller parts. Furthermore, Juby had a son baptized at St Saviour's Southwark on 1 May 1602, around the time of this plot. All this is consistent with a young man in his early twenties, as Juby would be if he had been in his late teens in 1597–8. Among the major female roles in *1 Tamar Cam*, no actor is specified for Tarmia, but Jack Jones appears to have played Palmeda. Jones later appears in the registers of St. Botolph Aldgate from 1607 to 1615, but he is nowhere to be found in Henslowe's Diary; thus he was almost certainly not an adult member of the company in 1602. If we turn to lesser female roles, Thomas Parsons played a nurse and a hermaphrodite, as well as several minor male parts. Parsons had played the androgynous role of a fury in *The Battle of Alcazar*, and had been identified by Henslowe in 1599 as Thomas Downton's 'boy'; now, three years later, he was playing both female and male roles, just as Dick Juby and James had done. A 'James' also appears here, playing a hermaphrodite. This may be the same James from either of the other plots noted above, or it could also be Philip Henslowe's boy James Bristow, whom Henslowe had bought from William Augustine on 18 December 1598.[53]

Before we leave Henslowe and the Admiral's Men, there is one more (apparent) player of female parts to consider, namely John Pig. He appears in two of the plots we have looked at, playing minor male roles: Andreo, a youth, in *Frederick and Basilea* (June 1597) and a beggar in *Troilus and Cressida* (1599). However, on 8 December 1597, Henslowe lent the Admiral's *6s 7d*. 'for makynge & a payer of yeare sleavse of the bodeyes of pyges gowne', and an inventory of apparel belonging to the company, taken in March 1598, includes both male and female items of clothing specified as Pig's. There is 'j red sewte of cloth for pyge, layed with whitt lace'; 'Pyges damask gowne', 'j harcoller tafitie sewte of pygges', 'j white tafitie sewte of pygges', and 'j littell

[49] On 1 December 1597, Henslowe lent Robert Shaa money 'to bye tensell for bornes womones gowne', and presumably this gown belonged to 'little will Barne', as opposed to the adult player William Borne/Bird. Greg, *Henslowe Papers*, p. 136; W. W. Greg, *Dramatic Documents from the Elizabethan Playhouse: Commentary* (Oxford, 1931), p. 66; Foakes, *Henslowe's Diary*, 72.

[50] Greg, *Henslowe Papers*, p. 137.

[51] Greg, *Henslowe Papers*, pp. 138–41, provides a transcript.

[52] Greg, *Henslowe Papers*, pp. 145–8, provides a transcript.

[53] Greg, *Dramatic Documents*, p. 56 and pp. 66–7, discusses the possibilities.

gacket for Pygge'.[54] It appears that Pig was playing some substantial female roles, or had recently done so, around the same time that he was playing minor male roles. His exact age is uncertain, but he seems to have been an apprentice like the others we have seen. There survives a playful letter, undated but apparently from the 1593 tour of Strange's Men, in which Pig refers to 'my good master hinsley' [Henslowe] and also alludes to Edward Alleyn as his master. On 27 March 1598, Pig witnessed a loan along with 'Jemes', presumably the Admirals' boy of that name.[55]

The final plot surviving from around this time, *The Second Part of the Seven Deadly Sins*, did not originate with the Admiral's Men. It is usually assumed to have been written for Strange's Men in the early 1590s, but I have shown elsewhere that it almost certainly represents the Lord Chamberlain's Men, Shakespeare's company, around 1597–8.[56] This plot identifies five actors with specific female roles: 'T Belt' played Panthea; 'Saunder' played Queen Videna and Procne; 'Nick' played a lady and Pompeia; 'Ro Go' played Aspatia and Philomela; and 'Ned' played Rodope. There was also a boy 'Will' who played Itis, a child, but since this is not a female role we will not worry about it here.

The lack of surnames makes some speculation inevitable in identifying these boys, but 'T Belt' can now be identified with a fair amount of certainty. He was Thomas Belte, who was bound as an apprentice on 12 November 1595 to John Heminges of the the Lord Chamberlain's Men, who, as we saw earlier, was a freeman of the Company of Grocers.[57] Heminges was among the most prominent of the many professional players who were free of London livery companies, and Belte is the earliest of the boys apprenticed to these freemen-players whose presence on stage can be documented.[58] Belte may have been the son of Thomas Belte, a Norwich city wait who was expelled from the city along with his wife and children on 16 November 1594, almost exactly a year before Heminges bound the apprentice of that name.[59]

The 'Saunder' and 'Nick' of the *2 Seven Deadly Sins* plot are most likely Alexander Cooke and Nicholas Tooley, both of whom eventually became sharers in the King's Men. Cooke was bound as Heminges's second apprentice on 26 January 1597, and Tooley refers in his will to 'my late Mr [i.e. master] Richard Burbage', suggesting that he had been apprenticed to Burbage.[60] Cooke is probably the Alexander Cooke who was baptized at Sandwich, Kent on 15 December 1583, along with a twin sister Anna, and Mary Edmond has made a good case that Tooley was born in 1582–3 in Antwerp, the son of a wealthy merchant-adventurer and freeman of the Leathersellers who died when Nicholas was an infant.[61] If these identifications are correct, then Cooke and Tooley were about fourteen and fifteen years old respectively when they played the lead female roles in *2 Seven Deadly Sins*. Though we are dealing with several levels of uncertainty here, these ages are entirely consistent with what we saw earlier with the Caroline cast lists.

The other two performers to play female roles in *2 Seven Deadly Sins* were 'Ro Go' and 'Ned'. The first of these was probably Robert Gough, who first shows up with the King's Men in 1603 when he married Augustine Phillips's sister and was a legatee in the will of Thomas Pope. Some have speculated that he was Pope's apprentice, but in any case he

---

54 Foakes, *Henslowe's Diary*, pp. 73, 318, 321, 323.

55 Foakes, *Henslowe's Diary*, pp. 119, 282–3.

56 David Kathman, 'Reconsidering *The Seven Deadly Sins*', *Early Theatre* 7.1 (2004), 13–44.

57 Guildhall Library MS 11571/8, f.508r.

58 This is mainly due to the fact that no professional cast lists exist before the late 1590s, and livery company apprenticeship records are more scanty. On 14 October 1584, Richard Haywarde was apprenticed as a Vintner to the famous clown Richard Tarlton (Guildhall Library MS 15211/1, f.171v), but we have no proof that Haywarde appeared on stage.

59 David Galloway, ed., *Records of Early English Drama: Norwich, 1540–1642* (Toronto, 1984), 107.

60 Guildhall Library MS 11571/8, f.545v (Cooke's binding); E. A. J. Honigmann and Susan Brock, *Playhouse Wills 1558–1642* (Manchester and New York, 1993), 125 (Tooley's will). My paper on *2 Seven Deadly Sins*, cited above, has more detail on the evidence for identifying these boys as Cooke and Tooley.

61 Mary Edmond, 'Yeomen, Citizens, Gentlemen, and Players: The Burbages and Their Connections', *Elizabethan Theatre: Essays in Honor of Samuel Schoenbaum* (Delaware, 1996), 36–9.

must have been with the company for some time before 1603 (as a non-sharer) in order to form such close bonds. The 'Ned' of the plot is tougher to identify, but one intriguing hypothesis is that he was Edmund Shakespeare, William Shakespeare's younger brother. Edmund was a player at the time of his death in 1607, and it is reasonable to think that he had experience before that. He was baptized on 3 May 1580, and thus was seventeen or eighteen years old when the plot was made. This age was, as we have seen, an age at which a boy might play either female or (minor) male roles. However, the name 'Edward/Edmund' is common enough that this identification must remain an interesting conjecture.[62]

To sum up: the evidence in these Elizabethan plots, taken as a whole, paints a picture that is virtually identical to what we saw earlier for the 1620s and 1630s. No person identifiable as an adult, let alone a sharer, is ever shown playing a female role, whereas several people specifically identified as 'boys' are shown playing such roles. Several of these 'boys' doubled small male roles, suggesting that they were in their late teens at the time. At least one and probably two of the performers who took female roles (Thomas Belte and Alexander Cooke) were formally apprenticed to an adult player at the time, indicating that they were between their early teens and their early twenties.

## JACOBEAN EVIDENCE

When we move into the Jacobean era (1603–25), the evidence about players of female roles becomes more diffuse. There are no more theatrical 'plots', but there are a few play manuscripts, and one printed folio, with some of the actors' names written in. Toward the end of this period, we also find the first printed cast list to pair up actors with specific roles, anticipating the many such lists from the Caroline period. As it happens, all the relevant evidence from this period comes from the King's Men, whose roster of apprentices can be reconstructed with surprising thoroughness. To the extent that we can identify the players behind the names, the evidence is all consistent with what we saw for the earlier period: female roles were played by teenage apprentices and never (as far as we can tell) by adults.

The first name to consider is John Rice, who, like most of the other boys we will encounter, eventually became an adult player. On 16 July 1607, the Company of Merchant Taylors put on an entertainment in their hall for King James, including 'a very proper Child, well spoken, being clothed like an angel of gladness' who delivered an eighteen-line speech written by Ben Jonson. The Merchant Taylors paid forty shillings to John Heminges of the King's Men 'for his direccion of his boy that made the speech to his Maiestie', and five shillings 'to John Rise the speaker'.[63] On 31 May 1610, in a city pageant honoring Henry's creation as Prince of Wales, Rice played Corinea of Cornwall, 'a very fayre and beautifull Nimphe . . . with a Coronet of Pearles and Cockle Shelles on her head', alongside Richard Burbage's Amphion, 'a graue and iudicious Prophet-like personage'.[64] The 'angel of gladness' might have been androgynous, but here Rice's character is explicitly female. Given that he was chosen for these two special performances, it is reasonable to believe that Rice was one of the King's Men's leading performers of female roles around this time.

Although Rice was identified in 1607 as Heminges's 'boy', there is no record of his being apprenticed to Heminges as a Grocer, as Belte and Cooke were. It is possible that he was formally apprenticed to some third party and Heminges was only his master within the acting company, a situation similar to what we will see below in connection with Stephen Hammerton. We do not know for sure how old Rice was, but we can make a good guess. Although he had been called a 'boy' in 1607, he signed a bond as one of twelve sharers in the newly formed Lady Elizabeth's Men on 29 August 1611, fifteen months after his appearance

62 I discuss 'Ro Go' and 'Ned' more fully in the *2 Seven Deadly Sins* paper cited above.

63 Chambers, *Elizabethan Stage*, vol. 2, p. 213n1.

64 T. W. Baldwin, *The Organization and Personnel of the Shakespearean Company* (Princeton, 1927), p. 423.

as Corinea in the water pageant. This was a young company; one of the other sharers, Giles Gary, had performed with the Children of the Queen's Revels in 1609, and two others, William Barkstead and William Ecclestone, were both twenty or twenty-one years old.[65] It is not unreasonable to think that Rice was about the same age. Of the numerous John Rices baptized in England around the appropriate time, perhaps the most promising is the one christened in St. Bride's Fleet Street on 22 September 1591; he would have been fifteen at the time of the 1607 entertainment, eighteen in the 1610 pageant, and a few weeks short of twenty for the 1611 bond.[66] Regardless of whether this is the right John Rice, the player of that name was most likely in his mid-to-late teens in 1607–10.

Next we have Richard Robinson, another boy who later graduated to adult roles and sharer status. Robinson first appears with the King's Men in 1611 in two different plays: in the Folio cast list of Jonson's *Catiline*, where his role is not specified, and in the manuscript play *The Second Maiden's Tragedy*, where a stage direction indicates that he played the substantial part of the Lady.[67] In Jonson's *The Devil is an Ass*, written and performed in 1616, Merecraft expresses a desire for 'a witty boy' to impersonate a lady, and Engine suggests getting one of the players, some of whom 'are very honest lads'. He specifically recommends 'Dick Robinson, / A very pretty fellow, and comes often / To a gentleman's chamber, a friend's of mine'. Engine tells how the gentleman had brought Robinson to a feast dressed as a lawyer's wife and fooled everybody, whereupon Merecraft exclaims, 'They say he's an ingenious youth!'[68] Robinson is directly or indirectly called a 'boy', 'lad', 'fellow' and 'youth', terms which collectively are most consistent with a boy in his late teens. Though the name is quite common, he may be the 'Richard Robenson', son of Richard, baptized at St. Leonard Shoreditch on 15 February 1598; that was the home parish of Richard Burbage, to whom Robinson was probably apprenticed, and Robinson definitely lived there as an adult.[69] If so, he was thirteen at the time of *The Second Maiden's Tragedy* and eighteen when he was praised by Jonson. Robinson was a sharer in the King's Men by 27 March 1619, when he is named in the company's new patent. Baldwin plausibly suggests that Robinson had taken the place of Richard Cowley, who had just been buried on 12 March.[70]

Our next piece of evidence is a copy of the 1616 Ben Jonson folio in which a contemporary hand has annotated the character lists for two of Jonson's plays, indicating which actors played which roles in revivals by the King's Men dating from 1616–19.[71] These cast lists are of great interest for theatre historians but for our purposes the most interesting notations are those indicating that 'Richard Birch' played the major female roles of Fine Madam Would-Bee in *Volpone* and Doll Common in *The Alchemist*. No player of that name is known, but the King's Men did have a boy named George Birch, who was apprenticed to John Heminges for

---

65 There are actually two surviving versions of the 1611 bond, transcribed by Greg, *Henslowe Papers*, 18, 111. For Gary, see Edwin Nungezer, *A Dictionary of Actors* (New Haven, 1929), p. 85; for Barkstead, Mark Eccles, 'Brief Lives: Tudor and Stuart Authors', *Studies in Philology*, 79.4 (1982), 10; for Ecclestone, Mark Eccles, "Elizabethan Actors II: E–J", *Notes & Queries* 236 (1991), 454.

66 St. Bride's Fleet Street baptisms, 1587/8–1653 (Guildhall Library MS 6536). There was also a John Rice baptized at St Martin in the Fields on 1 September 1594, but he was seventeen at the time of the 1611 bond, which seems a bit young.

67 Nungezer, *Dictionary of Actors*, p. 300.

68 Peter Happé (ed.), *The Devil is an Ass* (Manchester and New York, 1994), 2.7.57–75.

69 St Leonard Shoreditch baptisms and marriages, 1558–1653 (Guildhall Library MS 7493). The register also shows the baptism of this Richard Robinson's two younger brothers: Daniel (20 April 1600) and Ralph (14 May 1601). For Robinson's probable apprenticeship to Burbage, see Bentley, *Jacobean and Caroline Stage*, vol. 2, p. 550. A Richard Robinson was apprenticed as a Draper to William Risby on 2 May 1610 (Drapers' MS +287/F.B. 1), but the name is common enough that we cannot assume this to be the player, absent any evidence connecting Risby with the King's Men.

70 Baldwin, *Organization*, p. 51.

71 James A. Riddell, 'Some Actors in Ben Jonson's Plays', *Shakespeare Studies*, 5 (1969), 285–98. The same hand also wrote character names next to two of the actors' names in the cast list for *The Silent Woman*, performed by the Children of the Queen's Revels, and similarly annotated the cast list for *The Alchemist*.

eight years on 4 July 1610 (as 'George Burgh') and was an adult member of the company from 1619 until his death in 1625.[72] Riddell suggested that the annotator meant George Birch but misremembered his first name, a suggestion that seems eminently plausible. Adding to the plausibility is the fact that the company had another boy at the time named Richard (Sharpe), as noted below.

In August 1619, the King's Men performed a topical play called *Sir John Van Olden Barnavelt*, about the Dutch patriot of that name. A manuscript of this play survives as British Library MS Add. 18653, mostly written by Ralph Crane but with the names of several minor players added by a prompter.[73] Among the roles paired with players' names are two female ones: 'T Holc' played the Provost's wife, and 'Nick' played Barnavelt's wife. The first of these must be Thomas Holcombe, who was apprenticed to Heminges on 22 April 1618 for a term of eight years. This apprentice may be the 'Thomas Hollocomb' who was baptized in Shobrooke, Devonshire, on 7 April 1605, in which case he would have been fourteen in August 1619.[74] In any case, he cannot be much younger, for 'George sonne of Thomas Holcome Plaier' was christened at St Giles Cripplegate on 24 July 1624, and Holcombe was buried there on 1 September 1625.[75] The 'Nick' of *Barnavelt* is most likely Nicholas Crosse, who was apprenticed to Heminges on 25 May 1614. Bentley suggested that Nick was Nicholas Underhill, but Underhill was not apprenticed in the company (to Ambrose Beeland, as a Draper) until 13 October 1620.[76]

Now we come to the cast list in the 1623 quarto of John Webster's *Duchess of Malfi*, the first printed cast list in English to give the names both of actors and of the roles they played. There are actually two names given for three of the roles, and from our knowledge of these players' biographies it is clear that these must refer to separate productions, one from 1613 to 1614 and one from between 1620 and 1623.[77] Three female roles are assigned: 'R. Sharpe' played the Duchess, 'I. Tomson' played the Cardinal's mistress, and 'R. Pallant' played Cariola.[78] 'I. Tomson' is John Thompson, whom we saw earlier in the King's cast list for *The Roman Actor*. The other two names belong to boys who were apprenticed to John Heminges.

Richard Sharpe, who played the lead female role in this production, was apprenticed as a Grocer to Heminges on 21 February 1616 for eight years. He had been baptized at St. Leonard Shoreditch on 18 October 1601 as the son of Peter Sharpe, so he was fourteen at the time of his binding.[79] The cast lists in the 1679 Beaumont and Fletcher folio show him acting in many plays with the King's Men between 1616 and 1623, though without roles specified; his role as the Duchess came during the second half of his apprenticeship, when he was between seventeen and twenty-one years old. By 1626 he was playing male roles for the King's Men, and he continued to do so until his death in 1632.[80]

Robert Pallant was also apprenticed to Heminges, for eight years beginning 9 February 1620. He was the son of the minor player Robert Pallant Sr, and had been christened at St Saviour's Southwark on 28 September 1605; thus, he was

72 Guildhall Library MS 11571/9, f. 344r (Birch's binding); Bentley, *Jacobean and Caroline Stage*, vol. 2, p. 377 (Birch's later career).

73 Bentley, *Jacobean and Caroline Stage*, vol. 3, pp. 415–17.

74 Shobrooke parish register, Devon Record Office, Exeter. I am grateful to Eliza Newton of the Devon Record Office for copying the record of Holcomb's baptism record for me.

75 Bentley, *Jacobean and Caroline Stage*, vol. 2, p. 475.

76 Guildhall Library MS 11571/10, f. 111v (Crosse's binding); Drapers' MS +288/F.B. 2 (Underhill's binding).

77 The actors listed for Ferdinand are Richard Burbage, who died in 1619, and Joseph Taylor, who replaced him in the company; those listed for Antonio are William Ostler, who died in 1614, and Robert Benfield, who does not appear in the company until 1619. The list is reproduced in E. K. Chambers, *William Shakespeare*, vol. 2 (Oxford, 1930), p. 76.

78 The quarto actually brackets Pallant's name with 'The Doctor' and 'Court officers' as well as Cariola, but since it would have been physically impossible to play all these roles, someone in the printing house probably added the bracket by mistake.

79 Guildhall Library MS 11571/10, f.198v (Sharpe's binding); Guildhall Library MS 7493 (Sharpe's baptism). The St. Leonard Shoreditch register of burials 1558–1654 (Guildhall Library MS 7499/1) shows that Sharpe's father, Peter, was buried there on 24 August 1603, at the height of that year's plague outbreak.

80 Bentley, *Jacobean and Caroline Stage*, vol. 2, pp. 569–71.

between fourteen and eighteen years old when he played Cariola. No other specific roles are recorded for him, but in 1624 he was listed among those 'imployed by the Kinges Maiesties servantes in theire quallity of Playinge as Musitions and other necessary attendantes.'[81]

## CAROLINE EVIDENCE

The Caroline period (1625–42) provides us with the most complete record by far of the actors who took female roles on the pre-Restoration professional stage, with a corresponding increase in biographical data. We already saw much of this evidence in the cast lists for *Holland's Leaguer* and *The Roman Actor*, and the Elizabethan and Jacobean evidence has added to the picture without changing it in any significant way. The remaining Caroline evidence provides further details, though it also includes a few puzzling bits of information which have to be taken into account.

### KING'S MEN

As we saw in our earlier discussion, seven cast lists pairing actors with roles survive for the King's Men from 1626–32: Massinger's *The Roman Actor* (licensed 1626, printed 1629), Carlell's *The Deserving Favourite* (printed 1629), Massinger's *The Picture* (licensed 1629, printed 1630), Clavell's *The Soddered Citizen* (MS *c.* 1630), Arthur Wilson's *The Swisser* (MS 1631), Massinger's *Believe As You List* (licensed 1631), and Fletcher's *The Wild Goose Chase* (performed 1632, printed 1652). The four boys named in the cast of *The Roman Actor* – John Thompson, William Trigge, Alexander Gough, and John Honeyman – played the bulk of the female roles in all of these plays, but a few others also made appearances.

The 1629 quarto of *The Deserving Favourite* says that the minor part of Mariana was played by Edward Horton. Very little is known of Horton outside this cast list and the name was a fairly common one, making it impossible to pin down his birth date with any confidence. However, his name does also appear in the 1647 Beaumont and Fletcher folio. A stage direction in *The Mad Lover* says 'Enter Stremon and his Boy Ed. Hor.', after which Horton's character is addressed as 'small Tom Treble', and later in the play he apparently sings a song. As Bentley points out, the manuscript underlying the printed text presumably dates from a known revival of the play in 1630, just a year after the *Deserving Favourite* quarto.[82] If Horton was 'small' and a 'boy' in 1630, then obviously he must have also been a boy in 1628–9 when he played Mariana.

Two of the remaining King's female roles have connections to John Shank. According to the MS of *The Soddered Citizen* (*c.* 1629–30), the part of Miniona's maid was played by 'John: Shanks Boy'. Though the boy's name is not given, the fact that he is identified as a boy is enough for our purposes. He was presumably an apprentice of Shank, who played Hodge in the same production, and might even have been Shanks's son John, later known to have been an actor.[83] In the printed cast list for the 1632 revival of *The Wild-Goose Chase*, a line near the bottom reads 'Petella, their waiting-woman. Their Servant Mr. *Shanck*'. ('Their' refers to Rosalura and Lillia-Bianca, the two main female characters of the play.) Bentley, following Baldwin, took this to mean that Shank had played Petella, which would be a virtually unique example of a sharer playing a woman.[84] However, it is more likely that 'Petella, their waiting-woman' and 'Their servant' are two distinct roles, with Shank taking only the second one. Petella appears in only one scene (Act 2, Scene 2) and speaks no lines. Later (Act 5, Scene 4), Rosalura and Lillia appear along with a male servant who makes humorous, bawdy remarks. This scene-stealing servant inherently seems a much more likely role to be identified in a cast list than a mute such as Petella. Given that the role is entirely in keeping with the clowns typically played by

---

[81] Guildhall Library MS 11571/10, f.381v; Bentley, *Jacobean and Caroline Stage*, vol. 2, pp. 519–20.

[82] Bentley, *Jacobean and Caroline Stage*, vol. 2, p. 479; vol. 3, p. 375.

[83] Bentley, *Jacobean and Caroline Stage*, vol. 2, p. 566.

[84] Bentley, *Profession of Player*, pp. 114 note 1 and 257–8; Baldwin, *Organization*, p. 176.

Shank, I think we can say with some confidence that Shank was 'Their Servant', and that the actor playing Petella is unidentified.

The final female role in the King's casts is Oriana, a relatively small but important part in *The Wild Goose-Chase*, which was played by Stephen Hammerton. In 1699, James Wright wrote that Hammerton 'was at first a most noted and beautiful Woman Actor, but afterwards he acted with equal Grace and Applause, a Young Lover's Part'. Wright's statement is ambiguous about Hammerton's age, but in fact we know that he was an apprentice in 1632, and quite a bit of information about the circumstances of his apprenticeship emerges from a lawsuit filed in that year.

On 12 June 1632, William Blagrave, deputy Master of the Revels and co-financier of the new Salisbury Court playhouse, filed suit in the Court of Requests against Christopher Babham, previously an investor in Salisbury Court but now associated with the King's Men at the Blackfriars.[85] Blagrave claimed that Hammerton had been apprenticed to William Perry, a freeman of the Drapers who led a series of playing companies, and that Perry had turned over Hammerton to Blagrave for the remaining nine years of his apprenticeship by a deed dated 15 October 1629. Blagrave charged that around November 1631, Babham had stolen both the deed and Hammerton, whom he was now using for his own 'great gain and advantage'. Babham denied this, claiming that Hammerton was actually apprenticed to William Waverly, citizen and merchant taylor of London. The Merchant Taylors' records back up Babham's statement by revealing that on 5 December 1631, Stephen Hammerton, son of Richard Hammerton of Hellifield, Yorkshire, gentleman, was apprenticed to William Waverly of the Strand, Merchant Taylor, for a term of eight years.[86] The Drapers' records show no trace of Hammerton, but he had probably been bound to Perry in a less formal capacity, which was trumped by Waverly binding him in a livery company.

We cannot determine Hammerton's exact age, because the registers for the parish of Long Preston, Yorkshire (which includes Hellifield) are missing between 1608 and 1622, when we would expect to find his baptism.[87] But he was probably about sixteen when he was apprenticed to Waverly, since apprenticeships were often timed to end around age twenty-four. He was called a 'boy' numerous times in the court documents and, in November 1632, Blagrave again called him a 'boy' when he complained to the Lord Chamberlain that Hammerton was still with Babham and 'by him employed at the Blackfriars playhouse'.[88] Hammerton never returned to Salisbury Court, going on to a successful career as a young leading man with the King's Men.

## QUEEN HENRIETTA'S MEN

After the King's Men, the second most prestigious Caroline acting company was Queen Henrietta's Men, who played under Christopher Beeston at the Cockpit. This company generated several cast lists specifying who played women, and enough is known about these players to provide us with some more evidence about ages. Unfortunately, this evidence is not as clear as we might hope, because the exact dates of some of the lists are uncertain. These lists also include the only apparent example of a sharer playing a woman but this example is not without its problems.

Fortunately, no such problems are presented by the last of these cast lists, for Thomas Nabbes's *Hannibal and Scipio*. The play was printed in quarto in 1637, and the title page helpfully tells us that it was 'Acted in the yeare 1635. by the Queenes Majesties Servants, at their Private house in *Drury*

85 The following description is based on G. E. Bentley, 'The Salisbury Court Theatre and Its Boy Players', *Huntington Library Quarterly*, 40 (1977), 129–49. I discuss the case more fully in Kathman, 'Grocers, Goldsmiths, and Drapers'. The original bill and answer of the suit are now Public Record Office REQ-2-681.

86 Merchant Taylors' Apprentice Binding Books, 1629–1635 (Guildhall Library MS 34038/10), p. 180, and Presentment Books, 1629–37 (Guildhall Library MS 34018/2).

87 I am grateful to Mrs Judith A. Smeaton, Acting County Archivist of North Yorkshire, for undertaking a search of the surviving archives on my behalf.

88 Bentley, 'The Salisbury Court Theatre', 143.

*Lane*'.[89] Twelve different actors are named, but only one in a female role: Ezekiel Fenn, who played the female lead, Sophonisba. Fenn was baptized at St Martin in the Fields on 9 April 1620, so he was about fifteen years old when he played the important role of Sophonisba. He apparently also played the female lead Winifred in a revival of Dekker and Rowley's *The Witch of Edmonton*, since the 1658 quarto of that play includes an epilogue spoken by that character and signed 'Phen'. The exact date of this revival is not known, but it is not likely to have been after 1637, when Fenn was listed among the leaders of Beeston's Boys at the Cockpit. The 1639 quarto of Henry Glapthorne's *Poems* includes a poem entitled 'For *Ezekial Fen* at his first Acting a Mans Part', in the form of a prologue to be spoken by Fenn.[90] Thus the timeline for Fenn's career is unusually clear: he was playing a demanding female role at the age of fifteen, and another when he was no older than seventeen, but by the age of nineteen he had started playing men.

Several of the actors playing male roles alongside Fenn in that 1635 production of *Hannibal and Scipio* had earlier played women for the company. The best-known of these is Theophilus Bird, alias Borne, who played Sophonisba's lover, Massanissa. Bird was baptized as 'Theophilus Borne' on 7 December 1608 at St. Leonard's Shoreditch in London, the son of the actor William Bird (alias Borne). On 6 December 1623, Sir Edward Dering paid 1*s* 6*d* to see a play, and gave a further 2*s* 6*d* 'to little Borne ye boy there'.[91] No other theatrical boy named Borne is known, so it seems probable that this was Theophilus, one day short of his fifteenth birthday; in fact, Dering's money may have been a birthday gift. The 1630 quarto of Massinger's *The Renegado* reveals that 'Theo. Bourne' played Paulina, sister to Vitelli, and the 1631 quarto of Heywood's *Fair Maid of the West, Part II* (printed along with Part I) reveals that 'Theophilus Bourne' played Toota, Queen of Fesse and wife of Mullisheg. Both cast lists apparently refer to performances some time before the publication dates, but exactly how far before is uncertain.

*The Renegado* was licensed for performance at the Cockpit on 17 April 1624, at which time Bird was fifteen and Lady Elizabeth's Men occupied the Cockpit. The quarto says that the play 'hath beene often played by the Queenes Maiesties seruants, at the priuate house in *Drurye-Lane*' (i.e. the Cockpit). This led Bentley to argue that the cast list refers not to the first performance, but to one by Queen Henrietta's Men in 1625–6, when Bird was seventeen.[92] I think the 1624 date is more likely, though the difference is not large.[93]

The quarto containing both parts of *The Fair Maid of the West* says that the play 'was lately acted before the King and Queen, with approved liking. *By the Queens Majesties Comedians*'. The prologue and epilogue were reprinted in Heywood's *Pleasant Dialogues and Dramas* (1637) with the further specification 'Spoken to their two Majesties at Hampton Court'. Bentley took this to mean that both parts had been performed together at Court between 10 October 1630 and 20 February 1631, when Queen Henrietta's are known to have performed three plays at Hampton Court.[94] This would make Bird about twenty-two when he played Toota, at the very upper end of the age range we have seen for actors playing women. However, this dating is far from certain; Queen Henrietta's also played at Court in the 1629–30 Christmas season, and most plays were printed at least two or three years after the first performance. About the best we can say is that Bird might have been as old as twenty-two when he played Toota but he may have been somewhat younger. The fact that his name does not have

89 Bentley, *Profession of Player*, p. 278.

90 Bentley, *Jacobean and Caroline Stage*, vol. 2, pp. 433–4. In vol. 1, p. 251 and vol. 3, pp. 271–2, Bentley discusses the date of the *Witch of Edmonton* revival. See also W. B. Streett, 'The Durability of Boy Actors', *Notes & Queries* 218 (1973), pp. 461–5.

91 Gibson, *REED* Kent, vol. 2, p. 921.

92 Bentley, *Jacobean and Caroline Stage*, vol. 4, pp. 812–14; vol. 1, pp. 220–2.

93 The evidence for the earlier date is summarized by Bill Lloyd in an unpublished paper.

94 Bentley, *Jacobean and Caroline Stage*, vol. 1, p. 249.

the honorific 'Mr' in the cast list suggests that he was not a sharer.[95]

Hugh Clarke played the medium-sized (male) role of Syphax and the smaller role of Nuntius in the 1635 production of *Hannibal and Scipio*, but some years earlier he had been the company's most important player of women's roles. In Shirley's *The Wedding* (acted probably in 1626 and printed in 1629), he played Gratiana and in *The Fair Maid of the West, Part I* (printed in 1631, as noted above) he played Bess Bridges.[96] These are the lead female roles, both requiring quite a bit of skill. We do not know Clarke's precise age, but on 6 May 1627, he married 'Judith Brown alias Robins' at St Giles in the Fields. Bentley doubted that the Hugh Clarke in this record was the actor, but Judith Brown alias Robins was the daughter of Robert Browne, a longtime traveling player in Europe, and the step-daughter of William Robins, a leading member of Queen Henrietta's Men.[97] If this is the right Hugh Clarke, he played Gratiana just a year before his wedding, and was very probably married when he played Bess Bridges. This is not as implausible as it might seem at first; if he got married at eighteen, Clarke would have been seventeen when he played Gratiana and about twenty or twenty-one when he played Bess. Early marriages were not uncommon in the London theatrical community. William Shakespeare got married at eighteen (albeit not in London), and so did Edward Kynaston; Henry Condell was married at twenty, and John Heminges at twenty-one; Thomas Holcombe had a child at nineteen; Alexander Cooke was probably married at nineteen and a father at twenty-one.[98] It would not be surprising for an older 'boy' of twenty-one or twenty-two to play Bess Bridges, for the character is a heroic woman who becomes a sea captain at the end of part 1. In any case, Clarke does not appear to have been a sharer at the time, for his name, like Bird/Bourne's, lacks the designation 'Mr' in the cast list.

After Ezekiel Fenn, Theophilus Bird/Bourne, and Hugh Clarke, information about the Queen Henrietta's boys becomes scantier, but there are some clues. Timothy Reade played Cardona in *The Wedding* (*c.* 1626), was one of the leaders at Salisbury Court by 1634, and become a well-known clown.[99] He may be the Timothy Reade, son of John, baptized at St. Mary Whitechapel on 2 November 1606, since there was a player named John Reade living in neighboring St. Botolph Aldgate in 1600.[100] This would make Reade nineteen when he acted in *The Wedding*, an appropriate age, though the evidence is not conclusive enough for certainty. John Page played Jane, Justice Landby's daughter (the second-largest female role) in *The Wedding* (*c.* 1626) and went on to play the minor male role of Lelius in *Hannibal and Scipio* (1635) and perform with Beeston's Boys at the Cockpit in 1639.[101] Bentley speculates that he might be the John Page baptized at St. James Clerkenwell in 1615 and buried there in 1641, but admits that the name is extremely common, even just in that parish. Edward Rogers played Donusa, niece to Amurath, in *The Renegado* (*c.* 1624–6), and Millicent, Carolina's daughter, in *The Wedding*

95 Bentley, *Profession of Player*, pp. 272–5, discusses the numerous oddities of the *Fair Maid* cast lists. Bentley unaccountably dates the production to 1626 in this book, though he had earlier dated it 1629–30 in *The Jacobean and Caroline Stage*. I do not know what evidence, if any, caused Bentley's change of mind.

96 Bentley, *Jacobean and Caroline Stage*, vol. 2, pp. 406–7.

97 See June Schlueter, 'English Actors in Kassel, Germany, during Shakespeare's Time', *Medieval and Renaissance Drama in England* 10 (1998), pp. 238–61, the appendix to which prints the will of Judith's brother Robert and disentangles the families of the two theatrical Robert Brownes who were active around the same time.

98 Condell was baptized on 5 September 1576 in Norwich and married Elizabeth Smart on 24 October 1596 at St. Lawrence Pountney; see David Honneyman, 'The Family Origins of Henry Condell', *Notes and Queries* 230 (1985), 467, and Mark Eccles, 'Elizabethan Actors I: A-D', *Notes and Queries*, 236 (1991), 44. For Heminges, see Eccles, 'Elizabethan Actors II', 457. For Holcombe and Cooke, see the discussion in the present paper, plus Nungezer, *Dictionary of Actors*, p. 102.

99 Bentley, *Jacobean and Caroline Stage*, vol. 2, pp. 540–1.

100 St. Mary Whitechapel parish register 1558–1645 (London Metropolitan Archive X024/090); Nungezer, *Dictionary of Actors*, p. 291.

101 Bentley, *Jacobean and Caroline Stage*, vol. 2, p. 518.

(*c.* 1626). Nothing else is known of him, and the name is far too common to guess at an identification in the absence of further evidence.

One other printed play besides those noted above contains a cast list for Queen Henrietta's Men: Robert Davenport's *King John and Matilda*, printed in 1655 with a cast list which must date from before 1634.[102] Ten actors are listed alongside their roles, but unfortunately, none of them are female roles. However, the publisher of the quarto, Andrew Pennycuicke, says in his dedication to the Earl of Lindsey that '*It past the Stage with generall Applause (my selfe being the last that that* [sic] *Acted* Matilda *in it*)'.[103] It is difficult to say whether Pennycuicke's claim is accurate; he does not appear in any theatrical record from the 1630s, but he did have theatrical friends, including Theophilus Bird of Queen Henrietta's and Beeston's Boys. If he did play Matilda, Pennycuicke's statement implies that he did not do so in the original production. Regardless of which production he performed in, he could not have been older than twenty-one at the time; he was baptized on 1 October 1620, and the theatres were closed in early September 1642, a month before his twenty-second birthday.[104] This is consistent with the upper age limit we have seen for boys playing women.

Finally, there is one other person who appears to have played a female role for Queen Henrietta's Men, and he presents an apparent counterexample to the idea that sharers never played women. The cast list in the 1631 quarto of *The Fair Maid of the West, Part I* indicates that 'Mr Anthony Furner' played 'a kitching Maid', a very minor role consisting of only three short speeches containing a total of thirty-five words. This must be a misprint for Anthony Turner, who was a sharer with Lady Elizabeth's Men as early as 1622 and with Queen Henrietta's Men from at least 1626 to 1641. It is a bit curious to see an actor's name attached to such a small role, especially since actors are only named for eleven of thirty-one roles in Part I. Furthermore, Turner is listed as playing Bashaw Alcade in Part II, a part which had been taken by William Wilbraham in Part I. Bentley lists numerous other oddities about these cast lists, including the seemingly random ordering of the roles and the inconsistent use of 'Mr' to indicate a sharer.[105] These oddities raise the possibility that there was some sort of mistake in the printing, but, like Bentley, I am reluctant to dismiss the evidence outright. If the list is accurate, it suggests that sharers may have occasionally taken very minor female roles of a non-sexual nature, perhaps for comic effect. The existence of just this one example out of all the evidence we have seen suggests that the practice was not widespread, though, and there are still no examples of leading women – or even significant supporting roles – being played by sharers.

## KING'S REVELS

The other Caroline playing company with cast lists relevant for our purposes is the King's Revels. This company was originally established at Salisbury Court in 1629 as an all-boy company designed as a sort of training ground for the King's Men at Blackfriars but that arrangement had started to unravel by 1632, when the two companies got into a dispute over the boy Stephen Hammerton, as described above. By 1634 the King's Revels had become an adult company, though perhaps one with a larger number of boys than usual. Of the two full King's Revels cast lists which survive, one (*Money is an Ass*) belongs to the earlier period and consists entirely of boys, while the other one (*Messalina*) belongs to the later period and includes both adults and boys. There also exists a manuscript play (*The Wasp*) containing the names of several King's Revels players from the later period.[106]

*Money is an Ass* was written by Thomas Jordan and brought to the press by him in 1668. Though the title page give no date or company ascription,

---

102 Bentley, *Profession of Player*, pp. 276–8.

103 Bentley, *Jacobean and Caroline Stage*, vol. 3, p. 233.

104 Bentley, *Jacobean and Caroline Stage*, vol. 2, pp. 524–5.

105 Bentley, *Profession of Player*, pp. 272–6.

106 Bentley, *Profession of Player*, pp. 281–6, discusses all three lists, though he was unaware of some of the evidence I present below. Information in the following paragraphs without a citation comes from these pages.

Jordan's dedicatory epistle says that 'This Play was writ by *Me* & pleas'd the Stage, / When I was not full fifteen Years of Age', and the play's prologue implies that it was originally performed by an all-boy cast. In a Chancery deposition in 1665, Jordan gave his age as forty-eight, meaning he was born about 1617.[107] If his claim in the epistle is correct, this would mean that the play was performed in about 1631–2, rather than in 1635 as Bentley speculated. The accompanying cast list contains eight names, including Jordan himself, who played Captain Penniless. Six of these eight, including Jordan, appear in a lengthy list of King's Revels players presented at Norwich on 10 March 1635.[108] Thus, the *Money is an Ass* cast list appears to represent a performance by the King's Revels company during the period before 1634 when it was still a boy company at Salisbury Court.

Even though this cast is all boys, it is still tangentially relevant for our inquiry because these boys were being bred to act women's roles potentially at the Blackfriars and at least one of their fellows (Hammerton) actually did so. As noted above, Thomas Jordan was born around 1617 and stated that he was 'not full fifteen Years of Age' at the time of the performance. Thomas Loveday, who played Clutch, went on to act on the Continent and in London in the 1640s and was a member of the King's Company after the Restoration. He gave his age as forty-nine in the same set of 1665 depositions in which Jordan testified, meaning he was a year older than Jordan (and thus born around 1616) and was fifteen or sixteen years old when *Money is an Ass* was performed.[109]

The other six boys in the cast were 'Wal. Williams', who played Mr. Featherbrain; 'Tho. Lovell', who played Money; 'Nich. Lowe', who played Credit; 'Tho. Sandes', who played Calumny; 'Amb. Matchit', who played Felixina; and 'Wil. Cherrington', who played Feminina. I have not found plausible baptismal records for Nicholas Lowe or Ambrose Matchit, but excellent candidates for the other four can be found in London parish registers. Walter Williams, son of John Williams, shoemaker, and his wife Alice, was baptized on 19 September 1619 at St Andrew Holborn, adjacent to the Salisbury Court playhouse; Thomas Lovell, son of John Lovell, shoemaker, and his wife Alice, was baptized on 23 August 1620 in the same parish; Thomas Sandes, son of Henry, was baptized on 24 March 1616 at St Margaret, Westminster; and William Charington, son of Anthony, was baptized on 18 May 1617 at St Olave Hart Street.[110] These were all reasonably common names, but in each case there was only one boy of that name baptized in London during the relevant ten-year period, and the baptisms of Williams and Lovell in the parish next to Salisbury Court is surely no coincidence. These four boys would have been between eleven and fifteen when *Money is an Ass* was produced; this is a bit younger than most of the boys we have seen in the adult companies, but right in line with the other all-boy companies such as the Children of the Chapel. The only one of the four known to have acted elsewhere is Thomas Lovell, who acted after the Restoration for the Duke's Company.[111]

The second full cast list for the King's Revels appears in the 1640 quarto of Nathaniel Richards's *The Tragedy of Messalina, the Roman Empress*. Here the male parts are played by adult actors and, based on their other known company affiliations, Bentley showed that this cast must date from between July 1634 and the plague closing of May 1636, which caused the dissolution of the company. Of the three

[107] PRO C24/903, cited by Judith Milhous and Robert D. Hume, 'New Light on English Acting Companies in 1646, 1648, and 1660', *Review of English Studies* New Series 42 (1991), p. 500, note 26.

[108] Bentley, *Jacobean and Caroline Stage*, vol. 1, pp. 286–9, reproduces and discusses this list, which contains names at the end which may not be King's Revels players.

[109] Philip H. Highfill, Jr, Kalman A. Burnim, and Edward A. Langhans, *A Biographical Dictionary of Actors, Actresses, Musicians, Dancers, Managers & Other Stage Personnel in London, 1660–1800*, vol. 9 (Carbondale and Edwardsville, Illinois, 1984), p. 365; Milhous and Hume, 'New Light', p. 490.

[110] St. Andrew Holborn baptisms, 1558–1623 (Guildhall Library MS 6667/1); St. Olave Hart Street baptisms, marriages, and burials, 1563–1631/3 (Guildhall Library MS 28867); Arthur Meredyth Burke, *Memorials of St Margaret's Church* (1914), p. 92.

[111] Highfill, Burnim, and Langhans, *Biographical Dictionary*, vol. 9, p. 368.

actors named for female roles, Matthias Morris, who played Sylvana, wife to Silvius, cannot be reasonably identified. Lepida, mother to Messalina, was played by Thomas Jordan. Since we saw above that Jordan was born about 1617, he was between seventeen and nineteen when he played Lepida. The lead female role of Messalina was played by John Barrett, who does not appear in the *Money is an Ass* cast list but does appear in the 1635 Norwich list. Barrett must have been at least in his mid-to-late teens when he played Messalina, for he had sons baptized at St. Giles Cripplegate (as of 'John Barrett, Player') on 12 November 1637, 11 November 1638, and 31 January 1640, and was himself buried there on 31 March 1640.[112] There are too many John Barretts to identify his baptism with certainty, but the most plausible candidate is the John Barrett, son of Thomas Barrett, fishmonger, baptized on 16 October 1616 at St Giles Cripplegate, the same parish where the player's children were later baptized.[113] This would make him between seventeen and nineteen when he played Messalina, twenty-one when his first child was baptized, and twenty-four at his death.

## RESTORATION EVIDENCE

The last batch of evidence we have to consider comes from after the Restoration. Some of this evidence deals with female roles before 1642, while some of it has to do with such roles in the early 1660s, as the English stage was making the transition from boys to actresses. Restoration theatrical practice did not necessarily correspond to pre-1642 practice, of course, and in some ways it demonstrably differed. Still, there was enough continuity that evidence of the transition can be instructive.

The first category of evidence consists mainly of a paragraph in James Wright's *Historia Histrionica* (1699), describing how various Restoration actors had been boy-actors before the civil war and had played women on the professional stage. This paragraph is part of a longer discourse on the history of English theatre, one which is fairly accurate to the extent that we can check its claims. The paragraph is worth quoting in full:

> 'Tis very true, *Hart* and *Clun*, were bred up Boys at the *Blackfriers*; and Acted Womens Parts, *Hart* was *Robinson*'s Boy or Apprentice: He Acted the Dutchess in the Tragedy of *the Cardinal*, which was the first Part that gave him Reputation. *Cartwright*, and *Wintershal* belong'd to the private House in *Salisbury-Court*, *Burt* was a Boy first under *Shank* at the *Black-friers*, then under *Beeston* at the *Cockpit*; and *Mohun*, and *Shatterel* were in the same Condition with him, at the last Place. There *Burt* used to Play the principal Women's Parts, in particular *Clariana* in *Love's Cruelty*; and at the same time *Mohun* Acted *Bellamente*, which Part he retain'd after the Restauration.[114]

Some of these claims can be checked against contemporary evidence from the 1630s and early 1640s, and all of them can be put into the context of the era's theatrical history. Doing so suggests that Wright's account is largely accurate, and that it is consistent with the evidence we have already seen about the ages of boy actors.

Wright's first claim, that '*Hart* and *Clun*, were bred up Boys at the *Blackfriers*; and Acted Womens Parts', is supported by a piece of evidence brought to light by David George in 1974.[115] It is a list of characters from the 1634 quarto of Beaumont and Fletcher's *Philaster*, annotated in a contemporary hand by the names of actors who were with the King's Men in the early 1640s. 'Clarke' and 'Bird' are listed as playing Philaster and Thrasaline, but Hugh Clarke and Theophilus Bird were with other companies until at least 1635–7, and do not certainly appear with the King's Men until 1641.[116] Four female roles are identified: 'Wat' played Arethusa, the king's daughter; 'White' played Gallatea, a wise modest lady attending the princess; 'Thomas' played Megra, a lascivious lady;

---

112 Bentley, *Jacobean and Caroline Stage*, vol. 2, p. 359.

113 St. Giles Cripplegate parish register, 1606/7–34 (Guildhall Library MS 6419/2).

114 [James Wright], *Historia Histrionica: An Historical Account of the English Stage, Shewing The ancient Use, Improvement, and Perfection, of Dramatick Representations, in this Nation. In a Dialogue, of Plays and Players* (London, 1699), p. 3. I have normalized long s in the transcription.

115 David George, 'Early Cast Lists for Two Beaumont and Fletcher Plays', *Theatre Notebook*, 38 (1974), 9–11.

116 Bentley, *Jacobean and Caroline Stage*, vol. 2, pp. 377–9, 406–7.

and 'Charles' played the lead role of Euphrasia, daughter of Dion, who disguises herself as a page named Bellario for most of the play. The identities of White and Thomas are uncertain, but 'Wat' and 'Charles' are most likely Walter Clun and Charles Hart, the Restoration actors mentioned by Wright. These were not especially common names, and the chance of different boys named Walter and Charles appearing together in a King's cast list at the appropriate time would seem to be rather small.

I have not been able to determine Clun's birthdate, but Hart's can be identified with a high degree of certainty. He was baptized at St. Giles Cripplegate on 11 December 1625, the son of William Hart, weaver.[117] 'Winifred dau. of William Harte, Weaver als Player' was baptized in the same parish on 29 July 1638, and buried there on 19 July 1639 as 'Winifred daugr of William Harte weaver', with 'als Player' added in the margin. Four months later, on 23 November 1639, 'Mary daugr of William Harte Player' was buried in the same parish. Collectively, these entries identify this William Hart with the actor of that name who was with the traveling King's Revels company in 1635 and with the King's Men in 1636–7.[118] Both Charles and William Hart (as well as Walter Clun) were among ten actor-sharers who signed a contract on 27 December 1648 with financier Robert Conway, a contract which became useless less than a week later when the Puritan authorities arrested all the players in a crackdown on illegal playing.[119] William Hart was buried in St Giles Cripplegate on 9 November 1650 as 'Willi Hart Player from the hospitall'.[120]

Thus, it appears that Charles Hart was a boy with the King's Men at the same time that his father was a hired man with the same company, and that father and son were still acting together in the late 1640s when plays were illegal. Wright tells us that Charles Hart was Richard Robinson's 'Boy or Apprentice', and we have no reason to doubt this, though further documentary evidence is lacking. Wright also tells us that Hart 'Acted the Dutchess in the Tragedy of *the Cardinal*, which was the first Part that gave him Reputation'. James Shirley's *The Cardinal* was licensed by Sir Henry Herbert on 25 November 1641, and the theatres were closed in September 1642, giving us a ten-month window when the play could have been performed.[121] If Wright's assertion is correct, Hart was sixteen years old when he played the important role of the Duchess – an age which fits comfortably with all the other evidence we have seen for boy actors in general.

Wright next tells us that '*Cartwright*, and *Wintershal* belong'd to the private House in *Salisbury-Court*', referring to the Restoration actors William Cartwright junior and William Wintershall. However, he does not say that they were boy actors, and Cartwright, at least, was about twenty-three years old when the Salisbury Court playhouse opened in 1629.[122] It is entirely possible that Cartwright and/or Wintershall were boy actors at some point, but Wright provides no good evidence on the matter. Wright was simply going through all the major Restoration players who had been active before 1642, and he referred to these two even though they had not been boys in the 1630s like the others.

Wright does explicitly say that Nicholas Burt had been a boy, 'first under *Shank* at the *Black-friers*, then under *Beeston* at the *Cockpit*'. He further specifies that '*Mohun*, and *Shatterel* were in the same condition with him, at the last place' [i.e. the Cockpit], and that 'There *Burt* used to Play the principal Women's Parts, in particular *Clariana* in *Love's Cruelty*; and at the same time *Mohun* Acted *Bellamente*, which Part he retain'd after the Restauration'. These details provide some valuable clues to the possible timing of the events described, though they are not without ambiguities.

117 Guildhall Library MS 6419/2. I am grateful to Martin Devereaux of the Guildhall Library staff for consulting the original register to confirm my reading of William Hart's occupation as 'Weaver'.

118 Bentley, *Jacobean and Caroline Stage*, vol. 2, pp. 463–4. Bentley missed the 1625 christening record of Charles Hart, so he did not make the connection between the players Charles and William Hart.

119 Milhous and Hume, 'New Light', p. 496.

120 Bentley, *Jacobean and Caroline Stage*, vol. 2, p. 464. For more on Charles Hart, see my article on him in the *Oxford Dictionary of National Biography* (Oxford, 2004).

121 Bentley, *Jacobean and Caroline Stage*, vol. 5, pp. 1084–7.

122 Bentley, *Jacobean and Caroline Stage*, vol. 2, pp. 404–5.

Since John Shank died in January 1636, Bentley suggested that Burt was originally apprenticed to Shank in the mid 1630s and transferred to Beeston's Boys at the Cockpit after Shank's death and the plague closure of 1636–7. James Shirley's play *Love's Cruelty* was originally licensed in 1631 but it was in the repertory of Beeston's Boys in 1639 and was published in 1640; thus, Burt could have played Clariana for that company at some point between 1637 and 1640.[123] Wright says that Mohun played Bellamente (the principal male part) in the same production; in fact, Mohun is known to have been one of the principal members of Beeston's Boys in the late 1630s.[124] Wright implies that Mohun had been a boy with Burt at the Cockpit while simultaneously attributing a male role to him, but this conundrum can be solved by assuming that Mohun had recently graduated to male roles and was only a 'boy' in the sense of being a member of 'Beeston's Boys', a company made up mostly of former apprentices. Mohun's exact age is unknown, but there was a Nicholas 'Bert', son of John Bert, christened at St Stephen, Norwich on 27 May 1621. This boy would have been between sixteen and nineteen in the late 1630s, right in line with the other performers of female roles that we have seen.

There is, however, a second possible scenario to consider. Wright says that both Mohun and 'Shatterel' were boys with Burt at the Cockpit. There were actually two brothers named Shatterell, Edward and Robert, who both acted with the King's Company after the Restoration. Robert was baptized on 10 November 1616 at St Botolph Aldgate, son of Robert and Emme, while Edward was baptized on 3 April 1620 at St. Andrew Holborn, the son of Robert Shatterell, cook, and Emma, 'out of Clement Neumans house in Cocke yard neare Holborne Bridge'.[125] Edward played only minor roles and died before 1665, while Robert was a prominent member of the company for two decades. Furthermore, Robert was definitely a player in the 1630s, for on 1 March 1636 he received a licence to marry Jane Brett, widow, describing himself as of St Giles in the Fields, 'player' and age twenty-one, even though he was actually only nineteen at the time.[126] Significantly, St Giles in the Fields was the parish of the Cockpit. Given all this, it seems likely that Wright is referring to Robert Shatterell rather than Edward, especially since the other actors named by Wright were all famous in the Restoration. But Robert Shatterell was almost twenty-one by the time the theatres reopened after the plague and Beeston's Boys were organized in 1637, so he was no longer a boy in the ordinary sense. He was probably around the same age as Mohun, who was an adult by this time.

These difficulties might be eliminated if Burt, Mohun and Shatterell were all boys at the Cockpit in the early, rather than late, 1630s, and the performance of *Love's Cruelty* described by Wright was the original production in 1631 or soon after. This would imply that Burt was at the Blackfriars in the late 1620s, and that he moved to the Cockpit for reasons unrelated to Shank's death. A Nicholas Burt, son of Robert Burt, butcher, was baptized on 4 December 1614 at St Andrew Holborn, the same parish where Robert Shatterell was baptized two years later.[127] This boy would have been sixteen or seventeen in 1631, an appropriate age to play Clariana. Robert Shatterell was fourteen or fifteen at the time, certainly a boy. The main fly in the ointment is Michael Mohun's statement in a 1682 petition to Charles II that he had faithfully served the king and his father '48 yeares in ye quality of an Actor', implying that his career had begun in 1634.[128] Also, the absence of Mohun from any of the printed Queen Henrietta's cast lists of the early 1630s makes it seem unlikely that he would have played a lead role such as Bellamente during that time. It is possible that Mohun was a few years off

123 Bentley, *Jacobean and Caroline Stage*, vol. 5, pp. 1129–32.

124 Bentley, *Jacobean and Caroline Stage*, vol. 2, pp. 511–12.

125 St Botolph Aldgate, baptisms and marriages 1558–1625 (Guildhall Library MS 9220); St. Andrew Holborn, baptisms 1558–1623 (Guildhall Library MS 6667/1).

126 Highfill, Burnim, and Langhans, *Biographical Dictionary*, vol. 13, pp. 287–9.

127 St. Andrew Holborn, baptisms 1558–1623 (Guildhall Library MS 6667/1).

128 Highfill, Burnim, and Langhans, *Biographical Dictionary*, vol. 10, p. 276.

in his recollection, or that Wright was confusing Robert and Edward Shatterell, but I am inclined to think that this second scenario is less likely than the first one. Whichever scenario is correct (if in fact either is correct), both involve Burt playing Clariana in his mid-to-late teens.

The evidence provided by Wright has to do with the period before plays were outlawed in 1642, but boys continued to play women right up until the introduction of actresses in 1660–1 and even a bit beyond. At least one of these can be identified from the eighteen-year period when plays were only acted surreptitiously in England. On 1 January 1649, Parliamentary soldiers simultaneously raided illegal performances at four London playhouses and arrested the players. A newsletter account of the raid described how the players arrested at Salisbury Court were paraded through the streets in their costumes: 'Abraham had a black Satten gown on, and before he came into the durt, he was very neat in his white lace pumps. The people not expecting such a pageant looked and laughed at all the rest, and not knowing who he was, they asked, what had that Lady done?'[129] This must have been Abraham Ivory, a Restoration actor who was said in 1704 to have 'formerly been a considerable Actor of Womens Parts' before deteriorating into alcoholism. If so, he cannot have been younger than his mid to late teens in 1649, for Ivory's first child, William, was christened at St. James Clerkenwell on 1 May 1652. Ivory and his wife had four more children christened in the same parish, and Ivory himself was buried there on 15 February 1680. Unfortunately, we cannot determine an upper limit for Ivory's age in 1649, but this evidence is consistent with what we have seen for other actors (such as John Barrett) who fathered children within a few years of playing women on stage.

When we come to the open re-establishment of the adult playing companies at the Restoration, we are on firmer ground. John Downes's *Roscius Anglicanus* (1708) lists several actors who played women's parts in 1659–61, and since Downes had been a prompter since the early 1660s, his testimony deserves to be trusted. In his account of the company formed by John Rhodes in 1659–60, he lists six players who 'commonly acted women's parts': William Betterton, Edward Kynaston, Edward Angell, James Nokes, Mr Floid and Mr Moseley.[130] The ages of the latter three are uncertain, but good information survives about Betterton, Kynaston and Angell. William Betterton, brother of the famous actor Thomas Betterton, was baptized on 4 September 1644 as the son of Matthew Betterton, and thus was about fifteen in 1659–60.[131] Kynaston and Angell were both apprenticed to Rhodes in the Drapers' Company, of which he was a freeman; Kynaston was bound on 5 July 1654 as the son of Thomas Kynaston of Oswestry, Shropshire, and Angell was bound on 15 October 1656 as the son of John Angell of St Martin in the Fields, Westminster.[132] Angell's exact age is not known, but Kynaston was born on 20 April 1643 in Oswestry, and thus was sixteen or seventeen in 1659–60.[133] He continued to act female roles until at least 7 January 1661, when Samuel Pepys saw him play the cross-dressing title role in Ben Jonson's *Epicoene*, being both 'the prettiest woman in the whole house' and 'the handsomest man in the house'.[134] Kynaston was seventeen years, eight

[129] Milhous and Hume, 'New Light', p. 495.

[130] John Downes, *Roscius Anglicanus* (London, 1708), p. 18.

[131] Highfill, Burnim, and Langhans, *Biographical Dictionary*, vol. 2, pp. 101–2.

[132] Drapers' Apprentice Bindings 1634–55 (Drapers' MS +289/F.B. 2) and Apprentice Bindings 1655–89 (Drapers' MS +290/F.B. 4), both unpaginated.

[133] Oswestry parish register, Shropshire Records and Research Centre MS P214/A/1/1. The register contains a genealogy of the family of Thomas Kynaston, mercer, and Sara Micklewright, written in a different hand from the other entries. This genealogy lists birth dates for the couple's eleven children between 1638 and 1656, including Edward on 20 April 1643. There were a surprising number of Edward Kynastons in Shropshire, but the record of Kynaston's binding to Rhodes allows us to identify the correct one. This identification confirms the birth date given by a note in the Burnley collection; see Highfill, Burnim, and Langhans, *Biographical Dictionary*, vol. 9, p. 79. I am grateful to Alison Healey of the Shropshire Records and Research Centre for so thoroughly answering my queries about the entry of Kynaston's birth.

[134] Robert Latham and William Matthews, eds., *The Diary of Samuel Pepys*, vol. 2 (Berkeley and Los Angeles, 1971), p. 7.

months, and eighteen days old when Pepys saw him play Epicoene. He may have played a few more female roles after that, but he was married at St Giles in the Fields on 27 February 1662, just short of his nineteenth birthday, and thereafter became a well-known adult actor.[135]

In the early eighteenth century, Colley Cibber related an anecdote wherein Kynaston was scheduled to play the female lead in a tragedy before Charles II, but the performance was delayed because 'the Queen was not *shav'd* yet'. Some critics have pounced on this story as supposed evidence that women were played by adults rather than boys; however, as we have just seen, Kynaston was in his late teens when he played such roles, an age when he had presumably started to shave already.[136] Another piece of evidence often cited by these critics is a poetical prologue written by Thomas Jordan to introduce the first play to use actresses rather than boys, a production of *Othello* in late 1660. This prologue, which was printed in 1664 in Jordan's *Royal Arbor of Loyal Poesie*, reads in part:

> But to the point: In this reforming age
> We have intents to civilize the stage.
> Our women are defective, and so siz'd
> You'd think they were some of the guard disguis'd:
> For (to speak truth) men act, that are between
> Forty and fifty, Wenches of Fifteen;
> With bone so large and nerve so incompliant,
> When you call Desdemona, enter Giant.[137]

First of all, note that in context, it is clear that Jordan is talking about present (i.e. Restoration) practice, not what happened before 1642. As we saw earlier, Jordan had been a boy actor himself in the 1630s, and had played female roles while in his late teens, a typical age. As we have just seen, the late teens was also a typical age to play women in 1660, based on the limited evidence we have. But talented boys were no doubt scarcer than they had been before the Civil War, and it is not difficult to imagine that adults sometimes played female roles in those early days of re-establishing the professional theatre. In fact, there is some documentary evidence for such a practice. One of the Halliwell-Phillipps scrapbooks at the Folger Shakespeare Library includes a title page of the sixth quarto of Beaumont and Fletcher's *The Maid's Tragedy*, dated 1650 but probably printed in 1660. In the dramatis personae, an early hand has written 'Hart' opposite Amintor, 'Wintersal' opposite Evadne (Amintor's wife), and 'Cartwrite' opposite Calianax. William Wintershall had acted at Salisbury Court before 1642, and must have been at least 40 in 1660; in fact, he played the King in *The Maid's Tragedy* for the King's Company just a few years later.[138] If the anonymous annotator is correct, this is an example of a clear adult, probably a sharer, playing a lead female role shortly after the Restoration.

While Jordan's poem and the *Maid's Tragedy* quarto suggest that adult men sometimes played female roles in the brief period between the reintroduction of legal theatre and the introduction of actresses, they do not suggest that adult men *always* played such roles nor do they suggest that they had done so with any regularity before 1642. To the contrary, the evidence from Downes points to such roles being ordinarily played by adolescent boys, and the situation described by Jordan would have been a notable (and comic) exception.

## SUMMING UP

With all the evidence before us, it might be useful to summarize the facts. Of the forty-plus named actors known to have played female roles for adult companies, those whose age we can determine were all between twelve and twenty-two years old, with the normal range being roughly thirteen to twenty-one. If the printed cast list for *The*

135 Highfill, Burnim, and Langhans, *Biographical Dictionary*, vol. 9, pp. 79–85.

136 Highfill, Burnim, and Langhans, *Biographical Dictionary*, vol. 9, p. 80. For citations of this anecdote by critics, see Forse, *Art Imitates Business*, p. 91, and Rosenberg, 'Shakespeare's Squeaking Boy Actor', p. 5.

137 Thomas Jordan, 'A Prologue to introduce the first Woman that came to Act on the Stage in the Tragedy, call'd the Moor of Venice', in *A Royal Arbor of Loyal Poesie* (London, 1664), p. 21.

138 George, 'Early Cast Lists', 10.

*Roman Actor* represents the first performance in October 1626, then Alexander Goughe was twelve when he played Canis and John Honeyman was thirteen. Robert Stratford was certainly thirteen when he played Triphoena in *Holland's Leaguer*, and William Trigge explicitly testified that he had been apprenticed to John Heminges at the age of thirteen. On the high end, Theophilus Bird may have been as old as twenty-two when he played Toota in *The Fair Maid of the West*, though he may well have been a bit younger. William Trigge was almost certainly twenty when he played Rosalura in *The Wild Goose-Chase*, and Richard Sharpe was between seventeen and twenty-one when he played the Duchess in *The Duchess of Malfi*. John Thompson and Hugh Clarke were probably in their very early twenties when they played Panopia and Bess Bridges respectively, though neither boy's age can be determined for certain. Clarke was probably married when he played Bess Bridges, the only known example of a married man playing a woman on stage.

The very youngest boys seem to have played only minor parts, but boys across the entire rest of the age range can be found playing demanding lead female roles. Alexander Cooke and Nicholas Tooley were probably fourteen and fifteen when they played the lead female roles in *2 Seven Deadly Sins*; Ezekiel Fenn was fifteen when he played Sophonisba in *Hannibal and Scipio*; Charles Hart was sixteen when he played the Duchess in *The Cardinal*. John Thompson was in the middle of his apprenticeship, and thus probably around seventeen, when he played the key role of Domitia in *The Roman Actor*. As noted above, Richard Sharpe was between seventeen and twenty-one when he played the even more demanding role of the Duchess of Malfi, and Hugh Clarke was probably in his very early twenties when he played Bess Bridges. The one apparent example of a female role being taken by a sharer, namely Anthony Turner in *The Fair Maid of the West, Part I*, involves a minor bit part of only a few lines.

It is also interesting to break down where these boys came from, when that information is known. Several of them were sons of professional players, a group which includes Robert Stratford, Alexander Goughe, Robert Pallant Jr, Theophilus Bird, (probably) Timothy Reade, and Charles Hart. More generally, they tended to come from London parishes with a high concentration of players, whatever their father's occupation. Thus, Stratford, John Wright, Charles Hart, and possibly John Barrett were from St Giles Cripplegate, one of the most theatrical parishes in London. Goughe and Pallant were both christened in St Saviour's Southwark, where many players for the Bankside playhouses lived.[139] Arthur Savill and possibly John Page were from St James Clerkenwell; Theophilus Bird, Richard Sharpe and possibly Richard Robinson were from St Leonard Shoreditch; John Honeyman was from St Botolph Bishopsgate; Robert Shatterell was from St Botolph Aldgate; Ezekiel Fenn was from St Martin in the Fields; and (probably) Timothy Reade was from St Mary Whitechapel. All of these parishes had significant concentrations of professional players.[140] Later, Walter Williams, Thomas Lovell, Edward Shatterell and possibly Nicholas Burt were all baptized in St Andrew Holborn, the parish next to the Salisbury Court playhouse and one which had a high concentration of players later in the seventeenth century.

Some boy actors came from outside London: Thomas Belte (probably) from Norwich, Alexander Cooke and William Trigge (probably) from Kent, Nicholas Tooley from Belgium via Warwickshire, Thomas Holcombe from Devonshire, Stephen Hammerton from Yorkshire, Edward Kynaston from Shropshire. Most of these boys were formally apprenticed to masters in livery companies, and all of them performed with the King's Men (save Kynaston, who came later). This latter

[139] See G. E. Bentley, 'Records of Players in the Parish of St Giles, Cripplegate', *Publications of the Modern Language Association*, 44 (1929), 789–826, and 'Shakespeare's Fellows', *Times Literary Supplement* (15 November 1928), p. 856.

[140] Bentley's *Jacobean and Caroline Stage*, vol. 2, provides numerous examples of players living in these parishes. See also Roslyn Knutson, *Playing Companies and Company Commerce in Shakespeare's Time* (Cambridge, 2001), pp. 29–35, focusing on St Saviour's Southwark, St Botolph Aldgate, St Leonard Shoreditch, St James Clerkenwell and St Giles Cripplegate.

fact is significant, since all of the boys for other companies whose origins we can trace were born in London. This does not mean that no boys from outside London ever performed with companies other than the King's Men – at least some of Andrew Cane's non-London apprentices probably appeared on stage – but it does suggest that such boys were much more likely to gravitate toward the premier playing company, leaving native London boys for the other companies.[141] As the case of Stephen Hammerton illustrates, the King's Men were powerful enough to appropriate just about any boy who showed promise, whatever his origins.

There are no doubt more facts waiting to be uncovered by further research, but I hope to have shown that the facts we do have about boy actors and pre-Restoration female roles show some clear and consistent patterns. No significant evidence supports the idea that such roles were played by adult sharers but a wealth of specific evidence demonstrates that they were played by adolescent boys no older than about twenty-one. These boys came from both London and the countryside, and many (perhaps most) were formally apprenticed in livery companies. As our knowledge about boy actors continues to grow, these essential facts should form the basis of any future discussions about the sexual and gender implications of boys playing women in Shakespeare's time.

[141] Cane's non-London apprentices included John Hilton from Fulham, Middlesex; Hugh Pusey of Pusey, Berkshire; and Thomas Gibbins of Hurley, Berkshire. None of them can be shown to have acted, but it seems highly likely that at least some of them, if not all, did perform on stage. See Kathman, 'Grocers, Goldsmiths, and Drapers'.

# MISTRESS TALEPORTER AND THE TRIUMPH OF TIME: SLANDER AND OLD WIVES' TALES IN *THE WINTER'S TALE*

MARION WELLS

Would some God unveil all lives to us, Slander would retire discomfited to the bottomless pit; for the illumination of truth would be over all.

Lucian, 'Slander, a Warning', lines 33–6.[1]

The main source for *The Winter's Tale* is, as is well known, Robert Greene's romance *Pandosto*, first published in 1588. The title page of the first edition of Pandosto reads as follows:

Pandosto. The Triumph of Time. Wherein is discovered by a pleasant History, that although by the means of sinister fortune Truth may be concealed, yet by Time, in spite of fortune, it is most manifestly revealed . . . *Temporis filia veritas.*

This motto – Truth is the Daughter of Time – had a good deal of cultural currency during the Renaissance, as is sufficiently illustrated by the fact that it forms the basis of important pageants in both Mary's and Elizabeth's coronation processions.[2] Importantly for my purposes here it also became associated with the Renaissance allegory of the classical Calumny of Apelles, based on Lucian's essay on slander cited above. An early and important instance of this association shows up, as Fritz Saxl has shown, in the woodcut of an edition of the *Cinque Messe* dedicated to Alessandro de Medici by the Venetian publisher Marcolino in 1536.[3] This woodcut bears the legend *Veritas Filia Temporis*, and shows Truth emerging with the aid of Saturn (as Father Time) from the clouds of obscurity even as she is beaten back by the winged monster identified by Saxl as *Calumnia*. Geoffrey Whitney, in his sixteenth-century book of emblems, illustrates *veritas filia temporis* with verses in which Slander is one of the causes of the disappearance of Truth. The motto thus gradually came to be associated specifically with the suppression of truth through slander.

In *Pandosto* Greene employs the motto as the structural principle of his romance: the story will show the gradual 'discovery' of a truth that will be fully revealed by the end. Though this is, in a basic sense, the structural principle of all narratives, the motto seems especially relevant to the working of romance, which characteristically depends on the occlusion of vital information – a separation of hitherto united parts (of families, friends, stories etc.) – during the 'tragic' sections of the text, and on the gradual 'discovery' of the truth by play's end. The pronouncements of Time in the shape of the chorus suggest the similar presence of the *veritas filia temporis* motto behind the plot of *The Winter's Tale*: 'let Time's news / Be known when 'tis brought forth. A shepherd's daughter / And what to her adheres, which follows after, / Is th'argument of time' (4.1.26–9). The 'argument of time' allows the 'shepherd's daughter' to make her timely return from her supposed death to the frozen world of Sicilia. In the context of the *veritas filia temporis*

1 The text is reproduced in *The Works of Lucian of Samosata*, trans. by H. W. Fowler and F. G. Fowler (Oxford, 1905), p. 11.

2 I am indebted for this discussion of the *Veritas Filia Temporis* motto to Fritz Saxl's seminal article 'Veritas Filia Temporis', in Raymond Klibansky, ed., *Philosophy and History: Essays Presented to Ernst Cassirer* (Oxford, 1936), pp. 197–222.

3 See Saxl, 'Veritas', 199.

motto, Perdita takes on a quasi-allegorical significance as the daughter of time who is also lost truth, *veritas perdita*. The oracle that declares Hermione's innocence of the charges against her also supports this narrative structure of occlusion and return: 'the King shall live without an heir if that *which is lost be not found*' (3.2.134–5, italics mine).

The motto lays bare the narrative principle that the play associates with the resolutions of romance and, significantly, with the lowly literary category of the 'tale', or 'old wives' tale'. As Mary Ellen Lamb has noted, the play consistently refers to itself and its actions as resembling 'an old tale': the death of Antigonus and the surprising reappearance of Perdita are both described as being like 'old tales' that strain their listeners' credulity. It is, then, precisely those events that designate the play as a tragicomedy (or as a romance) that signal their indebtedness to 'old tales'.[4] As the category 'old wives' tale' already indicates, tale-telling is historically the province of women – and especially lower-class serving-women – and for this reason alone dismissed as part of an unimportant or even harmful oral tradition.[5] Lamb suggests that the danger attributed to old wives' tales is due in part to their association with a feminine corporeality incompatible with early modern conceptions of masculine subjectivity.[6] I wish to argue that *The Winter's Tale*'s structure explores a more specific association between the narrative structure of tales (inscribed within the *veritas filia temporis* motto) and the time of pregnancy, from conception through gestation to birth. The particular emphasis on the power of Time as a narrative force that operates both in the 'masterplot' of life and the fictions of 'old tales' draws attention to the play's juxtaposition of female tales and the female experience of pregnancy and childbirth.[7] Not surprisingly, the *veritas filia temporis* motto sometimes depicts a feminized Time, rather than Father Time, so that Time can be *pregnant* with truth.[8] This juxtaposition is figured most clearly in Autolycus's passing reference to one Mistress *Taleporter*, a midwife, whose name suggests that her midwifery is connected to the tales she tells (tall tales, at that) about the births she witnesses.[9] I shall return below to the symbolic importance of the midwife Mistress Taleporter, whose alter ego in the play proper is Paulina.

If the play asserts a connection between tales and the feminine spheres of pregnancy, childbirth and midwifery, it also seems to suggest a dark masculine counterpart to the tale that works against Time: slander. Mistress Taleporter and her counterpart, Paulina, work with Time to produce not only children but also miraculous tales that the listeners disbelieve at their peril. Leontes, on the other hand, reacts against the power of women's tales – and female rhetoric more broadly – and impugns his wife's sexual honesty. The scene in which Leontes interrupts Mamillius and Hermione's intimate tale-telling is central to my argument. The interruption of the tale focuses our attention on the opposition between masculine sexual slander and female tale-telling: that is, between two distinctly gendered kinds of discourse which organize the tragic and romance phases of the play respectively. Using the history of the *veritas filia temporis* motto as my starting point, I shall explore the play's complex treatment of the relationship

4 See Mary Ellen Lamb's 'Engendering the Narrative Act: Old Wives' Tales in *The Winter's Tale, Macbeth*, and *The Tempest*', *Criticism*, 40 (1998), 529–555.

5 Lamb notes anxiety over the influence on young children of the women's tales: '[anxiety] appears as well in childrearing manuals, which warned against the widespread existence of this oral tradition and its harmful potential as a means by which women – whether mothers or lower-class wet nurses – could exert permanent influence over young minds' (p. 531).

6 Lamb's association between the tale and the female body remains quite general: 'Nostalgia for this childhood period of effeminacy and its pleasures, including its narrative pleasures, could not easily be reconciled with a self built upon the rejection of the feminine and the corporeal' (p. 531).

7 Peter Brooks' discussion of the psychological models for plots influences me here. See *Reading for the Plot: Design and Intention in Narrative* (Oxford, 1984), *passim*, but especially the chapter entitled 'Freud's Masterplot'.

8 See for example *Temporis Filia Veritas*, (London, 1589).

9 During his interruption of the sheep-shearing festival, Autolycus tells a tale about a 'usurer's wife . . . brought to bed of twenty money-bags at a burden' (4.4.261–2). Questioned about the tale's veracity, he replies: 'Here's the midwife's name to 't, one Mistress Taleporter, and five or six honest wives' that were present. Why should I carry lies abroad?' (4.4.267–9).

between these gendered discourses and the genre of romance.

### 'TONGUE-TIED, OUR QUEEN?'

Milton's version of the *veritas filia temporis* motto represents a striking appropriation of its central trope in the service of a fantasy of male parthenogenesis. It is not a woman in childbirth who (metaphorically) gives birth to truth but a man whose thoughts might literally bring forth Truth:

> this ill hap wait upon her [i.e., truth's] nativity, that she never comes into the world, but like a bastard, to the ignominy of him that brought her forth: till Time the midwife rather than the mother of Truth, have washed and salted the infant, declared her legitimate, and churched the father of his young Minerva, from the needless causes of his purgation.[10]

As Katharine Eisaman Maus argues, this appropriation of pregnancy and childbirth occurs in a context in which male nervousness about childbirth is inseparable from a desire to 'conflate intellectual originality with childbearing' (p. 370). This passage also betrays an anxiety about the role of the midwife, Time, who has the power to declare the 'infant' legitimate. These issues arise almost immediately in *The Winter's Tale*. Leontes's perhaps latent fears about Hermione's imminent confinement come to the surface in the context of her power to persuade his friend Polixenes to prolong his stay. Hermione's persuasiveness turns for Leontes into evidence of adultery, and when her child is born Leontes declares it the illegitimate offspring of Polixenes.[11] Like the 'truth' in Milton's passage, Perdita comes into the world 'like a bastard', and it is only Time that will prove her legitimate. Numerous recent critics have discussed the complex psychological dynamic of this crucial opening scene, reading Leontes's jealous rage in the context of a culture in which men were excluded from almost every stage of the birthing process.[12]

These issues are certainly central to an understanding of both Leontes's and Polixenes's anxiety about female sexuality. But I would like here to focus on the implications of this scene's conflation of female power over time and female speech. Polixenes's opening words tell us that the time of his visit is coterminous with the time of Hermione's pregnancy, which is almost at term. The mapping of the beginning and end of Polixenes's stay onto Hermione's pregnancy involves him in the narrative of her pregnancy, and it is perhaps to this strange coincidence that both Leontes's pressing requests and Polixenes's anxious desire to be gone respond. The fact that Polixenes initially advertises the power of Leontes's tongue to persuade ('no tongue that moves, none, none i'th' world / So soon as yours could win me', 1.2.20–1) only to capitulate to Hermione's tongue instead suggests moreover that Hermione's pregnancy informs both her rhetorical strength *and* her control over the staying of time: 'He'll stay, my lord'. (1.2.86) This scene suggests that it is because the time of pregnancy provides a natural model for the narrative process inscribed within the *veritas filia temporis* model that pregnancy and verbal power will be linked in the action of tale telling. For pregnancy illustrates clearly the relation between duration (gestation) and the inexorable emergence of issue – in both the narrative and bodily senses of the term.[13] Before moving to the scene that

---

[10] *The Doctrine and Discipline of Divorce*, in *The Works of John Milton*, vol. 3, part 2 (New York, 1931), quoted in Katharine Eisaman Maus, 'A Womb of his Own', *Inwardness and Theater in the English Renaissance* (Chicago, 1995), p. 189.

[11] See Lynn Enterline, '"You speak a language that I understand not": The Rhetoric of Animation in *The Winter's Tale*', *Shakespeare Quarterly*, 48 (1997), 17–44, which begins with a discussion of the relationship between Hermione's sexuality (made manifest in her pregnant body) and her rhetorical power.

[12] Janet Adelman's *Suffocating Mothers: Fantasies of Maternal Origin in Shakespeare's Plays, Hamlet to The Tempest* (New York, 1992), and Gail Kern Paster's *The Body Embarrassed: Drama and the Disciplines of Shame in Early Modern England* (Ithaca, 1993) both have excellent discussions of this play's involvement in historically contemporary discourses of maternity and childbirth. I am indebted to both pieces in this essay. See in particular Adelman, pp. 220–5, and Paster, pp. 261–5.

[13] See Carol Thomas Neely's *Broken Nuptials in Shakespeare's Plays* (New Haven, 1985) for an excellent discussion of the play on the word 'issue' in *The Winter's Tale*, pp. 192 ff.

suggests a profound symbolic connection between tale-telling and pregnancy, we should consider how historically contemporary theories of time might influence Shakespeare's presentation of the narrativity of time.

As Frank Kermode has argued, the New Testament establishes a crucial and influential distinction between two different kinds of time – time as duration, or 'chronos', and time as crisis or fulfilment, 'kairos'.[14] In early modern writing on time this distinction is apparent, though the terms are quite different. John Fox captures the distinction between what he calls the 'duration and succession of so many minutes' and the 'tempestivity of time' rather beautifully:

> Time is taken under a double notion; there is the space of time, and there is the opportunity of time: Time and opportunity differ: time is the duration or succession of so many minutes, hours, days or years, one after the other, from the beginning of a man's life to the end thereof . . . Opportunity is the time appointed and fitted, in order to this or that work or business, viz. A meeting of time and means together, to effect the end. This is called the season or tempestivity of time, when time, tide and wind meet and clasp together . . . Eccles. 3.1, 'to every thing there is a season', or opportunity of doing. Time may be continued when the season of time is ended; the sails of time may be aloft, when the gale of opportunity is lost. Every time is not a spring-time, a seed-time, a gaining-time; manna was not to be had but in the morning. The beauty of time is the opportunity of time . . . This part of time we are to redeem.[15]

Passing time is marked by moments of crisis or fulfilment that give retrospective meaning to those apparently endless moments of successive time. Hermione's pregnancy encompasses both duration – the 'Nine changes of the wat'ry star' (1.2.1) – and seasonal time, the definitive moment or turn in time as the birth itself approaches. Her pregnancy marks, as it were, the transformation of *chronos* into *kairos*, and the concern surrounding the issue of this pregnancy points up a concern with issue in a narrative sense – with, that is, the dynamic of *plot*.[16] The transformation from duration to *issue* (or kairos) is a natural process, neither impeded nor aided by human interference; the child is conceived, gestated and born according to the laws of nature, and brought forth by the action of time. Indeed Paulina's words as she leaves the prison after the child's birth emphasize the independence of the time of gestation from human constraints: 'This child was prisoner to the womb, and is / By law and process of great nature thence / Freed and enfranchised' (2.2.62–4).[17] The chorus of Time that ushers in the 'comic' resolution of the play reiterates Paulina's words within an explicitly narrative context. The same temporal necessity that ensured the birthing of Perdita also ensures her timely reappearance in the unfolding of the plot:

> but let Time's news
> Be known when 'tis brought forth. A shepherd's daughter,
> And what to her adheres, which follows after,
> Is th'argument of Time. (4.1.26–9)

Time's narrative – which he earlier calls 'my tale' (4.1.14) – seems to dramatize for us the crucial movement from *chronos* to *kairos* as a restitution of the 'issue', both narrative and generative, that was prematurely cut off by Leontes's attack on the 'seed-time' (Fox) of Hermione's pregnancy.

The bantering exchange between Hermione and Polixenes indicates a nostalgia, on Polixenes's side, for a time without the kinds of *kairoi*, or

---

14 See Frank Kermode, *The Sense of an Ending: Studies in the Theory of Fiction* (Oxford, 2000), pp. 35–64. Kermode does note that the interpretation he adopts of New Testament usage of 'chronos' and 'kairos' is controversial, pp. 48–9.

15 John Fox, *Time and The End of Time, in two discourses: The first on redemption of time, the second on the consideration of our latter end* (London, 1670).

16 Julia Kristeva, 'Women's Time', in *Feminisms: An Anthology of Literary Theory and Criticism*, eds. Robyn R. Warhol and Diane Price Herndl (New Brunswick, 1997), p. 863.

17 Gail Kern Paster has a slightly different reading of this moment: 'Leontes may imprison Hermione and disenfranchise her, but once her labor has begun he cannot prevent the prison from being resconstituted as a birthing chamber or the delivery of Hermione's baby from taking place' (p. 270). Paster's emphasis is on the power of the female space to reconstitute itself, even in prison, while I emphasize the irresistible power of time to bring forth 'issue'.

determining moments, with which we are concerned here: without, that is, births, departures, deaths, beginnings and endings of any kind. He says of his youthful association with Leontes: 'We were, fair Queen, / Two lads that thought there was no more behind / But such a day tomorrow as today, / And to be boy eternal' (1.2.63–6). A desire to be boy eternal is also a desire not to have fallen – into sin as into time:

> We were as twinned lambs that did frisk i'th' sun,
> And bleat the one at th'other. What we changed
> Was innocence for innocence. We knew not
> The doctrine of ill-doing, nor dreamed
> That any did. (1.2.69–73)

Polixenes is almost artless in his association of the fall from eternal boyishness with the intervention of women and sexuality into this male paradise:

> O my most sacred lady,
> Temptations have since then been born to's: for
> In those unfledged days was my wife a girl.
> Your precious self had then not crossed the eyes
> Of my young playfellow. (1.2.76–9)[18]

The implication of Polixenes's words is that the intrusion of women and sexuality into his boyhood friendship with Leontes has broken up eternal time and tripped them into mortal time. Tomorrow and tomorrow and tomorrow has given way to the time of plot, which, like the mortal life-span, is governed by the necessity of the end.[19] Hermione's powerful speech thus reinforces not only her potentially disruptive verbal power but also – and therefore – her intimate involvement in the movement of these two men from the 'timeless' era of childhood to the teleological time of adulthood.[20]

## 'A SAD TALE'S BEST FOR WINTER': TALE-TELLING AND THE SPACE OF CHILDHOOD

Leontes's violent separation of Mamillius and Hermione occurs just as Mamillius settles down to whisper his winter's tale to his mother.

> HERMIONE Come, sir, now
> I am for you again. Pray you sit by us,
> And tell's a tale.
> MAMILLIUS Merry or sad shall't be?
> HERMIONE As merry as you will.
> MAMILLIUS A sad tale's best for winter. I have one
> Of sprites and goblins . . .
> HERMIONE Nay, come sit down, then on . . .
> MAMILLIUS I will tell it softly,
> Yond crickets shall not hear it.
> HERMIONE Come on then, and give't me in mine
> ear. (2.1.22–33)

The scene establishes a close verbal and physical intimacy between Mamillius and his mother, and it does so within a context of comfortable female banter ('giv't me in mine ear'). Mamillius teases and is teased by two ladies who wait on him, and his precocious replies suggest how carefully he has listened to their gossiping: 'You'll kiss me hard, and speak to me as if / I were a baby still' (2.1.6–7). Since Mamillius's name links him to the female breast, the scene seems to explore the origins of the male subject in an exclusively female environment in which physical nurture and tales are indivisibly linked.[21] When Mamillius begins, at

---

18 See Adelman, *Suffocating Mothers*, who argues that Hermione's pregnancy raises anxiety about original sin: 'Both in Polixenes's opening speech and in his pastoral myth, the sexualized female body is the sign of male separation and loss' (p. 221).

19 See Peter Brooks, 'Freud's Masterplot,' in *Reading for the Plot*.

20 For a discussion of the threat posed by the 'woman on top', see Natalie Zemon Davis, *Society and Culture in Early Modern France* (Stanford, 1975), and David E. Underdown, 'The Taming of the Scold: the Enforcement of Patriarchal Authority in Early Modern England', in *Order and Disorder in Early Modern England*, eds. Anthony Fletcher and John Stevenson (Cambridge, 1985), p. 116. Underdown notes that the period 1560–1660 seems to have seen a new focus on the perceived unruliness of women, an unruliness including scolding, witchcraft and sexual licence.

21 Paster, *The Body Embarrassed*, notes the etymology of Mamillius's name, arguing that Leontes identifies with Mamillius partly as a result of 'his memory of his own early displacement from the maternal body, activated by the little boy's imminent displacement from his exclusive relation to his mother and by the semiotic links to the breast in the little boy's name'

Hermione's suggestion, to whisper a 'sad tale' to her, then, he demonstrates again how well he has absorbed the nourishment available in this female environment.[22] It is Leontes who sees the analogy between this whispered tale and the intimacy of nursing: 'Give me the boy. I am glad you did not nurse him' (2.1.58). Although Hermione has apparently not nursed Mamillius, this whispered exchange of an old wives' tale is evidence enough of a contamination of the boy by female influence. If we look forward to Hermione's bitter assertion in the courtroom that Perdita is 'haled out to murder' with '[t]he innocent milk still in it most innocent mouth' (3.2.100–1), we seem to see a recreation of that moment of interrupted nursing here, though this time the violence is against the oral tradition of women's narrative. Later, Mamillius's decline is described as the decline of one deprived of nourishment: 'He straight declined, drooped, took it deeply . . . / Threw off his spirit, his appetite, his sleep, / And downright languished' (2.3.14–16). Leontes has short-circuited the fruitful exchange between his wife and child by contaminating the 'innocent milk' of their colloquy.[23]

The contrast could not be clearer between the quiet intimacy of this female colloquy in which Mamillius, to his father's distaste, still participates, and the rude interruption of Leontes's too-public clamour. When Leontes and his circle burst into the scene we feel the sudden presence of a violent, or potentially violent, male power. Leontes has already indicated that the passage from boyhood to manhood is marked by the 'unmuzzling' of the phallic dagger: looking at his son's face, Leontes earlier remembers himself as a boy, 'my dagger muzzled, / Lest it should bite its master, and so prove, / As ornament oft does, too dangerous' (1.2.158–60). As Lamb points out, this image implies that since that time 'his masculinity, as represented by his now unmuzzled dagger/phallus, has become able to bite its master' (p. 534). Leontes's attack on Hermione, which appears to be an act of self-defence at first, of course becomes a kind of self-castration, as he causes the death of his first-born and the apparent death of his new baby. The weapon in question, though, is not any physical dagger but the rhetoric of sexual slander. When Paulina accuses Leontes of making himself scandalous, she invokes an image of slander as a kind of sword:

> for he,
> The sacred honour of himself, his queen's,
> His hopeful son's, his babe's, betrays to slander,
> Whose sting is sharper than the sword's
> (2.3.84–7).[24]

The circle created by the telling of a winter's tale is imagined as a vulnerable arena of safety, nourishment and care-taking that is torn apart by the male discourse of slander.

Interestingly, the earliest instances of literary versions of 'old wives' tales' emphasize the apotropaic capacity of the tale, as though these tales have always been imagined within a threatening context.[25] Apuleius, for instance, though aware that the 'fabula anilis' (old woman's tale) occupies the lowest rung on the ladder of literary genres, nevertheless gives to the old woman in the robbers' cave the powerful, luminous tale of Cupid and Psyche. In this episode, the old woman tells the story to a princess who is taken captive by dangerous robbers. The story is told to distract the

(p. 265). Though this reading certainly makes sense of the earlier scenes of the play, the interrupted tale-telling scene suggests that Leontes's primary relation to Mamillius at this point is jealousy, jealousy in particular of the physical intimacy present in this scene.

22 Though she does not note the scene's symbolic association of nursing and tale-telling, Mary Ellen Lamb does comment that the 'flight from the feminine' – including the feminine sphere of 'old wives' tales' – 'became a flight from corporeality itself' ('Engendering the Narrative Act', p. 530).

23 See Peter Erickson's useful account of the importance of nourishment in the play: *Patriarchal Structures in Shakespeare's Drama* (Berkeley, 1985).

24 M. Lindsay Kaplan and Katherine Eggert also note that it is self-destructiveness once again that is at issue here, as well as aggression toward others: 'Strikingly, [Paulina] focuses on the fact that his accusations harm not only his wife and children, but his own honor. The slander against Hermione transforms into self-slander' (106). See their essay "Good queen, my lord, good queen": Sexual Slander and the Trials of Female Authority in *The Winter's Tale*', in *Renaissance Drama, New Series*, 24 (1994), 89–118.

25 Scheherezade's stories in the *Arabian Nights*, for instance, actually save her from death.

princess rather than through any altruistic concern on the part of the old woman, yet the tale itself seems to create a space of safety around the princess while she listens. In George Peele's *The Old Wives Tale*, Gammer Madge says: 'I am content to drive away the time with an old wives winter's tale' (99). But her tale is interrupted by the unlooked for (and potentially dangerous) arrival of the tale's characters themselves: '*Madge*. God's me bones! Who comes here? / *Frolic*. Soft, Gammer, here some come to tell your tale for you' (121). Arguing that Shakespeare may have derived his title and other details of his play from Peele's play, Philip Edwards speculates that Shakespeare may remember Madge's interrupted tale when he has 'Leontes, the real-life man of winter, [storm] in'.[26] In any case, the broken tale in Shakespeare's play reveals even more clearly that the action of tale-telling performs an apotropaic function. The 'tale of winter,' according to Mamillius's playful introductory remarks, concerns churchyards, sprites and goblins: it is, in other words, a tale about fear and death, safely contained within the intimate safety of the mother–child dyad in which he tells his tale. With Leontes's violent irruption into this space, fear and death become real presences within the play. His violence against the tale seems to work its evil not only by splitting open the fictional frame of the tale, but more specifically by disrupting the relation between *chronos* and *kairos* implied by the juxtaposition of the tale of death with the body of the heavily pregnant Hermione. By attacking female sexuality in the body of the mother, Leontes's slander spills the seeds of what John Fox calls 'seasonal time' (or *kairos*) prematurely, prompting both the untimely birth of Hermione's baby (she 'is, something before her time, delivered', 2.2.28) and the death of Mamillius.

## 'SHE HATH BEEN PUBLICLY ACCUSED'

The destructiveness of sexual slander appears to depend in part on its public nature. When Leontes bursts in to break the circle of female colloquy that includes his son, he interrupts a private domestic scene with public defamation. As Lisa Jardine has noted in relation to Othello's act of calling Desdemona 'whore', the accusation of whoredom 'audiently' pronounced has a cultural and legal force that dramatizes the real vulnerability of women to the kind of violent 'phallic discourse' invoked by Paulina.[27] Leontes makes sure his followers are listening to his accusation, turning them into witnesses for the prosecution:

> You, my lords,
> Look on her, mark her well. Be but about
> To say she is a goodly lady, and
> The justice of your hearts will thereto add
> ''Tis pity she's not honest, honourable.'
> . . . But be't known
> From him that has most cause to grieve it should be,
> She's an adultress. (2.1.66–80)

Hermione herself protests what she calls Leontes's 'publication' of her: 'How will this grieve you / When you shall come to clearer knowledge, that / You thus have published me?' (2.1.98–100). The use of the word 'published' recalls another woman wounded by male discourse: Lucrece. The praise of Lucrece that her husband Collatine so unwisely utters in Tarquin's hearing makes him her 'publisher': 'Or why is Collatine the publisher / Of that rich jewel he should keep unknown / From thievish ears, because it is his own?' (*Rape of Lucrece*, 33–5). Collatine's 'rich jewel' is in one sense Lucrece's beauty, which he praises; but in another sense it is her chaste sexuality, which should be 'kept unknown'. In thus *publishing* her sexuality Collatine becomes the unwitting accessory to

[26] Philip Edwards, '"Seeing is believing": action and narration in *The Old Wives Tale* and *The Winter's Tale*', in *Shakespeare and his Contemporaries: Essays in Comparison*, ed. E. A. J. Honigmann (Manchester, 1986), p. 79.

[27] Lisa Jardine discusses the crucial difference that publicity makes to a slander against a woman's sexual integrity: defamation 'audiently' uttered becomes an event which the woman ignores at her peril. See Jardine, '"Why should he call her whore?": Defamation and Desdemona's Case,' in *Addressing Frank Kermode: Essays in Criticism and Interpretation*, eds. Margaret Tudeau-Clayton and Martin Warner (Urbana, 1991), p. 138.

Tarquin's rape.[28] In publishing Hermione in such brutal terms ('she's / A bed-swerver, even as bad as those / That vulgars give bold'st titles', 2.1.94–6), Leontes participates in the kind of sexualized, misogynistic discourse that prefigures Tarquin's actual rape.

Hermione also poignantly mourns the violation of her privacy in the court scene. Women recovering from childbirth traditionally enjoyed a 'green month' in which they rested and regained their strength. This period of sequestration and recovery came to a ceremonial close with the 'churching ceremony', in which the woman, accompanied by her midwife and female 'gossips', processed to the church to be blessed. In dragging Hermione into court to defend herself before the end of her 'green month', Leontes has once again forced her into the public arena as an explicitly sexual woman: motherhood is rewritten as adultery.[29] She is, as she herself recognizes,

> on every post
> Proclaimed a strumpet, with immodest hatred
> The childbed privilege denied, which 'longs
> To women of all fashion; lastly, hurried
> Here, to this place, i'th' open air, before
> I have got strength of limit. (3.2.100–5).

As M. Lindsay Kaplan and Katherine Eggert show in their essay on slander in *The Winter's Tale*, slander against women in the early modern period was predominantly of a sexual nature, suggesting that it was women's sexuality itself that was considered to be a threat to social stability.[30] Leontes's transformation of Hermione's rhetorical authority into evidence of sexual promiscuity certainly supports the notion that 'anxiety about female sexuality might be considered a displaced version of anxiety about female authority' (p. 90).[31] The focus of concern was of course on the legitimacy of the heir, and this is also one of Leontes's central concerns. But as Kaplan and Eggert emphasize, the play indicates not that defamation of women acts as a useful constraint on women's unruly sexuality but rather that it delegitimizes rightful heirs and thus radically undermines social continuity.[32] Indeed in the court scene, Shakespeare indicates a direct – almost magical – connection between sexual slander and the destruction of lineage. Mamillius seemingly dies as direct result of Leontes's obtuse refusal to believe in his wife's innocence even after the oracle is pronounced. In attacking (and 'publishing') his wife's sexuality, Leontes also attacks the generative process of time that both the time of pregnancy and the narrative structure of old tales represent. He is, as Stanley Cavell remarks after Nietzsche, attempting to take revenge on time and its 'it was'.[33] If the 'old wives' tale' writes childbirth and death into a single, cyclical tale, the unconscious goal of Leontes's slander seems to be to ensure that he will not see his power pass from himself to his son. And in interrupting the 'tale of winter' with a slanderous story of sexual misconduct, he performs on himself the kind of self-destruction later envisaged by Florizel:

> then
> Let nature crush the sides o'th' earth together
> And mar the seeds within! Lift up thy looks.
> From my succession wipe me, father!
> (4.4.477–80).[34]

---

[28] See Nancy Vickers, 'The Blazon of Sweet Beauty's Best: Shakespeare's Lucrece', in *Shakespeare and the Question of Theory*, eds. Patricia Parker and Geoffrey Hartman (Cambridge, MA, 1994). Vickers extensively discusses the ramifications of the use of the word 'publish' in this poem.

[29] For a discussion of this travesty of the churching ceremony, see Paster, *The Body Embarrassed*, p. 272.

[30] M. Lindsay Kaplan and Katherine Eggert, '"Good Queen, my lord, good queen"', pp. 89–119.

[31] See also Underdown, 'The Taming of the Scold', and J. A. Sharpe, 'Defamation and sexual slander in early modern England: the church courts at York', Borthwick Papers no. 58 (York, 1980).

[32] 'Breaking the link between women's authority and the sexual malfeasance, however, requires *The Winter's Tale* to represent slanders against women, such as the imputation of scolding, as crimes with negative consequences for the social order, a representation that runs counter to most legal understandings of the problem in early modern England.' Kaplan and Eggert, 'Sexual Slander,' p. 105.

[33] Stanley Cavell, *Disowning Knowledge in Six Plays of Shakespeare* (Cambridge, 1987): 'Nietzsche spotted us taking revenge on Time, Time and its "it was"' (p. 211).

[34] Kaplan and Eggert quote this passage in support of their own argument that Leontes's slanders 'have serious consequences

## MISTRESS TALEPORTER: MIDWIFERY AND TRUTH

The nexus of issues we have been considering thus far comes into focus in the figure of the aptly named *Mistress Taleporter*, who appears in Autolycus's humorous but not senseless recasting of the play's major themes to guarantee the truth of his story of monstrous birth. During the sheep-shearing festival, Autolycus relates a tale from a ballad about 'how a usurer's wife was brought to bed of twenty money-bags at a burden' (4.4.260–2). When the credulous Mopsa asks, 'Is it true, think you?' (4.4.264), Autolycus tellingly replies: 'Here's the midwife's name to't, one Mistress Taleporter, and five or six honest wives that were present. Why should I carry lies abroad?' (4.4.267–9). As her name indicates, Mistress Taleporter is, in addition to being a midwife, also a tale-bearer, facilitating the production of *issue* in both literary and physical contexts. Despite the frivolity of the context here, the theme of midwifery is far from frivolous, since the apparently trivial figure of Mistress Taleporter has a far more important alter ego in the person of Paulina, whose maieutic role in the play will finally make sense of the various 'issues' I have been tracing here. But before turning to Paulina's actual role in the play we should consider how the figure of the midwife might have been regarded by Shakespeare's audience.

Autolycus's words give us some idea: 'Here's the midwife's name to't, one Mistress Tail-Porter', (4.4.267–8). The use of a midwife's name to guarantee the truth of the offspring is well attested in contemporary documents: not only did the midwife assist at the birth of the offspring but she also gave a sworn deposition as to the identity of the father. The power of the midwife in this and other matters is revealed by a number of the strictures contained in the oath administered before licensing: 'yee shall neither cause nor suffer any woman to name, or put any other Father to the Childe, who is not indeed; neither to claime any other womans Childe for her owne'; and 'you shall not in any wise use or exercise any manner of Witchcraft, Charme; or Sorcery, Invocation, or other Prayers than may stand with Gods Laws and the Kings'.[35] I pull these two examples out of the oath because they both reveal a fear of the power of the midwife, who does after all preside over the very threshold of life, a threshold characterized by mystery and superstition, as the barest glance at contemporary midwifery manuals reveals.[36] The mystery of birth was certainly enhanced by the fact that this was an exclusively female event; it was rare, except in emergencies, for a male surgeon ever to attend the birth, and the woman's attendants (or her 'gossips') were all female.[37]

The midwife's 'tale', then, bore witness not only to her special authority and knowledge, but also to the secrecy of the events in the birthing chamber. We might understand Leontes's furious 'publication' of his wife's supposed sexual misdemeanours as a deliberate infraction of these rules of secrecy, an attempt to displace this female, secret discourse with a male, public one. Similarly, since one of the midwife's tasks was to attest to the identity of the baby's father, Leontes's proleptic certainty that the baby is not his seems once again to set itself against the voice of the midwife. In Milton's reworking of the *veritas filia temporis* motto, the figure of the midwife is directly identified with Time (Time the midwife). Leontes's resistance to the work of the midwife – most clearly undertaken by Paulina, who brings his child to him from the prison – also represents a refusal to accept the passing of time. His much later acceptance of the magically revived Hermione explicitly addresses this earlier refusal. Remarking that Hermione was 'not so much wrinkled, nothing / So agèd as this seems'

---

for his own reputation, his happiness, and the stability of his rule' (p. 106). In his case and in Polixenes's case (who slanders Perdita), they argue that 'sexual slanders against women are shown to pose dangerous national consequences' (p. 106).

35 Quoted in Thomas Rogers Forbes, *The Midwife and the Witch* (New Haven, 1966), p. 146.

36 See for example Thomas Raynalde, *The Byrth of Mankynd: Otherwise Named the Womans Booke*, 1545.

37 See Paster's excellent discussion of the conditions of childbirth in the early modern period, *The Body Embarrassed*, pp. 185–200. Paster also reads Paulina as symbolically fulfilling the function of the midwife, p. 271.

(5.3.28–9), Leontes seems at first to have learned little through his suffering. But Paulina points out that these wrinkles merely testify to 'the carver's excellence, / Which lets go by some sixteen years, and makes her / As she lived now' (5.3.30–2). Leontes's response to this rebuke represents the culmination of his transformation: 'As now she might have done, / So much to my good comfort as it is / Now piercing to my soul' (3.3.32–4).

The notion that Paulina is to be understood as a midwife figure is supported by Leontes's own furious accusations. Berating Antigonus for being unable to control his wife, Leontes says 'You, sir, come you hither, / You that have been so tenderly officious / With Lady Margery your midwife there' (2.3.158–60).[38] Paulina's words when she hands Perdita over to Leontes follow quite closely the traditional words accompanying the midwife's ritualized transmission of the child to the father; she says, 'The good queen – / For she is good – hath brought you forth a daughter – / Here 'tis – commends it to your blessing' (2.3.65–7), and this is clearly a rendering of the midwife's usual words: 'Father, see there is your child, god give you much joy with it, or take it speedily to his bliss'.[39] Paulina has brought the baby to him, swearing that it is his own, and thus fulfilling the midwife's most important and potentially most controversial social function: she ritually reasserts, and thus gives legitimacy to, the mother's claim as to the baby's parentage. Leontes's rage explodes most violently at this point, as though he is responding to precisely this specifically female social power: 'Out! / A mankind witch! Hence with her, out o'door – / A most intelligencing bawd' (2.3.67–9).

In speaking out strongly for Hermione, as she does at her own peril, Paulina fits into the conventional role of the 'gossip': a woman's female friends, known as her gossips, attended during her lying-in and were popularly rendered as vociferous in their denunciations of the husband's meanness, cruelty etc.[40] But Shakespeare's portrayal of Paulina differs crucially from these popular portrayals of scolding, gossiping women in that she is presented as both dangerously vociferous and *right*. Similarly, although many satirical treatises reflected male fear of female power during the time of childbirth, Leontes's power struggle in this scene is clearly pitifully misguided and self-destructive.[41]

If Paulina acts as a midwife in bringing the child to its father and guaranteeing its parentage, Antigonus, her husband, seems to become her opposite number. He is Leontes's servant, as Paulina is Hermione's, and if Paulina is midwife to Hermione and to the time she embodies, Antigonus becomes, albeit against his will, Leontes's representative as slanderous destroyer of time's natural course. His name means 'against life/creation', and he delivers Perdita to a supposed death just as Paulina tried to deliver her to life. Hermione, indeed, calls him the 'thrower-out /

---

38 This little scene between Leontes and Antigonus illustrates clearly David Underdown's contention that husbands of transgressing wives were as much the targets of social opprobrium as their wives, for not adequately controlling them. Describing a typical shaming ritual, Underdown writes: 'a rough-music procession headed by a drummer and a man wearing horns; the enlisting of the next-door neighbours as surrogates for the offending couple; the acting-out of the proscribed behaviour by the "husband" riding backwards on horse or donkey and holding a distaff, the symbol of female subjection, while the "wife" (usually a man in woman's clothes) beats him with a ladle. The husband, it should again be stressed, is as much the subject of disapproval – for tolerating the offence – as the "wife". Underdown, 'The Taming of the Scold', p. 128.

39 Quoted in David Cressy, *Birth, Marriage and Death: Ritual, Religion, and the Life-Cycle in Tudor and Stuart England* (Oxford, 1997), p. 62.

40 See particularly *The Batchelars Banquet* (London: For R. Bird, 1601), chapter 3.

41 See also, for example, Thomas Gataker's *Marriage Duties Briefly Couched Togither*, published in 1620, which makes clear its author's belief that 'a mankind woman or masterly wife is even a monster in nature', 9–10. See Linda Woodbridge, *Women and the English Renaissance: Literature and the Nature of Womankind, 1540–1620* (Brighton, 1984) for a full discussion of these matters. Kaplan and Eggert make a similar point about the play's revision of contemporary associations between verbal and sexual transgression: '*The Winter's Tale* explicitly counters this nexus, within the context of a recuperation of Elizabeth's heritage and authority, by showing female outspokenness as compatible with and appropriate to female virtue and chastity, linking instead male speech with shame and the disruption of patriarchal succession.' 'Sexual Slander', p. 104.

Of my poor babe' (3.3.28–9), and it is for this ill-deed that he himself must die. He also slanders Hermione (though not maliciously) by interpreting his dream of her as evidence that she did in fact have an affair with Polixenes and produce an illegitimate child. Even the means of his death fits into the pattern in which time is either embraced or rejected; the bear which rushes onstage and 'dines' on Antigonus seems to embody the Ovidian concept of devouring time, 'tempus edax'. This would also dramatize, in a humorously literal way, the notion that we are about to 'devour' sixteen years in 'one self-born hour'. Antigonus's implausible death is the onstage emblem of the overtly implausible passing of time necessitated by the shift into the marvellous realm of romance.

Exclusion from the scene of birth, like dependence on an 'old tale' rather than 'ocular proof' of events, tends to engender a fearful and/or sceptical response in the husband/hearer. The birth we have not seen may be monstrous; the tale we have only heard is probably untrue. The redemption of lost truth, in the person of Perdita, happens offstage and is reported by the courtiers in terms reminiscent of the original debate between Paulina and Leontes as to the 'truth' of her parentage: 'This news which is called true is so like an old tale that the verity of it is in strong suspicion' (5.2.27–9). The 'news which is called true', is the lost daughter, whose true name is revealed only now, when the 'argument of Time' has worked its magic. She is the lost truth (veritas) of the *veritas filia temporis* motto, abandoned when Leontes sets his face against the truth of Hermione's maternity. Like the birth of Perdita herself, the 'verity' of this tale is scarcely believable. But the kind of old wives' tale with which Shakespeare is concerned here is the tale of the midwife Mistress Taleporter, who assists at the mystery of birth and reports what she sees to a sceptical and fearful male world. The final scene of the play represents an initiation of Leontes into the mysterious female rites surrounding birth; simultaneously, the matter of the scene, worthy as Paulina says of 'an old tale', will dramatize the transformation of the old wives' tale into the stuff of romance.[42] Naturally enough it is Paulina, the midwife, witch, and 'intelligencing bawd' who presides over these rites of initiation and brings the 'statue' into life.

## 'WOMEN'S MATTERS': THE END OF THE TALE

The *veritas filia temporis* motto on a woodcut from William Marshall's *Goodly Prymer in Englyshe*, 1535, is accompanied by the legend from Matthew 10: 'Nothyng is covered that shall not be discovered'.[43] Paulina's actions in the final scene of the play as she gradually reveals to an astonished audience that Hermione still lives may certainly be understood as facilitating the 'discovery' of truth to the world of the play. But a necessary condition of this resolution is the initiation of Leontes into the female mystery he has so far rejected and the symbolic answering of the slander levelled at Hermione in the court scene. In order that our play *The Winter's Tale* may come to a close, the tale of winter interrupted by Leontes must be taken up and completed. The play's closing scene of animation and thanksgiving stands in for the churching ceremony that never took place, but it also brings Mamillius's *sad tale* of winter to a close, and in doing so returns the mother to the centre of the family circle from which she was abruptly taken when the tale was interrupted.[44]

If the female rituals of 'churching' and 'tale-telling' are symbolically connected in the final

[42] Mary Ellen Lamb also notes the use of the statue scene as a metaphor for the creation of theatre from old tales: 'it is this statue scene, often associated with the power of the playwright, which makes of this play a "winter's tale"' ('Engendering the Narrative Act', p. 536). What is important for me about this claim, though, is that it represents Leontes's initiation into the *time* of the tale, which is what Fox calls 'seasonal time', the time of ends and beginnings, and the time of *romance*.

[43] See Saxl, p. 203.

[44] The notion that this final scene may be understood as a reminder of the churching scene is noted by Paster: 'the ritualistic character of her unveiling symbolizes its function as a reminder of the churching ceremony that Leontes's trial prevented; accompanied by her gossips, the woman to be churched entered under a white veil'. *The Body Embarrassed*, p. 278.

scene, it will be useful to consider briefly how these rites combine to form the miraculous ending that is characteristic of Shakespeare's romances. A 1601 text written as a dialogue between a 'chancellor' and a kinswoman concerning the validity of churching tells us something of the conduct of the ceremony and thus indicates how Shakespeare's hints of this ritual might work in the play.[45] The woman remarks: 'neither the husband must joyne with his wife, nor the father with his daughter, nor the sonne with his mother, nor the brother with his sister', and the Chancellor says of the participants: 'It is fittest that they onely that were by the woman in her anguish and travell, should be by her also at her Thanksgiving. *What a Devill should men medle with womens matters* ?' (italics mine). The midwife, we learn elsewhere, will be the principal support to the wife during the ceremony, and certainly Paulina, as midwife, is the central figure here, presenting Hermione to Leontes as she had sixteen years earlier attempted to present Perdita. But the company surrounding Hermione is patently not that present at the birth of Perdita; these *women's matters* are now attended by the most significant male figures in the play as well as a group of lords and attendants, and, in spite of the injunction that 'the husband must [not] joyne with his wife', it is Leontes's joining with his wife (his renewed wooing of her) that immediately precedes the blessing of Perdita and the final resolution of the oracle ('Turn, good lady, / Our Perdita is found', 5.3.121–2). In the closing scene of the play, Shakespeare has transfigured the churching ceremony, which apparently emphasized a separation between the sexes mirroring that enforced at the birth itself, in order to re-establish the marital intimacy threatened, precisely, by the fact of childbirth.

The coming together of both sexes around the mother coincides with the entry of Leontes into the space of tale-telling that he hitherto vigorously rejected. The lords who attend on Leontes are now not set apart as witnesses against Hermione, but included in the rapt audience who listen to Paulina, now fully in her role as a *Mistress Tale-porter*. Following a scene that is dense with references to 'old tale[s]' (5.2.27–9; 5.2.61–3), we experience the entry into Paulina's chapel as an entry into the space of the lost 'tale of winter'. The broken creativity of the tale-telling scene is at least partly restored here, as Leontes acknowledges what he could not acknowledge before: the legitimate association between women's art and women's nurture: 'If this be magic, let it be an art / Lawful as eating' (5.3.110–11).[46] The creativity of this scene is also directly associated, as it is in the earlier tale-telling scene, with the generative power of time. Paulina's first words to Hermione, the words that call her into life, are surely not coincidentally also words that invoke the power of time: ''Tis time. Descend. Be stone no more. Approach. / Strike all that look upon with marvel' (5.3.99–100). Paulina's authoritative ''tis time' is an assertion of power over time, or more precisely of an ability to control the transition from *chronos* to *kairos* that we considered earlier. For her spiriting away of Hermione, and the consequent freezing of the winter prevailing in Sicilia, amount to a control over precisely the plotting of time that so incensed Leontes at the start of the play. In the statue scene Leontes confronts, and acknowledges, the irresistible mechanics of time: it is time that brings forth children, time that brings death, time that 'makes and unfolds error' (4.1.2) in the plots of plays and lives.

Invoked by Paulina, Hermione returns like the characters in Madge's 'old tale' who suddenly come to life and take over the scene. As Lamb argues, the power of old tales merges with the power of the playwright just when the play signals most clearly its movement toward comic (or romance) resolution:

---

45 *Certaine Questions by way of Conference betwixt a Chancelor and a Kinswoman of his concerning Churching of women* (London, 1601).

46 Paster, *The Body Embarrassed*, comments ruefully: 'eating in hunger is now safe only because the threat represented by Hermione's too-present maternity no longer obtains' (p. 278). But if we read this scene as a direct response to the interrupted tale scene, this line can be understood as an acknowledgement of the wrong done to the maternal figure whose art and whose nurture are one.

'it is the miraculous unlikelihood of the last three acts in which *The Winter's Tale* most resembles the oral narratives of childhood' (p. 535). But it is not just the unlikelihood of these events that draw them, by association, into the sphere of childhood tales. The play's movement into the recuperative phase of romance is predicated on the repetition or renewal of the interrupted scene of tale-telling. When Paulina remarks that the revival of Hermione 'should be hooted at / Like an old tale' (5.3.117–18) in the absence of ocular proof, she prepares us to see Hermione's return to speech (as the definitive sign of life) as a return to the earlier scene in which a 'sad tale of winter' was left untold. And indeed when Hermione does speak, she seems to invite her daughter to tell her own tale; she is eager, she says, to 'see the issue':

> Tell me, mine own,
> Where hast thou been preserved? Where lived?
> How found
> Thy father's court? For thou shalt hear that I,
> Knowing by Paulina that the oracle
> Gave hope thou wast in being, have preserved
> Myself to see the issue. (5.3.124–30)

This speech seems to prepare the way for a mutual exchange of 'tales' – between mother and daughter – that will recall, and perhaps repair, the earlier tale whose violent interruption transformed its listeners into actors in its 'sad tale of winter'.

# SHAKESPEARE PERFORMANCES IN IRELAND, 2002–2004

JANET CLARE

In one of the final scenes of Frank McGuinness's *Mutabilitie* (1997) located in Ireland, there is a parting speech between William (Shakespeare) and the Irish Bard, the File, before William returns to London intending to make 'another crooked sixpence in a crooked house among men as crooked as myself'. The File (Gaelic for poet) is disillusioned with Shakespeare; this jobbing playwright is not the poet of her prophecies. Shakespeare has come to Ireland with his players, not to fulfil a romantic, nationalist role, but to act and 'live like Lords in Ireland'. McGuinness, with the added richness of national contexts, explores, as did Edward Bond in *Bingo*, a discrepancy between the identity of the writer and the art: 'I do exist but not as you imagine', claims William to File. The perplexing question of Shakespeare's identity – colonial and postcolonial – in Ireland frames *Mutabilitie*. Equally resonant is the clash of cultures epitomized in the contrast between the pragmatism of Shakespeare and the desperate, pessimistic romanticism of the File. Something of these issues underlies the performance of Shakespeare's plays in Ireland – and here my discussion is limited to the Republic. On the one hand, its national theatre, the Abbey, which last year celebrated its centenary, performs Shakespeare quite rarely. On the other hand, Shakespeare, while not compulsory, remains central to the school curriculum. There has been a strong tradition of amateur productions of Shakespeare, notably that of the Dublin Shakespeare Society, formerly the British Empire Shakespeare Society. However, the choice of text for large auditorium productions is largely dictated by the limited range of the school syllabus, since it is this that will guarantee an audience. When a professional Irish theatre company decides to do Shakespeare, other than for schools, it is faced with the task of making a creative discovery that is its own and interesting risks are often taken.

Whether the relationship between schools and theatres is working to the benefit of everyone concerned is a question articulated in the Irish press and on the boards of theatre companies. The exploration of Text and Performance is not a routine aspect of classroom practice, so the emphasis in production is very much on telling the story and on attempting to strike a chord with a young audience through the contemporary gloss of its design. The Second Age Theatre Company, as its name suggests, produces plays to attract school audiences and in the last two years there have been productions of three examination-prescribed texts, *Romeo and Juliet*, *Hamlet* and *Macbeth*. Again, as is frequently acknowledged, an audience largely comprised of school children can be as restless as the auditory Elizabethan and Jacobean playwrights occasionally complained about. Alan Stanford, one of the co-founders of the company in 1989, bravely elected to direct *Romeo and Juliet*, performed first at the Gaiety Theatre in Dublin in September 2002 and then in Cork and Athlone, with a Junior Certificate audience in mind. One of the outstanding features of this production was Bruno Schwengl's sharp, linear and versatile stage design. There was throughout the production an arresting visual focus on an uncluttered stage: a bed becomes a bier and a tomb; the balcony window the moon; a spire-like tree allows Romeo to scale the balcony to reach Juliet.

The Chorus was dispensed with and we are immediately drawn into a Verona where a church liturgy is murmuring in the background. This is ignored by the adolescents of the city. Eschewing the temptation to suggest a more contemporary Irish resonance of sectarian warfare, Stanford's production was notable for the extreme youthfulness of the young people of Verona. Youth and age were more sharply defined and opposed than that of family and lineage, so that Romeo and his friends were easily assimilated into and paired off at the Capulets' party. These young Montagues and Capulets (helpfully dressed in red and blue respectively) are bored by familial disputes (for them, they are indeed a plague on both houses); instead, they are absorbed by partying and their awakening desires, with an occasional, yet fatal, knee-jerk reaction to the festering and tedious feud of their elders. The problem was that the youthful actors approached their parts in naturalistic vein and spoke their lines at pace and with lack of enunciation, such that much of the meaning could only have been lost on the audience. The exceptions to this fear of eloquence were Michael Grennell's Prince and Merrina Millsap's nurse. Grennell's experience as a radio actor – he was a member of the Radio Eireann Players for four years – was apparent and the Prince's final pronouncement, taking in the survivors of the feud, carried a sobering authority often missed if we are left with the impression only of the play's final couplet.

Second Age also produced two productions of *Macbeth* during the period of this review to cater for the Leaving Certificate syllabus. The first was performed in November 2002, directed by Alan Stanford, while the second was an interesting collaboration between Second Age and the Theatreworks (now Ouroboros) company directed by Michael Craven. Theatreworks in the past has produced a dramatization of *Venus and Adonis*, Ted Hughes's *Tales from Ovid* and the first-ever Irish production of *Troilus and Cressida*. The company states that its artistic policy is to choose texts that 'tell epic and transforming tales of the profundity of the human spirit'. The transformations wrought in *Macbeth* are of course hideous in their spiralling destructiveness. To underscore this, the production exploited stage images to disturbing effect. Its visual focus was the crib, which also served as a cauldron for the bearded male witches, set behind an oriental style transparent screen. The crib is empty when Lady Macbeth refers to having given suck and Macbeth reaches over to comfort her. Entering the Macduffs' castle, one of the murderers rocks it before murdering the baby in it and the crib is again spotlit when Fleance escapes from Banquo's murderers. Altogether, this was a suggestive and intelligently directed production which captured well the precipitate, elided action of the play. Macbeth is silhouetted on the screen crowned at Scone while the thanes articulate their unease at his rise to power. Banquo's body is left on the stage to rise as the ghost at Macbeth's feast and throw it into disarray. Visual images were resonant. Olwen Fouère as Lady Macbeth crouched over a burner, the flames lightening up her face as she read and registered the contents of Macbeth's letter. As if to emphasize the Macbeths' nightmarish collapse, Denis Conway's Macbeth knelt in the same spot with the same lighting effects as when he had snatched at the air to grasp the imagined dagger. Fouère recaptured her earlier pose and posture as, in her sleepwalking, she knelt to wash her hands obsessively. Possibly one is being over-ingenious in suggesting a comic conceit of the desperate wish of Macbeth and Lady Macbeth to wash away their crime when the porter enters with a mop and bucket and mops the stage as he improvises his role at hell's gate.

Theatre venues in Dublin can certainly test the physical resources and resourcefulness of a company. Second Age's production of *Hamlet*, directed by Alan Stanford, was performed in January 2004 at the SFX City Theatre, a comfortless and cavernous space, formerly a community hall. Again, the production had the Leaving Certificate audiences in mind. The cast, one learned, had read John Updike's *Gertrude and Claudius* and there was something of this – and Updike's acknowledged influence, Wilson Knight's 'Embassy of Death' essay in *The Wheel of Fire* – in a production that was quick-paced and narrative driven. The ghost with

11 *Hamlet*. Second Age, dir. Alan Stanford, SFX City Theatre, Dublin, 2004. Simon Coury as Claudius, Helene Montague as Gertrude and Rory Keenan as Hamlet.

his impossible demand was the malign force in Stanford's interpretation; Old Hamlet was vindictive rather than sorrowing. Simon Coury as Claudius gave the impression of a sensible, rational, balanced king, always solicitous about Gertrude. The covert glances between Helene Montague's Gertrude and Coury's Claudius indicated that this was a couple with a past. The Elsinore court approved of their new monarch, closing ranks behind him, embarrassed by Hamlet's mocking, disruptive, adolescent behaviour. When Hamlet remarked to Guildenstern that 'The king is a thing', Guildenstern's incredulous, angered response 'A thing, my lord?' (4.2.28) more than compensated for the earlier cut of Rosencrantz's 'cess of majesty' speech. If Rory Keenan failed to evince the full emotional register of Hamlet, he did convey the sense that it is only through bantering humour that Hamlet can retain any sanity. This supposition dominated in the graveyard where the ironic matter of fact tones of the gravediggers were matched by that of Hamlet. As Fintan O'Toole pointed out in an *Irish Times* article 'The playwright for the globe', Irish actors such as Charles Macklin, Spranger Barry and Peg Woffington, by demonstrating that Shakespeare's lines could be delivered with a natural tone, have helped to shape the theatrical legacy of Shakespeare. It is a pity then that there is some tendency in Irish Shakespeare for comic parts to be played as 'Irish'. The gravediggers, ponderously eating their sandwiches and drinking tea from their flasks while speaking with a working-class Dublin accent, wonderfully convey how firmly rooted these characters are in everyday life, as well as perpetuating the stereotype of the stage Irishman. Yet another kind of stage Irishman gave subtle humour to this production. Barry McGovern, celebrated for his acting of Beckett, presented a Polonius unswervingly loyal to his monarch, so uncomprehendingly unfeeling toward Ophelia as to be bleakly comic and enjoying every officious moment as Elsinore's chief minister.

Second Age Theatre Company work on a tight budget and there was nothing wasteful in this production. Alan Stanford directed and doubled as the ghost and the Player King, the latter an orotund Edwardian thespian with a stock of speeches at his disposal. As with the *Romeo and Juliet*, the stage set was simple and uncluttered, with plain high-backed chairs and table suggesting an impoverished Eastern European dictatorship and two rear doors enabling fluid entrances and exits. Considering the considerable cut to the part played by Fortinbras, the rationale for costuming Claudius, Polonius and the court in military kitsch with Hamlet and Horatio evidently representative of the young audience, was not, however, immediately apparent.

If Second Age's audience consisted predominantly of school pupils, the audience for the Birmingham Repertory visiting production of *Hamlet* at the Olympia, directed by Calixto Bieito, staged during the 2003 Dublin Theatre festival did not. Publicity carried warnings that this was a disturbing production, not suitable for children. Perhaps it is missing the point to ask for the rationale in Bieito's hybrid version with George Anton's drugged-up Hamlet and his rape of Ophelia, an incestuous Polonius and a glitzy 'good-time girl' Gertrude. The text was a neon-lit collage with the transposition of soliloquies ('To be or not to be' followed the death of Polonius), and Horatio singing his lines at the piano. 'Where is the tragedy?' one member of the audience was heard asking on leaving the theatre, and there was none. In this re-imagining of *Hamlet* misogyny and sexual abuse were, instead, the keynotes.

The small Peacock theatre, adjoining the Abbey, was the first venue for the Dublin Gate founded by Micheál MacLiammóir and Hilton Edwards in 1928. The Gate, founded to complement the Abbey by performing European and American drama, moved the following year to the Rotunda, while the Peacock has been used intermittently as a venue for some new writing commissioned by the national theatre as well as non-Irish theatre. In the late 1970s there were several notable Shakespeare productions directed by Patrick Mason. In the period of this review, there was one Shakespeare production at the Peacock, that of *Henry IV Part 1* in November 2002, commissioned by the national theatre and directed by Jimmy Fay, a former associate director of the Abbey. This was an edited version by the young Dublin playwright Mark O'Rowe, whose plays *Made in China* and *Howie the Rookie* are set among the violent streets of gangland Dublin and offer an almost exclusively male terrain. O'Rowe did some unobtrusive editing to produce a version of the play that looked and felt very macho. Niamh Linehan doubled as the two female parts, Mistress Quickly and Lady Percy, and demonstrated her versatility by playing Vernon as well. Tavern scenes were cut, notably Hal's guying of Francis, so that there was little sense of popular community in contradistinction to the court. Approaching theatre in the round, the set was reminiscent of the Royal National Theatre's production of *Richard II* with Fiona Shaw as the king. The stage was positioned between two facing blocks of seating with entrances and exits at each end and additional hatch entrances in use for the battle at Shrewsbury.

In the Peacock's small studio theatre *Henry IV* inevitably lost something of its panoramic scope as the play moved from court to tavern to the Percy camp. The loss of a sense of national epic was to some extent compensated for by intense focus on the male protagonists: ambition, rivalry and a jostling for power are starkly exposed. As the King, Nick Dunning probed the subtext of the opening address. Beginning on a note of world-weariness, his crown in his hands, the speech gathered force as he moved across stage, sat on the throne and put on the crown with a renewed sense of purpose at the prospect of his crusade. All the other characters spoke with local or regional accents. The second scene opened with Sean Kearns, a majestic rather than corpulent Falstaff, carrying a drunken Hal over his shoulder and then bantering in resonant Irish borderlands with his royal drinking companion. Falstaff's insecurity soon became apparent. When Hal reveals his presence at the Gadshill robbery and exposes all Falstaff's shenanigans, Kearns gave the longest pause I have heard before Falstaff's riposte; nervously sipping his beer, registering panic, he hit on his get-out clause, 'I knew you'. Consternation – real not feigned – greeted Hal's promise in the tavern charade to banish Falstaff. Tom Murphy's nasal, punkish Hal was not yet, though, entirely intent on rejecting Falstaff. He was happy enough to go along with Falstaff's preposterous claim to have killed Hotspur and there was felt generosity in his readiness after the battle of Shrewsbury to 'gild' Falstaff's lie. The production confidently rejected any stereotyping of the male protagonists. As Hotspur, Declan Conlon gave a wonderfully suggestive interpretation of a mind engaged elsewhere as he restlessly weighed up what history might deliver him. Conlon was no rash, latter-day chivalric hero, but, except when in the presence of his wife, a man brooding intensely on becoming king. Self-conscious forgetfulness seemed a condition of all-consuming ambition. It was with expressive and profound irritation that he greeted the correction that it was at Berkeley Castle not Ravenspurgh where he met Bolingbroke

(1.3.246) and also the thought, when he is with Mortimer and Glendower, that he has forgotten the map demonstrative of his ambition to divide the kingdom.

There have been two notable small theatre productions of Shakespeare, both attracting appreciative audiences, during the period of this review. *Twelfth Night*, directed by Donnacadh O'Briain, was performed by Natural Shocks in the tiny performance space of The Crypt in Dublin Castle during the 2002 Dublin Theatre Festival. The Crypt is darkened at the time of writing. In its considerable cutting, the production was textually irreverent and, inevitably, linearity was achieved at the cost of the play's tonal range. The duping of Malvolio was gone, along with any anti-puritan, anti-festive impulse, so that the production concentrated on cross-wooing and romantic excess. The cast, with help from Charles Lamb, prefaced each of the acts with a lively resume of events, anticipating audience incredulities in their knowing delivery. Gesturing toward commedia dell'arte in Chisato Yoshimi's vivid, non-realistic costume and in its mannered acting style, the production was fast-moving, accessible comedy without being disturbing. Since there was no revenge against Malvolio, there might seem little to ruffle the play's happy ending. The ending did, however, undermine the predominantly comic tone of the production in two suggestive visual details. Antonio was left alone, abandoned by the lovers, his hands still rope-bound until he is untied by Feste. Olivia's lingering farewell to Viola/Cesario, whom she must now call 'sister', suggested something of the sexual ambivalence which had been little developed in the performance overall. These were rare nuanced moments in a production which went for broad and, in the case of Myles Breen's Andrew Aguecheek in the mode of Kenneth Williams, camp comedy.

*Measure for Measure* was a bold choice for the small surburban community theatre The Loose End in Tallaght, Dublin, performed in October–November, 2002 (Rattlebag Theatre, directed by Joe Devlin). To set *Measure for Measure* in 1950s Ireland when Church and State had such a grip on the hearts and minds of the people might seem a predictable enough idea, but in Rattlebag Theatre's sparse production it was an inspired decision. The various locations of the play were simply differentiated by changing the hanging portraits: in Angelo's state room a portrait of a figure suggestive of Eamon de Valera and a picture of the Sacred Heart, in the convent the Virgin Mary and in the monastery one of the popes. Angelo and Isabella were no longer mirror images of characters theologically divided: she the noviate nun intent on greater, not lesser, restraint, he the abstemious puritan whose only concept of mercy is to execute a man to prevent further sin. Both were now representatives of a rigid, absolute Catholic morality. Waiting for Isabella to make her second appeal for her brother's life, Aidan Condron represented a distraught Angelo, on his knees saying the rosary, before angrily and despairingly throwing the rosary beads into the desk drawer. He wore a pioneer pin in his lapel (the Pioneer Association was a Catholic group for men only who took a vow of total abstinence from alcohol) and, in a play that for many in the audience would have been unfamiliar Shakespeare, this was a neat way of locating him. Isabel Claffey's Isabella was a young woman who had apparently always been destined for the convent; she voices a real moral abhorrence at Claudio's 'sin' and when Angelo implies that she is being morally lax in her attitude to her brother's 'vice', she painfully extenuates herself. All she knows is what she has been taught and unquestioningly imbibed. Claffey was moving in her encounters with Angelo, not because of impassioned flights of rhetoric, but through her unchallenging simplicity: until faced with the choice of saving her brother or her soul, morality has for her been fairly unproblematic. Throughout, Claffey accentuated Isabella's vulnerability, shocked as she is by the perfidious ways of men. First Angelo and then Claudio betray her trust. In the prison she sank into Claudio's arms, expecting that he will be resolute in facing death, but then, as his will weakened, she was overwhelmed by a sense of male depravity: 'Thy sin's not accidental, but a trade' are the words of a woman discovering the threatening aspect of

12 *All's Well That Ends Well.* Classic Stage Ireland, dir. Andy Hinds, Helix, Dublin, 2004. Bertram (Peter Gaynor) and Helena (Janet Moran).

male sexuality. It is no wonder then that she turned trustingly to the friar, eagerly grasping his hands as he offers a way out of a hideous situation that she can barely comprehend. It would have been interesting if she had seemingly rejected his overtures of marriage at the end of the play as yet another experience of male deceit and betrayal, but in one of the most unambiguous endings of the play I have seen, she appeared to accept his proposal happily. In apparently ironic counterpoint to his assertion that he has never been affected by love, John Murphy as the Duke betrayed his interest in Isabella from the moment he overheard the prison dialogue. Almost as buttoned-up as Angelo in the opening scene as friar, he also appeared almost as overwhelmed as Angelo by the power of his attractions.

Joe Devlin cut the parts of Pompey, Froth and Elbow, so that much discursive interplay about the underworld of Vienna was lost. But we lost no sense of the sexual licence of the city. The second scene shifted to the brothel, the walls of which displayed the same religious iconography as the previous state scene. The dialogue between Lucio and the gentlemen had gone, to be replaced by one between Mistress Overdone and Lucio, caught *in flagrante*. The dialogue was cleverly transposed so that Lucio's 'I have purchased as many diseases under [your] roof' became his opening words as he got up from the bed. To emphasize the hypocrisy of the city's rulers, one of the officers in attendance on Angelo was then seen entering the brothel, compensating for the omitted line about the preservation of the brothels in the city but not the suburbs: 'a wise burgher put in for them' (1.2. 92). Sean Duggan played Lucio with a touch of Christy Mahon of *Playboy of the Western World*, relishing every moment of his encounter with the friar and telling lie after lie about the Duke. This was a man

13 *All's Well That Ends Well*. Classic Stage Ireland, dir. Andy Hinds, Helix, Dublin, 2004. Stella McCusker as the Countess.

transgressive of authority, who would chance his arm while in the economy of the production he incorporated all that Pompey represents.

The final production of this review was the inaugural production of Classic Stage Ireland and the Irish premiere of *All's Well That Ends Well*, directed by Andy Hinds in June 2004 at the Helix, Ireland's newest arts centre, on the campus of Dublin City University. *All's Well* was a bold choice with which to inaugurate the company and Andy Hinds produced a wonderfully lucid and ungimmicky interpretation of the play. The key to the production was that all the characters evidently desire Bertram and are driven variously to worship, impress, manipulate or trap him. Peter Gaynor's immature Bertram, locked blindly into his hero worship of Parolles, is frantically trying to escape this attention. His panic is palpable when in the French court, Helena, making her choice of husband, proclaims 'This is the man' (2.3.105). The idea that Bertram has to undergo rites of passage before he is mature enough to reciprocate Helena's love and devotion leads to a denouement that is unambiguously celebratory. The general shiftiness which often seems the only way to play Bertram in the final scenes was not much in evidence in Gaynor's Bertram, as he called out urgently for pardon and gladly embraced his wife, whose pregnancy was scarcely visible. The production created a closure that was in mood anticipatory of the reunions and reconciliations of the last plays.

In Anne-Marie Wood's set, Roussillon is evidently a very devout place and this lent Helena's healing gifts a religious aspect. A Byzantine-like icon of Christ hung at the rear of the stage. Supernumerary nuns were constantly in attendance. The play opened on a ritualistic scene of mourning as the mourners gathered round the grave of Bertram's father and threw earth on it. There was a strong sense in the first scene of characters isolated by their private grief, capturing what the Countess alludes to as Helena's 'mystery' of loneliness. Janet Moran's Helena appeared abstracted as she tolerated Parolles's intrusive and mocking commentary. In Roussillon, Moran, her hair braided, resembled nothing but a gawky, awkward schoolgirl. She was transformed by a dawning awareness of her own autonomy over her fate and by the recognition of her power in curing the king. In 2.3, the contrast with her earlier self could not have been more marked as Moran entered dancing with the king in a court that no longer resembled a hospital ward. Stella McCusker's Countess too portrayed a woman slowly emerging from mourning. The first sign was when with the smartly suited Lavatch, played by the black actor John Jeffery Rolle, she sprang to life as she assumed momentarily the part of the fool in the mock question-and-answer game (2.2). There was an almost flirtatious quality in McCusker's delivery as she joked about being young again and as her agile movements interacted with those of Lavatch.

One hesitates before making so provocative a pronouncement that, of all the Shakespeares under review, Hinds's *All's Well* was 'more Shakespeare'. In its confidence and belief in the riddling text this was undoubtedly the case. It is impressive to find such an inadequately funded company devoting time to voice workshops and master classes. On the strength of their first Shakespeare production, Classic Stage Ireland represent a strong ensemble and, more importantly, signify that post-colonial Ireland can claim Shakespeare for itself, no longer deterred by a sense of his English 'otherness'.

# SHAKESPEARE PERFORMANCES IN ENGLAND, 2004

MICHAEL DOBSON

2004 was another year for grief, horror and distress in the English Shakespearian theatre in general, and in Stratford-upon-Avon in particular, but for once I can report that this was for all the right reasons. With Michael Boyd firmly established as the RSC's new artistic director, the company's ample helpings of doom and gloom were in 2004 mainly confined to its stages instead of permeating the entire organization, taking the form of an ambitious all-tragedy repertory season in a Royal Shakespeare Theatre reprieved from the threat of demolition and instead scheduled for a long-overdue internal remodelling of the auditorium. The spring and summer's *Macbeth*, *Romeo and Juliet*, *King Lear* and *Hamlet*, all of which transferred in turns to the Albery theatre in London during the winter 2004–5 season, were prefaced by a fine stand-alone *Othello* in the Swan (which itself transferred to a new venue, the Trafalgar Studios on Whitehall, in the early summer), and elsewhere too the tragedies were in special favour. Cheek by Jowl offered the year's other striking *Othello* (which spent most of the year touring the world, to close at the Riverside Studios in Hammersmith in December); the Globe presented their own *Romeo and Juliet*, and Vesturport's high-wire Icelandic *Romeo and Juliet* (described in the previous *Survey*) made a welcome return to London, this time to the Playhouse on Northumberland Avenue (and this time with special guest celebrity cameos). Meanwhile *Hamlet*, the play Michael Boyd had chosen for his first RSC production as artistic director, found itself receiving rival attentions from two longer-established heavyweights among directors: one of Boyd's forbears as head of the RSC, Trevor Nunn, perhaps mischievously, opened a *Hamlet* of his own at the Old Vic just a few weeks in advance of Boyd's Stratford press night, and later Yukio Ninagawa brought what was essentially a revival of his 1998 account of the play to the RSC's former auditorium at the Barbican, just between Boyd's production's Stratford run in the summer and its London transfer in the late autumn. *Macbeth* was in even greater demand, given a lacklustre, penny-plain studio revival by Shakespeare at the Tobacco Factory in the RSC's other forsaken London home, the Pit, and a much more engaging, promenade production by Out of Joint (on tour, at the Arcola theatre in Islington, and subsequently at the nearby Wilton's Music Hall), and yet another major London *Macbeth* went into rehearsal at the end of the year, for the Almeida company, with Simon Russell Beale in the title role and Emma Fielding as his Lady (scheduled to open in January 2005). So at least there will be some pleasant reasons too why the year which saw the re-election of George W. Bush as president of the United States may be remembered as a notable one for tragedy.

It's very striking how collective waves of feeling like this can run through the Shakespearian repertory: in this boom year for catharsis, for example, no one in England seemed remotely interested in the histories. The sole exception who proved the rule was Alan Strachan at Regent's Park, who directed what was surprisingly the Open-Air Theatre's first ever *Henry IV Part 1*: predictably in this setting the play turned primarily into a genial vehicle for Falstaff, ably played by Christopher Benjamin, and although Christopher Godwin as the King did what he could to keep the audience interested in matters of state the underpopulated battle scenes convinced few and Jordan Frieda's Hal fewer, and I imagine that Falstaff's next Regent's Park outing will be in *The Merry Wives of Windsor* as usual.

### COMEDIES

If history was displaced by tragedy in 2004, comedy was at very least coloured by it. Both of 2004's principal accounts of *Twelfth Night*, at the Albery and on the road with the English Touring Theatre respectively, found plenty for Illyria to be unhappy about, and a Nottingham Playhouse *The Tempest*, despite an old-fashioned desert island set that would have served perfectly well as a travel agent's window display, was memorable primarily for the sunless gloom of its Prospero, Clive Francis; elsewhere a touring *Merchant of Venice* by Northern Broadsides, similarly, was about as light on light relief as it could well have been. Despite the summer's accustomed cheerful crop of *A Midsummer Night's Dream*s, *Much Ado About Nothing*s and *Love's Labour's Lost*s the most important revivals in this genre were of the dark comedies themselves, *All's Well That Ends Well* and *Measure for Measure*. The former received a handsome Jacobean-dress RSC production, by Gregory Doran, which opened at the Swan in November 2003 and subsequently transferred for a sold-out run at the Gielgud, while the latter appeared in two contrasting incarnations on the South Bank in the summer, one at the Globe and the other, a National Theatre/Complicite co-production directed by Simon McBurney, at the Olivier auditorium of the National.

It makes sense to start with the *All's Well That Ends Well*, not only because it was the first of these comedies to open but because it was in some respects the most melancholy of them all, despite some not always well-judged directorial attempts to inject some extra jollity and comfort into this most austere, ironic and controlled of the problem plays. I've commented elsewhere in this volume on the production's determination to underline as heavily as possible the poignancy of what will

14 *All's Well That Ends Well*. RSC, dir. Gregory Doran, Swan Theatre, 2003. Judi Dench as the Countess.

probably be Dame Judi Dench's last stage appearance in a Shakespeare play, from her unscripted arrival in 1.1 in advance of the other characters onwards, and her performance as the Countess would undoubtedly have been extremely affecting even without the 'cello music which warned us to be prepared to be tastefully moved every time she appeared. It remains true, however, that the Countess isn't nearly so central to this play as is Helena, and some younger London reviewers unfamiliar with the piece, arriving at the Gielgud to find its exterior plastered with an enormous photograph of Dame Judi and the words 'JUDI DENCH IN *ALL's WELL THAT ENDS WELL*' above the main door, professed considerable surprise when the Countess remained offstage for much of the first half and most of the second and then wasn't even given a line by which to express a view about the dénouement. What the play did give Dench to do, though, she of course did beautifully: her sole soliloquy, a mere quatrain and two couplets at 1.3.124 ('Even so was it with me when I was young . . .'), was like a sudden flashback to her Viola (had she only become Countess in the first place after making a willow cabin at the then Count's gate?), and her subsequent questioning of the lovesick Helena – part teasing, part probing, her support for her ward in visible conflict with a genuine impulse to reproach her which finally gave place to a completely uncritical identification with her romantic plight – was as finely gradated and supple a piece of playing as one could hope to see. What enriched this scene was an underlying sense, on Dench's part, of the sheer indecorum of what the Countess was doing, the more welcome here in that as Helena, Claudia Blakley didn't convey anything like the same keen awareness of the taboos which her proposed pursuit of Bertram was violating, nor anything like the same nuanced sense of the distinctions between different levels of public and private speech. This was a Helena whose tears in 1.1 seemed to express only disappointment and frustration rather than complete abjection, a Helena perfectly convincing when voicing the cheerful persistence of her second soliloquy, 'Our remedies oft in ourselves do lie' (1.1.212–25), but whose delivery of the first ('O were that all!', 1.1.78–97) didn't give the impression that she had ever truly felt that her desire for Bertram was as impossible or self-destructive as that of a hind for a lion. In this production, Helena's passion wasn't obviously a disaster from the outset (not for Helena, at least), partly because no one except Bertram seemed especially bothered about the social gap between the poor physician's daughter and the count (which didn't even show up much at the level of costume, since both of them looked sumptuously courtly), and partly because although this Helena briefly doubted whether she would win Bertram she never seemed to doubt her eligibility to try. Both the production and the performance seemed to think that Helena was perfectly normal – not so much a ruthless stalker armed with a medical textbook as a nicely dressed, plucky, straightforward blonde with wide eyes and large teeth. Perhaps she just wasn't Bertram's physical type. In any case, she was never very interesting, despite the extraordinary plot of which she still had to provide the motor.

It's hard to criticize such a highly polished and consistently entertaining production as this one without sounding at best ungrateful and at worst carping, but there were times when Doran seemed definitely to be adding effects to the surface of the play, sometimes in defiance of its text, rather than finding them latent in its depths. Apparently in quest of easy accessibility and easy laughs, some minor roles were coloured to within an inch of their lives. Both Lafeu and Lavache, one written as dry and the other as bitter, were played as out-and-out clowns: Charles Kay made Lafeu into a humours-comedy pantaloon (who practically launched himself downstage into a spotlight to deliver 'Good Tom Drum, lend me a handkerchief' in the last scene as if it were a music-hall gag line, regardless of the relative position of Parolles at the time), and Mark Lambert made Lavache into a full-on twinkling Irish jester of the hey-nonny-nonny school, complete with bladder on stick, and completely without the serious religious self-disgust and misogyny implied by most of his lines. Since the only funny thing about most of Lavache's jokes is that they are actually about as funny as Eeyore's, this was as counterproductive as it could well have been, and Lambert's performance, extra comedy music cues and all (complete with full accompaniment and a jig for his offensive little song about Helen of Troy in 1.3), neatly summed up everything which gives Shakespearian comedy a bad name in the culture at large. Doran's decision to play 2.2, the sending off of Lavache to the court, as a merry folk-music-backed romp in which all the servants and even the Countess participated in his forced bathing was certainly the production's most obvious violation of the spirit of the play. But if this vision of Roussillon as an egalitarian paradise suggested that the problem of social class was all in Bertram's head, the production elsewhere seemed to go out of its way to exonerate him, prepared to represent the women of Italy entirely through the lens of his retrospective account of them. In the second half of the play (introduced by the sole non-realist touch in the production, the playing of 3.3, Bertram's installation as general of the Florentine cavalry, as a little tableau in which Bertram shouted his lines over battle sound-effects while mounted centre-stage

15 *All's Well That Ends Well.* RSC, dir. Gregory Doran, Swan Theatre, 2003. 1.1: Helena (Claudia Blakley), Lafeu (Charles Kay), the Countess (Judi Dench) and Bertram (Jamie Glover).

on a simulated horse), the Tuscan widow and her friend Mariana, so far from looking like the estimable, respectable proprietresses of a religious bed-and-breakfast establishment, looked like gipsies out of an operetta, artfully muddied faces and all, and Shelley Conn's Diana resembled nothing so much as an amateur Carmen, flirting and simpering and generally behaving exactly like the exploitative, calculating minx described in Bertram's clumsily mendacious attempts at self-exculpation in Act 5.

It's just as well, then, that the King, Parolles and Bertram were all so strong in this show, as otherwise there'd have been some risk of this production suggesting that nothing very much was really at stake in the plot of *All's Well That Ends Well* after all. As the King, Gary Waldhorn sustained the perfect balance between comic self-importance and near-tragic dignity: his genuinely touching display of recovering faith in the possibility of being cured of his fistula, for example, saved 2.1, Helena's promise of a cure, from being swamped by quasi-magic lighting effects and incidental music. Similarly it was largely thanks to the conviction and force of the King's mounting anger with Bertram in 2.3 that the choosing scene was able to recover from the flippant game of musical chairs into which it had fallen during the normally tense sequence of Helena's choice itself, here played as a dance from which the Lords she indicated she would not be choosing absented themselves one by one. This scene risked lapsing irrevocably into trivial homophobic comedy when the last clause by which Helena dismisses one Lord, 'if you ever wed' (2.3.93), was taken as a cue to play him as flagrantly camp and to treat Helena's remark as a waspish allusion to his apparent homosexuality, upon which another Lord still in the dance then began to mince strenuously in the hopes of being let off on the same grounds. Even Helena, rather than being too apprehensive for light comedy at this point in the action, enjoyed taking a further share of this cheap laugh: 'happy' in her subsequent non-choosing of this next candidate, 'You are too young, too happy . . .' (2.3.97), was given a little prefatory pause and audible inverted commas so as to make it into a euphemism for 'gay.' But this Larry Graysonesque collective giggle, which risked making Helena seem almost unconcerned about the implications and risks of what she was doing, was mercifully brought up short by Bertram's horror at finding himself the last potential partner left in the dance and by the King's growing sense of outrage at his subsequent refusal of his self-appointed bride: both the younger and the older party to the masculine face-off into which this scene resolves itself knew that it was a serious matter, at any rate. In fact what happened to Blakley's Helena in this production consistently looked far less traumatic than what happened to Jamie Glover's wonderfully straightforward, unselfconscious Bertram: he was comprehensively destroyed, while she just had an adventure.

The one character who was instead comprehensively made by his experience of the play's events, in this reading, was Guy Henry's Parolles, a gangling miracle of self-consciousness for whom every tiny social encounter had already been a nerve-racking matter of precariously-maintained bluff well before his promise to recover the Florentines' drum. He only found himself left on stage to have his first conversation with Helena at all in 1.1 because he was unable to attract sufficient notice from any of the servants to get his trunk carried off in Bertram and Lafeu's train (in the end, after restoring his sense of his own viability as well as he could by his inept man-of-the-world attempts at flirtation, he gave up and dragged it away himself), and it was only Bertram's naive faith in him that kept him afloat at all during the court scenes. Although the scene of his nocturnal interrogation was handled relatively clumsily and rather too fast, the discomfiture of Parolles was a real high point of this *All's Well*, since here, unusually, it looked not so much like social disgrace as like personal salvation. The soliloquy at 4.3.332–42, 'Yet am I thankful', was a revelation: this was a Parolles who was overjoyed to realize that now he had been discredited as a soldier he could shed his accustomed intolerable daily burden of pretence, and Henry managed to make the words 'Simply the thing I am / Shall make me live' sound like the sun coming out. Back in Roussillon, he was handed Lavache's bladder-on-a-stick to signify his investment in his new social role of public laughingstock, and he seemed quite contented with it, or at least quite happy to play up his accustomed crippling embarrassment for the amusement of others instead of having to try to keep it to himself as before. This was a virtuoso comic performance that was also a feat of psychological intuition, and a real coup of well-judged casting.

With Parolles already on this upward trajectory, where did that leave the further revelations and irresolutions of the last scene? With such an irritating Diana giving evidence on behalf of such an undercomplicated Helena, a good deal of the burden in its last movement fell on the King, and Waldhorn as ever carried the keynote perfectly, his genuine concern as to Helena's fate never allowing him to lose sight of the King's narrowness of vision and touches of self-importance ('Take her away, I do not like her now', 5.3.283, got a well-deserved laugh that was sympathetic as well as mocking), while his responses to each successive riddle focused and carried the audience's desire to see the plot properly resolved. Glover's Bertram, meanwhile, was progressively immobilized into a dumbstruck rigidity downstage left as his public identity was pulled slowly and excruciatingly apart, until after Helena declared herself and his position became finally untenable he abruptly broke and collapsed onto his knees, his voice cracking into a despairing sob, on 'Both, both. O, pardon!' (5.3.310). Glover gave a superb rendering here of an unimaginative, unreflective and largely inarticulate young man realizing too late that his attempts at achieving liberty have only betrayed him into a permanent version of exactly the 'subjection' he had resented back in 1.1: his performance never made the mistake of trying to make Bertram likeable, but I've never seen the young Count's situation illuminated so fully and so desolately.

It's a pity, I think, that after making such a good job of the spectacle of this unwilling bridegroom's public entrapment – made the more painful here by Helena's apparent insensitivity to the mortifying destruction of his reputation by which it had been achieved – Doran should have chosen to close the plot down on a note of pure saccharine. Having addressed herself solely to the King and to Bertram since her entrance, concentrating on establishing her identity, her fulfilment of Bertram's impossible conditions and the now-unbreakable legal force of her marriage, Helena finally acknowledges the presence of the Countess only at 5.3.321, with the words 'O my dear mother, do I see you living?' There is surely something potentially dismissive about this remark, as well as something affectionate: the line makes a private reference back to their dialogue in 1.3, in that Helena here calls the Countess 'mother' at long last in the sense of 'mother-in-law', but that 'do I see you living?' seems already to be wondering how long the estate of which Helena has now unassailably made herself mistress is going to be burdened with the older woman who has just definitively become the *Dowager* Countess of Roussillon. The Countess, tellingly, makes no answer at all to this overture, and it is the ever-diplomatic Lafeu who smooths the moment over by deciding that it should officially be regarded as touching, making his tactful little joke about borrowing Parolles's handkerchief. In Doran's production, though, Helena's line was played not as the formal acknowledgment of the sidelined in-law in whom she has conspicuously declined to confide her scheme for re-ensnaring Bertram (a scheme which has even involved tricking the Countess into thinking her dead), but as the joyous instigation of a reunion toward which the whole plan had apparently been oriented from the outset. Turning upstage as if in relief from the stammering, numbed, just-recovering Bertram, as though now that piece of business had been sorted out she could at last greet the person she had most wanted to see all along, Helena spoke these words in tremulous joy, her happiness at seeing the Countess again tinged by only the slightest hinted apprehension that she might consider her daughter-in-law's recent conduct a little *outré*. For Doran the real conclusion of the play came not with Bertram's response to the reappearance of Helena but with his mother's, for which, in the absence of a single line, a heavy-handed music cue had to be supplied. As Dench hesitated upstage centre, gazing into Blakley's eyes and silently registering as best she could an unspoken conflict between her pleasure at seeing Helena again (and pregnant with her grandchild at that) and her misgivings about the strategy by which this hitherto underestimated daughter-in-law had secured her social resurrection, the 'cello trembled on a suspense-filled low fifth (unfortunately reminiscent of the first note of the *Blackadder 2* theme music), a note which at last resolved into a ringing major chord as Dench slowly raised her arms and Blakley rushed into a heartwarming embrace. It was about what could be done, I suppose, to make the Countess look like the centre of a scene which really has much more to do with her displacement from that position, but it looked considerably more facile and sentimental than does Shakespeare's script. Doran, however, did have the tact to finish not on this cosy and implausible vision of female bonding but on an image of the young couple now faced with the prospect of making a marriage out of the consequences of that memorable night in Italy: after the King had made his gloriously obtuse promise to supply Diana too with a husband of her choice, the other players except Helena and Bertram dispersed, and the last two lines of the King's speech (here, with the epilogue cut, 'All yet seems well . . . more welcome is the sweet', 5.3.334–5), were addressed confidingly and placatingly to the Countess, as the monarch and the dowager made a graceful withdrawal upstage left, their eyes turning back toward their juniors. The lights faded on Helena and Bertram looking warily at one another, circling each other, a pace apart, in a recapitulation of the choosing scene's dance that was perhaps itself a recapitulation of the ending of Trevor Nunn's production in the RST twenty-two years earlier. This was *All's Well That Ends Well* Lite, perhaps, but it deservedly filled the Swan and the Gielgud (for an extended run, at the latter), and it will be interesting to see whether the next time anyone revives *All's Well* they will once more bill it as a 'neglected' play, as usual.

There was nothing light about Simon McBurney's *Measure for Measure* at the National, which shared with this show only very high production values and a surprising sense that the male party to the bed-trick may have suffered a greater blow to his integrity than did either of the women involved. Like all of Complicite's work, this was very much an ensemble piece, rehearsed and re-rehearsed to a nicety, and many of the 21-strong cast remained visible in the shadows around the edge of a small, squared raised central acting area even when not involved in the action – in fact one mannerism of this show, which reviewers found either impressive or maddening, was that characters leaving at the end of one scene would continue to leave but would go into unlit slow-motion as the next began all around them. Behind the acting area was a gauzy curtain, onto which shadows could be projected from behind and video images from in front: candles for the convent in 1.4, for example and, most arrestingly, a whole visionary sequence enacting the bereavement and jilting of Mariana while it was narrated at 3.1.210–33, acted by supine players on the floor behind the standing figures of Isabella and the Duke but projected onto the curtain from a camera directly above them so as to give full-length images. Around the stage, principally downstage right, were a number of video monitors, and by the use of one fixed video camera on a tripod, usually placed stage left, the faces of characters on stage could be subjected to ruthless close-up inspection.

In a play so preoccupied with surveillance, produced in modern dress in a year when the state's determination to maintain public order by every technological means at its disposal seemed seriously to be risking the individual liberties of the citizen, this equipment never looked irrelevant or intrusive, and it was often incorporated naturalistically into scenes. The newly promoted Angelo's harried but excited face appeared on the monitors at the end of 1.1, held there by the lens of a journalist as the Duke and his bodyguards left Vienna by helicopter; in the brothel in 1.2 the monitors showed pornographic videos, until Lucio, illustrating 1.2.7, changed the channel to show, as a portrait of 'the sanctimonious pirate', a picture of George Bush Jr; Angelo's courtroom featured a microphone by which he might impart his official responses to Isabella's petition; at the prison, Isabella and Claudio could only speak to one another through an imaginary perspex screen fitted with another microphone, and the Duke eavesdropped on their private conference through

16 *Measure for Measure.* National Theatre/Complicite, dir. Simon McBurney, Olivier Theatre, 2004. Isabella (Naomi Frederick) and Angelo (Paul Rhys).

earphones while watching them on CCTV. The ground-bass of the production, then, was topicality: the prisoners wore orange overalls *a la* Guantanamo Bay, and the word 'security' in the Duke's cryptic remark to Escalus at 3.1.485, 'There is scarce truth enough to make societies secure, but security enough to make fellowships accursed', sounded like a comment on the anti-terrorism precautions in force all around the West End at the time of the production.

This said, McBurney's *Measure for Measure* was memorable not only for the ways in which it used Shakespeare's play as the source for a series of arresting images of our own troubled times but for the singular clarity and force with which it rendered the psychological states of the play's chief characters. This was the darkest *Measure for Measure* I've ever seen, its sole glimpses of comedy arising less from its Lucio (played as a very un-fantastic, pimp-like lout by Toby Jones) than from Richard Katz's fine 70s-moustached Pompey (given an extremely meticulous part-slapstick sequence of visiting his former associates in their respective briefly-spotlit prison cells), and from the farcical discomfiture experienced by Angus Wright's earnest, bespectacled Provost over the problem of dealing with the corpse of Ragozine in 4.3 (which, produced on stage, prove unmanageably to be entering rigor mortis, and which had to be decapitated with a saw just off-stage, the process gruesomely visible in shadow-play on the curtain). Elbow started as a comic Latino in 2.1, his malapropisms the result of imperfectly learned English, but he had ceased to be funny altogether when he returned in 3.1, metamorphosed into a prisoner-kicking fascist. All this gloom, violence and bad faith seemed to originate within one character, and it wasn't Angelo. Despite a programme note which identified the central riddle of the play as 'Is the Duke a good man or a bad man?', McBurney seemed to have decided unambiguously for the latter conclusion: this production played out in full the perspective on *Measure for Measure*, more familiar in academic criticism than on the stage, that identifies Vincentio as the source and centre of all Vienna's problems. David Troughton played the Duke as an ageing, unsmiling Stalin in heavy greatcoat, sunglasses and Homburg hat, a brooding dictator who underwent a sinister rejuvenation in the process of scapegoating Angelo with all his own failings. His interview with Claudio in prison, so far from being an inert and irrelevant piece of sententious poetry, seemed here to be a typical sample of this Duke's behaviour: 'Be absolute for death', instead of being intoned as a piece of noble sermonizing, was heavy-breathed down the microphone into Claudio's cell as though the Duke were taking the opportunity to unload all his own world-weariness and self-disgust onto this helpless condemned prisoner, committing suicide by proxy. Understandably, as the Duke grew ever more agitated and aroused with his own death-wish, Claudio eventually collapsed onto the floor of his cell in horror, blocking his ears.

By contrast, Naomi Frederick's Isabella seemed positively light-hearted, and indeed her performance worked beautifully precisely because she was so unlike the familiar operatic kind of Isabella who seems to have arrived in the play solely in order to suffer. This short-haired, brisk, confident girl wasn't a particularly spiritual or introverted nun, just someone serenely confident that if she was good and pleased her superiors all would be well, in this world and the next, and while she was bitterly shocked and upset by Angelo's proposition and her brother's perceived apostasy neither experience appeared fundamentally to violate her sense of her self. It was Paul Rhys's Angelo who underwent the deepest trauma in this production, his identity quite fractured by his forbidden and increasingly criminal desire for Isabella. Before her arrival in 2.2 he looked neurotically in control, but in control nonetheless – fastidiously disinfecting the lip of a glass of water brought by a servant with a sterile white handkerchief – but this was a control he was never to regain hereafter. Aghast and troubled after her departure, he began to rise from his judicial swivel chair, and only then realized to his shock that he had developed an erection during the novice's pleading – a very literal reading of 'What's this? What's this? Is this her fault or mine?' (2.2.168), but it certainly worked. His subsequent decision to put his mind and will into the service of this carnal longing looked like a desperate and doomed attempt to bring all the different aspects of his personality back into line with one another. By 2.4 he was already a twitching wreck when left in private, actually rolling up his shirt cuff and cutting his arm with a razor blade on 'Blood, thou art blood' (2.4.15) before hastily concealing this curious, baffled piece of self-harm when the servant arrived to announce Isabella, and we watched him descend yet further into tormented, self-watching moral collapse throughout the ensuing scene. When, on 'Redeem thy brother . . .' (2.4.163ff), Angelo slowly unzipped his fly and forced Isabella's stiff and unwilling hand awkwardly inside, the extreme discomfort of the audience was as much in empathy with Angelo's horror at seeing himself behaving like this as it was with Isabella's disgust. This was a remarkable piece of acting – taking Angelo's puritanism almost to the level of hysteria, but carrying the audience throughout – albeit supported by some cunning textual editing. The play, cut and with some transpositions of scenes in the third and fourth acts, was given without an interval, obviating the way in which Angelo can sometimes seem to get forgotten during the second half, and his enormous shadow often towered above the actors even during sequences from which he was absent, one arm stretched out in the imperious beckoning gesture by which he had propositioned Isabella. That gesture, frighteningly, was repeated at the end of the play. Vincentio's self-restoration was a solemnly gleeful affair, during which Angelo, facing upstage, gradually shrank, clutching his knees, into the judicial chair in which he had been placed to hear his own cause centre stage, biting the fingers of one hand in abject, infantilized horror, only to be swivelled slowly and deliberately into the full view of the audience by the Duke, who leaned over his shoulder to deliver 'Sir, by your leave' (5.1.359) with a horrible mock-avuncular intimacy. Reclaiming the place of authority from Angelo, the Duke took over his gesture too: during his proposal to Isabella, he too stretched out an imperiously inviting right hand, and suddenly in the direction that hand indicated a hitherto unseen acting area was lit up beyond the curtain – a hygienically spotless bedroom, the white linen sheets of the double bed turned down in readiness. The words 'and what is yours is mine' (5.1.536) can never have sounded so ominous or so possessive: and on that,

17 *Measure for Measure*. Shakespeare's Globe, dir. John Dove, 2004. Isabella (Sophie Thompson) and the Duke (Mark Rylance).

all froze, and the lights faded. This was a powerful and searching *Measure for Measure*, and, at a mere £10 a ticket thanks to a sponsorship deal with Travelex, a sold-out one, even in the Olivier. The main complaint raised against it was simply that it ran for very few performances, but since Complicite generally revive their shows over a period of years those who missed it can live in hopes of having another opportunity to catch it in the future.

It is very easy to describe the Globe's rival *Measure for Measure* after this: it was simply the diametrical opposite in every respect, quite the most harmless and cheerful rendering of this play I can well imagine. In colourful, mainly tawny Jacobean costumes, with a panto Dame of a Mistress Overdone from Peter Shorey, it couldn't have seemed further from the political anxieties of 2004, a lone hint of topicality coming from the Scots accent that Liam Brennan employed as Angelo, which made him sound quite like Gordon Brown. But Angelo seemed nowhere near the centre of this show, and he never looked half as threatening as the brothel and prison scenes looked jolly: he was in any case dressed in such elaborate all-black recreated-clothing-of-the-period that even his brief, clumsy physical assault on Isabella during 2.4 looked more comically impractical than menacing. The show was instead stolen, delightfully enough, by Mark Rylance's Vincentio, a stuttering, under-confident, unworldly bachelor in round glasses who fell touchingly in love with Sophie Thompson's spinsterish Isabella in between just about keeping ahead of the plot. While one wouldn't necessarily accuse the director John Dove of having decided to try playing *Measure for Measure* purely for laughs, he might as well have done so, since it was this production's comedy which worked and its gestures toward serious moral debate which didn't. If a *Measure for Measure* fails to persuade its audience that prostitution, attempted rape, judicial murder and a police state are anything to get very upset about, it transpires, they can settle down to enjoy this play solely as an unusual but quite satisfying piece of farce. It was all rather sweet, but it made Doran's *All's Well That Ends Well* look like *King Lear* by contrast.

*Twelfth Night* received two contrasting revivals this year too, one stunningly designed but poorly acted and the other beautifully acted but if anything slightly under-designed. At the Albery Stephen Beresford had the simple and extremely promising idea of setting the play in India, an idea vividly brought to life by Jonathan Fenson's design. An elaborately carved wooden proscenium-within-a-proscenium, leaning markedly to the right and bearing a string of ancient coloured light bulbs along its cross-beam, framed two opposing walls which might have been those of temples or of houses, the space between them not committed to being either interior or exterior save by the provision of extra props and lighting from one scene to another (in Olivia's house, a little memorial shrine to her brother; for the box-tree scene, drying laundry). 'Everything we discovered in India seemed to make sense of the play', commented Beresford in the programme, 'its vibrancy, its passion, its cruelty, the irreverent humour that informs every interaction, the public nature of people's emotional lives.' It's a lovely idea, and it looked terrific – Neha Dubey, for example, made a ravishing veiled, sari-clad entrance as Olivia, and Raza Jaffrey's Orsino looked very fetching in polo kit (though the tightness of his jodphurs got some unintended laughs from a school party, when I saw them). But most of these effects were thrown away whenever the actors opened their mouths: as Viola, Shereen Martineau was in such painful need of a voice coach that listening to her almost gave you a sore throat, and Paul Bhattarcharjee took Malvolio's lines so rapidly and with such an impoverished sense of timing and occasion that so far from emerging as a fascinating tragic victim of the caste system he seemed like the least interesting character on the stage. The one really charismatic performer in the cast was Kulvinder Ghir, who played Feste as a Baul singer, a semi-religious nomadic Bengali minstrel, and enlivened the beginning of the second half with a terrific cod-Bollywood dance routine. It was interesting to hear Shakespeare's lines supplemented by Urdu from time to time – Sir Toby's 'pickled herrings', for example, were replaced by the name of a subcontinental fish dish which I didn't recognize but which many south Londoners in the audience clearly did – and it was usually clear what the emotional point of a scene was supposed to be (at the end of the play, for instance, this mournful Olivia was still a good deal more interested in Cesario than she was in Sebastian). But an all-Indian *Twelfth Night* remained a good idea rather than an actual achievement (pleasing though it was to see a comparatively young audience including a high proportion from London's Asian diaspora turning out to see Shakespeare), and it will continue to do so until London boasts a crop of Anglo-Indian actors rather more accomplished at stage work than were this particular cast.

Stephen Unwin's production for English Touring Theatre was a jewel of technique by comparison, and it's a mark of the strengh in depth of its casting that Maria was played by the excellent Susan Brown, whose rendition of this waiting-gentlewoman was comic, vengeful and always grounded in a real sense of lived social relations. The younger players looked like genuine finds: Geraldine Rich, straight out of RADA, made a fine, poised Viola (especially good in 1.5 at sounding affectingly irritated by Olivia's perceived ingratitude in rejecting Orsino), Catherine Walker was a fountain wistfully stirred as Olivia, and Gareth David-Lloyd made an interestingly overwrought, vulnerable Sebastian. The subplot was dominated by a fine pair of antagonists, an impossible Sir Toby on the crusty verges of senility, Michael Cronin, and a stiff, officious Malvolio, Des McAleer, and the one puzzling piece of casting in this show was that of Alan Williams as a crabbed, dowdy, middle-aged Feste who could neither sing nor make witty remarks with any great aplomb and thus seemed to be in rather the wrong line of work. The costumes were expensively late Elizabethan, with a good deal of blue and yellow satin here and there – apart from lacking a three-cornered hat, Geoffrey Beevers's Sir Andrew looked rather like the Francis Wheatley painting of James William Dodd in the role in the 1770s – but they were redeemed from looking merely olde-worlde by the clean-lined post-modern clarity of Becs Andrews's well-nigh minimal set. A low, flat, polished wooden platform was framed by a proscenium of its own, and behind it another frame could be either curtained in maroon plush (for some interiors, such as Orsino's court) or left open to reveal a backdrop of blue sky and sea (for much of the rest of the time). This was pleasantly clear, but somehow insufficient: these two alternatives didn't seem to do justice to the range of spaces the play suggests, especially not to Olivia's territory, and having Sir Toby, Sir Andrew and Fabian hide not behind a potted box tree but merely below the far rim of the platform gave the garden scene a curious bleakness and agoraphobia that didn't help it at all. But this was a touching and very funny account of the play, with the alternation between comedy and pathos in the reunion scene especially well-judged, and I'm not at all sorry that this should have been the first *Twelfth Night* my own identical twins should ever have seen. It is to the show's credit, I think, that they found it a very truthful and satisfying depiction of how incompetent singletons can be at telling twins apart.

There is far less to say about the rest of the year's revivals of comedies. Barrie Rutter's Northern Broadsides *Merchant of Venice*, which toured extensively in the spring, seemed to have been given a larger costume budget than many of this company's earlier productions, but the play seemed ill-suited to the company's chosen aesthetic. On a simple set (two white platforms with a space between them which might occasionally be read as a canal, in front of a white crucifix on black curtains), the Venetian gentlemen wore blue Burtons suits, Morocco a linen suit with a green cummerbund, green cravat, panama hat and moccasins, Aragon a long black velvet drape coat with silver and grey striped waistcoat and a cane, and Portia an elaborate red gown, while only Rutter's would-be tragic Shylock wore plain black. If anything, this elaboration of visible differences between groups only made it the stranger that everyone on stage spoke in a similar Yorkshire accent (for 'aught' read 'owt', as ever), and it still isn't obvious to me that playing Shakespeare's depictions of social conflict as though they all took place in some classless Pennine utopia is any more illuminating or any less flattening than was the long-abandoned convention by which all his characters except the comic peasants used to speak in RP. The acting in this production never quite lifted the show above such reservations: Clare Calbraith's inflexible Portia sounded monotonously put-upon for the entire first half, Paul Barnhill's Bassanio was a smug bully whose response to the ring plot was one of simple aggression (driving Portia and Nerissa backwards off the platform so that their revelation that the doctor and the clerk had been them in disguise all along hastily conceded the upper hand rather than securing it), and Barrie Rutter's performance as Shylock, all bending waist and waving arms, moved from one staring signpost to another, with only his very last line, 'I am content' (4.9.391), delivered at anything below a shout. Only Jo Theaker's performance as Jessica stood out, largely because she didn't seem to have been directed at all: instead of part-building herself a little off-line portrait of a Jewish daughter tormented by guilt at having abandoned her father and her faith, as has been the custom in recent productions, she looked blithely unconcerned about the whole business, blandly faithful to the completely underwritten nature of the role.

*A Midsummer Night's Dream* suffered from a large budget this year too, in Gale Edwards's production at the Chichester Festival Theatre. Alison Chitty's glossy, hard set – a circular white acting area onto which nine doorways opened through a curved back wall, with a balconied upper level above them, and electric stars visible above that and through some of the doorways – gave a harsh, flat echo like a quarry whenever anyone turned upstage, and the spheres that descended to suggest the forest, together with the shiny purple of Oberon's costume and some very hackneyed injections of dry ice, gave the whole show a distinctly ITV1 feeling. The fairies wore dayglo tutus and had blue hair, and indulged in fidgety pieces of business whenever Edwards grew anxious that the audience might listen to the poetry: the mechanicals acquitted themselves better, especially Jonathan Cullen as a Quince touchingly divided between earnest admiration for Bottom's acting and exasperation at his refusal to be managed, but the play-within-the-play was hopelessly sabotaged by being placed high up on the balcony at the back of the set, much too far from either the onstage audience or the paying one. Karen Louise Hebden's production at the Derby Playhouse was in a similarly vulgar overall style, resembling at times a modern provincial pantomime with its four stage-school child fairies and its intrusive use of plastic, Pontins-like keyboard music played from a small orchestra pit, but since Rosie Alabaster's design budget hadn't gone much further than the purchase of a data projector which shone twirling flowers onto the set throughout the forest scenes none of this was able to obstruct the actors to anything like the same extent. The result was a warm-hearted production, more at home in the muddy woods than at court, with an extremely funny, young Irish Bottom at its centre (Conor Moloney) and a lithe, Caliban-like Puck from Paul Ewing.

Warm-hearted vulgarity was the main thing the Globe's *Much Ado About Nothing*, directed by Tamara Harvey, had to offer: this was an all-female production in Elizabethan dress, all unflattering breeches and stuck-on moustaches, with Josie Lawrence as an inexplicably Brummie Benedick and Yolanda Vazquez as an unchangingly fierce, unattractive Beatrice who would have been too angry as Katherine but might just have made a passable Sycorax. It was easily outclassed in every respect by Creation's outdoor production in Oxford, directed by Charlotte Conquest with a cast of only nine: Tom Peters pulled off the remarkable doubling of Benedick and Verges, and Elizabeth Hopley was a subtle and intelligent Beatrice, capable of compassion as well as resentment. Peters was responsible, among much else, for the best piece of ad-libbing I saw during what was the wettest English summer since records began: when a downpour abruptly began in the middle of his best soliloquy, 'This can be no trick' (2.3.209ff), and the audience began to reach for hoods and umbrellas, he simply paused in mid-sentence, looked puzzled and mildly offended, and said 'What?' This single monosyllable, half taunt and half lament, carried two completely contrary meanings, making a double-edged joke about the entire peculiar situation of outdoor Shakespeare: it said 'here am I, Benedick, enjoying a perfect fictitious sunny day in Messina whatever discomfort you may be fussing about', but it also said 'here am I, Tom Peters, having to pretend not to notice the rain at all while you at least get to wear waterproof coats instead of a lightweight Spanish lounge suit'. This is a player exceptionally good at working an audience, even in extreme weather conditions, and I hope to see more of his work (preferably indoors) in the future.

Before I move on to the tragedies, this is probably the place to mention the most unusual Shakespeare production of the year, Gregory Doran's adaptation of *Venus and Adonis* as 'A Masque for Puppets'. This co-production with the Little Angel Theatre, the RSC's contribution to the current minor boom in bunraku represented elsewhere by *The Lion King* and *His Dark Materials*, opened in London in the autumn and then transferred for a short run at the Other Place in Stratford in November and December. Michael Pennington sat stage right, reading out a slightly abbreviated text of the poem (prefaced by sonnet 26 and the Dedication, while a puppet Shakespeare presented a puppet Southampton with a puppet copy of the poem); stage left sat the guitarist Steve Russell, accompanying the action with Elizabethan music; and in between sat an exquisite little puppet-sized proscenium arch theatre, about twenty feet wide. Approximately quarter-life-size marionette puppets performed behind the proscenium, to be replaced by more like third-size bunraku doubles (and two horses, and a boar) operated by a team of black-clad, masked puppeteers in front of it for the bulk of the poem. It isn't often that you overhear someone in a Stratford audience saying that the heroine reminds them of Marina and realize that they are referring not to *Pericles* but to *Stingray*, so this was an occasion to cherish. It's a pity, perhaps, given how much of the text of *Venus and Adonis* is spoken by Venus, that Pennington's voice, admirable as it is, wasn't supplemented by that of an actress for the goddess's speeches proper. Even so, this hour-long show was undeniably very charming (relentlessly so, complained some), right down to her exit by dove-drawn chariot, though it has to be admitted that watching Venus's unsuccessful attempts to copulate with Adonis being enacted in minute anatomical detail by bunraku puppeteers could seem at times rather like watching masked fetishists having incompetent sex in public using elaborate prosthetics. Let us hope that the RSC at least have the sense

18 *Othello*. RSC, dir. Gregory Doran, Swan Theatre, 2004. A tale of two marriages: Othello (Sello-Maake ka Ncube), Desdemona (Lisa Dillon), Iago (Anthony Sher) and Emilia (Amanda Harris).

not to follow this show up with a similar treatment of *The Rape of Lucrece*. *Hero and Leander* with a water tank, and Gerry Anderson as a consultant? It could happen.

## TRAGEDIES

Doran's most impressive achievement this year, though, puppets or no, will remain his *Othello*, the curtain-raiser to the Tragedies summer season in the RST, which opened at the Swan in February and eventually closed at the Trafalgar Studios in London in June. In its design (by Doran's usual collaborator, Stephen Brimson-Lewis), this was in the mainstream of productions of this play over the last three decades, particularly reminiscent of the last National Theatre revival (in 1997, with David Harewood and Simon Russell Beale). The costumes were roughly late 1940s, the military uniforms British; ceiling fans rotated above the set in Cyprus; wire fences across the back of the stage marked this out as a play set on the dangerously male terrain of the military; and all was more or less naturalistic. What distinguished this *Othello* from its predecessors was an unusual emphasis on the interrelations between the two marriages at the centre of the play – quite apart from the sheer intelligence brought to each of the four roles involved by Sello-Maake ka-Ncube as Othello, Lisa Dillon as Desdemona, Amanda Harris as Emilia and, producing the kind of virtuoso, transformative performance one has come to take for granted from this actor, Anthony Sher as Iago.

This was a production, first of all, which recognized Othello and Desdemona as a pair of aristocrats, and potentially a very spoiled pair at that. Ncube, who is originally from Soweto and played Aaron in the Market Theatre *Titus Andronicus* described in Doran and Sher's *Woza Shakespeare!*, played a consciously African Othello with hints of the glamorous chieftain, hints which made some commentators anxious that the play was once more going to present the spectacle of an exotic outsider lapsing into barbarism under pressure. In the senate scene, he rolled his eyes and laughed as he spoke of the Anthropophagi (1.3.141ff), as if letting the Venetians into the secret of the hackneyed, touristic African mumbo-jumbo which he had played

19 *Othello*. RSC, dir. Gregory Doran, Swan Theatre, 2004. 'Was not that Cassio parted from your wife?': Othello (Sello-Maake ka Ncube) and Iago (Anthony Sher).

up in order to flirt with Desdemona, but there was no irony later in the play when on a comparable passage of grand-sounding geography, 'Like to the Pontic Sea' (3.4.456), Ncube began to perform a strange, high-stepping, stamping tribal dance, a movement which returned more emphatically for the epileptic fit in 4.1. It was as though this Othello, from being confidently able to joke about the stereotype of the credulous Moor, was gradually manoeuvred into inhabiting it. It wasn't that either the play or the production believed in it as an essential truth, simply that both recognized it as an available pattern of behaviour under these cultural circumstances. If anything it was Othello's arrogance which stood out in this performance, both before and after the poison with which he is dosed by Iago, a sense of privilege which made him into something above and beyond the dupe he is made of by the plot: he had eloped with Desdemona because he knew he could get away with it, delivering the shocking line 'That I have ta'en away this old man's daughter' (1.3.78) to Brabantio's face without even sounding provoked into this offensive way of referring to his father-in-law by anger or rejection, and hence his implicit belief later in the play that he would be able to get away with killing her too seemed less incongruous. Desdemona, similarly, had run off with Othello out of a serene sense of her own unlimited entitlement, and it is greatly to Lisa Dillon's credit that she never threatened to play the role as the model of cloying sacrificial wifeliness it can sometimes become. By not treating the senate scene as if she thought Desdemona was behaving like a paragon – instead presenting her as a pampered, wilful good girl who had clearly been brought up to feel that she innately deserved to have anything she wanted, including her father's prize dinner guest if she so chose – Dillon produced the most convincing and affecting performance in this role which I've yet seen. In Cyprus she was actively affronted when Othello abruptly turned against her, rather than just pathetically hurt, and as a result what eventually happened to Desdemona seemed tragic rather than merely an exercise in formulaic pathos. You cried for her death without feeling for a moment that your tears were somehow being mechanically induced, and it was a death made the more upsetting by not seeming wholly inevitable: in 4.2, for example, the 'brothel' scene, Othello seemed briefly to regain his faith in his wife's innocence at 4.2.90, and the two embraced on Desdemona's 'Heaven forgive us!', pausing for long enough to give the audience a chance to imagine what might happen now if Othello had the sense to trust her after all before he abruptly lapsed into his supposedly righteous indignation against 'the cunning whore of Venice / That married with Othello' and stormed off once more toward tragedy.

What happened between the senate scene and this terrible interview was presented as in part the result of a leakage from the other marriage with which this union of touchingly like-minded egotists was brought into dangerous proximity, a relationship I've rarely seen given such sustained attention. Amanda Harris's Emilia, rather than looking, as sometimes happens, like Desdemona's more downtrodden sister, was of the different class which her marriage to a mere ensign implies, someone used to being posted with her husband from one barracks to another and sufficiently at home in the company of soldiers for Iago's paranoid fantasies about her, which can seem to spring from thin air, to have plenty to work on. Doran allowed her to join the carousing soldiers in 2.3 as a sort of incidental mistress of ceremonies, helping pass around the drinks and even participating in the debagging of Justin Avoth's inebriated Cassio (an unusually gauche Florentine who in this production looked practically interchangeable with the gormless Roderigo). This prompted Iago to stare in horror at the audience, nodding in shock and pointing, as if to indicate that this incident just proved what he had already told us about his wife's unacceptable familiarity with other men's underwear. Harris's Emilia was both tough and, at first, relatively unscrupulous, not just stupidly obedient in providing Iago with the handkerchief (at 3.3.294–320) but making a rational, hard-nosed calculation of her own best interests: it clearly wasn't the first time this couple had been complicit in some such petty crime against their superiors, nor the first time he had mistrusted her. Emilia could still put Iago's request above Desdemona's rights to her own property at this stage of the play because, as this production beautifully illustrated, though her marriage grew even less satisfactory at the same time as her relationship with Desdemona grew tentatively closer, at this stage the two women were still only professionally acquainted. This is the first time I've seen the scenes between Desdemona and Emilia played as though the two really were complete strangers until Emilia got assigned to Desdemona as her attendant for the voyage to Cyprus (at 1.3.296), and they were greatly enhanced by it. The relationship became not an established mistress-confidante pairing but a fleeting, fatal, cross-class intimacy. It was first brought to the audience's attention in a lovely little piece of business in 2.1, during the banter with Cassio immediately after the women's arrival in Cyprus, when Emilia fumbled anxiously in her handbag to produce a hip-flask, then nervously crossed the stage in order to add some whisky from it to the seasick Desdemona's coffee, not sure whether her sense that this was what Desdemona physically needed was quite sufficient to warrant such a familiar and presumptuous gesture toward a social superior. This gift was received with similarly provisional gratitude, and there the relations between the two remained, until their friendship came to a tiny, short-lived flowering in the willow song scene, 4.3. At first there seemed every possibility that this interview might be a complete non-event: the two gossiped almost absently for the first part of the scene, and Desdemona really did want to dismiss Emilia at 'So, get thee gone' (4.3.56). Emilia was on her way out until Desdemona, letting her guard down as she found herself alone, suddenly sighed 'O, these men, these men!', at which Emilia decided to return and try to comfort her, and so it was that she came back in and settled, with a cigarette (Desdemona refused one herself), to talk more intimately than the two ever had done before or ever would again. It was only when Emilia grew confidentially upset during her speech about wives' rights to avenge themselves on faithless husbands – clearly understood by Desdemona as a confession just too far – that Desdemona was able to bring the conversation to a close, having regained the position of the consoler rather than the consoled: 'Good night, good night' (4.3.102) brought the encounter to a rather awkward and abrupt ending, with Emilia slightly embarrassed at having confided so much and Desdemona equally unsure as to whether she should have heard it. This was acting of the highest possible order, minutely observant and perfectly communicated.

It goes without saying that Sher's Iago was well up to this standard of detailed, original playing throughout. His ensign's peaked cap was at first reminiscent of Ian McKellen's fourteen years earlier, but his Iago had nothing of McKellen's blank, satanic impassivity. Instead he seethed throughout with a barely contained overplus of obsessive sexual curiosity and disgust – a seething nonetheless covered by a dapper, suave, military precision of movement that made him appear pert as well as vicious. (This was an Iago who actually stood to attention and adopted a sergeant-major's parade-ground voice, for example, as if issuing orders, on 'Strangle her in her bed, even the bed she hath contaminated', 4.1.202–3.) Our first glimpse of Iago found him helping a slightly drunk, dinner-suited Roderigo into a raincoat on their apparently casual way back from a party on the rainy night of Othello's elopement, and his first sly acknowledgement of an audience to his superior cleverness came at 1.1.74, Roderigo's 'Here is her father's house. I'll call aloud'. So far from the two men having agreed before the dialogue began that this was the objective of their walk, in this reading Iago had been steering Roderigo in this direction for this purpose all along without Roderigo ever realizing it, and on Roderigo's remark he rose on tiptoe behind his back, raised his palms and gave a little 'O!' of sarcastic mock-surprise. (This production made nicely visible, incidentally, the way in which it is only the foolish Roderigo, admirably played by Mark Lockyer, who is allowed to express any scepticism about the plausibility of the play's plot, notably at 2.1.220, where he at first can't believe that Desdemona can possibly have already cuckolded Othello with Cassio.) A similar moment of relished superiority of strategy came after the cashiering of Cassio, when, at the close of the dialogue in which he advised the ex-lieutenant to petition Desdemona for his reinstatement, Iago feigned to forget not to salute him – clicking his heels, half raising his hand to his brow, and then hurriedly putting it to his side again with a pseudo-apologetic smirk that to the audience was obviously a taunt but which Cassio himself might just have read as a symptom of embarrassment. It provided the perfect reinforcement for Cassio's hangdog exit, and the ideal transition into 'And what's he then that says I play the villain?' (2.3.327ff).

This was an Iago with a genuine erotic fixation on Desdemona – at 2.3.290 his 'Now I do love her too, / Not out of absolute lust – though peradventure I stand accountant for as great a sin' was illustrated by a fascinated, lingering sip at her abandoned cup of cold whisky-laced coffee, and 4.2 found him, left briefly alone after the exit of Desdemona and Emilia at line 176, rummaging voluptuously in the vertical military packing case that held her clothes (before he was startled by the arrival of a felonious Roderigo, looking for his jewels among her personal effects). But then again he had an erotic fixation on Cassio too, growing so visibly excited in 3.4 while describing the supposed erotic dream during which the lieutenant had allegedly climbed on top of him that at 3.4.40 he unthinkingly dabbed his brow with the stolen handkerchief before, reminded, cramming it hastily back into his pocket and getting on with the crucial line of persuasion for which it would provide the vital prop. Perhaps it would be more accurate to say that Sher's Iago was fixated on other people's sexuality in general, and driven to attack it wherever he could: ingeniously, for example, this production found a reason why Cassio, instead of being efficiently murdered, only suffers a leg wound, since Sher's Iago was too busy trying manically to castrate him in the dark to get on with delivering the *coup de grace* before the hue and cry arrived on the scene. This, indeed, was Iago's signature wound: shortly afterwards his 'Come, mistress, you must tell's another tale' (5.1.127) was delivered with a nod and a wink as a tacit instruction to the party of soldiers who were restraining Bianca to feel free to rape and brutalize her while she was in their custody, and Iago's conflation of sexuality with

20 *Othello*. Cheek by Jowl, dir. Declan Donnellan (world tour, culminating at Riverside Studios, Hammersmith), 2004. Othello (Nonso Anozie) and Iago (Jonny Phillips).

violence reached its horrible culmination in the following scene when he killed Emilia with a knife-thrust between the legs. This wasn't a cold Machiavellian with some rational master-plan but a full-blooded psychopath: ''Tis here, but yet confused' (2.3.310) was delivered with more than ordinary puzzlement and discomfort, as if by someone who didn't want to think nearly as often as he did about why he was engaging on the appalling course of action he was trying to formulate. In short, this was a production as busy as ever at the game of diagnosing Iago and hunting for his motives, and very adept at it too. Perhaps predictably, its final image was of Sher: sitting wounded downstage left, head down and silent ever since vowing never to speak word, he abruptly sat bolt upright after the final couplet of the play was pronounced and raised his head, eyes staring wildly out into the auditorium. Was he suddenly realizing the full horror of what he had done or suddenly realizing that he needed to come up with another plan, and quickly? You didn't know – of course you didn't know – but you could go on thinking fruitfully about it for months.

Declan Donnellan's production, for Cheek by Jowl, was another kind of *Othello* entirely. It had no set to speak of, just five brocade-draped wooden boxes (ammunition cases? coffins?), and every proscenium-arch theatre to which it toured was stripped bare to the wings and to the back wall. (It has to be admitted that this show was better suited to being played in the round in small venues like the Riverside Studios; at the Oxford Playhouse, for instance, this treatment simply produced an overlarge acting area with poor acoustics.) Realism as conventionally understood was replaced by the sorts of ensemble, rehearsal-exercise-like techniques at which Donnellan excels. At the opening of the play, for example, the entire cast entered and began walking about on the stage, but all save Iago and Roderigo froze into a tableau centring on Othello facing Desdemona while the two disgruntled men, still pacing among their immobile and invisible colleagues, discussed the elopement. A dumb show of Cassio's promotion followed, as Iago outlined his ostensible reasons for hating Othello, and the tableau of Othello and Desdemona as perfect couple would recur as an illustration at subsequent points in the action (in 'And what's he then that says I play the villain?', 2.3.327ff, for example). During Iago's scenes of persuasion, the ideas he placed in Othello's imagination were made visible to us on the stage, with Desdemona lying on her back and simulating orgasm during 'But how, how satisfied, my lord? / Would you, the supervisor, grossly gape on, / Behold her topped?' (3.3.399–401), and she and Cassio acted out the encounter implied by Iago's subsequent account of Cassio's dream (415–30).

As all this may suggest, this was a production interested above all in the play's depictions of people in thrall to pre-fabricated scenarios, an *Othello* inflected by hints of Genet; there was an odd sense in which Desdemona and Emilia (Caroline Martin and Jaye Griffiths) didn't seem to be immersed in the real action of the story at all, a relaxed, modern pair of friends (distinguished only by the fact that one of them, Emilia, chain-smoked) who nonetheless found themselves the object of murderous male fantasies. Bianca was only the most striking instance of this tendency, a woman who was here allowed only to be a creature of male fantasy, by trade at least: Kirsty Besterman played her not as an unmarried sexual partner called 'whore' only by malign convention but as a fully fledged career dominatrix, who in 3.4 took money from Cassio to beat him while he pleasured himself, mopping himself afterwards with the handkerchief, and thereby supplied the play with what was almost a miniature comic-sub-plot version of the fatal instance of domination and submission that is Desdemona's murder. It wasn't always easy to know in what spirit to read any of this – where was this version of Cyprus? which actions were we supposed to read literally, which as fantasies? – and as a result the production depended very heavily for its continuing emotional purchase on the figure seen here as the most literal-minded on the stage, Othello himself. While Jonny Phillips's Iago, forever swaggering and slinking his way around the edges of the stage, seemed stereotypically weaselly and villainous – so much so that it was almost impossible to believe that Jaye Griffiths's blithe Emilia had even noticed she was married to him – Nonso Anozie held the centre of this production with a huge, eloquent performance of grief, bafflement and rage. Whatever else was happening, he was in earnest throughout, insisting on being heard: in the senate scene, for example, the governors of Venice would happily have got on with their war against the Turks and ignored Brabantio entirely had Othello not demanded a hearing for the tale of his wooing. In a post-modern production, his was a surprisingly old-fashioned Othello – slightly self-important, potentially even a little stupid, but essentially better-intentioned than anyone else in the cast – and the killing of Desdemona was made as atrocious a spectacle as it has ever been: enraged, Othello actually lifted her into the air above him by the neck as he strangled her, before dropping her back onto the bed. He did not, however, attempt to rewrite himself as a great lover with his last breath, since his couplet about dying upon a kiss was cut, and this piece of editing seemed if anything designed to make him more sympathetic rather than less so. More than twenty years since their first *Othello*, it's a tribute to Cheek by Jowl that they should still be producing such consistently provocative and exploratory work as this show.

None of the RSC's summer season of tragedies in the Royal Shakespeare Theatre (*Macbeth*, *Romeo and Juliet*, *King Lear*, *Hamlet*) were anything like this innovative, though the enterprise of putting these four plays on with a single repertory company (with most actors appearing in at least two shows) seemed, for today's RSC, laudably ambitious. It's a shame, perhaps, that the company assembled for this project wasn't stronger: although most of the principals did well, some of the acting in the lesser roles was as poor as I've ever seen in this theatre. Pal Aron, for example, made both the weakest Malcolm and the most undisciplined and incoherent Edgar the RST can ever have seen, and his former performance, in Dominic Cooke's *Macbeth*, was saved only by a directorial decision to play Malcolm, interestingly, as though he really had gone to pieces during his English exile (shivering unshaven and apparently on the edge of the DTs under a blanket), so that it was only the arrival of Clive Wood's strong Macduff that prompted him into talking himself eliptically back into action. This *Macbeth*, the first tragedy of the RSC season to open, was for the most part serviceable – with a

21 *Macbeth*. RSC, dir. Dominic Cooke, Royal Shakespeare Theatre, 2004. Sian Thomas as Lady Macbeth.

simple, effective design by Robert Innes Hopkins that used a lot of under-lighting along the front of the stage, straightforward greatcoated witches who held a rope like the Fates, a brisk pace, and no interval – but it was as striking for what it didn't do as much as for what it did. It did not, for example, present a compelling portrait of a close marriage. As Macbeth, Greg Hicks already looked steely and remote from the outset, with little in the way of human warmth and social belonging to lose, and one got a strong sense from his early scenes with Sian Thomas's Lady – from whom he developed a bad habit of recoiling, repeatedly, with his chin up, whenever she sounded too keen about killing Richard Cordery's amiable Duncan – that she was goading him into committing the murder primarily in the hopes that a little homicidal complicity might spice their marriage up a bit. Sadly, it didn't work: theirs was the picture of a relationship which might have been, rather than of one being tested to destruction, and with Macbeth so tight-lipped it fell to his Lady to do most of the visible emoting. Sian Thomas made a rather feminine Lady Macbeth as a result, and, once more in this year of unexpected flashbacks, a remarkably old-fashioned one, issued with a hairstyle and a nightdress which seemed to be based on those worn by Sarah Siddons. The Macbeths were in this reading isolated from one another all along, and consequently they seemed most at home in the play's last movement, when actually separated, in the sleepwalking scene and in 'Tomorrow, and tomorrow, and tomorrow'. Indeed the whole production closed on another aborted intimacy, when Fleance (here present for the final battle, a piece of adaptation that goes back all the way to William Davenant) was left alone with Macduff beside the corpse of Macbeth, after the departure of Malcolm and his thanes/earls. The fatherless son and the childless father looked briefly at one another, as if about to compare notes about their respective situations, but then they couldn't quite face it, and Macduff awkwardly left – leaving Fleance on the verge of being accosted, instead, by the reappearing witches.

Max Stafford-Clark's production for Out of Joint was a good deal more exciting and considerably more violent than this one, but surprisingly it had a far simpler and more triumphalist ending. It billed itself as a promenade production, but if that term is taken to imply a show in which the audience are kept in almost constant movement around an acting area while the play takes place among them it was that only intermittently. The bulk of the play – from 'They met me in the day of success' (1.5) through to the end of 3.3 (the killing of Banquo), and from the apparition scene (3.5) to the ending – was actually played out in a single room with the audience seated on benches around three sides of a demarcated acting area, as in any studio production, but the use of other spaces for the opening movement, for the banquet scene and for a brief nasty moment after the killing of Macduff's family in 4.2 was striking enough. On tour at the orthodox, proscenium-arch Oxford Playhouse, the play began with the audience (only 80 strong, despite the 600-plus capacity of the house) being led out into the street from the foyer and round to the rear of the building, where they were made to queue to enter the scenery dock while being inspected and intermittently hassled by a pair of African-looking youths in combat fatigues carrying AK47 rifles. The rough, cavernous space to which we were grudgingly admitted was emphatically not our territory: in this noisy, smoky, dimly lit space piled with crates, some more heavily armed African soldiers (some wearing kilts with their combat gear) and some of their womenfolk were smoking, beating drums, dancing, and it was some time before two more soldiers, played by Danny Sapani and Chu Omambala, pushing their way across the room between the apprehensive spectators, were accosted by three tribal-looking witches, whose lines were drawn from both 1.1 and 1.3 but were spoken, by two out of the three, in an African dialect of French. In this play about disputed national boundaries, where Norway and England each seek to intervene in Scottish affairs, Sapani's Macbeth was bilingual too, responding quickly to their promises and riddles, and so this *Macbeth* was under way, transposed to a contemporary Africa of child-soldiers and rival warlords, and haunted by memories of Idi Amin's incongruous enthusiasm for Scottish nationalism.

An edited version of 1.2 followed, conflated with 1.4, all played around the scenery dock in the midst of the crowd, and this treatment worked extremely well for Macbeth's asides, with Sapani pacing among the audience and eyeballing individual spectators as he thought aloud about the possibility of killing the Duncan who had just promoted Malcolm above his head to be Prince of Cumberland. It was only at the transition to 1.5 that we were ushered through a doorway into a new space – the backstage area itself, fitted up as a perfectly ordinary studio theatre like a small reflection of the larger auditorium beyond the safety curtain which provided its back wall. Here, in front of a loyal official portrait of the fly-switch-bearing Duncan, was Monica Dolan's Lady Macbeth, the sole white principal in this cast. Despite a programme note citing the real-life case of a white aid worker, Emma McCune, who married a warlord in the Sudan in 1990 and was nicknamed 'Lady Em' thereafter, it has to be admitted that Dolan and Sapani seemed to be in completely different productions. Hers was a rather patronizing Lady Macbeth, heavily inflected by Ayckbourn, sounding, with her Northern-based cut-glass tones, more like a socially ambitious Liverpool suburbanite than a participant in a guerrilla war. Toward the end of the dagger scene, as the prospect of imminent discovery loomed offstage, she pronounced the words 'I hear a knocking / At the south entry' (2.2.63–4) as though even this emergency could not diminish her self-congratulation at already being the mistress of a house which boasted not a mere back door but a *south entry*. (This attitude seemed the more incongruous in that the Porter manning that entry was rewritten entirely to fit the African *mise-en-scène*, becoming a young odd-job employee who begged the audience for money to pay for him to study abroad.) It was only to be expected that the apogee of Dolan's performance would be the banquet scene, where she played the aspiring hostess discomfited at her moment of triumph to perfection. She got to play hostess not just to the thanes, either: for this passage the whole audience were briefly shepherded out onto the Playhouse stage proper, where a table was laid, and a lucky few even got to sit among the guests of honour and share the wine. After Banquo's disconcerting appearance (from underneath it), 'Stand not upon the order of your going, / But go at once' (3.4.116–17) had to be repeated personally to almost every member of the audience, as Lady Macbeth shooed us back into the improvised studio, where the remainder of the scene, her desultory, depressed conversation with Macbeth (from 'It will have blood', 3.4.121) was played as if after a lapse of time.

The most provocative use of this other space, though, came during 4.2, the killing of the Macduffs. While two murderers dragged Lady Macduff and her son out of sight (onto the stage proper), another had found the terrified Ross who had tried to warn them to flee, and he held Ross prisoner and forced him to listen (with us) to the sounds of rape and butchery coming from just beyond the safety curtain. When the two killers returned, the sound of a lone baby crying indicated that one member of Macduff's family still survived, and, horribly, the murderers slowly handed Ross one of their bloodstained machetes. It was perfectly clear that he could either demonstrate his loyalty by killing the baby himself or be killed alongside it. Kevin Harvey handled this moment extremely well, shaking as he took the knife and left toward the crying: then, after a long moment, the crying stopped, and he returned, almost vomiting, and the awful scene was over. Except that it wasn't: after Ross's exit, the murderers urged us to our feet, beckoned us forwards, and offered to let us peep through the safety curtain at their victims in exchange for small sums of money. This was the one really intriguing, self-reflexive moment in what was otherwise almost a straightforward exercise in naive realism, and it made a more forceful point about the nature of tragedy as a genre than did any of the RSC's tragedies-only season. What exactly is the difference between paying to see *Macbeth* and paying to see images of real murder? Would it have been more inappropriate to accept these feigned murderers' invitation to become fully fledged voyeurs of their handiwork, or to refuse it, as the theatrical contract involving this bloody piece of drama stood? After this vivid and troubling scene, the rest of Stafford-Clark's production almost came as an anticlimax: Malcolm and his followers returned to power wearing UN armbands and making speeches through megaphones, and the whole cast beat drums and played bagpipes to give a long rousing African version of 'Scotland the Brave' before the curtain call. It seemed glib and facile after what had preceded it, but this was still a powerful and disturbing account of the play, and another intriguing addition to the long, controversial and surprising relationship between *Macbeth* and Africa.

The year's two major productions of *Romeo and Juliet* had far less to recommend them, displaying less passion between them than did any single scene of this *Macbeth*. Peter Gill's RSC production looked like a tasteful re-run of Zeffirelli's, only without the energy. Nice-looking young men stood about in tights in front of a pale blue set on which Italianate architecture was sketched as if in Old Master drawings, but nothing seemed to spark between the performers at all: it was like watching an unusually well-funded school production, and not even a performance at that but the first off-book walk-through. In the aubade scene, 3.5, Romeo and Juliet (Matthew Rhys and Sian Brooke) faced outwards beside one another on the balcony bickering idly and sarcastically about whether it was a lark or a nightingale for all the world like near-strangers passing the time while waiting for a bus, and in the tragic scenes which followed both indicated when they thought their characters might be upset by shouting a little, without actually seeming to feel anything at all. June Watson did what practically amounted to a solo turn as the Nurse, but this was one of those productions you have the odd sensation of having forgotten while it is still in progress, the one unmitigated dud of the RSC's season. The Globe's rendition, directed by Tim Carroll, at least had more bustle to it, but such zest as it displayed was dissipated in jolly asides to the crowd, and from its flippant rewriting of the opening brawl onwards – which here was supposed to originate from a dispute as to whether it was the turn of the Capulet servants or the Montagues to make the customary opening announcement about switching off mobile phones – it didn't seem to want to be taken in earnest. Even the balcony scene was dominated by giggling over Tom Burke's inept attempts, as Romeo, to climb the pillars to the upper level. Three performances in June were at least enlivened by a professed attempt to give the play in a reconstruction of Elizabethan pronunciation as well as of Elizabethan clothing, but, while the cast did well not to be more distracted by this phonetic challenge than they were, the result was simply a random mix of stage Irish, stage West Country and stage West Indian, ranging from Melanie Jessop's 'This noight yer shall be'old 'im at wor fest' (1.3.82) to Kananu Kirimi's 'Me onnli lov sprong from me onnli het!' (1.5.137). The lesson that should be drawn from this, perhaps, is that it's probably less important to act with the pronunciation of an Elizabethan player than with the commitment and expertise which Shakespeare's fellows must surely have brought to this text.

Back in Stratford, Bill Alexander's *King Lear* was an infinitely more serious and estimable piece of

22 *King Lear*. RSC, dir. Bill Alexander, Royal Shakespeare Theatre, 2004. Kent (Louis Hilyer), Lear (Corin Redgrave) and the Fool (John Normington).

work, and boasted in Corin Redgrave's Lear what was probably the most compelling single performance of the summer season. Beautifully lit by Tim Mitchell and designed with elegant simplicity by Tom Piper – on a long, deep, rectangular acting area, the only objects composing the set were benches and refectory tables, piled with increasing disorder at its back and sides as the action progressed – this was, however, a production that managed to be very fine only while nonetheless displaying, here and there, some sadly undistinguished acting. I've already registered an official complaint about Pal Aron's Edgar, who began the evening as a bespectacled, caricatured bookish ninny in plus-fours before metamorphosing into an indiscriminately barking Poor Tom who never seemed to have thought about which aspects of his behaviour were motivated by the need for disguise and which weren't, and who as a result ought in justice to have been recognized by his father any number of times during the storm scenes; but he was not the only member of this cast who seemed well below standard. As Goneril and Regan, Emily Raymond and Ruth Gemmell were unvaryingly cross and bad throughout, and while the understatement which made Sian Brooke such an underwhelming Juliet made her rather an effective Cordelia, Matthew Rhys was if anything even less qualified to play Edmund than he was to impersonate Romeo, forever breaking up his longer and more complex sentences into often nonsensical and unmetrical shorter units and swallowing crucial consonants. To crown it all, Sean Hannaway managed somehow to throw away that gem of a small role, Oswald, to no effect whatsoever. The announcement in this season's inconveniently oversized programmes that some of the 2004 company will again be employed by the RSC in 2005 already has some Stratford habituees anxiously guessing which ones.

Fortunately, Alexander's production had such clarity of outline, and had teased such detailed, nuanced performances from the remaining key players, that it was able to carry all this: between them Lear, Gloucester, Kent and the Fool were easily capable of distracting an audience from the cruder performances around them, and as a result this *Lear* was especially strong in the heath scenes. Not that it didn't make an impressively authoritative and original stab at the opening love-test, too. At the very opening of the play, the whole cast for 1.1 were found seated around the stage, with the principal members of Lear's family at a white-draped table set along its front, picked out in turn by spotlights as the house-lights dimmed: the occasion, as the lighting stabilized and Edmund was introduced to Kent downstage front, might have been the tense annual meeting of a present-day family-run restaurant business. Lear's first entrance was a real coup: instead of arriving with the rest of his family in his train, he appeared from the back of the stage and tottered slowly and solemnly downstage to join them, a bent old man in a red waistcoat who had to lean uncertainly on two walking sticks as he picked his way agonizingly toward them, and they all silently registered their horror and apprehension at his condition (has he really grown so feeble since we last saw him?) – until, infuriatingly, he stopped a little way short of the table, stood upright with what he took to be a mischievously twinkling smile, and threw the sticks away. From the polite laughter and applause that greeted this hubristic little joke, it was clear that this King Lear had always regarded himself as the life and soul of the family party – it wasn't for nothing that his longest-serving companion was an old music-hall comic of a Fool, warmly and percipiently played by John Normington – and his tyranny at first consisted as much in his complete insistence on his children's smiling, amused attention as it did in his actions. Playing Lear not as already gloomily tragic for his first entrance but in irritatingly ebullient high spirits about his impending retirement made enormous sense, and the first two-thirds of the love-test – an impossible piece of behaviour on exactly the same level as the joke entrance with the sticks – went with a swing and a good many self-congratulatory chuckles. At first Redgrave's Lear delighted in keeping his children in suspense even about how many of them would be receiving a share of the family estate: calling for a projector to be switched on to shine an image of Britain onto a flip-chart screen on 'Give me the map there' (1.1.37), he then artfully paused, fumbling with a set of notes, at a crucial point in his next sentence: 'Know that we have divided / In *[riffles, looking down, half-smirking]* . . . three our kingdom'. Drawing felt-pen lines vigorously on the map, he was having the time of his life: after issuing Goneril with Scotland and much of the North of England, he responded to Regan's dutiful protestations by scribbling a line from the Mersey to the Severn to give her Wales during 'To thee and thine hereditary ever' (1.1.79–82), and then, as if only reminded to throw in a free bonus by recalling the name of her husband, looked up at the anxious, craning faces of the dependent couple, gave a little amused 'O!' at his own pretended forgetfulness, and extended the line southwards to the Channel to add the duchy of Cornwall to their share, laughingly pointing first at the map and then at the man as he crowed 'Cornwall!' under his breath as though it were a Basil Brush punch line.

The ensuing transition into anger with the uncooperative Cordelia was exquisitely registered: Lear at first thought that she too was joking on 'Nothing will come of nothing', and 'Speak again' sounded like an invitation to her to tell him another. He took her aside, warning her with confiding affection that he was serious on 'How, how, Cordelia?', then moved through a sort of saddened, head-shaking disbelief before reserving the full force of his rage for Kent. At Cordelia's subsequent plea that he should let Burgundy and France understand that she wasn't being disowned for any crime except an aversion to flattery, he came tenderly to her and held her, cradling her head, so that we almost thought that father and youngest child were about to be reconciled after all, but after pronouncing 'Better thou / Hadst not been born than not t'have pleased me better' (1.1.233–4) in tones of wounded sorrow Lear practically let her fall to the floor and stumped off across the stage, contenting himself with a sarcastic slow handclap on Cordelia's betrothal to France and absently giving Burgundy an approving, conciliatory pat on the head to show which son-in-law he would really have preferred, had things gone according to plan. This was already a performance of complete conviction and complete authority – yes, this was clearly how this old devil would behave, and we felt that we had known him for years. Between them, Alexander and Redgrave had found a way of making the love-test and its aftermath psychologically convincing without needing to shroud it in cod ancient ritual or any anxious signs that we were only supposed to read it at the level of fairytale.

Over the last four or five years, Corin Redgrave, remembered around Stratford as rather a clumsy actor when last with the RSC in the early 1970s, has suddenly come into his own, and his recent stage and screen work – notably in Harold Pinter's own revival of *No Man's Land* – has revealed him to be capable of roles of hardness and of vulnerability. Lear is of course both, and of all the performers I have seen in this role Redgrave was perhaps the best at rendering both the savage anger of the first three acts and the softened, reconciled pathos of the last. This was a production interested above all in Lear himself as a psychological and moral case history: the storm scene wasn't titanic or even very loud, but the emotional force of its minute portrait of a calcified personality cracking into humanity via madness was no less intense for that, and 'Poor naked wretches' (3.4.28–36) made a direct, visceral appeal to the consciences of its audience. Some critics were irritated by the little interjections of 'hmm?' which Redgrave favoured, often in mid-sentence, as at 'Then let them anatomize Regan, mm? See what breeds about her heart. Is there any cause in nature that makes this hardness, hmm?' (13.70–2; as so often nowadays, this was primarily a Folio-based acting text, but with the joint-stool scene added from the quarto). But it was precisely through little touches like this that Redgrave illuminated the thought-processes of his Lear, as in the reconciliation scene, which was made the more moving by the little semi-comic, naturalistic touch Redgrave introduced when he paused to rack his brain before hesitantly attempting to ask his anxious question at 4.5.79 in the appropriate language: 'Am I . . . suis-je . . . en France?' This wasn't the most eloquently well-spoken or the most consistently well-acted *Lear* of recent years, but it gave an exceptionally clear and fully realized account of its protagonist's progress, and the last scene was as crushing as always. Instead of risking his back by cradling her corpse in his arms, Redgrave's Lear dragged Cordelia slowly onto the stage to take her place beside the bodies of her sisters – bodies which he, heartbreakingly, inspected with uncomprehending curiosity while the other survivors were speaking about him – and after his death (from a naturalistic heart attack, with Louis Hillyer's Kent practically fighting Edgar off to prevent him trying to resuscitate him) the remaining characters, their inconclusive elegies spoken, trailed away, leaving only Kent seated on the stage, weeping among the bodies as the lights faded.

Of the year's three versions of *Hamlet*, the most satisfying was easily Michael Boyd's, despite the publicity attracted by Trevor Nunn's at the Old Vic and the gravitas surrounding Yukio Ninagawa's at the Barbican. Nunn cast a young newcomer in the title role, Ben Whishaw, who was hailed as a major discovery by some of the newspaper critics and who might even have deserved these accolades had his performance only thought of somewhere new to go after a plausibly snivelling rendition of 'O that this too too solid flesh would melt' (1.2.129–58). This was a modern-dress production: the rucksack worn by its beefy Laertes, Rory Kinnear, and a number of other minor props, were strongly reminiscent of Stephen Pimlott's RSC production of 2001, but the show's set (dominated by an immense concrete staircase descending at its rear) didn't resemble any contemporary centre of power and overall Nunn's account of the play lacked both the cogency and the topical political resonances of Pimlott's. Instead we were given only a study in adolescent inadequacy, a *Hamlet* centred on a Prince who never rose to any of the occasions the play offered him but instead sulked and whinged his way gracelessly about the

23 *Hamlet*. Old Vic, dir. Trevor Nunn, 2004. The closet scene: Gertrude (Imogen Stubbs) and Hamlet (Ben Whishaw).

stage hoping that someone else, ideally his mother, would solve his problems for him. Never has 'O cursed spite / That ever I was born to set it right!' (1.5.189–90) so monotonously set the tone for a performance in this wonderful and here substantially wasted role. 'To be or not to be', transposed to the earlier position it occupies in the first quarto, was played as a scene of its own, with Hamlet coming and sitting on a bench, considering whether to end it all on the spot with an overdose of pills, and then leaving and, to be fair, Whishaw's hesitant, naturalistic performance of this soliloquy would have made a good drama-school exercise: but it characteristically reduced the speech's philosophical content to a mere whining personal complaint about what a miserable time Hamlet was having and how unfair it all was. The production, it's true, had a perfectly convincing diagnosis for all this tedious behaviour, in the person of Imogen Stubbs's Gertrude, a simpering blonde who kept fit by taking tennis lessons with Claudius in between affairs of state and whose highly maintained youthful good looks would undoubtedly have turned the heads of many of Hamlet's peers had she ever visited his Wittenberg hall of residence. Unfortunately she was far more interested in being thought charming than in belatedly bringing up her terminally spoiled son and she too turned out to be wholly inadequate to the situation in which she found herself, resorting to drink even before the expected full-on Oedipal closet scene and, rather wonderfully, draining the poisoned cup in the duel scene only to show Claudius that he had no business accusing her of being a lush in public. 'Gertrude, do not drink!', indeed! The last thing the dying Hamlet did, pathetically, was to lift her dead hand and tousle his own hair with it – as if all he'd really needed all along was a cuddle. This was, I suppose, a perceptive depiction of a mutually incapacitating, over-indulged mother and son, but you didn't really want to spend longer than four minutes with either of them, never mind a full four hours. Nunn hasn't directed a really successful Shakespeare now for more than five years, and while his previous thirty years of work in this field have given him a good many more laurels to rest on than most, there are murmurings abroad that he may be losing his touch.

Ninagawa's production, which was in its different way just as unsatisfying a *Hamlet*, toured extensively before arriving at the Barbican (it was produced in association with the Theatre Royal, Plymouth), by which time it looked slightly tired. If Nunn's Elsinore had looked like nowhere recognizable but was at least recognizably supposed to be somewhere in the present, Ninagawa's belonged to no time and no place, the set consisting solely of dangling vertical lengths of barbed wire and, above them, twelve naked light bulbs, which swung in agitation whenever the action beneath them grew violent. Like his RSC *King Lear* back in 1999, this English-language production suffered from an unfocused and portentous vagueness quite absent from his Japanese-language *Pericles* in 2003: in schematically colour-coded costumes which alluded at once to the Samurai period and to the European Renaissance without belonging legibly to either, the actors, with no realized society within which to interact, spoke at rather than to one another, as if from within their own individual follow-spots. Michael Maloney, hampered by a cassock-like black costume which made him resemble an eccentric trainee priest, managed some striking moments, but they always looked like so many striking moments, his performance an intermittent anthology of good poses struck in a vacuum rather than a sustained exploration of the role: at the end of the first half, for example, here placed just after the court's exit from the play scene (3.2.258), he stalked upstage to stand between the two chairs which had just been vacated by Claudius and Gertrude, paused, and then pushed them both over backwards, upon which the lights dimmed. There was a hint of kitsch self-congratulation about the mean, moody look on Maloney's face as he did this which rather devalued the gesture, a hint which persisted even through the duel scene, and once again I found myself leaving a tragedy disappointed that its players hadn't managed to seem to be wholly in earnest about what they were doing. Are all our younger actors too ironic and aloof and small-scale nowadays fully to inhabit

24 *Hamlet*. RSC, dir. Michael Boyd, Royal Shakespeare Theatre, 2004. Toby Stephens as Hamlet.

Shakespearian tragedy, or even to go through its motions without looking as though they are half sending them up?

The answer, to judge from Michael Boyd's RSC *Hamlet* at least, is not all of them. Toby Stephens took what was in every sense a good stab at the title role, offering a muscular, overwrought Prince who was a deadly serious player throughout in a lethal game of internal court politics. This Elsinore, its denizens clad in undistracting Renaissance costumes, was a claustrophobic place already on a knife-edge of political tension before the first scene even began: the set, by Tom Piper, offered a circular acting area confined at its rear by a curved wooden wall (into which concealed doors would open as required), and the Francisco who here challenged Barnardo clearly never quite stopped mistrusting the colleagues who relieved him – he later reappeared among Claudius's loyal bodyguard, for example, summoned by a quiet word from Polonius as the play-within-a-play threatened to become politically sensitive. This was a theocratic court as well as an absolutist one: 1.2 began with a chorus of 'Sanctus' as Gertrude and Claudius processed, bride-and-groom-like, to the centre of the stage beneath a shower of confetti, clad in opulent shades of red and gold which contrasted dramatically with the black robes of the dispossessed Prince who stood behind and between them. Clive Wood made a powerful, imposing Claudius, whose first, official speech to the court did not preclude some private flirtation with Sian Thomas's Gertrude: describing old Norway as 'impotent and bedrid' (1.2.29), he caught her eye and gave a tiny swaggering smile, to which she responded with a blushing downward grin, as though to confirm the implicit contrast he was drawing between the Norwegian monarch and the Danish. Hamlet was visibly disgusted by this, and in 'Seems, madam?' (1.2.76–86) his voice sounded almost on the edge of cracking into tears, an effect which Stephens sustained right through 'O that this too too solid flesh would melt' once he was left alone. If I were to criticize Stephens's performance at all it would be for the fact that his voice sounded on the edge of hysterical weeping like this for most of the play, rarely varying from this pitch of feeling save in greater and lesser degrees of the aristocratic sneering which made him such a superb Coriolanus ten years ago but which can grow a little tiring in other roles. He wasn't helped with this during the soliloquies by the production's austere shortage of props, which too often left him looking for something to focus on in the middle distance above the heads of the audience, and was liable to give his performance a generalized quality, but of all this year's Hamlets he still managed to be the only one who was animated not only by a desire to stay alive and, preferably, kill Claudius into the bargain, but by a reaching, restless curiosity about the nature of the universe around him.

Here he was amply backed-up by this production's overwhelming interest in that bourn from which no traveller returns, and given the distinctive colouring of Boyd's earlier work for the RSC – which has often been preoccupied with ghosts, even when producing plays whose scripts don't supply roles for them, as in the case of his *Romeo and Juliet* in 2000 – it was only to be expected that a highlight of this show would be its scenes with Hamlet senior, played by Greg Hicks. Indeed Boyd, unfortunately for this journal, seems to have anticipated considerable interest in the ghost, to such an extent that he forbade the official photographers from taking any dress-rehearsal or preview photographs of Hicks in the role so that the particular form his appearance took would come as a guaranteed surprise to playgoers, a move which has resulted in there being none extant by which to illustrate this account of his performance. Words, then, will have to suffice: picture a withered, whitened figure, naked save for the tattered remains of cereclothes dangling kilt-like from its waist, dragging from its immobile claw-like right hand a huge broadsword which makes an echoing, scraping sound as it trails along the ground, a sharp and silvery counterpoint to the lowing oriental drum which punctuates each of its appearances. Its eyes are hollow, its left arm stiffened and crooked, and it moves as if in slow motion, stretching out each foot before it in turn, toes pointed, in the creeping balletic ghost of a martial stalk. It is the uncanny shell of a performance, all technique, studiedly uninhabited except by the impersonal, leftover pain of the late king's death; it is certainly the most dead thing you have ever seen arrive on a stage by its own motion. In 1.1, in response to Horatio's horrified entreaties, this tormented, zombie-like remnant of a self manages briefly to reanimate the muscles of its face, slowly and agonizingly opening its mouth and trying to force one last breath from its dead lungs as though dying once more before the sentries' eyes, but then the cock crows and it is gone. With Hamlet in 1.4 it finally manages to achieve speech, but it is scarcely human speech, as deliberately mannered as its movements. The metallic voice drops almost an octave during the resonating last consonant of almost every word, and as it utters what almost constitutes a recorded message to Hamlet junior, so remote is the next world from which it speaks, it once more manages to seize the handle of the sword in both hands and swings it slowly around, raising it above its head on the line 'Revenge his foul and most unnatural murder' (1.4.25) and, keeping it there, hanging suspended above young Hamlet's head, through most of the narrative of the poisoning. On the words 'O horrible, O horrible, most horrible!' (1.4.80), it almost breaks down, and its auditor is almost sick, and when it scents the morning air and finally utters the words 'Adieu, adieu, Hamlet. Remember me' (1.4.91) it leaves not by stalking off but by leaping grotesquely into the grave which suddenly opens before it centre stage. This was an astounding piece of acting, and a real feat of dramatic imagination on Boyd's part, the other-worldliness of the ghost brilliantly rendered as an irruption from some other theatrical genre altogether – dance? the religious ritual of another culture? It was the more astounding in that this wasn't Hicks's only contribution to the production either: the revenant returned both as the Player (repeating that pose with the sword during the narrative of Pyhrrus's killing of Priam, to Hamlet's discomfort, and uncomfortably reminding Gertrude of her late husband during one pointed moment while standing before her as the Player King) and as the Gravedigger (troubling her memory again during one fleeting glance at Ophelia's funeral). Remember thee? This was a performance fit to haunt the audience's nightmares for years to come.

What constrained Hamlet from carrying out the ghost's injunction immediately in this production was very much the efficiency of his antagonist and his security apparatus. Hamlet seemed to be bracing himself for imminent action during the play scene – well-nigh taunting Claudius at one charged moment, when he detained the property crown from the players and put it on his own head – and there was every reason why the guards should have been summoned just as Lucianus was about to get to work. On Hamlet's 'You shall see anon how the murderer gets the love of Gonzago's wife', the action froze into a red-lit tableau and the Prince purposefully brandished a dagger at his uncle: but then a blackout signalled the interval, and afterwards Claudius regained the initiative, now aware of just who his enemies were (there was a nice little moment after Ophelia's funeral, for example, when Claudius gave a special, reproachful emphasis to the word 'Horatio' in 'I pray you, good Horatio, wait upon him' and Horatio, alarmed to have been recognized, sullenly removed the hood he had pulled up over his face at the court's entrance). Guards arrived with Rosencrantz and Guildenstern to disarm Hamlet during their dialogue at 3.2.279ff and, although the loyal Horatio then supplied him with his own dagger after their departure, its victim would only be Polonius (here stabbed rather implausibly through a wooden wall). Hamlet was genuinely distraught to find who he had killed and during the remainder of the closet scene he seemed genuinely concerned to persuade his mother to join him in resisting Claudius, rather than just getting sidetracked into wallowing in his feelings about her remarriage. It is to its credit that this production always kept its eyes on the practical politics of the court: although the text was elegantly cut, for example, some of 'How all occasions do inform against me' was retained, here treated not as a self-flagellating soliloquy but as a purposeful attempt by Hamlet, rapidly gagged by being dragged off stage by his captors and onwards toward England, to get word to Fortinbras via the Captain of the father killed and mother stained whom he was trying to avenge. The account of his escape from the ship was here given in the first quarto version, in the form of that little scene between Horatio and Gertrude in which the converted queen explicitly declares her allegiance to her son and her desire that he should succeed in killing Claudius, and taking her cue from this Sian Thomas completely reversed the conventional trajectory of her role. Instead of collapsing in on herself from the closet scene onwards, this Gertrude was redeemed from the self-indulgence her marriage to Claudius had represented and took a renewed interest in the people around her. She is the only Gertrude I've ever seen, for example, who sounded as though she would actively have liked to rescue the drowning Ophelia in her set piece at 4.7.135–55, and she seemed actually to want to help Laertes (interestingly played, by Gideon Turner, as a reformed libertine) with his grief.

This was a comparatively extroverted *Hamlet*, then, a plot-driven revenge thriller with an unusually developed interest in the death toward which it was propelling so many of its characters, its set a circular space around a grave. If it had any failings, they were a poorly conceived treatment of the relationship with Ophelia, which never looked very exciting on either of their parts (would this active young aristocrat really have taken an interest in Meg Fraser's oddly down-market virgin, someone who on going mad adopted the make-up of a Victorian prostitute and sang ribald songs in a cockney accent, like Nancy in *Oliver!*?), and a slightly self-contained quality. It was very distressing that the game ended as wastefully and mortally as it did; we felt very shaken and moved at the spectacle of this prince's death (at the end of an electrifying swordfight, to Terry King's credit) and chilled, as the lights faded on Fortinbras's takeover, to hear once more the relayed sound of the ghost's scraping swordpoint. But how did the world of this production, and indeed the worlds of the other productions in this season of tragedies, connect with our own? Perhaps the RSC will be more successful at regaining their place as a theatre company expert at making Shakespeare's plays relevant to the contemporary world in 2005, when they embark on a comparable season of comedies. (How pleasant it would be to think that we lived in a world closer in spirit to Shakespearian comedy than to Shakespearian tragedy!) But in the meantime, the rest is silence.

# PROFESSIONAL SHAKESPEARE PRODUCTIONS IN THE BRITISH ISLES JANUARY–DECEMBER 2003

JAMES SHAW

Most of the productions listed are by professional companies, but some amateur productions are included. The information is taken from *Touchstone* (www.touchstone.bham.ac.uk), a Shakespeare website maintained by the Shakespeare Institute Library. *Touchstone* includes a monthly list of current and forthcoming UK Shakespeare productions from listings information. *The Traffic of the Stage* database, also available on *Touchstone*, archives UK Shakespeare production information since January 1993, correlating information from listings with reviews held in the Shakespeare Institute Library. The websites provided for theatre companies were accurate at the time of going to press.

## ALL'S WELL THAT ENDS WELL

Royal Shakespeare Company. Swan Theatre, Stratford-upon-Avon, 3 December 2003–7 February 2004.
www.rsc.org.uk
Director: Gregory Doran
Countess: Dame Judi Dench
Helena: Claudie Blakley
Parolles: Guy Henry

## ANTONY AND CLEOPATRA

Glasgow Repertory Company. Botanic Gardens, Glasgow (Bard in the Botanics season). 15–27 July.
www.glasgowrep.org
Director: Scott Palmer
Set in 18th century India.

## AS YOU LIKE IT

Sphinx Theatre Company (formally Women's Theatre Group). Bridewell Theatre, London, 19–26 February and on tour.
Director: Sue Parrish
Rosalind: Danielle King

Royal Shakespeare Company. Swan Theatre, Stratford-upon-Avon, 13 March–8 November.
www.rsc.org.uk
Director: Gregory Thompson
Rosalind: Nina Sosanya

Shakespeare at the Tobacco Factory. Tobacco Factory, Bedminster, Bristol, 20 March–26 April.
www.shakespeareatthetobaccofactory.co.uk
Director: Andrew Hilton
Rosalind: Saskia Portway

R J Williamson Company. Nottingham Castle, Nottingham, 15 July–10 August and tour.
www.openairshakespeare.co.uk
Directors: Robert Williamson and Frank Jarvis
Rosalind: Martha Swann
Touchstone: Robert Williamson

Peter Hall Company. Theatre Royal, Bath, 11–30 August and international tour.
Director: Sir Peter Hall
Designer: John Gunter
Rosalind: Rebecca Hall
Touchstone: Michael Siberry
Jaques: Philip Voss

Oxford Stage Company. Lincoln's Inn, London, 14–16 August.
www.oxfordstage.co.uk
Director: Kevin Hosier

## THE COMEDY OF ERRORS

Bremer Shakespeare Company. Theatre Royal, Bath, 3–6 March. Part of the Bath Shakespeare Festival.
www.shakespeare-company.com
Director: Sebastian Kautz
In German with English surtitles.

Festival Players Theatre Company. Tour May–August.
www.festivalplayers.org.uk
Director: Michael Dyer
Cast of four. Includes 5 new songs with lyrics taken from *Venus and Adonis*, *Passionate Pilgrim* and Nicholas Brenton.

Two Minds Theatre Company. Rosemary Branch Theatre, London, 1–27 July.
Director: Robert Gillespie
Both sets of twins doubled.

Bristol Old Vic. Old Vic Theatre, Bristol, 3–25 October.
www.bristol-old-vic.co.uk
Director: David Farr

Court Company. Courtyard Theatre, London, 26 November–21 December.
www.thecourtyard.org.uk
Director: Christopher Geelan

*Adaptation*

*The Bomb-itty of Errors*
New Ambassadors Theatre, London, 24 April–12 July.
Director: Andrew Goldberg
Rap version written and performed by cast of four.

*Da Boyz*
Theatre Royal, Stratford East. 7 May–14 June.
Director: Ultz
'Hip-hop' updating of *The Boys from Syracuse*.

## CORIOLANUS

Royal Shakespeare Company. The Swan Theatre, November 2002–May 2003; Old Vic 6 June–23 August.
www.rsc.org.uk
Director: David Farr
Coriolanus: Greg Hicks

Top of the World Company. Tour of South West England, September–October.
www.top-of-the-world-theatre.com
Director: Tom Frankland.

## CYMBELINE

Royal Shakespeare Company. Swan Theatre, Stratford-upon-Avon, 30 July–7 November and tour
www.rsc.org.uk
Director: Dominic Cooke
Imogen: Emma Fielding
Iachimo: Anton Lesser

## EDWARD III

Royal Shakespeare Company. Gielgud Theatre, London, 17 December 2002–24 January 2003. Transfer from the Swan Theatre.
www.rsc.org.uk
Director: Anthony Clark
Edward III: David Rintoul

## HAMLET

Gateway Theatre Company. The Studio, Broadway Theatre, London, 28 January–22 February; Gateway Theatre, Chester, 24–26 April
Director: Tristan Brolly

Wild Thyme Theatre Company. Upstairs at the Gatehouse, London, May–June.
Director: Stephen Jameson
Hamlet: Miranda Cook
All female Hamlet set in Weimar Germany.

R J Williamson Company. Nottingham Castle, Nottingham, 17 July–8 August.
www.openairshakespeare.co.uk
Director and Hamlet: Robert Williamson
Ophelia: Emily Lloyd

Natural Perspectives Theatre Company. Royal Observatory Garden, Greenwich Park, London, 26 July–10 August.
Director: Matt Peover
Hamlet: Matthew Bulgo

Thelma Holt in association with Setagaya Public Theatre. Sadler's Wells Theatre, London, 28 August–6 September.
Director: Jonathan Kent
Hamlet: Nomura Mansai
All male production. In Japanese with English surtitles.

Birmingham Repertory Theatre & Edinburgh International Festival. Royal Lyceum Theatre, Edinburgh, 20–30 August; Birmingham Repertory Theatre, Birmingham, 9–20 September.
Director: Calixto Bieito
Hamlet: George Anton

Chapterhouse Theatre Company, Lincoln. Tour September–November.
www.chapterhouse.org
Director: Karen Crow
Hamlet: Philip Stevens

Nuffield Theatre Company, Southampton, 16–31 October.
www.nuffieldtheatre.co.uk
Director: Patrick Sandford
Hamlet: Stephen Noonan
Polonius: John Woodvine

Maddermarket Theatre Company, Norwich, 20–29 November.
www.maddermarket.co.uk
Director: Peter Beck
Hamlet: Charlie Hollins

*Adaptation*

*Hamlet*
Compagnie Mimodram (Georgia). Ustinov Studio, Theatre Royal, Bath, 6–8 March. Part of the Bath Shakespeare Festival.
www.bathshakespeare.org.uk
Wordless dance adaptation performed to a jazz score.

*Hamlet*
Arc Dance Company. UK tour April.
www.arcdance.com
Director: Kim Brandstrup
Dance adaptation that includes source material from *Prince Amlet*. Reworking of Brandstrup's 1993 production *Antic*.

*Hamlet*
Det Lille Turneteater Company. Children's international theatre festival. Glasgow Garage, Glasgow, 1–4 June.
www.detlilleturneteater.dk
80 minute version presented by two actors and aimed at an early teenage audience.

*La Tragédie d'Hamlet*
Théâtre des Bouffes du Nord/CICT. Warwick Arts Centre, Coventry, 11–14 June.
Director: Peter Brook
In French with English surtitles.

*Humble Boy*
Royal National Theatre. Tour October–December.
www.nationaltheatre.org.uk
Director: John Caird
Author: Charlotte Jones

*Opera*

*Hamlet*
Royal Opera Company. Royal Opera House, London, 12–30 May.
www.royaloperahouse.org.uk
Directors: Patrice Caurier and Moshe Leiser
Composer: Ambroise Thomas

## HENRY IV PART I

*Adaptation*

New York City Players. Barbican Centre, London, 11–15 November. Performances cancelled.
www.nycplayers.org
Director and Adaptor: Richard Maxwell

## HENRY V

Northern Broadsides. February–May, UK tour with *A Woman Killed with Kindness*.
www.northern-broadsides.co.uk
Director: Barrie Rutter
Henry: Conrad Nelson

Royal National Theatre. Olivier Theatre, London, 14 May–20 August and tour.
www.nationaltheatre.org.uk
Director: Nicholas Hytner
Henry: Adrian Lester
Chorus: Penny Downie

Mad Dogs and Englishmen. Tour June-August.
www.mad-dogs.freeserve.co.uk
Henry: Paul Lockyer

*Adaptation*

*Henry*
Glasgow Repertory Company. Botanic Gardens, Glasgow, July (Bard in the Botanics season).
www.glasgowrep.org
Director: Scott Palmer
A faithful adaptation setting the play in the First World War.

## JULIUS CAESAR

Royal Lyceum, Edinburgh, 19 September–18 October.
Director: Mark Thomson
Julius Caesar: Kern Falconer
Modern urban setting.

## KING LEAR

English Touring Theatre. Old Vic Theatre, London, 18 March–19 April and tour.
www.englishtouringtheatre.co.uk
Director: Stephen Unwin
Lear: Timothy West

Stamford Shakespeare Festival. Tolethorpe Hall, Stamford, 9 July–6 September (in repertory with *Twelfth Night* and *The Beaux Stratagem*)
www.stamfordshakespeare.co.uk

*Adaptation*

*Wicked Bitches–King Lear, the Daughters of a Madman*
Blue Mountain Theatre. City Varieties Music Hall, Leeds, 10 May and tour.
Playwright: Floyd Knight

*Lear's Daughters*
Yellow Earth Theatre Company, Tour October–November.
Director: David KS Tse
Devised by: Elaine Feinstein & Women's Theatre Group
90 minute prequel.

## LOVE'S LABOUR'S LOST

Royal National Theatre. Olivier Theatre, London, 15 February–18 March.
www.nationaltheatre.org.uk
Director: Trevor Nunn
Berowne: Joseph Fiennes
Rosalind: Kate Fleetwood

## MACBETH

Richmond Theatre, Richmond, 28 October–2 November 2002, transfer to Albery Theatre, November 2002–March 2003.
Director: Edward Hall
Macbeth: Sean Bean
Lady Macbeth: Samantha Bond

Crucible Studio, The Crucible Theatre, Sheffield, 30 January–22 February.
www.sheffieldtheatres.co.uk
Director: James Phillips
Macbeth: Finbar Lynch
Lady Macbeth: Lucy Whybrow
Eighty minute version performed by a cast of four.

*Adaptation*

*Elsie and Norm's Macbeth*. Playhouse, Salisbury, 12 December–4 January 2003.
Playwright: John Christopher Wood
Director: Charlotte Conquest

*From a Jack to a King*
Musical by Bob Carlton based on *Macbeth*.
Coliseum Theatre, Oldham, 30 January–22 February.
Follows the fortunes of Eric Glamis, an amateur rock star who has amibitions to make the big time.

*Makb3th*
Pirate Utopia Company. Tour April.
www.pirateutopia.org/macbeth
High-tech, multi-media event: 'Please bring your mobile phones.'

*Macbeth*
Teatre Romea, The Pit, London, 8–12 April.
Director: Calixto Bieito
Performed in Catalan and Spanish with English Surtitles. A mafia-based production that cut the witches.

*Sleep No More*
Punchdrunk Theatrical Experiences, Beaufoy Building, London, 8–20 December
Directors: Felix Barrett and Maxine Doyle
Unstructured promenade production set in a series of rooms without straightforward plot or narrative.

*Opera*
Edinburgh International Festival. Usher Hall, Edinburgh. September
Composer: Verdi
Conductor: Sir Charles Mackerras

## MEASURE FOR MEASURE

Royal Shakespeare Company. Royal Shakespeare Theatre, April–October.
www.rsc.org.uk
Director: Sean Holmes
Angelo: Daniel Evans
Isabella: Emma Fielding
Duke: Paul Higgins

Arcola Theatre, London 27 May–11 June.
www.arcolatheatre.com
Director: Jack Shepherd
Angelo: Scott Ainsle
Isabella: Rebecca Lenkiewicz
Duke: David Carter

Glasgow Repertory Company. Botanic Gardens, Glasgow, 25 June–6 July (Bard in the Botanics season.)
www.glasgowrep.org
Director: Kate Varney
Duke: David Caird

## THE MERCHANT OF VENICE

Illyria Theatre Company. Tour May-August.
www.illyria.uk.com
Company of seven actors.

Chichester Festival Theatre Company. Chichester Festival Theatre, 6 June–2 October.
www.cft.org.uk
Director: Gale Edwards
Shylock: Desmond Barrit
Portia: Niamh Cusack

Ludlow Festival. Ludlow Castle, 20 June–11 July.
In repertory with *The Winter's Tale*.
www.ludlowfestival.co.uk
Director: Michael Bogdanov
Designer: Chris Dyer
Shylock: Philip Madoc

## THE MERRY WIVES OF WINDSOR

The Royal Shakespeare Company. Tour October 2002–May 2003; Old Vic, 7 June–23 August.

www.rsc.org.uk
Director: Rachel Kavanaugh

Heartbreak Productions. Tour June-August.
www.heartbreakproductions.co.uk
Director: Peter Mimmack

*Opera*

*Falstaff*
Royal Opera Company. Royal Opera House, London, 11–26 February.
www.royaloperahouse.org.uk
Composer: Verdi
Director: Graham Vick
Falstaff: Bryn Terfel

*Falstaff*
Halle Orchestra, Bridgewater Hall, Manchester, May.
Composer: Verdi
Conductor: Mark Elder

*Falstaff*
Bampton Classical Opera, Bampton, Oxfordshire, July.
www.bamptonopera.org
Composer: Salieri

A MIDSUMMER NIGHT'S DREAM

Propeller Theatre Company. The Watermill Theatre, Newbury, 5 February–22 March; and tour.
Director: Edward Hall
All-male production.

Queen's Theatre, Hornchurch, 18 March–5 April.
Director: Bob Carlton

Playbox Theatre. Dream Factory, Warwick, 27 March–9 April and local tour.
www.playboxtheatre.com
Director: Stewart McGill

Bristol Old Vic. Main House, Bristol, 8 May–7 June.
www.bristol-old-vic.co.uk
Director: David Farr

Oskaras Korsunovas Theatre. Gardner Arts Centre, Brighton, 14–17 May; Riverside Studios, London, 20–4 May.
Director: Oskaras Korsunovas
Lithuanian Theatre Company
Adaptation where each actor carried a life-sized wooden board

Heartbreak Productions. Tour June–August.
www.heartbreakproductions.co.uk
Director: Peter Mimmack

New Shakespeare Company. Open Air Theatre, Regent's Park, London, 2 June–6 September.
http://openairtheatre.org
Director: Michael Pennington

Glasgow Repertory Company. Botanic Gardens, Glasgow, 25 June–6 July (Bard in the Botanics season).
www.glasgowrep.org
Director: Gordon Barr

Maddermarket Players. Maddermarket Theatre, Norwich, 26 June–5 July.
www.maddermarket.co.uk
Director: Tim Seely

Chapterhouse Theatre Company. Lincoln and on tour September–November.
www.chapterhouse.org
Director: Karen Crow

Sheffield Theatres. The Crucible Theatre, Sheffield, 24 September–1 November.
www.sheffieldtheatres.co.uk
Director: Michael Grandage

*Ballet*

*A Midsummer Night's Dream*
Northern Ballet Theatre. UK Tour September–November.
www.northernballettheatre.co.uk
Director: David Nixon

*Opera*

*A Midsummer Night's Dream*
British Youth Opera. Queen Elizabeth Hall
30 August–4 September.
Composer: Britten

MUCH ADO ABOUT NOTHING

Chapterhouse Theatre Company. Tour
June-August.
www.chapterhouse.org
Director: Karen Crow

Glasgow Repertory Company. Botanic Gardens, Glasgow, July (Bard in the Botanics season).
www.glasgowrep.org
Director: Kate Varney
Set in 1945 Britain.

OTHELLO

Haymarket Theatre and Concentric Circles Company. Haymarket Theatre, Basingstoke, 7–22; Theatre Royal, Bath, 7–8 March.
Director: Christopher Fettes
Othello: Ricky Fearon
Iago: Christopher Middleton
Cut Act V scene 1

Nottingham Playhouse Theatre Company. Playhouse, Nottingham, 31 October–22 November.
www.nottinghamplayhouse.co.uk
Director: Paul Savage
Othello: Leo Wringer

Royal & Derngate Theatres Northampton, October; Greenwich Theatre, Greenwich, 4–15 November.
Director: Rupert Gould
Othello: Ron Cephas Jones
Iago: Finbar Lynch

*Adaptation*

*Iago's Stories*
Gulbenkian Studio, Newcastle-upon-Tyne, 12–15 March.
Director: Annie Rigby

*The Tragedy of Othella, the Hip Hop Diva of Venice Beach*
HWS Rembiko Project. Rocket@Demarco Roxy Art House, Edinburgh, 1–15 August.

PERICLES

Ninagawa Theatre Company. Royal National Theatre. Olivier Theatre, London, 28 March–5 April.
Director: Yukio Ninagawa
Translator: Kazuko Matsuoka

Royal Shakespeare Company with Cardboard Citizens Company. The Warehouse, Southwark, 22 July–9 August.
www.rsc.org.uk
Director: Adrian Jackson
Promenade production including testimonies of asylum seekers.

Lyric Theatre Hammersmith. 18 September–18 October.
www.lyric.co.uk
Director: Neil Bartlett
Pericles: Will Keane
Modern-dress production.

RICHARD II

Shakespeare's Globe Theatre, London. 8 May–27 September.
www.shakespeares-globe.org
Director: Tim Carroll
Richard II: Mark Rylance
Bollingbroke: Liam Brennan
All-male company.

RICHARD III

Shakespeare's Globe Theatre, London, 25 May–27 September.
www.shakespeares-globe.org
Director: Barry Kyle
Richard: Kathryn Hunter
All-female company.

Royal Shakespeare Company. Royal Shakespeare Theatre, Stratford-upon-Avon, 11 July–8 November.
www.rsc.org.uk
Director: Sean Holmes
Richard: Henry Goodman

## ROMEO AND JULIET

Chapterhouse Theatre Company. Tour June–August.
www.chapterhouse.org
Director: Richard Main

English Touring Theatre. Tour September–December.
www.englishtouringtheatre.co.uk
Director: Stephen Unwin

Theatre Vesturport (Reykjavik). The Young Vic, London, 1–25 October.
www.vesturport.com
Director: Gisli Orn Gardarsson
Set in a circus environment.

*Adaptation*

*Ronnie and Julie*
The Outlookers. Gala Theare, Durham. 10–11 March.
Devised and performed by disabled actors to address issues for the disabled.

*Shakespeare's R&J*
Splinter Group (New York). Theatre Royal, Bath, 11–15 March; Arts Theatre, London September.
Adaptor and Director: Joe Calarco
Set in a repressive Catholic boarding school. Cast of 4, all male.

*Opera*

*I Capuleti e i Montecchi*
English National Opera. Barbican Centre, London, 8–10 October.
www.eno.org
Opera by Bellini.

*Ballet*

*Romeo and Juliet*
Royal Ballet of Flanders. Sadler's Wells, London, 6–10 May.
Choreographer: Andre Prokovsky
Composer: Prokofiev

*Romeo and Juliet*
Royal Opera House. Royal Opera House, London, 4–14 June.
www.royaloperahouse.org.uk
Choreographer: Kenneth Macmillan
Composer: Prokofiev

*Romeo and Juliet*
Northern Ballet Theatre. UK Tour September–November.
www.northernballettheatre.co.uk
Director: David Nixon

## THE TAMING OF THE SHREW

Over the Edge (Zimbabwe). Ustinov Studio, Theatre Royal, Bath, 12–15 March. Part of the Bath Shakespeare Festival.
www.bathshakespeare.org.uk

Royal Shakespeare Company. Royal Shakespeare Theatre, Stratford-upon-Avon, 31 March–8 November.
www.rsc.org.uk
Director: Gregory Doran
Katherine: Alexandra Gilbreath
Petruchio: Tony Britton

Shakespeare's Globe Theatre Company. Shakespeare's Globe Theatre, London, 10 August–28 September.
www.shakespeares-globe.org
Director: Phyllida Lloyd
Petruchio: Janet McTeer
Katherina: Kathryn Hunter
All female.

Theatre Royal Plymouth and Thelma Holt. UK Tour October–December
Director: Mark Rosenblatt
Kate: Nichola McAuliffe

Petruccio: Ross Kemp
Induction omitted.

*Adaptation*

*The Tamer Tamed*. Royal Shakespeare Company, Swan Theatre, Stratford-upon-Avon, 9 April–8 November.
www.rsc.org.uk
Playwright: John Fletcher
Director: Gregory Doran

*Taming of the Sista*
Millfield Theatre, Edmonton, London, 4 May.
www.millfieldtheatre.co.uk
Adaptor: Maurice Blackman
Black contemporary take on Shakespeare's *The Taming of the Shrew*, using rap, poetry, dance, music and monologue.

### THE TEMPEST

Sheffield Theatre Company. Old Vic Theatre, London, 13 January–15 March.
www.sheffieldtheatres.co.uk
Director: Michael Grandage
Prospero: Derek Jacobi

Royal National Theatre Education. Cottesloe Theatre, London, 19–20 March.
www.nationaltheatre.org.uk
Director: Mark Rosenblatt

Creation Theatre Company. Open Air Theatre, Headington Hill Park, Oxford, 1 July–13 September.
www.creationtheatre.co.uk
Director: Zoe Seaton

*Adaptation*

*The Little Tempest*
Royal National Theatre. Olivier Theatre, London, 15–21 March.
www.nationaltheatre.org.uk
Director: Rebecca Gould
Adaptor: Lesley Ross

*Ballet*

Independent Ballet Wales. UK Tour June–December.
www.welshballet.co.uk

### TIMON OF ATHENS

Ealing Shakespeare Players. Quaker Meeting House, Edinburgh, 11–23 August. Edinburgh Fringe Festival.

### TITUS ANDRONICUS

Royal Shakespeare Company. Royal Shakespeare Theatre, Stratford-upon-Avon, 12 September–7 November.
www.rsc.org.uk
Director: Bill Alexander

### TROILUS AND CRESSIDA

Shakespeare at The Tobacco Factory. Tobacco Factory, Bedminster, Bristol, 6 February–15 March.
www.shakespeareatthetobaccofactory.co.uk
Director: Andrew Hilton

### TWELFTH NIGHT

Isleworth Actors Company. Rose and Crown, London, 11–22 March.
Director: Arthur Horwood

Playbox Theatre. Dream Factory, Warwick, 13 March–8 April and local tour.
www.playboxtheatre.com
Director: Stewart McGill

Creation Theatre Company. Open Air Theatre, Headington Hill Park, Oxford, 6 June–28 July.
www.creationtheatre.co.uk
Director: Charlotte Conquest

Stamford Shakespeare Festival. Tolethorpe Hall, Stamford, 9 July–6 September.

www.stamfordshakespeare.co.uk
Courtyard Theatre Company. Courtyard Theatre, London, 10 and 17 August; 1–21 September.
www.thecourtyard.org.uk
Director: Toby Eddington

Dundee Repertory Theatre, Dundee, 3–20 September.
www.dundeereptheatre.co.uk
Director: Dominic Hill

Royal Exchange, Manchester. Royal Exchange, Manchester, 10 September–25 October.
www.royalexchange.co.uk
Director: Lucy Bailey

The White Company. Shakespeare's Globe Theatre, London, 2–12 October.
www.shakespeares-globe.org
Director: Tim Carroll
Olivia: Mark Rylance
Revival of 2002 production

*Adaptation*

*Meat and Two Veg*. Cartoon De Salvo.
19 February–6 March
Director: Alex Murdoch.
Adaptation set in the Second World War.

## TWO GENTLEMEN OF VERONA

Facsimile Productions. Pentameters, London, 25 March–13 April and tour.
www.facsimiletheatre.co.uk
Director: Lucy Gordon-Clark

New Shakespeare Company. Open Air Theatre, Regent's Park, London, 4 June–6 September.
http://openairtheatre.org
Director: Rachel Kavanaugh

Theatre Set-up. Tour June–August.
www.ts-u.co.uk
Director: Wendy McPhee

Northcott Theatre Company. Northcott Theatre, Exeter, 16 July–16 August.
www.northcott-theatre.co.uk
Director: Richard Beecham

## THE WINTER'S TALE

Dundee Repertory Theatre. His Majesty's Theatre, Aberdeen, 12–15 February.
www.dundeereptheatre.co.uk
Director: Dominic Hill
2001 revival.

Compass Theatre Company. Greenwich Theatre, London, 11–15 March; The Crucible Theatre, Sheffield, 15–19 April.
Director: Neil Sissons.

Ludlow Festival. Ludlow Castle 21 June–12 July.
www.ludlowfestival.co.uk
Director: Michael Bogdanov

Oxford Shakespeare Company. Lincoln's Inn, London, 31 July–31 August.
www.oxfordshakespearecompany.co.uk
Director: Chris Pickles

## MISCELLANEOUS

*Loves of Shakespeare's Women*
Jermyn Street Theatre, London, 21 January–2 February
One-woman show by Susannah York. First seen at 2002 Edinburgh Fringe Festival.

*Shakespeare's Italian Job*
Metro Gilded Balloon Treviot, Edinburgh, 1–25 August.
Director: Malachi Bogdanov
*The Italian Job* translated into Shakespeare's language.

*Shakespeare's Villains*
UK tour.
Director and performer: Steven Berkoff

# THE YEAR'S CONTRIBUTIONS TO SHAKESPEARE STUDIES

## 1. CRITICAL STUDIES

*reviewed by* RUTH MORSE

As I complete my three-year stint of reading and reviewing Shakespeare criticism, and as part of my annual general reflections, I want to acknowledge the invisible support which makes this article possible. I think I can speak for the other reviewers in saying how chastening it is to realize just how much Shakespearians depend upon the judgements in this section to keep abreast of what's going on, especially in places where access to books and periodicals is limited. The brute fact of wealth is repeatedly brought home to us, by which I mean not merely access but the freedom which comes with time, Pascal's sitting quietly in a room – time to read, to write, to think. Universities which appreciate, and subsidize, scholarship – and not all of them do – underwrite our writing, and not crudely as one component in our terms and conditions. Subsidy of journal publication through university presses, and university departments, enhances our conversation. It isn't all good news, however, and I have previously signalled the increase in what threatens to become a kind of institutional vanity publishing. Subsidy may soon be necessary for the publication of specialized monographs but it is already taken for granted with collections of conference papers or, indeed, collections of essays by individuals. For example, this year essays from the World Shakespeare Congress in Valencia and the Shakespeare in Europe meetings have begun to appear, courtesy of Ashgate's rare willingness to make them available – as long as someone else does all the preparation. The University of Delaware's commitment to Renaissance literature has long been exemplary and both presses have been laudably open to non-Anglo-Saxon scholars. For more miscellaneous collections, Ashgate and Boydell and Brewer may soon be the last homes of the English-language *festschrift*. I have tried to indicate both the positive, where subsidized labour or financial support has brought about a book which would otherwise not now have been possible (the proceedings of the Basel European Shakespeare conference and the excellent *festschrift* for Brian Gibbons, for example, which will appear in next year's pages), but also the dubious, where I believe that subventions by deans or departments have enabled certain local scholars to commit yet another publication. Could I put my hand on my heart and affirm that not all essays merit republication between hard covers? This year, in this essay, pressures on space have taken their toll but I hope I have listed everything I received in the bibliography which follows this essay (articles in collaborative volumes will be found in 'Collections').

I have worried, in previous years, that 'history' is tacitly replacing 'theory' as our butts and lists. I have written about my reservations that inadequate histories of religion, with present-minded categories about what 'must have' constituted one or other of two – merely – christian sects, have given us a false argument which is wrong-footed even when compromises (Shakespeare was both or neither Catholic or Protestant) appear on the horizon. Religion is not a chi-square, and we need finer-grained analyses not about what constituted 'puritan' or 'Gallican Catholic' but what ranges of belief were tolerated where and when. Religion is just too important to be left to believers. As I have read a series of contributions which engage with the language of post-industrial-revolution economics, I wonder if there is not a clear and present danger from belief in a unified *homo economicus* which too often entails the received idea that industrial capitalism replaced a collectivist, communitarian, customary tradition; that early-modern man [sic] turns from group to individual action which is all economic. Is this not *déjà vu* all over again? There is no time back in the mists in which there was an associated sensibility; the clear innovations of double-entry book keeping or paper credit began in the Middle Ages (among what we are pleased to call Arabs, Italians and Jews), when authors worried about the replacement with, or restriction of, exchange-values of many kinds by something merely monetarized. I suppose I am saying that there are important differences between a 'back-formation' and a 'back story', and that 'a' prior account may hide – at what we used to call a theoretical level – more varied and more complex views than any broken-backed Hegelianism always allows. We need an article, or a book, which might be titled 'Verbal Value: anxieties about exchange and money in the Age of whatever we're calling it this week' which is based on a close study of historical semantic shifts in more than one language.

In Shakespeare criticism there may be a cutting edge, but it is rare; the field moves more by opening out (one thinks of continental Shakespeares; Shakespeare prequels, sequels, and adaptations), partly under the influence of participants in our conversations. The influence of outstanding practitioners stimulates, resuscitates, opens and legitimates approaches of all kinds, as is manifest in essays acknowledging particular scholars in critical sequels and adaptations which appear below. So also, there are ideas whose time has come, as is evidenced by the ripples which have succeeded the publication of Lukas Erne's *Shakespeare as Literary Dramatist*, reviewed last year. New interest in adaptations, both in creative and in critical writing, is stimulating work which helps us understand both our pasts and our criticism; we are re-absorbing linguistic-literary approaches which include dictionaries, histories of the language, and guides which might once have been dismissed as reference books. These are not the clarion calls of wall-tumbling paradigm shifts, but rather the slow drum roll of recognition, where exemplary work asserts or reasserts its viability and fecundity. This year I continued to remark how much good work appears in books intended for teaching, or for common readers, particularly in the Arden and Oxford series; how both new respect for editing and textual bibliography, and new forms of 'close reading' (often modified by developments elsewhere), have had resurgences. Attention to the 'received text' and its traditions of commentary as determinants of criticism have helped us become more conscious of the burden of the past and the English Shakespeare critic. And, for the second year running, there is always *The Merchant of Venice*.

So let me begin with work on *Merchant*, which, conveniently enough, also illustrates some of these opening points. A rich and sparkling essay by Janet Adelman dissects and lays before us a tissue of conflicting points of view in which different characters voice a series of opinions which amount to a summary of the radical incoherences of attitudes to any 'Jewish question'. Her close readings are under-written by contemporary reading, by editorial correction between early editions, as well as by attentiveness to linguistic change and range in the period. She surveys ideas of descent, religion, rites or other practices which might (but might not, in the case, say, of suspiciously successful medical expertise) be allied to cult, 'nation' (in the sense of political or geographical origin), visible/sensible difference (or lack thereof) and the threat of *conversos* entering the greater population. This is fine-grained argument, very good on the joke on Aragon, which reveals anxieties explored within the play: purity of blood and descent as what Englishmen mocked in the Spanish aristocracy. She explores English ideas of the Spanish as, despite their protestations to the contrary, actually descended from the Moors and Jews they execrated, in effect realigning Shylock's invisible difference with the colour difference visible in the Prince of Morocco, whose insistence upon 'blood' returns later in the play; she uses this observation to show how the play distinguishes Jessica from her father by insisting upon her fairness as a contrast to his blackness. Extending her reading to the minor characters, Adelman then excavates the names of Chus and Tubal, to remind us that these grandsons of Noah were the ancestral founders of those post-Flood nations which correspond to Aragon and Morocco. Into this historical tapestry she is then able to weave Lancelot Gobbo's pregnant Moorish mistress. And it is this idea of Shakespeare's thinking about common ancestry, land and religion as the foundations of nation-hood which finally leads her to think about Jews as a figure of landless nationality. The upshot is to remake Belmont, as a borderland which is also a fantasy of England, with its hybrid happiness, balancing religion, descent and state.

*The Merchant of Venice* concludes Lisa Lampert's *Gender and Jewish Difference from Paul to Shakespeare*. This book has the great advantages of starting from the complexities of the Middle Ages and of situating the development of 'identities' in a nuanced and dynamic series of contexts which looks forward to modern social structures in the context of debates about universalism. Her view of *The Merchant of Venice* is thus part of an argument which questions periodizations and identities; for her the Venetians are exegetes struggling with spiritual and literal, inner and outer, the values of trade and those of Christian community, where the desire for profit undermines stable values and, above all, religion and race. Here she calls into question the fundamental categories which have occupied students of the play. I do not see how her work can succeed in changing several hundred years of presuppositions, but her interpretation invites us to think again in ways that have implications for study elsewhere. Her perspective is longer than our interest in one play, but in the context of humane letters – as we might once have called it – a book of importance.

Linda Woodbridge unites a series of essays which circulate around *The Merchant of Venice*. Most of the essays use Venice to illustrate ideas about capital and economic exchange, so that Shakespeare is called up to support a theoretical approach, rather than an 'economical' approach to revitalize interpretation of Shakespeare. A series of unresolved problems emerges: was there a change in economic circumstances or a perception that something was changing, more or faster than whatever it was had hitherto changed? (One longs for a discussion of labour shortage, inflation and increasing urbanization after the Black Death as a comparison. Or Shakespeare's almost complete failure to observe women's work in the home, with the exception of service. There is no essay on the merry wives and their laundry.) How did people discuss exchange, and were gifts or mutual obligations being monetarized, and, if they were, how did people react? But, finally, there is a problem about the status of metaphor and how we treat those perceived resemblances, at whatever level of abstraction. There is nothing less like identity than similarity, and metaphor is one of those hyphen-like exercises whose stunning, violent yoking demands that we question its effect, as its affect. To paraphrase Raymond Carver, what do we talk about when we talk about money? In this context the most important essay in the collection is Mark Netzloff's analysis of what we mean by capital, capitalism, and coin in the stage world of Venice, and the world stage of London. It is refreshing to find such an open reading of the challenge to think about what constitutes value in *The Merchant of Venice*. And there is an equally invigorating discussion of Lancelot Gobbo by Steven R. Mentz.

Less promising, because more prone to assertion of similarities and influences, is Eric Spencer's discovery of Aristotle's critique of money in *The Merchant of Venice*, which evades any need to show influence or connection between the two. Asserting and denying links contributes to the messiness in which Spencer declares himself interested; there is no need to hang familiar discussions about value on an ancient philosopher. And Robert Darcy strains at Freudian and other metaphors, suggesting, among other things, the equivalence between Shylock's moneybags (two, round) and his testicles; as well as that Portia's father is an incestuous hoarder of his daughter's sexual service. The economic advantage of marriage to such a wastrel as Bassanio is not explained.

Despite my reservations about 'economic' criticism, let me recommend the two Shakespearian chapters of Jonathan Gil Harris's *Sick Economies: Drama, Mercantilism, and Disease in Shakespeare's England*, one of which looks at *The Merchant of Venice*. Harris uses the examination of metaphors as armatures of thought, here the fiction of 'mercantilism' as a 'transnational typology', which he relates to invasive disease, in a synergy of anxiety. There is some swift moving on in the analyses, which sometimes threaten to overwhelm frail theatrical barks, whose tone seems to me at odds with the metaphors of xenophobia and disgust Harris finds. Shakespeare's comedies are, after all, funny. Intellectual historians have discussed many of the same issues, and it is a pity that in this fascinating book there is insufficient attention to their work. But the strength of such analysis from our side, as it were, of the engagement is our alertness to the styles of romance – or of comedy – in other aspects of writing, whether we call it political or economic. Harris wants the theatrical discourse to be pathological, and he wants to insist upon nationalisms and trade in his transnational discourses; he therefore gives disproportionate attention to sexually-transmitted disease (not, for example, plague, which surely had great community interest) which he finds homologous to the desire for wealth through commerce. He has the usual difficulties in both denying and then exploiting 'mercantilism' as a central theory. As he notes, in the humoural theory of medicine, analogous to the four elements, as well as with ideas of heavenly as human bodies, we are all always sick, because never in balance. In that sense existence itself is 'pathological', and there is nothing sinister in the pervasive exploitation of disease as metaphor, or dis-ease as a state of being. This is one of those strong readings which will provoke thought, whether or not it compels agreement.

Individual articles include James O'Rourke's exploration of the play in what he takes to be the contemporary context. In arguing that Shakespeare wrote an anti-racist response to the execution of Lopez (1594), he spins a web of high-political court intrigue and prejudice against Italian (Lombard) moneylenders, actually in London, rather than an attack on (absent) Jews, although 'Jews' turn out to be a screen for homosexuals (I compress), so that the play 'reflects', via a double scape-goating structure (Shylock sacrificed, Antonio in some way cast aside), a conspiracy which involved Essex's plotting against (the closet homosexual) Francis Bacon. This kind of interpretation depends on any number of encrypted references, which are quite like some recent Catholic-conspiracy fantasies. Along the way Portia ends up as a phallic mother. By contrast, there is Laurie Shannon on 'husbandry' and friendship in the play, examining interlocking language registers which indicate presuppositions, ideals, and contradictions. This well-argued essay builds from her work on friendship praised in these pages last year.

Despite my optimism about books for students, some seem to have been thrown together on the cheap, at speed, which will do nothing for reputations such as Routledge's. S. P. Cerasano's so-called 'sourcebook' on *The Merchant of Venice* is an apparently unselfconsciously marxisant introduction to the play, as seen in the topics by which it organizes its reading: its major socio-political contexts turns out to be economic, including the 'capitalist playhouse'. What is missing from this picture? Contemporary ideas about Venice; the family; structures within the play (including economic structures of marriage and choice). The criticism is mostly twentieth century, mostly American. By Shakespeare's day, the fictional idea of Venice was already anachronistic but, even so, one might help students to think better about a Catholic but tolerant trading city with large numbers of immigrants and possible social mobility for non-citizens. It will be news to many that 'the English saw the Venetians as a people to be emulated' or that 'they revered Venetian accomplishments' or 'hoped to model their own aspirations' on Venice. It is extraordinary that she prefers Jan Morris's lyricism on Venice to the fine scholarship collected, albeit on the continent, by Ton Hoenselaars, or Margaret Jones-Davies, or Manfred Pfister.

I have pleaded before for attention to worlds elsewhere. But let me caution voyagers to Lancashire. Two volumes of conference papers are collected under the tendentious sub-title 'Lancastrian Shakespeare', a pun which refers to the site of the conference event but which also implies the dubious claim that the Shakespeare's so-called 'lost years' were spent hiding in the open at Houghton in that county. Many of the essays concern Catholics in the region, few of the essays are directly about Shakespeare's work, and of those some are very sure about his hitherto unrecognized Catholic sources or encrypted allusions and allegories. These volumes are replete with associations, sometimes vague or distant, characterized as 'sinister'. They are not. In a world informed by the metaphors of religion, concepts of institutional chastity, for example, employed vocabulary which was already anachronistic in the Middle Ages. Among those not about Catholics, Philippa Berry's energetic essay on time and gender in *Romeo and Juliet* is based on work by Julia Kristeva which has not compelled assent, as she herself recognizes.

Books which explore 'foreign Shakespeare' include Murray J. Levith's on China. This is what it says on the packet, although Shakespeare has only been 'in' China since the twentieth century and often in an ambivalent combination of curiosity and suspicion of outside cultural forces – his work was banned from 1964 with the Cultural Revolution. Shakespeare has been used to support a variety of political agendas and that is the main thrust of the book, which is largely based on English-language sources. Some of the uses to which Shakespeare has been put recall eighteenth- and nineteenth-century adaptations in Europe (including use of the Lambs *Tales*), and there are obvious parallels to the experience of formerly-colonized anglophone countries which may interest post-colonialists. In *Writing Russia in the Age of Shakespeare*, Daryl W. Palmer puts Shakespeare in the title but discusses him very little. Palmer acknowledges that his approach is basically chronological and descriptive, as he shows that the clichés about 'Russia', especially its tyranny, are very old. Catherine O'Neil writes about Pushkin, and what he made of his reading, so her book may appeal only to those who read or study Russian, but as part of the history of Shakespeare reception it is a fascinating account of one great poet reading another and, particularly, of the traditional importance of character, especially in translation. Shakespeare in translation offered the known world a combination of character in action (or inaction), which created a serious, secular repository of reference. In that sense Roger Paulin's much larger, more ambitious study of Shakespeare in Germany illustrates how that repository grew and functioned. This a tripartite history. In the beginning, Shakespeare offered something against what was perceived as nothing: not an alternative to native traditions but a spur in the absence of native traditions (which means that the native past was not taken terribly seriously, viz., baroque tragedy); that Shakespeare was, at least, not French; that he offered romantic imagination, nature and verisimilitude so that, even when French arguments were important, they were interpreted in a German context. For students of Shakespeare and religion, the exploitation of 'incarnational language', which alludes, among other things, to Luther, will be of interest. This is not a book for beginners: Paulin assumes knowledge not only of the critical traditions of Britain and France, but also of the English received edition and something of theatrical reception and translation in France. It will be a pity if anglophone readers dismiss this book out of hand. Among other things, inside this fat book there are several thin ones waiting to be extracted: what plays were first to be translated (and from what texts, e.g. Garrick's *Romeo and Juliet* in 1758, Warburton's edition for Wieland just afterwards)? how did foreign tastes evaluate and select from the stock of Renaissance drama? what is it to be progressive about criticism? – to suggest only three.

Shakespeare appears in a variety of other European countries in two collections edited by Ton Hoenselaars, and by Hoenselaars and Angel-Luis

Pujante. Readers interested in translation, or in productions in Europe, will find the Arden book on translated Shakespeare stimulating (countries and languages are identifiable in the bibliography). Let me recommend Dirk Delabastita's Shakespeare companion to translation, indicating ways in which languages might be mixed within Shakespeare's own plays, and the purposes such multilingualism could serve, as well as his useful bibliography on translation. The survey of four hundred years of Shakespeare in Europe makes a good companion volume. These essays emanate from cultures whose approaches to texts are different enough from Anglocentric universities that they often offer places to stand from which to think about otherwise unquestioned assumptions or presuppositions. Just as Anglophone scholarship has recently begun to treat editors and editing with more respect, so Werner Brönnimann, in the context of the ongoing Germanophone bilingual series, explores the problem posed – not only for the non-English-speaking buyer – by the aura of authenticity which accrues to the three best-known annotated editions of Shakespeare. He emphasizes – with characteristic lightness of touch – the different styles of dual-language editing, basically what I've elsewhere called the 'replacement' (to be read independently) and the 'accompaniment' translation, which gives students considerable philological information. I shall return to these questions below. Anyone who is acquainted with French or other continental work on Shakespeare will be surprised by David Steinsaltz's assurance about Shakespeare's hostility to the French language, in an article which relies on the assumption that characters are always to be believed and that Shakespeare agrees with them. There is much better work on the subject in Dirk Delabastita's essays.

Two recent collections are unified, if that is the word, by geography, Scandinavia and Canada. The first puzzles me, since there isn't a 'Scandinavian' approach, there's no Icelander or Greenlander (or woman) among the contributors, and some of the essays reprint historical material surely available elsewhere. Nor is there much explanation of what Georg Brandes has to say to us now. The whiff of parochialism reaches worrying strength when the editor, Gunnar Sorelius, unselfconsciously refers several times to Shylock's race or 'the typical Jew' before pointing out in passing that meanings change. The first three essays are historical and Swedish: a retranslation of an extract from Strindberg, which is old-fashioned, loquacious and intelligent; some biographical-critical observations by the director Al Sjöberg (d. 1980); and a fifty-year-old essay by Gunnar Sjögren reviewing even older ideas about what kind of 'moor' Othello is (and a second essay unidentified). Keith Brown reconsiders what is 'renaissance' in Shakespeare and finds symmetrical construction to be a key to plays he might have equally have categorized as 'classicizing'. Roger D. Sell expands work from *Neuphilologische Mitteilungen*, with particular application to *Henry V*; but it must be said that his real concern is the debate between present-minded critics such as Terence Hawkes and a more historically-informed analysis of verbal action. *Hamlet* recurs often, as in Michael Srigley's fantasy that King Christian IV attended a specially-rewritten performance of the play (which would have held a mirror up to him); as well as national-character reputations for drinking. Kristian Smidt, surely Norway's foremost Shakespeare critic, refers to work already available in English in a piece on 'Improvisation and Revision' which looks at the inconsistencies he has highlighted.

'Is there a distinctly Canadian Shakespeare'? asks the jacket blurb to *Shakespeare in Canada: a world elsewhere?*. Well, yes and no. Should we expect a specific and unique national orientation? Or, rather, why are we asking this question, if not to imply that there ought to be, but that, equally, Canada's distinctiveness need not depend upon any such thing. By contrast to the Scandinavian volume, in which the origins of the authors are almost coincidental, this is a book emphatically about Canada; about its institutions of education, culture and Shakespeare; and Canadians reacting to Shakespeare. In that sense it is a Shakespeare companion to Post-colonial Canada rather than a Canadian contribution to Shakespeare, as Diana Brydon's afterward makes clear. There are articles on performance, institutions and adaptations, as well as a strident critique of Northrop Frye.

In *Material Shakespeare*, Lloyd Davis has collected essays from the conference of the Australian and New Zealand Shakespeare Association, but the only sense of 'elsewhere' is in surveys of local performances. In Sharon A. Beehler's paper on 'Kairos' as the principle of 'right' time, she suggests that clocks changed time for everyone, as if they superseded other measures for the whole, largely clockless, population. She finds in *Hamlet* moments when the right moment is also the opportune moment. Ann Blake's essay on social mobility in marriage argues that happy marriages appear to take place within a single social status but that Shakespeare is often intriguingly vague about what that status is. Her survey seems innocent of the traditions of discussions of true nobility. Lloyd Davis himself has some interesting reflections on how we might think about 'Shakespearian cultures' and a substantive essay about the court as a mixed cauldron of education, for good, but also of temptation. The high-status male was encouraged to learn self-control in the difficult circumstances of court life. He tries to draw a sympathetic portrait of Bertram trying to learn, but it doesn't seem to me that 'trying to learn' is exactly Bertram's idea of escaping surveillance. And there are some less familiar approaches to teaching experience, which are not criticism, but can be moving, on the seclusion of prisons or the openness of the web, via Simon C. Estock on ecocriticism of *The Winter's Tale*. In *Shakespeare's Illyrias: Heterotopias, Identities, (Counter) histories*, Martin Procházka collects papers from the World Shakespeare Congress in Valencia precisely on ideas of elsewhere, 'heterotopias', in the comedies and romances. His contributors write directly about the 'where' of Shakespeare's London stage settings, which they often refer to as a 'geographical fantasy' which takes advantage of historical geographies of considerable latitude where there be dragons.

'Elsewhere' also appears in a new translation of Yves Bonnefoy's Shakespeare criticism, criticism which proposes repetitive, maddening, magisterial, highly-rhetorical, self-absorbed, unrepentantly old-fashioned, deeply Catholic, and occasionally breath-taking series of reflections from a renowned French poet who has always recognized his own deepest preoccupations in his readings of Shakespeare. Bonnefoy's concern with 'presence' might well be read alongside Ingrid Habermann's essay on the passions, because the importance of understanding the philosophico-religious terminology concerns us all. Bonnefoy's translations, almost exclusively of the tragedies, are interpretations for the solitary, and philosophically-minded, reader in the study; he sees the plays as poems of character in the face of mortality, and is quite sure he knows the characters' motivations and anterior experiences, without ever balancing the functions of character in the complexities of plays as wholes. But, take his idea of Romeo as villain, a seducer who uses Juliet instrumentally in his own dreamily-idealistic misperception of what other people might want or need, so that in Bonnefoy's picture Rosaline has had a happy escape. Aside from a complete refusal to consider Juliet's autonomy or initiative, this is at least intriguing. The translator-in-chief wants us to think of Bonnefoy as a kind of feminist; heaven forfend. His preoccupations (remaking French poetry, above all) are not ours, yet this is a book full of often uncomfortable, plaguingly stimulating, ideas. Readers should be warned that among the exasperating features of this collection is the complete lack of acknowledgement of or reference to other scholars or critics, as these essays began as prefaces in high-popular paperbacks.

Poets, and other writers, reading, reinterpreting and recycling Shakespeare, have come to be of increasing interest. Let me call this 'Adaptation and Afterlife', and begin by praising, in passing, Stephen Orgel's excellent essay on Comus which reads Milton reading Shakespeare, both *The Tempest* and *Venus*, and uses his reading of Milton's reading to read back to Shakespeare, and to suggest, in passing, some almost startling counterfactuals. Nineteenth-century Shakespeare has had a boom this year. It is a pity for Robert Sawyer that his study of four Victorians reading Shakespeare should appear at the same time as Adrian Poole's Arden introduction to Victorian Shakespeare, as well as the marvellous two-volume collection on the same subject edited by Poole and Gail Marshall. Sawyer's assertions and confusions about George Eliot, Swinburne, Browning and Dickens make unhappy reading. These present-minded, anachronistic essays may be exemplified by the following: 'Yet if Hamlet may be said to represent the intellectual Everyman and Lear to represent the bad Victorian father, one might argue that Falstaff combines the two characters, possessing the intelligence of Hamlet, combined with the paternalism of Lear'. Everyman? Paternalism? Does the chronology not matter? or Falstaff's desire for, but lack of, power? Sawyer sidles up to the idea that if Prince Harry breaks Falstaff's heart (although it is only Mistress Quickly's sentimental view that this is so), it must be because the love between Falstaff and the prince dared not speak its name. He allies himself with Jonathan Goldberg's view of Harry's homsexuality but he wants Swinburne to be the idea's onlie begetter. It is not enough to 'find' allegory or parallel; Sawyer insists that Dickens himself becomes a figure like Polonius in relation to his own family; that in *Hard Times* Louisa is also Ophelia because she is left motherless, her marriage is arranged (just the opposite of forbidden), which leads to spiritual death. Her relationship with Tom is – like Laertes and Ophelia – potentially incestuous. I think there's a subtext throughout this book in which another book is trying to emerge, a book which would be a study of appropriations of *masculinity*, and the bisexuality of great writers.

Words such as 'conversation', 'complicity', 'partnership' suffuse Poole's *Shakespeare and the Victorians*, with its sections on theatrical experience, on painting and illustration (in which the erotic fantasy of the depiction – of women, especially, but also of children), where he concentrates on moments when the characters are poised before different possibilities, and 'the way artists can arrest a moment of crisis from the onward movement of text and performance'. He is at his best on the novel. He begins with the theatrical 'flash', which was used to characterize certain kinds of acting, and turns it to the ways that novelists focussed Shakespeare, and themselves in their uses of Shakespeare. He looks at what we now call the prequels, and at the sensitivity of the female character-analysts, as well as at Thackeray; he is particularly convincing on *Shirley*, that often-underestimated condition-of-England novel, where he explicates Charlotte Brontë's description of her heroine's 'crafty use' of *Coriolanus*, and intertextuality becomes a method of raising questions through deferral; he is especially good on Brontë's insight into misinterpretation when the characters are reading *Coriolanus* together. In the chapter on Dickens, Eliot and Hardy Poole teases out allusions, quotation, rewritings and reversals in ways which illuminate the three authors' conversations and quarrels with Shakespeare. In something which is more than 'influence', he shows them reading and returning to Shakespeare, including the discomforts of recognizing allusion; and Hardy's suspicion toward those who cite Shakespeare.

Marshall and Poole's two-volume collection (once again the result of a conference which clearly inspired much rethinking and rewriting among the participants) opens with an excellent introduction, which not only sets out the wares of the essays to follow, but sets the questions in context, making the editors' prefatory material a substantive contribution of its own. Just how 'performance' and 'the written' interact is a fascinating subject, which recalls Jack Goody's work on the interaction of the oral and the written. Goody argued that the complex syntactic possibilities in what we read aid us in increasing the potential complexities of what we hear; Poole insists that Shakespeare, read or performed, experienced directly or funnelled through Victorian rewritings and reinterpretations, created a substratum of conversation, secular reference and allusion of a complexity the individual contributors spell out in specific cases. Strong 'readings' invite us to rethink Trollope or Tennyson, but also Shakespeare, because 'strong' readings see him fresh. This is a collection which is genuinely a book (two books, in fact – the other will be discussed in the 'Shakespeare and Performance' review next year, with criss-crossing reflections on English cultures and *les lieux de mémoire*. If I have a reservation, it is that there is no third volume on European parallels, a point all the more important given the significance, throughout the collection, of Diane E. Henderson's essay, one of the year's best. In short compass, Henderson writes a nuanced study of Scott and 'race', in which Shakespeare becomes the source for an ethical tradition to support Scott's ideal of a British nation, which he emphasizes as distinct from the corruption of its political centre. Scott's position, literary, national and unificatory, was tremendously important in the formations of romantic nationalism, as of the novel as it subsequently developed in North Britain and in a variety of new national movements on the Continent. There is an important line from Scott to Dumas and Hugo (the former an 'editor' of Shakespeare, the latter the father of the translator and editor of Shakespeare, for whom he wrote a book-length preface), both of whom saw their prose as in some sense Shakespearian.

In the same volume, Philip Davis writes convincingly on George Eliot and the uses of 'Shakespearean' as a promotion to cultural iconicity. Eliot was assimilated to Shakespeare as another in a line of English writers who grasped and conveyed character as tragedy. Victorian thinkers perceived Shakespeare's prose as poetic in its compression and saw characters' speeches as his, in a kind of double pre-consciousness which showed the inner person in outer words and actions. At the same time, there was a widespread theory that poetry had been superseded by scientific progress which can be found in Carlyle and Emerson and Macaulay, but also in Newman. In George Eliot's characterizations prose no longer seemed explanatory and at second hand; her narrator in *Middlemarch* reflects on self-knowledge as a tangled web in her 'mixed' characters, whose reactions to each other are part of our perceptions. She was sympathetic and impartial, reading her Shakespeare perhaps through Scott (and Scott is the explicit undercurrent of this book), and, for her Victorian readers, offered a 'mind' in the same way Shakespeare did. There are equally complex essays by Christopher Decker on the ways that the Tennyson death-bed became apotheosized as Shakespearian, which consecrated them both as national poets. The implicit argument is that patterns of nationalism modified the old trajectory of greatness (minor poems, pastorals, then epics) developed for Homer, Virgil or Dante, into a different model. Decker doesn't consider the way the post-Romantic poets might escape the demand for pastorals (another topic enjoying attention this year), replacing them with a recreation of the emotional life, but he might have, since he goes on to look at Tennyson's identification with Shakespeare's anonymity, his privacy, in fierce resistance to revealing his autobiography to his reading public. Decker insists upon Tennyson's affinity, not his rivalry, and distinguishes – counter-intuitively, perhaps – Tennyson's sense of belonging to a craft and tradition from Goethe's discomfort with Shakespeare's shadow. Above all, he sees in Tennyson's affiliation a sign, like *In Memoriam* itself, of fidelity. Just as this essay finds a way around assumptions of contestatory 'appropriation', so Robert Douglas-Fairhurst discusses 'universalism', finding in Tennyson's habits of allusion a generalization about the ways that poets remember. Tennyson quoted Shakespeare's lines as embedded questions to which he replies; this invites the idea that certain ideas – as expressed – are timeless and shared. 'Because allusion suggests two writers speaking with one voice, it can express a community of response to events which divide people from one another, such as death'. In a move which would please Bonnefoy, he uses Tennyson's 'weeds' to express disgust with the fecundity of life; here allusion is reflexivity about writing itself, as well as a mise-en-abyme, since meaning multiplies and allusions to Shakespeare could be both culturally re- and de-generative. My point here is that the study of writers writing to writers, as well as about them, or with them, is a site of creativity which can tell us a great deal – in its specific detail – about approaches which may otherwise lack the test of detailed analysis. For readers interested in visual material (not here covered), let me recommend the wonderful catalogue mentioned all too briefly last year, *Shakespeare in Art* (London, 2003), with its wealth of further reference.

Kim C. Sturgess turns to Shakespeare in nineteenth-century America, in an interesting and useful book about popular appreciation of the foreign bard. It remains a question why we should think this enthusiasm problematic or sinister, as if, along with a song and a flag, new nations had to have their very own Homer. Americans didn't reject the religion(s), the style of education or the legal system that were established on British (not 'English') foundations, so why should they have rejected the history of English-language literature or theatre? And there was not 'just theatre' for entertainment: there were concerts, sermons, lectures, sport and special-interest associations of many kinds, not least animal- or flower-fanciers. European culture (painting and music were broader than merely 'British') was always distinguished from British political interests. Antagonism can be expressed as competition, on the playing field or in culture but sometimes sharing, affinity, allusion, is more complicated.

I mentioned at the outset the uses of detailed analysis to support larger arguments, as 'close reading' transforms itself. That *Representations* should publish Richard McCoy's tribute to Paul Alpers in an essay on *King Lear* is a sign of *rapprochement*. What begins as a look at parents and children (in the light of Alpers's '*King Lear* and the Theory of the Sight Pattern', 1963) becomes an analysis of the history of discussion of the play which followed it, tacitly as a history of literary-critical reading. The bent of the essay is toward a contextualization of the play in the language of Eucharist and sacrifice, at least in part to demonstrate the ways that different kinds or schools of reading can be brought together to enrich one another as well as the texts which are their starting point and justification. In the Rasmussen collection, Alpers himself writes about New Criticism and 'the Example of Shakespeare's Sonnets', concentrating on poetry's forms and formalisms of different kinds. In short compass this essay does far more than Frank Erik Pointner's attempt to 'revalue' the Sonnets. There is a characteristically trenchant essay by Heather Dubrow which rehearses the arguments about aesthetics commonly derived from Kant in ways which elegantly demonstrate both how little they represent Kant as well as how similar such attacks are to the traditional disruptions between generations, whatever the 'former age' position has been. The same fine ear for linguistic complexity applied to schools of literary criticism reveals patterns of aggression and evasion which are not simply generational. She speaks with calm authority of the many ways we employ intellectual positions to demonize each other, so that the politics of criticism becomes war by other means.

Juliet Dusinberre looks not at rivalry among critics but among poets in an essay on *As You Like It*. Rethinking the problems of intertextuality, which she finds too readerly for a play, she explores the presence, or resonances, of other writers of comedy and of pastoral. Significantly, she begins with Heaney and Primo Levi, thinking about exile and displacement, and how flight into a forest can evoke both comedy and criticism. She moves toward the politics of pastoral and the risks of discussion in 1599 of Ireland, circles back to encompass John Heywood's work for Queen Elizabeth's father and moves across the channel to absorb Erasmus and Rabelais. Dusinberre is currently editing the play, and her explorations suggest reciprocity, even fraternity in the poetic enterprise, making playwriting a space where one can be playful, serious and ironic about belief in both romantic love and in poetry.

Harry Berger Jr uses the occasion of reflecting on current approaches to Shakespeare studies to engage with current critical positions while demonstrating the strengths of detailed reading, in an essay on *Henry V* which begins from the propositions that 'any written play is intended as both a text for reading and a script for acting'; that because reading is an activity more complex than our experience in the theatre, what actors do can encompass hints in the text which lead them toward potential meanings; and, finally, that plays function in part as a kind of trailer, where the attraction which is coming is a printed book to be perused (the word is his) in the privacy of our own closets. This is not a new argument, as we all recognize, and Berger has contributed as much as anyone to the ways we think about it. As he acknowledges, Katharine Maus's *Inwardness and Theater in the English Renaissance*

(1996) suggested that some of the actors' work is always to suggest that there is more here than meets the eye, or the ear. Berger's defensiveness, of course, antedates the work of Lukas Erne on the dynamics of publication. That 'performance tells us it has a text within which passes show' is a fine formulation for the doubleness of theatre *and* text. The poetry of history – the English history plays, but epic above all – has always implied that there are events out there which underlie, messily, the structured content of writing; what is different about a theatrical text, however, is its invitation to visualize inwardly. Berger is excellent on the first part of the equation, the need to read well, to notice the non-semantic non-logic which carries so much meaning. He also makes the excellent point, immediately glaringly obvious, that Q printings emphasize *a* play as an independent entity, whereas F places *Henry V* within a quadripartite Henriad (that dangerously epic-izing title). He calls attention to changes of names, from Hal to Harry to Henry (though I see no reason why one wouldn't hear vocatives in the theatre), and to the question of Falstaff as an external conscience-ness raiser. Because some readers read exceptionally well (Harry Berger Jr, to take one instance) is no reason not to assume that some theatre-goers don't see equally well, with readerly attention to four plays or spectatorly memory of echoing responses. Berger's fine article is a reminder that reading *and* listening require concentration, but also conversation.

While I am praising good readers, let me call attention to a startling piece of 'hearing' by David L. Kranz, based on the metrical views of George T. Wright. He writes about the soundpatterns of *Macbeth*, how and where they occur, and how that might underlie and support meaning. He exposes a kind of poetic 'weird music' in the speeches in the play, in thick clusters of sound, repetitive formulae, as if there were really music underscoring the text. What is new and striking is the elaboration of how the tune patterns vary when their content shifts from the witches to, say, Scotland's sufferings or Malcolm's moral test of Macduff, where the sounds appear to be redeemed by their association with the forces of good. Kranz's care in assessing the threat of cyclical violence against the promise of redemption is part of what makes this such an exciting essay. He moves from the witches, to the Macbeths, to the least apparent reappearance of the 'tune' in the public scenes of orthodoxy, finally to the transcendent, *because* immanent, presence of the 'tune' at the end of the play. There is a numerological riff too complex to be explained here, which Kranz labels speculative, but which is well worth a pause, even if we finally reject it as extravagant. The ambiguities of diabolical and divine seem embedded in both the play's cohesions and coherences.

Despite Mark Womack's apparently serious title, his is an essay which celebrates triviality, exuberance, excess of meaning, and all the frivolous pleasures of paronomasia. Womack dares to suggest that sometimes puns are there for the hell of it. William Flesch looks at the function of markers which indicate someone speaking ('sayd she' or 'quod I'); he is acute on the function of quotation within poetry (someone else's speech), and the way speech tags can sometimes turn what was prose into verse, and often what appeared to be oral into writing. William Poole has been developing a linguistic approach which includes an earlier article in *Shakespeare Survey 54* (2001). This year's contribution begins by looking at stage directions as descriptions to a reader rather than as blocking instructions to an actor, to argue for the texts as something between written and oral (or both written and oral). He wants Shakespeare's linguistic moment to be peculiar in its syntactic openness, and uses this observation to rehabilitate older approaches to Shakespeare, in an argument which seems to promise to be a unified syntactic-field theory. He examines the dynamics of understanding a speech in the time of its utterance, when an audience suspend their comprehension while something complex is said. So far so good, but he also wants to attach this to hyperbaton, the mixing up of normal syntactical order. I am not sure I have followed all of his connections, nor whether he thinks the s.d.s Shakespeare's or not, but I am sure that Shakespeare's characters' idiolects in the context of Early Modern English merit more attention, as does stage context.

So let me recommend a series of books which bill themselves as dictionaries but which are much, much more. Each of Athlone's 'Shakespeare Dictionaries' is different, and each of them is an education in Early Modern English, as if someone had taken a series of registers or semantic fields and created a kind of Roget around them, embedded in explanatory prose. These are books which will while away a lot of hours, as a search becomes a session. If one wanted to explore 'stage directions', to take the immediate example, Hugh Macrae Richmond's *Shakespeare's Theatre* offers four packed pages of history, context, to directions in the play-book and on the line, as well as references for further reading. As one would expect, N. F. Blake's compendium of *Shakespeare's Non-Standard English* is the place to look for register variation, promising hours of instruction in useful categories with exhaustive listing. The sections on 'forms of address' alone are an education in manners, the good, the bad and the ugly. Charles Edelman's *Shakespeare's Military Language* covers all kinds of fighting, from fisticuffs to warfare, and is attentive to the metrical necessities which sometimes explain inaccurate naming (e.g. rapier has more syllables than sword). *Shakespeare's Legal Language*, compiled by B. J. Sokol and Mary Sokol, is also full of the exigencies of imprecision, as well as giving precise definitions. Here is our best chance to master 'praemunire'. The Latin and French terms of the English bar appear as and when, and are explained individually. Readers interested in the curious case of Law French will, however, find excellent suggestions for further reading. The authors – not in any sense simply compilers – of these volumes bring together material which is widely separated (of necessity) in Renaissance literature. They allow the curious to test hypotheses about meaning, not just by Shakespeare. Not the least important result of consulting these books will be more caution about interpreting cultural terms in dramatic context.

Among the excellent contributions this year is another modestly-titled work which should become part of every reader's, and certainly every teacher's, arsenal of central reference books. Shakespearians will all have remarked the changes in annotation which characterize the different series of the standard editions of the plays and poems, as well as the need – as we lose familiarity with older forms and styles of English – to say what the sentences mean. For over a hundred years, E. A. Abbott's *A Shakespearian Grammar* (first edn 1869, third edn 1870) has been the best detailed source for the curious; recently, there have been introductions such as C. L. Barber's indispensable *Early Modern English* (1976); the chapters in *The Cambridge History of the English Language* (1992, 1999) by Matti Rissanen and Olga Fischer; as well as Norman Blake's *A Grammar of Shakespeare's Language* (2002), praised in *Survey 56*. Abbott remains a source important enough to have been uploaded onto the web in what is in practice almost unusable form (www.perseus.tufts.edu), but even as an object in the hand (easily and cheaply available on the Web) the book has three major drawbacks: discrete descriptive paragraphs in alphabetical order (so that there is no linguistic model or overall analysis of Early Modern English), prescriptive views about correctness, and a very out-dated attitude to texts, which are quoted (or approximated) from long-superseded editions. The Arden series for students has commissioned Jonathan Hope to replace Abbott.

Readers habituated to assessments of the year's work in Shakespeare *criticism* may wonder in what follows if I have taken leave of my senses, so let me try to explain why I think Hope's *Shakespeare's Grammar* is such an important book, as important as last year's *Shakespeare as Literary Dramatist*. It isn't just that, as the blurb so accurately puts it, Shakespeare's language is an under-researched area. It is that in order to justify a reading, the bedrock of our interpretation must rely upon historically-inflected comprehension of the language. It is not just that *we* have forgotten a great deal about earlier periods of the English language (many features of which Hope explains along the way); nor that *we* sometimes find the vocabulary or the sentence-structure puzzling; surely there is every reason to suppose that Shakespeare's audiences and first readers found his characters' idiolects full of surprises, their syntax sometimes exceptionally condensed and often so difficult as to be almost beyond comprehension. Hope *systematically* explains how, and why and wherefore, with precision and clarity as well as the authority of a true language nerd. Among Hope's many convincing observations, I think the fine grain of his analyses constantly and consistently point to indications of characters thinking, and thinking about what they hear, where *that* they are thinking emerges from their styles, so that he also disproves Harry Berger Jr.'s scepticism about 'listening' cultures.

Although *Shakespeare's Grammar* appears to be intended for university students, they should be warned that it is stuffed with sigla, abbreviations and technical vocabulary, all laid out in those rebarbative numbered paragraphs so typical of linguistics research. It isn't an easy read; and it isn't for beginners who have no acquaintance with the vocabulary of grammar and syntax (Hope himself suggests that the uninitiated start with a trip to the Barber – indeed, I believe I see homage to some of the examples Barber made the classics of such complexities as 'thou' and 'you' and what they tell us about number, deference and blocking). Nonetheless, it should be required reading for us all, before we edit, or opine, or teach. Preferably now. With the appearance of this Grammar there can be no excuse for failing to base our ideas of *what* Shakespeare means upon *how* he could mean. From the opening example on the representation of Macbeth's and Lady Macbeth's thinking about murder, Hope always explains the linguistic aspects in the service of literary interpretation. Like Blake, Hope quotes directly from F and Q. Much more than Blake, Hope is sensitive to the ways that Shakespeare's language changed with characterization, under the pressure of metrics, and over time. Even with computers (even with total recall), think of the complex study from which grows the authority to say, 'Deletion [i.e. the suppression of 'a' or 'an'] seems to be particularly likely after *ever/never*' (32–3), meaning that he has distinguished the use of articles as functional or metric, or indicating dialect, or poetic archaism, or supported by parallel use elsewhere. His respect for Abbott appears in, for example, his readiness to support Abbott's hunches and hypotheses with his own evidence; but he corrects Abbott's errors or prescriptiveness in the light of historical language changes (such as the vexed 'his' genitive).

There are some contingent observations to be made: for one thing, Abbott's intended audience was schoolchildren (and the book sold in thousands); for another, the plays which Abbott quoted so frequently as to amount to a series of detailed commentaries, are remarkably similar to the ones schools still assign today: *As You Like It*, *Coriolanus*, *Hamlet*, *Henry V*, *Julius Caesar*, *King Lear*, *Macbeth*, *The Merchant of Venice*, *A Midsummer Night's Dream*, *Richard II*, *Richard III*. By contrast, Hope's examples come from the whole canon (very judicious selection from the agreed Shakespearian parts of *The Two Noble Kinsmen* and *Pericles*, though nothing from *Edward III*) including the poems (but not Shakespeare's will). Perhaps I may be one of the few readers to follow Hope sequentially through the whole text: readers of *Shakespeare Survey* may wish to trust my assurance that he covers the ground and develops some convincing generalizations about Shakespeare's language and its development. Unlike his predecessor, however, he gives no appendix with sample test questions useful for teaching.

From closely observed chains of utterance, let me pass to another area of current interest, or a current interest group: Shakespeare and religion, including Shakespeare's religion. Much of what passes for current coin, alas, is counterfeit, the kind of guilt (or innocence) by association which builds from hypothesis to assurance to rock-solid insistence in the course of a paragraph. Sounds of axe-grinding permeate too many articles which refer to the work of a small number of scholars as if publication made for acceptance and blossoming numbers to agreement. I read a number of pseudo-biographical fantasies which more and more depend either on unproven and badly-argued (if 'argued' is the word) ideas about the persistence of a monolithic Catholicism in which Shakespeare's distant cousins absorb him almost as far as the Gunpowder Plotters. I lamented the smell of burnt Bacon last year, and I continue to do so. Supposed 'circumstances' and their supposed 'influence' on Shakespeare's poems and plays can be tasted in work listed below by Patrick H. Martin and John Finnis on the supposed milieu behind the Sonnets, a number of the essays in the two-volumes from the Lancashire conference listed under Dutton, or, typically, James Ellison's attempt to argue that *Measure for Measure* is also addressed to threats to persecute Catholics. Ellison thinks Angelo is a puritan who executes the Catholic Claudio. Well, one could have puritanical Catholics, but the text doesn't call him a Puritan, but 'prenzie' (which he knows, as he knows the categories are problematic). Historians have a trade, which we ought to learn: Ellison mistakenly presumes that contemporary pamphlets offered true accounts of what was said and done at deaths. So, for him, the play only looks as if it's about sex and self-government. It's really about religion, with the Duke, like the English king, a figure of tolerance. By contrast, Natasha Korda (in Woodbridge, *Money*) knows more about the economic circumstances of Mariana and Juliet than the play does, and takes both women as emblematic of what not she, but the nineteenth century, would call 'surplus women' (although Vienna still has Catholic vocations). Nina Taunton and Valerie Hart attempt to link the QI *Lear* (which they believe was first performed before James VI and I), by adducing very dodgy parallels, to the Gunpowder plot. But they rely upon the much-criticized edition of Graham Holderness and upon much-criticized ideas expressed there. Hell makes an appearance in a number of the essays collected by François Laroque, though they are not always immediately criticism of Shakespeare's plays.

Some of the broader assessments of 'Shakespeare and Religion' to appear this year include Tom Bishop's essay in the Bradshaw collection, assessing where we are now. Although it is (like Frank Kermode's sensible paragraphs, discussed below) already out of date, given Robert Bearman's impressive analytic and detective – almost forensic – dismantling of John Shakespeare's 'testament' in *Survey 56*, it remains balanced in its attempts to deal with the dynamics of change in the sixteenth century while also dealing with the polemics of permanence in recent criticism. For the former, he emphasizes the slipperiness of doctrine and the defensive importance of ambiguity, and he is courteous about the vagaries of the latter. As also with other contributions in this volume, he emphasizes the need to read. And, one might add, to look at negative evidence. Maurice Hunt's most recent book (one of those generously subsidized by the author's home university) reprints five essays. Hunt believes that Shakespeare deliberately intervened in religious debate, particularly over spiritual reformation, merit and Providence, and that his position was an unusual mix of Protestant and Catholic. This assumes that there is a binary split between two static religious positions (which one can easily identify); that Shakespeare reveals his own (equally unchanging) views through his characters; that one can accordingly extract recognizable motifs, allusions, concepts from the plays. There is no negative control here either, viz., how much questions of individual character development, or puzzle in the face of fate, might be independent of specific religious positions, or even how it might be possible, in an age in which so much expression was necessarily religious in orientation, for anyone to write anything which couldn't be assimilated to the spectrum of Christian positioning. Among the question-begging presuppositions of this book are Shakespeare's tolerance, his universalism and his own biography as a source of his position. There is a great deal of listing occurrences and the 'criticism' can sound like this: 'Commentators on the play with few exceptions have not acknowledged that Sylvia's worth may derive primarily from certain Catholic values rather than from an unorthodox Neo-Platonism or from Scholasticism'. Indeed, the poetry of love exploited the intense language of religious longing and continued to do so but it did so in such different ways that its mere existence tells us nothing. I wish to end this section with a reflection on the understandable but worrying tendency, remarked last year by Brian Vickers in another context, to accept as authority, and as authoritative, scholars and scholarship to which attention has accrued, often because a book is controversial.

Of course, the history of religion is only one of the histories which must absorb our attention. This year I continued to read histories of gender; of economics (but not its related category, the law, including land tenure); histories of philosophy and its guilty partner, rhetoric. Historicisms of several kinds did battle. B. J. Sokol, whose Athlone Dictionary (with Mary Sokol) I praised above, now writes about *The Tempest* as entry into the latest natural philosophy (he calls it proto-science), in order to relate it to a supposed thick web of allusiveness to the new knowledge. His fascination with the history of epistemology does not always bear directly on a reading of the play, a line of country explored in Barbara Mowat's 'Prospero's Book', noticed last year, but is more a kind of natural philosopher's *Enquire Within*.

I'd like to mention as a cautionary tale, only obliquely Shakespearian criticism, Victoria Kahn's essay on Carl Schmitt. Schmitt was a right-wing German jurist, a Nazi and life-long anti-Semite, whose *Hamlet oder Hekuba* (1956, available also in French translation) significantly misreads Shakespeare as a hero not entirely unrelated to Schmitt himself, and *Hamlet* as an essay in political thinking for early modern confessional states. In Schmitt's anti-Benjamin definition of tragedy, the plot and characters always correspond to real persons and events, and his reading of Hamlet insists upon Hamlet as a version of King James. There is an object lesson here in the measure of mis-reading, since the concern with religion is not unfamiliar, and, as Kahn carefully demonstrates, the same problems of misunderstanding the contemporary dramatic context, with the specificities of its forms and genres, allowed Schmitt, as it does us, to distort through present-mindedness. Schmitt is also a warning against conscripting Shakespeare's plays to political arguments as symbols rather than as plays. The question of 'presences' poses itself here, too.

History comes in the title of James Hirsch's book on soliloquies. This is a much more ambitious book than its title suggests: it covers the representation of thought as speech, what is here called 'self-addressed speech', and 'guarded speech' in western literature, with special attention to theatrical conventions. Hirsch begins with a working definition of what soliloquy (and its related convention, the 'aside') has meant in the history of western theatre, with careful attention to changing fashion in sixteenth century (he largely ignores the Middle Ages, although characters have always spoken to themselves). He argues for the crucial distinction of realizing that in Shakespeare's day 'self-addressed speech' could be self-conscious, unconscious (more like praying), guarded, and overheard. The examples do not always seem to me to support a thesis which, broadly, sees capitalism and individualism take over from communalism; Roman drama was pre-capitalist but hardly communal. Much as I enjoyed the idea of a morphology of muttering, with characters talking to themselves, lying as well as crying out loud, I do not think this history remakes our habits of interpretation.

Rhetoric and rhetorical affect are treated historically by Robert Cockcroft, whose book is full of useful information about rhetorical expression of *pathos*, with some examples from Shakespeare. And the most recent *Shakespeare Jahrbuch* (2004) focuses on passion and rhetoric, reaching out to work in a variety of languages, and to theories of emotion now forgotten, or neglected, which treated Shakespeare as a *locus communis*. This is another reminder of secular texts (in Latin, then in the vernacular) as *loci communi* of cultural reference. It would be good to have a book on who quotes what kinds of texts (biblical or medical; histories or fables; poetry, prose, or plays) in what contexts. More historical knowledge of rhetoric would have been a help to Madhavi Menon, who has rediscovered the difficulties of distinguishing metonymy and metaphor, and allows her excitement about Roman rhetoricians to lead to the conclusion that Richard's crime is overuse of metonymy at the expense of metaphor. So also a claim to a historical approach to rhetoric and to political thought informs John Roe's discursive comparison of Shakespeare and Machiavelli. Roe isn't positing influence but similarity of interest. His approach is character-based, but character in 'morally dubious' situations which he likens to the rhetorical figure *paradiastole*: when negative evaluative language is susceptible to redescription which turns what looks negative to positive – like the Dark Lady's drawbacks. I cannot see that the avoidance or evasion of negative-evaluative language is either amoral or morally recuperative – it's a way of not calling a spade a spade, or avoiding the admission that rulers have always had to – or chosen to – do things of which we disapprove. That is not the same category as the villain with ruthless ambition. Nor do I see that it is *Shakespeare* who pauses at climactic moments of amorality, only to reassert conventional certainties. Roe's individual analyses focus on tragic politicians: Richard III, King John. He is at his best with the problem of tyrannicide when it is not regicide, in the Roman plays, but I scarcely think any political philosopher would have celebrated Antony's derelictions of duty because love is glorious. No one could argue that Antony or Cleopatra were good public rulers or good private citizens; their fascination lies elsewhere.

Derek Cohen's interest in character and history, and the pre-histories of Shakespeare's characters, appears in an article on Macbeth which, because of lag-time in publication, overlaps with his new book, a loosely-linked collection of studies (generously subsidized by his home university press) which turn on meanings of 'history', from the biography of the characters in the plays to the pre-histories of the plays' societies. Cohen's continuing interest in historical treatments of Jews in English literature reappears in his idea of tragedy, in which the exclusion of the tragic figure (particularly Shylock, but also Othello and Caliban) depends on his being an outsider. His method is close reading, but he often summarizes, with occasional quotations; nor is this a book at all engaged with current scholarship. It is serious, old-fashioned, and thoughtful – but I longed for more engagement with other scholars. Cohen is at his most interesting when dealing with character memory, though he tends to believe what the characters say they remember; he contrasts imagined pasts (e.g. Desdemona and Cassio) – but why are they historical? The trouble is that he's constantly running things together: the captain who takes the message to hang Cordelia is not the one who hangs Cordelia, although Edmund is clearly recruiting him to see that his order is carried out. Cohen wants there to be a difference between high- and low-class crime, but he's often describing differences in opportunity. The book's genesis as individual articles or essays is clear in its lack of conclusion.

Jennifer Low's book on duelling on stage, page and in society raises interesting questions which do not quite add up to the touchstone of masculinity she might have begun her work hoping to find. The book is honest enough to recognize that there are major incoherences which do not suit her desire to theorize masculinity. She asks, for example, if the extra-legal duel of honour, with rapiers, derives from medieval ideas of trial by combat, and if there was a rise in duelling, and, if so, why? (No figures, no discussions, no quotations to suggest that there was.) What is striking is that the supposed duels she wants to discuss don't take place – in *Much Ado* she makes a lot of Benedick's challenge as a kind of trial by combat, but of course there is no trial. Much turns on 'proxemic assumptions' (i.e. personal space) – how masculinity might be defined by how close you could get to someone else, but it looks as if pushing people around was about adult against boy or adult male against female. She asks how wounding could be articulated as sexual penetration and by characterization of the wounded as effeminate. This surely marks a big difference from war or combat, since we don't find those metaphors there. She takes the metaphors of penetration as phallic, and deriving from erotic registers – but they aren't: they are anxious euphemism, metaphors which come back to haunt men who have used them, as a kind of revenge upon male conquerors who promoted their sexual prowess only to find that its loss turned them not into women, but into incapable men. She does not distinguish 'duel' from battle combat, and I cannot see that Prince Harry suddenly becomes an 'unironic man on top' when he has killed Hotspur. Only when she starts talking about Hamlet does 'duel' as itself a metaphor arise. I think the problem is that all the works on duelling form one repertoire, including all plays: so, duels that don't take place aren't duels, are corrupted by the indignity of unworthy courtiers, involve cross-dressing, or are used mechanically (always a promising test of stereotype) – all come together. And although she wants her lady duellists to be didactic, the argument ultimately fails to convince. Nonetheless, this is a promising survey of an important subject.

Shakespeare and gender continues to interest many critics this year. Two books stood out, a little one and a long one. In one of those series-connected-to-a-big-edition (Cambridge), Stanley Wells turns three lectures into an important essay: the speaking voice remains, buttressed by an enviable breadth and specificity of reference. This is confidently sensible, and not at all *parti pris*. Wells begins, as one would expect, with perceptions of different audiences in different times and places. Then he defines and discusses 'lewd interpretation' – examining with care and kindness what makes for bad interpretation of, mainly, Shakespeare's bawdy: insistence upon unlikely meanings which are ahistorical, taken out of context, or multilingual where there is no reason to invoke more than one language. Substantive chapters on the Sonnets and on male characters in the plays follow. At every point he is generous. He has a good time with some of our editorial and critical ancestors and the constraints upon what they could and could not write. His historical sense for the development of literary study extends to the authority of our great, flawed, resource: the *OED*, on which we all rely. He assesses the strengths and weaknesses of other works of reference, from Partridge's pioneering study, to the extravagances of Frankie Rubenstein, and the successes of Onions and Williams. Above all, he is even-handed, and the greatest success of this little book is its clear-eyed understanding that the opposite of the 'non-dit' is not to say everything. Rather, to 'reveal' implies restrictions where silence opened interpretation to potential meanings and ironies nonetheless controlled by context. This book also illustrates my point about general books currently offering some of the best criticism around.

At a more scholarly, but no less readable, level, Carol Neely's new collection is one of my top books of the year. It's surprising that no such book exists, but excellent that the gap should be filled by this one. From the title we feel in the hands of somebody alert to historical category change: *Distracted Subjects* asks us to think again about the restrictions implied when we say 'madness'. Neely explores the plays, but also the distances and contradictions between the plays and the ambient culture, which reminds us how parlous it is to base so many of our ideas about the past upon literature. The illustrations are appropriate and well reproduced. She includes Shakespeare's *Macbeth, King Lear, The Two Noble Kinsmen, Comedy of Errors, Twelfth Night* and *The Merry Wives of Windsor* – all of which makes one reflect on just how much 'distraction' there was for bravura performances. She makes full and generous acknowledgement of Michael MacDonald's path-breaking (and grippingly readable) *Mystical Bedlam*. This book justifies long gestation, stringent rewriting and publishing the whole thing together. It is a complex, nuanced, analysis which corrects or modifies both medieval and early modern histories of medicine, Renaissance literature, and such luminaries as Freud and Foucault.

I read a lot of work this year which pointed out the horrors of rape, violence against women, and pornography. I do not think that it is coincidental that the now-universal availability of Web-porn is a current question of legal and social regulation. Using Shakespeare to castigate objectionable positions is hardly new, but readers will not find in what follows a great deal of Shakespeare criticism. Cynthia Marshall's wide-ranging work on early modern subjectivity contains a chapter on 'The pornographic economy of *Titus Andronicus*', which raises issues of dismemberment and gender within a Lacanian paradigm. The chapter is much more about modern discussions of subjectivity, pornography, and even criticism than it is about *Titus Andronicus*. The focus of the discussion is on what Lavinia might tell us about our own attitudes to women, eroticism, and aggression, so that Shakespeare's play becomes a, dare I say, disembodied example. As with the centrality of *The Merchant of Venice* for 'econo-criticism', the author's conceptualization of the problem itself creates problems: one character becomes an example in a larger argument about pornography. As a family, the Andronici cannot protect themselves; this does not make Lavinia a 'mutilated sex object', rather a woman who has been raped and mutilated, and is therefore 'between deaths', a daughter whose husband has been murdered, whose brothers are falsely accused, and whose father (also 'between two deaths') has lost his place in his world. I do not see that Lavinia's silence makes her subjectivity disappear – rather the contrary, as the actress's mute eloquence always shows. To say that the play 'feeds on her femininity' or to call Lavinia 'an emblem' (why is Titus not an emblem once he has only one hand? he could be a visual representation of castration as loss of power, after all) is to fall into the very metaphor trap which Marshall identifies elsewhere. The deaths of the Andronici are also, phoenix-like, the birth of a new emperor, as Julie Taymor's film emphasized. (Sometimes misreading a detail can be emblematic of a rush to judgement: Montaigne's reference to a traditional belief of superior sexual pleasure was not with a woman who is a cripple, physically incomplete, but a woman who limps.) Marshall insists that Lavinia's mutilated body is pornographic, fetishized to create perverse desire. Perhaps I'm old-fashioned, and perhaps there are always people in the audience who are turned on by a tongueless, handless, rape victim, but the idea that Lavinia is Shakespeare's 'hard-core' porn strikes me as itself perverse (but perhaps that's the point). Marshall invokes the visual imagery of martyrdom to argue that Shakespeare innovates by bringing it onstage (this would make Easter practices pornographic, because voyeuristic, too). But Lavinia is neither a criminal punished nor a witness tortured for her beliefs. If her family attempt to categorize her suffering as martyrdom, perhaps it is their attempt to give meaning to the senseless, and her dignity to the afflicted. Different characters not only treat her differently, but they talk differently, too, in ways Marshall does not analyze. This essay has the strengths of clear exposition, and a fierce moral polemic based on a universalist psychoanalytic paradigm; but it depends upon treating the script as an undifferentiated repertoire (by a young and sometimes clumsy writer) in which one character's precedence occludes the rest of the play. Other essays on the subject of women and violence are to be found in the collection in the Bibliography under Woodbridge and Beehler, where, I have to say, I found more use of Shakespeare as an illustration of his age's prejudices than criticism of the plays and poems.

And sometimes well-meaning revelation of potential perversity is just unhelpful, as in Jami Ake's attempt to argue that *Twelfth Night* articulates female-female (i.e. lesbian) desire: 'specifically, Viola spontaneously produces a poetry that undermines the courtly logic of Petrarchan circulation, establishing a space for female desire, and resisting Petrarchanism's silencing of women's voices in part by rejecting writing itself, even in its residual form as a "well penn'd" text'. Ake ignores the complete deception, that Olivia believes Cesario to be a man. Yet some of what purports to be criticism of feminist, post-modern, post-modern feminist, or post-feminist excesses falls into precisely the same traps. In the Bradshaw collection, Maurice Hunt imitates what he believes himself to be opposing, e.g. assuming monolithic contemporary criticism; not thinking about reception when interpreting pamphlets; presuming that Elizabeth herself protected *Twelfth Night* from censorship; he seems to think gender always immutable. It's easy to take the moral high ground if you start with a caricature of the argument you think you're rebutting – but important also to note that the moral high ground has never been celebrated for its sense of humour. So let me recommend Dympna Callaghan in characteristic vein in an essay exploring Adonis's misogyny and the risks of bestiality, and how they come together in the appetite for pig, via some thoughts about maternal incest, enjoying, along the way, the outrageousness of *epyllion*.

Gender has long been a favourite target of many critics of criticism, and it is clear that the culture wars of late-twentieth-century America hardened and exaggerated 'positions' of many orientations. As I have written above, not all essays, or controversies, merit republication in book form. The 'not-theory' label already palls. Collections by Richard Levin and Tom McAlindon are further evidence of how hard it is not to insist that one was always right; and also that indeed caricatural positions about 'history' have replaced 'theory'. All of Levin's essays have been published before, and some are republished with the reactions they provoked or inspired. As evidence of the culture wars of the American eighties they may have some interest, but as direct criticism of Shakespeare their main value remains a call to better reading, better argument, broader attention to negative evidence, and more close attention to texts. It is a question how often the demonstration that there's a lot of shoddy scholarship about belongs in a book at all, rather than in scholarly reviews – at length, when need be. The republication of scattered essays or articles can augment their value on first publication because, united, a larger argument appears. But McAlindon's incorrectly titled collection (if he doesn't have theories, he certainly has well-thought-out predispositions) also largely reprints critiques, corrections and rejoinders to a series of books and articles by self-styled 'radical' critics. McAlindon is obsessed by a version of the culture wars – not by 'theory', but by ultimately unconvincing work inspired by such notoriously unacceptable approaches as, among others, psychoanalysis and feminism. McAlindon's own orientation assumes a high degree of conscious, informed Protestant textualism and memory in Shakespeare's audiences which amounts to a degree of pre-supposition not entirely unfamiliar elsewhere. It is a pity that he has backed himself into an anti-theory corner, because the pose of beleaguered virtue detracts from the quality of his individual interpretations. This collection of nine essays (plus an anti-'theory' bibliography) brings together a series of critiques of various kinds of self-styled radical Shakespeare criticism. I am not sure who is going to read either of these books, which give *in toto* an ominous impression of righteous assurance – much too much like the critics they mean to counter. In a more positive analysis of the scholarship, and the controversies, which have opposed historicism and formalisms, Stephen Cohen traces the history of new historicism's apparent turn away from form, and asks us, persuasively, to think again about the possibilities of historically-inflected studies of form. This is an essay which sits very well with Andreas Höfele's article praised here two years ago.

Equally positive and stimulating is Edward Pechter's complex analysis of the scholarship on differences between bad Quartos and Folio texts, to identify unthought-through ideas about 'theatricality' (viz., that performances were cut for simplicity and speed). But Pechter's main polemic is against confusions in textual practice which he derives from acceptance or rejection of the tenets of the Romantic period's elevation of authorship. His strong point – about Shakespeare, and our understanding of Shakespeare's plays – is that the place where many of the cuts come, Act IV, is the 'pause' in which Shakespeare enlarges upon the central dilemmas, often by dilating upon the women's parts and shifting point of view upon the protagonist (thus implicit assumptions about 'theatricality' replace criticism of 'badness'). The bad quartos are bad because they lose all this. What is always striking about Pechter's scholarship is his willingness to use – his insistence upon using – words such as 'because', 'better', 'aesthetic', and 'value'. His is the kind of work which gives grumpy old men a good name.

Historically-orientated work on Shakespeare continues to grow. Joan Fitzpatrick's book-of-the-thesis recaps earlier scholarship and doesn't seem to indicate anything new about Spenser or Shakespeare or any growth of nationalism, and there is too little engagement with the quotations. Among the more energetic practitioners of this approach, Andrew Hadfield collects his scattered articles, and it is good to have his whole argument laid out: although Shakespeare is one among many writers who addresses the questions of nations, islands, and political union, Hadfield sees him in a context of anxious exploration of the cultural strains that union offered, or, perhaps, threatened. One can certainly argue that union was Uther Pendragon's project, as it was King Arthur's (although one which tended more toward European sovereignty than merely a greater Britain, on the model of Rome and its unifying empire), and after them King Alfred's. But at each step the terms mean quite different things, whether one writes of Geoffrey of

Monmouth or Anglo-Saxon Wessex. Hadfield is confident about the extent to which Shakespeare's plays address union, and he is more willing to read the history plays in specific political contexts than I think always convinces, but I am sure he is right to see in Shakespeare's many returns to legendary history, or historical legend, concerns with the sceptered isle's (or isles') political arrangements. Despite the 'can be read's, Hadfield has robust ideas about Shakespeare's orientation, if not his personal views, and sees him aligned first with Essex as a severe critic of Elizabeth and her policies and then, with King Lear and Cymbeline, as part of a general resistance to James. I find these readings strong to the point of tendentiousness, because they must assume visible pointers to immediately current events which then skew the plays as wholes towards specific moments of 'crisis', but other readers will make their own judgements. Willy Maley, too, addresses the national questions in essays which have all been published before, while one of them appears simultaneously in the Berry collection. John Kerrigan's Foreword engages with some of the issues, with characteristic acuity.

Also at book length, David Ruiter follows in the wake of François Laroque's *Shakespeare's Festive World* and Naomi Liebler's *Shakespeare's Festive Tragedy*, but is unlike either. He deals with three complex issues: time, history and great men, in the course of four plays. Whatever characters think, they are in time, part of history, and unable to determine, control or even always understand their places. Ruiter thinks these perceptions are linked and structured by feast days, festivals, and feasting. Certainly holydays and holidays punctuate any time-keeping, but whether they organize the plays is less clear. He keeps going back to G. K. Hunter's subtle formulations about the multi-valent and multi-vocal world of the plays and then tracing critical controversy about the balance of relaxation and riot. At this distance in time it is visible how many post-war critics were seduced into allegorizing Shakespeare's kings into Shakespeare's England in a march toward peace and unity (at whatever personal cost to the man as monarch). The agreed, but only apparent, festive suspension of ordinary life has always suffered from disapprobation and demurral, from St Benedict's legendary attempt to establish a rhythm by rule. Ruiter recognizes that his critical position is not new, and that the disorders sanctioned by festivity are not the same as the disruptions of civil war; the fluidity in his use of the 'fest' lexis is often fruitful but it always risks becoming a catch-all. He warns us against a binary polarity between monochordal order versus dialogic festivity as a simple struggle (the prince v. Falstaff), or as a tripartite slide from festival to misrule to malady, and emphasizes a dynamic community unified by the celebration of its own past. In that context, the yearly round of moveable and date-specific days of rest invites attention; it is curious how recognizable, within Shakespeare's reformed England, those days remained, and with them how much agreement about the license, conventions, and limits of celebration.

Dominique Goy-Blanquet's analysis of the movement from chronicle to stage is a narrative, English-language version of the sources of the first history tetralogy, part of a large project that already includes *Shakespeare et l'Invention de l'histoire*, which identified the agents of history, the sources, and Shakespeare's treatment of them (noticed in these pages two years ago). It is explicitly continental in orientation, agnostic about authorship and order, resolutely conservative about sources, and restricted largely to the familiar chronicle sources of Shakespeare's plays (unlike, say, Benjamin Griffin's *Playing the Past: Approaches to English Historical Drama 1385–1600*, noticed in 2002). Goy-Blanquet knows the editorial tradition well, and although her preferred editions are the newest Ardens for *1, 2, 3 Henry VI* and the new Oxford *Richard III*, she does not hesitate to take editors to task for unwarranted emendation and interference. She assumes considerable knowledge on the part of her readers as she proceeds through detailed analyses of how Shakespeare moved from the breadth of Hall and Holinshed to the focused structures of the stage. Her own structure is to identify a series of contrasts which are illustrated in her sub-sections: town and country; similar (tragic) trajectories for different characters; rearrangements of time and space to clarify issues of loyalty and betrayal, injury and revenge, above all, what she calls 'the progress of evil'. This book has clearly had a long gestation, and the scholarship is not always as up-to-date as one might hope (but, then, comprehensive bibliography in the North American style is no guarantee of historical or critical penetration). Donald Hedrick's essay on 'advantage', affect and history in *Henry V* begins by assuming that the wooing scene makes us uneasy, then that Freud can help us think about wooing and history. 'Advantage', Hedrick argues, is Shakespeare's own term throughout the play. 'Advantage' turns the number of French dead into English profit (I can't think why), and war with only a few men maximizes effort and glory. Although he mentions Pistol's comic conquest, he forgets that the French prisoners are all killed, so all 'advantage' is lost. He's really exploring economic and affective language. And history too is labour, so the play 'performs history as variously advantageable affective labor'. Thus, wooing Katherine, there is historical and erotic effort, but Henry meets his downfall in this comicohistoriopornographic wooing. Rulers, self-government and expansionism occupy David Scott Wilson-Okamura's look at ideas of colonization and Virgil in *The Tempest* via Virginia and Ireland. Intemperance becomes a problem specific to Dido (her love for Aeneas) and colony-building. But intemperance, in the play as a whole, has to do with self-control as a prerequisite for governing. Nor is the island a colony, or even a plantation. Let us have more historical work, but let it be better informed.

Sometimes, as I have noted above, more than one book appears in a year on the same, or overlapping, topic. There are two on 'romance' to be noted. Working with a generous definition of 'romance', and generic assertions which are equally broad, Michael L. Hays explores the rich tradition of medieval and contemporary 'romances' as sources for Shakespeare. The genesis of this book shows in the use of such insufficiently-examined categories as 'courtly love' or 'the chivalric tradition', and it is difficult (to take just one example) to see the men of *Macbeth* as 'chivalric knights' – famously vowed to protecting women and children. If there is more writing on the subject than he is aware of, it is certainly true that the subject is far from exhausted. Not everyone will agree with his avowedly bold attributions of influence, many of which strike me as coincidences or commonplaces, but the idea that there are motifs which had been, were and continued to be much exploited in Shakespeare's day is incontestable. By contrast, Helen Cooper's long-awaited study of *The English Romance in Time* gives us a wide-ranging book which will become a standard reference. Cooper's first book resituated Pastoral by showing how medieval pastorals not only survived, but created the conditions in which classical pastoral was read and understood, that is, Vergil through the lenses ground by centuries of accretion and habits of reading. The continuities she stressed in that book remind us how self-styled revolutions tend to invert the terms against which they think they are revolting. Here she turns to the great, sprawling 'romance', to illuminate continuities in a series of readings which explore the permutations and combinations of romance motifs in order to indicate exactly how protean the material continued to be. In the secular space of these kinds of fiction, authors worried, fantasized, hoped, instructed, exhorted and preserved incidents and categories which Spenser renewed, Bunyan preached, and Milton – ultimately – abandoned. The definitions are clear, the history is acknowledged from the outset and abetted by a useful Appendix of specific works. The chapters are organized by motifs whose combination of scope and specificity make this an unusually attractive book, well beyond the four Shakespearian plays now called 'Romances'.

Then, sometimes, from another discipline, comes new work which invites everyone to look afresh at something we didn't know there was more, much more, to know about. Ross W. Duffin's *Shakespeare's Songbook* is a work of reference, and much, much more. His collection gives commented, and sometimes illustrated, texts and musical notation of 160 songs connected with Shakespeare's plays, from sources as early (or as likely) as could be found. The accompanying CD offers some of the songs, some only in extracts (I found their brevity exquisitely frustrating): the rest can be accessed at www.wwnorton.com/nael/noa. Stephen Orgel's introduction is full of suggestive insights about Shakespeare the appropriator, absorbing old and contemporary songs which could speak to the situations of his characters; of the stage's transfer and transportability of songs and instrumental music. Duffin is sure that Shakespeare would have known over a hundred of the songs he includes (and he's very good on characters' bad memories of them); his argument that allusion to well-known songs, especially ballads, signals thematic material or likely plot events is consistent with Shakespeare's construction elsewhere, and often convincing. Even when the associations seem forced, the evidence enriches our sense of the available popular music of the day and emphasizes an aural source of shared cultural knowledge which included myths and legends as well as the staples of balladry lovers. There are, as always, reconstructions, which include the attempt to match words to existing music by finding close patterning; musicologists will have differing reactions to these. Performers will have the last word. Or tune.

Not quite last words, and far from least, a few brief comments on books for students and general readers. Further to my contention that much good work now appears in the guise of guides or collections for undergraduates, Frank Kermode offers a short introduction to three topics: Shakespeare as the outstanding playwright in the outstanding theatrical company in the age modern actors now call 'Jacobethan'. His thread winds and twists back upon itself, picking up themes like refrains. What makes this short introduction so good, and so exceptional, despite some longueurs and some assertions which will need revision, is its implicit emphasis on Shakespeare's inconsistencies and its explicit attention to what one might call the terrible pause, those moments of interim in action in which characters suffer the extremes of uncertainty. Kermode authoritatively compresses, without distorting, the social, political and religious context, nesting his narrative of historical – and current – contention within a virtual library of suggested further reading. He knows when to call a guess a guess, and describes major change without jargon or partisanship. His gift for elucidating what is not there is especially important for readers of Shakespeare, as he – to take a pertinent example – describes venture capital, trade and re-insurance in a historical Venice not reproduced in *The Merchant of Venice*. His eye for the new commodities sends him to King James against tobacco and Ben Jonson against most everything. Let me point out, additionally, that in Shakespeare the five great new luxury commodities never appear: in addition to the noxious weed, cane sugar, chocolate, coffee and tea seem to have been of no dramatic interest. Kermode's treatment of the lost years and of Shakespeare's religion is fair-minded but quite clear that specious arguments are fuelled by a mixture of irritation with the 'blank' in Shakespeare's biography, refusal to balance evidence (e.g. which Bible Shakespeare quoted or the popularity of such names as 'shakeshaft'), and the powerful annoyance of not knowing. He also treats the question of how much power and influence the theatres might have had, and leaves that a question, too. Along the way, of course, he is very good on understanding Elizabethan English.

The largest collection of new essays this year is *Shakespeare: an Oxford Guide*. At just over 700 pages, with forty-five chapters on many aspects of Shakespearian study by forty-three well-known contributors (accompanied by a mere eleven black and white illustrations, poorly produced and ill identified), this 'Enquire Within' proposes the most up-to-date, most comprehensive single-volume, blockbuster textbook currently on offer. In brief compass, it introduces Shakespeare's England, from biography to history to religion, 'Shakespeare's genres', and series of critical approaches, which are then applied in short critical readings of 17 plays and the poems, and a fourth section on 'afterlife'. Attenuated Bibliographies are appended to the individual essays. Particularly in the Life and Times section, the essays vary worryingly in quality, perhaps due to drastic cutting, but perhaps due to insufficient editing. No one (except me) is going to read this through, so the many repetitions are less problematic than the failures to give follow-ups or cross-references. However, these are complicated matters, and if reducing everything to bare bones replaces a body with a skeleton, it is not clear that such reduction *could* succeed. The more successful chapters are those which give pertinent examples for what they describe (Edmondson on tragicomedy, Gilbert on performance criticism, Lake on religion, Leggatt on the Roman plays, McDonald on verse, Maguire on textual bibliography, Smith on sexuality, Woodbridge on tragedy); the less happy remain a tissue of assertions (including the existence of powerful methodologies where 'orientation' might have done). More illustrations would have been helpful: tables and maps, *L/s/d* money, historical chronologies and genealogies, even mini-biographies, somewhere, to avoid the volume's otherwise difficult references to marital and dynastic complications. The Bible is the book's most serious blind spot, and there is a hole where classical texts ought to be. This volume merits our attention as a kind of resumé of 'where we are now', and it will no doubt function for years to come as an unattributed source for student essays. For many years I have felt able to spot plagiarism because the difference in style between what students can write themselves and what they lift has been so marked. Perhaps it is a sign of the editorial times, and an insistence on simplifying critical prose, but I have to say that I was startled by the inability of some of the writers to write complex sentences or express ideas using the full resources of the English language.

There is, however, a much larger compilation: Russ McDonald's one-volume collection of post-war criticism we cannot do without almost reaches 1000 pages. This anthology is useful not only for its selections, which cover fields, approach and the canon, but for its magisterial introductory paragraphs. I alert Shakespearians to these marvels of compression, because I foresee a long life for them in student essays. Other introductory guides are, I'm afraid, to be avoided: e.g., raw documents and extracts which are intended as 'background', as Faith Nostbakken's on *The Tempest*, with eclectic discussion topics at the end of each chapter. As an aide for teaching the play in schools, this collection illustrates why trickle-down has never been a satisfactory prediction. Stephen J. Lynch is dogmatic on *As You Like It: A Guide to the Play*. It is hard to write about teaching methodology and experience, as some of the essayists in the Davis collection illustrate. The Blocksidge education collection is at a low level, too much of 'how we do it at my school' for students of particular ages. And, at a higher level than the York or Penguin guides, Nicholas Marsh's introduction to the Problem Plays (in the series of which he is General Editor) is another kind of dogmatic. Intended to help students learn to read, it is authoritative, and, at least to my taste, just the sort of book which will come between students and their own reading. As a model Student Guide, what is particularly efficient is the way he laminates the readings, with close analysis in the service of different approaches (openings, gender in two chapters on men and on women, social control, wit and foolishness, drama), so that nothing is apparently intended to be final. At the end of each chapter he makes explicit what he has added to the previous analyses and suggests work for the student. But Marsh treats the characters as reachable human beings, and argues for his analyses of their inner lives as if there were only one way to play them. If I were desperate about my school or my students in League Tables, I might be tempted to use a book like this, because it's so sure about The Answers.

At last, just for fun, two books to give, or to receive. *The TLS on Shakespeare* is a delightful, exasperating collection of extracts from a century of the *Times Literary Supplement*, which was offered to subscribers, who could probably figure out some of the missing information (what is actually under review, which reviews appeared anonymously, criteria of choice, where to buy the *Macbeth* computer game). It's a jolly romp for a rainy afternoon, and it made me believe in progress in reviewing. At a higher level of seriousness (but not too high), one of the books published for Queen Elizabeth's anniversary year. Not the least interesting section of Michael Dobson and Nicola J. Watson's *England's Elizabeth*, on myths after Elizabeth, is the one on the queen and the playwright. My favourite Mark Twain essay is clearly far from the battiest of these. But the book is to be savoured right the way through, and not just for its insights into nostalgia, which seems always not to have been what it used to be. The connections they draw between Kapur's biopic and *Henry VIII* draw a forward march with eyes turned ever backwards, but seeing different things. Their pages on Judi Dench are multiply salutary: on *Shakespeare in Love*, on Dench's Elizabeth, but also on the place of this role within Dench's own career (and Dench's Victoria), an aspect often scanted in diachronic studies such as this one. In a sense Dench is the apotheosis of their argument, because, collapsing both period-eponymous monarchs, the actress embodies multiple ideas of a national past.

### WORKS REVIEWED


Adelman, Janet, 'Her Father's Blood: Race, Conversion, and Nation in *The Merchant of Venice*', *Representations*, 81 (2003), 4–30.

Ake, Jami, 'Glimpsing a Lesbian Poetics in *Twelfth Night*', *SEL*, 43 (2003), 375–94.

Alpers, Paul, 'Learning from the New Criticism: The Example of Shakespeare's Sonnets', in Rasmussen, *Renaissance Literature*, pp. 115–38.

Beehler, Sharon A., '"Confederate Season": Elizabethan Understanding of Kairos', in Davis, *Shakespeare Matters*, pp. 74–88.

Blake, Ann, 'Breaking Rank in Shakespearean Marriage Plots', in Davis, *Shakespeare Matters*, pp. 103–18.

Blake, N. F., *Shakespeare's Non-Standard English: a dictionary of his informal language*, Athlone Shakespeare Dictionaries (New York, 2004).

*Shakespeare in Education*, ed. Martin Blocksidge (London, 2003).

Bonnefoy, Yves, *Shakespeare and the French Poet*, ed. John Naughton (Chicago, 2004).

Brönnimann, Werner, 'Think-along edition: the bilingual *Studienausgabe* of Shakespeare', in Hoenselaars, *Language of Translation*, pp. 184–98.

*The TLS on Shakespeare*, ed. Michael Caines and Mick Imlah (np, nd, not for sale).

Callaghan, Dympna, '(Un)natural loving: swine, pets and flowers in *Venus and Adonis*', in Berry, *Textures*, pp. 58–80.

Cerasano, S. P., William Shakespeare's *The Merchant of Venice*, A Routledge Literary Sourcebook (London, 2004).

Cockcroft, Robert, *Rhetorical Affect in Early Modern Writing: Renaissance Passions Reconsidered* (Houndsmill, Basingstoke, 2003).

Cohen, Derek, *Searching Shakespeare: Studies in Culture and Authority* (Toronto, 2003).

'The Past of *Macbeth*', in Davis, *Shakespeare Matters*, pp. 46–61.

Cohen, Stephen, 'Between Form and Culture: New Historicism and the Promise of a Historical Formalism', in Rasmussen, *Renaissance Literature*, pp. 17–42.

Cooper, Helen, *The English Romance in Time: Transforming Motifs from Geoffrey of Monmouth to the Death of Shakespeare* (Oxford, 2004).

Davis, Lloyd, 'Shakespearean Cultures', in Davis, *Shakespeare Matters*, pp. 13–28.

Davis, Philip, 'Implicit and Explicit Reason: George Eliot and Shakespeare', Marshall, *Victorian Shakespeare*, pp. 84–99.

Decker, Christopher, 'Shakespeare and the Death of Tennyson', in Marshall, *Victorian Shakespeare*, pp. 131–49.

Delabastita, Dirk, '"If I know the letters and the language": translation as a dramatic device in Shakespeare's plays', in Hoenselaars, *Language of Translation*, pp. 31–52.

Douglas-Fairhurst, Robert, 'Shakespeare's Weeds: Tennyson, Elegy and Allusion', in Marshall, *Victorian Shakespeare*, pp. 114–30.

Dobson, Michael and Nicola J. Watson, *England's Elizabeth* (Oxford, 2002).

Dubrow, Heather, 'The Politics of Aesthetics: Recuperating Formalism and the Country House Poem', in Rasmussen, *Renaissance Literature*, pp. 67–88.

Duffin, Ross W., compiler and editor, *Shakespeare's Songbook* (New York, 2004).

Dusinberre, Juliet, 'Rival Poets in the Forest of Arden', *Shakespeare Jahrbuch*, 139 (2003), 71–83.

Edelman, Charles, *Shakespeare's Military Language* (London, 2000).

Ellison, James, '*Measure for Measure* and the Executions of Catholics in 1604', *English Literary Renaissance*, 33 (2003), 44–87.

Erne, Lukas, *Shakespeare as Literary Dramatist* (Cambridge, 2003).

Estok, Simon C., 'Teaching the Environment of *The Winter's Tale*: Ecocritical Theory and Pedagogy for

Shakespeare', in Davis, *Shakespeare Matters*, pp. 177–90.

Fitzpatrick, Joan, *Shakespeare, Spenser and the Contours of Britain: Reshaping the Atlantic Archipelago* (Hatfield, 2004).

Flesch, William, 'The Poetics of Speech Tags', in Rasmussen, *Renaissance Literature*, pp. 159–84.

Hadfield, Andrew, *Shakespeare, Spenser and the Matter of Britain* (Houndsmill, Basingstoke, 2003).

Harris, Jonathan Gil, *Sick Economies: Drama, Mercantilism, and Disease in Shakespeare's England* (Philadelphia, 2004).

Goy-Blanquet, Dominique, *Shakespeare's Early History Plays: From Chronicle to Stage* (Oxford, 2003).

Hays, Michael L., *Shakespearean Tragedy as Chivalric Romance: rethinking Macbeth, Hamlet, Othello, King Lear* (Cambridge, 2003).

Healy, Margaret, *Fictions of Disease in Early Modern England* (Basingstoke, 2001).

Hedrick, Donald, 'Advantage, Affect, History, *Henry V*', *PMLA*, 118 (2000), 470–87.

Henderson, Diana E., 'Othello Redux?: Scott's Kenilworth and the Trickiness of "Race" on the Nineteenth-Century Stage', in Marshall, *Victorian Shakespeare*, pp. 14–29.

Hirsch, James, *Shakespeare and the History of Soliloquies* (Madison and London, 2003).

Höfele, Andreas, 'Sackerson the Bear', *REAL: Yearbook of Research in English and American Literature*, 17 (2001), 161–77.

Hope, Jonathan, *Shakespeare's Grammar* (London, 2003).

Hunt, Maurice, *Shakespeare's Religious Allusiveness: Its Play and Tolerance* (Aldershot, 2004).

Kahn, Victoria, 'Hamlet or Hecuba: Carl Schmitt's Decision', *Representations*, 81 (2003), 67–96.

Kermode, Frank, *The Age of Shakespeare* (London, 2004).

Kranz, David L., 'The Sounds of Supernatural Soliciting in *Macbeth*', *Studies in Philology*, 100 (2003), 346–83.

Lampert, Lisa, *Gender and Jewish Difference from Paul to Shakespeare* (Philadelphia, 2004).

Levith, Murray J., *Shakespeare in China* (London, Continuum, 2004).

Levin, Richard, *Looking for an Argument: Critical Encounters with the New Approaches to the Criticism of Shakespeare and his Contemporaries* (Madison and London, 2003).

Low, Jennifer A., *Manhood and the Duel: Masculinity in Early Modern Drama and Culture* (Basingstoke, 2003).

Lynch, Stephen J., *As You Like It: A Guide to the Play*, Greenwood Guides to Shakespeare (Westport, Conn., 2003).

McCoy, Richard C., '"Look Upon me, Sir": Relationships in *King Lear*', *Representations*, 81 (2003), 46–60.

Maley, Willy, *Nation, State and Empire in English Renaissance Literature: Shakespeare to Milton* (Houndsmill, Basingstoke, 2003).

Marsh, Nicholas, *Shakespeare: Three Problem Plays*, Analysing Texts, (Basingstoke, 2003).

Marshall, Cynthia, *The Shattering of the Self: Violence, Subjectivity, & Early Modern Texts* (Baltimore and London, 2002).

Martin, Patrick H. and John Finnis, 'Thomas Thorpe, "W. S.", and the Catholic Intelligencers', *English Literary Renaissance*, 33 (2003), 3–43.

Menon, Madhavi, 'Richard II and the Taint of Metonymy', *ELH*, 70 (2003), 653–76.

Neely, Carol Thomas, *Distracted Subjects: Madness and Gender in Shakespeare and Early Modern Culture* (Ithaca, 2004).

Nostbakken, Faith, *Understanding The Tempest* (Westport, Conn. and London, 2004).

Nyusztay, Iván, *Myth, Telos, Identity: The Tragic Schema in Greek and Shakespearean Drama* (Amsterdam, 2002).

O'Neil, Catherine, *With Shakespeare's Eyes: Pushkin's Creative Appropriation of Shakespeare* (Newark and London, 2003).

O'Rourke, James, 'Racism and Homophobia in *The Merchant of Venice*', *ELH*, 70 (2003), 375–98.

Orgel, Stephen, 'The Case for Comus', *Representations*, 81 (2003), 31–45.

Palmer, Daryl W., *Writing Russia in the Age of Shakespeare* (Aldershot, 2004).

Parker, Barbara L., *Plato's Republic and Shakespeare's Rome: A Political Study of the Roman Works* (Newark, University of Delaware, 2004).

Paulin, Roger, *The Critical Reception of Shakespeare in Germany 1682–1914: Native Literature and Foreign Genius* (Hildesheim and New York, 2003).

Pechter, Edward, 'What's Wrong with Literature?', *Textual Practice*, 17 (2003), 505–26.

Pointner, Frank Erik, *Bawdy and Soul: A Revaluation of Shakespeare's Sonnets* (Heidelberg, 2003).

Poole, Adrian, *Shakespeare and the Victorians* (London, 2004).

Poole, William, '"Unpointed Words": Shakespeare's Syntax in Action', *Cambridge Quarterly*, 32 (2003), 27–48.

'All at Sea: Water, Syntax, and Character Dissolution in Shakespeare', *Shakespeare Survey 54* (Cambridge, 2001), pp. 191–200.

Reynolds, Bryan, *Becoming Criminal: Transversal Performance and Cultural Dissidence in Early Modern England* (Baltimore, 2002).

Rhodes, Neil, *Shakespeare and the Origins of English* (Oxford, 2004).

Richmond, Hugh Macrae, *Shakespeare's Theatre: A Dictionary of his Stage Context* (New York and London, 2002).

Roe, John, *Shakespeare and Machiavelli* (Cambridge, 2002).

Ruiter, David, *Shakespeare's Festive History: Feasting, Festivity, Fasting and Lent in the Second Henriad* (Aldershot, 2003).

Sawyer, Robert, *Victorian Appropriations of Shakespeare: George Eliot, A. C. Swinburne, Robert Browning, and Charles Dickens* (Cranbury, New Jersey and London, 2003).

Shannon, Laurie, 'Likenings: Rhetorical Husbandries and Portia's "True Conceit" of Friendship', *Renaissance Drama*, 31 (2002), 3–26.

Steinsaltz, David, 'The Politics of French Language in Shakespeare's History Plays', *Studies in English Literature*, 42 (2002), 317–34.

Sturgess, Kim C., *Shakespeare and the American Nation* (Cambridge, 2004).

Sokol, B. J., *A Brave New World of Knowledge: Shakespeare's The Tempest and Early Modern Epistemology* (Madison and London, 2003).

Sokol, B. J. and Mary Sokol, *Shakespeare's Legal Language* (London, 2000).

Taunton, Nina and Valerie Hart, '*King Lear*, King James and the Gunpowder Treason of 1605', *Renaissance Studies*, 17 (2003), 695–715.

Wells, Stanley, *Looking for Sex in Shakespeare* (Cambridge, 2004).

Wilson-Okamura, David Scott, 'Virgilian Models of Colonization In Shakespeare's *The Tempest*', *ELH*, 70 (2003), 709–38.

Womack, Mark, 'Undelivered Meanings: The Aesthetics of Shakespearean Wordplay', in Rasmussen, *Renaissance Literature*, pp. 139–58.

## COLLECTIONS

Berry, Philippa and Margaret Tudeau-Clayton, eds., Berry: *Textures of Renaissance Knowledge* (Manchester, 2003).

Bezzola, Ladina and Balz Engler, eds., *Shifting the Scene: Shakespeare in European Culture* (Newark, 2004).

Blocksidge, Martin, ed., *Shakespeare in Education* (London, 2003).

Bradshaw, Graham, John M. Mucciolo, Tom Bishop and Angus Fletcher, eds., *The Shakespearean International Yearbook 3, Where are we now in Shakespearean Studies?* (Aldershot, 2003).

Brydon, Diana and Irena R. Makaryk, eds., *Shakespeare in Canada: A World Elsewhere?* (Toronto, 2002).

Davis, Lloyd, ed., *Shakespeare Matters: History, Teaching, Performance* (Newark and London, 2003).

Dorval, Patricia, ed., *Shakespeare et le Moyen Âge* (Paris, Société française Shakespeare, 2002).

Dorval, Patricia, ed., *Shakespeare et ses contemporains* (Paris, Société française Shakespeare, 2002).

Dutton, Richard, Alison Findlay and Richard Wilson, eds., *Region, Religion and Patronage: Lancastrian Shakespeare* (Manchester, 2003).

Dutton, Richard, Alison Findlay and Richard Wilson, eds., *Theatre and Religion: Lancastrian Shakespeare* (Manchester, 2003).

Gheeraert-Graffeuille, Claire and Nathalie Vienne-Guerrin, eds., *Autour du Songe d'une nuit d'été de William Shakespeare* (Rouen, 2003).

Hoenselaars, Ton, ed., *Shakespeare and the Language of Translation* (London, 2004).

Laroque, François and Franck Lessay, eds., *Esthétiques de la nouveauté à la renaissance* (Paris, 2001).

*Enfers et Délices à la Renaissance* (Paris, 2003).

McDonald, Russ, ed., *Shakespeare, An Anthology of Criticism and Theory 1945–2000* (Oxford, 2004).

Marshall, Gail and Adrian Poole, eds., *Victorian Shakespeare, Volume 2: Literature and Culture* (Houndsmill, Basingstoke, 2003).

Mehl, Dieter, Angela Stock and Anne-Julia Zwierlein, eds., *Plotting Early Modern London: New Essays on Jacobean City Comedy* (Aldershot, 2004).

Pincombe, Mike, ed., *Travels and Translations in the Sixteenth Century: Selected Papers from the Second international Conference of the Tudor Symposium (2000)*, Studies in European Cultural Transition, 20 (London, 2004).

Procházka, Martin, ed., 'Shakespeare's Illyrias: Heterotopias, Identities, (Counter) histories', *Litterraria Pragensia*, 12 (2002).

Pujante, A. Luis and Ton Hoenselaars, eds., *Four Hundred Years of Shakespeare in Europe* (Newark, 2003).

Rasmussen, Mark David, ed., *Renaissance Literature and its Formal Engagements* (Houndsmill, Basingstoke, 2002).

Sorelius, Gunnar, ed., *Shakespeare and Scandinavia: a Collection of Nordic Studies* (Newark and London, 2002).

Wells, Stanley and Lena Cowen Orlin, eds., *Shakespeare: an Oxford Guide* (Oxford, 2003).

Woodbridge, Linda, ed., *Money and the Age of Shakespeare: Essays in New Economic Criticism*, Early Modern Cultural Studies, 1500–1700 (Houndsmill, Basingstoke, 2003).

Woodbridge, Linda and Sharon Beehler, eds., *Women, Violence, and English Renaissance Literature: Essays Honoring Paul Jorgensen* (Tempe, Arizona, 2003).

## 2. SHAKESPEARE IN PERFORMANCE
*reviewed by* EMMA SMITH

Of course you can't judge a book by its cover. But a pile of books on Shakespeare in performance encourages this kind of snapshot approach, and the semiotics of cover illustrations – like the semiotics of much recent performance – reveals an instinct towards a strongly framed visual concept. If we cannot judge the books by their covers, we can certainly answer certain questions by looking at them. Is Shakespeare in performance cool? Yes, says the cover to the achingly hip *Shakespeare, the Movie, II* (edited by Richard Burt and Lynda E. Boose), which shows us Ethan Hawke as moody rich boy Hamlet walking the streets of New York, his torso crossed with an urban bag strap, an ethnic knitted hat pulled down on his head, sunglasses and a downcast look of stylish alienation. Maybe, says Sarah Hatchuel's *Shakespeare, from Stage to Screen*, with a bearded Branagh, dressed in double breasted tunic and sword by his side, looking through the camera on the set of *Much Ado About Nothing*: it's film, so modern, but it has swords in it, so it's also old. No, says the uninspiring cover to Jonathan Holmes's *Merely Players*, which manages to suggest that his fascinating analysis of a range of actors' accounts of their work are the equivalent of the jacket's Jacobethan burgundy flock wallpaper. Is the field all olde-worlde doublet and hosery? No, says Cynthia Marshall's *Shakespeare in Production: As You Like It*, with its cut-out from Cheek by Jowl's all-male production where an arch Celia strokes Rosalind's flank. Not quite, says *Players of Shakespeare 6*, in which a sumptuously dressed king complete with crown who stands by his queen, looking stage-left in consternation, is played by a black actor. Yes, says Tiffany Stern's *Making Shakespeare* which opts for the marbled Shakespeare, chin on fist, regarding Westminster Abbey.

Most of this year's books on performance go for a high contrast, close-up stage image, a picture derived from the theatre but not of it, from which the rest of the characters and the space of the stage are cropped. The style of image thus contributes to the cult of actor celebrity encouraged in much mainstream Shakespearian production, and offers the visual counterpart to the cult of character criticism revivified by the academic field of Shakespeare-in-performance. Pascale Aebischer's iconic image for *Shakespeare's Violated Bodies* is Brian Cox as a bearded King Lear, hand raised in anger, as a blurred and moving Cordelia stumbles towards the camera; Henry Fuseli's version of David Garrick's Macbeth holding the bloodied daggers, recoiling from the fearsomely crinolined Hannah Pritchard is highlighted on the cover of John Wilders's *Shakespeare in Production: Macbeth*; an image of the dead Gertrude, in a red dress with arm outstretched, adorns the front of Li Ruru's *Shashibiya: Staging Shakespeare in China*; a comical image of a bespectacled Hal and a trim Falstaff in a metal crown from a play called *Schlachten* gives a cartoonish, out-of-*Asterix* tone to Ton Hoenselaars's *Shakespeare's History Plays*. Collectively, the images chosen to represent the books work sustainedly to stress character rather than stage, monochrome rather than colour, personality rather than theme, individual rather than ensemble, emotions of face rather than space. Only Colin Chambers's kiss-and-tell book *Inside the Royal Shakespeare Company* shows us an uncropped stage image in which the shape of the stage is a visible context for the action played out upon it: the fact that the image is of the Battle of Agincourt rendered as a stylized fight sequence in Matthew Warchus's *Henry V* (1994) suggests it should be read as metaphorical rather than representational.

The role of images in books on Shakespeare in performance seems indicative of our current disciplinary priorities. While there are reasons for the relative paucity of reproduced images in performance criticism – it is expensive to reproduce images and, as anyone who has tried to get permissions to reproduce film or production stills knows, a considerable hassle – the ratio of words about performance to pictures from performance is always heavily skewed. This makes the choice of illustrations particularly crucial. Robert Smallwood's *Players of Shakespeare*, a wonderful series the fifth and sixth volumes of which are under consideration here, illustrates each performance essay with two black-and-white photographs from the production. In each case these are of the actor writing the essay. In volume 5, for example, Philip Voss's account of Prospero has one picture of him cradling Miranda – the most interesting thing for an understanding of the play conveyed by this is that the actor, Nikki Amuki-Bird, is black, although no one mentions this as an aspect of the production – and another of him in a top hat, ringmaster-style, for his re-entry as Duke of Milan in Act 5. Nigel Hawthorne's performance of Lear is illustrated with an Old-Testament-prophet shot of the white-haired monarch in a white robe with a hand raised to heaven, and an image of him in a sunburst metallic crown while a puzzled Cordelia in girlish plaits looks concernedly from the edge of the frame. The pictures illustrating Alexandra Gilbreath's Hermione are refreshingly different: both offer a middle-shot tableau in which the emotional separation between Leontes and Hermione is imaged in the stage space between them. The two images make a suggestive visual link, largely through blocking and lighting effects, between Hermione's trial and the statue scene – a link which doesn't come out of Gilbreath's own account of her performance, although she is interesting on how the actor deals with Hermione's absence from the stage: 'So what did I do for the next two hours? Keeping in touch with the play was essential, just listening over the tannoy, trying to keep the momentum in place' (p. 88). In volume 6, the unillustrated introduction concerns itself with the visual description of the productions as a prefatory context for the actors' own words. Three actors discuss the Royal Shakespeare Company's *King John:* Guy Henry, who took the title role; Kelly Hunter, playing Constance; and Jo Stone-Fewings as the Bastard. These are collectively and individually revealing about the production and their approach to the play. It is the strength of Smallwood's editing of these contributions that actors' voices come through, from Henry's anecdotes and ironic self-deprecation ('Much comment was passed by audience members I spoke to about what a brilliantly symbolic masterstroke my wobbly crown was and how, in its wobbliness, it so perfectly suited such an imperfect king, [but] its wobbliness was more accident than symbol . . . it just didn't fit very well' (p. 27)) to Kelly Hunter's awkward, rather gauche parallel between the events of September 11th 2001 and the RSC's shocking announcement it would disband its traditional ensemble company system. Ultimately, however, their endeavour is as close to academic criticism as it could be: the focus is the script, the words, what they mean, and how an actor can make them mean what they mean. The illustrations to the volumes draw out the uneasy actorly and scholarly tension between the sentimentalised idea of the company ensemble and the iconography of the star, as words and images refocus stage productions through the perspective of their major characters.

The contents lists of *Players of Shakespeare* 5 and 6 might usefully be added to the appendix for volumes 1–4 in Jonathan Holmes's *Merely Players?* Holmes's concern with actors is verbal not visual. Indeed, he argues that his subjects are the accounts of performances by actors as a specific genre, the rhetorical embodiment of the performance for specific purposes, including the *Players of Shakespeare* series. Holmes's aim is also recuperative, wanting to allow the silenced actor's voice to be heard as a corrective to the prevailing current: 'Shakespearian performance is portrayed as having been impoverished from its lack of contact with criticism, which operates as a kind of benevolent patriarch, guiding the children of the stage in the right direction' (p. 8). Perhaps this overstates the case: academic Shakespearians seem increasingly in awe of their theatrical counterparts as performance criticism, or at least a gesture towards it, becomes more integrated in scholarly practice. The question mark in Holmes's title indicates a rhetorical question, but it's his question, not Jacques's: it may be a straw man rather than a real argument. And if he wants to interrogate *Players of Shakespeare*, he also wants to defend it: the careful initial categorization of actors' accounts as rhetorical sometimes shades into a cruder page and stage debate: 'What is happening in the theatre is at least as illuminating and as compelling as what is happening in the study' (p. 180). This may be true, but Holmes's own work is not about what is happening in the theatre, but about how some of its practitioners write – probably in the study – about the theatre. To make the writing transparent is to reinscribe a theoretical blindspot that, elsewhere, Holmes is keen to review. The book does, however, attempt to conceptualize in an invigorating way the routes, practices and texts by which theatre and study can cross-pollinate, and his book is a sophisticated and thought-provoking contribution to the field, not least because of its direct engagement with the specifically verbal and rhetorical texture of our accounts of, and interventions into, performance criticism.

Pictures are important as metaphor and synecdoche in Pascale Aebischer's *Shakespeare's Violated Bodies*. Aebischer's provocative credo, 'it is the white male subject of tragedy who will be marginalized in this study' (p. 5), isn't quite supported by that cover in which a violent Lear dominates the frame over a fuzzy, pushed Cordelia. There are some wonderful moments in this book. Discussing spectacular and occluded representations of violence in *Titus Andronicus*, Aebischer focuses on Lavinia's rape and her functionally disconcerting presence on stage afterwards. In the context of Antony Sher and Greg Doran's South African production of *Titus*, Aebischer notes parallels with a novel by Sher in which a raped and mutilated woman is interpreted as a Lavinia figure: she identifies how disturbing Sher and Doran's *Woza Shakespeare!* – an example of what Jonathan Holmes would identify as the rhetorical embodiment of practitioners' insights into Shakespeare – is in this regard. On *Hamlet* she discusses a production of Q1 in which doubling, dummies and absent present ghosts multiplied promiscuously; and is deft on the implications of André Tchaikovsky's bequest of his own skull to the Royal Shakespeare Company as a permanent Yorick and the queasiness of the company in making use of this unsolicited prop. Sometimes the tone of analysis is one of disappointment. Adrian Noble's reputation as a 'boys' director' (the quotation is from his Cordelia, Abigail McKern) is seamlessly elided with his 1993 production's depiction of the sisters as stereotypes (but aren't they?) and 'the dominant reactionary reading strategies of the conflated playtext he was working with' (p. 153): all of these are, the critical voice makes clear, to be regretted. The book tends towards a valorization of alternative or fringe theatre over established theatre and occasionally its real hermeneutic sophistication is blurred into academic agitprop. Aebischer's is a provocative voice in the field, however, as one of the few performance critics willing to critique the assumptions of mainstream theatrical praxis. Things are not going well for that Stratford boys' club, however. Former RSC Literary Manager Colin Chambers's *Inside the Royal Shakespeare Company* promises to be the critical equivalent of a staple of recent British television: the fly-on-the-wall documentary in which a public institution or company lets in the cameras, making unlikely cultural heroes of its more quirky employees and lacerating the management in the process. This popular genre understands that institutions are rarely interesting in themselves but their individuals are: it's a lesson not learned by Chambers, whose analysis of the RSC's fortunes is structured around the reigns of its artistic directors but fails to catch fire in human terms, as the collective body it anatomizes slouches from internal to external crisis with little grace, idiosyncrasy or humour. Chambers's admiration for the company values of Peter Hall's founding leadership is clear. He describes in detail the moves by which Hall established the theatre, fought for its public funding, differentiated himself from Olivier's National Theatre, and negotiated the running tension between creativity and the institution. It has aspects of a stock story that could be analysed through Propp's functions: a struggle with various Goliaths, or at various Agincourts, sees Hall increase audiences, champion new plays, establish 'a distinctive verse-speaking style [and bring] Shakespeare into the contemporary world' (p. 51), bequeathing to his heir Trevor Nunn a world-class theatre and the anxiety of how to improve it. Son Nunn in turn leaves to Terry Hands 'an almighty mess' (p. 92), and etiolated grandson Hands can only preside over its further decline: Sher's much-lauded Richard III in 1984 is cited as one of the outbreaks of individualism that fatally threatens the company ethic. Adrian Noble inherits as Peggy Ashcroft dies: the auguries are not good, and Chambers has begun to call the RSC 'the monster' (p. 96). The open verdict on Michael Boyd's recent appointment forms an unconvincing epilogue: by now, Chambers's jeremiad of decline is so clearly established that there is no narrative commitment to the idea of future development. Anyone interested in Shakespearian production in the UK is by definition interested in the Royal Shakespeare Company, so Chambers is assured of some readership, but to call his account, as the book jacket does, 'a vital document of our times' is to succumb to the new Stratfordianism of RSC-centric cultural analysis. Is it heretical to wonder whether the RSC's decline might not, in fact, be an *a priori* cause for weeping and gnashing of teeth?

The two volumes out this year in the *Shakespeare in Production* series, Cynthia Marshall's on *As You Like It* and John Wilders's on *Macbeth*, encourage us to take the longer view and wider view of theatrical hotspots. Marshall covers a chronological range from first performances to the end of the twentieth century, including American and British stage productions as well as film and television adaptations. She begins with Johnson's description of the play as 'wild and pleasing', and uses this combination of adjectives to think about challenging and conservative performance readings, emblematized in representations of the Forest of Arden as, variously, classical pastoral, as home to a stuffed stag which became a mascot of late Victorian Stratford productions, in the vogue for outdoor productions, as a surreally erotic set by Salvador Dali, or as a dream version of the duke's court with furniture covered by pale dustsheets. Details, from promptbooks, reviews and actors' reminiscences makes the narrative introduction consistently engaging. Earlier illustrations – an engraving of Ellen Terry in plumed hat, carrying a spear, and showing a finely turned ankle, or a mischievous-looking Touchstone in harlequin costume played by J. P. Harley – attest to the historical role of the picture in managing a performer's career. Neither has any relation to the play, only to the representation of the character, showing the actor in costume and pose in a frame uncluttered by stage scenery, plot structure or professional rivals in a fantasy of thespian autonomy. Wilders's account of *Macbeth* opens by carefully locating the play in the Jacobean context, then tracing the reinventions of this tragedy of regicide through Davenant's Restoration version, via 'Old Caledonian' eighteenth-century settings and the movement for historical accuracy, into expressionistic modernist versions. There is a brief but unconvinced section on films in the introduction, and a significant bias towards mainstream English production history. All the examples of productions of the last fifty years, bar one premiered at the Edinburgh Festival and one (predictably unsuccessful) at the Royal Court, hail from Stratford or the National Theatre. Wilders eschews any wider critical framework so that it is hard to connect production examples to other forms of criticism, such as revisionist readings of the character of Lady Macbeth, for example. It is a production history of *Macbeth* which domesticates this most politically challenging of plays.

Neither of the *Shakespeare in Production* volumes discusses productions outside the English-speaking world: a few lines on Kurosawa's *Throne of Blood* are thus sandwiched, culturally decontextualized, between Welles and Polanski in Wilders's account of *Macbeth*. The premise of three books on Shakespeare in, respectively, China, Ukraine, and, to a lesser extent, Canada – that their national engagement with the plays has been ignored by Shakespearians – is apparently ratified. Li Ruru's book *Shashibiya: Staging Shakespeare in China* is a fascinating analysis. Her appendices make clear that, since the end of the Cultural Revolution, versions of some twenty plays, largely comedies and tragedies, by 'Old Man Sha' have been performed, largely in the *huaju* mode of spoken drama. *The Merchant of Venice* is an unexpected Chinese favourite, and Zhang Qihong's 1980 production, in which onstage kissing provoked much public discussion, is discussed as a colourful romantic fantasy of escape from Maoist mundanity. An illustration shows Bassanio in flame-coloured Elizabethan costume wooing a pearlescent Portia: both actors are adopting non-Chinese physical stances and gestures while wearing prosthetic noses to look more westernized. The image would not look out of place from a 1950s British production, and Li notes that, unlike many communist countries in East Europe, China does not have a tradition of deploying Shakespeare for political purposes. Juxtaposing the image of *The Merchant of Venice* with one derived from *Macbeth* amply demonstrates the range of Chinese production styles. *Macbeth* – or *Xie shou ji* (*Blood-stained Hands*) is performed in traditional *kunju* style, with red and pink costumes, elaborate headdresses, and makeup designed to exaggerate facial expressions. Versions of *Macbeth* do, however, have political resonances: Xu Xiaozhong's 1980 production in Beijing echoed the director's memories of the Cultural Revolution, while stressing that Macbeth's was a national, historical tragedy as well as an individual one: 'we hope that our performance will ring a warning bell . . . Desire for individual power and ambition can change a virtuous general to a villain . . . What we say and do should be measured by Socialist moral and legal beliefs' (p. 73). Li notes that there are still few experimental productions of Shakespeare in China and that a combination of residual Soviet cultural influence, respect for authority, isolation and the conservatism of *huaju* performance style have tended towards stagnation of Shakespearean theatre. Li's book ends: 'Shakespeare, then, is not dead. But he is in a fitful slumber. Currently, Shakespeare productions do not enjoy consistent support, nor is the cultural atmosphere very receptive to him' (p. 230). She notes, however, that signs of interest among youth theatre groups and university drama courses may be a source of future regeneration.

At the time of writing, the unresolved presidential election in Ukraine is widely represented as a battle between a future facing towards Russia and one facing towards Europe and the West. Irena R. Makaryk's book *Shakespeare in the Undiscovered Bourn: Les Kurbas, Ukrainian Modernism, and Early Soviet Cultural Politics* uses extensive archival research to discuss a cultural moment rather like the present political stasis, as she analyses the Soviet director Les Kurbas's avant-garde Shakespeare productions in early twentieth-century Ukraine. Kurbas's own fate, sentenced to the gulag in 1933, is emblematic of that of Ukrainian Shakespeare: ignored in the West and forcibly co-opted into histories of Soviet theatre in the USSR. Makaryk's book disaggregates these totalising accounts of 'Soviet' Shakespeare, just as separatist nationalist movements have disaggregated the Soviet Union itself, focusing instead on the specific significance of Shakespeare in Ukraine amid its changing political landscape. Celebrating Shakespeare's birthday in 1939, a Ukrainian newspaper claimed that 'the great humanist, Shakespeare, is close to us, the citizens of this young socialist country' (p. 202). As in China, *Macbeth* plays a prominent role: Kurbas's discontinuous, modernist *Macbeth* of 1924 is at the heart of Makaryk's account. His use of moveable screens, raised and lowered at the sound of a gong, as a backdrop to the scenes is discussed with particular visual fluency which establishes rhythm, rather than continuous character narrative, as the production's key diachronic axis. A Fool/Porter character, making extempore topical references culled from the day's newspapers, serves to integrate Ukrainian popular tradition and circus performance with Western actor/audience dynamics to great effect: at

Malcolm's coronation it is the Fool, in his grinning, mocking make-up and dressed in bishop's robes, who blesses the new king. As Malcolm kneels for the episcopal blessing, a new pretender entered, killed him and took the crown. The fool-bishop solemnly blesses the new king, whereupon he, too, is assassinated and the ritual is repeated, thus questioning the play's assumption that order has been restored. The book ends with more recent *Macbeths* in 1991, and an optimism that the cultural partnership between Ukraine and Shakespeare might be a source of artistic and political dialogue in the future.

Both Li and Makaryk discuss a specific country's engagement with Shakespeare via the preposition 'in'. Ric Knowles goes consciously for 'and': in his *Shakespeare and Canada* he considers 'the two terms of my title as both shifting and mutually exclusive' (p. 12). Knowles discusses a range of those 'and' relationships: the Stratford Ontario festival founded in 1953, the role of Shakespearian stories in the late twentieth-century renaissance of Native theatre and varieties of Shakespearian production in non-anglo Canadian culture. The Stratford festival gives a prism through which to view four decades of Canadian nationalism: taking the 1993 festival as an example, Knowles is alert to the paratext of programme notes, advertising, material conditions of performance on the Moiseiwitsch stage, ticket prices and audience demography, as well as to the production detail of *Antony and Cleopatra*, costumed as 'an uncomfortable meeting of the Arabian Nights with fascist Italy' (p. 61, the suggestion seems to be that this discomfort is inappropriate to the play) or *A Midsummer Night's Dream* set among some inflatable forest objects variously experienced as a dismantled ham and Swiss cheese sandwich (this by an academic, naturally) and oversized rubber genitalia. The institutional context of the festival functions as an 'Ideological State Apparatus' (p. 68), and thus Knowles argues that the conditions that shape the theatrical production should be as susceptible to analysis as those productions themselves. Theories of language, translation and nationalism are key to the section on Shakespeare and Québec, with some interesting analysis of scenes from a quebecois *The Taming of the Shrew*. On adaptations of Shakespeare, Knowles works with African-Canadian playwright Djanet Sears's culturally and generically hybrid *Harlem Duet* to untangle racialized and gendered Canadian identities at the end of the twentieth century. Knowles's theorizing is eclectic and sometimes, as the Althusserian example suggests, rather majuscule clunky, but it is also stimulating.

Ton Hoenselaars's edited collection on *Shakespeare's History Plays* moves the discussion on, by including Shakespeare's own techniques of alienation alongside the translated and appropriated text in different cultural contexts: in Italy, Bulgaria, Japan, at the Viennese Burgtheater or the Avignon Festival. Since the history plays hardly feature in the accounts by Li, Makaryk or Knowles, it is particularly interesting here to focus a generic lens as well as a national one. Dennis Kennedy's introduction suggests that the history plays are not, in fact, at home in England either and that the novelty of the genre at the time Shakespeare was writing, as well as its peculiarities of genealogy and location, mean that the plays were always somehow unfamiliar. The contributors amplify this exciting sense of strangeness in a collection with unusual coherence and cumulative weight. Jean-Michel Déprats's assertion that 'French directors shirk from staging *Henry V* because of its dominant heroic note and jingoistic politics' (p. 75) may not seem a particularly striking intervention, but his analysis of Jean-Louis Benoit's production of the play at Avignon in 1999 works with different ideas of translation to discuss this play so insistently concerned with languages and with making English itself foreign. Images in this book are revelatory. James N. Loehlin's work on Peter Palitzsch's Brechtian *Der Krieg der Rosen* in Stuttgart in 1967, part of an informed view of the critical rehabilitation of *Henry VI* in a non-naturalistic politicized theatrical context, has a 'portrait' rather than 'landscape' illustration. This vertical orientation stresses the white space of the set and the gap between a frieze of human and horse skeletons and armour across the top of the stage, and a heavy figure in the foreground lumbering across a battlefield littered with bodies. A striking image of the bleak set of *Richard III* at the Burgtheater in 1987 (dir. Claus Peymann) shows two skeletal dark figures upstage, the crutches of Richard mirrored by the stick on which the Duchess of York leans, amplified in a range of metal poles cordoning off areas of the stage, and echoed downstage by stiffly armoured guards and a harsh horizon on which a metallic bird – perhaps a vulture – is perched.

It is in film studies that the visual has most scholarly and aesthetic authority, and in the study of Shakespeare on film that visual aspects of performance might carry most weight. *Shakespeare, the Movie, II* ought, like many of the cinematic sequels it imitates, to be a disappointment. It capitalizes on the 'phenomenally successful' *Shakespeare, the Movie* (1997) and recapitulates with the same editorial team of Burt and Boose and a similar line-up of contributors, including, for example, Barbara Hodgdon offering a second go at her own essay on *Othello* in the earlier volume. In fact, this is less sequel than new release: a unique paean to the particular commercial value of this publishing sector, which can present a book which is neither second edition nor sequel. The analogy with the directors' cut or reissued DVD format film is archly present: the introduction is knowingly headed 'Editors' cut' and includes Richard Burt discussing the menu formats of DVDs as a way of dehistoricizing Shakespeare film criticism. Here multiple versions controlled by the viewer replace the event or moment of first release, the textual metaphor of 'chapters' divides films into segments just as increasingly dispersed modes of viewing, on personal computer, home DVD or cellphone, privatize the experience of consumption; 'film reception has become posthistorical' (p. 4). Those who buy this book not realizing they have already bought much of it will perforce particularly relish the new articles. Katherine Rowe's discussion of Michael Almereyda's *Hamlet* (2000) is one of these fresh pieces and gives the book its up-to-date cover image: here she discusses forms of textuality in both film and play, arguing that the film investigates different technologies of memory. Rowe's self-reflexive argument about quoting from films brings out some of the difficulties in visual quotation that the books on stage performance encounter: 'without a medium that quotes the work in its own material dimensions, this essay has no cinematic text to close read' (p. 53). Shakespeare on film has often been presented as a pragmatic pedagogic encounter with the plays in performance: here, Rowe argues that the aesthetic entirety of the film text may be made unavailable through copyright in a manner analogous to the lost materiality of the stage performance. Laurie Osborne's essay on animated Shakespeares is also new to the collection: here a residual defensiveness about the coupling of Shakespeare and animation is parried via Sergei Eisenstein's writing on Disney's 'literalization of metaphor'. Her account of the way Brutus's decision to join the conspirators is visualized with feigned filmic jump-cuts in Yuri Yulakov's *Julius Caesar* (1996) is exciting, as is the description of the use of puppets in the *Animated Taming of the Shrew* (dir. Aida Ziablikova, 1996). Self-conscious technique in the animation is used to foreground Shakespearian self-consciousness. *Shakespeare, the Movie II* is concerned with the multiplying textual forms of Shakespeare in new media, and its modernity is both refreshing and perplexing. Rowe offers a hypermedia version of her essay online 'for as long as it remains feasible to host' (p. 53), alerting us that the apparent materiality of book and the film are countered by the exigencies of the internet: the virtual essay on the Shakespeare film becomes closer to the stage performance – catch it while you can.

Whether and how we can quote Shakespeare films are questions also at the heart of Bernice Kliman's article in Sarah Hatchuel and Nathalie Vienne-Guerrin's *Shakespeare on Screen: 'A Midsummer Night's Dream'*. Kliman defends the pedagogical technique of sampling Shakespeare films – her example is Michael Hoffman's version of *Dream* – through showing clips in the classroom, arguing that it is possible and necessary to interrogate a selected quotation, from a film as from any other text. The most interesting part of the volume is the transcript of the questions after the papers, although the papers don't show many of the techniques of oral delivery one might expect. Only a quoted student says 'Yeah' (p. 52), otherwise the linguistic level of academic discussion is very lucid. Illustrations here range from stills of films, including a number of grainy ones, to Richard Burt's analysis of *Dream* in pornography ('bardcore *Dreams*, or perhaps I should say, *Creams*', p. 60), and a brilliantly superfluous snap of Burt, arms round a polished-torsoed Puck in PVC trousers. The caption reads 'Puck and author at *The Donkey Show* (photo by Jean Howard)': Friday night at the SAA. There was apparently little discussion after Burt's paper, although Jay Halio gamely offers that the 1909 silent *Dream*, in which Penelope replaces Shakespeare's Oberon, might allow a lesbian reading. Burt's cheerful 'why not?' is followed by Kenneth Rothwell's 'Or they may not have had any male actor at the time' (p. 85): it's an exchange that seems, somehow, a miniature of many arguments in which material conditions of performance are adduced in support of conservative readings. Perhaps Rothwell thought better of it. Having poured cold water on the lesbian action, he attempts to regain some credibility with a cluster of louche signifiers: 'The first Shakespeare porn film I ever saw was at the Ritzy Brixton theatre in East London'. The discussion of the pornographic material bleeds uneasily into a session on Christine Edzard's *The Children's Midsummer Night's Dream*. Other contributors discuss Hoffman, Reinhardt and a forgotten 1960s television version. The editors are to be thanked for an excellent detailed film bibliography.

'Page to stage' has become a kind of performance criticism cliché, a conservative inscription of textual priorities masked by the apparent dynamism of the word 'to'. Two books refigure the formulation in different ways. Tiffany Stern's is an inversion: in her *Making Shakespeare: From Stage to Page* she focuses on the ways in which early modern conditions of production bear on Shakespeare's plays. Sarah Hatchuel's book on film is called *Shakespeare: From Stage to Screen* and, in beginning with a historical narrative of theatrical presentation, suggests that screen is a development of stage aesthetics. Stern's book begins by destabilizing the singular 'performance', reminding us that Shakespeare's works were in progress through their production, shaped by censorship, actors, audience, theatre building, political context, and that fluidity is thus a condition of their being. Written in lively style – taking us across the Thames to the Globe either on foot or by boat, via the cries of the watermen and the heads of traitors on spikes at the gatehouse – Stern's connections are refreshing and engaging. 'Black Othello' would have been strikingly similar to the tarred heads of those executed traitors; the image of Cymbeline on Ludgate is subliminally present in the references to arches and gates in the play; the Ghost's emergence from the trap in the stage identifies him as a denizen of Hell. The chapter on music is particularly interesting. This would be an excellent book for teaching with: it has the capacity to prompt discussion, to support speculation with acute scholarship, to model sophisticated and lucid academic prose, and provides vivid detail in order to bring a world of artisans and actors into enlightening collision with more deferential critical procedures. Hatchuel's book makes the move from stage to screen in more Whiggish terms, asserting that the theatre 'progressively introduced elements and techniques that foreshadowed (or were appropriated by) cinematic devices' (p. 1). Hatchuel's taxonomy of four types of Shakespeare films includes adaptations that use the original text (including films by Olivier and Branagh); free adaptations using a translation of the text (for example films by Kozintsev and Kurosawa); films inspired by Shakespeare plays (such as *West Side Story* or *Forbidden Planet*); and films in which characters are involved in Shakespeare roles or plays (*Last Action Hero, In the Bleak Midwinter*). Her focus is the first two. Using narratology to analyse the transformation of the Shakespeare play into a film draws out a theatrical mode of 'showing' and a cinematic mode of 'telling', in which the plays' original metatheatrical mode is transformed into an essentially realist cinematic world. Hatchuel works systematically and deftly with different cinematic concepts and theories, building up to more sustained 'case studies'. On Branagh's *Hamlet*, for example, she notes generic echoes to B-movies, to Mozart's *Don Giovanni* and to Darth Vader; comparing Welles and Parker's versions of the 'fainting' scene in *Othello*, she discusses the management of cinematic tension through subjective/objective shots and visual metaphor; different camera angles illustrate the shifting power dynamics in Act 3 of *Julius Caesar* with reference to films by Burge and Mankiewicz. Hatchuel is even-handed and unevaluative: the book would have benefited from illustrations and a filmography.

All this emphasis on the visual means that the final book can only appear in contrast. Perhaps performed music, however, is the counterpart to performed text, and in this respect it's a treat to have an audio CD of examples from *Shakespeare's Songbook* as part of Ross W. Duffin's study. Duffin, too, is quoting: giving snippets from a range of songs rather than complete performances. The singers are excellent, and mercifully disinclined – except in the songs to *Macbeth* – to overdramatic intonation. The entries are particularly interesting in identifying the ways new settings for songs might update a revived play, and on the ways in which already-known, popular songs with particular associations, are deployed in, for example, *Twelfth Night* and *Othello*. It covers songs within plays as well as songs alluded to. In most cases, Duffin gives considerably more information than the plays' recent editors: on *Twelfth Night*, for example, he offers two versions of a song 'O the twelfth day of December', Toby Belch's abortive song which gives us the play's closest approximation to its title. Neither has anything to do with Christmas or festivity and the most likely is 'Upon the Scots being Beaten at Musselburgh Field' which seems relevant largely in that its chorus, 'for a down, down, derry derry down, hey down a down, down, down a down, derry' has obvious applications to a heavy drinking session. The recent Oxford edition has no reference to any known tune, but it does offer a more thorough investigation of the possibilities for 'O Mistress Mine' than does Duffin. By gathering fragmentary evidence into a substantial work of reference *Shakespeare's Songbook* offers a compendium of information for readers and musicians: more than any other book here this is intended for practitioners and, as such, will influence future performance even as it memorializes past ones.

## WORKS REVIEWED


Aebischer, Pascale, *Shakespeare's Violated Bodies: Stage and Screen Performance* (Cambridge, 2004).

Aebischer, Pascale, Edward J. Esche and Nigel Wheale, eds., *Remaking Shakespeare: Performance Across Media, Genres, and Cultures* (Basingstoke and New York, 2003).

Burt, Richard and Lynda E. Boose, eds., *Shakespeare, the Movie, II: Popularising the Plays on Film, TV, Video and DVD* (London and New York, 2003).

Chambers, Colin, *Inside the Royal Shakespeare Company* (London and New York, 2004).

Duffin, Ross W., *Shakespeare's Songbook* (New York and London, 2004).

Hatchuel, Sarah, *Shakespeare, from Stage to Screen* (Cambridge, 2004).

*Shakespeare on Screen: 'A Midsummer Night's Dream'* (Rouen, 2004).

Hoenselaars, Ton, ed., *Shakespeare's History Plays: Performance, Translation and Adaptation in Britain and Abroad* (Cambridge, 2004).

Holmes, Jonathan, *Merely Players? Actors' Accounts of Performing Shakespeare* (London and New York, 2004).

Knowles, Ric, *Shakespeare and Canada: Essays on Production, Translation, and Adaptation* (Brussels, 2004).

Makaryk, Irena R., *Shakespeare and the Undiscovered Bourn: Les Kurbas, Ukrainian Modernism, and Early Soviet Politics* (Toronto, 2004).

Marshall, Cynthia, ed., *Shakespeare in Production: 'As You Like It'* (Cambridge, 2004).

Ruru, Li, *Shashibiya: Staging Shakespeare in China* (Hong Kong, 2003).

Smallwood, Robert, ed., *Players of Shakespeare 5* (Cambridge, 2003).

(ed.), *Players of Shakespeare 6: Essays in the Performance of Shakespeare's History Plays* (Cambridge, 2004).

Stern, Tiffany, *Making Shakespeare: From Stage to Page* (London and New York, 2004).

Wilders, John, ed., *Shakespeare in Production: 'Macbeth'* (Cambridge, 2004).

# 3. EDITIONS AND TEXTUAL STUDIES

*reviewed by* ERIC RASMUSSEN

## EDITIONS

There is an uncanny connection between the Arden Shakespeare and the Oxford Shakespeare. An Arden editor and an Oxford editor can be at work on the same play for many years, have virtually no contact with one another and yet produce their separate editions nearly simultaneously. Such was the case when the Arden2 *Troilus* and the Oxford *Troilus* both appeared in 1982, and again when the Arden3 *Henry VI Part Three* appeared within weeks of the Oxford edition in 2001. Since it seems implausible that the two publishers would conspire to flood the market with new editions of relatively unpopular plays, I take it that these are coincidences rather than instances of collusion. This year has brought one more: the appearance of the Arden3 *Pericles*, edited by Suzanne Gossett, and of the Oxford *Pericles*, edited by Roger Warren.

Comparison of such twins is inevitable, and seems particularly called for here. Gossett presents her edition, in part, as a response to the 'conjectural reconstruction' of the play in the Oxford *Complete Works*, which she views as an 'extreme' example of rewriting that often 'cannot be justified'. Adopting what she describes as 'a moderate approach, neither reconstructing nor refusing to emend', Gossett seeks 'to create a credible, bibliographically defensible, reading and performance script'. Warren, in marked contrast, offers 'a conjectural reconstruction of the play that lies behind the corrupt text of the Quarto', basing his text on the previous Oxford reconstruction. Whereas the Arden3 title-page advertises a single-handed encounter between the editor and her text – 'PERICLES, Edited by Suzanne Gossett' – the Oxford title-page is awash in authorial and editorial agents: 'A reconstructed text of *Pericles, Prince of Tyre*, by William Shakespeare and George Wilkins, edited by Roger Warren on the basis of a text prepared by Gary Taylor and MacD. P. Jackson'.

Since Warren's is a reconstructed text of the 'grossly corrupt' quarto, one might expect it to be heavily emended throughout. In fact, Warren sometimes preserves the Q reading in places where Gossett emends (e.g., 1.2.90, 2.1.152, 2.4.33, 4.3.43). The two editors also differ in their manner of defending their emendations: whereas Warren writes confidently, even dogmatically, Gossett is more reflective. Consider, for instance, what Warren calls 'the obvious emendation' *Unscissored* for Q's 'nonsensical' *vnsistered* in 'Unscissored shall this hair of mine remain' (13.29 in Warren's numbering; 3.3.30 in Gossett's). In her discussion of the line, Gossett observes that the emendation in question confirms Pericles's later vow 'Never to wash his face nor cut his hairs' (4.4.27–8), but she finds it problematic that the second vow unnecessarily reiterates the first. She therefore suggests that perhaps Pericles first vows that his daughter will remain his only 'heir, all unsistered' because, like Leontes, he will refuse to remarry, and only later swears to remain unwashed and unshorn. Given her further objection that 'editors have methodically discounted the play's persistent but buried concern with sisterhood', Gossett seems prepared to retain the Q reading, and it comes as something of a disappointment when instead she adopts the emendation 'Unscissored'.

In keeping with Gossett's previous exemplary work as a textual editor, she has here produced a superb text, in which I spotted only two trivial errors: for 'ere' read 'e'er' (2.5.67) and for '*with* Pirates' read '*with the* Pirates' (4.2.36 SD).[1] She attends to the textual issues, moreover, without ever losing sight of theatrical considerations. For example, Gossett offers a detailed bibliographical

With thanks to my ever perspicacious editor, Arthur Evenchik.

[1] There are few typographic errors in the collations: at 1.1.12.1 for '*Daughter*' read '*daughter*' in the Q reading; 2.2.43–4 for '*viuo*' read '*viuo.*'; 3.2.49–53 for 'vpon't;' read 'vpon't.'; 3.2.81–5 for 'recouered;' read 'recouered.'; a note is needed for the lineation change at 3.2.40–1 where Q lines 'or / Bagges'; Epi.12 for 'deed' read 'deede'; syllabic è should have been noted in 'distressed' (2.5.45), 'learned' (Epi. 10), and 'seemed' (Epi. 15).

discussion of reimposition – the use of standing type from Q1 in the printing of Q2 – a practice which suggests a very rapid reprinting and no doubt attests to the play's relatively large readership. But she is equally attuned to the ways in which audiences would have heard the text. In commenting on the 'aurally indeterminate moment' in 'in marriage pleasures playfellow' (1.0.34), she observes that 'in the theatre the line could be heard either as "in marriage, pleasure's playfellow", that is, marriage becomes companion to a personified "pleasure", or as "in marriage pleasures, playfellow" that is, as a companion in the pleasures of marriage' and concludes that it would be 'a mistake to limit the interpretation by introducing a hyphen between *marriage* and *pleasures*'.

Gossett's engaging introduction, illustrated with well-chosen woodcuts, alerts us to the play's distinctive features: *Pericles* provides the only instance in which a 'bad quarto' of a Shakespeare play was not followed by a 'good' text, and it is the only Shakespearian romance that depicts three distinct generations. The description of the three members of the family all being 'enclosed' at the end of the play (Marina in the brothel, Pericles on his ship, Thaisa in the temple) is particularly fine, as is the analysis of structural similarities to the court masque, suggesting that the brothel 'forms an anti-masque of sexual misrule in the play'.

Surprisingly, Gossett indulges in some conjectural reconstruction of her own:

> It is not difficult to imagine Wilkins prodding Shakespeare to consider a collaboration during the slack period when the theatres were closed . . . one night Shakespeare chats about travel tales with Wilkins . . . Susanna Shakespeare delivers a daughter in the week of 21 February 1608. Shakespeare, with painful memories of losing a child revived by the death of [his brother] Edmund's son and obsessed with the possibility that Susanna will die in childbirth, is relieved. Around this time he takes over the play, pouring his grief over the deaths of Edmund and his infant son, his fears for Susanna and his delight at his granddaughter's birth into the scenes of birth and apparent death.

Fans of Greenblatt's *Will in the World* will find similar things to admire in Gossett's exploration of the ways in which specific events in Shakespeare's life might have informed the composition of *Pericles*; other readers may find this flight of fancy to be an unnecessary distraction in an otherwise superior edition.

Although Roger Warren bases his text of *Pericles* on Taylor and Jackson's Oxford reconstruction, he doesn't follow it slavishly, drawing instead on his experience using the Oxford text in rehearsal when he served as dramaturg for productions of the play in Stratford, Ontario, in 1986 and Stratford-upon-Avon in 1989. As in Warren's previous editions, his commentary is alive with theatrical nuance: he defends the emendation of 'doo't, as no doubt he doth' to 'doubt – as doubt no doubt he doth' (2.91) by noting that 'the repeated "doubts" – far from facing the actor with a tongue-twister – help him to "anchor" the line, giving it a bite and edge in another passage of humdrum verse'.

Observing that *Pericles* has become 'if not a regular presence in the repertory, at least a frequent visitor', Warren devotes much of his introduction to the play in performance. Yet this theatrical history incorporates the authorship issue in unexpected ways, as in the wonderful report of a 1947 Stratford production that omitted the first four scenes on the grounds 'that the Shakespeare Memorial Theatre owed no hospitality to what Shakespeare evidently had not written'.

Gossett and Warren provide curiously differing accounts of Adrian Noble's 2002 RSC production. Gossett sees it as a fairly 'traditional' reading of the play, save that 'Noble had just directed a musical, and one of his notable interventions was the addition of a "theme song"' sung at various points in the play by Pericles, Thaisa, Lychorida and Marina. According to Gossett, 'some critics and a significant part of the audience' found the song 'over-obtrusive' and decidedly un-Shakespearian: she cites Paul Taylor's criticism that the song 'would not sound out of place in a Disney version of the play'. Gossett does not mention that this production was based entirely on the Oxford reconstruction. Warren, who could hardly be guilty of such an oversight, happily avers that the Oxford text 'proved its value in providing a secure basis for the production'. He also maintains that it was the reconstruction which provided the inspiration for the song: 'Responding to Oxford's restoration of a song for Pericles (Scene 8a), Noble developed this into a duet between Pericles and Thaisa . . . later, this was the song that Marina sang to Pericles . . . and it became the unifying feature of the production'. And according to Warren (who apparently reads the *Guardian* rather than the *Independent*), the recurrent song was a hit: 'Michael Billington reported that "the audience went wild at the end"'.

Warren's discussion of the text occasionally slips into the terms of the now widely discredited 'Pirate' narrative: Q is posited as an 'unauthorized publication' by the 'less [than] reputable Henry Gosson', and we are told that 'the chaotic copy from which it was evidently printed suggests that it was obtained surreptitiously'. But more troubling is the decision to break with series convention regarding the textual notes. Warren explains that 'since the Quarto is reprinted in full and without any alteration in Appendix A, thus enabling any change made in the present edition to be easily identified, collations in the normal sense become superfluous'. In lieu of standard collations, Warren offers, in Appendix C, a list entitled 'attribution of emendations'. Here, he cites the source of many emended readings but notes that 'unlisted changes' are adopted from the Oxford *Complete Works*; these latter emendations are generally discussed in the commentary.

This weird system is a terrible idea in a scholarly edition. A reader interested in tracking the points at which Warren departs from Q must flip back and forth between the edited text and the Q transcription; moreover, the transcription's through-line-numbers bear no relation to the scene and line numbers in the edited text. Under these circumstances, one can hardly describe the textual changes as 'easily identified'. For example, at 1.186 (page 102), the edited text reads 'for the which we mean', whereas the Q transcript at through-line-number 213 (page 237) reads 'For which we mean'. Turning to the list of emendations in Appendix C (page 291), one finds that the change is not listed, which means (by process of elimination) that it must derive from the Oxford *Complete Works*. Turning back to page 102, one finds a commentary note that reads, in part, 'Oxford's emendation of Q's "which" restores the metre'. At this point, the serious student of Shakespeare's text (knowing that the emendation actually originated with Malone) may well toss aside the Oxford *Pericles* and reach for Gossett's Arden3.

John Jowett has previously edited *Timon of Athens* for both the Oxford Shakespeare *Complete Works* and the Oxford Middleton *Collected Works*, and now for the Oxford single-text series. But any concerns that he might simply be going through the motions in preparing yet another edition of the play would be misplaced. Jowett has produced an outstanding critical edition. Locating *Timon* firmly within a context of collaboration between Shakespeare and Middleton, Jowett details the linguistic/stylistic case for divided authorship and points to some previously unnoted lexical differences, such as Middleton's tendency to equate money with 'debt' whereas Shakespeare equates it with 'gold' (a word that occurs 33 times in Shakespeare's section of *Timon*, more than in any other Shakespeare play, but only three times in Middleton's section). Jowett's readings of differences in dramatic characterization are brilliant in their subtlety. He sees Shakespeare's Timon, in the first scene, as 'quietly benevolent', undertaking common forms of philanthropy; Middleton's Timon, by contrast, is prodigal, parting needlessly, in the second scene, with vast amounts and offering gifts 'without utility'.

Jowett provides an impressive performance history, running to more than thirty pages, as well as a useful chronological listing of major productions. His discussions of production choices often segue nicely into explorations of the play's ambiguities. For instance, Trevor Nunn's 1990 Young Vic production began with a dumb-show of thieves burying loot and being shot at by police; thus, when Timon later finds gold, 'he unearths a product of the violent society he had attempted to leave behind'. Yet Jowett also points out that this gold comes from the earth, as if it were unrefined ore – a gift of nature that Timon had mined. Jowett views the gold's contradictory qualities as crucial to the play's representation of nature in its relation to human activity:

> if nature is prodigal, Timon is more justified in being prodigal himself: fortune favours him, and the generosity of the earth is limitless even when its gifts are not wanted. On the other hand, if Timon stumbles on someone else's hoard, the total resources available to humanity have not increased; Timon recirculates wealth that has circulated before and so paradoxically he finds himself in the very middle of economic culture at the very point when he was most sure that he had escaped it.

Jowett observes that the Folio's enigmatic title, *The Life of Timon of Athens*, does not conform to the 'Life and Death' formula of the history plays – no doubt because Timon's death is not presented on stage. For the same reason, the play is unusual among the tragedies with which it is grouped. Indeed, only at a relatively late stage in the printing of the Folio was *Timon* selected to fill a space that had been reserved for *Troilus and Cressida*. Jowett presents the complex printing history of the play's 'unscheduled inclusion' with admirable clarity. He speculates that the original intention was not to publish the play at all but to exclude it along with Shakespeare's other collaborative plays, *Pericles* and *The Two Noble Kinsmen*.

Jowett is a superlative editor. As always, his text is supremely accurate and I found no errors in the collations. (The introduction slips ever so slightly when it renders Greene's famous epithet for Shakespeare – 'an upstart Crow, beautified with our feathers' – as 'Aesop's crow'.) It goes without saying that Jowett's *Timon* is now the best edition currently available, and it sets a very high standard for future editions as well.

Jowett characterizes *Timon* as Shakespeare's 'least loved play', a distinction that is challenged by Michael Taylor's Oxford edition of *Henry VI Part One*, which identifies *that* play as Shakespeare's 'least liked and least played'. Yet *1H6* was enormously popular in its time: it occasioned 'the first glowing review' of a Shakespeare production (Nashe's praise of the Talbot character in *Piers Penniless*) and proved to be Henslowe's second most profitable play. Only in later centuries did it fall out of favour, not receiving its first unadapted, full-fledged production in Stratford-upon-Avon until 1977.

Taylor sees *1H6* as the sixteenth-century equivalent of Hollywood's biblical epics of the 1930s and 1940s, occasionally using a full stage to richly comic effect, as when the French soldiers '*half ready and half unready*' (2.1.39.3) leap over the walls of Orleans. Observing that 'the play's words seem to play second fiddle to its percussion', Taylor points to fourteen separate instances of stage combat, which he identifies as something of a Shakespearian innovation. Before this play, there were only three instances in which important characters indulged in sword fighting on the English stage – twice in Greene's *Alphonsus* (*c.* 1587) and once in Peele's *The Battle of Alcazar* (*c.* 1589).

In an introduction that adopts a conversational tone ('You had to be there, I suppose, to understand the emotions of Londoners at those first performances') without dumbing down its vocabulary (e.g., 'atavistic xenophobia'), Taylor reminds us that Shakespeare wrote more plays on English history than any of his fellow dramatists. He argues that the three parts of *Henry VI* constitute 'a critical response to Marlowe's glorification of ruthless foreign individualism' and later describes the stance of the first tetralogy toward 'official history' as 'a questioning, complicated one, critical, subversive, and ironic'. Taylor also recognizes that female characters in these early history plays are central to the 'spirit of subversion that stalks the land': when one disappears, another takes her place. The last act of *1H6* helps to establish the pattern, with Joan's exit in 5.5 immediately followed by Margaret's entrance in 5.6. This raises the intriguing possibility that the same actor could have played both roles, as Fiona Bell did in Michael Boyd's 2000 RSC production.

There are a number of errors in Taylor's text, some of them serious – for 'my' read 'mine' (2.1.69), for 'suffer' read 'study' (3.1.112), for 'pleases' read 'pleaseth' (3.2.128), for 'has' read 'hath' (4.1.50), for 'you' read 'thou' (4.5.21) – and numerous errors in the collations.[2] Other typographical errors suggest a general carelessness in the preparation of this edition.[3] Although not rising to the level of error, Taylor's emendation of the Folio line 'Or with light skirmishes enfeeblèd' to 'Or with light skirmishes be enfeeblèd' (1.5.47), restoring what he takes to be a missing foot, seems unnecessary. The F reading is a perfect pentameter, assuming that 'enfeeblèd' is pronounced with four syllables.

William C. Carroll begins his Arden3 edition of *The Two Gentlemen of Verona* by drawing attention to the play's largely overlooked presence in *Shakespeare in Love* (1998). Early on we see Viola (Gwyneth Paltrow) listening to the opening lines of *Two Gentlemen*, which is unnamed in the film, thrilled by the romantic language; Queen Elizabeth (Judi Dench) laughs at the comic scenes with Lance feeding the dog; for his part, however, Shakespeare (Joseph Fiennes), watching offstage, shakes his head at the audience's low taste. Carroll cites the use of *Two Gentlemen* in the film as a testament to 'Shakespeare's richly exuberant comic powers', but the self-critical attitude of Fiennes's Shakespeare might as easily be seen as representing the view held by those who dismiss the play as aesthetically inferior to Shakespeare's later work.

Carroll aims to challenge the 'critical cycle' which assumes that since *Two Gentlemen* is an 'early' play, it must be 'immature' and hence 'incompetent'. Such severe judgements often center on Proteus's attempted rape of Silvia and Valentine's forgiveness of his friend – a scene that Carroll describes as 'one of the most controversial in the Shakespeare canon', and one often disparaged as a dramaturgical blunder made by 'a callow and inexperienced playwright'. Carroll provides a context for Valentine's behavior by offering an extended discussion of early modern male friendship, in which he ranges widely and learnedly from Cicero and Erasmus to queer theory. Carroll argues that Shakespeare's response to the sixteenth-century discourses on friendship is 'more complicated and indeed more searching' than is generally realized. Specifically, he sees the ending of the play as pressing the social demands of male friendship to absurd limits, 'deliberately unsettling the audience by providing the form of closure but also leaving unresolved disturbing questions about desire, friendship and identity'. Such a reading dignifies *The Two Gentlemen of Verona* as an instructive precursor to *The Two Noble Kinsmen*, a late play that 'deploys . . . a comparable ambivalence about the friendship tradition, and suggests, as *Two Gentlemen* does, that romantic desire is a vastly stronger power than male–male friendship'.

Carroll's introduction skilfully modulates between sophisticated analyses of textuality in the play – identifying the six or seven love letters that circulate in *Two Gentlemen* as 'metonymies for sexual desire, their errant and self-referential paths effectively reflect[ing] the confusions and failures of the main love plots' – and more prosaic considerations, such as the breed of Lance's dog. With respect to the latter, Carroll cites a colorful description of one Crab, 'a beast of markedly indeterminate breed but vaguely resembling a beagle on stilts that had passed through the hands of a headshrinker'. Carroll nicely details the long tradition of invariably 'deadpan' Crabs that steal the show – and, more seriously, the lack of any theatrical consensus on how the attempted rape should be staged.

Carroll's text is letter perfect. The only errors I found in this edition are confined to the collations

---

[2] In the collation at 1.1.131 for 'Falstaffe' read '*Falstaffe*'; 1.2.37 for 'Towne' read 'Towne,'; 1.2.37 for 'Slaues' read 'Slaues,'; 1.2.100 the expansion of F's 'S.' to 'Saint' should have been collated, as was done at 1.2.143; 1.3.29 for 'Vmpheir' read '*Vmpheir*' ; 1.3.60 for 'Beauford' read '*Beauford*'; the textual note at 1.5.11 credits Theobald with the emendation whereas the commentary note gives it to Pope; 2.1.7.2 for '*their*' read '*Their*'; 2.1.39 for '*Talbot*' read '*Talbot.*'; 2.4.78 for 'Poole' read '*Poole*'; 2.5.19 for 'unto' read 'vnto'; collation note needed for the speech-heading 'GENERAL' at 4.2.15 where F reads '*Cap.*'; 5.2.17 for 'fear' read 'feare'; 5.5.13 for 'bach'lorship' read 'Bach'ler-ship' (5.5.13).

[3] The Oxford *Complete Works* is dated '1988' for '1986' on p. 80; a place-holder 'pp. **-**' survives on p. 92; 'MALONE' is all caps rather than small caps at 2.4.26, as is 'CAPELL' at 2.5.121.1; an 'Exit' direction is not italicized at 4.1.77; textual notes at 1.5.43, 1.5.43.1 and 1.7.2 are printed on different pages from the text to which they refer.

and hardly worth mentioning.[4] In his discussion of the text, Carroll revisits Clifford Leech's theory of a four-stage process of revision, and finds evidence for one revision only. Entertaining the possibility that the role of Lance was interpolated into the play after the romantic plot was completed, Carroll suggests a plausible date and motive for this revision: when Will Kemp joined the Chamberlain's Men in 1594, Shakespeare perhaps had to write a clown's part for him to play and so added the Lance scenes to a script he had originally written in the early 1590s. Carroll also explores the issue of why *Two Gentlemen* is given such a prominent place in the First Folio (second after *The Tempest*) and finds probable cause in the fact that the play was grouped with the other Crane transcripts. Then again, since an effort was apparently made to ensure that each section of the First Folio began with a play that had not previously appeared in quarto (*The Tempest, King John, Coriolanus*), one may also speculate that the placement of *Two Gentlemen* was occasioned by a desire to begin the collection with two new plays.

Inspired by the innovations of Michael Warren's *Complete King Lear* (1989) and Bernice W. Kliman's *Enfolded Hamlet* (1996), and heeding Steven Urkowitz's call for editions that offer readers 'the richness of alternative versions of works instead of burying them under eclectic texts', Jesús Tronch-Pérez has produced a genuinely unique edition: *A Synoptic 'Hamlet': a Critical-Synoptic Edition of the Second Quarto and First Folio Texts of 'Hamlet'*. Tronch-Pérez explored various possibilities for 'multi-textual presentation' and ultimately devised a system of 'synoptic superimposition'. In its simplest form, Q2 readings float above the line of text while F1 readings appear below it:

hath face, yourselves<br>
God given you one and you make another<br>
has pace, yourself

This arrangement achieves its goal of pointing readers 'directly and immediately towards the significant variants'. And Tronch-Pérez's formal innovation in presenting the text is accompanied by rigorous standards of accuracy (I haven't found a textual error), detailed textual notes and a magnificent bibliography.

Although there is much to admire in the *Synoptic Hamlet*, Tronch-Pérez's decision to produce a critical edition, with readings modernized and emended, may confuse users who assume that it presents a diplomatic reprint of the originals. At TLN 541, for instance, Tronch-Pérez emends Q2's 'loue' to 'lone', modernizes it to 'loan', encloses it in pointy brackets to signal that it is an emendation, and then provides the emended Q2 reading as supposedly variant from the identical F1 reading:

<loan><br>
For oft loses both itself and friend<br>
loan

One can see the logic in this, but since 'love' makes sense in the context of the line (although not, as Tronch-Pérez points out, in the context of the following lines on borrowing), perhaps the Q2 variant ought to have been preserved in the synoptic comparison. Emendation is also problematic in TLN 79, where Q2 reads 'sleaded pollax' and F1 has 'sledded Pollax', which is rendered here:

<sledded> pole-axe<br>
He smote the on the ice<br>
sledded <Polacks>

Tronch-Pérez notes that the F1 reading could also be modernized as 'sledded pole-axe', but 'for the sake of variety, fitting the character of the present edition', he opts for Malone's emendation, 'sledded Polacks'. In the *loue/loan* example, emendation has the net effect of hiding the variant rather than foregrounding it; in the instance of *Pollax/Polacks*, emendation actually creates a Q2/F1 variant. In both cases, emendation can certainly be defended, but one wonders if the reader's encounter with the richness of the original versions is not somewhat diminished.

Shakespeare has long been underrepresented in the Norton Critical Editions series, which for many years included only *Hamlet* and *1 Henry IV*,

[4] In the collation at 1.1.123 for 'brief' read 'briefe'; 1.2.88 for 'Song:' read 'Song.'; 2.1.90 for 'eu'n' read 'ev'n'; 4.4.187 for 'dog:' read 'dog.'; 4.4.187 for 'Aburne' read '*Aburne*'.

edited by Cyrus Hoy and James L. Sanderson, respectively. With the publication this year of new editions of *Macbeth* (edited by Robert S. Miola), *Othello* (edited by Edward Pechter), *The Tempest* (edited by Peter Hulme and William H. Sherman) and of an updated *1 Henry IV* (edited by Gordon McMullan), the series is now a powerful force in the battle for adoption in Shakespeare courses, especially at American universities. Each of the Norton Critical Editions under review offers a text – sometimes annoyingly announced on the title-page to be the 'Authoritative Text' – source materials and criticism, but the editions also differ in important respects: Miola's *Macbeth* includes a substantial critical introduction, whereas Hulme and Sherman's *Tempest* simply provides a prefatory plot summary, and Pechter's few introductory pages to *Othello* focus primarily on the play's reception history. (Although I trust Pechter implicitly – a courtesy afforded to fellow *Shakespeare Survey* reviewers past and present – his claim that 'during the past twenty-five years or so, *Othello* has become the Shakespearian tragedy of choice, replacing *King Lear* in the way *Lear* had earlier replaced *Hamlet* as the play that speaks more directly and powerfully to current interests' runs counter to the testimony of the *MLA Bibliography*, which records that, during the last twenty-five years, 2418 books and articles were written about *Hamlet*, compared to 1093 on *King Lear* and 878 on *Othello*.)

McMullan relates that since 'a great deal of work' had been done on *1 Henry IV* since Sanderson's 1962 edition, he was instructed to retain Sanderson's text but 'to select a new set of essays representative both of the history and of the current state of play in critical analysis'. Given that a great deal of work has also been done by textual scholars over the last four decades, there is no warrant for assuming that the text – however 'authoritative' – remains static while criticism marches forward. Still, McMullan is only following orders and he does reproduce important textual essays by Gary Taylor and David Scott Kastan on the 'Falstaff/Oldcastle' controversy. Indeed, one of the great benefits of McMullan's edition is the careful pairing of several essays in which the second engages and responds to the first (e.g., Harold Jenkins and Paul Yachnin offer a point-counterpoint on the 'structural problem', or lack thereof, in the play/tetralogy).

Determined to represent 'the continuities as well as significant ruptures between recent and traditional interpretations', Pechter's *Othello* includes the *de rigueur* selections from Rymer, Johnson, Hazlitt and Coleridge alongside equally trenchant analyses by Mark Rose, Michael Neill, Patricia Parker, Michael Bristol and Pechter himself, essays intended to be 'edifying' in Richard Rorty's sense of the term, 'useful for building new kinds of ideas'. Many of the selections in these new Norton texts are unexpected: Miola's *Macbeth* includes Welcome Msomi's South African *uMabatha* (1996); McMullan offers an interview with Gus Van Sant about *My Own Private Idaho* paired with an analysis of the film by Susan Wiseman; Hulme and Sherman provide excerpts from a number of 'Rewritings and Appropriations' of *The Tempest*, ranging from Fletcher and Massinger's *The Sea Voyage* to Peter Greenaway's *Prospero's Books* and Ted Hughes's 'Setebos'. Although one can understand the frustration behind the editors' note of regret that 'the fees requested by some publishers put a few crucial essays and rewritings out of our (and your) reach', it would have been an act of scholarly generosity – as well as a means to circumvent the obstacle imposed by the miserliness of these unnamed publishers – if the editors had identified the essays in question so that interested readers could locate them elsewhere.

Readers should welcome the sprinkling of new material in these editions. Peter Holland contributes an original essay to Miola's edition, exploring (with characteristic panache) the locations of *Macbeth* in recent film adaptations: not only *Scotland, PA*, but Illinois, New York, Utah, Wales and Japan as well. Stephen Orgel provides an intriguing new coda to his 'Prospero's Wife' essay for Hulme and Sherman's edition. In the original version in *Representations* (1984), Orgel observed that the famous textual crux *wise/wife* (4.1.123) had been solved by Jeanne Roberts's discovery, in 1978, of two copies of F1 that read 'wife', and concluded: 'Obviously it is a reading whose time has come'.

In the intervening years, however, Peter Blayney examined the two copies of F1 under high magnification and reported that what Roberts saw was probably an inked piece of lint. Orgel's essay in the Norton Critical Edition now concludes:

> Obviously in 1978, this was a reading whose time had come. And whose time, at the beginning of the twenty-first century, may already be past. . . . Typography, it now appears, will not rescue Shakespeare from patriarchy and male chauvinism after all. Prospero's wife – and Ferdinand's – remain invisible.

It's reassuring that progress in textual studies is reflected not only in this revised essay but also in Hulme and Sherman's text, which wisely reads 'wise'.

Scott McMillin's introduction to his edition of *The First Quarto of Othello* in Cambridge's Early Quartos series offers a fascinating discussion of 'the withheld period' – a phenomenon associated with dramatic texts in which the speech (not the sentence) is the only recognized complete rhetorical unit. In these texts, each speech is punctuated with a period at the end but no periods appear in the body. McMillin identifies four dramatic texts that exhibit this method of punctuation: *Othello, Philaster, The Maid's Tragedy* and *A King and No King*. All four of these plays belonged to the King's Men, all were first published by Thomas Walkley and Nicholas Okes, all were published in two editions between 1619 and 1625 and all were subsequently published in third editions by Richard Hawkins. Furthermore, McMillin contends that all four plays show signs of theatrical abridgement and that several have readings which appear to have resulted from mishearing. Not all readers will accept McMillin's conclusion that Q1 *Othello* was printed from a theatrical script taken from dictation by a scribe listening to actors perform an abridged version. But McMillin is certainly correct that Q1 *Othello* needs to be considered in the context of these King's Men plays of 1609–12 rather than solely in the context of other Shakespearian quartos. There is at least one error in McMillin's text: for 'trip' read 'strip' at 2.1.181; at 1.2.5 McMillin prints 'yerk'd' (the Folio reading) rather than Q1's 'ierk'd', but this may be an intentional emendation that escaped collation.

The New Cambridge Shakespeare is producing some interesting hybrids in its 'updated editions' series. The updated *Othello* provides a supplement of 'Criticism and Productions of *Othello* since 1984', written by Scott McMillin, while the rest of Norman Sanders's original introduction, text and commentary remains unchanged. The updated *Twelfth Night*, on the other hand, provides a completely new introductory essay by Penny Gay, which now supplants Elizabeth Story Donno's original introduction – although Donno's text and commentary remain intact. Similarly, Alexander Leggatt's introduction to the updated *All's Well* replaces Russell Fraser's (curiously, space is afforded for Fraser's original prefatory acknowledgements but Leggatt has none). The 'updating' of T. S. Dorsch's *The Comedy of Errors* is the most thoroughgoing: Ros King not only wrote a new introduction but revised the text and commentary as well; it sounds as though little of Dorsch's original may remain, although his name – and not King's – still appears on the book's front cover.

Of all the Cambridge updates produced this year, I found the most food for thought in McMillin's pithy ten-page addendum to *Othello*, which gives pride of place to recent criticism and performance in South Africa. As Martin Orkin's 1987 *Shakespeare Against Apartheid* observes, South African Shakespeare scholars in the 1980s were paying no attention to new historicist or cultural materialist critics, whereas 'the famous critics from earlier in the century, who *were* being attended to, could be quoted to reveal racist assumptions'. Orkin's book, arguing that such outdated scholarship only served to prop up the apartheid regime, appeared at the same time as a Johannesburg production directed by Janet Suzman with a white Desdemona and a black actor as Othello, deliberately challenged the prevailing standards in which 'black actors did not play roles in which they seemed to kiss or strangle white women'; the book and the production thereby epitomize what has come to be known as 'postcolonial Shakespeare' in South Africa.

In reviewing other performances, McMillin highlights a 1991 blackface production in Vienna where the 'make-up was intentionally *made* to rub onto the other characters' and the 1997 'photo-negative' production in Washington, DC, with a white actor, Patrick Stewart, playing Othello against a cast of black actors in the other speaking parts. McMillin draws appropriate attention to close readings by Michael Neill, Stanley Cavell, and Patricia Parker, readings he characterizes as 'intensely political . . . not because they study the play as though it were about politics but because they study its words in the belief that literature is about language at the same time as it is about race or gender or postcolonialism'.

In Penny Gay's new introduction to *Twelfth Night*, the focus is squarely on performance. 'Critical fashions' are discussed in less than two pages, whereas sixteen pages are devoted to 'Stage history'. Gay castigates the 'English tendency to read the play as an intrinsically melancholy piece', implying that American and Australian productions are both more lighthearted and truer to the text. Gay provides a lively discussion of 'M.O.A.I.', noting that Peter J. Smith's solution to the riddle as a reference to Sir John Harington's *Metamorphosis Of a Iakes* finds support in some recent productions where 'Malvolio has had the contents of a chamber-pot emptied over him in the "dark house"'. In this instance, the disconnect between the new introduction and the original commentary is particularly unfortunate, in that Donno provides no commentary note on the 'M.O.A.I.' riddle, and there is no cross-reference to Gay's discussion.

The lone brand-new edition in the New Cambridge Shakespeare this year is Anthony Dawson's *Troilus and Cressida*, which opens with a playful heading: 'Style and genre: heap of rubbish, salty comedy, or what?' This promises a breezy irreverence – entirely appropriate to the spirit of the play – that never quite materializes. Still, Dawson's critical account is solid and substantial. Particularly worthy of note is his discussion of symmetrical pairings of parallel characters (Helen/Cressida, Troilus/Diomedes, Pandarus/Thersites), his overview of the 'strong political notes' sounded in late twentieth-century productions, his identification of moments when the play's characters 'watch each other like spectators at a play', and his inclusion of a striking 1902 art nouveau illustration of Cassandra bursting in on the Trojan council.

In the current era of version-based editing of two-text plays, in which conflation is anathema and 'conflationist' a term of derision, Dawson takes a principled stand. Given the 'complexity, even insolubility' of the textual situation presented by Q and F *Troilus*, Dawson insists not merely that there is 'ample justification for an eclectic text', but that 'to refuse conflation altogether would be to shirk one's editorial responsibility'. Because he believes that, on balance, Q contains more 'superior' readings, Dawson 'hesitantly and with due caution' chose Q as copy-text. However, he writes, 'I have felt free to draw from both texts, selecting readings from F that I consider to be superior to those offered by Q'. One would assume that with Q as his control text, Dawson would defend in his commentary any 'superior' readings imported from F, but this is not always the case: dozens of F readings are adopted without comment throughout (e.g., 1.3.1, 1.3.253, 1.3.303, 2.1.14, 2.3.49–53, 2.3.59, 2.3.65–6, 4.1.17, 4.5.132, 4.5.178, 4.5.206, 5.1.18, 5.1.51, 5.2.41, 5.2.48, 5.2.117, 5.2.122, 5.3.23–5, 5.3.85, 5.4.3, 5.10.1, 5.11.48). I note in passing that the emendation of the Q/F reading 'Kings, disarme' at 3.1.134 to 'you shall do more / Than all the island kings t'disarm great Hector' is inspired.

Dawson takes collation seriously and even provides a brief guide that explains the conventions of textual notes. This primer, which ought to be emulated in all critical editions, should prove useful not only to beginning students but also to more advanced literary critics who have never quite understood what was going on in 'the band of terror'. Dawson's collations themselves, however, do not provide the best object lesson. At 3.2.29, the F reading 'sprite' is adopted without collation (Q reads 'spirite'); several relineations are not collated and there are a number of errors in the typography of the Q readings cited in the notes;[5] a textual note should have recorded that Q's 'trauell' is rendered 'travail' at 1.1.66; and although it is possible to see 'marvellous' at 1.2.120 as a simple modernization of Q's spelling 'maruel's', a note providing the Q reading might have been appropriate, given that 'marvel's' makes sense in context ('she has a marvel's white hand') and has been retained by some editors. Similarly, a note on the change of Q's 'biles' and 'byles' to 'boils' (2.1.2, 2.1.4) would have been welcome.

Finally, in the unofficial competition that emerges among this year's editors concerning whose play has been 'least liked', 'least played', and most neglected over the centuries, Dawson trumps Gossett's claim for *Pericles* (which 'disappeared from the stage for almost two hundred years') by observing that 'for just over three hundred years Shakespeare's *Troilus and Cressida* was absent from the English stage'. Then, in a slip, he points to another, unexpected contender: 'only *3H4* seems to have been absent from the stage for longer'. No performance history can prove this sentence wrong. Then again, a nonexistent play, although eternally absent from the stage, cannot be said to bear the stigma of unpopularity.

## TEXTUAL STUDIES

*Textual Performances: The Modern Reproduction of Shakespeare's Drama*, edited by Lukas Erne and Margaret Jane Kidnie, may well prove to be this year's most lasting contribution to Shakespeare textual studies. Intent upon surveying the current textual scene, two decades after the publication of *The Division of the Kingdoms* (1983), Erne and Kidnie solicited essays from the leading players in the field. The resulting collection has a unity that is often lacking in festschriften or volumes of conference papers: the contributions to *Textual Performances* are uniformly excellent.

The collection's opening essay is also its most provocative. Leah Marcus points out that the key passages in *Othello* that have been repeatedly cited by critics to define the play's attitude towards 'blackness, miscegenation, and sexual pollution' only appear in the Folio text, which, she argues, contains 'the play's most racially charged language'. Marcus detects an 'unease' that previous textual scholars have 'felt but could not directly express toward the more benign construction of racial difference offered in Q', a discomfort that found strikingly apt metaphorical expression in Alice Walker's reference to Q's 'contamination' of the Folio, which had 'taken colour in linguistic forms' from the Quarto: 'the pollution holds in the exchange'. There is, of course, no way of knowing whether Walker, with 'obliquity and suppressed shame', was 'subliminally reacting against' the recognition that 'Q does not rein in the cultural danger represented by Othello's blackness and sexuality with anything like the virulence of F'. Some may choose not to follow Marcus on her journey into the subconscious thoughts of previous editors. Nonetheless, it is clear that future editorial thinking will have to attend to these fascinating racial/textual differences.

Michael Warren and Paul Werstine, the only veterans from *The Division of the Kingdoms* represented here, both continue to challenge traditional editorial and textual assumptions. Warren explores the usual re-assignment of the Second Citizen's speeches in 1.1 *Coriolanus* to the First Citizen by puckishly asking 'what if, denying the editorial impulse to detect and manage error, one were to assume that the text is correct?' Having served recently as dramaturg for a production of the play, Warren observes that, in this instance and more generally, 'experience of performance often reveals

[5] Relineations not collated include those at 3.3.142–4 'I . . . me / As . . . me / Good . . . forgot?' Q lines 'I . . . it, / For . . . beggars, / Neither . . . looke: / What . . . forgot?'; 4.1.49–50 'The . . . time / Will . . . you.' Q lines 'The . . . so: / On . . . you.'; 4.1.79–80 'We'll . . . sell. / Here . . . way.' Q lines 'Heere lyes' on line 79; and 4.2.16–17 'Prithee . . . tarry' as one line in Q. In the collation at 1.3.239 for 'and' in Q quotation read '&'; 2.2.27 for 'fathers' read 'father's'; 3.1.102 for 'shafts confound' read '*shafts confound*'; 3.2.0.SD for '*Pandarus Troylus*' read '*P*andarus *T*roylus'; 3.3.272 for 'Agamemnon' read '*Agamemnon*'; 4.2.72 for 'neighbour' read 'neighbor'; 4.4.49–50 for 'Genius' read '*Genius*'; 5.1.23 for 'means' read 'meanes'.

that what presents problems in reading may present few upon the stage'.

For his part, Werstine revisits the paradigmatic example of the 'false start' in the Player Queen's speech as a key indicator of 'foul paper' copy behind Q2 *Hamlet*:

> 2034 That I distrust you, yet though I distrust,
> 2035 Discomfort you my Lord it nothing must.
> 2035+1 For women feare too much, euen as they loue,
> 2036 And womens fear and loue hold quantitie
> 2037 Eyther none, in neither ought, or in extremitie.

Editors from John Dover Wilson to Harold Jenkins have pointed to the unrhymed line (TLN 2035 + 1) and the extra-metrical 'Eyther none' in 2037, which do not appear in F, as clear instances of authorial false starts, rejected words that were deleted '*currente calamo*' but with deletion marks that were unclear to the compositor who was later faced with foul paper copy. Werstine, however, observes that both Samuel Johnson and Charles Jennens conjectured that a line written to rhyme with Q2's 'For . . . loue' had been dropped from Q2's copy – a possibility also entertained by the Cambridge editors, who noted that, since the extant unrhymed line appears at the top of a page (sig. H2r), a line could have been dropped from the bottom of the preceding page. George Steevens, imagining instead that the line originally formed a triplet with the preceding two, suggested that the final word in 2035 + 1 should perhaps read 'lust' rather than 'loue'. Thus, Werstine concludes, 'the history of Q2's reception shows the matter to be one of interpretation, hardly the basis for establishing a text of the play'.

Ernst Honigmann identifies 'four generations' of New Bibliographers: (1) Pollard, McKerrow, Greg; (2) Chambers, Alexander, Wilson; (3) Bowers, Prouty, Honigmann himself; and (4) Taylor, Warren, Werstine. This is a deeply personal history, in which Honigmann plays a role. While still an undergraduate, he heard Alexander speak on the problems of the King John plays, a problem that resonated with Honigmann and to which he returned in his Oxford B.Litt thesis, 'Studies in the Chronology of Shakespeare's Plays' (1950) and in his Arden2 edition of *King John* (1954). Moreover, Honigmann writes, 'one of the examiners of my thesis was F. P. Wilson, and I believe it influenced his thinking when he declared in 1951 that "the fact is that the chronology of Shakespeare's earliest plays is so uncertain that it has no right to harden into an orthodoxy"'.

In an important respect, bibliographers of the fourth generation have followed Honigmann's example: they see uncertainty in matters where orthodoxy had formerly prevailed. Thus, whereas scholars once assumed that in instances of two-text plays, such as *Hamlet*, the quarto was probably based on a 'foul paper' manuscript and the Folio on a playhouse manuscript (or vice versa), Werstine and others have pointed to the fact that no extant play survives in two such versions. Honigmann's thinking remains uninfluenced by such evidentiary obstacles: 'let us be clear', he writes, 'that most performed plays must once have existed as foul papers and promptbooks, however we name and define these texts'. Such pronouncements fail to advance the debate between some members of the third generation and their successors.

Honigmann concludes, on a more positive note, with a celebration of 'the truly impressive achievement' of the New Bibliography: 'the steady advance of scholarship and knowledge over a period of almost a hundred years', in which Greg is singled out as 'the hero of the movement'.

Henry Woudhuysen continues the praise of Greg in his brief history of the Malone Society, pointing out that Greg had a hand in each of the ninety volumes ('an astonishing number') that the Society produced from 1906 to 1939, when he was its general editor. Woudhuysen also lauds the Society's 'extraordinarily high standards of accuracy and correct scholarship' and fittingly quotes A. E. Housman: 'Accuracy is a duty, not a virtue' (a dry maxim that I'd like to appropriate as an epigraph for this annual review). Greg has been criticized by some for his 'willful' failure to record the marginal markings in the manuscript of *The Second Maiden's Tragedy* in his 1909 edition but Woudhuysen comes to his defense, pointing out that in this and other Malone Society editions, Greg 'was editing the plays as literary works in manuscript, not as dramatic documents'. Since Greg viewed the marginal markings as later additions, not as part of the original, he had no reason to include them.

John Jowett, who has edited *Measure for Measure* for the Oxford Middleton and is currently editing *Sir Thomas More* for the Arden3 Shakespeare, rightly notes in his essay that many readers will be surprised to see these plays 'transported into new authorial environments'. In each case, however, editorial practice calls attention to the plays' dual or multiple authorship. The Arden3 *Sir Thomas More* will adopt a parallel-text format to reflect the 'two crucial stages' in the genesis of the manuscript – the text as originally written and then as 'radically altered'. For *Measure for Measure*, Jowett decided that in those instances where there is reason to believe that an original (Shakespearian) passage was marked for deletion but inadvertently set in the Folio along with the (Middletonian) passage that was intended to replace it, the Oxford edition will set the 'deleted' text in grey type and the 'added' text in bold, such that 'the superseded text is placed under erasure'. Although the document of F1 *Measure* is 'textually singular', the text, 'viewed as something represented rather than simply existent in the document', is 'divisible'. Given the theoretical sophistication with which Jowett discusses these editorial decisions, one would like to hear more about differences in his handling of *Timon of Athens* when he prepared that text for the authorial environments of the Oxford Shakespeare and the Oxford Middleton.

Sonia Massai, who is currently editing *Edward III* for the Internet Shakespeare Editions series, discusses the theoretical underpinnings of preparing an electronic edition. She draws an important distinction between a critical *edition*, which 'privileges the modern text over other textual alternatives', and a critical *archive*, which 'provides accurate and searchable digital versions of the editions from which those textual alternatives derive'. As Massai rightly points out, the nature of the electronic archive 'radically affects both the way in which editors envisage the editorial task and the way in which readers approach the materials which the editor provides'. In a related essay, John Lavagnino astutely observes that one of the long-promised benefits of digital commentary, that 'you would simply click on a word and you'd see the notes for it', could prove in many case to be 'less simple than glancing down the page or across the opening at the notes'.

M. J. Kidnie urges editors to experiment more freely with the layout of the edited page, particularly in regard to stage directions. Current conventions for indicating stage action require that an editor specify the precise moment at which the action takes place, though the action might, in fact, be appropriate at any number of moments. Kidnie proposes a new set of conventions: stage directions could be placed in the margins – as they are in many early dramatic manuscripts and some printed texts – with markings, such as arrows, to show readers the range of possible options. In cases where there is uncertainty about the point at which a character should enter, as in the example Kidnie gives from *Troilus & Cressida* (4.6), an editor could provide multiple directions:

[Enter Diomedes and Cressida ▼]
ACHILLES 'Tis but early days
AGAMEMNON Is not yond Diomed with Calchas' daughter?
ULYSSES 'Tis he. I ken the manner of his gait.
He rises on the toe: that spirit of his
In aspiration lifts him from the ground.
[Enter Diomends and Cressida▲]
AGAMEMNON Is this the lady Cressid?
DIOMEDES Even she.

Kidnie concludes that 'this is no derogation of editorial responsibility; instead, it is to recognize that there can be no "right" choice, and to locate the interpretative decision firmly with the reader'.

The difficulty of challenging long-standing conventions, however, is well illustrated by John Cox's essay, in which he recounts the fortunes of the initial decision that he and I made *not* to include added stage directions in our Arden3 *3H6* but rather to discuss staging possibilities in the commentary.

Our plan was ultimately scuttled by the general editors on the grounds that Arden style required that an edition clarify stage action and that added stage directions were the most efficient way to do so.

The fact that such editorial labours are frequently ignored or cancelled out by theatre practitioners is the topic of Barbara Hodgdon's polemical essay, which aptly cites Nigel Hawthorne's impatience with editorial stage directions, manifested in the marginal annotation he made in his copy of *King Lear* next to '*He takes off his coronet of flowers*' and '*He throws down flowers and stamps on them*': 'No, he doesn't!' Elsewhere in the volume, David Bevington relates a story about Joseph Papp complaining to an interviewer about 'some hair-brained editor (meaning me)' who called Don Armado's petite squire 'Mote' rather than 'Moth' in *Love's Labour's Lost*.

Hodgdon maintains that traditional codes of editorial commentary 'serve neither performers nor performance', largely because one of the functions of such commentary is 'to converse (and often to quarrel) with previous editors, faulting injudicious choices, and thus engage with the text's history'. Nor is she satisfied with forms of annotation that give specific details of past performances – readings of particular lines or stage business – because to do so is to 'select moments from the constructed flow of performance of which they are a part, effectively "doing" to performance what the atomizing dictionary-based gloss does to text'. Hodgdon calls for a new set of protocols for 'performance commentary' in which the Shakespearian text would be viewed as 'a site combining a limited number of textual obligations with a wide range of performative options'.

Ann Thompson and Neil Taylor discuss the importance of 'casting charts'. An often overlooked feature of critical editions, casting charts are included in many Arden3 editions (especially the history plays) but do not appear, oddly enough, in any Oxford or Cambridge edition – not even those oriented toward performance issues. As Thompson and Taylor argue, casting charts have much to teach us about the potential doubling of roles and should therefore be of interest both to scholars concerned with early playhouse practices and to theatre directors wondering how many actors they may need for a given play. The charts of Q1, Q2, and F1 *Hamlet* that Thompson and Taylor prepared for their forthcoming Arden3 edition reveal that the three texts are 'extraordinarily similar in their casting patterns', provide 'virtually the same doubling possibilities', and 'need exactly the same number of actors to cover all the parts': eight men and three boys. The revelation that the three textual versions of *Hamlet* 'share essentially the same structure' is an unexpected payoff of these casting charts, and one that may encourage future editors to undertake them.

Erne and Kidnie are sure to be two stars of the 'fifth generation' of Shakespearian bibliographers. (The only disappointing feature of *Textual Performances* is that Erne has not contributed an essay of his own.) This outstanding collection not only attests to the vitality of our wing of the profession at the present historical moment but promises an exceptionally bright and bold future as well.

Andrew Murphy's *Shakespeare in Print: A History and Chronology of Shakespeare Publishing* is an extraordinary work of bibliographical scholarship, at once scrupulously accurate and thoroughly entertaining. Murphy's archival research has yielded a wealth of informative detail that enlivens his narrative account of the history of Shakespearian editing. Among the pleasantly gossipy tidbits, we learn that at least one contemporary found Capell 'too *opiniatre* and dictatorial' in conversation – which would explain why he alienated his few friends and became, in later life, 'almost an anchorite'; another contemporary characterized Malone as 'dull' and Steevens as 'clever', but observed that 'the dullness was accompanied by candour and a love of truth, the cleverness by a total absence of both'; David Nichol Smith found the growth of Shakespearian scholarship in America 'disgusting', while Oxford University Press warned McKerrow not to be 'too rigorous' in the standard of learning assumed for potential users of the Oxford Shakespeare 'because we shall hope to sell some copies to retired American business men'; McKerrow, for his part, determined that original punctuation should be retained 'when it isn't a nuisance', while Arthur Quiller-Couch proposed that each volume of the New Cambridge Shakespeare 'should be a pretty little book that ladies could carry to picnics'.

In the second half of his 500-page study, Murphy provides a full chronological listing of all single-text editions of Shakespeare published through 1709, all complete plays/collected-works editions published through 1821 and most collected-works editions published from 1821 to the present. I've gone over Murphy's 1712-item list with considerable care and have not found a single error.[6] And Murphy makes impressive use of this chronology. For instance, although it is standard to view the closing of the theatres as a time when readers turned to printed dramatic texts as a substitute for performances, I don't know of anyone before Murphy who has noticed that, for Shakespeare, 'the theatrical interregnum largely coincided with a significant decline in publishing activity. None of Shakespeare's plays was published during the course of the 1640s and only three plays appeared in print in the following decade'.[7] This startling observation has important implications, it would seem, for our evolving understanding of Shakespeare as literary dramatist.

## WORKS REVIEWED

Bevington, David, 'Modern Spelling: The Hard Choices', in Erne and Kidnie, *Textual Performances*, pp. 143–57.

Cox, John D., 'Open Stage, Open Page? Editing Stage Directions in Early Dramatic Texts', in Erne and Kidnie, *Textual Performances*, pp. 178–93.

Erne, Lukas, and Margaret Jane Kidnie, eds., *Textual Performances: The Modern Reproduction of Shakespeare's Drama* (Cambridge, 2004).

Hodgdon, Barbara, 'New Collaborations with Old Plays: The (Textual) Politics of Performance Commentary', in Erne and Kidnie, *Textual Performances*, pp. 210–23.

Honigmann, Ernst, 'The New Bibliography and its Critics', in Erne and Kidnie, *Textual Performances*, pp. 77–93.

Jowett, John, 'Addressing Adaptation: *Measure for Measure* and *Sir Thomas More*', in Erne and Kidnie, *Textual Performances*, pp. 63–76.

Kidnie, Margaret Jane, 'The Staging of Shakespeare's Drama in Print Editions', in Erne and Kidnie, *Textual Performances*, pp. 158–77.

Lavagnino, John, 'Two Varieties of Digital Commentary', in Erne and Kidnie, *Textual Performances*, pp. 194–209.

Marcus, Leah S., 'The Two Texts of *Othello* and Early Modern Constructions of Race', in Erne and Kidnie, *Textual Performances*, pp. 21–36.

Massai, Sonia, 'Scholarly Editing and the Shift from Print to Electronic Cultures', in Erne and Kidnie, *Textual Performances*, pp. 94–110.

Murphy, Andrew, *Shakespeare in Print: A History and Chronology of Shakespeare Publishing* (Cambridge, 2003).

Shakespeare, William, *All's Well That Ends Well*, ed. Russell Fraser, updated edition with a new introduction by Alexander Leggatt, New Cambridge Shakespeare (Cambridge, 2003).

*The Comedy of Errors*, ed. T. S. Dorsch, updated edition with a revised text and commentary and a new introduction by Ros King, New Cambridge Shakespeare (Cambridge, 2004).

*1 Henry IV*, ed. Gordon McMullan, Norton Critical Edition (New York and London, 2003).

*Henry VI Part 1*, ed. Michael Taylor, Oxford Shakespeare (Oxford, 2003).

*Macbeth*, ed. Robert S. Miola, Norton Critical Edition (New York and London, 2004).

*The First Quarto of Othello*, ed. Scott McMillin, Cambridge Early Quartos (Cambridge, 2001).

---

[6] The one slip in Murphy's narrative is the assertion that 'the only Shakespeare text which Bowers himself produced was an edition of *The Merry Wives of Windsor*, which he published in Alfred Harbage's Pelican series'. Bowers also edited *The Two Noble Kinsmen* for *The Dramatic Works in the Beaumont and Fletcher Canon* (Cambridge, 1989), item 1609 in Murphy's chronological list.

[7] The rule-proving exception may be the Second Folio, which may have been reissued by Richard Cotes *circa* 1640 (see William B. Todd, 'The Issues and States of the Second Folio and Milton's Epitaph on Shakespeare', *Studies in Bibliography*, 5 (1952–3), 82–109). In any case, an F2 published in 1640 would still precede the closing of the theatres, which began as a temporary ban in September of 1642 and was made permanent in 1647.

*Othello*, ed. Edward Pechter, Norton Critical Edition (New York and London, 2004).

*Othello*, ed. Norman Sanders, updated edition with a new section of the introduction by Scott McMillin, New Cambridge Shakespeare (Cambridge, 2003).

*Pericles*, ed. Suzanne Gossett, Arden3 (London, 2004).

*A Synoptic 'Hamlet': A Critical-Synoptic Edition of the Second Quarto and First Folio Texts of 'Hamlet'*, ed. Jesús Tronch-Pérez (Valencia, 2002).

*The Tempest*, ed. Peter Hulme and William H. Sherman, Norton Critical Edition (New York and London, 2004).

*Troilus and Cressida*, ed. Anthony B. Dawson, New Cambridge Shakespeare (Cambridge, 2003).

*Twelfth Night*, ed. Elizabeth Story Donno, updated edition with a new introduction by Penny Gay, New Cambridge Shakespeare (Cambridge, 2004).

*The Two Gentlemen of Verona*, ed. William C. Carroll, Arden3 (London, 2004).

Shakespeare, William and Thomas Middleton, *Timon of Athens*, ed. John Jowett, Oxford Shakespeare (Oxford, 2004).

Shakespeare, William and George Wilkins, *Pericles*, ed. Roger Warren on the basis of a text prepared by Gary Taylor and MacD. P. Jackson, Oxford Shakespeare (Oxford, 2003).

Thompson, Ann and Neil Taylor, '"Your sum of parts": doubling in *Hamlet*', in Erne and Kidnie, *Textual Performances*, pp. 111–126.

Warren, Michael, 'The Perception of Error: The Editing and the Performance of the Opening of *Coriolanus*', in Erne and Kidnie, *Textual Performances*, pp. 127–142.

Werstine, Paul, 'Housmania: Episodes in Twentieth-Century "Critical" Editing of Shakespeare', in Erne and Kidnie, *Textual Performances*, pp. 49–62.

Woudhuysen, H. R., '"Work of Permanent Utility": Editors and Texts, Authorities and Originals', in Erne and Kidnie, *Textual Performances*, pp. 37–48.

# BOOKS RECEIVED

This list includes all books received between September 2003 and September 2004 which are not reviewed in this volume of *Shakespeare Survey*. The appearance of a book in this list does not preclude its review in a subsequent volume.

Bachchielli, Rolando, ed., *Polidoro Virgili e la Cultura Umanistica Europea* (Urbino, 2003).

Barker, Howard, *Death, the One and the Art of Theatre* (Abingdon and New York, 2005).

Boon, Richard and Jane Plastow, eds., *Theatre and Empowerment: Community Drama on the World Stage* (Cambridge, 2004).

Cheney, Patrick, ed., *The Cambridge Companion to Christopher Marlowe* (Cambridge, 2004).

Davis, Madison J. and A. Daniel Frankforter, *The Shakespeare Name Dictionary* (New York and London, 2004).

George, David, *Coriolanus. Shakespeare: the Critical Tradition* (Bristol and New York, 2004).

Giannachi, Gabriella, *Virtual Theatres: An Introduction* (London and New York, 2004).

Greig, Noël, *Playwrighting: A Practical Guide* (Abingdon and New York, 2005).

Gurr, Andrew, ed., *Philaster, or Love Lies a-Bleeding* by Francis Beaumont and John Fletcher (Manchester, 2003).

Innes, Christopher, *Henrik Ibsen's Hedda Gabler: A Routledge Literary Sourcebook* (London and New York, 2003).

Jones, Robert Edmond, *The Dramatic Imagination: Reflections and Speculations on the Art of Theatre* (New York, 2004).

Kruger, Loren, *Post-Imperial Brecht: Politics, Performance, East and South* (Cambridge, 2004).

Lord, Suzanne, *Music from the Age of Shakespeare: A Cultural History* (Westport, CT, 2003).

Martin, John, *The Intercultural Performance Reader* (London and New York, 2004).

McGrath, John E., *Loving Big Brother: Performance, Privacy and Surveillance Space* (London and New York, 2004).

Ostovich, Helen and Elizabeth Sauer, eds., *Reading Early Modern Women: An Anthology of Texts in Manuscript and Print, 1550–1700* (New York and London, 2004).

Scheer, Edward, ed., *Antonin Artaud: a Critical Reader* (London and New York, 2004).

Shaughnessy, Robert, ed., *Four Renaissance Comedies* (Basingstoke, 2004).

Shevtsova, Maria, *Dodin and the Maly Drama Theatre: Process to Performance* (London and New York, 2004).

Spiller, Elizabeth, *Science, Reading, and Renaissance Literature: The Art of Making Knowledge, 1580–1670* (Cambridge, 2004).

Staniewski, Wlodzimierz with Alison Hodge, *Hidden Territories: the theatre of Gardzienice* (London and New York, 2004).

Steggle, Matthew, *Richard Brome: Place and Politics on the Caroline Stage* (Manchester, 2004).

Steible, Mary, *Coriolanus: A Guide to the Play* (Westport, CT, 2004).

Turner, Jane, *Routledge Performance Practitioners: Eugenio Barba* (London, 2004).

Woodford, Donna, *Understanding King Lear* (Westport, CT, and London, 2004).

Zitner, Sheldon P., ed., *The Knight of the Burning Pestle* by Francis Beaumont (Manchester, 2004).

# INDEX

No book titles or play titles, other than Shakespeare's, are included in this index, but the names of the authors are given. Book titles in review articles are listed, alphabetically by author, at the end of each section.

# INDEX

# INDEX

# INDEX

# INDEX

# INDEX